MW01026901

COUP IN DALLAS

The Decisive Investigation into Who Killed JFK

H. P. ALBARELLI JR.

With Leslie Sharp and Alan Kent

Organizational and Character Maps by Pete Sattler

FOREWORD BY DICK RUSSELL

Skyhorse Publishing

Copyright © 2021 by H. P. Albarelli Jr. and Linda O'Hara

All rights reserved. No part of this book may be reproduced in any manner
without the express written consent of the publisher, except in the case of brief
excerpts in critical reviews or articles. All inquiries should be addressed to Arcade
Publishing, 307 West 36th Street, 11th Floor, New York, NY 10018.

Skyhorse Publishing books may be purchased in bulk at special discounts for
sales promotion, corporate gifts, fund-raising, or educational purposes. Special
editions can also be created to specifications. For details, contact the Special Sales
Department, Arcade Publishing, 307 West 36th Street, 11th Floor, New York,
NY 10018 or info@skyhorsepublishing.com.

Skyhorse® and Skyhorse Publishing® is a registered trademark of Skyhorse
Publishing, Inc.®, a Delaware corporation.

Visit our website at www.skyhorsepublishing.com.

10 9 8 7 6 5 4 3 2 1

Library of Congress Cataloging-in-Publication Data is available on file.

Print ISBN: 978-1-5107-4031-0
Ebook ISBN: 978-1-5107-4034-1

Printed in the United States of America

CONTENTS

FOREWORD
BY DICK RUSSELL

The book you are about to read contains the strongest evidence ever published of a high-level conspiracy by the military-industrial complex and its ultra-right-wing allies to assassinate President John F. Kennedy on November 22, 1963. As an author who has spent years researching and writing three books on the subject, I state that unequivocally.

The narrative by H. P. Albarelli Jr., coauthored with Leslie Sharp and Alan Kent, is based upon a 1963 datebook, or desk diary, kept by a mysterious, deep-cover intelligence operative named Jean Pierre Lafitte. Albarelli had written about Lafitte's connection to the CIA in his 2009 book, *A Terrible Mistake*. I'll let the authors describe how he gained access to the datebook.

It is eerie to see this come to light after all these years—a template, albeit intentionally cryptic, for the diabolical planning resulting in a coup d'état that haunts our national psyche. Albarelli, author of previous books probing the US government's efforts to control human behavior as well as on the JFK case, died of complications from a stroke in June 2019. He was a zealous researcher who spent years developing the context that underlies the datebook revelations. This traces back to relationships spawned in World War Two, including those with Nazis subsequently utilized by US intelligence during the Cold War.

Some of the people identified as apparent conspirators in the datebook will be familiar to students of the Kennedy assassination. Others are named for the first time publicly. The interlocking connections between Texas oil interests and intelligence operatives are examined in detail, as well as the global reach involving fascist elements threatened by the Kennedy administration's move toward peaceful coexistence with the Soviet Union.

Here established beyond doubt is that the real perpetrators needed a fall guy to take the rap as a lone, Left-leaning gunman. The setup of Lee Harvey Oswald began many months before, carefully orchestrated by a cabal of evil geniuses in espionage. One of these was James Angleton, then-chief of CIA Counterintelligence. Another was Charles Willoughby, who formerly served as spymaster for

General Douglas MacArthur. A third was Otto Skorzeny, Hitler's favorite commando, aided by the US to establish a postwar domicile in Franco's Spain, where he created secret camps to train assassins.

In implicating Willoughby (whose possible role was first raised in my book *The Man Who Knew Too Much*), French hitman Jean Rene Souetre, soldier-of-fortune Thomas Eli Davis, Jr., and oil industrialist Jack Crichton, *Coup in Dallas* opens wider doors to which researchers have been seeking keys for years.

Albarelli's book also adds corroboration to my own work as an investigative journalist, including knowledge imparted to me by double agent Richard Case Nagell. While Nagell is not named in the datebook, it provides substantiation for his stressing Mexico City's Hotel Luma as a planning site and offers up the name of a Willoughby associate (Jack Canon) who Nagell had hinted was among several shooters in Dealey Plaza.

Coup in Dallas examines other layers of intrigue: the utilization by the conspirators of an East German call girl (Ellen Rometsch) in an effort to compromise JFK, and the alleged suicides of *Washington Post* publisher Philip Graham and Kennedy confidante Grant Stockdale.

Readers should not expect that *Coup in Dallas* means "case closed." By design of Lafitte, himself very much part of the plot, his entries are thin on detail and sometimes confined to initials. Doubtless, analysis of their content will occupy researchers in search of the truth for the *next* fifty years. But the clues are numerous, and sometimes explicit—for example, this chilling notation two weeks before the assassination: "On the wings of murder. The pigeon way for unsuspecting Lee. Clip, clip his wings."

Lafitte had died by the time the datebook was made accessible to author Hank Albarelli. It raises the question of why he would leave behind such a legacy. To assuage his guilty conscience? As a final puzzle that would tantalize and frustrate future historians? We will never know the motivation of a man who, in the words of a CIA official who knew Lafitte well, "gives a whole new meaning to the label 'spook.'" Regardless, Lafitte's datebook, a faux leather-bound red volume with a vintage Nazi coin taped to the inside front cover, is of immeasurable importance toward unraveling the takeover that took place that terrible day in Dallas—with ramifications that reverberate in our times. The assassination operation, Project Lancelot, is finally being exposed.

—Dick Russell is the bestselling author of thirteen books, including *The Man Who Knew Too Much*, *On the Trail of the JFK Assassins*, and *They Killed Our President!* with Jesse Ventura

PUBLISHER'S STATEMENT

We are proud to bring to readers, researchers, and scholars Hank Albarelli Jr.'s book *Coup in Dallas*, a comprehensive analysis of the machinations behind the John F. Kennedy assassination.

We do not have a definitive position on the authorship of the Jean Pierre Lafitte 1963 datebook and make no representation or warranty as to the veracity of its entries. However, we feel that Hank was a serious and dedicated researcher with absolute faith in the legitimacy of the datebooks, and his analysis ought to be part of the public record.

—Tony Lyons, Publisher
Skyhorse Publishing, Inc.

THE LAFITTE DATEBOOK:
A LIMITED ANALYSIS
BY DICK RUSSELL

Submitted September 13, 2018, upon request of a film production company interested in developing a documentary focused on the book initially titled *Coup in Dallas: Who Killed JFK and Why*.

Pending verification by forensic document specialists and handwriting experts, I have carefully reviewed the 1963 datebook allegedly written by Jean Pierre Lafitte. Based on the entries I have seen, cryptic as many of them are (no doubt intentionally), this is a crucial piece of new evidence indicating a high-level conspiracy that resulted in the assassination that November 22 of President John F. Kennedy. Many of the names mentioned are familiar to me as someone who has researched and published numerous articles and three books on the assassination over the past forty-plus years. A number of these names, however, were **not** known publicly in 1963 and for more than a decade thereafter. Thus, assuming the datebook entries were indeed set down at that time by Lafitte, this adds substantial credibility to the likelihood that the document contains never-before-revealed information about a conspiracy involving accused assassin Lee Harvey Oswald as well as his own killer, Jack Ruby.

My first book on the subject, *The Man Who Knew Too Much*, initially appeared in 1992. It does not mention Lafitte, whose name was not known to me at the time (or to any other assassination researchers that I'm aware of). He turns out to have been a deep-cover contract operative for the CIA and U.S. drug enforcement agencies. It's my understanding that the datebook, or desk diary, was kept secret by Lafitte's family after his death, until author Hank Albarelli was granted access and ultimately given permission to use certain information from the datebook under terms and conditions.

Let me here offer my insights into some of the names and dates in the datebook, and their potential significance in revealing the identities of the perpetrators behind what's been called "the crime of the century." I should add that the datebook also contains references to individuals whose names have not appeared before in assassination-related documents. From the datebook, it can only be concluded that Lafitte was directly involved with a number of people covertly connected to the assassination.

SOUETRE: This clearly is Jean Rene Souetre, whose name appears in a number of entries between April 25 and December 4. It appears that Souetre was part of a "kill squad" who showed up for meetings in New Orleans, Madrid, and Mexico City prior to the assassination. Souetre's name first appeared in the "assassination literature" following a 1977 release of CIA documents, which stated that "he had been expelled from the U.S. at Fort Worth or Dallas 48 hours after the assassination . . . to either Mexico or Canada." According to what the FBI told a Souetre acquaintance whom I interviewed, he'd been "flown out that afternoon by a private pilot . . . in a government plane." Souetre was a known hitman for the OAS, a terrorist group in France that had targeted President de Gaulle.

WILLOUGHBY: Until my first book came out in 1992, assembling circumstantial evidence linking retired General Charles Willoughby as a possible "mastermind" of the assassination, no one had raised such a possibility before. The datebook cites the far-right General Willoughby numerous times, specifying: "Nov 22 – Willoughby backup – team [with a strikethrough of the word team] squad – tech building – phone booth/bridge." Prior to that, an April 12 entry states: "Willoughby soldier kill squads."

SILVERTHORNE: That same datebook entry says: "Silverthorne – Ft. Worth – Airport – Mexico." The name of Silverthorne did not appear publicly until the late 1970s, when CIA officer William Harvey's handwritten notes about the agency's QJ/WIN assassination program were released. Silverthorne was a pilot who traveled "for a certain federal agency" to "countless countries" for "reasons best left unsaid," according to author Albarelli's 1996 interview with him.

ANGLETON: Listed in the datebook by his last name as well as initials (JA and JJA), the then-head of Counterintelligence for the CIA appears to have been involved in "high-level gathering in DC" during which "Lancelot planning" was discussed. The Lancelot reference is to a plot to kill JFK. The datebook's final mention of James Angleton (December 5, 1963) states: "JA – CLOSE OUT LANCELOT." Angleton's name was not generally known until the mid-1970s, when he was forced out of the CIA following revelations that he'd organized an illegal domestic spying program.

GEORGE W.: The several references in the datebook including one (August 29) regarding "shipment of LSD for New Orleans & Dallas – Texas laws?" are clearly referencing George White. He was a key operative in the CIA's top-secret MKULTRA program to control human behavior using drugs, hypnosis, and other means. He worked undercover for the same narcotics agency as Lafitte. White's name never came to light until 1977 during a congressional investigation.

TOM D.: Also referred to in several entries, this was Thomas Eli Davis, Jr., first mentioned in 1978 in the assassination literature as having trained anti-Castro Cubans and had been acquainted with Jack Ruby. The September 27 entry about Mexico City says: "Oswald – Comercio Hotel – meet with Tom D. at Luma." It was stated by the Warren Commission that Oswald had been to the Comercio; the Hotel Luma was first mentioned in my 1992 book as a meeting point. The September 29 datebook implies ("Tom at embassy – done") that Davis, who resembled Oswald, had impersonated him in visiting either the Cuban or Russian embassies in Mexico City.

CRICHTON: The name of Jack Crichton, who was connected to Military Intelligence and arranged the first translators for Marina Oswald after the assassination, appears several times in datebook entries in advance of the assassination.

A. L. EHRMAN: This July 30 entry clearly refers to Anita L. Ehrman, a foreign correspondent whose body was found that day in her Washington apartment. The only other reference to this appears in my 1992 book, citing a notebook seized from Richard Case Nagell by the FBI on September 20, 1963, but not released until 1975. That entry says: "ANITA L. EHRMAN. 7-30-63 WASHINGTON, D.C." Nagell was involved with Oswald in an assassination plot.

I believe that this datebook fills in many gaps about what really happened on November 22, 1963, and in the months leading up to it. This will be particularly evident to students of the assassination.

- There was a high-level conspiracy to assassinate President Kennedy involving meetings in and officials from Washington, D.C., as well as in other parts of the U.S., Mexico City, and Madrid.
- That Lee Harvey Oswald was just as he claimed after his arrest—a patsy set up to take the fall ("October 25: Oswald set in place," meaning that he was set in place in the Texas School Book Depository building; November 9: "On the wings of murder. The Pigeon way for unsuspecting Lee").

- That Oswald's rifle was apparently planted ahead of time ("November 20: rifle into building – yes/ok/DPD"; DPD stands for Dallas Police Department).
- That the shooting of police officer J. D. Tippitt after the assassination was apparently not part of anyone's plan: November 22: "O Tippett [*sic*] (why?) – ask JA who is Tippet?"
- That Jack Ruby did not metamorphose out of nowhere to kill Oswald. The name "Ruby" appears in June 7 and October 30 entries.
- That a cover-up was in place prior to the assassination that included a legal team (Robert Storey and Judge Duvall) as well as a translator for Marina Oswald.
- That a Dallas airport previously speculated as a rendezvous point for escaping assassins was listed in the datebook on November 24: "Red [Bird] Airport."
- That the plan involving Oswald was in place for some time. On September 16: "T. says L.O. is 'idiot' but w[ill] be used regardless. Set-up Complete." On October 5, JFK's visit to Dallas was announced in the press. The next day, the datebook says: "Oswald – issue (!). Check with Caretaker." On October 16, Oswald went to work at the Book Depository.
- That there are references to Oswald traveling to Mexico City in late September. Some have questioned whether he actually went there. The datebook indicates that he assuredly did, but also that Tommy Davis was there simultaneously.
- That prior to this, apparently Oswald was being shadowed in New Orleans: "May 10: T. says tail LO – No direct contact." Oswald had moved to New Orleans on April 24.
- That the name of WALKER appears more than once, initially concerning the shooting attempt on his life that Oswald was later accused of: "April 7 – Walker – Lee and pictures. Planned soon – can he do it? Won't." (It's possible that the word is *Wait*.) The indication is, someone was setting up Oswald to do this, but he didn't want to. The shot was fired at Walker on April 10. Later references indicate that General Walker was in fact aware of, if not in on, the plot to kill JFK:
- That other extreme right-wingers are notated at different times: Mitch WerBell, a known arms dealer; Otto Skorzeny, ex-Hitler operative living in Madrid; Willoughby compatriot Pedro del Valle.

- That two mentions of SHAW, in connection with New Orleans, most likely refer to Clay Shaw, named by Jim Garrison as a coconspirator in 1967.

In summary, it is possible from this datebook to piece together many things about the assassination that could be merely educated guesses until now. I believe, presuming the datebook is verified as having been written by Lafitte in 1963, that this constitutes probably the strongest evidence that has ever come to light of a conspiracy to kill President Kennedy.

INTRODUCTION
BY H. P. ALBARELLI JR.

For a little over ten years, from 1997 to 2008, I investigated the strange death of US Army biochemist Dr. Frank Rudolph Olson. My intense, obsessive inquiry into Olson's death resulted in a book that, in no small part, relied on the letters and datebooks of infamous and legendary United States Federal Bureau of Narcotics agent and CIA contractor George Hunter White. Through my exploitation of White's personal papers and datebooks, I also became extremely aware of the existence and importance of an obscure and fascinating character, Jean Pierre Lafitte.

Pierre Lafitte, as he preferred to be called, worked very closely with George White during the mystery-filled days of the Bedford Street CIA safe house in New York City's Greenwich Village. Later, during the 1960s and 1970s, Lafitte worked mostly on his own as a CIA contractor, hand-picked by Agency Counterintelligence chief James Jesus Angleton, and sometimes as an INS and FBI asset, engaged in cryptic projects worldwide. The enigmatic, shape-shifting Lafitte would appear in unexpected places: Europe, the Belgian Congo, South Africa, Latin America, Cuba, Mexico City, Canada, rural Maine, Las Vegas, and other locations. Lafitte's work for the federal government always appeared most intriguing, but difficult to decipher. Lafitte was a master impersonator, infiltrator, investigator, and conman. It has become near-commonplace today to refer to notoriously elusive characters as "ghost-like," but the term applies to nobody better than Jean Pierre Lafitte. My fascination with Lafitte exceeded the bounds of deep interest.

Amid my research on the book about Frank Olson's murder, I was summoned to New York City to meet with investigators for the doyen of American district attorneys, Robert Morgenthau. There, I had a day-long discussion about the Olson case with Morgenthau's Assistant District Attorneys Steve Sarocco and Dan Bibb.

During our meeting, I related that I had discovered evidence of an ultrasecret agreement between the US Department of Justice (DOJ) and Allen Dulles's

xvi   Coup in Dallas

CIA. The secret agreement, consummated in 1954, granted legal immunity to any qualified CIA employee, operative or agent, who committed a capital crime, including murder, while working on Agency operations.

To say the least, I was stunned that such an agreement existed, as were Sarocco and Bibb, who moved to confirm the agreement's existence on their own. The implications of the agreement on Frank Olson's death were astounding, but now, working on a book dealing with the assassination of President John F. Kennedy, I was left to seriously contemplate the possibility that if the CIA had directly participated in JFK's murder, or any murder, that possibly meant the Agency's personnel carrying out the murder could be granted immunity from prosecution. I discussed this with my friend attorney Steve Rosen, and we went back and reviewed the details of the secret agreement and found that in the absence of any official revocation of the agreement, this immunity could indeed be the case. I wasn't the first to raise this issue.

In July 1975, United States Congresswoman Bella S. Abzug, a fiery Democrat representing New York, took part in a special Congressional hearing to investigate, in part, this DOJ-CIA hidden agreement. Said Congresswoman Abzug to hearing witness CIA General Counsel Lawrence Houston: "In other words, this [secret agreement] in your judgment gave authority to the CIA to make decisions to give immunity to individuals who happened to work for the CIA for all kinds of crimes, including possible murder."

CIA attorney Houston craftily replied: "It was not designed to give immunity to individuals. It was designed to protect operations or information of the Agency, which [is] highly sensitive."

Abzug easily saw through Houston's duplicity and persisted, asking again if in fact the agreement—which some officials at the CIA today claim is still in effect, having never been revoked—had the effect of granting immunity to CIA employees who commit murder.

Answered CIA attorney Houston: "In effect it does."

Before I completed my book on Frank Olson's murder, I had the opportunity to meet the one person who was quite close to Lafitte, his wife. I had been informed by a highly respected journalist for the *New York Times*, John Crewdson, that Lafitte had been living in a small town in New England for at least twelve years. By chance, I had relatives in a nearby town, and I turned to them for help in locating Lafitte. As it turned out, he was living openly with his wife. Understandably, I traveled as quickly as possible to the place where they resided, which was quite easy because I was still living in Vermont, where I'd gone to write the Olson book. Of course, I shared the location and address with the DA's office in Manhattan but ventured there on my own.

I was too late to find Pierre. He had passed away before my arrival. But, as said, I had the opportunity to meet his wife, Rene. Our meeting was a cautious one, but I felt that by being honest about my interests and objectives, an initial bond of friendship was formed. That bond grew steadily stronger through the time when Rene relocated to the Miami, Florida, area. As far as I know, nobody from the Manhattan District Attorney's office ever made the same trip I did.

Through additional meetings with Rene, I became aware that Pierre, like George White, had kept datebooks within which he would jot down certain things, often specific to matters he was working on at the time. It was a practice that was expressly forbidden by the CIA, but Pierre and George were notorious for bending and breaking the rules. Said Rene, "He would sometimes emulate George, mainly for financial reasons, not out of any admiration or the like."

As I'm sure you can imagine, I was especially interested in viewing and reading Lafitte's personal writings. I respectfully made my interest known to Rene. She had agreed after thinking about it for what seemed a painfully long time. About two weeks later, she called again and said that she had become concerned about certain findings in Pierre's materials and that she now wanted to talk with "her family's attorney" about her concerns and liability issues. Oh, Lord, I thought, an attorney: that will surely mess everything up. But, perhaps thanks to the alignment of the stars, Rene called about a week later with good news.

I had learned through my Olson research that Pierre and his family lived in New Orleans during the 1960s and that Pierre had been briefly employed by the William Reily Coffee Company, where alleged JFK assassin Lee Harvey Oswald had also briefly worked in May and June 1963. I had been warned several times by writer Peter Janney, and other close friends who were also writers, to stay clear of the Kennedy assassination. "It's a black hole that draws you in deeper and deeper, until you cannot extract yourself," said Janney. He was right. But that's another story that can be discussed at another time.

What is important here is that I eventually gained conditional access to several of Lafitte's datebooks and a precious handful of his letters. I would guess that you can imagine my surprise when I was able to make out Lee Harvey Oswald's name in the 1963 datebook. Over a short period, I found other names connected to Oswald's. Some identified only by initials: "O," "OS," "JA," and "T." To make a long and convoluted story short, I was able to study Lafitte's 1963 datebook. And as expected, although for entirely different reasons from my initial expectations, it was remarkable for its contents. Perhaps "remarkable" is not a strong enough word.

There, in a worn, but well-preserved, leather-bound datebook, was a stunning parade of names: Angleton, Oswald, Joannides, Labadie, Martin—some under aliases, some coded, some not, some as bold as day, others scribbled in a hurried or tired hand, some of which I had no idea about, or even a clue as to who they were. Occasionally, I depended on expert assassination researchers like Steve Rosen, Malcolm Blunt, Dick Russell, and Stuart Wexler, and my cowriters Leslie Sharp and Alan Kent, to identify but a handful and for making sense of certain entries. At the start, I was nearly completely unfamiliar with the names R. G. Storey, Charles Willoughby, and Ilse Skorzeny. Through the datebook, the story of Lafitte's involvement in the events of 1963 rolled out page by page. As hopefully will become clear to readers of this book, Lafitte played what, no doubt, was a crucial role in the assassination of President John F. Kennedy.

One thing, however, should be made clear: I, as the author of this book, do not own any of Lafitte's datebooks or letters. Fortunately, I have been granted the right to reproduce certain selections from the 1963 datebook. But there are contents in those datebooks that the Lafitte family does not want published. Rene Lafitte was adamant about this and would not agree to anything else. It took considerable effort to convince her and others that I be allowed to reproduce her insightful comment about JFK's death recorded in a November 23, 1963, entry: "Rene says, coup de grâce."

Rene was a beautiful, petite woman who remarkably resembled actor Geneviève Bujold. Indeed, she was a former and successful fashion model. She was from a prominent French family and had been well educated in France, England, and Brussels. She spoke and moved with an unearthly grace. She told me, "I fell hopelessly in love with Pierre from the moment I met him. He [radiated] mystery and grace, at the same time. His eyes always sparkled with joy and adventure. His smile conveyed that he understood more about the mysteries of life than anyone. The French say, '*L'amour est l'emblème de l'éternité, il confond toute la notion du temps, efface toute la mémoire d'un commencement, toute la crainte d'une extrémité.*'"

Rene explained: "I'm sharing parts of the datebooks with you because [there's] a story that should be told. Pierre did many things in his life, inexplicable things, things I didn't understand but always trusted him to know that they were wise and well chosen. The story of President Kennedy's death may be one of those stories."

Significantly, Rene was not only well aware of Pierre's entries in his datebooks—and in a few cases helped early on in deciphering his handwriting because, as she explained, Pierre had had a "mild stroke" in 1962 that affected his handwriting, which she said at one time was "near beautiful"—but in many cases, she lived alongside Pierre during the instances he wrote about. Rene clearly remembered Otto Skorzeny: "He was imposing; his presence dominated a room, any room." Ilse Skorzeny: "She was all business. Maybe the woman behind the man, meaning the brains." Lee Harvey Oswald: "I only saw him a few times. Pierre didn't care for him. A confused young man. Pierre always said: 'He's always *déséquilibré*.'" Marina Oswald: "We felt sorry for her. She had no idea what was going on. He seemed to stick to her like glue but shared nothing with her." Jean Souetre: "Oh, he was very handsome, but a modest person, and very serious about his beliefs." Thomas Eli Davis, Jr.: "You couldn't help but like him." Charles Willoughby: "A dedicated soldier. A little too dedicated, with a sky-is-falling mindset."

When I first received an email message out of the blue from Ralph Ganis in North Carolina, I was skeptical, but intrigued. Ralph explained that he had exclusive papers that were "incredibly connected to JFK's murder." Ralph asked me about the chapter on Thomas Eli Davis, Jr. he had read in a book I had written, *A Secret Order*. The book had been my first book-length foray into the JFK assassination. I had been fascinated by what I learned about Thomas Eli Davis, Jr. I instinctively knew there was far more to Davis's story and that it was closely connected to the events of Dallas, November 22, 1963. I was also fascinated with certain events in Mexico City concerning Lee Harvey Oswald: a well-known poet and author Elena Garro, and her daughter; Warren Broglie at the Hotel Luma and its cast of unsavory characters, seemingly right out of a Humphrey Bogart film; Charles William Thomas, CIA and State Department employee; and, last but far from least, CIA Mexico City asset, Viola June Cobb, with whom I became a very good friend. In fact, June is the godmother of my grandson, Dylan Jackson Albarelli Centellas. June helped Dylan learn his ABCs and to count past one hundred. [Here in the interest of full disclosure, I should also state that my mother's family was quite close to Robert C. Hill, former ambassador to Mexico, Spain, El Salvador, and several other South American countries. Robert's brother, Richard "Uncle Dick" Hill, was a renowned veterinarian in New Hampshire. A wonderful man.]

At the time that Ralph contacted me, I had read Dick Russell's book, *The Man Who Knew Too Much*, at least four times, marking it up so much that I had to buy two additional copies. From Russell's amazing research and work, combined with what I had discovered at this juncture, I knew we were tantalizingly close to uncovering the real story behind the assassination, but I wasn't the least confident, nor did I feel like we were wading into hubris. Nonetheless, during my first few conversations with Ralph, I didn't mention anything about what I had learned from Lafitte's datebooks and from my hundreds of hours talking to and interviewing June Cobb.

When Ralph Ganis and I eventually met in North Carolina, where I would soon move for two years to work on this book, he allowed me access to his Otto Skorzeny archives. There were thousands of pages. I spent over a week at his home carefully reviewing and reading through several hundred documents. We stayed up late into the night discussing the secrets these papers held. We wallpapered several rooms of Ralph's house with link-analysis charts that, within days, resembled the assiduous maps created by artist Mark Lombardi. Stepping back and viewing these graphic displays of previously unknown global networks, we could clearly see that the narrative they spelled out was a virtual game changer that could provide a real accounting of who had killed President John F. Kennedy and explain the rationale, as well as exposing a huge and sophisticated cabal that controlled many of the world's events.

In a renewed discussion with Ralph about Thomas Eli Davis, Jr. and arms trafficker Victor Oswald, two intriguing characters in the JFK assassination, I revealed the existence of Lafitte's datebooks to Ralph. I told him what the 1963 datebook had to say about Davis, and many other subjects directly related to the JFK assassination. I explained to him how difficult it had been to gain access to the datebook and the applicable terms and conditions, and we decided that we would negotiate for further use of the datebook. I believe it was at this moment that we fully realized the actual dimensions and importance of the story that lay before us. It was exhilarating and frightening at once. I began writing a few days later.

Eventually, out of the blue, Ralph decided it was better that only he alone write a book about Otto Skorzeny. It was a setback timewise, but the book you have before you exclusively gives all the answers one may have about who killed JFK. I should say here that our [Albarelli, Sharp, Kent] approach to the Kennedy assassination may differ greatly from that of other serious researchers and writers. Our motive for writing this book did not turn on hubris, achieving grand recognition, or hero worship of President Kennedy. As with my book on Frank Olson, our motive was simply to present facts related to solving what was a long-seated mystery. We are quite aware of the contentiousness at play in tackling subjects widely regarded as "conspiracy theories."

I am also quite cognizant of the rules of what has become a sort of JFK assassination parlor game. We are not members of the perceived elite group of writers who have staked out the assassination as their exclusive terra ferma. We have no axe to grind politically. We worship at no politician's altar. We respect JFK as a man and admire his foresight and caring for the less unfortunate and, like many before us, recognize that he played an extremely dangerous game in regard to his sexual antics and womanizing. We condemn JFK for nothing.

This book is complex in places and presents many heretofore completely unknown, or unfamiliar, names and entities to the assassination annals. It is based solely on fact. We made a concerted effort not to speculate on anything unless completely unavoidable. Wherever possible, we relied on primary sources or secondary sources that also relied solely on primary sources. Wherever possible, we avoided quoting from books that are widely perceived as speculative and biased in composition. Whenever and wherever possible, we interviewed primary human sources, and, in a few cases, we had to mask true identities.

Last, I would like to recount a visit I made to Skyhorse Publishing's New York building in early March 2017. I had walked across Manhattan in the rain with my grandson Dylan and attorney Steve Rosen to meet with Skyhorse executives Tony Lyons and Hector Carosso. Once there, then-five-year-old Dylan sat with me in Tony's modest office looking fascinated at the many books that filled a wall. Scanning each title, Dylan soon focused on one that he asked to look at. It was *The Plot to Seize the White House* by Jules Archer. I handed him one of the several copies of the book from the shelf. He sat studying the cover, which graphically displayed a dollar sign and swastika, and the subtitle: *The Shocking TRUE Story of the Conspiracy to Overthrow FDR.*

Dylan had been quietly listening to our conversation about my book on Otto Skorzeny and the JFK assassination. He had also listened attentively to Tony's taped replaying of President Kennedy's famous March 27, 1961, speech on secret societies. After a moment, Dylan leaned over toward me and, pointing at the Archer book cover, whispered a question: "So, the same thing happened in your book?"

—H. P. Albarelli Jr.

A ROADMAP

Coup in Dallas is not a "whodunit" in the traditional sense. Investigative journalist H. P. Albarelli Jr. was not in active pursuit of the identities of those who actually fired the shots that took the life of President John F. Kennedy. Yes, the explosive new source material that Albarelli was granted exclusive access to includes the names of skilled assassins recruited to kill JFK in Dealey Plaza that Friday in November 1963. But his original pursuit was the more decisive investigation into who was behind the coup d'état—forces direct and indirect—which was by definition the overthrow of a democratic elected government that took place in the fertile anti-Kennedy landscape of Dallas, Texas.

Esteemed historians have argued that November 22 was a "systemic adjustment" more than a coup. Albarelli makes the case that the assassination was indeed a coup d'état by demonstrating that among the planners and perpetrators were mutinous elements within US intelligence, military ranks, and industry who held immense power and influence sufficient to overturn the democratic election of John F. Kennedy and get away with it. He presents persuasive evidence—much of it ignored or misunderstood previously—to prove that the assassination cabal, including holdovers from Hitler's Third Reich and Texas-based powers, passed deadly judgment on Kennedy's platform, which at its core was a commitment to full democracy on a global scale.

Toward the end of his life, Albarelli was reexamining the controversial question of *why* President Kennedy had to be removed permanently and in such a spectacular fashion, only to conclude that the answer is indistinguishable from, and indelibly merged with, the answers to *who* conspired, *who* approved, *who* strategized, *who* executed, and *who* orchestrated the cover-up. Yes, Albarelli had acquired evidence that a salacious political scandal had been staged in the summer of 1963 to expose Kennedy's reckless conduct and serve as the excuse for many in the highest echelon of US military, government, and industry to concede that he had to go, soon. However, he argues that the deep-rooted justification—the *why* of his assassination—was cumulative, and prioritized depending on which camp of historians or theorists one consulted. Arguments that have stood the test of time include: revenge for Kennedy's failure at the Bay of Pigs, his attempt at détente with the leader of Communist Soviet Union, his announced intention to incrementally withdraw US personnel from Vietnam, his aggressive pursuit of corporate monopolies and reversal of his initial position on the oil depletion allowance, his March 1963 commitment to deter Israel's nuclear program, the significant steps to end segregation, and his administration's increasingly hard line on organized crime. The official record of the rationale behind the assassination, including the lone assassin argument, seemed to Albarelli to be severely fragmented, often contradictory, and thus in much need of a more holistic approach.

Only an all-encompassing ideological remit of those who were involved, directly and indirectly, could effectively explain the motivation of the plot, the approval, the execution, and the cover-up. Although the concept remains controversial in some quarters—*how could so many be involved, or stand by as the coup unfolded?*—during Albarelli's investigation an inescapable conclusion emerged: *these individuals and the causes they served had been ideologically aligned since WWII and in ways that collectively compelled them to regard JFK's removal as both necessary and inevitable.* Further, Albarelli argues that those interests and organizations operated in tandem with the development and dramatic expansion of US intelligence, while cloaking themselves in nationalist movements, and in distorted religiosity on a global scale to disguise their true aims.

With that in mind, readers should anticipate they will encounter literally dozens of names and entities, many of them obscure, that were responsible for weaving what Albarelli's indispensable editor for this book, Hector Carosso, described as a tangle of spiderwebs that spanned two decades in the lead-up to the murder of the president in Dallas on November 22, 1963.

CHAPTER 1: WWII, SPECIAL OPS, AND ASSASSINATIONS

Author Albarelli deftly opens this book with the 1942 political assassination of WWII Vichy France's de facto prime minister, Admiral François Darlan. His murder assuredly involved personnel from America's Office of Strategic Services. As the war in Europe had escalated, the OSS, headed by General William J. Donovan, had assumed a role previously filled by the office of Coordinator of Information, the nation's first peacetime nondepartmental intelligence organization. Melding tactics derived from a French terrorist group known as La Cagoule, or "the Hooded Ones," with the expertise of operatives from Gen. Donovan's OSS, Admiral Darlan was vanquished in an operation in which a vulnerable young man, Fernand Bonnier de la Chapelle, was designated the patsy who was meant to be captured and then abandoned. Albarelli astutely draws parallels between the setup of de la Chapelle and that of Lee Harvey Oswald in the murder of President Kennedy in Dallas two decades later.

The readers learn that La Cagoule, a secret Roman Catholic, anticommunist, anti-Semitic French fascist organization intent on employing terrorism as a form of intimidation, engaged in heroin trafficking and marketeering until Hitler's invasion of Poland. Those same elements then organized the French version of his Gestapo, The Malice, whose support of the invaders tormented Vichy France for a half decade. After Hitler's defeat and the liberation of Paris, General Charles de Gaulle ordered the execution of its leader, marking the beginning of what would escalate into a virulent animus toward the French president that persisted through de Gaulle's own dangerous fall of 1963.

The details of this history may seem irrelevant to the assassination of Kennedy until Albarelli introduces the SS officer exiled in Madrid, Otto Skorzeny, best known as the mastermind behind the rescue of Italy's fascist dictator Benito Mussolini, a feat that established his bona fides as a brilliant tactician. It is Skorzeny who provides a critical link in the chain of events from fascist Europe of the 1930s and 1940s to the racist, anti-Semitic politics that permeated Texas well into in the early 1960s. Confirmed in a series of letters sent from a Parisian amateur detective to FBI Director J. Edgar Hoover, in which he identified facts that were not yet in the public domain at the time of his writing, "only the former director of the CIA, Allen Dulles could clear Otto Skorzeny of his critical role in the assassination."

We also meet a stateless character using the alias Jean Pierre Lafitte, who served alongside a near-psychopathic killer, one of Skorzeny's prized postwar trainers at his camp outside Madrid. Both men would end up in Dallas on November 22, 1963. Lafitte's previously inaccessible and remarkable records further elucidate those connections by introducing us to the Secret Organization of National Revolutionary Action (OSARN), closely aligned with both Hitler and Mussolini, with a singular stated agenda: "We want to build a new Europe in cooperation with national socialist Germany and all other European nations freed from liberal capitalism, Judaism, Bolshevism and French Masons . . . to regenerate France and the French race . . . to ensure that Jews who stay in France are subject to harsh laws, preventing them from infesting our race. . . ."

Returning to the aftermath of the murder of Admiral Darlan, we begin to understand how murder and mayhem infected US policy. OSS head Bill Donovan continued to seriously explore their use within his Division 19, which encompassed "assassination and elimination" programs as an extension of national security policy. As noted in a 1949 memorandum archived at the CIA (OSS's successor): "Let's get into the technology of assassination, figure most effective ways to kill. . . ."

CHAPTER 2: HOLDING COMPANIES, INTEL OPS, AND THE COLD WAR

Appreciating the path of development and expansion of US intelligence, operating in tandem with corporate interests and organizations, is key to understanding this investigation into the murder of President Kennedy. Readers are encouraged to persist as the web of names of individuals and entities, clandestine and legitimate, unfold—being assured that as the book progresses, their collective impact will be revealed.

Gen. Bill Donovan's evolution from the postwar dissolution of the OSS to the creation of the World Commerce Corporation extended his personal commitment to national security *at all costs* throughout the Cold War. A brainchild shared with a former OSS agent and Manhattan-based international corporate lawyer Allen Dulles, and with Britain's infamous intelligence expert William Stephenson, the WCC was a multitiered conglomerate made up of hundreds of international front companies and lawful private corporations collaborating with the government/military/intelligence apparatus to protect and advance interests around the world that might otherwise be vulnerable to mass revolt against predatory capitalism. While Donovan was operating the WCC, the Central Intelligence Agency, successor organization to his OSS, had taken up where "Wild Bill" left off and quickly adapted the deadly urgent mindset of World War II to manipulate the Cold War. Allen Dulles would soon head the CIA.

As the WCC built an effective, privatized global spy network, at the same time benefiting financially, even more sinister elements within US intelligence were in play, including cooperation with a highly secret criminal cabal, the Corsican Brotherhood, that played both sides during the Cold War. We also encounter names familiar to assassination researchers like Conein, Harvey, Shackley, Hunt, and Pash; and we first meet the elusive character Jean Rene Souetre, whose role in the ultraright dissident paramilitary group Organisation Armée Secrète (OAS) during the Algerian War takes center stage as we approach the 1960s. Albarelli also offers a fresh look at aspects of New Orleans District Attorney Jim Garrison's investigation into Clay Laverne Shaw and a virtually impenetrable organization at the time, Permindex, a godchild of the WCC with ties to French politician Jacques Soustelle's OAS and close personal connections between "Hitler's banker" and "Hitler's favorite commando."

It's a complex read, but without this framework, the investigation would remain stalled in the vacuum of the alleged personal agenda of one young (allegedly) procommunist agitator who was sympathetic to a Cuban revolutionary, or worse, stuck in the accumulation of decades of competing and contradictory conspiracy theories.

CHAPTER 3: THE PROJECT MANAGER AND THE PATRON

During his lengthy investigation of the 1953 death of CIA research scientist Frank Olson, which culminated in his 2009 book *A Terrible Mistake: The Murder of Frank Olson and the CIA's Secret Cold War Experiments*, Albarelli discovered a treasure trove of information in the diary and letters of Federal Bureau of Narcotics agent and CIA contractor George Hunter White. Through White's papers, Albarelli became aware of the importance of operative Pierre Lafitte, who was the "special employee" of White during the Greenwich Village LSD-laced adventures that White ran as a part of the CIA's MKULTRA program. Both White and Lafitte defied agency protocol and maintained personal records of their exploits, confident that the norms did not apply to those involved in their level of operations. Those private papers were roadmaps for Albarelli's investigation.

Lafitte, who resided with his family in New Orleans in 1963 under the name Jean Martin, was far more than a sidekick to White. He had been an actual FBN employee during the Cold War, serving the CIA and FBI during his long and bizarre career. By 1952, Lafitte was of such value that he was soon meeting with some of the CIA's top officials, developing personal friendships along the way, including that with CIA head of Counterintelligence James Angleton, who would become his patron, a relationship that would have dire consequences for John Kennedy and America in 1963.

Over the years, Lafitte was able to skillfully juggle his contact with White and others within Angleton's circles at the CIA, including his protégé Tracy Barnes, who warrants an entire essay as presented in the Appendix of this book; the notorious CIA officer William King Harvey; and organized crime members including Meyer Lansky and Santo Trafficante, Jr. This combined history compelled Albarelli to advance his investigations to events in Dallas.

Readers learn more about figures familiar to Lafitte since the war, including Jean Souetre, who was one of Otto Skorzeny's prized marksman and postwar trainer in the arts of sabotage, explosives, and assassinations. By the early 1960s, the former French Air Force Captain Souetre had joined the OAS in bitter opposition to President de Gaulle's position on Algeria, a North African country defined by *Time* magazine in its October 18, 1963, issue as "The Cuba of Africa." And we learn that October 18 happened also to be a date critical to the assassination plot. An example of the significance of timing, a prominent feature in the analysis of the exclusive material secured by Albarelli, it was only ten days later that former CIA director Allen Dulles was in Dallas, Texas, alerting his audience to the geopolitical threat posed by the fall of Algeria to the Algerians.

CHAPTER 4: SUICIDES AND CALL GIRLS

Albarelli next applies his unique method of inquiry by changing course from the broad milieu of individuals and constructs that led to the coup, to concentrate on the implications of that salacious scandal unfolding in the months before the assassination.

Speculation of Kennedy's alleged proclivity for extramarital sexual liaisons with beautiful and oftentimes interesting women had become a D.C. parlor game. His history of what many charged were reckless encounters provided the strategists a perfect and obvious opportunity for exploitation. Most recently, Ellen Rometsch, a beautiful femme fatale from East Germany known to Pierre Lafitte as "Ella," had been introduced to the president of the United States in late spring of 1963. It is apparent that Lafitte was at the very least privy to specific dates and a degree of detail of the circumstances of her time in the US with the president. We pursue the evidence that as early as June 16, Ella was on Lafitte's mind and that within a few weeks, he was aware of her imminent deportation, the timing of which coincides with intelligence reports that indicate Ellen Rometsch had become a problem for the Kennedy administration.

Across the Pond, another scandal with similar potentially devastating repercussions for Western intelligence was unfolding in London involving women a young Jack Kennedy had bedded, as well. Among elements within archconservative America, the sex-and-security scandals embodied an "excuse" to remove the president. By late October 1963, a credible exposé of Kennedy's sexual encounter with the alleged Communist spy fueled the righteous indignation of the far right. More deadly was the reaction of certain high-level officials within the military-industrial complex who were finally provided the rationale for a radical solution that might include permanent, lethal action.

Albarelli's coverage of the impact of the scandal also includes the high-profile and highly suspicious suicides of two prominent members of JFK's inner circle—including a renowned newsman and a former US ambassador—both of whom appear amidst Lafitte's numerous notebook entries. Lafitte is obviously well informed of aspects of Kennedy's personal world.

CHAPTER 5: JACKS-OF-ALL-TRADES

A week or so after the news of Ella Rometsch as *Communist seductress* broke, another distinctive character in this investigation had flown to Madrid to engage directly with Otto Skorzeny and his business associates. Thomas Eli Davis III or, as he preferred, Tom Jr., one of several somewhat obscure characters, played a complex role in this saga and is best described as one of the "Jacks-of-All-Trades" in the investigation. Albarelli compares Davis with other programmed intelligence assets he had researched for several decades.

By the spring and summer of 1963, Davis was engaging in numerous new adventures that align with the records of Lafitte, including one related to a Dallas mobster close to Jack Ruby and another tied to the head of French intelligence. The purpose of the Davis couple's early November trip to Madrid, directly related to Dallas and the upcoming assassination, is also revealed.

With Davis as the pivot, along with his wife, who was the daughter of New England bankers closely tied to the oil industry and military contractors, another massive web is unveiled to expose their direct connections with arms manufacturers, arms dealers, gunrunners, and assassination conspirators.

CHAPTER 6: LONG SHADOWS

From Tom Davis, and his ilk, we move to the implications of the shadows cast by so many who were on the periphery of the plot to kill the president. The datebook reveals Lafitte as a multitasker, quite capable of shuffling from one venture to another, all while managing details as the assassination plot began to take shape, including the setup of Lee Oswald. We also meet a figure shrouded in mystery for decades, the self-styled journalist who was imprisoned by Castro. According to Lafitte, the journalist was acquainted with Albert Osborne a.k.a. John Howard Bowen, an itinerant preacher and alleged operator of an assassin training camp who is known to have traveled to Mexico in late September 1963 on the same bus as Lee Oswald. Both men, whom Lafitte records on the same date along with the name Ruby, compel us to consider still another web of intrigue.

This chapter also provides provocative leads to the deeply entrenched propaganda machine whose editors and publishers included former OSS officers, military brass, extreme-right tacticians, and evangelical leaders that coalesce under one common theme: fascist sympathies masked as anticommunism, casting a decades-long shadow over America that culminated in Dealey Plaza.

We begin to recognize that, instead of periodic house cleaning, these spiderwebs had been left to thrive and accumulate in America's political ecosystem long before President Kennedy took office.

CHAPTER 7: THE GENERALS, THE TEAMS, AND THE KILL SQUADS

The shadow of General Douglas MacArthur emerges—not as having been directly involved in the plot to permanently remove Kennedy, nor is he identified by Pierre Lafitte—but as having found cover since the assassination in spite of being a symbol of archconservative anticommunism. We also meet a Marine Corps general who was liaising with elements on the fringes of the most fanatical global political movements, and through him, we meet several vile characters determined to use all means necessary to achieve religious dominance over US politics. These roads, some originating in South Texas, lead to Madrid, Spain, which was a home base for those committed to restoration of the Reich and strategizing the assassination of John Kennedy.

Most prominent among those propagandists identified in Chapter 6 were Generals Charles Willoughby and Edwin Walker, both of whom have long been recognized, even by those less steeped in this research, as prime suspects in the assassination. Further proof is now presented that the two highly controversial retired generals were among those directly responsible for the murder of John Kennedy.

Pierre Lafitte finally lays out for us the timing and the circumstances of the involvement of Willoughby and Walker and leads us to the cast of kill squads and teams known particularly to Willoughby for more than a decade, including two retired colonels who acted under the retired general's orders, who evaded scrutiny for decades.

We learn of a vast and tightly woven web of international organizations on the extreme right, driven primarily by religious ideology aligned with attempts to revive the Reich and disguised by populist political action groups in America like the John Birch Society, which had been advanced by Gen. Walker among the military troops under his command. The reader also gets a better sense of the significance of Willoughby's decades-long relationship with Allen Dulles, who was a former international lawyer for German corporations, the director of the CIA, and a pivotal member of the Warren Commission. Their friendship, and the fact that both had known Otto Skorzeny since the inception of the World

Commerce Corporation, prompted the authors to delve further into their written exchanges during the 1960s.

CHAPTER 8: THE SKORZENYS

Hitler's favorite commando, SS Otto Skorzeny caught the eye of shrewd assassination researcher Mae Brussell as early as the 1980s. For whatever reasons, Brussell's research was dismissed for decades by some of the most esteemed investigators of their day. Even before Albarelli had access to evidence that implicated Skorzeny and his wife, Ilse, he had paid close attention to Brussell's extensive material, including her exposés on the CIA-backed Gehlen Organization and, by extension, SS Otto Skorzeny.

Albarelli also draws from Major Ralph Ganis's *The Skorzeny Papers: Evidence of the Plot to Kill JFK,* which reveals information culled from a portion of Skorzeny's private collection Ganis acquired, some of which confirmed details found in Pierre Lafitte's records. These authors further tracked the history of the Skorzenys' remarkable postwar revival and recalibration, including Ilse's role in the decade-long business endeavors that she and Otto pursued with international real estate developers and with some of the most influential oilmen in Texas.

The reader learns that Ilse, serving as Otto's arms and legs for the logistics and finances underpinning the operation to kill Kennedy, traveled frequently from postwar residences in both Madrid and Co. Kildare, Ireland, to the US during 1963. Her front in intelligence parlance since at least 1957 had been a Manhattan-based international real estate firm that coincidentally opened offices in Dallas in the spring of 1963. From that location, we uncover names of other Dallasites whose collective history further exposes the deep roots of the Skorzenys in Texas.

We read about Ilse's colleague, a former OSS agent, who was a longtime associate of both Bill Donovan and Donovan's head of security at the OSS who was first on the scene to investigate the Amerasia Spy Case. Some historians suspect that the Amerasia scandal was key to the launch of the Cold War. This particular web includes the Tolstoy Foundation, a Dallas petroleum geologist, an air industry titan, and New England ties to Thomas Eli Davis. We also encounter "Hitler's banker," who by the early 1960s was engaged in schemes in the Bahamas that involved Dallas powerbrokers and who appears in Dallas just weeks before the assassination to suggest that financing was in play.

We then dig deep into the reasons that the Skorzeny couple (and fellow Nazis intent on establishing a new base outside of continental Europe) experienced such a warm welcome and a degree of solace in the Republic of Ireland while Otto was being pursued by authorities in Europe. We trace those ideological sympathies to powerful players in the state of Texas, especially those circulating around Dallas.

CHAPTER 9: DALLAS . . . LAY OF THE LAND

Rene Lafitte's reference to Dallas as the "lay of the land," recorded in her husband's datebook, was both literal and metaphorical: the tangible environs and a political climate imbued by virulent anti-Kennedy sentiment. Five of those environs became central to our investigation and provide the framework for the chapter: The Texas School Book Depository and surrounds; the University of Dallas; the Meadows Building; the Oak Plaza Building in Oak Lawn; and the Republic National Bank building, which Albarelli confirms housed an essential branch of the Central Intelligence Agency.

Since the war, the Dallas economy had been propelled by the state's petroleum industry, by military contractors moving into the region, and by concomitant financial and legal sectors. Officials of those businesses, operating beneath the radar in the lead-up to the assassination, had in fact tilled the ideological soil in Dallas for two decades. As with many relatively homogenous cities of its size in the South, Dallas also embodied a fierce resistance to government interference and generally embraced the fundamentalism and fervent anticommunist ideology of the Southern Baptists.

Such a highly charged environment held inherent operational appeal for the CIA, which by law was not allowed to spy or conduct missions within the United States. However, the agency found a way around those prohibitions through collaboration. Of particular interest to our investigation was an organization devoted to assisting refugees of WWII, utilizing agents in Soviet bloc countries to destabilize their governments after the war, and often exfiltrating valued individuals from Iron Curtain countries, many of whom were experts in the area of petroleum engineering and landed in Dallas. With that, we begin to understand Rene Lafitte's other phrase, "oil smooths the way . . ."

Among those Dallas notables implicated by Lafitte was an attorney who served as counsel during the Nuremberg Trials, an oilman who had been a close business colleague of Otto Skorzeny since the early 1950s, and his petroleum industry colleague in those schemes whose role in the assassination, according to a retired colonel interviewed by Albarelli, "had never been fully understood." We believe that has been remedied with this book.

We also meet that Russian-born petroleum expert; a recently retired president of a US military contractor and close friend of Allen Dulles; and the fabled, archconservative eccentric who at the time was designated one of the world's richest men, H. L. Hunt. This entangled cast of characters is archetypal of Dallas as a web of ardent capitalists who sincerely believed that the spread of communism was at their door, and that Kennedy was, at best, ignoring the threats.

CHAPTER 10: D'AFFAIRE KENNEDY

The final chapter of Albarelli's investigation opens with the stonewalling by the French government of an aggressive investigation by D.C. attorney Bernard Fensterwald in the early 1980s pertaining to official US records that "three Frenchmen, one or more of whom may have been in Dallas on November 22, 1963, and who were expelled by the American Government . . . presumably to Mexico . . . the next day. At least two of the three Frenchmen were hardcore OAS veterans, who were capable of all sorts of mayhem, and who had no 'legitimate business' in Dallas on the day of the murder."

The reader comes full circle as the authors pursue the trail of Jean Rene Souetre and his fellow assassins—members of homicidal terrorist groups since WWII and trained under SS Otto Skorzeny—who had joined forces with US intelligence. With a single entry on October 9, 1963, Lafitte also implicates Generals Willoughby and Walker, "kill squads" that included trusted seasoned assassins from Texas, and additional support teams possibly culled from vengeful Cuban exiles and American soldiers of fortune at the Bay of Pigs, all of whom converged in Dallas on November 22, 1963.

Albarelli and his coauthors leave behind speculation of the specifics that took place in the minutes before Kennedy was seen to grab his throat and choose instead to close the chapter hours before this disparate lethal cadre of skilled killers took their respective positions in Dealey Plaza.

EPILOGUE

The investigation concludes in unison with the December entries in Pierre Lafitte's 1963 datebook—with a Russian born, virulent profascist, anticommunist propagandist whose task was to "deal with Marina" Oswald in the immediate aftermath of her husband's murder by mobster Jack Ruby while in Dallas police custody. Within weeks, the writer had received the imprimatur of Allen Dulles, whose ties to the CIA had never been severed, and John Jay McCloy, consigliere to the vast fortunes of one of America's richest families. Both men were holdovers from America's disastrous collaboration with "former" Nazis. Their blessing assured that the Warren Commission would see to it that theories of Oswald's Communist motives would guarantee that the patsy had fulfilled his purpose. Regardless of eventual publication, the propagandist had served to bolster the cover-up of the conspiracy until the commission could report.

The ideology, shared with protofasciast architects of the Cold War, that drove the early phase of the cleanup operation could not be ignored, and it is that history, brought into focus with the chaos of contemporary American politics and the policies of the administration of the 45th president of the United States, that advanced the decisive investigation undertaken by H. P. Albarelli Jr.

ESSAYS

Much of Albarelli's research, as well as that of his cowriters, and the resultant draft manuscripts were "works in progress." Before his untimely passing, we had elevated aspects of this particular investigation from the category of "inconclusive" to "most likely." For that reason, Albarelli and his coauthors decided to present certain research in essay form to indicate that, while there is sufficient justification to share the valuable clues left behind by Pierre Lafitte—along with the rationale behind our deductions—there are lingering questions. The titles of the essays, presented by coauthors Sharp and Kent and guest essayist Anthony Thorne (Australian filmmaker and student of history), are straightforward, and the reader is encouraged to pursue the leads presented and to challenge accordingly.

ORGANIZATIONAL AND CHARACTER MAPS

Albarelli and his coauthor, Sharp, recognized very early on the complexity of presenting literally dozens of personal names and their alliances in narrative form with the attendant challenge for the reader to "keep it all straight." However, it was also untenable to oversimplify the depth and breadth of the forces behind the criminal, violent removal of the elected president. How best, then, could the propinquity of the innermost circles of those behind the assassination plot be depicted? The solution was the character-link analysis, labeled "Organizational Charts and Character Maps," found in the appendix of this book, created by graphics designer Pete Sattler, who grasped the significance of this project at its inception.

PIERRE LAFITTE DATEBOOK—SELECT ENTRIES AND IMAGES

The terms and conditions of access to the exclusive collection of private papers of Pierre Lafitte, including his 1963 datebook, impacted the determination of which screenshots from the datebook could be reproduced for this book. We analyzed the entire collection and determined to prioritize certain of those entries that are highlighted in the narrative. The resulting screenshots, found in Exhibits, should give readers an idea of the challenges in deciphering the handwriting and interpretation of the meaning of the text. The next challenge was to provide readers sufficient images of the surrounding entries—even those that include only a name and a number that are not mentioned in the narrative—to provide context, and to reveal to some extent the day-to-day world of the author of the datebook, the project manager of the assassination, Pierre Lafitte. We hope we have successfully met the challenge.

NOTES

Due to the evolution of this project, which spanned almost a decade, the chapter notes of *Coup* will conform with the format adopted by author H. P. Albarelli Jr. in his major manuscripts, *A Terrible Mistake* and *A Secret Order*. Notes are not numbered through the narrative; they are presented in sequence and/or by relevance, chapter by chapter, at the end of the book. The reader is encouraged to pause periodically and refer to those supplementary notes—some of which are lengthy by standards—and in particular when the primary text indicates that there are levels of understanding of any given area of research that simply could not be woven into the main narrative.

CHAPTER 1
WWII, SPECIAL OPS, AND ASSASSINATIONS

The past is never dead. It's not even past.

—WILLIAM FAULKNER

But more than wild was the man with the wile of Odysseus,
Like the King of Assassins, he welded together
An army of desperate, invisible soldiers
Each as bold as himself in single deeds . . .

—CARLETON S. COON, JUNE 2, 1959

It is still an open question whether an operator in OSS or in CIA
can ever again become a wholly honorable man.
We deserve to go to hell when we die.

—WILLIAM ALFRED EDDY, 1957

On the wings of murder. The pigeon way for unsuspecting Lee.
Clip, clip his wings.
—Lafitte datebook, November 9, 1963

What do France in December 1942, World War II, and the French Resistance—precisely where our story begins—have to do with the assassination of the 35th president of the United States, John F. Kennedy, the event that shattered the American landscape? This chapter will begin to reveal that the roots of our great American tragedy dive deeply into European soil two decades back, at a time when democracies and monarchies hung by mere threads in the face of Nazi Germany's military juggernaut and when all hands and all means were called upon to save the Allies from defeat.

As we shall read, the comrades in this monumental effort produced strange bedfellows and shifting expedient alliances that joined anti-Nazis with French profascist terrorists and gangsters, anticommunists, antimonarchists, and Allied commandos, all of whom exploited the means of assassination to advance their collective and sometimes contradictory ends. It's clear from the outset that this chapter, and the fullness of the book, will not argue that the assassination in Dallas was a new weapon in the arsenal of war and international affairs. Far from it. The beginnings, described here, establish the foundation for what eventually evolved into a complex set of interrelated aims, enterprises, individuals, and methods that ultimately triggered the murder of an American president. The events described in this chapter provided the tip of the spear for what ultimately became a kind of assassination incorporated.

SUMMER PALACE, ALGIERS, ALGERIA, DECEMBER 24, 1942, CHRISTMAS EVE, ABOUT 2:45 P.M.

The dark-haired, thin young man seated in the anteroom shifts about in his chair, nervously running his right hand along the shape of the Colt .45 caliber handgun concealed in his overcoat pocket. In his coat's inner breast pocket, he has $2,000 in US currency, a fake Algerian passport bearing the surname "Mornard," and forged papers, on pilfered stationery, stating that he has an official appointment with a civil servant in the Palace building that afternoon. The young man, dressed in all black, is waiting for the arrival of his target, Admiral François "Jean" Darlan.

* * *

Darlan, a lightning rod for controversy, was born in Nerac, France, in 1881. After graduating from the École Navale in 1902, he enlisted in the French Navy and, driven by a fierce ambition, became a rear admiral by 1929. Less than two years later, Darlan became admiral, in command of all French naval vessels. In 1936, he became chief of the French Navy's general staff and responsible for all French maritime operations worldwide. Historian and prolific author Peter Kross, who has also published respected books related to the assassination of President Kennedy, underscores that Darlan was not only ambitious, but also "an opportunist of the first order, and he showed his true colors shortly after the fall of France in June 1940."

Writes Kross: "With France now in his grasp, [Hitler] appointed Marshal Philippe Pétain as the head of the Vichy government. Pétain was a mere figurehead, doing the bidding of his German masters. Darlan was given wide powers within the Pétain administration, the most important being control of the large French fleet that was still virtually untouched by the war. Later, decisive action by the British Royal Navy crippled elements of the French fleet and assured the Allies that these ships would not fall into German hands."

Kross continues, "When the allies invaded North Africa in 1942, an enraged Hitler canceled the peace accord he had arranged with Vichy in 1940 and took measures to occupy all of France. Darlan believed that the Germans would inevitably win the war and did all he could to keep the Vichy regime in Hitler's good graces. By 1941, Darlan had assumed two new posts: Minister of the Interior and Minister of Defense. It was Vichy policy to support the Germans as much as possible, going so far as to offer them the use of the former French colonies with their strategic locations and vital raw materials. In the United States, the Roosevelt administration received information from the OSS about covert Vichy operations in Central and South America. According to the government website of the Central Intelligence Agency, its forerunner, the Office of Strategic Services (OSS), formerly known as the Office of Coordination of Information established in 1941, "consisted of men and women from many areas and backgrounds—lawyers, historians, bankers, baseball players, actors, and businessmen. Their assignment was to conduct espionage, sabotage, and morale operations against the Axis powers, and conduct in-depth research and analysis on the nation's enemies and their capabilities.'"

Its chief, General William J. Donovan, who had led the 165th Regiment of the US Army during WWI, received reports that Vichy agents were infiltrating the Caribbean island of Martinique, then prowling around the region while the port was being used as a refueling base for German U-boats. For all of Darlan's German sympathies, he drew the line in advance of full cooperation and made contact with the United States in the months leading up to Operation Torch. All his intrigues came once he was designated Pétain's successor on February 10, 1941. Darlan was now playing both ends against the middle in his dealings with the Allies and the Germans. During a visit to French Algeria in October 1941, he ordered his subordinates in the Navy to counter any Allied attack on Dakar, Senegal. At the same time, he contacted the Americans telling them he was prepared to cooperate "when the Torch landings took place."

* * *

The young man shifts nervously in his chair again and then stands and begins to pace the small anteroom. Darlan will be returning from a late lunch any minute now, and the young man's weeks of arduous small arms and evasive techniques training at a secret paramilitary camp will be put to the ultimate test. Two days earlier, the young man told two close friends, who, like him, were members of a small secret group called Hydra: "Darlan is a traitor who must be killed. He must disappear and I, as a member of Hydra, will be the one to make him disappear from this earth."

* * *

But what, if anything, might the just-turned twenty-year-old would-be assassin Fernand Bonnier de la Chapelle have in common with a twenty-four-year-old former US defector who two decades later would be arrested and subsequently charged with the broad-daylight assassination of the president of the United States?

Fernand de la Chapelle, reported to be an ardent monarchist and antifascist, was strongly opposed to the Vichy government and its supporters. Fernand had been a student until recently, dropping out of school to attend the paramilitary camp in Aïn Taya, an outlying area of Algiers graced with beautiful beaches. Aïn Taya camp was operated jointly by Britain's Special Operations Executive (SOE) and the US Office of Strategic Services (OSS). Lee Harvey Oswald exhibits a similar profile of the young ardent idealist when at age sixteen he joins the Civil Air Patrol, a youth auxiliary of the US Air Force, and upon turning seventeen, enlists in the US Marines.

* * *

Fernand belongs to a recently formed, tightly controlled commando unit called Corps Franc d'Afrique. The unit consists of about one hundred men, and its training concentrates on small arms fire, hand-to-hand combat, and escape and evasion. OSS Major Carleton Coon, who the reader will learn had a storied career as a trained anthropologist promulgating racial superiority, directs Fernand's unit. The lead trainer under Coon was French Army Master Sergeant Gilbert Sabatier, thirty-five years old at the time. Sabatier oversees a team of four highly skilled trainers, who concentrate especially on the use of firearms. At Coon's direction, Sabatier issues each of his trainees a Colt .45 caliber automatic pistol.

Fernand again sits in the chair, lights a cigarette, inhales deeply, and stands and paces once more. Through one of several large windows in the room overlooking a palm-tree-lined courtyard, he sees two Palace security officers standing, smoking, and talking to each other.

Christmas Eve, Fernand thinks, is ideal for lax security. Per his plan, he will kill Darlan and then attempt a faux escape during which he will be quickly apprehended, held briefly, and then released. Perhaps I'll become a national hero, Fernand thinks.

Fernand's thoughts are interrupted by the sound of moving tires on the gravel driveway outside. He sees that it's a large, dark sedan, Darlan's aide's car. He's here, Fernand thinks, returning to his chair, sitting on the edge of the seat. He runs his hand again over the gun in his pocket. He's here. He'll be up any minute now, Fernand thinks, and, as if on cue, he sees Admiral Darlan and his chief of staff, Jean Hourcade, come around a dimly lit corridor corner. They are walking down the hallway toward him, approaching the door to the Admiral's office. The two men are talking animatedly and laughing. Fernand stands, grinds his cigarette out on the floor, takes the gun from his coat pocket, and moves toward the two men, who haven't yet noticed him.

Fernand thinks, Should I say something? Should I make a declaration of some sort before firing or as I fire?

As Fernand raises his gun to fire, Darlan sees him and instinctively raises his own arm to protect himself from the coming bullet. Fernand pulls the trigger, and the bullet strikes Darlan in his head. There is a spray of teeth, skin, and blood, and Darlan is pushed back a few feet. He utters a low moan, and Fernand fires again. This time he hits the admiral center in the chest. Darlan crumbles to the floor, blood pumping from his chest wound, and a widening stain quickly overtakes his entire front. Darlan's eyes glaze over, and he never regains consciousness, dying an hour later in the hospital. Fernand turns to flee, but Hourcade is quickly on him, knocking him backward onto the marble floor. Fernand pushes the chief of staff away enough so that he can raise his gun and fire. The round hits Hourcade in his upper thigh and he cries out. Not surprisingly, the gunshots and sounds of human pain attract nearby people to the scene, all of whom come running.

Hourcade is still struggling to restrain Fernand, and the floor is slick with blood. Fernand breaks loose from Hourcade's grip, stands, slips and slides in blood, gains his footing, and bolts for the room's largest window—his planned escape. He smashes the glass with the butt of his pistol, but the window is barred tightly—the metal making it impossible to pass through. A uniformed Spahi cavalryman (Algerian cavalry), who heard the murderous commotion, comes running, throws his arm around Fernand's neck, and yanks him backward, as another security man hoists a chair and smashes Fernand over the head with it. Several hands yank Fernand farther away from the window and pull the gun from his hand. He is pinned to the floor by a heavier man. Another security guard begins to strike Fernand about the head and face. Fernand cries out, "*Tu me tues, tu me tues.*" ["You're killing me. You're killing me."]

Fernand is dragged to his feet, his arms held behind his back. A security guard begins to lead him down the hallway that Darlan had come from. Fernand is quietly sobbing and says, "*Je n'essaie pas de ficher le camp.*" ["I'm not trying to get away."] As he is led by Darlan's motionless body, he says, "*A présent il est mort.*" ["He's gone now."]

* * *

At the police station, Fernand talks to officers of the Algiers judicial police, who surround him. He is remarkably calm now, an air of confidence about him. Here again, we spot a similar reaction once Lee Oswald is brought to police headquarters, Dallas, TX, November 22, 1963. Some observers would later remark that Fernand appeared to be in a trance-like state, but his outward appearance seemed understandable, since he had been beaten about his head and, additionally, was most likely suffering the early manifestations of posttraumatic stress. He confesses to the Algerian officers, "I must tell you that I went every day to the home of Mr. Henri Astier, who was liaison to the Franc Corps. In the Corps, we had formed a hard group of us. We called this group Hydra." Fernand doesn't mention it, but the name "Hydra" was also used at the commando camp for a small elite group of marksmen and snipers. Was Oswald caught up in "hard groups" with similar code names?

Fernand goes on and explains to the police that "Mr. Astier" [Henri d'Astier] and Father Cordier, who lived with Astier, "made me realize what the future would be with Admiral Darlan as head of government."

Explains Fernand, "Gradually, I understood that because of the greatness of Darlan's vision, he would have to be countered by a historical action: his removal . . . his disappearance . . . an act of purification. I was made to understand that the disappearance of Darlan through execution would have to happen on Christmas Eve, 1942. . . . Father Cordier gave me an appointment on the morning of December 24 in his church. I went there, and he said he needed me to confess before acting [to assassinate Darlan]. In the name of Jesus Christ, he had me make my confession. I had barely made the sign of the cross before Father Cordier said, 'Here are the plans of action.' Cordier explained the process I must use to enter Darlan's office and the place where I had to post it. He handed me a large caliber handgun, loaded, and invited me to confess what I was doing, and he gave me absolution." Bonnier also reportedly told police that the $2,000 US found in his overcoat pocket came from Henri d'Astier.

Fernand continues with his confession and states that after Father Cordier gave him absolution, he met up with his "companions," Jean-Bernard d'Astier, Sabatier, and Mario Faivre. Says Fernand: "We were always four." The four young men then drove "to the gates of the Summer Palace." Once they were there, says Fernand, "It was about eleven thirty, early afternoon, when I entered without any difficulty into the place and went to be near Darlan's offices." There, Fernand recalls, "I stared at the spot decided by Father Cordier and then learned that the Admiral would not be there for at least two hours." Fernand went back outside, where his three companions waited, and they drove him to have lunch at the nearby Le Paris restaurant with Henri d'Astier and Father Cordier. Fernand tells police that Cordier spent most of the lunch time encouraging him "not to change his line of conduct."

At "about three o'clock" after lunch, Fernand recalls, "My friends came back to me with the same car. They took me to the same place [the Summer Palace]. I stood at a place and, upon arrival of Admiral Darlan, I was able to accomplish the mission which I was charged with."

Following Fernand's statement to the police, on December 25, Christmas Day, a judge declares that he would be subjected to a military court-martial before a tribunal in Algiers. Amazingly, the military tribunal convenes within hours and meets for only about an hour, hears all the evidence, rejects Fernand's lawyer's request for further investigation, and sentences Fernand to death. Fernand's attorney immediately pleads for clemency, but the plea is rejected, and it is ordered that Fernand be executed the next morning, December 26.

By this time, Fernand is beginning to have serious doubts about assurances he had been given that he would be released, and he asks to speak to the judicial police once again. He tells police Commissioner Garidacci that he did not act alone and that Abbe Cordier and Henri d'Astier were well aware of his plans to kill Darlan in advance of the act. Garidacci does nothing with Fernand's additional statement. Fernand is growing frantic with the realization that nobody is going to come forward to help him and that he is soon to shuffle off this mortal coil. Did Lee Harvey Oswald come to a similar realization, and far more quickly, within twenty-four hours of his arrest and a day before being led in cuffs to his death at the hand of Jack Ruby in the basement of police headquarters? We do know that Fernand was right. At 7:30 a.m. the next day, December 26, he is taken to a square called Hussein Dey and executed by a firing squad. Nobody records his last words. Oswald did not have the opportunity to offer his "last words."

Further implications of de la Chapelle as a precursor to Lee Harvey Oswald, the accused assassin of President John F. Kennedy in 1963, are pursued later in the chapter. For now, days after Fernand's execution, it is discovered that the $2,000 US he had in his overcoat pocket did indeed come from Henri d'Astier de la Vigerie, a fascinating character. Before the war, d'Astier had joined La Cagoule, a secret Catholic, anticommunist, anti-Semitic French fascist organization.

LA CAGOULE AND THE MALICE

Members of La Cagoule were sometimes called Cagoulards. French writer Rene Pierre-Goss, in a rare 1945 volume on "the conspiracy in Algiers," wrote with equally rare perception that Henri d'Astier was "in fact the occult leader of most of the elements resisting in Algiers." Pierre-Goss goes on:

He [Henri d'Astier] was a Cagoulard; people repeat it, and he does not try to hide the fact. His innate taste for intrigue, his urge to make trouble, to act as an outlaw, and to expend his strength recklessly, make him a kind of musketeer quite out of place in our century. An aristocrat, sprung from an ancient line, he is the enfant terrible of his family. He willingly talks of his disagreements with his two brothers. He is inclined toward the right, of course, but he does not conceal that he is much more royalist than monarchist. His personal tendencies lead him to devote himself more to the man than to an idea. . . . Henri d'Astier is more than a condottiere. He is completely sincere, entirely disinterested, and attached with every fiber of his being to the land of France. He suffers to see France in eclipse and the salt of the land—her best sons—losing its savor. He has the character of a leader and its essential capacity to arouse passionate devotion around him. Sometimes he has done mad things, extravagant, incredible things, but never second-rate.

La Cagoule, very much like today's jihadist groups in composition, was founded in 1936 by Eugène Deloncle, an unattractive, short, squat man who had been blessed with unusual hypnotic and persuasive powers, along with several other people, including French industrialist and ultrarightist, Jacques Lemaigre Dubreuil. Deloncle, an engineer who spoke precious little in public about La Cagoule, said the purpose of the group was to restore the Catholic monarchy to France. Deloncle didn't speak of the ways La Cagoule would achieve its aim, but history informs us that the organization was expert in carrying out assassinations, blowing up buildings, kidnapping, wiretapping, and torture. La Cagoule means "the hood" or "the hooded ones," due to the fact that members at most of their meetings wore face-covering masks to conceal their identities.

Historians Gaylek Brunelle and Annette Finlay-Croswhite aptly write in their brilliant volume on La Cagoule, *Murder in the Metro*: "Most scholars dismiss the Cagoule as a group of half-hearted, often comical street thugs whose inexperience doomed their farfetched plan to overthrow the French government and bring Mussolini-style fascism to France. . . . We contend that historians have underestimated the significance of Cagoulard violence and as a result have failed to perceive the group's purposeful terrorist action for what it was—a form of public discourse that quite successfully engaged the French populace in a dialogue about the fate of the Third Republic and, in the process, left a chilling trail of bloodshed." Brunelle and Finley-Croswhite continue:

> In the police reports and legal files associated with their activities, members of the Cagoule were identified as "terrorists." The terms "terrorist" and "terrorism," however, have proven extremely difficult for scholars to define, resulting in a multitude of possible definitions that the events in the United States on September 11, 2001, and the resulting outpouring of literature on terrorism, have complicated and problematized even more. "Terrorism" is a pejorative, but one with a long history. Terrorist acts inspiring widespread fear have been written about since at least the time of Xenophon, but ironically the word "terrorism" was coined in the French Revolution and is specifically associated with governance through intimidation. The first terrorists were the Jacobins, who sought to influence political behavior through terror, and their instrument of execution, the guillotine, became a symbol of terrorism or at least a method of behavior control. "Terrorism" was introduced into the English language in 1794.

Brunelle and Finley-Croswhite's contention that the Cagoule "perpetuated terrorism" is precisely on the mark, and, upon close examination, as we shall see, the alliance of Cagoule, the *hooded ones*, with the Nazis, combined with the actions of the OSS in North Africa, strongly set the initial stage for JFK's assassination.

* * *

We turn now to what matters most to this investigation, those *hooded ones* directly relevant to the murder of Kennedy in Dallas in 1963.

Jean Pierre Lafitte, author of the documents central to our story, enters the following in his loosely constructed day by day account of what was going on in his world in 1963:

Lamy -Filiol at hotel

One of La Cagoule's most notorious assassins, who often dealt with d'Astier, was Jean Paul Robert Filliol, spelled consistently with a single *l* by Lafitte. With the Vichy government formed in France, Filliol became the Cagoule's chief and most trusted assassin, an infamous killer known throughout Europe. Filliol, a tall, athletic man with classic features and intense dark eyes—who, during the 1940s, sported a Hitler-like mustache and always wore a black glove on his near-useless right hand— was born into a working-class family in Bergerac, France. Filliol served briefly during World War I and then worked as a salesman for the newspaper and publishing company Hachette. Around 1935, he opened a bookstore and had the time to cofound the Cagoule alongside Eugène Deloncle. Like Deloncle, Jean Paul was a virulent racist and anti-Semite who could spout noxious rants on demand. Filliol was also a man of sharp contradictions who faithfully attended Roman Catholic Mass weekly and claimed to love his brothers and sisters as God intended, provided they weren't nonwhite or Jewish. He was said to enjoy good food and wine and had a foul mouth and violent nature that often teetered into blood lust.

Shortly after the Cagoule was founded, Filliol began moving about Paris with "his own assassination team, which included twenty-seven-year-old Fernand Jakubiez and twenty-eight-year-old André Tenaille, both of whom shared Filliol's penchant for action but lacked his intelligence. Weapons and violence obsessed Filliol, who was a risk-taker by nature and always inclined toward overkill. He seems to have been a true terrorist in outlook, who sought to use violence to make a terrifying statement to those who witnessed the crime scenes he left behind."

Within months of La Cagoule's formation, Filliol became head of the group's Section Terroriste, and many of his fledgling assassins were in their late teens or early twenties. Beyond debate, Filliol was a pathological, homicidal assassin who appeared perfectly suited to the job of murder and was dissatisfied if he wasn't either killing someone or planning a lethal attack on targeted victims, regardless of their age or sex. Filliol was notorious for kneeling over his dead victims and asking: "Lord, must we cut all their throats?" In his vicious escapades, he was often accompanied by his beautiful, mysterious mistress and eventual wife, Alice Lamy, who, by all accounts, shared his maniacal ways.

Illustrative of Filliol's viciousness and tendency toward excess are the murders of high-profile brothers Nello and Carlo Rosselli, both born in Italy to a prominent Jewish family. Ardent, antifascists, and strong advocates for liberal socialism, the brothers were brutally murdered on June 9, 1937, in the French resort town of Bagnoles-de-l'Orne. Filliol and several young aspiring Cagoulard assassins ambushed the brothers by making it appear that their car had broken down by the side of the road. When the Rossellis stopped to help, they were attacked and stabbed multiple times, shot multiple times, and had their throats cut. Their funeral drew nearly 200,000 people.

Especially germane to this book is the discovery that Jean Paul Robert Filliol was closely associated with Jean Pierre Lafitte, an integral contributor to the successful execution of what many consider to be the crime of the century, the assassination of Kennedy. And perhaps equally significant is Filliol's history with Nazi SS Sturmbannführer Otto Skorzeny, who in some quarters continues to be benignly and often affectionately identified as Hitler's "favorite commando." We now know that Skorzeny played the crucial role of logistical mastermind of the hit in Dealey Plaza.

Throughout the 1930s, "Pierre Lafitte" often went by the aliases Jean Pierre Mornard and Jean Monard, as well as by Pierre Jean Martin during the time that he was closely aligned with the French Gestapo-like group called the Malice. Lafitte's surviving personal effects act to support the claim and contain a few French SS badges as well as two Malice identity cards under the name of Martin.

The Malice was established on January 30, 1943, by Pierre Laval, another close associate of Lafitte. Laval had served as Prime Minister of France in 1931 and 1932. Far right in his politics, Laval, after the Germans seized control, served the Vichy government as vice president of its Council of Ministers and then as head of the government. When France was liberated in 1944, the government of General Charles de Gaulle had him arrested for treason. He was tried and sentenced to death. After attempting suicide, Laval was executed by firing squad.

Laval put La Cagoule member and Vichy Secretary General Joseph Darnand, yet another Lafitte associate, in charge of the Malice. Darnand (sometimes mistakenly spelled "Danard") was a thirty-seven-year-old former World War I French army officer and a transportation company director. When World War II began, he again joined the French army and soon founded a Vichy anti-Resistance militia. In August 1943, Darnand became an officer in the Nazi SS because he was disgusted with the Vichy authorities after they refused to arm his Malice soldiers who had all been targeted by the Resistance for assassination.

French Sûreté Commissioner Jean Belin also revealed that SS Otto Skorzeny played an earlier role in Vichy affairs. Belin writes that in September 1940, he "was personally instructed by the Minister of the Interior [Vichy government] to proceed to the Château de Châteldon with a strong force of police and a whole battalion of cyclists." Belin states, "There was a strong belief that the Nazis were about to kidnap Pierre Laval and remove him by air, just as they had rescued Mussolini after the invasion of Italy." Commissioner Belin had firm orders that any brazen Skorzeny-type action to snatch Laval be prevented. Belin further stated that within twenty-four hours of going to the Château, "the German Ambassador to Vichy France, Otto Abetz, had arrived in the provisional capital, accompanied by a force of SS men armed with machine guns."

Belin explained: "At first Marshall Pétain had apparently refused to see Hitler's envoy but later relented. He had, however, persisted that Laval remain under house arrest. Abetz lost his temper and declared that he would liberate the Vice-Premiere by force, only to be told that, if he attempted any such thing, his men would be fired on as they approached the Château." Belin soon returned Laval to Vichy, and Skorzeny apparently was never called on to assist Ambassador Abetz.

In time, Joseph Darnand put Filliol in charge of the Limoges [city in southwestern-central France] branch of the Malice. The blithe psychopath Filliol quickly developed whole new dimensions to his homicidal psyche, not the least of which were enhanced interrogation techniques featuring brutal torture and the drugging of subjects. Historians Brunelle and Finley-Croswhite inform us that Filliol and his mistress, Alice Lamy, a name that surfaces in Lafitte's datebook, interrogated and tortured over one hundred people in one day alone at an abandoned movie theater called the Palace in Périgueux, France. This extraordinary act of sustained torture would pale in consideration of Filliol's next horrific act, the destruction of the town of Oradour-sur-Glane in Limousin (France). There the Nazis, with Filliol's close assistance, murdered over six hundred people, including two hundred children.

Pierre Lafitte would also cross paths with Filliol—who like Lafitte would use at least twenty aliases—when in 1944 he was associated with the SS Waffen Charlemagne Division, a French unit aiding the Nazis in their occupation of France. It is reported by surviving members of Lafitte's family that he was with the SS Brigadeführer Krukenenberg in April 1945, just prior to its being moved to Berlin to defend Hitler in his final bunker days, but independent confirmation of this remains elusive. There is no evidence that Lafitte was ever captured, let alone brought to trial; however, at the end of World War II, Filliol was tried in absentia and sentenced to death. His sentence was never carried out because he escaped to Spain, and fascist dictator General Francisco Franco refused to extradite the killer.

Once in Spain, Filliol soon established contact with Nazi Otto Skorzeny, who had been "resettled" for the benefit of US intelligence interests in the country's capital.

Unfortunately, the full extent of Filliol's dealings with Skorzeny remain sketchy. We do however have enough details to paint a graphic portrait of the Cagoule assassin in Spain. There, Filliol quickly landed a secure and well-paid executive job with the international division of L'Oréal, a cosmetic and beauty products company. Today a very well-known company, L'Oréal was founded and operated by Eugène Schueller, a passionate anti-Semite and ultraright-winger. Schueller, during the 1930s and the war years, financially supported La Cagoule and Deloncle's 1940 political group, Mouvement Social Revolutionnaire (MSR). MSR, like La Cagoule, was ultranationalistic, anticommunist, and anti-Semitic and featured Filliol as chief of intelligence and Schueller as a group director and central source of funds.

As noted, when Filliol settled in Spain after the war, he quickly resumed the relationship with Skorzeny stemming from their shared experiences during WWII, and while details of that association are sparse, we do know that Lafitte was included in their tight circle, a history that has been consistently overlooked. Beginning in October 1944, after holding a series of conferences with German and French advisors, Joseph Darnand, a forty-six-year-old prominent La Cagoule member, virulent anti-Bolshevist, Malice founder, and Nazi SS officer, founded a "special service" called the Organisation Technique (OT), which was made up of about 200 volunteers. Filliol was placed in charge of OT's training division. His first major project was to take on the training of about 150 paramilitary parachutists. We begin to grasp the impact of Filliol's history with Otto Skorzeny.

Not sure how best to go about the task of training the OTs, Filliol sent a telegram requesting assistance from Nazi Sturmbannführer Skorzeny, whom he had first encountered in Paris. Filliol had remained greatly impressed by the Nazi officer's level of self-confidence and the depth of his knowledge about creating effective and expert paramilitary groups. With Skorzeny's assistance, Filliol established an OT headquarters at Wilflinger (Germany) and three training camps at Hausen, Wald, and Mengen, all in Germany. Professor and respected author Perry Biddiscombe informs us that the Hausen camp was focused exclusively on sabotage and offered special training in "reconnaissance, map reading, and the use of explosives, although SD advisors complained that the discourse at all three camps was mainly political." Prof. Biddiscombe goes on to reveal that "morale in the OT was poor, particularly since some of the activists fancied themselves anti-German nationalists, although the prospect of surrendering to the ascendant Gaullists seemed sure to result in execution or a prolonged prison sentence at hard labour."

Otto Skorzeny was soon disappointed by the sagging morale of Filliol's men, as he had been when inspecting the trainees he was responsible for in Denmark—a subject that is pursued later in the book—but, "hoping to heighten its enthusiasm," he allowed Filliol "to run a number of independent operations aimed at provoking right-wing resistance in France." Filliol formed "four three-man groups of agents from the OT's sabotage and propaganda section" and "had them parachute behind enemy lines in early 1945, two on 6 January (in southwestern France) and two on 9 February (in the northern part of the country)."

Today, sources in France and Spain report that "sometimes" and "occasionally" Filliol and Skorzeny acted together on Skorzeny's numerous covert activities in Spain and elsewhere. These sources include former Madrid police official Iago Serrano; however, two additional sources have requested to not be identified herein because of fears of "reprisals from corporate interests in both countries." Pierre Lafitte elected to leave Europe for Canada and the United States not long after Skorzeny settled in Spain.

Perhaps most unsettling about Filliol today is that Serrano staunchly maintains that Filliol traveled to Dallas, Texas, several times in the early 1960s and that "he was present in Dallas on November 22, 1963." This claim is both supported, although somewhat clouded, by Pierre Lafitte's November 20, 1963, datebook entry highlighted earlier in the chapter, *Lamy—Filiol at hotel . . .*

Background of Jean Pierre Filliol's life is found in the chapter Endnotes, and the provocative nature of the entry and Filliol's strong association with Lafitte and Otto Skorzeny is pursued in later chapters.

OSARN

On October 9, 1963, Pierre Lafitte, while in New Orleans, Louisiana, wrote in his datebook, "OSARN- OSARN-OSARN . . ." before getting down to the business of progressing the operation destined for the city of Dallas.

Another close associate of the murderous Filliol was Jacques Corrèze, a man who over the past half-century has consistently been labeled a bloodthirsty racist and shapeshifter who causally oversaw Filliol's homicidal activities. Corrèze had been a high-ranking member of La Cagoule and the personal assistant of Eugène Deloncle and served as a critical link in the funding of La Cagoule by Eugène Schuller, founder of the L'Oréal cosmetic company.

During World War II, Jacques Corrèze and Eugène Schuller were staunch supporters of the pro-Nazi Vichy regime. Earlier on, Corrèze was associated with the profascist militant groups, Camelots du Roi, the Secret Organization of National Revolutionary Action (OSARN), and the Knights of Gladiators, whose members wore costumes whose design was taken from the Ku Klux Klan in the United States. OSARN was closely aligned with Benito Mussolini and Hitler. OSARN's purpose was stated: "We want to build a new Europe in cooperation with national socialist German and all other European nations freed from liberal capitalism, Judaism, Bolshevism and French Masons . . . to regenerate France and the French race . . . to ensure that Jews who stay in France are subject to harsh laws, preventing them from infesting our race . . . to create a socialist economy which guarantees a fair distribution of production by simultaneously increasing both wages and production." OSARN was also closely associated with Reinhardt Heydrich, head of Hitler's dreaded Nazi Gestapo whom Otto Skorzeny had occasion to interact with.

Following the close of World War II, Corrèze was convicted of several war crimes and sentenced to ten years in a French prison. Jacques Corrèze was freed in 1949 after only five years in prison. Shortly thereafter, he was hired by then-L'Oréal company president François Dalle. One of Corrèze's first assignments for the company was to help better organize Procasa, L'Oréal's Spanish marketing firm. While in Spain, naturally Corrèze became friends with Otto Skorzeny after being introduced to his fellow SS officer by former La Cagoule assassin Jean Filliol, by now the vice president of international marketing for L'Oréal.

After several years with Procasa, Corrèze was dispatched to the United States, where he was charged with directing Cosmair, a division of L'Oréal. He successfully built the division to a very prosperous market position, but in 1991, the US Department of Justice, Office of Special Investigations, announced that it was opening an investigation "to determine whether the chairman [Corrèze] of the

$1 billion American affiliate of L'Oréal, the French cosmetic company, should be barred from the United States for his pro-Nazi activities during World War II."

The Justice Department's interest in Corrèze was sparked by articles in two prominent Parisian newspapers, *Libération* and *Le Monde*. The articles focused on Corrèze's strong Nazi-linked past. Following their publication, the leaders of several Jewish organizations in the US and France provided the Justice Department with numerous documents related to Corrèze's nefarious wartime activities and requested that the department place him on the agency's formal watch list and that he be banned from entry into the United States.

According to two former employees of the department's Office of Special Investigations, both of whom declined to be identified in this book, the examination of Corrèze's past quickly unearthed unexpected details about his links to Jean Filliol, Gerard Litt, and Otto Skorzeny, inclusive of detailed suspicions about Filliol's and Litt's presence in Dallas, Texas, at the time of the JFK assassination. A formal request by author Albarelli to the US Department of Justice for documentation concerning these suspicions remained unanswered in 2019. A similar request to the CIA also remained unanswered. Corrèze died suddenly in June 1991, and the Justice Department suspended its investigation into his activities.

* * *

But who was Gerald Litt? According to historian Perry Biddiscombe, Litt was "Skorzeny's main ally . . . a black marketer who controlled a group of ex-Cagoulards and gangsters called the 'National French.' Something of a human toad, with a corpulent frame and an oversized head, Litt was described as a glutton, a coward, and a bloodthirsty anti-Semite, with a personality as brutish as his physical composition. He had begun working for the Paris station of the *Abwehr* in 1942, assembling an intelligence and strong-arm unit and becoming one of the Germans' most trusted informers."

Litt was also very much engaged in drug trafficking, pushing heroin processed in Marseilles to Allied troops; these were many of the same heroin processors that Pierre Lafitte would work with when Litt arrived in Montreal, Canada, and the United States. Litt had been highly recommended to Skorzeny by Nazi SS officer Hauptsturmführer Doering, whom he had met in North Africa in 1943, and who soon thereafter brought Litt to Berlin to meet with Skorzeny. Litt agreed with Skorzeny to form anticommunist groups that would square off with the French Resistance. He also agreed to organize stay-behind networks in France and elsewhere. Guerrilla members of these networks were to be trained at "a special school near The Hague."

Biddiscombe writes: "The project was code-named 'Jeanne,' perhaps after Litt's wife's name, although the name was also meant to refer to 'Jeanne d'Arc,' whose image and legacy French right-wingers had attempted to expropriate." While a member of the small, vicious team of assassins referred to as the "Richard Group" behind project 'Jeanne,' madman Gerard Litt lived in the apartment of its leader, located less than a five-minute walk from an office space on the Champs-Élysées occupied by the future wife of SS Otto Skorzeny, Ilse Luthje (who had joined the Hitler Youth as a young girl), while she maintained operational connections with the Sûreté, the French security forces. Litt is named in Lafitte's October 9, 1963, datebook entry, just forty-four days before the assassination. We also learn more about the Sûreté and Ilse's stint with the French agency later.

* * *

How do we know that these experienced assassins, who emerged from the ranks of La Cagoule to deal directly with Otto Skorzeny, coalesced in 1963 specific to our investigation of events in Dallas? Some of the answers reside in a series of obscure postassassination letters addressed to FBI Director J. Edgar Hoover from a Mr. Paul Gluc, 112 General Leclerc Avenue, Boulogne Billancourt (92), France. According to one of the letters, Mr. Gluc, a self-described benevolent detective, was employed by French automobile manufacturer Régie Renault and lived in a populous suburb five miles from the center of Paris.

A detailed account of this strange and revealing correspondence over a span of nine years, and the subsequent FBI memo traffic that attempted to discredit its significance and impugn the character of the author, is available to the reader in the Endnotes to this chapter. For now, the following excerpts serve to not only validate the aforementioned history of assassins directly associated with one another, and by inference with Otto Skorzeny, but they also provide Gluc's independent confirmation of certain entries in the 1963 datebook of Pierre Lafitte essential to the investigation of the assassination of John Kennedy.

Mr. Director, only you can clear OTTO SKORZENY of guilt of being (an) agent in the Dallas operation with (the) passive complicity of Allen W. Dulles.

—Paul Gluc, March 14, 1975

The 1975 letter was Gluc's fourth and final correspondence with the FBI. The first letter, dated March 18, 1964, just four months after the assassination of President John F. Kennedy and later claimed by the FBI to be either lost or misplaced, was hand-written in English to "Mr. Hoover, director of the FBI." It reads:

> I understand you are very close to the solution of all the mysteries of President Kennedy's assassination, but I suspect you are without key information. This information concerns the holders of many of the missing cards, Jean Souetre, as well as Jean Paul Filliol, both known to have been in Dallas on 22 November 1963. . . . Included in this knowledge are Mme. Lamy and M. Litt, all mentioned before, and extremely distasteful individuals. . . . I am anxious to spell this out for you by coming to Washington, D.C.

The letter was signed: "Mr. Gluc."

Author Albarelli is grateful to Mr. Gluc's son, Thierry Baudin, for providing a photocopy of the carbon copy of his father's first letter to Director Hoover, the contents of which suggest Hoover's Bureau had every reason to misplace it.

With his letter, Gluc has provided us independent corroboration that Filliol, Lamy, and Litt were known associates and that they were in Dallas, and, as noted, he did so as early as March 1964. We also see, perhaps for the first time outside of cryptic reports that revealed a smattering of facts, that the FBI was made aware of the possibility that known assassin Jean Souetre had been in Dallas. Yes, Gluc could have simply picked up on the obscure rumors about Souetre being expelled from the Dallas-Fort Worth area, but there was no known trail in the public domain of the presence of Filliol, Lamy, and/or Litt in Dallas that would tie the three to Jean Souetre.

* * *

A brief introductory sketch of both Souetre and Skorzeny, characters who loom large throughout our story, is in order.

Otto Skorzeny, made infamous for his role in the 1945 daring rescue of Italian fascist dictator Benito Mussolini at the behest of his Führer, Adolf Hitler, was a native of Austria. Born in 1908, his father, an architect and engineer, operated the successful Viennese construction company he founded around the turn of the century. As a student, Otto was more drawn to mathematics than the social sciences, and although he showed little interest in academics, he developed an ear for languages. His real prowess resided in athletics, and the art of fencing in particular.

As British journalist Stuart Smith reveals in his excellent exposé, *Otto Skorzeny: The Devil's Disciple*, by age nineteen, Otto was immersed in the dueling society at his engineering sciences university. Smith writes, "Built around ritualistic duels with the Schlager sword (in which the object was to gain and inflict impressive facial scars, not to kill one's opponent) and gargantuan drinking sessions, such societies were a fixture of German and Austrian universities, and membership constituted a rite of passage for a certain kind of macho student." According to Smith, Otto excelled and became a target for those who wished to test their mettle. Eventually he received the slash from ear to chin on the left side that would mark him for life, a permanent and striking addition to the impression his 6'4" frame made on any he encountered.

Smith observes, "Like his scar, Otto Skorzeny acquired his politics in student clubs. Austro-German student associations were originally a product of the nationalistic fervor stirred up during the Napoleonic Wars. By the 1920s many had acquired a reactionary ethos dressed up as ardent patriotism." As we will learn, Otto lived a life guided by that deceptive philosophy.

Reflecting on that scar that served as a kind of trademark, Skorzeny wrote, "I was to be grateful for the self-discipline we learned in our student clubs. I never felt so bad under fire as I did at eighteen when I had to fight my first duel, under the sharp eye of my fellow students. My knowledge of pain, learned with the sabre, taught me not to be afraid of fear. *And just as in dueling you must fix your mind on striking the enemy's head, so, too, in war. You cannot waste time feinting and sidestepping. You must decide on your target and go in.*"

Some might argue this was a reflective metaphor for the logistics he applied to the assassination in Dallas.

* * *

In light of Skorzeny's lead instructor at his camps outside Madrid, Jean Rene Souetre, being identified by Gluc, a brief introduction of the Frenchman who will dominate the final pages of this book is also in order.

Born Jean Rene Marie Souetre in 1930 in France, like so many in our saga, Souetre adopted at least eleven aliases during this life, several of which he shared with Pierre Lafitte. Described as being quite handsome with dark, slightly curly hair, startling eyes, and an infectious smile, Souetre was said to have been a lover of women.

At age twenty, he joined the French Air Force, and by 1953, he was captain with the Security branch of the French 4th Air Force, stationed near Reims.] It was there that he encountered an army captain from Texas, and as we will learn in Chapter 10, Souetre remained in annual contact with the former US military officer until the events of November 22, 1963, permanently severed communication. By 1954, Souetre had succeeded in becoming a master parachutist and airborne soldier, an equivalent in America to being an Airborne Ranger. He also volunteered for a new commando unit that was being formed by the air force Fusiliers Commandos de l'Air. Souetre received the Chevalier de la Legion d'Honneur and the Croix de la Valeur Militaire while serving in Algiers in 1955–1959. Both medals were revoked after Souetre joined the Organisation Armée Secrète, more widely known as the OAS.

SPIES, KILLERS, SOLDIERS, AND IDEOLOGUES

Joining Otto Skorzeny, and his band of assassins in Madrid, were former wartime Nazis of special note to this book, Léon Degrelle and Junio Valerio Borghese. Léon Joseph Marie Ignace Degrelle was a notorious Nazi collaborator born in Belgium in 1906 to a wealthy Catholic family. Young Léon studied at a prestigious Jesuit college and received a law doctorate from the Catholic University in Louvain. Following his schooling, Degrelle organized his own political party in Belgium, the Rexist Party, a Christian-based social justice group with deep-seated fascist, anticommunist, anti-Semite, and antibourgeois underpinnings. Degrelle also became Belgium's chief supporter and collaborator with Hitler, forming a military brigade of non-German Waffen SS members to fight in World War II.

Following the end of the war, Degrelle, along with many of his brigade members, fled to Spain. The Belgian government accused Degrelle of treason and demanded that Franco's government hand him over to them. Franco refused and helped Degrelle seek refuge and settle in his country. The Belgians, who had tried Degrelle in absentia and condemned him to death by a firing squad, were outraged by Spain's refusal and ordered that all of Degrelle's supporters and family members in Belgium be rounded up and arrested. Nearly twenty of his supporters were executed, and several of his children were beaten and tortured in prison. The Belgian intelligence services sent several covert teams into Spain to kidnap Degrelle, but all failed. The Jewish community in Israel and America applied pressure for Degrelle's extradition and claimed that he was responsible for the wartime deportations and deaths of over thirty-five thousand Jews in Belgium.

Skorzeny, who had first met Degrelle when he was in command of his Belgium SS division, welcomed Degrelle to Spain with open arms, helping him financially to form a construction company that received a large amount of Spanish government work, as well as lucrative contracts from the US government and Pentagon to build military airfields throughout Spain. We have reason to pursue Degrelle later in the book, based on a remark made by a family member of Pierre Lafitte to author Albarelli that Léon Degrelle funded a small part of the JFK hit, "*only because he despised Kennedy so much . . .*"

Prince Junio Valerio Borghese was another highly esteemed member of this cadres of fascists. Said Degrelle of Borghese, "he was a very impressive man," adding, "the most important man of post-Fascist Italy" (Martin Lee interview with Léon Degrelle, May 23, 1993). Valerio Borghese was born at the turn of the century into a noble Italian family. The family's heritage can be traced back to the days of Julius Caesar. Handsome, self-assured, and ever-restless, Borghese enlisted in the Italian Navy before World War II and was assigned to "an elite naval sabotage unit that eventually became known as the Decima Flottiglia MAS." Decima MAS, or X-Mas, was a highly successful wartime group that was responsible for sinking many British warships. Borghese's exploits with the Italian Navy quickly became near legendary.

In July 1943, Mussolini's Axis government was shaken when Italian royalists seized Mussolini and threw him into a remote, inaccessible stone prison in the Apennine Mountains. Spectacularly, his seemingly hopeless situation was reversed when he was freed and returned to power through a daring raid on the prison by Hitler's favorite Nazi commando, Otto Skorzeny.

Following Mussolini's return to power, the Nazis demilitarized Italy's army and navy, and Borghese took his X-Mas subordinates to operate on the land where they became infamous for rounding up Italian civilians and torturing them before publicly executing many. Slow on the uptake, Mussolini eventually realized that Borghese's operations were happening apart from his overall strategy and that the Black Prince was also keeping close contact with Nazi SS officers, British intelligence officers, and OSS officers Allen Dulles and James Jesus Angleton.

Impulsively, Mussolini decided to arrest Borghese but quickly released him, and by late 1944, the Italian fascist dictator and his mistress had been killed and viciously mutilated by frenzied Italian crowds. Allen Dulles quickly requested that US Vice Admiral Ellery Stone act to protect the Black Prince from any harm. Records indicate that a few months later, on May 9, 1945, OSS officer James Jesus Angleton spirited Borghese, dressed in an American soldier's uniform, away to safety in Rome. About a week later, Borghese was arrested, tried, and convicted of minor wartime crimes by the Allies. He served only about two years in prison and was then released to become an active force advancing international terrorist activities designed to promote the cause of fascism.

Eventually, Borghese was joined in his activities by the notorious terrorist and assassin Stefano Delle Chiaie. Says author Martin Lee in his groundbreaking work, *The Beast Reawakens*, "Borghese often spoke highly of the five-foot fascist phenom, referring to Delle Chiaie as 'one of the few men capable of putting things in order in Italy.'" The reader encounters Delle Chiaie in depth later in the chapter, but for now it's important to note that it was Delle Chiaie who accompanied the Black Prince when they fled Italy for Spain following the botched putsch known as Golph Borghese in December 1970, where they rendezvoused with Otto Skorzeny. According to Lee, "Delle Chiaie glorified violence as a hygienic outburst capable of cutting through the postwar bourgeois morass. During the 1960s, his organization, Avanguardia Nazionale (National Vanguard) came to be regarded as the cudgel of Italian right-wing extremism. For guidance and inspiration, Delle Chiaie looked to Julius Evola, the reactionary intellectual who emerged as the gray eminence of postwar Italian fascism."

The Black Prince also held an ideology he believed strongly in, unlike James Jesus Angleton, who was wrapped up in the beauty of words and professionally obscuring their use. When he first met Borghese, Angleton was a painfully thin, well-schooled, aspiring poet whose androgynous qualities seemed to anticipate David Bowie. While Borghese was shrewd and finely attuned to wartime reality, Angleton was a neophyte to war and world counterintelligence. In time, however, Angleton would become well known as the longtime head of CIA Counterintelligence, moving beneath the protective umbrella of his patron, Allen Dulles, and involve himself in the early 1950s CIA-sanctioned MKULTRA experiments that brought him into contact with Federal Bureau of Narcotics "special employee" Pierre Lafitte.

Esteemed writer Kevin Coogan notes in his brilliant biography of political philosopher and white nationalist Francis Parker Yockey that "planning for Operation Gladio's stay-behind network couldn't succeed without Borghese's tacit approval." Writes Coogan, "The CIA then created an underground army of ex-fascist combat veterans in an operation code-named 'Operation Gladio' [Gladio being the name for a Roman double-edged sword]."

According to Coogan, Julius Evola (who we now recognize was the inspiration of both Valerio Borghese and Stefano Delle Chiaie) was an admirer of Yockey, the top American fascist of the day whom we explore later in this chapter, and Evola himself had become involved in the Nazi underground SD (Sicherheidsdienst). In his book, Coogan claims, "Evola's SD work at the end of the war is shrouded in mystery. Historian Richard Drake says that while he was in Vienna, 'Evola performed vital liaisons for the SS as Nazi Germany sought to recruit a European army for the defense of the Continent against the Soviet Union and the United States.'" This organization was linked to the Otto Skorzeny underground Nazi headquarters in Madrid and Buenos Aires. (The reader is urged to consider the Chapter Endnotes focused on Evola.)

* * *

We would be remiss if we didn't pause to acknowledge Britain's leading fascist at the time, Oswald Mosley, and his anti-Semitic, nationalistic Union Movement of Fascists, which was formed in October 1932. Mosley's movement was ideologically aligned Skorzeny's network. In 1951, Mosley, due to tax problems, relocated to [Clonfert Palace near Eyrecourt] Co. Galway Ireland. He and his wife, Diana Mitford, one of the infamous Mitford Sisters and also an unrepentant fascist to her death in 2003, were deeply ensconced in Ileclash, Fermoy, Co. Cork when the Skorzenys began visiting the country in 1957. Otto and Ilse's lodge and farm in Ballysax, the Curragh, Co. Kildare, was located less than two hours north of Ileclash. According to his book, *Oswald Mosley*, historian Robert Skildesky offers, "After an internment, with his wife Diana Mitford, during WW II, Mosley adopted the pro-US 'united Europe' position of Franz-Josef Strauss and hung around with such characters as Otto Skorzeny, a top Nazi incorporated into Western intelligence work." (See Chapter 8 for further detail on Oswald and Diana Mosley.) And while there is no written evidence thus far, author Albarelli was confident that Mosley eventually became closely involved with Otto and his wife, Ilse (a claim supported by their close geographic proximity in Ireland), Pierre Lafitte, and Lee Harvey Oswald's mother, Marguerite Oswald.

* * *

American fascist and neo-Nazi Francis Parker Yockey and his admirer and colleague H. Keith Thompson were both politically and literally aligned with Valerio Borghese as well as Otto and Ilse Skorzeny. Equally intriguing is the peculiar relationship Yockey's ideological cohort Thompson had with Lee Oswald's mother, Marguerite. In the aftermath of the Kennedy assassination and subsequent murder of her son while he was in police custody, Marguerite was approached by Thompson to "manage her affairs." One such effort was securing Marguerite's appearance on the Irv Kupcinet talk show, *At Random*, in Chicago in the spring of 1964. Kupcinet is known to many assassination researchers as the father of Karyn Kupcinet, who died under mysterious circumstances on November 28, 1963, just six days after the assassination. It is reported that she had made an incoherent call suggesting she knew something about the assassination.

Kupcinet's format for his show was to comb the city on an ad hoc basis for celebrities, persons of public interest, and/or obscure but interesting personalities to join his panel to discuss anything and everything. Among the participants of this particular panel were a popular Chicago area Catholic priest; Marguerite, the mother of the accused lone assassin; and, in an extraordinary coincidence, Hjalmar Schacht, known as "Hitler's banker." Schacht, and in particular his financial skills, is as pertinent to our investigation as is Marguerite.

(Note: the audiotape of this episode of *At Random* is available through the Museum of Broadcast Communication, Chicago, IL.)

As mentioned, there are reported meetings between Lee Oswald and Francis Yockey, philosophical mentor of Thompson. The authors have identified a very tight window in Oswald's timeline when in mid-September 1959, he spent three days in New Orleans waiting to sail to Le Havre en route to his alleged final destination, the Soviet Union. According to hotel records, he stayed at the Liberty Hotel. The same records indicate that a "Mr. and Mrs. Smith" from Houma, LA, and a "Mr. and Mrs. Jal Vial" from Baton Rouge were also checked in. Of note, three months earlier, Oswald had applied for admittance to the Albert Schweitzer College located in Switzerland via correspondence with Robert Schacht, the college's NY-based admissions officer. By coincidence, Robert was a blood relative of Kupcinet's guest in the spring of 1964, Hjalmar Schacht. (See Endnotes for excerpts of a thorough analysis.)

Remembered as the father of Holocaust denial, Yockey is known to have used Corrine Dunbar's, a popular New Orleans restaurant, as a mail drop and to have checked into a New Orleans hotel with an unidentified female before his final trip to California in June 1960. Whether or not he was in the Crescent City at the same time as Oswald before the latter left for Russia has not been confirmed. On arrival in California, Yockey was arrested for possession of multiple passports. While incarcerated, he committed suicide by cyanide rather than face interrogation. Among his final visitors was admirer Willis Carto, a rabid anti-communist who briefly served in a similar capacity as Thompson for Lee's wife, which will close out our saga.

The *San Francisco Chronicle* declared Yockey "as important a figure in world Fascism as we know today."

* * *

Returning now to the assassination of Darlan, which serves as template for the future setup of Lee Harvey Oswald as "the perfect patsy" on November 22, 1963, soon after the execution of François Darlan's assassin, Fernand Bonnier, there were scattered and persistent reports that the young Frenchman had been a patsy of sorts and that he was not an avid monarchist, but was only an impressionable, somewhat naive, youth who had been manipulated toward murderous ends by skillful others. This belief stems from the fact that Bonnier's "friend," Henri d'Astier, while active in La Cagoule, on several occasions joined Filliol in carrying out a devious tactic for ridding La Cagoule of suspected double-agent members by manipulating them into veiled assassination efforts during which it would be highly likely that they would be captured or killed. Filliol dubbed this manipulation "the pigeon way." Here, one is easily reminded of the quote by CIA official Miles Copeland: "You can sometimes gain points in the war of dirty tricks by killing an expendable person on your own side and blaming it on the other when considering this type of lethal deception." And in mid-November 1963, Pierre Lafitte, in New Orleans, would jot down in his datebook: *"On the wings of murder. The pigeon way for unsuspecting Lee [Oswald]. Clip, clip his wings,"* no doubt a reference to Jean Filliol's tactic of manipulation within his assassin camps.

For this reason, and others, the authors regard Fernand Bonnier as the human, or operational, template for future patsy assassins. Meaning not that Bonnier didn't shoot Darlan, as he clearly did, but instead that he was cleverly manipulated into performing the murder. Bonnier was in good company: students acting as assassins were nearly commonplace in the 1930s and 1940s. Swiss-Jewish medical student David Frankfurter failed in his attempt to assassinate Hitler in 1935 but in 1936 managed to kill Wilhelm Gusloff, anti-Semite and Nazi leader, in Switzerland. Maurice Bavaud, a Catholic theology student, tried to assassinate Hitler in 1938. Bavaud is often presented as the quintessential lone assassin, but careful examination reveals that he was part of a broad conspiracy. In 1941, the

Nazis executed Bavaud by beheading him. Georg Elser, a part-time student and construction worker, tried to blow Hitler up at a reunion celebration.

Surely, if the media at the time of Darlan's assassination had been advanced to its current stage, we would know every detail about Fernand Bonnier, just as we know details about Oswald that have been twisted beyond recognition as relevant to the investigation of the Kennedy assassination, including his preference in underwear, his deep-seated political beliefs, as well as the psychology of his mother, father, and siblings; however, the age of the antihero had yet to arrive. Fernand the media subject in 1943, and subsequent years, was reduced to the hand that held and fired the murder weapon. His hand was but a tool holding an instrument of death, and his being, so to speak, was little more than the machine that powered his hand. In this regard, the tenor of the press at the time of Darlan's murder was a compliant accomplice of Bonnier's. Indeed, in some lengthy accounts of Darlan's assassination, readers learn nothing about Bonnier, other than his name, and even less about his last forty-eight hours on Earth. He has fired his weapon, killed his target, and left the stage. His part is over, but that, of course, is not what he wanted; that was the result of the dictates of the times. Darlan was killed by politics and political intrigue created by bigger fish—not by some guppy like Fernand Bonnier, or Lee Harvey Oswald, who both would ultimately be examined and dissected in countless ways a million times over.

THE OSS

It is these authors' hard-and-fast position that the OSS, on orders or a wink and nod from General Dwight Eisenhower, accomplished the murder of Darlan. This act enjoys many parallels to the murder of President Kennedy. While we reached this conclusion independently, perhaps it is best to show here the subsequent conclusions of esteemed historian Stephen Ambrose. Readers may also want to keep in mind that, nearly eighteen years later, President Eisenhower would order the assassinations of both Patrice Lumumba and Fidel Castro. We also know that Otto Skorzeny spent time in the Congo, as revealed in Maj. Ralph Ganis's *The Skorzeny Papers: Evidence for the Plot to Kill JFK*, as was Jean Pierre Voyatzis, whom we will meet later in this chapter.

Ambrose queries: "Was Darlan's murder the first assassination for the American secret service? Was Ike himself in on the plot? Does that explain the rather curious circumstance that at the moment it was committed the commanding general of all Allied operations in North Africa was at a corps headquarters on a farm more than a day's drive from Algiers?"

Ambrose goes on: "At the time, in 1942, few Americans would have believed it possible for their government to be involved in such dastardly work; a generation later, however, millions of Americans would take it for granted that if there was foul play, and the predecessor of the CIA was in the area, and if the Americans benefited from the foul play, then the OSS must have been involved."

Stephen Ambrose aptly centers much of his discussion about Darlan's assassination on Jacques Lemaigre Dubreuil, whom readers remember as a founder of La Cagoule. Dubreuil had high political aspirations and hoped to become finance minister, even prime minister, in the Giraud government. Henri Giraud, whom we will encounter in depth shortly, had served in the 4th Zouave Regiment in North Africa and eventually joined the staff of General Franchet d'Espèrey in Constantinople. At the outbreak of WWII, Giraud, by then a member of the Superior War Council, was given command of the 7th Army. When Darlan was assassinated, Giraud became his successor as the civil and military chief of French North Africa.

The trouble with all of this was that Charles de Gaulle hated Dubreuil, and Dubreuil was a very close friend of an extraordinary diplomat and confidant of Ike Eisenhower's, OSS Robert D. Murphy, mentioned earlier in the chapter. When de Gaulle united with Giraud in January 1943, and then in the spring of 1943 became head of government in Algeria, he declared Dubreuil a Nazi collaborator. Dubreuil quickly fled to Madrid, Spain, where he joined a group of former La Cagoule assassins who would eventually join up with Otto Skorzeny after the former Nazi SS officer relocated to Madrid. When in 1944, Dubreuil attempted to reenter France after the liberation, De Gaulle had him arrested and wanted to place him on trial for treason. Incredibly, Dubreuil's friend Robert Murphy convinced the French "to drop charges against Dubreuil and held a party in Paris in celebration of Dubreuil's freedom." Three years later, Dubreuil was tried for treason but was acquitted. On July 12, 1955, after moving to the Rabat district of Casablanca, he was assassinated in the entryway to his home by persons unknown.

Not long after the Darlan assassination, in early January 1943, another violent incident acted to push American officials further away from any meaningful alliance with Charles de Gaulle. This incident came to be called the "Duke Street Murder." As historian Anthony Cave Brown has underscored, OSS director Donovan, knowing that supporters of de Gaulle were aggressively trying to remove Giraud, thought it might be prudent to explore an alliance with de Gaulle's intelligence service, the Bureau Central de Renseignements, but "was quickly dissuaded" by advice from both the US State Department and the White

House. Known by the men in his battalion during WWI as "Wild Bill" out of admiration for his coolness and resourcefulness during combat, Donovan will assume a role almost larger than life as our opening chapters unfold.

In January 1943, on the heels of Admiral Darlan's murder, an incident known now as "the Duke Street Murder" cemented Director Donovan's beliefs that Prime Minister Charles de Gaulle's secret service director, Andre Dewavrin, while very competent, might be more unpredictable and untrustworthy as himself. America's powers already regarded de Gaulle as equally unpredictable and untrustworthy, but, more concerning, they concluded that he was unduly inclined to compromise with leftists.

Dewavrin commanded the Bureau Central de Renseignments et d'Action (BCAR), which maintained its headquarters at 10 Duke Street in London. Despite his being viewed as a secret La Cagoule member, the US State Department thought it could work with Dewavrin, as did Donovan, until the Duke Street incident acted to alter thinking. On January 20, 1943, Donovan sent a telegram to Col. William Eddy, his chief African representative in Algiers, that read in part:

> The utmost secrecy must be maintained regarding this information. In October (1942), an Alsatian named Paul Manuel [*sic*: it was Manoel] left France and, in Lisbon, received provisional approval by the Free French and British for services with the former in London. He is reported to have broken down under examination in England, by both the Free French and the British, and to have made the following admissions: (a) Manuel [*sic*] was an assumed name. (b) The Germans sent him here to join the Free French after training him in a school of espionage. His roles in Free French circles were to be those of spy, saboteur, and agent provocateur. Reports received from the Free French state that after the departure of his interrogators, the Alsatian committed suicide by means of a slip noose fashioned from his belts and placed around his neck.

Donovan soon learned that there was far more to the incident concerning Paul Manoel than outlined in his telegram. Writer Anthony Cave Brown states that the OSS director indeed began to believe that Dewavrin "was no better than a Sicherheitsdienst thug." (Sicherheitsdienst, or SD, was the intelligence and security agency for the Nazi SS and the Nazi Party.) Through his own investigation of the Manoel case, Donovan learned that the BCRA had secretly set up what he termed "an inquisitorial chamber" in the basement of its Duke Street headquarters and that the French secret service was using "black methods" of interrogation. The British secret service learned this at the same time as Donovan and ordered the French to shut down the chamber of torture immediately. The French ignored the order, and, soon thereafter, the British and Director Donovan learned that a Frenchman named Dufour, after having been cleared of any suspicions of being a double agent by the British, was brutally tortured by BCRA agents at Duke Street. Also revealed, in the early autumn of 1942 a man named Paul Manoel arrived in London and was also suspected of being a double agent. Manoel was interrogated by the BCRA in the Duke Street basement, and it was discovered that he had "two magnificent swastikas tattooed on his arms." According to the French secret service, Manoel then admitted to being "an officer of the Sicherheitsdienst." After he was placed in a holding cell, the French claimed Manoel hung himself hours later.

The "Duke Street Murder" didn't escape the attention of FBI director J. Edgar Hoover in the United States. At about the same time that the incident occurred, things between the Bureau and OSS were strained. The FBI had just set up shop in Paris and was becoming a real bother to Donovan's agency. Tangled up in the ongoing jurisdictional conflict were diplomatic relations with the French government and the intelligence service. In September 1944, Donovan had "befriended" Andre Dewavrin, mostly out of necessity and good politics, but Hoover became outraged when he learned that the OSS chief had invited Dewavrin to the United States, where he was to be awarded the Distinguished Service Cross. Hoover demanded that the invitation be withdrawn and that no award be given, citing the Duke Street Murder as his main reason. General Eisenhower sided with Hoover, and a compromise was struck whereby Dewavrin could still came to visit provided there was no publicity about his presence. Dewavrin met briefly with President Roosevelt, but his reception "was chilly." Observes writer Mark Riebling: "Offended, the French spy chief blamed Donovan, who had been formally charged with arranging the visit. Returning to his 'strange and ruthless' homeland (as Hoover had snidely dubbed it), Dewavrin promptly ordered the OSS out of Paris."

While in custody, accused assassin Fernand Bonnier made no mention to the Algerian police about his OSS commando training, the ultimate responsibility of Bill Donovan, and said nothing about the camp he attended shortly before he assassinated François Darlan. This was intentional, as he did not want to draw any attention to American intelligence units and personnel, the training camp in Aïn Taya, or to his lead instructor, OSS Major Carleton Coon.

Because this book's subject is the world's most notorious assassination and because of Coon's instrumental role in promoting and advancing assassination as a tool of statecraft, we shall look at him here, as well as his close associates in North Africa.

* * *

Carleton Stevens Coon, born in Massachusetts in 1904, was raised north of Boston and attended Phillips Academy, Andover, and then went on to Harvard University, where he studied anthropology under Professor Earnest A. Hooton. After graduating magna cum laude, twenty-year-old Coon, in the summer of 1924, traveled to Morocco with Gordon H. Browne, who, like Coon, felt an irresistible pull toward Northern Africa. Coon's utter fascination with "supposedly Nordic African tribes," called the Riffians, under the leadership of Abd el-Krim, as they fiercely battled Spain for their independence, turned "into addiction," according to writer Mark Saxton. Coon made a half-dozen journeys into Rif lands, often "fearlessly accompanied" by his first wife, a strikingly beautiful woman named Mary Goodale. Coon, ruggedly handsome and permanently tanned from the African elements, could never satiate his obsession with Northern Africa.

By 1939, Coon held a unique knowledge of Spanish Morocco and was widely regarded as an expert on the country and its surrounding regions. When the Second World War began, Coon and Browne, who had settled in Morocco to run a Boston-based importing company, joined the Army's intelligence unit, G-2. Then, in 1942, they enlisted in the Coordinator of Information (COI) and then the Office of Strategic Services (OSS), both outfits precursors to today's CIA. After the war, Browne's business in North Africa became part of William Donovan's World Commerce Corporation's network of intelligence gathering and international trade, as we shall soon examine.

In 1941, desperate to be stationed in Morocco, but frustrated in his efforts because of a 1933 clashing with an American minister in Ethiopia that resulted in his being blacklisted by the US State Department, Coon was able to easily convince OSS officer Colonel Robert Solborg of his and Browne's value to the war efforts in Morocco. Coon recalled: "Solborg led Browne and myself into his private office and asked us if we were willing to go to Morocco, make contacts with the Riffian tribes, and hide out in the mountains when the Germans came in. We agreed. Then I told Colonel Solborg about the State Department's attitude toward me, and he spoke to Mr. [Wallace] Phillips. Mr. Phillips slid his glasses halfway down his nose, looked at me over his lenses, and said, 'I will fix that.' He did. How he persuaded the State Department Brahmins and Pharisees to relent, I do not know."

Coon, now approved for duty in Morocco, first had to attend intensive OSS paramilitary training at the ultrasecret Camp X in Canada. Camp X was overseen by Sir William Stephenson for the Government of Canada and the British Security Coordination service. The camp was located near the Whitby/Oshawa border in Ontario, about 30 miles from the United States line. At Camp X, Coon shared quarters with several men who eventually became legendary for their various wartime and postwar exploits: George Hunter White, Garland Williams, Gregory Bateson, Philip Strong, Louis Cohen, and Kenneth Downs. Schooling at Camp X was a round-the-clock and included intensive courses in silent killing, assassination and elimination, knife fighting, hand-to-hand combat, small arms handling, explosives, and Hydra-radio operation.

After completing his training in Canada, Coon was dispatched to Lisbon, Portugal, where he acted as a coding clerk for Col. Solborg and patiently awaited his orders to go to Morocco. About two weeks later, Coon received orders to travel to Tangier, where he was to meet with OSS Marine Corps Colonel William A. Eddy, a man he grew to greatly admire. Col. Eddy was Bill Donovan's chief African representative, had grown up in the Middle East, and was fluent in Arabic. He had a PhD from Princeton University. Eddy was a World War I veteran who had lost a leg in combat. His OSS associates touted that "no American knew more about Arabs or about power politics in Africa than did Eddy." Following the end of World War II, Eddy quickly joined the staff of the CIA.

Said Coon a few years after he first met Eddy: "Now I was to begin an association with a person whom I consider one of the greatest men I have ever met, one of the happiest associations of my life."

"Colonel Eddy was a man of extraordinary ability combined with personal qualities that completely commanded Coon's loyalty and affection," states Mark Saxton, editor of Coon's wartime memoirs, *A North Africa Story*. "Eddy's professional reputation was deservedly prodigious, although he was hard to classify. He served both the OSS and the State Department at various times. His military rank, although in a sense a cover, was real, well earned, and acquired in a normal way. Grandson of the founder of the American University of Beirut and born in Sidon [Lebanon] of a missionary family, Eddy was a student at Princeton at the beginning of World War I. He joined the Marine Corps, was wounded in France, and decorated for bravery in action. When peace came, he took up teaching in

Egypt and then, for several years, was president of Hobart College in upper New York State. Eddy rejoined the Marines during World War II. [Following Eddy's time in Algeria with Coon] Eddy was named minister plenipotentiary to Saudi Arabia and went to live in Jidda, the port of Mecca. From there, in 1945, he was the man who made possible the almost unbelievable voyage of the old, crippled King Ibn Sa'ud on the American destroyer Murphy to a meeting with President Roosevelt on the Great Bitter Lake in the Suez Canal."

Col. William Eddy and Carleton Coon were often supported in their intelligence activities in Morocco by American Henry Winthrop Buckingham, a covert OSS agent who ran the Hotel El Fahar, a pension hotel in Morocco. Buckingham, a Yale University graduate, would later turn up in the Warren Commission investigation of JFK's assassination. At that time, as readers shall see, Buckingham was reported by the FBI as having possibly seen, and dealt with, Lee Harvey Oswald when Oswald was alleged by several other individuals to have been in Morocco. (See Chapter 5, Thomas Eli Davis, Jr.)

In Tangier, during late summer 1942 through early October of the same year, Coon reveals: "I became a commuter between Gibraltar and Tangier. My business was to load .45 pistols, ammunition, Sten guns, flares, and other useful objects into British diplomatic pouches and to see that they got to the British Legation, after which I had to shift them to our Legation and then tote them down to Casablanca in a US navy pouch. [Gordon] Browne also made some of these trips. My chief obstacle was the British foreign office. On several occasions, I had the pouches loaded and, at the last minute, I had to reduce the weight by half, remove all pistols, etc., etc., and this increased the frequency of my visits and made them all the more conspicuous."

After Coon moved from Tangier to OSS headquarters in Algiers in late October 1942, only two months before Darlan's assassination, accounts about his activities, including his own writings, become very vague. Coon appears to have deliberately downplayed his involvement in several critical areas. Fortunately, we do know from scant accounts of other OSS officers, and the diligent and recent research of several historians, and from Coon himself in his North African memoirs, about his time at the training camp. Coon tells us that prior to going to the camp he was bedbound for a week in Marrakech with exhaustion and pneumonia. He then journeyed to Tangier to confer with Colonel Eddy. After three days, Eddy told Coon that he was assigning him "definitely to Algiers, where I joined the Massingham mess [British military area] at Cape Matifou [cape area of Algeria]. There I stayed until Christmas." Coon continues:

I was assigned to [Cape Matifou], where there was doubt whether it was to be purely British or Anglo-American; meanwhile I was assigned to it as Colonel Eddy's personal representative, and as the only American. I ate and slept at the mess but, in the daytime, served as instructor for the Corps Franc d'Afrique at Aïn Taya. The British took me in very warm-heartedly, and I enjoyed my association with them very much. In fact, I liked them immensely and look back upon that period as a very pleasant one.

At the beginning, I understudied Major Bruce and Captain Gubbins [British instructors] in their instruction at Aïn Taya. I had little training in this and was very awkward. They were very tolerant and tried to help me. Soon it appeared that they were going to pull out and start instructing Massingham personnel at their new location at Club des Pins; I was to be left with the Corps Franc alone. Hence I chose six Frenchmen to serve as instructors and proceeded to train them intensively, but we had trouble because of the lack of materials. I arranged for these to be delivered and got permission to blow up a wrecked landing barge on the beach. Meanwhile the pupils were sent forward, and we were awaiting a new lot.

At the time, I wore British battle dress with a blue Corps Franc cap. When I went to Algiers I went in civilian dress. I drove my Studebaker with Consulat d'Amerique plates; all in all, I occupied an extremely anomalous position and often had to go into lengthy explanations with British MPs to get past them into the Matifou mess.

My work instructing at Aïn Taya was brought to an abrupt end on the day before Christmas. A former member of our camp at Aïn Taya assassinated Darlan; Captain Sabatier, the head of the camp, hid for several days and then went to jail; my instructors either hid or were jailed, and the camp and my instruction program blew up.

Oddly, this is Coon's extremely brief and implicit account of Darlan's murder. He makes no mention of the fact that he was very close, several blocks away, to the scene of the crime in the hour it took place. There is also the issue of where the gun came from that Bonnier shot Darlan with. Like the infamous Mannlicher-Carcano rifle that Lee Oswald allegedly used in Dallas, the chain of custody of the Darlan murder weapon, reported initially to be a Colt Woodsman .22 pistol, is disputed. The weapon was not used, or issued, by the American or British troops in Algiers as some claimed, but, coincidentally, Carleton Coon had brought such a gun to Algiers with him. Coon maintained, after the assassination, that his Colt Woodsman .22 had been stolen. However, most authorities said that Bonnier had used a Colt .45 caliber automatic, a handgun that had been issued to him and others in his group by his head trainer, Sabatier.

Like the Lee Harvey Oswald case—which had more than its share of odd and prominent personages involved in addition to Coon—there was another unexplained person on the scene of Darlan's murder. This was the British head of intelligence, Sir Stewart Menzies, who was widely known to have despised Darlan. Menzies, known in the trade as "C," rarely traveled to North Africa and reportedly had no reason to be in Algiers the day Darlan was assassinated. Menzies's presence in Algiers has never been explained and remains a mystery. His special assistant, Patrick Reilly, stated a few days after the assassination that Menzies had told him to take a brief and unexpected vacation just before Darlan was killed and that, when he returned, Menzies was there and made no mention of his Algiers trip. Again, like the Kennedy assassination, newspaper accounts identifying Bonnier as the lone assassin, with no known accomplices, appeared almost instantly.

It should be noted here that in Algiers, Eddy and Coon became notorious for their creative and extensive enlistment of Tangier prostitutes in their covert operations. Wrote Eddy after the war: "[We] would enlist the cooperation of Tangier prostitutes who, for a consideration, would earlier stroll around and take the Spanish sentry off into the woods for half an hour to (1) the saving of Allied lives, (2) the delight of the Spanish soldier, and (3) double pay, if not the delight of the prostitute. Well, she worked anyway, and why not in the woods as well as in the sheets?" In the early 1950s, officials at the CIA and US Federal Bureau of Narcotics emulated some of the Coon-Eddy tactics, employing prostitutes in New York, Chicago, and San Francisco.

* * *

Greatly overlooked in the dynamics of OSS interactions and activities with Admiral Darlan, as well as in directing the official duties of William Eddy and Carleton Coon, is Robert Daniel Murphy.

Murphy, despite his critical importance to FDR, General Eisenhower, and William Donovan, nearly always dwelt in the shadows of the significant history he helped create, mold, and shape. He was a natural diplomat, a born negotiator, pragmatic, wise, fearless, and uncanny in his foresight, willing to always go the extra mile to win the seemingly unwinnable. Reads a cover blurb for his book, *Diplomat Among Warriors*, "Whether in striped pants or cloak-and-dagger, Bob Murphy managed to be where the trouble was—and his story of his foreign service career is a unique combination of colorful personal experience and an absorbing, startling account of America's role in a turbulent world."

Born the son of a railroad worker in 1894 in Milwaukee, Wisconsin, Irish-American Catholic Robert Murphy studied prelaw at Marquette University, a Jesuit school in his hometown, and received his law degree from George Washington University in 1920. Following a position as a cipher clerk at the American Legation in Bern, Switzerland, Murphy became a foreign service officer in 1921 and served in Zurich, Munich, Seville, and Paris. In Munich, "When a noisy ruffian named Adolf Hitler fired a shot at the ceiling in the now-famous beer hall putsch, Mr. Murphy was on hand and taking notes."

In 1940, Murphy was counselor and ranking diplomat at the US Embassy in Paris. In 1941, when the Nazis entered Paris, Murphy became chargé d'affaires in Vichy, France. He was dispatched by FDR to Algeria to negotiate an agreement that became known as the Murphy-Weygand accords, which allowed the Roosevelt administration to grant Marshal Pétain's Vichy government licenses to import American food products and manufactured goods into French North Africa, despite a British blockade.

In autumn 1942, President Roosevelt asked Murphy, who had been granted the title Minister to French North Africa, to assess the situation with North Africa as part of secret preparations for the Allied invasion. Murphy was instrumental in gaining the agreement of key French army officers in supporting Operation Torch, the invasion of French North Africa. Despite the fact that Murphy despised the Vichy regime and most of its leaders, he never lost sight of the ultimate aims of President Roosevelt, General Eisenhower, and OSS director Donovan. When he struck an agreement with Admiral Darlan for his support of Allied forces, regardless of Darlan's unpopularity, Anglophobia, and anti-Semitism, the American and British media screamed bloody murder, but Eisenhower and Roosevelt knew the deal with Darlan was the key to victory.

THE VICHY

Murphy's *New York Times* obituary of 1978 reads: "Great care had been taken by Mr. Murphy and others to prevent the impending North African invasion from becoming known to Gen. Charles de Gaulle, who had raised the Free French standard in Jondon. Instead of General de Gaulle, the Allies selected Gen. Henri Honoré Giraud to head the French effort in North Africa after the [invasion] landings, but General Giraud turned out to have no following at all. No act of Mr. Murphy's was as violently criticized as his concurrence in the appointment as Governor General of Algeria of Marcel Peyrouton, a former Vichy Minister of the Interior who had signed the death warrant for General de Gaulle. Mr. Murphy wrote in his memoirs: "Some imaginative, but not well-informed, American journalists depicted me as the American Machiavelli, who had conspired with Peyrouton during those Vichy days and who had worked with him behind the scenes ever since. But such reports gave me and the State Department too much credit for guile."

The *New York Times* article is a bit off about General Giraud not having popular support. Indeed, Giraud was a national hero who had served in the French army for forty-six years, through both world wars. American diplomat Robert Murphy said of Giraud, "This extraordinary old soldier had a brilliant service record as a young officer in North Africa. He knew the country well, and he knew Arabs well and was generally respected by them. Giraud was somewhat of a specialist in escape."

In 1914, at the Battle of St. Quentin, Giraud was severely wounded in bayonet-to-bayonet fighting and then was captured by the Germans. Taken to a POW hospital in Belgium, he escaped seven weeks later by donning the disguise of a circus laborer. Later, in 1933, Giraud led several military operations against Rif rebels in Morocco. During World War II, he was captured in Wassigny, France, while leading a reconnaissance patrol against the Nazis. He was held at Kenigstein Castle outside of Dresden, and, after he was court-martialed "for ordering the execution of two German saboteurs" and acquitted, he then spent nearly two years planning his successful escape by lowering himself down the castle's surrounding and treacherous cliffs using torn bed sheets he tied together.

Returned to France, Giraud was widely hailed for his bravery, but some in the Vichy government attempted to talk him into returning to Germany. Giraud flatly refused, and an enraged Heinrich Himmler, Nazi Waffen SS chief, ordered the Gestapo to assassinate Giraud and to take as many members as possible of the general's family as hostages. In all, seventeen members of Giraud's family were forcibly held by the Nazis. Giraud still refused to surrender himself, and the Allies, aware of his daring escape, quickly contacted him. At a secret meeting on October 23, 1942, Giraud sat down with diplomat Robert Murphy and US Army General Mark W. Clark. Said Murphy of the meeting: "Some French military leaders holding African commands had been released by their captors after assurances that they would not take up arms against the Germans during the period of the Armistice. Giraud had made no promise, nor had he sworn allegiance to Marshal Pétain. So, he was free to set about organizing French resistance against the Germans, preparing for the day he confidently anticipated when American forces would arrive."

Giraud asked Murphy and Clark for a written commitment that he would be named commander of all French forces within two days of all landings in North Africa and France. On November 7, 1942, Giraud met with US General Dwight Eisenhower in Gibraltar. Eisenhower asked Giraud to take command of French North African troops for Operation Torch and to order them to fight for the Allies. Giraud, always fiercely proud and confident, told Eisenhower that if he didn't have the freedom to command the entire operation, he would not participate on any level and would sit the invasion out. Eisenhower held his ground. Giraud reluctantly gave in to Eisenhower's pleas and flew to Algiers on November 9. However, his attempt to take command of French forces was rebuffed because Admiral Darlan, already in Algiers, had craftily taken authority. Within several days, after Darlan ordered French troops to join the Allies, he was appointed high commissioner of French North and West Africa, and Giraud was named commander of all French forces under Darlan. After Darlan was assassinated, Giraud was elected to succeed Darlan.

MORE OSS SPECIAL OPS

Pertinent to the North African "Darlan affair" is the involvement of OSS officer C. D. Jackson. Charles Douglas Jackson, deputy director of the Office of War Information and deputy chief of the Psychological Warfare Division, was dispatched to Algiers to "ameliorate . . . the public relations disaster caused by the Americans with Admiral Jean Louis Darlan, a Vichy French collaborator with the Nazis." Many in America and the media were upset that the Eisenhower administration was "doing business with a Vichy Frenchman way too close to the Nazis." Jackson was the consummate propagandist even before the US entered the war, serving as president and emissary for his boss, news mogul Henry Luce of Time, Inc., of the Council for Democracy, founded in 1940 with primary funding by Luce to counter the America First Committee made up of isolationists that opposed America's entry into the war.

By the early '50s, Jackson was serving as president of the Free Europe Committee, the anticommunist propaganda machine under the control of then-deputy director of the CIA, Allen Dulles. Jackson oversaw the broadcast service Radio Free Europe. In 1952, he served as speech writer for General Eisenhower's first run for president, placing him in close proximity to two characters of particular interest, adman Rosser Reeves and US Ambassador to NATO and former

OSS agent Charles Spofford. Both Spofford and Reeves appear in the private papers of Pierre Lafitte in the context of money. Around the same time, Jackson also helped cofound the Bilderberg Group, the oft-reviled annual conference of international elites including monarchy, government leaders, military brass, the cream of academe and media, and above all global corporatists. The ground floor Bilderberg Steering Committee included Robert D. Murphy, as noted, a great friend of Ike Eisenhower and roving diplomat who had been in league with Jackson in North Africa.

Some readers may recall that C. D. Jackson—who most researchers believe, justifiably, was a trusted, longtime CIA asset—played a central role in taking possession of the original, infamous Zapruder motion picture film that graphically depicted the shooting of JFK. By Monday following the assassination, Richard B. Stolley, an editor for *LIFE* magazine who had arrived on the scene within hours of Kennedy's murder, had purchased all rights to the film from Abraham Zapruder on behalf of his employer. Inexplicably, Dallas authorities failed to seize the film as evidence in a crime, and Stolley's boss at *Time-LIFE*, C. D. Jackson, in an arrogant act of impudence, decided that the film be "withheld from public viewing."

As an expert in propaganda and psychological operations who would eventually serve as President Eisenhower's Special Assistant, working closely with the White House's Psychological Strategy Board and Operations Coordinating Board, Jackson is now widely viewed as the central player in establishing the bedrock for this nation's propaganda and psychological warfare programs, inclusive of the CIA's notorious Operation Mockingbird, a covert program begun in the early 1950s and overseen by Frank Wisner (Directorate of Plans), Allen Dulles (named DCI in 1953), and Cord Meyer (Office of Policy Coordination). The operation acted to recruit prominent American journalists to promote the CIA's positions on various policies and activities. Mockingbird also covertly funded an unknown but suspected sizable number of journals and magazines to publish articles written to influence the media and populations of other countries, as well as readers in the United States. At the top of the list of the Mockingbird network in the 1960s were *Time* and *LIFE* magazines, *Reader's Digest*, and Katherine Graham's *Washington Post* newspaper.

About a year after *Time-Life* decided to keep the Zapruder film under wraps, the Warren Commission, in October 1964, issued its instantly controversial report that concluded Lee Harvey Oswald was the lone gunman in the assassination. Surely, C. D. Jackson would have agreed with the Commission, but he passed away on September 18, 1964. One can only wonder what he would have thought about *Time-Life* having helped finance Oliver Stone's sensational feature film *JFK*.

* * *

In 1943, Major Coon handed OSS director William Donovan a detailed report he had written advocating agency adoption of political assassination as an instrument of state policy and the formalization of an ultraelite assassination bureau. Coon rationalized:

> The world is now too small and too tight to permit continuation of the process of trial and error. . . . A mistake made in one quarter will, of necessity, spread rapidly all over the world, for all our apples are now in one barrel, and if one rots the lot is destroyed. . . . We cannot be sure that the clear and objective scholars who study the existing social systems, and draw blueprints for a society to suit our technology, will always be heard, or that their plans will be put into operations. We can almost be sure that this will not be the case.
>
> Therefore, some other power, some third class of individuals aside from the leaders and scholars, must exist, and this third-class must have the task of thwarting mistakes, diagnosing areas of political world disequilibrium, and nipping the causes of potential disturbances in the bud. There must be a body of men whose task it is to throw out the rotten apples as soon as the first spots of decay appear. A body of this nature must exist undercover. It must either be a power unto itself or be given the broadest discretionary powers by the highest human authorities.

About ten years after Coon's assassination proposal was submitted to Donovan, it would appear in a slightly refined form in a 1955 study of the US State Department by Hans Morgenthau. Morgenthau was the father of Henry Morgenthau, a New Dealer who was FDR's secretary of the treasury and grandfather to Robert Morris Morgenthau, legendary and longtime New York County and Manhattan District Attorney. In his study, Hans Morgenthau discussed the existence in the United States of a "dual state." He wrote that the United States "includes both a 'regular state hierarchy' that acts according to the rule of law and a more or less hidden 'security hierarchy' that not only acts in parallel to the former but also monitors and exerts control over it." In Morgenthau's view, the "secret hierarchy" is able "to exert an effective veto over the decisions of the regular state governed by the rule of law."

Swedish research professor Ola Tunander aptly refers to the secret hierarchy as the "security state," arguing that ". . . the democratic state and the more autocratic security state always march side by side. While the democratic state offers legitimacy to security politics, the security state intervenes where necessary by limiting the range of democratic politics." According to Tunander, the democratic state seeks political alternatives, but when no alternative exists, the security state enters the scene to securitize the subsequent emergency. In fact, Tunander asserts, "the security state is the very apparatus that defines when and whether a state of emergency will emerge." Professor Tunander continues:

> Logically speaking, one might argue that Morgenthau's "dual state" is derived from the same duality as that described in Ernst Fraenkel's conception as typifying the Nazi regime of Hitler's Germany. In the Nazi case, though, this duality was overt, combining the "regular" legal state with a parallel "prerogative state," an autocratic paramilitary emergency state, or *Machtstaat* [dictatorship] that operated outside or "above" the legal system, with its philosophical foundation in the Schmittian "sovereign." Fraenkel refers to Emil Lederer, who argues that the *Machtstaat* ("power state," as distinct from the *Rechtstaat*) has its historical origins in the European aristocratic elite, which still played an important role within European society after the triumph of democracy. This elite acted behind the scenes in the 1920s to prevent a possible socialist takeover. However, this *Machtstaat*—the Nazi SS state—was arbitrary because of its individualized command.

In his analysis, Morgenthau draws a parallel between Nazi Germany and the US dual state. Indeed, in his view, the autocratic "security state" may be less visible and less arbitrary in democratic societies such as the US, but it is no less important. Morgenthau argues:

> . . . the power of making decisions remains with the authorities charged by law with making them, while, as a matter of fact, by virtue of their power over life and death, the agents of the secret police [and the security state] at the very least exert an effective veto over [these] decisions.

Many readers, at this point, may recognize in the novel state structures fashioned by Coon and Morgenthau the sturdy foundation for what is regarded today as "deep politics" or the "deep state."

According to William Donovan's biographer, Anthony Cave Brown, to whom Coon graciously gave a copy of his assassination corps proposal long missing from OSS files and archives, Donovan perhaps "gauged it imprudent and undesirable" to create Coon's "undercover, third class of assassin." However, the author disagrees with this assessment and believes there is ample evidence that the OSS and its successor agency, the CIA, with or without Donovan's official sanction, nonetheless created an assassination corps. In support of this is Major Coon's own keen experience with the Admiral Darlan assassination, which well exceeded the bounds of scholarly or political mutterings. There is also Coon's firsthand exposure to, and attendance at, the secret Camp X, which was dubbed a "school for mayhem and murder" by George Hunter White, an OSS officer who carried out at least two wartime assassinations.

Finally, under secret orders from OSS director Donovan, Coon, in September 1943, following the Darlan assassination, went to Corsica, an excursion that easily can be regarded as his continuation down the geopolitical trail of assassination. That month, Coon and a handpicked team of sabotage, demolition, and lethal skills experts boarded a French light cruiser called the *Fantasque* in Algeria and were swiftly carried to Corsica. There, Coon and his team rendezvoused with a soon-to-be legendary French army officer, Lucien Conien. Along with infamous QJ/WIN and US Army officer Boris Pash, Conien shares the upper tier of actors in the practice of state-sponsored murder, or assassination. Indeed, Conien has been greatly overlooked concerning his early history involving assassination.

According to declassified CIA and FBI files, Conien was "a former member of the Corsican Brotherhood." This despite the fact that the group's code was "once a member always a member." The Brotherhood was a shadowy, ultrasecret group that financed its operations through drug trafficking and contract killings, and which reportedly still exists today. People familiar with the Corsican Brotherhood say that it "makes the Mafia look like the Kiwanis Club" and that "the entire concept and practice of *omertà* originated with the Corsicans." Said Conien of the Corsicans:

When the Sicilians put out a contract [to kill], it's usually limited to the continental United States, or maybe Canada or Mexico. But with the Corsicans, it's international. They'll go anywhere. There's an old Corsican proverb "if you want revenge and you act in twenty years, you're acting in haste."

Lucien Conien appeared to be a natural swashbuckler with an overabundance of bravado. Born in Paris, France, in 1923, Lucien Emile Philippe Conien grew up in Kansas City, Kansas. In 1939, at the age of seventeen, he enlisted in the French army and was sent to France to fight. When France fell to the Germans in 1940, Conien returned to the United States and quickly enlisted in the US Army. Because of his combat experience in France, and his fluency in the French language, he was assigned to the OSS.

The OSS sent Conien stateside for jump school and counterinsurgency training and then dropped him by parachute behind enemy lines in Vichy France, with orders to assist the French Resistance launch assassination and to sabotage operations against their Nazi occupiers. It was in France, at this time, that Conien first encountered Jean Pierre Lafitte, then operating under the alias Jean Pierre Voyatzis, who was apparently working both sides of the fence. Through Lafitte, Conien was introduced to key members of the Corsican Brotherhood, the highly secret criminal cabal, which worked closely with the Resistance. Conien would later proudly reveal that he was made an honorary member of the Brotherhood—this about the same time that he met OSS officer Carleton Coon in Corsica.

British historian John Simkin writes: "In 1951, Gordon Stewart, the CIA chief of espionage in West Germany, sent Conien to establish a base in Nuremberg. The following year [CIA official] Ted Shackley arrived to help Conien with his work. The main purpose of this base was to send agents into Warsaw Pact countries to gather information needed to fight the Soviet Union during the Cold War. . . . Later, Conien worked with [CIA official] William Harvey in Berlin." It was at this time that Conien first encountered Otto Skorzeny, who was also covertly assisting Berlin Station Chief Harvey. Conien's next assignment was in Southeast Asia, where, earlier in 1945, he had parachuted into Vietnam and where he organized attacks against the Japanese Army. In 1947, Conien joined the staff of the CIA on the recommendation of CIA officer Richard Helms.

THE OAS AND THE AGINTER PRESS

Before being air-dropped into Vietnam again in 1954, Lucien Conien spent a few weeks at Otto Skorzeny's training camp outside of Madrid. It is the same camp where multiple French ultraright *guerre révolutionnaire* tacticians who would meld into the OAS were going through intensive warfare training before being dispatched to Vietnam. By 1957, they had become bitterly opposed to Senator John Kennedy from Massachusetts when he advocated for Algerian independence. The training was rigorous, even brutal at times. Skorzeny's chief trainers at the camp, Jean Rene Souetre, mentioned in the mysterious correspondence of Frenchman Paul Gluc, and fellow Frenchman Yves Guiliou, who widely used the alias Ralf Guerin-Serac, were relentless in their objective to shape their trainees into thoroughly trained professional soldiers. Conien met every several days with the former SS officer for drinks, dinner, and an occasional choice cigar.

Not surprisingly, and especially germane to one of this investigation's central characters, is that Lucian Conien knew Otto Skorzeny quite well. His initial links to Skorzeny can be found in La Cagoule, the French Resistance, and the long-standing, mysterious, and Portugal-based Aginter Press. Ostensibly a press or media agency, Aginter Press fronted for what CIA officials privately called "assassination central." Often wrongly cited as being founded in 1966, Aginter Press was first organized in 1962 by Skorzeny's prized trainer, Guérin-Serac, as a "counterinsurgency, counter-guerrilla center with support of the CIA, of the paramilitary Portuguese Legion, and especially of PIDE, the feared Portuguese secret police, which supposedly financed Aginter Press at the tune of two million escudos per month. Aginter Press was a sizable operation. Between 1962 and 1965, it organized and established an important network of informers linked, through PIDE, to the CIA and to the security services of such countries as West Germany, Spain, Greece, and South Africa," as well as numerous Latin American and several other European countries.

Significantly, as readers will learn in detail later—regardless of the fact that today the CIA maintains that it knows nothing about Guillou and that he does not appear in their voluminous files—we know that, only about six months before the JFK assassination, on May 23, 1963, Guillou, under the alias Guerin-Serac, accompanied by OAS member and trained assassin Captain Jean Rene Souetre, met with CIA representatives in Lisbon, Portugal. A brief glimpse at Captain Souetre before we encounter him in full in Chapter 10 tells us that a detailed once-secret memorandum by CIA Deputy Director of Plans Richard Helms identified the purpose of the Lisbon meeting, as described in at least two declassified CIA documents, which was to enlist the CIA in OAS efforts to assassinate French leader Charles de Gaulle.

Reads one of the CIA documents: [Souetre] said that after de Gaulle, there would be only two choices in France: Communism or the OAS. Therefore, the OAS believed that it was important to allow de Gaulle to remain in power while the OAS strengthened its organization. "Souetre pointed out, however, that the OAS must be prepared to counter a Communist plot at any time, as de Gaulle was an old man and also since he could easily meet with an accident. Souetre smiled as he made the last statement but hastened to add that the Communists might see fit to assassinate de Gaulle in order to precipitate the revolution. Soue-tre claimed that the OAS had a list of the Communist penetrations of the French Government and expressed the belief of the OAS that the de Gaulle government was aiding the Communist takeover by seeking a rapprochement with the USSR."

The July 10, 1963, memorandum sent to the US Department of State's Intelligence Bureau reveals that Souetre also told the CIA in Lisbon that "he intended to provide some information about the activities of [the OAS] which would be of interest to the US." Souetre also stated, "in answer to a question on his status in Portugal," that *he traveled on various passports, one of them being a US passport.* Helms writes that Souetre "claimed to be documented as a naturalized citizen from Martinique" and that *he had US contacts who could arrange documentation.* [Italics added.]

Souetre's claim that he traveled sometimes on a US passport is, of course, quite important to later sections of this book because of credible, subsequent reports that he traveled to Louisiana, Florida, and Dallas in 1963, prior to the JFK assassination. It has been reported that Souetre met with CIA official and assassination chief William King Harvey at Plantation Key, Florida, months before JFK was killed. It has also been alleged that Souetre met Lee Harvey Oswald at a CIA training camp in Florida prior to the assassination. At this meeting, Souetre is reported to have introduced himself to Oswald as "Alfred from Cuba." These claims will be explored in detail in the final chapters.

Significantly, in 1980, author and expert JFK researcher Dick Russell spoke to Mike Ewing, an investigator for the US House Select Committee on Assassinations, just as the committee was closing operations. Ewing told Russell that Jean Souetre "was connected with people involved with murders or political assassinations in Europe."

Continued Ewing: "[Souetre] was most definitely in the same circles of OAS-connected killers. The agency [CIA] admits that its own handlers of QJ/WIN and WI/ROUGE were afraid of them; that they were not following CIA directives; and that they were off on assassination plots of their own. The CIA was trying to keep them on a leash because it was afraid to cut them off."

Souetre's companion at the meeting in Lisbon was his compatriot Guerin-Serac, who, before he established Aginter Press, had been a French soldier serving in France, before fighting in the Korean Conflict in the early 1950s, and "possibly served as a liaison man between the CIA and the French services." Guillou/Guerin-Serac had also been a master parachutist in Algeria, "before he deserted the French army and joined the OAS rebellion. (This at the very same time as Jean Rene Souetre.) After Algerian independence and the OAS's defeat, he emigrated to Spain and then to Portugal, the last colonial empire that appeared willing to fight for Western values over 'Communist imperialism.'"

Historians Michael Bale and Franco Ferraresi have emphasized Guerin-Serac's instructive writings for novice terrorists, which, although written over fifty years ago, appear tailor-made for today's senior terrorists. Some apt excerpts from Guerin-Serac's manual *Missions Spéciales* are:

—Subversion acts with appropriate means upon the minds and wills in order to induce them to act outside all logic, against all rules, against all laws. In this way, it conditions individuals and enables one to make use of them as one wishes.

—*Action psychologique* [is] a nonviolent weapon [used] to condition public opinion through the use of the press, the radio, conferences, demonstrations, etc. . . . with the goal of uniting the masses against the authorities.

—Terrorism breaks the population's resistance, obtains its submission, and provokes a rupture between the population and the authorities. . . . There is a seizure of power over the masses through the creation of a climate of anxiety, insecurity, and danger.

—Selective terrorism . . . destroys the political and administrative apparatus by eliminating the cadres of those organs.

—Indiscriminate terrorism . . . destroys the confidence of the people by disorganizing the masses so as to manipulate them more effectively.

As mentioned, the two years before forming Aginter, Guerin-Serac both trained and served as a trainer in the arts of sabotage, explosives, and assassination at Otto Skorzeny's secret training camps outside of Madrid. Indeed, Guerin-Serac, along with Jean Rene Souetre, were considered Skorzeny's most competent trainers, and they were often called upon to work with US Special Forces who attended the camps. About this same time, claim several European historians, "US Army special forces began a program of targeting Western/NATO installations in Belgium, while disguising themselves as terrorists."

* * *

In early 1962, when Guerin-Serac first moved to establish Aginter Press, he acted in concert with Robert Leroy, a French SS officer during the war and WWII

Nazi SS officer Otto Skorzeny, both of whom served as the strategic leadership for Aginter. Leroy was a prewar member of Charles Maurras's Action Française, a Far-Right political group, and then an active member of La Cagoule's terrorist underground. He took part in the Carlist Requetés militia forces during the Spanish Civil War and then served as a Vichy intelligence operative. He was also a member of the Waffen SS Charlemagne division and was a key member of Otto Skorzeny's commando forces, where he served as an instructor. Along with Skorzeny, following the end of the war, Leroy served as a lead instructor with Skorzeny's efforts to train Egyptian leader Abd al-Nasir's intelligence and security services, after recruiting a hundred German advisers from Nazi soldiers serving during WWII, the SS underground, and from among technical experts with military industries. The purpose was to train Arab guerrillas in commando tactics and to protect the former Nazi technicians working for Nasir from Israeli "hit" teams. The job was carried out at the CIA's bequest."

Professor Ola Tunander writes revealingly of Aginter:

> [The] international fascist intelligence network, Aginter Press, was established to implement the Strategy of Tension, with support from the Portuguese security service PIDE and the CIA. This network included a unit specializing in the infiltration of anarchist and pro-Chinese groups, and its "correspondents" would use such organizations as a cover for carrying out bombings and other violent attacks. Aginter Press also included a strategic centre for subversion and intoxication [drugging and poisonings] operations, along with an executive action organization that carried out assassinations (most likely the same "pool of assassins" that William Harvey, CIA station Chief in Italy, had recruited in Europe for the CIA's "Executive Action Capability"). All of these divisions of Aginter Press were under the leadership of French OAS officer and former US liaison officer Captain Yves Guillou (alias Yves Guerin Serac), in collaboration with Robert Leroy, a former French SS officer, and *Otto Skorzeny, a senior German SS officer.* [Italics added.]

A portentous January 1968 affidavit sworn by Aginter Press assassin and Jean Rene Souetre associate Jacques Godard reveals the group's relationship with certain American persons and organizations: "In the course of our services we had relations with certain persons and organizations like, for example, President Tschombe and with Biafra. We likewise were in charge of relations with the John Birch Society, which was an American political group financed especially by

Texas oil producers whose activity is absolutely anti-communist. Everywhere where there is a struggle, either open or covert, with Communists, the John Birch Society [JBS] lends its financial aid to the people who are struggling against international communism."

The reader encounters the significance of the Texas oil producers and the Dallas branch of the JBS in Chapter 9, "Lay of the Land," to further understand the width and breadth of influence of Aginter Press and similar fascist organizations.

* * *

Readers will soon learn about two other far-reaching organizations quite similar to Aginter Press. These are the postwar World Commerce Corporation and the Nazi-created Spain-based SOFINDUS group, both ubiquitous commercial organizations that served as multifaceted intelligence operations and assassination bureaus.

Underscoring all these facts is the OSS's official War Report, as well as other declassified OSS documents, which reveal the agency's deep concerns, at one point, that it was "recruiting Mafiosi and, on a smaller scale, hit men from the ranks of Murder, Inc., and the infamous Philadelphia Purple Gang." According to the report: "[The OSS Operational Group] consisted of tough little boys from New York and Chicago, with a few live hoods mixed in. . . . Their one desire adds that, by 1943, 'there were several murders' and that 'these guys were considered to be so dangerous' that the Allied High Command ordered them 'confined to a castle near Spezia [Italy].'"

THE BLACK ORCHESTRA

No overview of the annals of State-sponsored violence and assassination would be complete without coverage of Stefano Delle Chiaie. Known variously throughout Europe as *"Umbra Mortis"* ("the Shadow of Death"), "the Black Pimpernel," and *"Il Caccola"* ("Shorty" in Italian slang), Delle Chiaie was also widely regarded as primary coordinator of political assassinations for the notorious "Black Orchestra" (*L'Orchestre Noir*). This was the name given to an ultrasecret, but loose-knit, organization of old-guard Nazis, neofascists, and racist Rightists, who were pro-Hitler Nazist and committed anticommunist. Born in 1936 into a "staunchly pro-fascist household" in Italy, Stefano "first appears to have been recruited into secret service work as an auxiliary agent" in "early summer of

1960." However, in 1958, Delle Chiaie, at the age of twenty-two, joined the ultrafascist group Ordine Nuovo (New Order), which had as its motto "Our Honor is Our Loyalty," adopted from the Nazi SS creed. About a year later, Delle Chiaie organized his own group, the Avanguardia, which was responsible for numerous assassinations and bombings throughout Italy. Said Delle Chiaie at the time: "We are for man-to-man engagements. Before setting out, our men are morally prepared so that they learn to break the bones even of somebody who keels down and cries."

Beginning in 1960, Delle Chiaie began carrying out his terrorist activities beyond Italian borders. Stuart Christie writes of Delle Chiaie:

> Outside Italy, Delle Chiaie and his accomplices have been responsible for the murders of exiled political dissidents, the setting up of death squads both in Europe and in Latin America, and the provision of mercenaries for right-wing plotters in Africa and Asia, while they have been partners in crime to international drug dealers and kidnappers. Delle Chiaie is also alleged to have acted as "regulator" for the sinister "P2" masonic lodge in Italy with the Vatican and various Latin American dictatorships.

Senior Official of the European Parliament Geoffrey Harris informs us that after Delle Chiaie fled his base in Italy, he journeyed to Madrid, Spain, where he joined up with Otto Skorzeny and Aginter Press leader Yves Guerin-Serac. Skorzeny placed Delle Chiaie under the tutelage of Guerin-Serac, and Delle Chiaie quickly became a trusted "correspondent" (assassin) under the aliases Roberto Martelli and Roberto Martin, often doing "wet work" (assassination) assigned by Skorzeny. Some of that work involved Skorzeny's band of mercenaries in Africa, the Organisation Armée Contre le Communisme International. According to French secret service documents, Delle Chiaie also planned and executed several murderous excursions into South America and the United States.

Stuart Christie, one of the very few historians who has covered Delle Chiaie, writes: "Delle Chiaie [was] welcomed to Spain by numerous friends of the 'Black Orchestra,' in particular Otto Skorzeny, the Duke of Valencia, Jose Antonio Giron, a former Franco minister who provided them with accommodation at his villa in Fuengirol, and Mariano Sanchez Covisa, an influential Madrid business-man and father of the notorious 'Guerrillas of Christ the King,' the Spanish death squads. Spain was to provide new opportunities for Stefano Delle Chiaie with his special skills, his considerable influence over his friendship circle and his small army of dedicated followers in both Italy and Spain. His leadership qualities were immediately recognized by Skorzeny, who took him under his wing as his protégé. Skorzeny's business operations also provided useful cover for the real life's work of Delle Chiaie, which was now entering a new and more international phase." Christie points out that Skorzeny and Delle Chiaie would pursue their fascist driven operations well into the late 1960s via the far-right mercenary organization Paladin Group in Françoist Spain. Writes Christie:

> The spirit of "contestation" which marked the late sixties and early seventies throughout the western world inspired resurgence in the activities of the anti-Françoist movements in Spain. The terrorist campaign initiated by the Basque separatist organization ETA was a particularly aggravating thorn in the flesh of the dictatorship. Obsessed with the threat of communism and inspired by the ideas of SAS founder David Stirling, Skorzeny had, since the early fifties, been toying with the idea of setting up an "international directorship of strategic assault personnel" [shades of the early OSS proposals] whose terms of reference would enable it to "Straddle the watershed between the paramilitary operations carried out by the troops in uniform and the political warfare which is conducted by civilian agents.

Christie explains that the Spanish Interior Ministry had given Skorzeny carte blanche to neutralize perceived enemies of Françoism. By 1968, he was recruiting his former Waffen SS men. Other recruits were former members of the OAS, the later outlawed Service d'Action Civique (SAC), as well as South Tyrolean and exiled Yugoslav fascists, Anti-Castro Cubans, and Portuguese exile fascists. According to Christie, "The day to day running of the Paladin organization, as it was named, was entrusted by Skorzeny to an old colleague from the Third Reich, Dr. Gerhardt Harmut von Schubert . . . . The public face of the Paladin organization was that of a legitimate security consultancy [similar to British Special Air Services founder, David Stirling's private military organization Watchguard] but this was only to provide cover for its real function of recruiting mercenaries and killers for dictators and failing colonialist regimes." The model of these private mercenary companies later inspired creation of similar, loosely regulated security firms in the US, most infamous being Blackwater Security in 1997.

Shortly after arriving in Spain and undergoing training at one of Skorzeny's camps, Delle Chiaie and Guerin-Serac developed "a new political theory" termed the "strategy of tension." British *Observer* newspaper editor Magnus Linklater describes the strategy as an idea that viewed "acts of terrorism . . . carried out and then blamed on left-wing groups." These terrorist acts would "gradually lead to the kind of instability that threatened the democratic state. If this continued long enough, the army might finally be encouraged to step in and take over, thus laying the ideal breeding-ground for Fascism—a military dictatorship."

In the 1970s, Delle Chiaie opened an incredible chapter to his violent life when he joined murderous forces with American assassin Michael Vernon Townley. Townley, in league with CIA officials and the Chilean secret police, carried out a shocking assassination in 1976 in Washington, D.C., when he blew up the car carrying Orlando Letelier, former Chilean ambassador to the United States, and his associate, Ronnie Moffitt, an American woman with the Institute for Policy Studies. (This author, Albarelli, witnessed the immediate aftermath of that horrific explosion.) The explosion rocked Washington's historic Dupont Circle and sent car fragments and bloody body parts flying for over a block. Townley was responsible for several other assassinations. He was convicted in absentia by an Italian court for an assassination attempt in 1975 in Rome. His assassination tools varied and included explosives, guns, brute force, and biochemicals.

Like the OSS, the US Army also maintained more than a passing interest in assassination, especially given the chaotic situation in Berlin and Eastern Europe at the end of the war. Thus, the Army, primarily through its Counter Intelligence Corps, made concerted efforts to recruit from its existing ranks any serviceman who had been imprisoned for murder or other violent crimes.

As author Albarelli has documented elsewhere in his body of work, from 1949 through the mid-1950s, the fledging CIA aggressively studied assassination history and techniques. A particularly blunt 1949 Agency memorandum reads:

> Let's get into the technology of assassination, figure most effective ways to kill—like Empress Agrippina—do you want your people to be able to get out of the room? Do you want it traced?

Empress Agrippina was the wife of Roman Emperor Claudius, whom the Empress wanted to murder so that her son Nero could attain the throne. Claudius had a fondness for eating mushrooms—a trait that most likely initially drew CIA's attention—and the Empress decided to poison him by mixing lethal mushrooms in with those he most favored eating. Among the Empress's concerns, according to Gordon and Valentina Wasson—two of the Agency's contractors most knowledgeable about mushrooms worldwide—was that the poison she employed could not be "sudden and instantaneous in its operation, lest the desperate achievement should be discovered." Or, as the CIA's memorandum casually expressed, the Empress "had to have time to get out of the room before Claudius keeled over." So, she chose the deadly *Amanita phalloides* mushroom, which the Wassons wrote was an excellent choice.

> The victim would not give away the game by normal indispositions at the meal, but when the seizure came, he would be so severely stricken that thereafter he would no longer be in command of his own affairs.

Suffice it to say, Nero took the throne.

ADVANCES IN TECHNIQUE

Incredibly, Carleton Coon's assassination proposal was not wholly original. It came on the heels of another secret memorandum to OSS director Donovan from Coon's friend, Col. William A. Eddy. In August 1942, Eddy sent Donovan a detailed proposal for an "assassination program," under which American and French agents would assassinate "all members of the German and Italian Armistice Commission in Morocco, with the appearance of a 'reprisal' unconnected to the OSS."

Additional evidence that Wild Bill Donovan moved forward with Coon's assassination proposal comes in the form of a November 1949 personal-and-confidential letter sent to him from an unidentified friend to whom he had issued a challenge several months earlier. Although the letter writer's name is redacted in declassified OSS documents, the author is certain that it was written by Dr. James Alexander Hamilton, an OSS official stationed at various stateside training sites.

The letter's author opens his missive with the greeting "Dear Bill" and apologizes for taking so long to get back to Donovan with his "thoughts on the problem which you raised when I saw you last." The letter then gets right to the task at hand, setting out "the means that I think might be most efficacious." Beginning with the intended outcomes, the writer is stunningly specific:

> You will recall that I mentioned that the local circumstance under which a given means might be used might suggest the technique to be used in that case. I think that gross divisions in presenting this subject might be (1)

bodies left with no hope of the cause of death being determined by the most complete autopsy and chemical examination, (2) bodies left in such circumstances as to simulate accidental death, (3) bodies left in such circumstances as to simulate suicidal death, and (4) bodies left with residua that simulate those caused by natural diseases.

Continuing his dispassionate survey, the writer proceeds to elaborate various detailed protocols for disguising, concealing, or avoiding trace evidence of cause of death, enabling undetected assassination. The letter states:

I believe that there are two chemical substances which would be most useful in that they would leave no characteristic pathologic findings, and the quantities needed could easily be transported to the places where they were to be used. One of these, sodium fluoroacetate, when ingested in sufficient quantities to cause death, does not cause characteristic pathologic lesions nor does it increase the amount of fluorine in the body to such a degree that it can be detected by quantitative methods. The other chemical substance which I have in mind is tetraethyl lead which, as you know, could be dropped on the skin in very small quantities, producing no local lesion, and after a quick death no specific pathologic evidence of the tetraethyl lead would be present.

If an individual could be placed into a relatively tightly sealed small room with a block of CO_2 ice, it is highly probable that his death would result and that there would be no chances of the circumstances being detected. It is highly probable, though, that there would be a period of hyperactivity in the course of such a death.

Another possibility would be the exposure of the entire individual to X-ray. When the whole of the body is exposed, a relatively small amount of radiation is sufficient to produce effects that would lead to death within a few weeks, and it is highly probable that sporadic deaths of this kind would be considered as due to blood dyscrasias.

If it were possible to subject the individual to a cold environment, he would freeze to death when his body temperature reached 70 degrees, and there is no anatomic lesion that is diagnostic in such cases.

There are other techniques which I believe should be mentioned since they require no special equipment besides a strong arm to smother the victim with a pillow or to strangle him with a wide piece of cloth, such as a bath towel. In such cases, there is no specific anatomic change to indicate the cause of death, though there may be serosal petechiae and marled visceral congestion which would suggest strangulation along with some other possibilities.

A shorter, second letter to "Bill" from Dr. Hamilton, dated three months later and presumed written to follow up the first, reads:

Due to work pressures here, I haven't had adequate time to pursue your questions regarding visceral congestion and strangulation. Assembly and review of available literature, which I am presently accomplishing for you, best answer the other issue you raised related to simulated suicide. I agree with your assumption that falls from high places are simplest to carry out and more effective. . . . [The] treatment of coffee or a drink beforehand, thus allowing others to participate in the scenario as described, is encouraged. In the proper settings, simulated suicide is foolproof.

Other evidence reveals that the OSS, in the final days of the war, closely examined the bioterrorism techniques explored by the Cagoule in France. As with all creative endeavors, the efficiency of assassination evolved, including the critical element of concealment. In 1952, the US Army's Special Operations Division at Camp Detrick in Frederick, Maryland, at the request of the CIA, performed a secret and formal study of assassins and their various techniques. Significantly boosting Camp Detrick's interest were the greatly overlooked efforts at bioterrorism and bioassassination that were conducted by La Cagoule's Henri Philippe Roidot, a high-level Cagoule assassin, who headed a three-member "execution team."

Historians Brunelle and Finlay-Croswhite reveal that Roidot "enrolled in a course at the famous Institut Pasteur," where he wanted to learn how to "cultivate typhus and botulism bacilli in test tubes" to be used for killing targeted subjects. Roidot went so far as to slip some of his concocted and assumed lethal substances into the drinks of enemies, but he had fallen short of creating anything toxic enough to kill. The latter Roidot also was less than discreet with his professors at the Institut, and he was dismissed from classes. Nonetheless, Henri Roidot appears to have been well ahead of the curve in biowarfare. During World War II, the OSS research and development department, after reviewing files on La Cagoule under the direction of Stanley Lovell, developed a covert program whereby Chinese prostitutes were enlisted to assassinate high-ranking Japanese officers with botulism-loaded capsules that were "less than the size of the head of a common pin." The program was quite effective.

And decades after the war, it was revealed during a 1977 Congressional hearing on the CIA that OSS agents used biological compounds to poison a number of targeted Nazis. Chief among these targets was the head of Germany's Reichbank, Hjalmar Schacht. The CIA, commenting on what it had seen in OSS files, said that the incident was "an example of the successful use of biological warfare materials." The Agency went on to say, "the biological material Staph enterotoxin was given to Schacht to make him so sick that he could not attend" an important meeting. Staph enterotoxin is an easily aerosolized bacterium that produces toxins that cause a variety of diseases, such as food poisoning and toxic shock syndrome. Central among the reasons the Schacht incident is cited here is his still-to-come and peculiar relationship with Lee Harvey Oswald's mother, which will be covered in detail later in this book, and, of course, Schacht's very close association to a critical subject in this book, Otto Skorzeny, and his wife, Ilse Skorzeny.

Last, there is the little-known and highly secret existence of Division 19. This was the OSS's launching pad for "assassination and elimination" programs. It was Division 19 that provided the bedrock for all the CIA's executive action [assassination] to come. First organized on June 28, 1941, by Executive Order number 8807 from President Roosevelt, Division 19 was initially run by Dr. H. Marshall Chadwell. Dr. Chadwell would eventually go on to become assistant director of Scientific Intelligence at the CIA, following stints at the Rockefeller Foundation in New York and the US Atomic Energy Commission. Division 19 was secreted within the National Defense Research Committee's [NDRC] Office of Scientific Research and Development. Under the Committee's structure, which maintained 19 divisions, Division 19 was headed "Miscellaneous" on purpose to obscure its true objectives. Dr. Vannevar Bush was chairperson of NDRC. (Bush is named extensively in an essay, Graduate Research Center of the Southwest, available in the appendix of this book.)

Readers should also be aware that closely following the end of World War II, the US Army's Col. Boris Pash, through his secret Alsos Mission, reported that the biowarfare capabilities of Nazi Germany were centered "on more than 70 bio-warfare research and development sites, including 16 universities; 10 commercial firms; 2 chemical warfare institutions; and 4 concentration camps which conducted experiments on human subjects." Pash's report revealed that "the only high-ranking Nazi to take an active interest in bio-warfare was Heinrich Himmler." Reads Pash's report: "Himmler's Waffen SS established a laboratory near Posen, Poland, in 1943, where it was intended to perform extensive experiments using human subjects. However, the laboratory would be abandoned before it could be completed, and a new laboratory in Geraburg, Thüringen, was still being built when Germany surrendered."

It is also pertinent to note here that OSS Major Carleton Coon was well acquainted with Dr. James Hamilton, author of the graphic assassination missives to Donovan. In February 1944, Coon traveled to the United States for the purpose of visiting Area S, a secret 100-acre OSS training compound in Fairfax County, Virginia. There he received special training in a wide range of specialized intelligence-related matters. OSS staff at the training compound who worked closely with Coon were Dr. James A. Hamilton, Camp S chief; Dr. Richard Lyman, the camp's "head psychiatrist"; Dr. Harry "Henry" Murray; and "Dr. Belachi and Dr. Gingerellli."

Dr. Hamilton, following World War II, had a significant history in peacetime psychological and behavior modification projects, inclusive of the CIA Projects MK/ULTRA and ARTICHOKE. Dr. Hamilton had also been a central member of the OSS Truth Drug project that was partially overseen by infamous federal narcotics agent George Hunter White, who mentored Pierre Lafitte for over a decade.

Interviewed in Hawaii, Dr. Hamilton told this author: "George White, as I'm sure you're aware, was not a scientist, nowhere near being one . . . his boasts about using THC as a truth drug on Del Grazio and others were laughable. We all knew that . . . Little Augie certainly knew when he was smoking anything other than tobacco. He was a connoisseur with hash . . . the entire truth was tremendously overblown. We were sincere in our efforts, but it never worked at all. White eventually arrived at experiments with more serious drugs under the CIA banner. Then things became serious."

And as things became serious for the Americans, Hunter-White pursued his tradecraft with delight while two other characters with leading roles in our saga—one of whom who helped create an ingenious system of interlocking front companies known as World Commerce Corp. and the other, a larger than life Nazi—together launched the varied and consequential postwar activities that ultimately left their mark on Dallas in November 1963. We move now to the effective and lucrative arrangement between Wild Bill Donovan and Otto Skorzeny and the attendant impact on the Cold War.

CHAPTER 2

HOLDING COMPANIES, INTEL OPS, AND THE COLD WAR

I t's a secret OSS gathering. The group of twelve is meeting in New York City at the Hotel Biltmore. The year is 1943. It is the height of the Second World War. Aline Griffith has volunteered for "hazardous duty" at the age of twenty-one. She will soon become known only as Aline, Countess of Romanoff.

Aline is staring at a photograph. The picture of the naked, bloody woman did not unduly impact her. It was the hopelessness of the situation. The sheer hopelessness of being surrounded by four sadistic SS officers.

I never want to find myself in such a situation, Aline thought.

Never.

"Are you sure you're willing to risk your life, Tiger [the code name she was assigned]?" she's asked, fully expecting the answer.

"Yes," she said.

"We have your assignment then" was the reply

Already? Aline thinks. She stiffed her back and took one last look at the photo.

"We need you in Spain."

Spain? She almost said it aloud.

Did she hear correctly? She had no idea but just didn't expect it.

France, Sweden, Switzerland, but not Spain. Spain.

It seemed like only moments ago she had been told to think about her assignment.

"You'll be there for some time," she was told. "Years, maybe longer, if everything works out."

* * *

To begin, in Madrid, operations are conducted out of a small section in the Calle Alcala Galiano, 4, twelve blocks from the embassy offices. Cover is the American

Oil Office, despite that the work has nothing to do with oil. Until September 1947 (when the CIA was founded), this "interim group" operated under the name of the World Commerce Corporation (WCC) with main offices in the Hotel Plaza Athénée in Paris. It was financed by several of Bill Donovan's wealthy OSS colleagues within New York-based Bache & Company and its global network.

Bache was a leading brokerage firm founded in 1879. In its early years, it was steered by oil industry magnate John D. Rockefeller, whose son Laurance makes an appearance later in our Madrid story. At its peak, Bache had 176 offices worldwide.

Said Aline of the OSS: "Before World War Two, the United States had no foreign intelligence service; only the American State Department had been responsible for collecting intelligence. [After I temporarily worked in the Paris office] Frank Ryan, who had been the OSS officer in Washington, D.C., in charge of Portugal and Spain during the War, was the person who directed our activities. We renewed contacts with agents in Czechoslovakia, Switzerland, West and East Germany, and the Scandinavian countries. The Cold War was already underway, and we were contacting agents and preserving experience that had been built up during the war."

At the time of this meeting at the Biltmore, Nazi SS officer Otto Skorzeny is still nearly five years away from working with peacetime Allied forces, including Donovan's OSS, but we've learned his focus is already directed at covert operations and assassinations. Soon, Otto and Hjalmar Schacht, the latter known widely as "Hitler's banker" and the close relative of Otto's soon-to-be (third) wife, Ilse, who would involve herself daily in the overall Skorzeny operations, would make significant contributions to the development of a number of corporations under the umbrella of the World Commerce Corporation (WCC), but we get ahead of ourselves.

THE OSS IS SHUTTERED

At the end of World War II, with the United States and Britain flush with victory and yearning for peace, the need for continued covert, national intelligence services was seriously questioned by both American and British leadership.

In late fall of 1944, OSS director William "Wild Bill" Donovan, who expectedly was staunchly in support of a continued role for his intelligence organization, handed President Roosevelt a secret memorandum proposing the creation of a permanent and centralized American intelligence agency modeled on the best of the OSS. Donovan's proposal also featured agency representation from the Army,

Navy, and Department of State, and retaining all specialized OSS personnel. Unfortunately, before it could receive a fair review, Donovan's proposal was leaked to the press, which claimed it would create a "super-spy system" and "American Gestapo." The chief suspect in the leak was FBI director J. Edgar Hoover. As intended, Hoover's behind-the-scene actions ignited a wildfire in the hotbed of Washington's cutthroat culture.

It was no secret that Roosevelt always had his doubts about Donovan, and in early 1945, he ordered Col. Richard Park, Jr., his chief White House military aide, to conduct a secret investigation into the wartime operations of the OSS. On March 12, 1945, Colonel Park handed Major General Clayton Lawrence Bissell, acting Chief of Staff for Army Intelligence, a top-secret, 58-page evaluation of OSS activities that Roosevelt had quietly asked him to compile. Said Bissell's memorandum for the record on Park's evaluation: "[Park] suggested I should read the first two pages, which I did. The paper recommended a rather thorough OSS housecleaning was desirable."

Bissell's housecleaning comment was an understatement. Had Col. Park's report drawn a line in the sand of an impending turf war between Donovan, the military, and Hoover's FBI? He certainly had far more drastic action proposed against the OSS. Wrote Col. Park at the front of his evaluation: *"If the OSS is permitted to continue with its present organization, it may do further serious harm to citizens, business interests, and national interests of the United States."* [Italics added.] Following these damning words, Park continued to pile it on:

It appears probable that many improper persons have penetrated into OSS—some who cannot handle themselves, some with questionable backgrounds, and some who may be plants for foreign intelligence and counterintelligence agencies. The Communist element in OSS is believed to be of dangerously large proportions. This will be revealed by a thorough investigation. OSS is hopelessly compromised to foreign governments, particularly the British, rendering it useless as a prospective independent postwar espionage agency. Further questioning of British intelligence authorities will evince nothing but praise because the OSS is like putty in their hands and they would be reluctant to forfeit a good tool. If the OSS is investigated after the war it may easily prove to have been relatively the most expensive and wasteful agency of the government. With a $57,000,000 budget, $37,000,000 of which may be expended without provision of law governing use of public funds for material and personnel, the possibilities of waste are apparent. There are indications that some official investigation of OSS may be forced after the war. It is believed the organization would have a difficult time justifying the expenditure of extremely large sums of money by result accomplished.

Having decisively whittled down the many-branched OSS tree to but a stubby stump, Park then recommended:

It is therefore recommended that General Donovan be replaced at the earliest possible moment by a person who shall be recommended by the Joint Chiefs of Staff [JCS], and who shall be instructed by the Joint Chiefs of Staff to re-examine the organization with the end of weeding out personnel and other elements of the OSS detrimental to the interests on the US . . . It is recommended that, although a world-wide secret intelligence coverage for the benefit of this government in the postwar period is necessary, a new agency with such superstructure as Donovan proposes be vetoed in favor of an organization along the lines of the one now in operation in the Western Hemisphere in which President Roosevelt appointed the Directors of Military Intelligence, Naval Intelligence, and the Federal Bureau of Investigation to cooperate. Such a plan however should have the approval of the JCS, FBI, and others whom the President sees fit.

Contained within the Park Report to Roosevelt were numerous examples of alleged OSS abuses and wrongdoings. In many ways, the report constituted a "Family jewels"-type document, like the one that would impact the CIA decades later, except that the Park report contained a fair amount of poorly written rumor, gossip, innuendo and semitruthful information, some quite pertinent to this book.

First is an item in the report that gives brief mention to a little-known and alleged OSS employee named Victor Oswald, whom readers will encounter again. Reads the section:

In August 1944, it was learned that one Victor Oswald, a Swiss national, married to a Dutch national, was coming to the U.S. A reliable source relates Oswald's statement that his trip was connected with a U.S. corporation for whom he was to handle all fertilizer matters. It was not known whether he planned to remain in the U.S. or whether he would return to Spain, where he formerly resided and worked in the Iberian Peninsula. It is reliably reported that he had been working for British intelligence and was, if fact, a British agent. It was also reported that he was an OSS employee.

Another item concerns the future head of the Central Intelligence Agency. It reads: "Mr. Allen Dulles, Chief of the OSS in Switzerland, is strongly influenced, particularly on Hungarian affairs, by a Mr. Royall Tyler who is also a member of the OSS. This has been confirmed. Mr. Tyler is in charge of Hungarian affairs and has had a channel to Hungary for some time. He also sent some US officers into Hungary, via parachute, two days before the Nazi occupation. Tyler is listed as a British secret agent of the Foreign Office in the top-secret files of the British S.I. in Istanbul and London. The story of his enrollment into British Secret Service is known to a number of persons in the US."

Another item is: "Late in 1943 a representative of the OSS reportedly approached a Washington widow possessing unusual social connections and background and employed in a government agency at a salary of $600 per month. The representative proposed that she lease a large apartment and undertake an extensive program of entertainment in an attempt to gain information from individuals whom OSS would ask her to invite to such parties. She was told that all expenses would be paid, including rental of the apartment, a suitable wardrobe, cost of entertainment, etc., and also her existing salary, as 'money means nothing.'"

Last: "In June 1943, a prominent businessman was told, at a formal dinner in Washington, by a member of the OSS, that they had just received an increase in authorized strength of 1,000 officers, 3,000 enlisted men and 5,000 WACs, two-thirds for foreign service and one-third for duty within this country. He asked why the large number of people for the US, when OSS already had so many personnel in Washington. He was told that the OSS planned to enter the field of domestic investigation and would be sort of a US Gestapo with power to penetrate every government agency, trade union, large corporation, etc." By the end of the war, the OSS had over 30,000 agents and paid assets worldwide.

Roosevelt deftly put Wild Bill's proposal aside until the media's fervor died down. He revived his interest in Donovan's memorandum in April 1945, only to die one week later, without taking any action on it. His successor, President Harry S. Truman, declared the OSS unnecessary in an era of peace and terminated it by executive order on September 20, 1945. Truman believed the central mission of any intelligence service should be to provide the commander in chief with daily reports and briefings on world events, and *not* the conduct of covert activities. His decision to eliminate the OSS was supported by certain senior military officials and FBI director Hoover, all of whom held a personal disdain for Donovan. In fact, a group linked to Army G-2 fabricated a White House paper highlighting damaging information compiled from every federal agency that had lodged a complaint against the OSS.

Donovan was aware of the strong animosity toward him but still struggled unsuccessfully to save the OSS. A few branches of the organization did survive, and on September 26, 1945, Brigadier General John Magruder, was former OSS Deputy Director for Intelligence, and John J. McCloy, who served as Assistant Secretary of War—a man many readers will recognize as having played a pivotal role in the Warren Commission—countermanded the presidential order to totally disband the organization. Thus, OSS officers were able to transfer to a new organization, the Strategic Services Unit. The transfer included the OSS Counter Espionage branch known as X-2.

Following the disbandment of the OSS, in May 1945, Donovan headed for Nuremberg at the invitation of Supreme Court Justice Robert Jackson, recently named by Truman to serve as chief US counsel at the trials. According to Douglas Waller, General Donovan's biographer, it was Donovan who selected Nuremberg, Germany, for the location of the trials, which he is alleged to have advocated for as early as October 1943.

Prior to his appointment, Jackson, on April 13, 1945, had given a speech before the American Society of International Law that captured President Truman's attention and resulted in Truman's quickly deciding to place US participation in the Nuremberg trials into Jackson's hands. In his April 13 speech, Jackson took exception with the proposed disposition of Nazi war criminals of US Treasury Secretary Henry Morgenthau and US Secretary of State Cordell Hull. Morgenthau and Hull "favored drumhead courts martial designed primarily to convict and execute" Nazi defendants.

In direct contrast, Jackson instead "favored a trial of the Nazis based on justice." Jackson said he "wanted convictions based on solid evidence." He was particularly upset over the US Justice Department's proposal "to turn over to the Soviet Union as many as half a million Germans regardless of personal guilt for 'reparations.'" In his position as US chief prosecutor at Nuremberg, Jackson also insisted that Nazis on trial be given the right to counsel "of their own choosing."

Writes Henry T. King, Jr., a former member of the US prosecuting team in Nuremberg: "In the evidentiary phase of the Nuremberg trials Jackson's approach offered fairness to the defendants. Jackson wanted the primary Nuremberg case against the Nazis to be substantiated by their own documents. He wanted less reliance on the testimony of witnesses and this approach precipitated a critical dispute with William J. Donovan, his presumed deputy, who wanted the case to be based on greater use of witnesses. Jackson prevailed, and Donovan went home."

For the purpose of this investigation, also serving the US prosecution team under Jackson were attorneys Robert G. Storey and Leon Jaworski. It is significant to note that both men became esteemed Texas attorneys and advanced lucrative practices with special emphasis on their oil industry expertise. Later, the two Texans not only served as assisting lawyers to the Warren Commission investigating JFK's assassination, but they were appointed to the formal group created by Texas Attorney General Waggoner Carr that produced its own report on the assassination, essentially a "ringing endorsement" of the Warren Commission Report. Readers will encounter the significance of Jaworski and Storey in a later chapter.

AMERICAN INTELLIGENCE CHOOSES SIDES

At the time of Donovan's arrival in Nuremberg, SS officer Skorzeny was being held in a Nuremberg witness wing, having been transferred there by aircraft from Wiesbaden, Germany. In a stroke of fate, he was one of the very first Nazis to be interrogated by Bill Donovan in November 1945. Recalled Skorzeny in 1957 on the encounter:

> One day I was called into an especially large interrogation room. A number of older gentlemen in uniform, among them a US Army general awaited me. Once again, I had to go over my mission in Italy at great length. At the end the general posed a few supplementary questions which revealed considerable knowledge. Unfortunately, I only learned much later that it had been Major General William Donovan who had interrogated me.

In another of several editions of Skorzeny's memoirs, he wrote a different account of his encounter with Donovan. Perhaps he met with the OSS chief more than once, or he had forgotten the earlier account. However, oddly, in the official Nuremberg record there is no documentation of the Donovan "interrogation" of Skorzeny. According to Skorzeny's private papers secured at auction by collector Major Ralph Ganis, this so-called interrogation did take place and included a long discussion of a secret business enterprise, World Commerce Corporation, that Donovan was helping create. According to Major Ganis in his book *The Skorzeny Papers: Evidence for the Plot to Kill JFK*, "it is likely Donovan's meeting with Skorzeny was not a routine interrogation but rather a sounding out. He was there to see firsthand the man entrusted to carry out Germany's most secret missions and evaluate his inside knowledge of Nazi assets for possible inclusion in asset recovery operations." Subsequently, Skorzeny was invited to partake as a chief covert operative. As mentioned previously, his acceptance of Donovan's invite would become more than apparent in the coming months and years. Said Skorzeny:

> Donovan asked to see me during my time in Nuremberg Prison. The meeting was very cordial; there was neither victor nor vanquished, just two soldiers, both rather dare devilish and inventive, who had served their countries to the best of their ability.

REMNANTS OF THE OSS AND SOE CONVERGE

Similar to Donovan's OSS, the British Special Operations Executive (SOE) would undergo an unceremonious dissolution. Like Donovan, his brother in spycraft, William Stephenson proposed saving the SOE after the war. Winston Churchill, who had been the biggest advocate of the SOE, seriously considered keeping the organization, realizing that the Soviet Union was becoming a major adversary to the West. But Churchill's loss in a general election in July 1945 removed the fate of the SOE from his purview. The new prime minister, Clement Attlee, held similar opinions to those of President Truman and summarily ordered the SOE shuttered practically overnight.

To their credit, Stephenson and Donovan had not only created efficient intelligence and covert operations services, but they also achieved the difficult task of creating organizations that worked well together. In numerous ways, the OSS and SOE were one and the same, and it was this effective coordination and blending that emerged as a unique capability. Unity of effort is one of the main principles of war, something both men understood well. When the war ended, the close relationship that had existed between the two organizations was exploited severely by Donovan's critics as a central security risk.

THE BACC ON THE ROAD TO THE WCC

Donovan and Stephenson were wise men who could ignore and rise above silly criticism. They were also loath to relinquish the hard-fought capacities of their organizations and their unique bond of trust and camaraderie. Taking matters into their own hands, the two men began to methodically and secretly implement a plan to save what they could of the OSS and SOE through the creation of a private intelligence service by using the existing structures and networks rejected by their governments. Thus was born one of the most remarkable intelligence organizations in the annals of the Cold War, the British-American-Canadian Company S.A. (BACC).

BACC, which soon was renamed the World Commerce Corporation, was initially based in Manhattan and registered in Panama. The quasi-government organization was formed in April 1945 by William Stephenson [known by his code name *Intrepid*, his code name] along with a handful of trusted former SOE officials, including Sir Charles Hambro (chief of the SOE). Hambro had been head of the SOE's first assassination unit, Section X; George Muhle Merten, who had run Donovan's highly secret and exceptionally well-funded Project George, concerned with enemy penetration of South America); David Mackenzie Ogilvy (one of Intrepid's staff officers); and John Arthur Reid Pepper (Intrepid's deputy). Stephenson listed his address as Plaza Hotel, New York City, with his legal residence in Jamaica, and listed himself as chairman of the board of Caribbean Cement Co. and Bermuda Hotels Corp.

Historian Anthony Cave Brown writes: "The BACC officers contemplated at formation were Pepper (president), Ogilvy and Merten (vice presidents), and Thomas William Hill (secretary). Hill gave his address Room 3606, 30 Rockefeller Plaza, New York City—the same address as that of Intrepid's British Security Coordination organization, although other reliable records indicate that while indeed located in Rockefeller Plaza, the BSC offices were at 600 Fifth Ave., the International Building (located in the complex with architectural twins La Maison Française and the British Empire Building) where Allen Dulles leased a private office when he was ousted from the CIA."

At first, Donovan appears to have played no formal part in the establishment of either BACC or WCC, although his law firm, at that time known as Donovan Leisure Newton Lombard & Irvine, acted as legal advisers. (A few amateur historians have written that Allen Dulles's law firm, Sullivan and Cromwell, served as advisers to BACC and WCC, but we found no hard evidence of that. Additionally, it has been written that Dulles encouraged Donovan to participate in BACC and WCC, but again no hard evidence of that was found.) This leads us to speculate that Donovan may have initially been the "face" of WCC rather than the inspiration, as those listed in early documents for WCC include Harry Beaston Lake and W. W. Cumberland, both investment bankers at the firm Ladenburg Thalmann, 25 Broad St. NYC.

In 1879, American banker Ernst Thalmann teamed up with Adolph Ladenburg, the scion of a German banking family. As confirmed in "History of Ladenburg Thalmann," by World War II the firm was providing banking services for British Security Coordination (BSC), including acquisition of foreign currency, which was required in small denominations by a plethora of British covert wartime agencies as well as escape packs for Allied aircrew. The SOE turned to the BSC, and the close links between the BSC and Donovan's OSS meant that there was continual collaboration between all three entities in support of this task. Harry Lake and Bill Donovan shared an address at the exclusive One Sutton Place for a number of years. It should be noted that Lake was on the board of the American Moroccan Corporation, which will have greater relevance as we pursue the role of Thomas Eli Davis, Jr. in Chapter 5.

In a convenient web of other addresses, Donovan's law partner, George Stanley Leisure, lived at 640-660 Park, sharing a prestigious address with J. Russell Forgan, another founding board member of World Commerce. Leisure was on the board of financial investment giant Empire Trust, whose web extends over time to those active on the ground in Dallas that managed the immediate aftermath of the assassination. Forgan's company, Glore Forgan, was heavily invested in J. Peter Grace's W. R. Grace & Co., a global maritime shipping concern. Grace, the first grand master of the Sovereign Military Order of Malta, a.k.a. the Knights of Malta, in America, sat on Forgan's board for decades.

Of note, at the height of the war, the man at the official helm of the SOE, Roundell Palmer, the 3rd Earl of Selborne, was also in charge of economic warfare, placing him in close proximity to decisions involving the services Ladenburg Thalmann provided. Reporting directly to Lord Selborne was Viscount Frederick Leathers, a former Minister of Transport who was placed in charge of war support. For those more familiar with the esotericism that preoccupied the shadows of power at the time, both in the US and Britain, both men were alleged members of the Prieuré de Sion, a neochivalric fraternal order with alleged roots in the Crusades, established legally in 1956 in France. In an instance of continuity, Viscount Leathers later appears in the roster of board members of the World Commerce Corporation.

Brown explains that among those legal advisers (Donovan and Leisure's firm) was Lt. Col. Otto C. Doering, Donovan's second in command at the OSS. Donovan only became an official director of WCC in October 1947. At the same time, Edward R. Stettinius, Secretary of State from November 1944 to July 1945, who had substantial holdings in WCC, joined the board. According to Brown, in due course a number of other people prominent in intelligence and special operations joined the firm, as directors, officer, or shareholders. They included J. Russell Forgan of the Glore Forgan group of merchant bankers (and future career ambassador David Bruce's successor as chief of OSS Europe); Lester Armour (former deputy chief mission to Moscow who would inherit the chairmanship of the Swift Armour packing company of Chicago); W.K. Eliscu (a member of Donovan's OSS staff); Lieutenant Colonel Rex L. Benson (staff member of the British Secret Intelligence Service and chairman of merchant bankers Robert Benson and Company of London). Here it should be noted that Benson was the lead SOE interrogator of Otto Skorzeny after his surrender. Brown adds that the WCC board also included several persons who had been prominent in the Canadian intelligence services.

In addition, Brown tells us that people with intelligence connections, but not formally members of any intelligence service, took an interest in the corporation. They included Nelson Rockefeller (son of John D. and former coordinator of Inter-American Affairs, an organization with intelligence responsibilities and associations in South America); John Jay McCloy (former undersecretary of the War Department and high commissioner in Germany); Richard Mellon (of Gulf Oil corporation); and Sir Victor Sassoon. The list of WCC board members and "interested parties" reflects America and Britain's future power brokers that would influence matters on a global scale as the Cold War escalated.

With so many powerful corporate titans interested in the WCC, in hindsight the holding company emerges as a quango, an acronym for 'quasi-autonomous nongovernmental organization, a term coined in the 1970s inspired by remarks of the president of Carnegie Corporation in 1967 describing *"a genus of organization which represents a noteworthy experiment in the art of government."* Were the founders of the WCC following European models established under fascist regimes for the control of and profit from global supply chains and markets, and did that agenda require the services of the sophisticated intelligence apparatus established by Donovan and Stephenson being shuttered by democratically elected government officials after the war? A former employee of WCC recounts, "The idea was to take advantage of the organization and international contacts that were set up during the war . . . The goal was to set up various companies, mostly in Central and South America." And as British writer and wartime intelligence officer Roald Dahl argued in support of the creation of WCC, "we all needed jobs in civilian life."

It is believed that BACC/WCC was initially funded in part with about $10 million that was in the accounts of the OSS London office at the time of Germany's surrender. Eustice Mullins writes: "This money could not be 'returned' to the U.S. Government without stating where it had come from. As proceeds from dealings in gold and jewels, an inquiry could provoke a Congressional investigation."

FOLLOW THE MONEY AND THE ARMS

About the same time that Donovan and Stephenson began seriously organizing BACC, word began to leak out in certain Washington, D.C., quarters about nefarious activities of certain OSS officials and agents who had been involved in the wartime looting of enormous amounts of gold, gems, diamonds, antiquities, and art. Some credible reports centered on what appeared to be a large number of OSS officials who had stolen millions in gold from captured Nazi stockpiles and hidden warehouses. Some prestigious banks in Europe and North Africa were said to have amassed millions of dollars in gold and diamonds. Eventually these reports linked up to postwar accounts concerning former SS officer Otto Skorzeny, and a few of his fellow officers, who had been given substantial amounts of gold, some of which had come from OSS-looted coffers. Substantial amounts of gold also flowed from other sources. There can be little doubt that these rumors either influenced, or made their way into, Col. Richard Park's report.

When Frank T. Ryan, who had been stationed in Spain as the Chief of SI (Secret Intelligence), became president of World Commerce in place of Pepper, who remained as executive vice president, Intrepid arranged for him to see in London a group of men prominent in government, intelligence, and finance. Ryan, who later managed the activities of the Countess of Romanones and came to know Otto Skorzeny quite well, is elaborated upon later in the chapter as the story of the Countess continues. For now, the men Ryan would be introduced to by Intrepid comprised a virtual who's-who of high finance in the United Kingdom. They were connected to virtually every large financial institution in the U.K. and the United States. A result of the inspired symbiosis, within a five-year period following the founding of the BACC, its successor, the WCC, had organized at least 275 additional corporations worldwide under its umbrella. Many of these enterprises appear to have been aligned with the Swiss-based holding company Permanent Industrial Exposition or "Permindex," alleged to be a trade organization that many researchers argue served as a CIA front. Permindex is studied in more depth as we close this chapter.

* * *

By all indications in the Skorzeny private papers, Victor Oswald was not only a close colleague of his, but both men knew Frank Ryan, the hands-on director of the WCC. Oswald was a Swiss citizen, married to a Dutch National, who often traveled to the United States but resided in Madrid, where he had gone into business with Otto Skorzeny. Some reliable reports have Oswald working as a covert British agent during the war, as well as the OSS. Perhaps like Viscount Leathers, Oswald served as liaison. According to Pierre Lafitte's 1962 datebook, Oswald had a hand in arms shipments to CIA training camps outside of New Orleans, Louisiana.

Important to also note here is that Oswald maintained a number of ownership positions with a number of Mexico- and Germany-headquartered firms, including at least one that appeared to involve Warren Broglie, a Swiss national, and Franz Waehauf, a German, respectively the manager and an employee at the Luma Hotel in 1963, when Lee Harvey Oswald visited both Mexico City and the hotel. Equally relevant is an October 1, 1963, datebook entry, *"tell Tom D. O says come to Madrid,"* the importance of which will be made clear in Chapter 5, focused on a gunrunning soldier of fortune by the name of Thomas Eli Davis, Jr.

Interesting to reveal here is that Victor Oswald was also a constant object for observation by the US Embassy in Madrid. In May 1949, Paul T. Culbertson, chargé d'affaires, US Embassy in Spain, sent a "Confidential" letter to US Secretary of State Dean Acheson displaying a keen interest in Oswald's affairs. The letter addressed the embassy's concern over several German firms operating in Spain.

Reads the letter in part:

I have the honor to report that the embassy is in receipt of several communications from the Office of the Political Adviser for Germany at Frankfurt commenting on evidence received that the firm Empresas Reunidas Comercio Exterior S.A., Madrid, sometimes known as ERCESA, is a cover for Johannes BERNHARDT, former SS General and operator of the German state holding company, SOFINDUS, and on intimations that Bernhardt also has some connection with the firm of H.V. Oswald Company, of which the principal proprietor is Mr. Victor OSWALD, a Swiss national resident in Madrid. This embassy has thoroughly investigated this natter, utilizing the facilities of a controlled American source, normal credit agencies, and available files. It is found that Empresas Reunidas Comercio Exterior, S. A., is unquestionably controlled by or serving in the interests of Johannes Bernhardt. The management has changed hands at least twice in the last two years. All three of the present Spanish directors are known to have been former pro-Nazis. Two of them, Gregorio PEREZ Huidobro, an officer of the Madrid police department, and Federico CARUNCHO Astrey [on the list of blocked nationals by US Dept of Treasury Office of Foreign Assets Control], have long been known to be intimates and employees of Bernhardt. Evidence is available indicating that Bernhardt owns all of the capital of the company.

According to a document generated by the US State Department Secret Security Information titled "German Nationalist and Neo-Nazi Activities in Argentina": ". . . The scattered neo-Nazis also have in common a certain optimism as to the future, and appear to have ample financial backing. They receive support from such industrialists and financiers as Ludwig Freude, and possibly, Fritz Mandl in Argentina and Johannes Bernhardt in Spain. Nazi war veterans like Otto Skorzeny and air ace Col. Hans-Ulrich Rudel serve or are used by unknown leaders to stimulate interest in and coordinate organizational efforts. During the past five years Skorzeny and Rudel have traveled in an orbit touching Buenos Aires, Madrid, Cairo, Munich, Vienna, Dublin, and Paris. The reasons for Dublin will be better understood later in our story."

An additional government report titled "Pattern of Post-War Nazi "Survival" Operation" reveals that "1947 and 1948 showed continuing growth in Spain of a secret international Nazi-Fascist movement. Information conveyed through a reliable source in Brussels told that the movement was to be called 'The New Socialist Europe'; for the moment, however, it was more realistically designated the 'Shelter for the Downcast' (Hogar de los Desperados)."

The Brussels report mentioned three leaders of this movement. The first of the leaders named appears to be Guido Beck, a Czech physicist, who had been in Argentina since 1948. The second leader named can be clearly identified as Johannes G.F. Bernhardt. Bernhardt, since 1936, had occupied a position of peculiar advantage in Spain and commanded a large private fortune. He was the principal agent for the German Government in its transactions with the Spanish Nationalists regarding delivery of war supplies during the Spanish Civil War and was consulted by the German Embassy regarding the charges and payments.

A 1937 memorandum of the Director of Economic Policy Division in the German Foreign Office shows that Hermann Goering intended "to appoint Herr Bernhardt as his special representative for economic questions in Nationalist Spain. . . . Spain's war debt to Germany was estimated at 400 million RM. Part of the settlement was to be made through Spanish Government investments in the SOFINDUS (Sociedad Financiera Industrial) headed by Bernhardt. . . . The third member of the trio of leaders named in the Brussels report perhaps was none other than Otto Skorzeny."

In spite of these reports, which in fairness to Paul Culbertson may not have been widely distributed, the chargé d'affaires at the American Embassy in Madrid concluded: "With regard to any financial or business connections between Bernhardt and Victor Oswald or his firm, the embassy has been unable to secure any evidence. Oswald is known to be acquainted with Bernhardt and readily admits such acquaintance but disclaims any connection or dealings with him whatever. From evidence at hand, it is my opinion that Oswald is too intelligent and too well-connected to either wish or need to have any dealings with Bernhardt." Bernhardt's history suggests that Culbertson was not fully informed about the position he held, which brought Victor Oswald's friend and business partner, Otto Skorzeny into his realm.

SOFINDUS

Further study of the Madrid-based Sociedad Financiera Industrial (SOFINDUS) emphasizes the extraordinary reach of umbrella holding companies similar to World Commerce Corp. It could be argued that SOFINDUS provided the model for WCC. According to a document released by the CIA, "Nazi War Crimes Disclosure Act," composed in June 1945, at the outbreak of the Spanish Civil War in 1936, German-born businessman and Nazi Johannes Bernhardt offered his services to Franco, a personal friend of his. It was arranged that the subject handle the exchange of Spanish products for German war material.

The report continues to document that in 1938, under his direction, in addition to serving as a purchasing agency for wolfram (tungsten) and other strategic commodities, Bernhardt handled foreign exchange transactions for the German Government and the German intelligence services; provided cover employment for Hitler's SiPo [security police] and SD agents, sometimes paying a part of their salaries; facilitated the granting of Spanish visas to Abwehr agents, promising employment; set up bank deposits (probably in Spanish names) to provide for Abwehr expenses in case of diplomatic break between Spain and Germany; and assisted the German intelligence services in other ways. SOFINDUS also handled foreign exchange for the Nazi Government and the intelligence services. During the German domination of France, Bernhardt had held extraordinary powers to control transportation for the more efficient delivery of goods, not only in Germany, but in France, as well.

The report adds that Bernhardt is also said to have a substantial camouflaged interest in Prodag (Productos Agricolas, S.A.), import-export of agricultural products headquartered in Valencia, Spain, whose board included at least one former Nazi SS staff officer.

"Evidence of intention to carry on Nazi activities, and of belief in eventual resurgence of Nazism, has been apparent among Germans in Argentina since 1946. Shadow organizations left behind by officials of the Nazi Party and Third Reich upon the break in diplomatic relations between Argentina and Germany, in 1944, have continued to function." Thus reads the introduction of a 1953 State Department report referred to previously, "German Nationalist and Neo-Nazi Activities in Argentina," and designated "Secret Security Information," finally released by the CIA in 2000. As mentioned, according to the US State Dept. report, the neo-Nazis were optimistic that fascism would prevail on a global scale and received support from: Nazi Ludwig Freude—alleged to have been Peron's close German confidant and the most important Nazi in Argentina who, while his son as Peron's private secretary shepherded Nazis into the country, Ludwig smuggled in their money; Friederich "Fritz" Mandl, a Viennese-born munitions king and dealer in the precious wartime commodity of iron, closely aligned with Peron during the Cold War; and Johannes Bernhardt, the mastermind of SOFINDUS, all employing the organizational skills of SS Otto Skorzeny and Hans Rudel.

The State Department advised Eisenhower's White House division that while both the neo-Nazi movement in Argentina and the radical nationalist organizations in Germany lack unity and dominant leadership, "they are generally guided, however, by a single basic aim, which is to destroy or invalidate democratic capitalism and establish planned economy on a global scale through the agency of strong totalitarian governments."

According to Ralph Ganis, author of *The Skorzeny Papers: Evidence for the Plot to Kill JFK*, Otto Skorzeny was aware of all operational aspects of Bernhardt's SOFINDUS and its agent network. The seizure of Nazi assets in Spain by the Allies, made public in news reports on September 25, 1945, included those held by Johannes Bernhardt's SOFINDUS, which Ganis says also provided cover for a vast Nazi network that extended into South America, and the timing of the seizure of assets in Spain coincides with the foundation of the BACC, soon to be named WCC, which took advantage of Skorzeny's particular skills.

Before pursuing WCC in depth, in 1953, Bernhardt of SOFINDUS, whose expertise included export-import of agricultural products and attendant commodities futures, established a major operation in Buenos Aires, Argentina, prompting our interest in what came to be called "the great salad oil swindle," the financial scandal that had been brewing since 1962 but culminated the morning of November 22, 1963, just two hours and fifteen minutes before Kennedy was gunned down in Dallas. The alleged swindle, reported in depth by Pulitzer Prize-winning journalist Norman C. Miller of the *Wall Street Journal*, implicated the Buenos Aires-based agribusiness conglomerate Bunge Corporation, the largest customer of New Jersey-based Allied Crude Vegetable Oil. Allied's president, Toni DeAngelis, guilty of a bizarre scheme to mislead inspectors responsible for measuring the amount of oil stored in massive tanks with American Express Field Warehousing Corp, claimed that Bunge had started short selling his stock around November 15. Bunge executives denied the claim. As reported in "Mind Control, Oswald & JFK: Were We Controlled?" by Kenn Thomas and Lawrence Lincoln, the underanalyzed financial crisis on the morning of November 22 that had been triggered by the salad oil scandal and the assassination of Kennedy cannot be coincidental. Their research provides us a distinct thread to warrant reasonable suspicion that Skorzeny's fellow Nazi and close business associate, Johannes Bernhardt, was likely involved in the near collapse of the US commodity market as part of a greater agenda—an agenda summed up in a cautionary State Department memo of the period—*to destroy or invalidate democratic capitalism and establish planned economy on a global scale through the agency of strong totalitarian governments.* [Italics added.]

THE WORLD COMMERCE CORPORATION

On April 2, 1947, BACC officially changed its name to the World Commerce Corporation (WCC), maintaining its headquarters in New York. States Brown: *"What was remarkable about the corporation was that all but one of its first directors, and about everyone associated with it, had had intelligence connections with the American and British governments during World War II and that all the officers were former members of Donovan's and Intrepid's services."* [Italics added.]

An April 4, 1952, memorandum to the US Secretary of State reveals some of the financial dynamics, governmental cooperation, and business reach of WCC when it reported that WCC officials were having discussions for over a year "with the Czechs looking toward the purchase of a German steel company of a Czechoslovak strip mill, which has been under a blocking order of the US Treasury since January 17 [1952]." It just so happens that this former Nazi company involved our primary subject, Otto Skorzeny.

As mentioned, the level of Donovan's initial involvement in the operational BACC is difficult to determine, but clearly the fledgling company was legally represented by Donovan's New York law firm. Also clear is that Donovan had begun secretly transferring his government organization over to a private cover company even before the formal decision had been made to disband the OSS.

Evidence of Donovan's transferring organizational assets is found in the recollections of one of Donovan's more fascinating agents, Aline, Countess of Romanones, the femme fatale who opened our chapter. As noted, the Countess was a former OSS agent, born in Pearl River, New York, in 1923 as Aline Griffith. After graduating from college in 1943, and working as a model, she was recruited, as described in our opening vignette, by the OSS.

Aline's assignment in Madrid, January 1944 to August 1945, meant that she worked for OSS officer Frank T. Ryan. As mentioned, Ryan, the son of wealthy industrialist John J. Ryan, was the OSS chief of SI for Spain. At the end of the war, in April 1945, we now know that Frank Ryan helped his boss, William Donovan, and William Stephenson (Intrepid), formerly of the SOE, form the BACC, the first incarnation of the World Commerce Corp.

Countess Aline's recollections of the formation of BACC and WCC, written in 1991, are especially insightful and raise several intriguing issues:

> In August 1945, a cable came in from Washington ordering the immediate return of all OSS employees in Spain and the termination of all networks that had been working for us. It was a hasty move and created much distress among our staff. The same week, I received a surprise. An OSS official from Washington visited and informed me that I was the only one of our SI group to be kept on for work in a super-secret organization inside Spain. I was told this would depend on my being able to get my visa extended to permit me to remain in the country.

Aline explains that she was instructed to prolong her visa by reopening offices for John J. Ryan and Sons, where she would obtain bona fide sales to Catalan manufacturers. Then, abruptly, she was ordered to Paris to work for World Commerce Corporation, in a similar role she had filled in Madrid, but focused on French firms and their business in Czechoslovakia and Sweden. Six months later, she was sent to Zurich, Switzerland, where she would again work for World Commerce to establish a similar office. The future countess writes:

> My boss at the time was Frank Ryan, who had been the Chief of SI for Spain and Portugal in Washington. I had the impression that I would eventually be organizing networks for information on Soviet intelligence

activities. I was scheduled to move to Prague to open offices there when I married. Only 40 years later [approximately 1990] did I learn that this company [WCC] was not openly being used as a cover for US government intelligence, even though everybody I saw and worked with during the two years in that job had been an OSS agent in one country or another. The company's set-up seems to have been a precursor to the Iran-Contra situation, where sales from private companies were used to bolster pro-US groups in a foreign country.

Said Aline shortly before she died on December 11, 2017:

> It was [different] after eight or nine years. Otto [Skorzeny] came in as leader and everything changed . . . everything went through him. For me it was for the better. With the [assassination] transfer to Otto we were far more sophisticated. More weapons at our use . . . anything really . . . staff I didn't know we had use of . . it became very sophisticated, more widespread. I was soon out of it. . . . I didn't want to know half of what we were doing.

A page from the financial ledger maintained by Pierre Lafitte brings the Countess's story full circle. He writes, "*Using old American Oil Mission cover with Harvey (JA)*," which is clear reference to Aline's American Oil Office. That particular ledger sheet also includes the names of Willoughby, a primary suspect in this investigation; Conrad Hilton (Hilton Hotels and board member of General Dynamics behind the F-111 scandal, which Bobby Baker was embroiled in during the fall of '63; adman Rosser Reeves, who was the brother-in-law of David Ogilvy, who authored the mission statement for Bill Donovan's WCC; and Charles Spofford, Gen. Eisenhower's trusted confidant, who along with Ogilvy ran Ike's presidential campaign, coining the tag "I Like Ike." The other name, "Rothermel," can be safely assumed to refer to Paul Rothermel, confidential assistant to Dallas oilman H. L. Hunt. Aline's service to Frank Ryan and the World Commerce Corp. and reference to her old cover, American Oil, indicate a certain continuity of intelligence operations throughout the Cold War.

* * *

How might Otto Skorzeny and his new bride, Ilse, have purchased a place at the table among the business elites that formed the World Commerce Corp, aside from skills honed during the war? Donovan's OSS secretly reported that the Reichsbank gave "two to three sacks of gold to [Otto] Skorzeny," and that an additional "approximately 2 million Reichsmarks and a considerable quantity of dollars were probably given to Skorzeny." And, added the OSS, Skorzeny was "presumed to have transported, during the first days of May 1945, and on mule back, considerable quantities of gold coins and precious stones contained in leather sacks, and to have buried them in the immediate neighborhood of Theodor Kornerhutte in a hut located under the Dachstien (Austria-US Zone). These gold coins and precious stones, presumably stolen from the main part of France during the occupation, are supposed to have represented the war treasure of the Sonderverband and to have been buried at this spot on the orders of Skorzeny himself and his three lieutenants."

As evidenced in his private papers, by the early 1950s, Skorzeny was very much involved financially and operationally with the WCC. Over the years, the WCC had acquired the majority stock in worldwide trading group Biddle Sawyer Corp., headquartered in NYC, which dealt in chemicals, pharmaceuticals, botanical drugs, waxes, gums, and essential oils. The transaction secured Anthony J. Drexel Biddle a membership on the board of WCC. In 1961, Biddle became US Ambassador to Spain, placing him in close proximity to Otto and Ilse Skorzeny, arms merchant Victor Oswald, and Johannes Bernhardt, among various other "former" Nazis ensconced in Madrid.

Biddle returned to the US in April '62, and World Commerce folded, allegedly for tax reasons, on August 31st of that year with reported gross income from trading—commodities included—to commissions and interest to just under $1 million with a total net income of $514,000, a far cry from its first year of operation, 1947, when it posted a $50,000 loss. This history of conglomerates tied directly to global commodities markets while at the same time serving as fronts for political and intelligence operations, contributes to the argument that the stock scandal with the valued food commodity vegetable oil—mostly soybean—at its center, brewing since 1962 and climaxing hours before the assassination, deserves greater coverage whether tied directly to this investigation or not.

Prior to its folding, from 1950 through to 1958, Otto Skorzeny was in written communication with WCC President Frank Ryan and Vice President, as well as international playboy and one of Bill Donovan's OSS agents, Ricardo Sicre. Named in Otto's private papers, Sicre (frequently using the alias Richard Stickler) had established a training school for spies who crossed from Vichy France into Spain. After the war, Sicre was installed as a vice president of WCC, adding to a body of evidence that WCC was being used as a privately controlled international espionage and assassination network. In time, he would arrange countless covert arms shipments facilitated under the auspices of WCC, often directly linked to US Military Assistance Advisor Groups. Much of this covert work in which Sicre played a major role involved former CIA Madrid Station Chiefs Alfonzo Rodriquez (1951) and James A. Noel (1963). Rodriguez, a.k.a. Earle Williamson and Wallace Growery, and Noel, a.k.a. Woodrow Olien, each had a lengthy history in agency operations in Cuba as well as Spain (see End-notes). Whether they were witting participants or not, Rodriguez and Noel serve as a segue between WCC and any serious exposition of the maneuvers among elements of the CIA hierarchy that contributed to the assassination plot.

PERMINDEX (PERMANENT INTERNATIONAL INDUSTRIAL EXPOSITION)

Pravda, 7 March 1967 published an article by V. Yermakov titled "as above" [Clay Shaw of the CIA] which was datelined Rome, 6 March 1967.

Thus begins an agency document labeled "Foreign Documents Division, Special Handling—1415 17 March 1967." The referenced article reads in part,

> The US Central Intelligence Agency made use of the services of Clay Shaw for their own interests in Italy. The District Attorney of New Orleans is accusing him of participation in the conspiracy which resulted in the assassination of President Kennedy. Newspapers in Rome recounted this in materials carried on the front pages.
>
> Clay Shaw spent some years in the Italian capital, as one of the leaders of the so-called "World-Wide Trade Center," which was located in a very fashionable district of Rome. This "Center" was least of all concerned with trade operations and the development of commercial ties. Its purpose was something else entirely. It specialized, in the words of the newspaper, in financing "bigoted anti-communist groups." Clay Shaw and the US Agent Major Blumenfeld [*sic*], who appears now in the capacity of a businessman from Canada, entered into secret relations with political circles in Rome, among deputies of the Christian-Democratic Social-Democratic, and Neo-fascist parties. They also deeply penetrated the business world of Italy. Shaw was given the task of establishing contacts with the extreme rightist groups in Rome, including the representatives of the neofascist organizations . . ."

The article continues to assert that Permindex was a Swiss-based "criminal operation" that financed OAS groups in France, and that its branches in Italy were no more than screens covering one of the subsidiary branches of the Central Intelligence Agency. It should be noted that Canadian-born lawyer and businessman Louis Bloomfield, who rose to the rank of major in the Royal Canadian Army Service Corps and was named in the reports as having been involved in the foundation of Permindex, was the attorney/representative of the Bronfman dynasty, alleged to have been significant investors in Permindex. The Bronfmans were also the primary investors in Empire Trust. The NY financial firm had, in 1953, employed Dallas oilman John Alston "Jack" Crichton to oversee its convoluted web of petroleum assets. A decade later, Crichton would represent a central component in the strategic plan to assassinate the president of the United States.

It should also be noted that the OAS, under military leadership of General Raul Salan (a name that appears in the Lafitte material) and with financial backing from several involved with Permindex, attempted what is known as the "Generals putsch" launched on April 21, just two days after the tragic climax of the Bay of Pigs debacle on April 19. According to a *New York Times* report, a meeting had been held in Madrid on April 12, nine days prior to the Algerian putsch, between Salan and emissaries of the CIA. The emissaries are reported to have conveyed to Salan that the US would recognize a new French Government in Algeria within forty-eight hours if no attack was made against either Tunisia or Morocco. It should be noted that Major Bloomfield maintained an office in Tangier. (See Chapters 5 and 8 for the further implications.)

Critics and detractors of New Orleans District Attorney Jim Garrison's 1967 indictment of Clay Shaw as being involved in the plot to assassinate Kennedy have argued that because *Pravda* served as Communist Russia's primary propaganda publication, and reports of Permindex as a nefarious front were picked up from far-left Italian publication *Paesa Sera*, all of the facts were disinformation. More informed researchers recognize that the CIA's own documents prove that over the years, former OSS agent Col. Shaw had participated on a contract basis in agency activities. Thus far, no documents have surfaced to dispute the fact that Shaw joined the board of Permindex in the late 1950s, allegedly at the behest of the brother of Giorgio Mantello, a.k.a. George Mandel, a Hungarian-born businessman then based in Switzerland. Most records agree that Mandel was a significant factor in the creation of CMC (Centro Mondiale Commerciale), the firm that CIA documents assert was identical with Permindex. Agency documents are clear that Ferenc Nagy, a fellow Hungarian and close friend to Mandel, contacted the agency to invite their utilization of and involvement in the real estate development and management firm Permindex.

Absent Lafitte datebook entries naming *Shaw*, there would be no reason to venture into the labyrinth of New Orleans man-about-town Clay LaVerne Shaw. From the outset of this research, the possibility that the entries refer to Robert Tyler Shaw, a.k.a L. F. Barker, was not discounted out of hand. According to author Peter Dale Scott, who the reader encounters frequently in this book, Robert Shaw oversaw Cuban operatives and reported directly to the CIA's David Atlee Phillips in Mexico City. However, the question persists: why would Pierre know him as Shaw rather than Barker, and, setting aside the possibility that Thomas Eli Davis knew Shaw in Mexico City, what other circumstances might have involved Robert Shaw/L. F. Barker with Willoughby or Souetre? We therefore proceeded with the likelihood that Pierre meant Clay Shaw; in fact, there is reason to believe Pierre worked for Shaw long before being hired in 1967 as chef of the Plimsoll Club in the International Trade Mart, and as we read in a later chapter, Shaw also had a major investment in play involving the metal nickel, as did Pierre Lafitte and his cohorts.

Volumes of research have been made accessible to the interested public related to Jim Garrison's investigation into Clay Shaw, David Ferrie, Guy Banister, and their unique New Orleans milieu pursued by the New Orleans district attorney, from media coverage of the trial itself to director Oliver Stone's excellent, if somewhat embellished and entertaining, record of the spectacle. Now, with Lafitte's datebook as evidence, Clay Shaw's nexus cannot and should not be ignored or dismissed out of hand.

Records prove that in 1958, Shaw was named to the board of directors of the Rome World Trade Center—Centro Mondiale Commerciale (CMC), affiliated with Swiss-based holding company, Permindex. One of the stated goals of the CMC was that *"Rome will recover once again her position as center of the civilized world."* According to intrepid researcher Mae Brussell, "its [CMC] location was frequently moved, its presidents rotated; its modus operandi altered. CMC included Italian fascists, elements of the European paramilitary right, the CIA, and the US Defense Department. There were major shareholders with banks located in Switzerland, Miami, Basel and other major cities."

CMC affiliate Permindex had been established in Bern, Switzerland, in 1956 and progressed beyond a holding company on paper to investment in a proposed multistory building meant to establish a physical address in Rome, Italy. According to a March 12, 1959, A.A.P.-Reuters headline. "A Market Place for All the World," "A group of ambitious financiers are busy converting a 'phantom' city, built by Benito Mussolini near Rome, into a site for Europe's first international shopping centre for businessmen. The project, designed to compete with the international trade mart at New Orleans and other similar schemes in the United States, will give Europe a single show window where private businessmen can display, or order, goods manufactured in all parts of the world. The organizers, Permanent Industrial Exhibitions, 'Permindex,' have taken four large, abandoned palaces . . . that were part of *a dream world of the Italian Fascist dictator who planned them as the focus point of a grandiose world fair and monument to the external glory of Fascism. . . .*" [Italics added.]

Informed researchers assert that Permindex was a direct extension of Bill Donovan and William Stephenson's World Commerce Corporation and that WCC worked closely with the World Trade Mart of New Orleans, nominally to promote world trade. Better recognized under the title International Trade Mart of New Orleans, ITM was founded by Col. Clay Shaw, who during WWII served under Donovan as an OSS liaison officer to Winston Churchill's headquarters. It was in front of the ITM building that Lee Oswald staged one of his Fair Play for Cuba leaflet demonstrations in August 1963.

After the war, Donovan's comrade in arms Stephenson established a haven in Montego Bay, Jamaica. Dubbed the "Tryall Club," the enclave served as a protected planning center for global corporatists and ideologues, including the chairman of Houston-based Schlumberger Well Services, Jean de Menil—a good friend of George de Mohrenschildt as well as Jacques Soustelle, financial patron of his OAS.

Others in the milieu at the Tryall Club included Montreal lawyer Major Louis Mortimer Bloomfield, alleged to have been recruited into the British SOE in 1938 and who later served Donovan's OSS, as well. Bloomfield's name appears on a number of Permindex related documents, and most agree that he was the original chairman when the holding company was based in Bern, Switzerland. Bloomfield was attorney and representative of the Bronfman dynasty behind liquor distiller Seagram's fortune. The family was represented on the Permindex board by Baron Alain de Gunzberg, of Mumm's Champagne. The Baron was the brother-in-law of heir to the fortune Edgar Bronfman, who was a major investor and board member of the prestigious US financial firm Empire Trust Co., mentioned earlier as boasting Bill Donovan's law partner on its board. In the early 1950s, Empire tapped a young Texan, James Alston Crichton, who had served in the OSS during the war, to oversee their oil interests under numerous company names including Dorchester Gas, Whitehall Corp., and Oil & Gas Management. As the reader will learn, Lafitte's datebook confirms much of what researchers have contended for decades, that Crichton played a crucial on-the-ground role in Dallas leading up to and immediately following the assassination.

Whether nominal or not, Ferenc Nagy presented himself as president of Permindex. Nagy (not to be confused with the committed Communist who served as prime minister of Hungary from 1953 to 1955, Imre Nagy) was the erstwhile leader of the Hungarian Small Landholders party and the Hungarian Peasants Association (HPA) who served as the prime minister of Hungary from 1946 until forced resignation in June 1947. Nagy's antifascism never overshadowed his lifelong aggressive anticommunist stance.

THE POND

In 1947, according to author Anna Mazurkiewiz in her persuasive Vol. 2 "East Central Europe in Exile: Transatlantic Identities," "As the Communists consolidated their power in Hungary, the former trickle of emigrating Hungarian political figures became a flood that included Prime Minister Ferenc Nagy. . . . These departures were facilitated by the American intelligence officers staff: 74 of them were arranged by James McCargar, who was posted with the US Department of State in Budapest for 18 months, beginning in 1946. McCargar, whose title was Secretary of Legation, Chief of the Political Section was also an operative of The Pond."

Hungary best symbolizes Communist resistance with the uprising of 1956, an event that informed the choices of Hungarian leaders in exile, former Prime Minister Ferenc Nagy included. Nagy's path to the United States after the war had been paved by the Department of State. James McCargar, under the umbrella of State, facilitated Nagy's entry and welcome to the US. McCargar was also an operative for an obscure semiprivate spy agency created almost ad hoc in the early 1940s.

Referred to by historians at the CIA as "this other espionage organization," The Pond filled a vacuum while Gen. Donovan was securing legitimate financing from the Roosevelt administration for America's new and official spy agency, the OSS.

In his own words, James McCargar wrote, "I first saw Budapest in the summer of 1946. I came as a covert agent, a member of an *American intelligence organization—there then being no CIA—which has since ceased to exist.*" [Italics added.] That independent intelligence operation, established by New Orleans native Colonel John Valentine "Frenchy" Grombach, was known as "The Pond."

On the heels of groundbreaking work by historians of the caliber of Francis Stoner Saunders, whose *Who Paid the Piper: The and Cultural Cold War* cracked open long sealed doors, the CIA eventually acknowledged that semiprivate entities like The Pond existed. Their version says, "Sadly, most of the Pond's 13-year history is lost. This obscurity was intentional. When the Pond was created in early 1942, the United States had very little experience with intelligence, and the notion of a spy agency which would be not only officially unacknowledged, but actually unknown, appealed to some people in Washington. These people were repelled by the larger-than-life publicity hound William Donovan and his 'Oh So Social' intelligence agency. For a precedent they looked instead to foreign intelligence services such as the British MI-6, which they thought was more discreet and whose chief was never named in the press. In accordance with this philosophy, the Pond spent most of its existence not as a government agency, but as a private sector organization, operating within real companies with names such as the Universal Service Corporation. This practice contributed substantially to obscurity and security. However, three successive government agencies found that having such an independent intelligence operation—and, worse yet, one run by a pugnacious, conspiratorial ideologue—was more trouble than it was worth, and the notion of having a truly secret intelligence organization never did catch on in the United States."

In what has been reported as a vicious competition for status and financing, Donovan's OSS won out over Frenchy Grombach's The Pond. Ironically, later Donovan's World Commerce Corp. would assume a structure and profile similar to those of Grombach's organization, serving as cover for what was tantamount to a semiprivate/government front for espionage and global intel operations.

The minor thread in the tapestry, from Grombach to our investigation, can best be condensed in a vignette of his history in New Orleans. "Frenchy" was the son of the French Consul in New Orleans, and as a young man, he was famous for his boxing skills, shared with the son of an executive of Southern Cotton Oil Co. in New Orleans, Herschel V. Williams. Years later, former OSS agent and Air Force Col. Williams was hired as a senior executive of NYC Previews Inc., the international real estate firm that provided Otto Skorzeny's wife, Ilse, a cover as she maneuvered the globe in the decade leading to the assassination in Dallas.

PERMINDEX CONTINUED

By 1963, Ferenc Nagy had established an office and a residence in Dallas, Texas, for reasons yet to be fully understood. Among Nagy's benefactors was Dallas oilman Clint W. Murchison, whose DC lobbyist, Bobby Baker, was a key figure identified in the unfolding scandal that threatened the political future of native

Texan and Kennedy's vice president, Lyndon B. Johnson. Johnson's team had convinced the Kennedy team that a swing through Texas in the fall of 1963 was critical to the reelection outcome. Baker, LBJ's faithful servant, was a cofounder of DC's Quorum Club in 1961, an environment designed to meet the needs of certain senators, congressmen, lobbyists, Capitol Hill staffers, and others well connected, whether they were "looking for drinks, meals, poker games, or an opportunity to share secrets in private accommodations." Baker was also a lobbyist for Dallasite Clint W. Murchison, the quintessential archetype of Texas independent oil who is well known for having significantly enhanced the private lifestyle of FBI Director J. Edgar Hoover for years. Less known is that Murchison was an early investor in Otto Skorzeny's oil scheme in Spain.

As acting president of Permanent International Industrial Expositions while New Orleans businessman Clay Shaw served on his board, Nagy's role at Permindex must also be considered in the context of its affiliate, parent company, or both, Centro Mondiale Commerciale. According to Italian journalist Michele Metta, who reported persuasively on political intrigue and machinations in Italy in 1963 but who suffered decades of criticism from American assassination researchers, the fascist Valerio Borghese (named in Chapter 1) was tied directly to CMC as president of Italian financial entity Credito Commerciale e Industriale. Metta insists that "Credicomin," headed by Borghese, who according to ally and Belgian fascist leader Léon Degrelle was the most important fascist in Italy and whose close relative appears in the address book of Clay Shaw, came into the hands of the son of Dominican Republic dictator Rafael Trujillo.

According to Gerry Hemming, the ex-Marine who worked for the Castro regime before changing sides and whom some consider a controversial source, Trujillo's son, Ramfis, and his former intel director "met in Haiti in February of 1963 to finance Kennedy's assassination." Although financing Kennedy's assassination is far more complex than Hemming asserts, some of his claims align with several clues left by Pierre Lafitte and the pursuant research into dynamics in the Dominican Republic and Haiti in 1963, outlined later in this book.

Michele Metta delved into CIA documents that confirm Nagy, as head of Permindex, had indeed proposed that an American businessman join the board and that a CIA agent be placed on the staff of Permindex. Nagy's request was summarized for agency superiors by Chief of International Organizations Division Cord Meyer, Jr., indicating it was not dismissed out of hand. Meyer's role in the events of November 1963 has been pursued at length by dedicated researchers. Further inquiry by these authors is reserved for the paperback edition of this book, as intended by author Albarelli. The clues left by Lafitte indicate that he was somehow privy to if not involved in the death of Cord Meyer's former wife, Mary Pinchot Meyer, the alleged confidante and paramour of President Kennedy, in 1963.

Over the years, variant sources have offered names of Permindex executives and board members. Among them were prominent Canadian, Swiss, and Italian businessmen and financiers, including aristocracy and their representatives. At one point, the board included American attorney Roy Cohn, who served as general counsel to rabid anticommunist Senator Joe McCarthy. Emblematic of the strength of the webs being spun during the Cold War, the political strategist would later mentor the future US president Donald Trump. Cohn and the impact of his ideology on the business mogul who would become the 45th President is pursued in the Epilogue of this book.

Other board members of Permindex held various levels of intelligence pedigrees, including the president of the Fascist National Association for Militia Arms, Giuseppe Zigiotti. Also identified is Italian Carlo d'Amelio, lawyer and administrator for the House of Savoy whose interests included dealings with King Farouk of Egypt, who also had a representative seated on the board of Permindex. Carlo d'Amelio served as founding president of Permindex affiliate Centro Mondiale Commerciale (CMC). Other evidence of continuity between World Commerce Corp and Permindex includes the presence of John S. Schlesinger on the board of Permindex when operations were relocated to Johannesburg. Schlesinger was a partner in Hambros Bank, named in the WCC records.

For this investigation, Permindex board members who stand out include: Jean de Menil, who had known French anthropologist Jacques Soustelle years prior to Soustelle's personal revolt against de Gaulle and joining the OAS; Paul Raigorodsky, a White Russian with experience in the Soviet Union's oil industry who landed in Dallas after the war; and Prince Guiterez di Spadafora, Sicilian-Italian industrialist and landowner.

* * *

Descended from 13th-century Sicilian peerage, Prince Spadafora was the former undersecretary of agriculture to Italy's fascist dictator Benito Mussolini. His son, Don Michele, married a young German woman, Konstanze Schacht, in Munich in July 1964, the bride being given away by her father, Hjalmar Horace Greeley Schacht.

Hjalmar is now infamous for having served as president of Germany's Reichs-bank and Hitler's minister of economics when the extermination of Jews was determined to be essential to the economic survival of the Reich. Regarded as "Hitler's Banker," Hjalmar was closely aligned throughout the Cold War with Otto and Ilse Skorzeny. The exact relationship, whether biological or financially and ideologically driven, remains a mystery, but there's no doubt that both Otto and Ilse knew Schacht as "Uncle Hjalmar."

Hjalmar's other daughter, Munich attorney Cordula Schacht, made headlines in 2015 when she represented the family of Joseph Goebbels, Adolf Hitler's min-ister of propaganda and one of closest and most devout Nazis. In headier days, Goebbels hosted the marriage ceremony of British fascist Sir Oswald Mosely to Diana Mitford in his Berlin home with the Führer as honored guest. Years later, the rights to Goebbels' writings were transferred by his siblings to a mysterious Swiss Nazi financier, François Genoud, who later transferred the rights to Cor-dula Schacht, the sister of Konstanze Schacht Spadafora. Ms. Cordula Schacht reportedly refused the publisher's conditional offer of royalties that stipulated the funds be paid out to a Holocaust charity, insisting the monies be paid to the Goebbels family. Cordula prevailed, and the courts ruled in favor of the Goeb-bels family.

The Thursday, November 7, datebook entry printed horizontally on the page reads:

11:30 meet Warsaw (+hotel) with T. and Hjalman / Ilse - Get - $.

Considering the timing and the surrounding entries, we know that Ilse Skorzeny was in Dallas, and from there we deduce that she was having lunch with Uncle Hjalmar Schacht at the Old Warsaw, a posh restaurant known for its old-world European ambiance and cuisine located in the Oak Lawn/Maple Terrace neigh-borhood north of downtown Dallas. For reasons that will be made clear, we know that the hotel in question was The Stoneleigh.

Schacht's fellow board member at Permindex Paul Raigorodsky resided in the Maple Terrace apartments next door to The Stoneleigh, one of many Dallas addresses of George de Mohrenschildt, now infamous for having befriended Lee Oswald. Both were a stone's throw from the Old Warsaw. Raigorodsky, studied in depth later in the book, was known as the "godfather" of the White Russian community in Dallas.

Permindex member Jean de Menil, who married into the Schlumberger fam-ily and assumed charge of the global oil well services company, had served in

Venezuela during the war, running Gen. Charles de Gaulle's Free French forces alongside Soustelle. Disillusioned with de Gaulle over the questions of Algerian independence, Soustelle joined the OAS, which would attempt (on numerous occasions) to assassinate Charles de Gaulle. Jena de Menil had aligned with Soustelle over de Gaulle. It was President de Gaulle who raised alarms that Permindex was serving as a front for operations designed to topple his Republic and kill him in the process.

* * *

Having confirmed that holding companies—including CMC and Permindex—served as fronts for intelligence operations, including sanctioned assassinations executed from WWII through the height of the Cold War, we turn to profiles of persons of interest who until now have skirted appreciable scrutiny, beginning with our chronicler Jean Pierre Lafitte—familiar to Clay Shaw—who would be selected as project manager for "Lancelot," the plot to kill JFK:

> Hard 2 believe that it will
> go forward . . . but it will, it is
> me?
> —Lafitte datebook, October 19, 1963

CHAPTER 3

THE PROJECT MANAGER AND THE PATRON

I thought I had led a damn interesting life, but compared to Pierre my times were tame. I've done it all, but he's done even more, and before some of it was ever done he invented it.
— George Hunter White, Federal Bureau of Narcotics,
June 18, 1960

T says tail LO [Lee Oswald]— no direct contacts- calls? No.
Report to Angleton + not here (wife?) Rene says A looks
like cadaver— Mexico City?
—Lafitte datebook, May 1, 1963

Rene says 'Coup de grâce.'
—Lafitte datebook, November 23, 1963

Gretna, Louisiana: The modest, three-bedroom, suburban dwelling sitting on a small lot in the Terrytown section of Gretna mirrors the many homes that surround it: nondescript, cookie-cutter structures, many built shortly after World War II and bought up through postwar veteran benefits. Situated on the west bank of the Mississippi River, Gretna is the second-largest city in Jefferson Parish, Louisiana, and only five miles away by car from New Orleans proper.

In 1963, a man named Jean M. Martin, along with his wife and children, resided in the new development within Gretna. By some accounts, the Martins first moved into the house in early 1962. Neighbors knew Martin as a chef employed in nearby downtown New Orleans. By 1967, he would become more widely known as the manager and executive chef of New Orleans's prestigious Plimsoll Club, located in the well-known International Trade Mart that had recently moved from the corner of Camp and Common to its spanking new location at the foot of Canal St. between Canal and Poydras. Jean Martin's Gretna address was conveniently situated about eight miles from the Trade Mart.

Sometimes Jean Martin drove on the nearby Pierre Lafitte highway, which because of its name gave him an especial amusement. In New York City, as well as several other places, he was well known as Jean Pierre Lafitte, a namesake he cribbed from the notorious pirate over three decades before he embarked on a surreptitious career that would make him a renowned undercover investigator, informer, imposter, and con artist among insiders.

Jean Martin, along with his family, arrived in New Orleans, his alleged place of birth, in either mid-1961 or early 1962. Using one of his many aliases, he briefly took a job as a maintenance man at the Standard Coffee Co. (more widely known as the Wm. Reily Coffee Co.) and then after about three months became the sous-chef at one the best French restaurants in New Orleans. Eventually, he became viewed throughout the region as an excellent French chef.

Besides residing in the New Orleans area, Martin/Lafitte also sometimes lived in New York City, where he maintained a small apartment and owned a restaurant in the West Village. As Pierre Lafitte, Martin also frequently traveled throughout the United States and Europe, sometimes under other aliases. The FBI and CIA, respectively, underwrote many of his trips. Truth be told, either Martin or Lafitte are his given surnames. In all, Lafitte/Martin maintained over thirty aliases, which he adroitly juggled on his countless covert government-sponsored missions.

Following nearly seven years working closely with George Hunter White, Lafitte, like White, took to maintaining a daybook, or desk diary. The practice was greatly frowned upon by the Federal Narcotics Bureau and expressly forbidden by the CIA, but neither man seemed to be the least inhibited by the Agency's taboo. White's datebooks, which span nearly twenty-five years, were discovered in the late 1970s and have subsequently become a virtual goldmine of information for any researcher willing to devote the time and effort to deciphering his often-difficult-to-read handwriting and researching the overflowing cornucopia of names and places that riddle the datebooks. Pierre Lafitte's datebooks, which, as best as can be determined, only cover four years, 1961 to 1964, were discovered in 2008 and, as has been explained, were gained access to on a limited basis about three years later. Lafitte's 1963 datebook and a handful of related letters and ledger entries, some in French and others frustrating due their brevity and use of single letters in place of full names, proved to be a goldmine detailing an incredible saga leading to the assassination of the president of the United States.

On May 10, 1963, he wrote in what appears to be a hurried hand that he had been assigned by a mysterious "T" to "tail" Lee Harvey Oswald and to report directly to James Jesus Angleton. In the same note, he asks, "Mexico City?"

Thus began Pierre Lafitte's incredible activities related to Lee Harvey Oswald and the assassination of JFK.

ALARM BELLS WENT OFF

Six years after President Kennedy was assassinated, on December 9, 1969, alarm bells went off loudly at the CIA. Technical Service Division Chief Dr. Sidney Gottlieb announced at an Agency directors meeting that the FBI had arrested Pierre Lafitte in New Orleans, where he was working as manager-chef for the posh Plimsoll Club in the International Trade Mart.

Unbelievable, came the incredulous response, *how could that be? Doesn't he often work for the FBI, not to mention us?* Richard Helms, now director, ordered, *Find out what's going on! Make certain there are no photos of him in the newspapers or any magazine. Go out and spend whatever time needed and sweep up all his photographs. Deliver to me.* In spite of weeks spent complying with his direct command, one photo escaped the effort.

As a result, apparently the FBI had had little choice but to pick Lafitte up. Six years earlier, he had swindled an unfortunate speculator named Ralph L. Loomis out of nearly $350,000. Ironically, the elaborate scheme involving diamond mines in Africa had originated out of an FBI sting operation, which the Bureau had called Lafitte in on to do undercover work. Lafitte had made investments under the alias drug dealer Anthony Shillitani while in the Belgian Congo in 1960 and early 1961, on another deep-cover assignment for the CIA. Lafitte adds to his legend. Donning surgical garb, he walked into a crammed OR in Boston and calmly fired rounds in a "nonprotected" operating room. In Kansas City, he earned a place in a thinly disguised novel. Dressed in a plain-tweed suit and a wig that fit expertly, he shot a Missouri judge on his way from washing his hands.

Here also it is important to point out that Lafitte turned up in yet another tangle of historic proportions during the 1960s. Two years prior to the JFK assassination, as mentioned, Lafitte had worked for the Standard Coffee Co., best recognized as the Reily Coffee Co. founded by New Orleans native William B. Reily, Jr., an avid anticommunist closely connected to McCarthyite and far-right New Orleans ideologue and radio commentator Edward Scannell Butler. Both Reily and Butler were close to CIA Assistant Director Charles Cabell, Chief of

CIA Security Research Staff (former) Brig. Gen. Paul Gaynor, and Agency ARTICHOKE Project Official Morse Allen. Readers may recall that alleged JFK assassin Lee Harvey Oswald also worked as a "maintenance man" for the Reily Coffee Co. in the summer of 1963—the same position that Lafitte had filled at Reily in late 1961–early 1962. Indeed, Oswald was hired by the company on the same day Lafitte was instructed to begin tailing him.

LAFITTE'S ARREST

According to FBI documents, during its six-year "search" for Pierre Lafitte, the notorious operative had used dozens of aliases, including Louis Romano, Frank Maceo, Paul Maceo, Jean Martin, Peter Martin, John Martin, Jack Martin, Paul Martino, Paul Mertz, Jean Mondolini, Louis Hidell, Paul Jehan, Jean Jehan, Louis Mancuso, Jacques Montaine, Peter Orsini, and Louis Tabet.

Lafitte had been arrested by a team of five FBI agents at his home in Gretna on December 8, 1969, charged with being a fugitive from justice, and then was transported to Boston, Massachusetts, for arraignment before US District Court Judge Francis J.W. Ford for allegedly defaulting on bail posted seven years earlier. Lafitte had been indicted in 1962 in Boston on fifteen counts of mail fraud and transportation of stolen property after he allegedly swindled an investor, Ralph L. Loomis of Kittery Point, Maine, out of $350,000 through an alleged scheme aimed at financing mineral mining rights and diamond mines in Africa, as well as nickel mining rights, and fraudulent stock transfers involving Canadian Javelin Ltd., a conglomerate that will be considered in greater depth later in this book. Convenient in assisting Lafitte's plea of innocence was that Loomis had died about one year earlier.

When the FBI team arrested Lafitte at his New Orleans home, another team of agents visited and searched the relatively new and hugely popular Plimsoll Club, where Lafitte had been hired as manager and executive chef under the alias of Jean M. Martin. Local newspapers on the Lafitte/Martin arrest stated, "Lafitte has developed a wide reputation for the food served at the Plimsoll Club in the International Trade Mart in downtown New Orleans. He has received [written] compliments from Mrs. Lyndon B. Johnson and numerous state and city officials for the French cuisine served at the club, and was made a Louisiana 'colonel' by Gov. John J. McKeithen." It was not long after joining the Plimsoll that Martin was inducted into the Confrérie de la Chaîne des Rôtisseurs, the elite gastronomic society whose international roster boasted social and diplomatic luminaries including David K.E. Bruce, then Ambassador to the Court of Saint James.

Other newspaper articles underscored that Lafitte/Martin's cuisine had been a favorite of Clay LaVerne Shaw, the International Trade Mart's founder and managing director who had by then retired from his post as director of ITM. In March 1967, Shaw would be arrested and charged with conspiracy to assassinate President Kennedy by New Orleans District Attorney James Garrison.

The day after Lafitte's arrest, the *New Orleans States-Item* newspaper reported: "A spokesman for the Plimsoll Club said Lafitte has had no involvement in financial affairs of the club. 'He has not signed checks, handled cash or otherwise served in a position to affect the club's finances,' the spokesman said." The same publication stated on December 22: "Lafitte once served for several as an informant for the FBI in its investigation of swindling operations. According to federal officials, he had used several names." Lafitte told *States-Item* reporters that he was "a South Louisiana native and learned his culinary arts while living for a number of years in France." The following day, the *States-Item* stated that "court records in Boston show that Lafitte is from Armonk, New York, a small Westchester County town near New York City." In January 1970, the trial of Jeanne Pierre Lafitte was postponed indefinitely.

LAFITTE'S MYSTERIOUS HISTORY

In his later years, after retiring from the Federal Bureau of Narcotics, legendary agent George Hunter White said of Pierre Lafitte:

> I thought I had led a damn interesting life, but compared to Pierre my times were pretty tame. I've done it all, but he's done even more, and before some of it was ever done he invented it. He was what you would call a changeling. I don't mean master of disguises, I mean an actual chameleon, a man that had the ability to transform himself right in front of you. He could go from good to bad, from rich to poor, from royalty to commoner, from intellectual to simpleton, from hoodlum to police officer. He would disappear for months or years at a time and then he would show up, knock on your door, like only a day or two had passed. He mastered time as it affected him, it was as if time waited for him. I liked him but I never trusted him because he was always in the game. He only loved and cared for his wife and children, everyone else was fair game in the scheme of things. He was the greatest imposter and confidence man that ever lived, not because he was a good actor but because he was a hundred different people in one. . . . There's a side to Pierre that rarely reveals itself, but is

always there. A dark, abysmal side, and once you become aware of it, it's almost impossible to be completely at ease with him.

James Phelan, who wrote for the *New York Times*, *Paris Match*, and the *Saturday Evening Post* (which published his article "The Vice Man Cometh" in June 1963, a piece some refer to as a Valentine to New Orleans DA Jim Garrison), was one of the few people, besides George White, who were able to get close to Lafitte. Phelan had traveled to New Orleans to cover the bold cleanup operation of the city's seedier clip joints by the new district attorney. In the June 8th article, Phelan mentions that he had spent a "leisurely ten days" with Garrison and his investigator. We soon learn that by the time Phelan showed up in New Orleans, he was well acquainted with Pierre Lafitte, the man who at that very time was orchestrating preliminary plans for the assassination of President Kennedy from his base in the Crescent City.

Here we should also mention that Phelan, according to JFK authorities Lisa Pease and James DiEugenio, occasionally served as an FBI informant, and perhaps also a CIA informant. Phelan was a good friend of Robert Maheu, a former FBI agent and CIA employee, as well as the CIA's go-to guy and go-between for special projects, Pierre Lafitte. At any rate, Phelan believed Lafitte was perhaps the most unique person he had even encountered.

"When I first heard of a man who called himself Pierre Lafitte," Phelan wrote, "my credulity was strained beyond the most elastic boundaries. Even after I met him, I had difficulty believing that he was even semi-real, or that he had done any other of the things that he said he had done." Out of respect for Lafitte's privacy, Phelan always described him in general, and sometimes deceptive, terms: "He was a short, bald man with cold blue eyes and a French or Italian accent." Aside from the accuracy that he could adapt accents, at the time Lafitte had a full head of hair, was not short, and had dark eyes.

Phelan claimed to have first met Lafitte several months after Lafitte's undercover Las Vegas work for newspaper owner Hank Greenspun. Phelan explained that the *Las Vegas Sun* articles about the entire affair that ran in Greenspun's newspaper never mentioned Lafitte or his role in bringing down a corrupt law enforcement officer or any others. But as a seasoned investigative reporter, Phelan instinctively knew that despite the amazing story publicly revealed, there was more, far more, to it all. Phelan met with Greenspun, and the feisty editor told him all about the story's missing Lafitte part. "The story was even more amazing than I had imagined," said Phelan. "I asked Greenspun, 'How do I get to talk with Lafitte?' He said, 'I have no idea where he is or how to reach him. He calls here once in a while to see how things are going. I can tell him you're interested in talking with him.'" Phelan said that he told Greenspun he would deeply appreciate that.

After the Greenspun case, and publication of Phelan's article "The Man Who Took Las Vegas" in *True* magazine, Phelan flew to New York at the behest of editor Doug Kennedy and lived with Lafitte for three weeks in Riverdale, NY, to record more of his exploits for a follow-up series for Kennedy's magazine. Subsequently, Lafitte would also visit Phelan periodically at his California home. Phelan's wife, Amalie, a highly trained psychologist, recalled:

> It wasn't uncommon for Pierre to come by . . . but always unannounced, at any time of the day or night. Jim didn't mind. He enjoyed his time with Pierre. They would sit up for hours on end talking. Once, late, around midnight I looked out the kitchen window and there was Pierre sitting on a bench in the backyard waiting for someone to notice him out there. That was Pierre—there one moment, gone the next.

Asked about Lafitte's mysterious lifestyle, Amalie said:

> There was no question that he lived a life of intrigue. Jim would get odd little postcards from him from places all over the world. . . . There was a sense of danger always around . . . I asked Jim once if there was any reason to be concerned in having Pierre come around. Jim said, "It's a good question. I don't imagine he goes anywhere without a shadow.

Amalie and Jim's daughter, Janet, also remembers Lafitte: "I was pretty young, but yes, I remember him. He was very mysterious, always appearing out of nowhere to talk to my father. I couldn't help but be fascinated by him. He put off airs like a movie star. There was just something about him."

Said James Phelan of Lafitte: "He used dozens of different names—and occupations—in dealing with mobsters around the country, and somehow kept his identities straight in his mind. Years later, he sent me a birthday card from the Belgian Congo—where he was engaged in God knows what. It had forty of his names—like Orsini, Monaco, Tabet, Shillitani—on it, but not the name Pierre Lafitte."

Phelan's Belgian Congo line about Lafitte was a crafty citation. What the investigative reporter did not mention was that Lafitte was in the Congo at the very same time that the CIA had slated Patrice Lumumba for assassination, a fact that surely did not escape Phelan's notice. Was Lafitte the never-identified CIA operative WI/ROUGE? It appears quite likely that he was, and we know, without doubt, that he was close to QJ/WIN, who was also there at the same time.

Some thirty months after the assassination of Lumumba in January 1961, James Phelan was in New Orleans interviewing Garrison about his early successes as DA, giving him ample opportunity to bump into the sender of that postcard from the Congo, Pierre Lafitte—his host in Riverdale, after which he had clearly developed more than a casual acquaintance. Four years later, around the time Lafitte returned to New Orleans to fill the role of chef at the International Trade Mart's Plimsoll Club, Phelan was also back in town to pursue the leak that a valiant effort to open a local investigation into the Kennedy assassination was underway. In his May 6, 1967, article for the *Saturday Evening Post* titled "A Plot to Kill Kennedy? Rush to Judgment in New Orleans," Phelan—who would later testify on behalf of the defense—rocked the early foundations of Garrison's case against the founder of the International Trade Mart, Clay LaVergne Shaw.

* * *

Not only had James Phelan consistently asserted that he did not know Lafitte until the Greenspun case, he had also failed to mention that he was a good friend of George Hunter White. Indeed, he had written a number of popular men's adventure magazine articles about White's Federal Narcotics Bureau maneuvers. Phelan knew George White long before he had ever spoken to Hank Greenspun, and he had met White, along with Pierre Lafitte, on several occasions well before the Las Vegas affair was ever conceived, but, of course, out of respect for both men, Phelan kept this information to himself. His silence added to the mystery and intrigue that hung about the exploits of White and Lafitte, who had known each other since the late 1940s. As we will learn, Pierre was in communication with George White throughout 1963, including a time frame that coincided with their mutual friend James Phelan's visit to New Orleans.

In June 1952, according to a letter by George White, the CIA officially recruited Lafitte as a "special employee" after he was summoned to Washington, D.C., to meet with CIA officials Dr. Sidney Gottlieb and James Jesus Angleton. Wrote White: "Expecting to be at CIA only a day, Lafitte was held over for a few days. I hope to hell they know what they are in for. I suspect even to that crew that he's one of a kind." While at CIA headquarters, Lafitte also met Agency Security Chief Sheffield Edwards, Frank Wisner, and Richard Helms.

Subsequently, Lafitte undertook a number of covert domestic and international assignments for the CIA, including a trip to the Republic of Congo in December 1960, which, as noted, coincided with the January 1961 CIA-assisted assassination of Patrice Lumumba. Lafitte's work for the CIA lasted until about 1978.

Longtime CIA MK/ULTRA czar Dr. Gottlieb was more guarded about his words on Pierre Lafitte. "I'm not even sure he exists in the epistemology of the CIA," said Gottlieb. "He gives whole new meaning to the label 'spook.'" Gottlieb continued:

> It's widely known that he worked with George [White] in New York and San Francisco. That's no secret at all today. But . . . he did . . . he did a lot more than that. He traveled extensively for the Agency . . . I would encounter him in unexpected places, completely . . . I'd see him but I wasn't privy to what he was doing. Often I would ignore his presence as he would mine.

As reported in *A Terrible Mistake* by author Albarelli, "In 1952, the CIA inaugurated 'Project Artichoke,' in an attempt to answer the question 'Can we get control of an individual to the point where he will do our bidding against his will?' as posed by the head of CIA's Security Research Staff of the Office of Security, Paul Gaynor. The major tool of choice in the pursuit of this goal was LSD, ample supplies being doled out by Sid Gottlieb, and the creation of scenarios for the use of the drug on unwitting subjects was handled through coordination with Federal Bureau of Narcotics top agent George Hunter White, who made frequent use of FBN 'special employee' Pierre Lafitte."

These activities—and the personnel involved in them—were carefully vetted by CIA Counterintelligence head Jim Angleton. White became a "CIA consultant," and Gottlieb was soon informed that Angleton and CIA Deputy Director of Plans Frank Wisner were very interested in retaining the services of Pierre Lafitte, for "special projects." Lafitte's unique skill set was understandably intriguing to these men, and soon Lafitte was engaging in meetings with officers at the top echelon of the Agency. On the evening of June 23, 1952, Lafitte's wife, Rene, telephoned White at home and informed him that Pierre was being held overnight in Washington, D.C., for meetings with Wisner, Office of Security head Sheffield Edwards, and Wisner's Chief of Operations Richard Helms.

Thus began Lafitte's long-term relationship with operatives at the core of CIA's clandestine operations. There would be dinners with Angleton, who would become a close friend, coded communications, and Agency-assisted passports issued to Lafitte in the coming years.

Former Army Colonel Albert R. Haney—who was a close and valuable source for this author's investigation into Dr. Frank Olson's murder and was also quite close to CIA director Allen Dulles, after he valiantly assisted in bringing Dulles's wounded son, Sonny, home from Korea—said [to Albarelli in Florida]: "I never met Lafitte, or whatever his name was, but I'd heard so much about him that I felt like I knew him. I'll tell you this right up front: there were very few people like him, very few . . . I was told a story once, about an amazing incident where Angleton had somehow challenged Lafitte to try and fool him somehow. Anyway, a while later Angleton went to lunch one day and a very gracious maître d' greeted him and took him to his table, where a most attentive waiter took his order and brought him his drinks. Angleton was there for about an hour or so and never once had any clue that the maître d' and waiter were Pierre Lafitte, who greeted him on the sidewalk smiling broadly and still dressed as the waiter."

* * *

Former FBN agent and high-ranking US Treasury Department official Malachi L. Harney made some studied observations of Lafitte in his little-known book devoted to the subject of classic informers and law enforcement officials. Harney introduced Lafitte as a "most interesting character" and the "type of person sometimes of invaluable assistance to the law enforcement officer, who is an outsider, but must be in a compartment of his own. This is a sort of 'private eye' individual but a very special variety of that genus." Claimed Harney, conforming to the cover story put out by the FBN about Lafitte's beginnings with the Bureau and embellishing some on his own with the infamous Joseph Orsini drug-case story:

> As an indication of his versatility, this man, who never had any previous contact with the narcotic traffic [*sic*], was able, when released from [Ellis Island] under security bond, to make a case resulting in the disclosure of a ring importing seventeen kilograms of heroin monthly through the Port of New York, through connivance of crewmen of the French Lines, who were members of a Corsican smuggling mob. Cooperation of the Federal Bureau of Narcotics with the French police brought about the seizure of a large clandestine heroin conversion plant in the outskirts of Paris. In addition to its magnitude, this case was highly important for its timing and for its revelation as to the source of a flood of heroin into New York. Lafitte, with Narcotic's Bureau District Supervisor George H. White, went on from there to develop a case against a leading narcotics distributor in New

England—a Mafia character who, as a sideline, had connections which enabled him to filch a steady supply of revolvers from a factory before the registry numbers of the weapons were recorded.

Harney then speculated: "Lafitte would have been a great detective in any organization, combining a tremendously keen mind with a histrionic ability which made him an undercover operator par excellence. Some of his motivation to assist the law is quite simple. He had been able to make a good living at it, when one considers the rewards for recovering property and similar emoluments. He had a special reason for coming to us, in that he was anxious to enlist some official sympathy on trying to clarify an obscure, nationality status."

Harney does not explain this status, nor does he tell us how Lafitte's immigration status was ultimately resolved (the CIA resolved it, under pressure from Lafitte), but we do know that in 1957 Bernard Fensterwald, a former State Department employee and highly regarded attorney who had just been hired by US Senator Thomas C. Hennings, Jr., contacted the FBI at the direction of Hennings to inquire about the Bureau's reaction to a request to Hennings to sponsor legislation to block the deportation of Lafitte. FBI official Louis B. Nichols responded: "I told Fensterwald that this, of course, was a matter for the Immigration Service and, on a purely personal and confidential basis, the Senator should be exceedingly cautious before he got out on a limb; that if he inquired into Lafitte's background he would find an extensive record; and that under no circumstances would the Bureau support Lafitte. I told him officially, of course, we could not take a position but that, personally, we would hate to see some friend embarrassed and that he should be very cautious. Fensterwald stated that was enough for him."

All of this, of course, significantly adds to the overall mystery that still, to this day, surrounds the man known as Pierre Lafitte; but here it is important to note that Bernard Fensterwald later, during the mid-1970s, launched a thorough investigation of his own into the assassination of President Kennedy that in part focused strongly on French soldier and OAS coordinator Jean Rene Souetre (and the then-unidentified CIA operative OJ/WIN), as well as several other foreign assassins, who had been expertly trained in Spain by Otto Skorzeny. It seems highly likely that Fensterwald's initial exposure to Pierre Lafitte may have led him to these strong JFK assassination leads. It also seems highly probable that at the same time Fensterwald was aware that Lafitte had been tasked with undercover work in France attempting to unearth Soviet moles burrowed into the French government.

* * *

Author Dick Russell in 1992 prophetically wrote about CIA Counterintelligence Chief James Jesus Angleton's deep concerns about Jean Souetre's June 1963 alleged offer to the CIA of a "list of the Communist penetrations of the French government." Russell reveals that Angleton was especially concerned after his "only trusted [Soviet] defector, Anatoly Golitsin, had informed [him] in 1963 that the SDECE had been penetrated by a KGB spy ring of some twelve agents."

Continued Russell: "More KGB spies were said to be concealed within the top echelons of several French ministries, and Golitsin claimed that even de Gaulle's entourage had been penetrated by a senior KGB official. The result of Golitsin's charges was Angleton's recruitment of the SDECE's intelligence boss In Washington, Philippe de Vosjoli, to spy on his own embassy and pass along classified information. Sometime in mid-1963, de Vosjoli even allowed Angleton inside the French Embassy to perform a personal after hours 'black bag job'—purloining French cipher traffic and other data."

In his 1970 memoir, *LAMIA*, Vosjoli writes: "*Solving political difficulties* [in the early 1960s] *by assassination had become a habit in Paris. . .*" Shortly after resigning from French intelligence work on October 18, 1963, Vosjoli planned on traveling from the United States, where he was at the time, to Paris, but, as he revealed in his memoir:"[On] *November 22, 1963, an hour after the assassination of President Kennedy, I received a cable from SDECE ordering me to fly at once to Paris. The airports were closed, no immediate transportation was available, and I decided to think it over until the following day. That night a very dear friend called me from Paris, with a serious warning, 'You are now in a free country. The minute you are sent back to France you will no longer be free. Orders have been given to silence you by any means.'*" [Italics added.]

Vosjoli had been targeted for assassination himself by the intelligence service he once headed, apparently because he had been unwittingly exposed to information about JFK's assassination through his association with Angleton and other assassinations carried out by the French. In short, Vosjoli, the day after JFK's death, became well aware of who masterminded the hit on Kennedy and who the actual three shooters were. Moreover, he had to worry about being targeted for assassination himself.

Lafitte's records in the spring of 1963 indicate that he knew Vosjoli was, at the very least, acquainted with actors that he himself was directing, including Thomas Eli Davis and wife Carolyn. These relationships are pursued further in Chapter 5.

* * *

That Lafitte was often in dicey, but critically needed, situations, where his presence was carefully concealed and rarely noted, is perhaps the best testament to his extraordinary ability to remain invisible whenever he so chose and attests to the desire of those who contracted with him to keep his activities secret. When writer James Phelan revealed that Lafitte had spent time in the Belgian Congo, nobody seemed to notice that it had been at the same time that Patrice Lumumba was murdered. The fact that Lafitte was employed in New Orleans at the same place as Lee Harvey Oswald is beyond provocative; and the fact that Lafitte was charged to "tail," "dog," and "keep an eye on" Oswald in the months leading up to the assassination of JFK by a character he disguises with the code "T" is especially revealing when he is then advised to report to "Angleton," the patron of the project to assassinate the president. The datebook entries confirm long-standing suspicions that Oswald was indeed the "patsy" set up to take the fall for the assassination.

Lafitte maintained an outstanding record in countless secret government cases where his undercover role was never breached, making his selection as a sort of handler for Lee Harvey Oswald only natural.

That Lafitte was all over the high-profile drug cases involving Eugene Giannini, Joe Valachi, and the legendary French Connection case without any detection of his presence at all tells of his extraordinary skills and deep connections; that he shadowed George Hunter White and Charles Siragusa throughout New York City after being vetted and trained personally by CIA counterintelligence chief James Jesus Angleton relays much about what his objectives were; that a United States Senator would go to great lengths to protect him from law enforcement and deportation, and that the CIA and FBI cooperated in these efforts, all underscore his extreme importance. The fact that Pierre Lafitte was there in November 1953 at a Manhattan hotel with Dr. Frank Olson only moments before Olson's death through a fatal fall tells us a great deal about his being privy to the machinations of the CIA and FBI, but his role in Olson's death is another story, and here we are focusing on his CIA-given task in 1963 to handle Lee Harvey Oswald. Here, more on Pierre Lafitte's background and doings for the United States government will be helpful.

LAFITTE'S BEGINNINGS

In 1952, several federal agencies, including the CIA, FBI, and FBN (Federal Bureau of Narcotics), began widely planting the cover story that Jean Pierre Lafitte had first arrived illegally in the United States in 1951 from Europe and that he had been promptly arrested and imprisoned. However, the truth about how Lafitte first set foot on American soil is far more fascinating.

As alluded to earlier, the name "Lafitte" belonged to two brothers, Pierre and Jean, born in 19th-century France. The brothers were notorious and celebrated for pirating Spanish, French, and British ships in the Gulf of Mexico and looting cargo holds of vast booty that they sold in New Orleans's open-air markets and bazaars. The brothers operated a livery stable as a front and engaged heavily in the slave trade, selling captives at a dollar a pound to legendary Jim Bowie. While their exact birth dates and causes of death are subjects of debate, it is well established that the Lafitte brothers were urbane, well-read, multilingual Beau Brummels who were very much involved in espionage, serving as double agents for Spain and America. Throughout his life, our Jean-Pierre Lafitte, who generally used only the name Pierre, would claim that he was a direct descendant of the Lafitte brothers.

On several occasions, Lafitte claimed he had been born in 1902 or 1907, and even 1912, in the United States, the illegitimate son of a Louisiana madam named Sabina, who ran a string of brothels and carried him as a baby from parish to parish on her hip, supported by the holstered pistol she also always carried. Later, some people who claimed to know Lafitte would say he had been born in Corsica, while others said he was born in Sicily, and still others said he was a native of Belgium. They were all wrong, according to Lafitte himself, who said when he was about seven years old, his mother's Louisiana business holding had gone sour and she left the United States with him and traveled to France. Said Lafitte's son 2017: "It was alright for a madam to be a madam back then, but to be a business madam, meaning having a keen business sense and to actually make money, was not alright. That's why she had to leave."

After spending a few months in Paris, Lafitte's mother settled in Marseilles with her young son. In the early 1900s, Marseilles was a thriving center of commerce on the Mediterranean Sea. Already one of the oldest and most culturally diverse cities in Europe, it was also France's undisputed capital of crime. By the 1930s, huge quantities of raw opium, transported to Marseilles from Turkey through Munich, Basel, and Strasbourg, were being transformed into heroin. The best heroin in the world, the best money could buy, was in Marseilles. And there were tremendous profits in dealing heroin, tremendous recurring profits. Many Corsicans migrated to Marseilles from their island home a little over one hundred miles southeast of the port city. By the late 1960s, over 600,000 Corsicans would populate Marseilles.

About a year after settling in Marseilles, Lafitte's mother vanished. Later, Pierre would tell people she had abandoned him after she had returned from a trip to Shanghai with Pierre in tow. However, from sketchy French accounts, it appears that Sabina was murdered, although her body was never found. Less than sympathetic relatives, who thought they had inherited a prepubescent servant, took in homeless Pierre. Not surprisingly, Lafitte ran away within a year, after "taking all that I could and then some more." The young boy survived for three years living on the streets and working in some of the many restaurant kitchens that operated in the city. Lafitte described it years later:

> For me it was common sense to seek out such work. I never had to worry about where my next meal was coming from, and the kitchens were always warm, dry and safe. That I would learn a skill which would be useful later in life never crossed my mind, but that is how I came to know my way around a kitchen so well.

Lafitte developed a real culinary talent, and by the age of fourteen, after he had secured permanent living quarters on the floor above a notorious seaman's tavern, he was routinely called upon to fill in for errant and truant chefs. During his non-working hours, he laboriously honed his skills at larceny and other illicit crafts. In the process, he encountered other boys his age, nearly all of whom were equally busy on the wrong side of the law. Among his closest companions were François Spirito, who had come to Marseilles from Naples, and Paul Bonaventure, Antoine D'Agostino, and Joseph Orsini, later Spirito's lieutenant, and all Corsicans. By the 1930s, Spirito and Carbone ruled the Marseilles underworld and operated an international heroin network that reached French Indochina, Egypt, Turkey, Greece, Germany, Yugoslavia, and South America. According to Lafitte, during his prewar years in Marseilles, he briefly fell under the tutelage of Jean Voyatzis, a major international drug smuggler and "the greatest importer of manufactured Chinese opium into Europe." Lafitte's world at that time also included illicit traffickers Elie Eliopoulos from Greece and August Del Grazio from America.

Sometime between late-1936 and 1938, Lafitte decided to return to America. French authorities claim that it was because he was wanted for desertion from the French Foreign Legion, in addition to several arrests for smuggling, as well as opium and heroin trafficking. Reportedly, Lafitte deserted the Legion "at least six times." He denied it. By the time Lafitte departed Europe for America, according to his own account, he "could fluently speak five languages, get by with another two or three, and pass without question or any suspicion as a citizen of any of a dozen countries." He modestly added, "However, I never thought of myself as an imposter. I was a master impersonator."

The late 1930s found Lafitte traveling back and forth between New York City, Montreal, Boston, Paris, and Marseilles. In France in the early 1940s, he had dealings with Henri Dericourt, double agent extraordinaire, who sold drugs and black market goods for François Spirito. Dericourt was an accomplished pilot who, from 1951 through to his disappearance in Laos in 1962, flew loads of gold and heroin out of Indochina for Air Opium, operated by drug kingpin Bonaventure "Rock" Francisi. According to FBI files, Lafitte maintained contact with Dericourt even after setting up shop in the United States.

Before his death in 1975, George White, who for decades adhered strictly to the FBI-CIA cover story about Lafitte's first coming to the US in 1952, wrote to former colleague Garland Williams about "how absolutely amazing it is that everyone and their brother has swallowed hook-line-and-sinker the myth of Lafitte's arrival here . . . if I didn't know that he'd been around since before they invented iced tea I'd probably believe it myself. The assumed truth becomes clearer over time but a central repository for the real story is more helpful. I'll keep my own when it is necessary."

As with FBN agent George Hunter White, the year 1953 was a seminal one for Pierre Lafitte, with both men finding themselves in Cuba at the beginning of 1953 and again in 1954, 1955, and later. As was the case with White, we are uncertain what specifically took Lafitte to the island nation; however, some things are clear. Interviews with Lafitte's family reveal that he was well acquainted with Amleto Battisti y Lora, a wealthy Corsican who had come to Cuba via Uruguay. Battisti, a tall, slim man who shaved and waxed his head, was often referred to as a "Mafia kingpin" and "Mafia Family head." He was a member of Cuba's House of Representatives, owned a bank in Havana, and operated Havana's luxurious Hotel Sevilla Biltmore, built in 1908 at a cost of millions and within which criminal mastermind Meyer Lansky held a silent partnership. Battisti, always cunning, extremely intelligent, and the quintessential ladies' man, took special pride in regularly importing new groups of prostitutes from abroad "for the exclusive enjoyment" of his guests at his hotel, which he had taken over in 1939. He also opened at least two casinos in Cuba and several bolita gaming operations in Florida, in partnership with Santo Trafficante, Jr., the head of the Florida Mafia.

Pierre Lafitte had known and worked with Battisti in France, where the two had teamed up with François Spirito to operate an extensive white slavery and prostitution ring that extended from France to Egypt, and beyond. Few Americans in the 1950s had heard of Battisti. The few who had were mostly movie actors, entertainers, and writers. In Cuba, Battisti was a hotelier to celebrities, hosting Frank Sinatra, George Raft, Robert Mitchum, Lana Turner, Ava Gardner, Enrico Caruso, Josephine Baker, Errol Flynn, Gloria Swanson, Georges Simenon, and Graham Greene.

Battisti was also very much involved in drug trafficking, with some law enforcement officials claiming he was a major dealer in heroin. Indeed, it was Battisti who convinced Lucky Luciano, following his deportation form the United States, that Cuba was the ideal location from which to establish his main heroin distribution route into North America. Cuban writer Enrique Cirules states that Battisti was head of one of several Mafia families headquartered in Cuba. Battisti was also quite close to Meyer Lansky, who maintained a home in Cuba. A 1958 US Treasury special investigation report on Battisti stated: "Mr. Battisti, in the opinion of the undersigned, is capable of anything." Ironically, Battisti, who on occasion employed Lafitte in Cuba to carry out sensitive jobs, once quipped: "[Pierre] is a little too untrustworthy to deal with, except for when the need arises, and unfortunately it does on occasion."

In addition to Battisti in Cuba, Lafitte also dealt with Amedeo Barletta and Paul Damien Mondolini. Barletta, a Calabrian, was Mussolini's counsel and "administrator of Mussolini's family in the United States" and, according to the FBI, had been a wartime double agent planted by the Italians in Latin America. This, of course, put him close to Otto Skorzeny, as the former SS officer's private papers reflect.

In 1942, the Bureau ordered Barletta's arrest in the Dominican Republic, but he fled to Argentina, where he remained until the end of the war. Soon thereafter, he turned up in Havana, as a representative for several large American automobile and pharmaceutical companies, including, according to writer Cirules, General Motors. Before the war, Barletta had been a General Motors sales manager in the Dominican Republic, where he clashed with dictator Rafael Trujillo, who claimed that Barletta was plotting to assassinate him. Cirules also claims that Barletta, alongside Lansky and Battisti, headed a "Mafia family" and was involved in drug trafficking.

Paul Mondolini, a.k.a. Paul Marie Bejin, Jacques Desmarais, and Eduardo Dubian, was born in Corsica in 1916. In wartime Marseilles, where he migrated at an early age, he worked, like many morally ambidextrous bandits, for the Resistance and, at the same time, collaborated with the Germans during the Nazi occupation of France. Remarkably, Mondolini later served as chief of police in Saigon, Vietnam, before he went on to gain worldwide notoriety when he took part in the sensational 1949 robbery of the royal jewelry of the wife of the Ismailian prince Aga Khan, an operation that, according to a disgruntled former deputy of France's intelligence chief Roger Wybot, involved Wybot himself, along with at least four unidentified gunmen, one of whom was allegedly Pierre Lafitte. Otto Skorzeny was very involved with Wybot, as was Otto's wife, Ilse.

Mondolini's association with Pierre Lafitte extended back to their days of drug running in Marseilles and Indochina for François Spirito and Paul Carbone. In Cuba, where he did not well establish himself until 1955, Mondolini, in partnership with Corsicans Antoine D'Agostino and Jean Baptiste Croce, who owned two nightclubs in Havana, became a major player in moving heroin via Cuba to Montreal, Canada. Interesting to note here is that Mondolini's prominent activities in Cuba coincided almost day by day with numerous trips to Cuba taken by CIA Inspector General Lyman B. Kirkpatrick. Kirkpatrick said in 1968 that his Cuban trips were "an effort to help the [Cuban] government establish an effective organization to fight Communism." Kirkpatrick would also say that at the time the CIA was flush with money. "There basically wasn't a limit," he said. "We got what we asked for." And nearly two-thirds of the money went for covert operations.

British crime historian Charles Wighton significantly noted in 1960, "The overseas section of the Corsican gang working in the closest collaboration with the American Mafia in Montreal, Havana, and Mexico City [is] run by [Antoine] D'Agostino and the notorious Paul Mondolini." Indeed, it was Mondolini, along with fellow Corsican Jean Jehan, who masterminded the infamous international heroin caper popularized by the hit film *The French Connection*. Worth noting here is that Jehan, according to CIA records produced in 1976, was thought to be the off-the-record owner of the Bedford Street building in New York City, where George Hunter White, with steady sidekick Pierre Lafitte, operated his CIA-funded safe house, an urban abode of erotic pleasures melded with the horrors brought on by unguided psychedelic journeys. Throughout his drug trafficking career, multilingual Mondolini was considered one of the shrewdest and most intelligent dealers that the FBN confronted.

In Cuba, Lafitte was also well acquainted with Santo Trafficante, Jr., whom he initially knew from his days in Tampa and St. Petersburg, Florida. Trafficante, beginning in 1955, spent a lot of time in Cuba looking after his numerous casino and hotel properties, including the Sans Souci, Havana's oldest gambling casino, the Hotel Deauville, the nightclub Capri, the Havana Hilton, and one of Havana's most popular casinos, the Tropicana. Trafficante was no stranger to Cuba. His father, Santo, Sr., born in Sicily and godfather of the Florida mob, had gambling and bolita operations there that predated World War II and that Santo, Jr., had helped operate since the early 1940s.

Santo Trafficante, Jr., much like his close partner in crime Meyer Lansky, maintained an elusive yet steadfast relationship with the CIA. Some former government officials have observed that Trafficante's cautious alliance with the intelligence community was based "on a quid pro quo relationship whereby both sides prospered in their frequently similar objectives." Perhaps Trafficante's close relationship with Lansky insured his relative immunity from law enforcement and prosecution. (Santo, Jr., was never convicted of breaking any federal law.) Lansky's alliance with the CIA extended back to the days of the OSS and the long-kept secret Operation Underworld.

In 1950, Lansky opened a major new heroin avenue between Turkey, Marseilles's sophisticated processing labs, and America's ever-expanding demand for the drug. Chief among Lansky's suppliers were Paul Mondolini and Antoine D'Agostino. Often facilitating the reliable and uninterrupted flow of heroin to its ultimate sales points on America's streets was Pierre Lafitte, who played a brokering role in many of the larger shipments that were routed to Lansky's dealers. We can only assume that Lafitte's other life as an undercover federal informer and investigator significantly helped his darker deeds involving drug trafficking. Wrote two of this country's finest journalists and writers, Sally Denton and Roger Morris, who rank among the very few investigative writers who are aware of Lafitte:

> As so often in his career, Lansky in his new French connection enjoyed the U.S. government as a de facto silent partner. He trafficked with the secret sanction, protection, and sometimes collaboration of the CIA, the FBN, and other Washington agencies. From its OSS roots during the war, the CIA was now in expedient alliance with organized crime against Communism's influence around the world. CIA stations in Turkey and elsewhere in the Middle East discouraged or even suppressed investigations of opium-growing or smuggling by local politicians, military, and other officials enlisted as allies or even intelligence assets against the Soviets. By the same rationale of national security, successive American administrations refused to confront the known collusion with drug traffickers of allied governments in France and North Africa. From the Mediterranean, the new heroin supply routes soon extended as well to Indochina, where U.S. intelligence and drug enforcement agencies first clashed among themselves and ultimately colluded, in what would become by the end of the sixties a vast new channel of the Syndicate's narcotic trade, with momentous consequences.

At the same time he was launching his French connection pipeline, Lansky decided to relocate from Florida to Havana, Cuba, where he thought he could more easily manage his drug trafficking because Cuba was far more accessible for the tight-knit group of Corsicans and Frenchmen that served him. (Many of these men were on the watch or wanted lists put out by the FBN and FBI.)

It is significant to note here that Lafitte also knew the enigmatic John Maples Spirito (no relation to François Spirito), one of the most mysterious characters in Cuba's revolutionary history, and Frank Sturgis and Sturgis's much over-looked comrade in arms, Richard "Rex" Sanderlin, as well as soldiers of fortune William Alexander Morgan and Herman "the Butcher" Marks. All five characters are listed in Lafitte's book outline on Cuba, with the introductory line "Never was there a more brave and fascinating (some would argue foolhardy and opportunistic) band of men than those I encountered in Cuba during the budding revolution there."

Last and of significance, there was John Martino. Martino's name is found in several of George Hunter White's address books and in Lafitte's notes concerning his trips to Florida and Cuba. Martino, a self-described small businessman in Miami, was virtually unknown until Castro's Revolutionary Guards arrested him on July 23, 1959, for illegally entering Cuba. Lafitte had known Martino for at least seven years prior to his arrest. From about 1950 through to 1959, Martino had maintained a close association with Santo Trafficante, Jr., to whom he supplied gambling and electronic equipment for Trafficante's Havana hotels and casinos. Beginning about 1955, Martino partnered with former Army Counter Intelligence Corp. and CIA Technical Service Staff employee Allan Hughes in his Cuban electronics ventures. (As some readers may recall, Hughes was present at the fateful Deep Creek Lake, Maryland, meeting where Frank Olson was allegedly dosed with LSD.)

Only recently has Martino been given any real attention vis-à-vis his activities in Cuba and the assassination of JFK. Noted historian David Kaiser writes that Martino was close to Santo, Jr., and, prior to his arrest, had been hoping to open a brothel in Havana. Kaiser also reports that Trafficante was in contact with Frank Sturgis and William Morgan. Martino was imprisoned in Cuba's notorious La Cabana fortress, where his fellow prisoners eventually included Morgan, arrested and executed by firing squad for betraying Castro, and three CIA officials who had been arrested for attempting to either bug or bomb the Chinese Embassy in Havana.

Lafitte, operating under the alias Jean Pierre Martin, visited Martino in prison on at least one occasion in 1961. This is known only because of a notation made by George Hunter White: "Pierre to see Martino Cuba—call Rene." [Rene being Pierre's wife.] A subsequent notation by Lafitte reads: "Siragusa re Martino Cuba." This pertains to former OSS officials and Federal Narcotics Bureau agent Charles Siragusa, who was approached by the CIA in 1960 about contracting American Mafia figures in Cuba, and elsewhere, to help three CIA employees imprisoned with Martino to escape. It is thought that perhaps Siragusa contacted White and Lafitte for help with this request.

According to a January 1978 report by investigative journalist Jack Anderson, Siragusa said that he had met with CIA-TSS officials in 1960 about "three Spanish-speaking CIA operatives [who] had been arrested while pulling a Watergate-style break-in at the Chinese Communist News Agency in Havana." The CIA authorized Siragusa "to spend up to $1 million to affect [*sic*] the rescue of the imprisoned agents." Interesting to note is that the three CIA operatives were employees of the Agency's Technical Services Division, at the time under the direction of Dr. Sidney Gottlieb. The three men, David Lemar Christ, Thornton J. Anderson, and Walter E. Szuminski, according to CIA records, were audio and electronic specialists highly trained in bugging devices. (See Endnotes for more detail of negotiations for the release of the three men.) According   to former CIA officials, all three men had also worked closely with Allan Hughes, and according to Gottlieb, Hughes was assigned by the Air Force to the CIA. Gottlieb confirmed that the three men had entered Cuba under aliases and false indemnification papers issued by the Agency's Technical Services Division. Also, while the three were imprisoned in Cuba, Gottlieb's Technical Services shop seriously considered secreting an unnamed "former Air Force officer," who was an expert in hypnosis, into their cells to either hypnotize them or to assassinate them before they could be interrogated. Knowledgeable, confidential sources reveal that this was Allan Hughes. However, this is unverified, and the CIA declined to comment on the matter.

Last, Gerry Hemming, a soldier of fortune to whom the CIA may have contracted work and who was imprisoned with the three men briefly, said: "They were all scared out of their minds. They knew that other Americans had been executed by Castro, and they were scared shitless they were going to be lined up at the wall and shot."

A WIDER CAST OF CHARACTERS

About this same time, in the summer of 1960, another CIA official approached Charles Siragusa. This was Vincent Thill, who had worked earlier in Berlin with

William King Harvey. It is clear from the Lafitte datebook that Bill Harvey was a prominent fixture in Pierre's world in 1963. Described as everything from "One of the greatest intelligence officers I have ever known. . . ." (David Murphy, CIA Soviet specialist) to "the hard-drinking gun nut who figured prominently in a number of the Agency's assassination jobs" (author David Talbot), Harvey was in turn brilliant, incredibly driven, and extremely difficult to control. Harvey bolted Hoover's FBI in 1947 and was recruited into the new CIA soon thereafter. Demonstrating a keen talent for counterespionage, Harvey worked his way to the head of CIA's Staff C, "C" denoting counterintelligence.

In the wake of his role in exposing Soviet spy Kim Philby, Harvey was awarded the lead in what was then the most significant CIA post in the world, the Berlin Operating Base. In 1959, Director Allen Dulles brought Harvey back to Washington, D.C., to head Staff D, formally concerned with signals intelligence, but due to the extraordinary level of secrecy surrounding the office—Staff D regularly liaised with the National Security Agency—was utilized as a secure place to park operations that the Agency did not care to chat about in front of a Congressional committee. ZR/RIFLE was one of those projects. In 1962, Harvey was promoted to the head of Task Force W, running the CIA's entire Cuban operation. There he planned the "splitting" of the Castro regime and the assassination of Fidel Castro and continually battled with the Kennedy administration's anti-Castro policies.

Harvey regarded the mix of sabotage, psychological warfare, and political action that constituted most of "Operation Mongoose" as being a weak, bureaucratic effort that wasted time and money and endangered US national security.

According to testimony before a US Senate committee in October 1977, Siragusa stated that Thill requested his help in recruiting Mafia figures for the purposes of assembling an assassination team. Remarkably, Siragusa testified that Thill promised that "each team member" would "be paid $1 million in fees and expenses" for each kill. Siragusa testified that he declined to assist Thill, but CIA documents have emerged that indicate otherwise.

A January 1961 Agency file reveals that Harold Meltzer, a close associate of Meyer Lansky, was among those seriously considered for the CIA's assassination team, a seeming extension of the Agency's QJ/WIN program. The cryptonym QJ/WIN first appeared publicly in 1975, during the Church Committee's investigation of the CIA and its various assassination programs. QJ/WIN was initially thought to be one single operational asset of the CIA's "Executive Action" program, crypted as ZR/RIFLE, a project under the direction of CIA legend

William K. Harvey. ZR/RIFLE was formally constituted in November 1961, but the QJ/WIN program traces back well before that time. According to the "Harvey notes," well known by now to researchers in this field of study, in 1958 the Chief of Station in Luxembourg made contact with "QJ/WIN" in connection with an illegal narcotics operation in the United States. For a year and a half, he was "contracted sporadically by COS Luxembourg, on behalf of the Bureau of Narcotics. . . . In October 1960 [portion blanked out] . . ." The redacted portion relates to the use of QJ/WIN in the Agency's participation in efforts to assassinate Congolese Premier Patrice Lumumba, a grim episode that the Church Committee delved into in some detail.

Harvey Meltzer had been arrested in the past by the Narcotics Bureau and had cooperated with agents White and Siragusa on an unidentified "project" in New York in 1956 and 1957. During this period, Meltzer, called "Happy" by his friends, also had business dealings with Pierre Lafitte in Los Angeles, where Meltzer lived and owned a sportswear company and several automobile dealerships. Lafitte and Meltzer operated and partly owned together two restaurants at about the same time that Lafitte had talked Meltzer into investing in a diamond mine in South Africa and in a nickel smuggling scheme also based somewhere in Africa. (The relevance of nickel to our story will be pursued in Chapter 6.)

Meltzer's name also comes up prominently in several other intriguing documents and ways. In 2006, writer Thomas Bass, a professor at the University of Albany, stated in a radio interview: "Many spies have worked for *Time* magazine, at least spies that we know of, were, in fact, working for the Central Intelligence Agency. There's that very famous example of *Time* magazine Bureau Chief, Mr. Enno Hobbing, who was, in 1954, moved from Paris to Guatemala where he led the coup d'état while working out of the offices of *Time*."

Indeed, US Department of State and US Army Project Paperclip files reveal that First Lieutenant Enno Hobbing escorted former Nazi scientist Alexander Lippisch, designer of prototype German jet fighter planes including the deadly Messerschmitt ME-163 jet fighter, to America's Wright Field in Ohio. Hobbing was also involved, along with Col. Boris Pash, in the transport of former Nazi scientist Wernher von Braun to the United States.

The CIA has consistently claimed that Hobbing resigned from the Agency around 1955, but the Agency also declines to explain why Enno Hobbing's name appears on several CIA reports and cables from 1962 and 1963. Some of the Hobbing-related cable traffic is found in the file of Agency asset Viola June Cobb without explanation. Cobb was working for the CIA in Mexico City in 1962 and in 1963, at the time of Lee Harvey Oswald's visit there.

Special markings on Hobbing-related cables reveal that his involvement in Mexico City intelligence activities may have been connected to Project ZR/AWARD, a top-secret operation the CIA refuses to define, but that may have been connected to the Agency's ongoing hypnosis and behavior-modification activities under Project ZR/ALERT, in Mexico and possibly New Orleans. Additionally, ZR/ALERT appears to have had an undefined operational connection with CIA assassination program QJ/WIN and ZR/RIFLE. These connections involved two CIA possible assassins, Harold Meltzer and Hanna Yazbeck, recruited by the CIA through the efforts of William Harvey. (Some FBI files seem to suggest that Meltzer's real name may have been Harold Fried.)

Both Meltzer and Yazbeck were recruited initially for the Agency's QJ/WIN program. QJ/WIN is often cited by researchers as only the code name for an individual CIA assassin. This single citing is erroneous, because the cryptonym also refers to a CIA program under which multiple people were recruited by the Agency. Author Albarelli helped identify at least twelve such individuals recruited by the Agency under the QJ/WIN cryptonym. In addition, there were multiple QJ/WIN offices run by the CIA across the United States and the world.

The digraph "QJ" designates Spain, meaning the QJ/WIN program was based in Spain, where, of course, Otto Skorzeny lived. This is underscored by the much-overlooked testimony of the CIA's Theodore Shackley, associate deputy director for clandestine operations, testifying under the alias "Mr. Halley," before the Senate Select Committee to Study Governmental Operations with Respect to Intelligence Activities, US Senate Select Committee on Intelligence, in Washington, D.C., on August 19, 1975. Twice, Shackley directly linked Spain to the QJ/WIN program, after he was asked: "Do you recall a CIA asset who went by the cryptonym QJ/WIN?"

Answered Shackley: *"No, I do not. Knowing the system, and so forth, normally it would have something to do with Spain. It does not ring any bells with me. That is all I can give you, a sort of Pavlovian response. You flash QJ/WIN on the screen, I am telling you now I do not know, but it probably has something to do with Spain."* [Italics added.]

The letters WIN indicate the broad program cryptonym, and often individuals were given numbers after these three letters. For example: QJ/WIN-1, QJ/WIN-2, QJ/WIN-3, and so on.

An October 1976 CIA memorandum concerning a "review of the ZR/RIFLE file" reveals the following:

In 1959, [Harold Meltzer] furnished information to our QJ/WIN California office but has not since cooperated with us. N.B. he has the background and talent for the matter we discussed but it is not known whether he would be receptive. [This the review took from a December 1960 CIA document.] YAZBECK lived in Beirut and worked for QJ/WIN's office intermittently during the past 10 years (dates not given-possibly during 51-61.) YAZBECK's chief bodyguard from 50-58 (not named) was a convicted murderer. The bodyguard was murdered. States that YAZBECK has an available pool of assassins.

Harold Meltzer first came to the attention of the CIA after mobster Johnny Rosselli had a conversation about him in 1959 with Agency Security Office chief Sheffield Edwards. Earlier the same year, according to a letter from FBN supervisory agent and CIA contractor George Hunter White to Garland Williams, also a FBN supervisor and a close friend to White, White and Charles Siragusa had discussed Meltzer with Rosselli during a meeting in Miami. It appears that Meltzer was not initially recruited by the CIA to perform assassinations but instead was slated to help spot and recruit potential candidates for the Agency's ZR/RIFLE and QJ/WIN programs.

However, Meltzer's skills as a hitman for Rosselli were notorious in mob circles.

That the CIA, as exposed in the above quoted memorandum, maintained a "QJ/WIN California office" is intriguing and, of course, summons up all sorts of theories about the assassination of Robert F. Kennedy.

Worth noting is Harold Meltzer's deep involvement in drug trafficking, especially through illicit routes originating in Mexico City, which extended back to the mid-1940s, when Meltzer was protected by high-ranking associates in the US Embassy in Mexico City. By the 1950s, Meltzer's extensive trafficking involved two wealthy young South American brothers, one of whom was madly in love with young Viola June Cobb, an eventual CIA asset in Cuba and Mexico. (Cobb eventually turned the brother, who had become her fiancé, in to the FBN as a way of getting him to shed his drug addiction.) Meltzer and his trafficking associates, according to FBN sources, would sometimes fly to and from Mexico City in private, chartered Tri-Cities Flying Service planes owned by Evelyn "Pinky" Brier, a former wartime Woman's Auxiliary Air Force pilot. Included among Pinky Brier's other clients were CIA DCI John McCone and US Supreme Court Justice Earl Warren.

A revealing December 19, 1960, FBN bio-sheet contained in Hanna Yazbeck's CIA 201 file, most likely written by FBN supervisor Garland Williams, who also worked for the CIA's Amazon Natural Drug Company, reads: "Yazbeck lives in Beirut, Lebanon and worked for my office intermittently during the past ten years. I have often visited his home, but I cannot remember the address. However, he is quite well known in Beirut as the leader of a gambling syndicate. He often heads up a hatchet squad when disputes arise between the Moslem and Christian underworld factions in Beirut. Yazbeck is of the Christian faith. During the period, I was in Europe (1950–1958), his chief bodyguard was a convicted murderer who owed his release from prison to Yazbeck's power. This bodyguard has since been murdered, but Yazbeck has an available pool of assassins. He has been convicted in an Egyptian Court at Cairo Alexandria on a charge of smuggling hashish. Since then, he has had a passionate hatred for Egyptians and Arabs in that order. In addition to his very wide circle of criminal friends in Lebanon, Syria, Turkey and Egypt, he also has many friends in high political positions in these countries. YAZBECK lives ostentatiously. He has a beautiful home and both he and his wife are loaded with jewelry. He has a stable of girls for his own private enjoyment. I suspect that during the summer holiday season he is a procurer for wealthy Arabs in various Middle Eastern countries who visit the mountain resorts adjoining Beirut. Rumors were constantly received regarding his importance as a narcotics trafficker but we have been unable to develop a successful narcotic case against him. I have always strongly suspected he has been, and will continue to be, engaged in any criminal activity that is profitable. YAZBECK is about sixty years old but has the appearance of 50. He is 6' tall and heavily built, ruddy complexion and has very charming manners. He speaks a little French but no English."

An undated FBN typed document (perhaps in follow-up to the above) on Hanna Yazbeck reads in part: "YAZBECK is well known to Garland Williams as a major drug trafficker operating in Turkey, Syria, and Egypt, according to FBN official Charles Siragusa. . . . Siragusa says that if anyone could assemble a reliable team of murderers, Yazbeck is the man. Obviously, there is a need for close coordination with other agencies here and abroad, if Yazbeck, as assumed, is to continue his narcotics and sex-trafficking activities. Siragusa says it may be necessary to brief, to whatever extent needed, George White, now in San Francisco. White once conducted an investigation targeting Yazbeck and others and developed a deep dislike for the man. Siragusa can handle the appropriate people within the Narcotics Bureau without drawing any attention to our use of Yazbeck."

* * *

Finally, in regard to other CIA-recruited QJ/WIN participants with whom Pierre Lafitte interacted, there was Edward Lawton Smith, a Canadian born in Nova Scotia on April 5, 1921, and who came to the United States sometime in the early 1950s and, on occasion, worked in Europe with QJ/WIN-2, Jose Marie Mankel, an alias used sometimes by Lafitte:

848 - Harvey - . . .
White – Smith (Canada)
—Lafitte datebook, January 24, 1963

Smith was reported to look like Lee Harvey Oswald, and he often traveled to Mexico City in the early 1960s. According to FBN and CIA documents, Smith had been in the Canadian army during World War II, serving in Germany, France, and Belgium, as well as serving four years with the Argyle and Sutherland Highlanders, Canadian Army. Records indicate that he "received an honorable discharge despite a court martial which involved the killing of a fellow Canadian soldier during a fist fight. The victim crashed into a plate glass window. Smith was convicted and sentenced to be shot. However, the conviction was reversed by Criminal Court Appeals and Smith was returned to duty."

After his military service, Smith "acquired a petty criminal record in Montreal and has spent most of his adult life there. He earned himself a reputation as a muscle man for various Canadian mobs. About two years ago his association with a Canadian Mafia group became known to our New York office. Because of the absence of any adult criminal record, his past service as a muscle man and his reliability to the criminal code, he was used as a courier to smuggle large quantities of illicit drugs from Montreal to the United States, principally New York City,"

Smith was recruited in New York City around 1957 by Lafitte to be an undercover, paid special employee reporting to George White and Garland Williams: "He succeeded in introducing an undercover US Narcotic Agent to the principal Canadian gangsters from whom large evidential narcotic purchases were made followed by coordinated arrests of both the Canadian suppliers and the New York distributors." In 1959, Smith had mysterious dealings with June Cobb and Warren Broglie in New York City, perhaps related to a drug-trafficking ring based in New Orleans.

Because of Smith's undercover work, "a major international narcotic drug smuggling and distributing conspiracy case was developed. Smith as of this date [1960] is still testifying in Federal Court in New York City against the many criminals involved. His conduct as a witness has been exemplary even under severe cross examination by highly talented criminal defense lawyers. SMITH has no criminal record in the United States and his Canadian criminal record is not available. He is about 5'10", very handsome, flashy dresser, lives flamboyantly and is the lady-killer type. We do not have a photograph of him. Although he is presently married to a former stripteaser, divorce proceedings are pending. He has been temporarily living at the St. George Hotel in Brooklyn but will leave there shortly upon termination of Federal Trial in New York. He expects to make his home in New Jersey but can always be reached, even at a later date, through the New York office. The Armstrong Circle Theatre Television Program and *Reader's Digest* magazine are interested in dramatizing his accomplishments for law enforcement."

Smith's daughter, who declined to be identified in this book due to her serious concerns about possible retaliation, says of her father: "He led a strange and secret life. We know he worked for the CIA, but really have no idea what he did."

SCENES FROM LAFITTE'S NEW ORLEANS

In 1961, with significant funding from Californian industrialist Patrick J. Frawley and Dallas oilman Clint Murchison, mentioned previously as a financial benefactor of Ferenc Nagy's Permindex, and with financial support from his friends at International Trade Mart, Lloyd Cobb and Director Clay Shaw, twenty-seven-year-old Ed Butler founded the Information Council of the Americas (INCA). His publications under that banner were relied on by the CIA in a blitz of propaganda just prior to the invasion at the Bay of Pigs, which could explain his association with Deputy Director CIA Charles Cabell. Some of their money went toward a film titled *Hitler in Havana*, reviewed as a "tasteless affront to minimum journalistic standards" by the *New York Times*. Researchers will be aware that Butler was a member of "Free Voice of Latin America" for a short time before being ousted for his extreme right political views. Its own secretary treasurer, William Klein, who filed incorporation papers that designated a young Cuban student at Tulane University as president and a shy, intelligent former citizen of Belize Honduras as vice president, wrote in a recap of the organization for DA Jim Garrison, "The life of the Free Voice as a corporate entity was ephemeral and uneventful. For my own part it was an absolute bore."

The letter states that Ed Butler's globe-encircling Communist conspiracy theory quickly made his removal from office mandatory. According to Grand Jury testimony, the originator of the concept of Free Voice was William Dalzell. He testified that along with Klein (who according to an investigator present during

Grand Jury later went to work at the Office of Naval Intelligence in DC), he wanted to "warn Latin America of what has transpired here since Castro has been in power for the last few years." Klein's dismissive remarks about the organization, as well as his version of Butler's role at Free Voice, contradicts Dalzell's testimony in several areas, including that Butler was never active because INCA was in effect competing with Free Voice. However, there is no doubt that Butler and Dalzell were well acquainted in spite of his claims.

In a memo from Orleans Parish prosecutor Andrew Sciambra to DA Garrison, William Dalzell worked "undercover as a petroleum consultant." This comports with a Lafitte note on April 17, 1963, *"-Dalzell - $money for drilling."* Several months later on July 17 he writes, *"Dalzell crazy?"* and in parentheses, (*Rene says ignore his antics*). Indeed, sources indicate that Dalzell had a mental breakdown in New Orleans around that time. In his article "The Friends of Democratic Cuba," published in the Fall/Winter 1993/4 issue of *Back Channels*, researcher William Davy provided a summary of the numerous hats worn by Dalzell. According to Davy, ". . . Another incorporator was William Dalzell. Dalzell was a private investigator closely associated with Guy Banister Associates. Dalzell was a Navy veteran who also worked as a cryptographer for the Department of Defense. He later shows up in Ethiopia and Yemen as a petroleum advisor with the Agency for International Development, whose links to the CIA have been amply documented." Davy continues, "According to Garrison's files, Dalzell also operated out of the American Embassy in Rome for a time and spoke about a half dozen languages, including Swahili. *Some of his activities in the early 1960s included attempting to obtain weapons for revolutionaries in Honduras as well as a PT boat and submarine for the anti-Castro Cubans.* [Italics added.]

Davy asserts that although the group was ostensibly made up of New Orleans civic personalities incorporated for the purpose of collecting funds to aid the anti-Castro cause, The Friends of Democratic Cuba was strictly a dummy front for intelligence operations. An informant for DA Garrison claimed that it was "an undercover operation in conjunction with the CIA and FBI which involved the shipment and transportation of individuals and supplies in and out of Cuba." The organization disbanded within a month of its inception, and the splinter group became Dalzell's Free Voice of Latin America.

"T"

A prominent figure in the life of Pierre Lafitte in 1963—the character he carefully disguises as "T"—was mentioned in the early pages of this chapter. It is clear from

Pierre's records that "T" served as liaison for the top echelon of the conspiracy. Exhaustive consideration including more than twenty-four months of deliberations drew these authors to believe that the *most logical candidate* was CIA's Tracey Barnes, head of Domestic Operations Division. As Alan Kent writes in his analysis "A Well Concealed 'T'" available in the Appendix of this book:

> [Barnes's secretary Alice McIlvaine said] "When Angleton called, Tracy ran to his office." . . . Tracy Barnes moved beneath the radar through the most dramatic covert events that the CIA was involved in between 1953 and 1963. Rather than being the "corporate liberal" . . . Barnes was a daring, frequently "over-the-top," hard-core cold warrior. Barnes was arguably more directly involved with operations that included political assassination than was any other high-ranking CIA officer of his era. By comparison, the man many of us have been most interested in over years of studying the assassination (of JFK), William K. Harvey, is not even close. . . . [Barnes] was bitter about the Kennedys following the Bay of Pigs, and remained so for the rest of his life. Personalizing the tragedy of the "brilliant disaster," Barnes is quoted by [author Evan] Thomas as telling a friend late in his life that "Kennedy let me down."

In August 1963, Ed Butler, who at the very least knew Dalzell while a founding member of Free Voice, joined in a radio debate that all assassination researchers should be familiar with. On August 9, 1963, Oswald had been handing out Fair Play for Cuba Committee leaflets, when he became involved in a confrontation with Carlos Bringuier, a twenty-seven-year-old Cuban exile and member of the DRE, a militant right-wing, anticommunist, anti-Castro, anti-Kennedy group. Oswald had been arrested, and while in jail he was visited by FBI agent John L. Quigley. On August 21, Oswald debated the issue of Fidel Castro and Cuba with Bringuier and Bringuier's friend Ed Butler on the Bill Stuckey Radio Show. Later that month, Oswald was seen in the company of David Ferrie and Clay Shaw.

A month after Rene Lafitte tells her husband to ignore Bill Dalzell's antics, which appear to have been related to Ed Butler, and just days after Oswald paid a fine for the August 9 demonstration, Pierre makes a note on August 16:

> Antoine's Room – Martello,
> E. Joanides [sic] and Labadie. Quigly [*sic*]
> Interview st. demonstration
> Call Holdout

Martello is a reference to New Orleans Police Department officer Lt. Francis L. Martello (not to be confused with Francis "Monk" Martello). Lt. Martello happened to pass by as the August 9th confrontation between Oswald and Brin-guier—described as nothing more than shadowboxing—broke out. According to Martello's incident report, "[Oswald] seemed to have set them up, so to speak, to create an incident, but when the incident occurred, he remained absolutely peaceful and gentle."

Although official records do not explain why Tampa-based FBI Special Agent Stephen J. Labadie might have been in the French Quarter in New Orleans on August 16, a Lafitte entry of the following month, on September 24, reads "-*Oswald D/T (Labadie/Florida),*" indicating that SA Labadie was directly engaged in matters of keen interest to Pierre Lafitte and his superiors.

Quigly is a misspelling of the name Quigley, FBI Special Agent John L. Quigley, who interviewed Oswald in the New Orleans jail before he paid a $10 fine and was released.

Holdout was a mystery. Perhaps Lafitte was referencing a confidential informer, or perhaps a code name for a program. There are also reasons to speculate "holdout" could be a high-level double agent whose identity was so significant to a much larger set of circumstances that were unfolding under Angleton's control that Lafitte dare not speak or write his name. In the following chapter of this investigation, we consider the possibility that "holdout" was the moniker of someone in the highest echelon of domestic intelligence who, having been persuaded that there was "righteous" justification for an assassination that would impact global politics for decades, came on board with the plot to permanently remove John Kennedy from that stage.

As noted previously, some datebook entries may have been created after the fact—a reflection on prior events, or notes for future reference—so we can't know with certainty that Lafitte was present at this meeting at Antoine's, nor is it clear that the meeting was held on the 16th. We do know, however, that on the 16th, Oswald was less than a fifteen-minute walk from Antoine's, this time standing in front of Clay Shaw's International Trade Mart, passing out leaflets again.

Lafitte's datebook remains dormant for the next four days; then on August 21st, the day of the radio debate hosted by Bill Stuckey, he records:

Talk Joannides Cuba –
he refer to K org. in
Mex – similar setup now.

Discuss with King – Geo
+Charles about Havana
Mx trips. (Holdout) [followed with a check mark]

The cornerstone of the two entries made within a week of each other is George Joannides, who maintained addresses in both Miami and, for a period in 1963, New Orleans. Investigative journalist Jefferson Morley, whose groundbreaking lawsuit against the CIA continues to reverberate, pursued George Joannides's role as agency liaison to the House Select Committee on Assassinations in 1978. Morley revealed that the agency personnel file for Joannides indicates that in 1963 he served as the chief of the Psychological Warfare branch of the Miami station with a staff of twenty-four and a budget of $1.5 million. As such, Joannides was also in charge of handling the anti-Castro student group that Lee Harvey Oswald had tried to infiltrate in New Orleans in August 1963. Known as the Directorio Revolucionario Estudiantil (the Student Revolutionary Directorate), Joannides was responsible for guiding and monitoring the young Cuban exiles. According to the Directorate's leaders in Miami, funding also supported the DRE chapters in New Orleans and other cities.

Morley shares that at least two leaders recall having had a close but stormy relationship with George Joannides, whom they knew only as "Howard." The records of the Directorate, now in the University of Miami archives, support their memories. The group's archives show that "Howard" worked closely with the Directorate on a wide variety of issues. In his essay "What Jane Roman Said," Morley writes:

While the details of Joannides' motivations remain concealed, the results of his actions in 1963 are well documented. According to a Kennedy White House memo, the CIA "guided and monitored" the Cuban Student Directorate in mid-1963. Declassified CIA cables show that "Howard" demanded that the group clear their public statements with him. In his job evaluation from the summer of 1963, Joannides was credited having established control over the group. He dispensed funds from the AMSPELL budget, which the Directorate's leaders in Miami and New Orleans used to publicly identify Oswald as a supporter of the Castro government in August 1963. AMSPELL funds were also used within hours of the [sic] Kennedy's death to link Oswald to Castro.

The results of his expenditures, it must be said, were consistent with US policy. The former Directorate leaders say their purpose in launching a propaganda blitz against Oswald was to discredit the Castro regime and create public pressure for a US attack on Cuba . . .

Morley also writes that Joannides "kept his hand in all of this secret. Joannides certainly knew of the Directorate's contacts with Oswald within hours of Kennedy's death, *if not earlier.*" [Italics added.]

Also according to Morley, "Joannides did not report his knowledge in written documents. Such records might have been turned over to law enforcement and thus exposed the agency's operations to public view. His actions were consistent with his duty to protect 'sources and methods' and with Jane Roman's observation that SAS was keeping information about Oswald 'under their tight control.'"

With Lafitte's August 16 entry, those questions are laid partially to rest. We now know that Joannides met with the FBI and New Orleans police on the heels of Oswald's street demonstration of the 9th. Whether Joannides turned over records during that meeting, or merely gave FBI SA Labadie and SA Quigley, along with NOPD Martello, a verbal update on agency operations, is unknown.

ANOTHER MEETING

Lafitte's calendar for the month of August was full indeed. On August 13, three days before the meeting at Antoine's, he made a note that "T w/Silverthorne to fly in here with Harvey – meet Trafficante tomorrow." It's clear that Lafitte is in New Orleans, and that something of significance has drawn the CIA's William King Harvey and Mafia boss Santo Trafficante to the Crescent City for a meeting with "T." (Joseph Silverthorne was a favored pilot within the agency.)

The following Wednesday, as emphasized, George Joannides was still on Lafitte's mind as he made a note related to the "K. org. and Havana - MC trips and Joannides." In the same entry, Lafitte also mentions "discuss with King - Geo. + Charles." It is doubtful that King is a reference to Lafitte's friend William King Harvey because he is identified throughout the datebook as "Harvey." It is, however, reasonable to suspect that "King" was George Joannides's boss, J. C. King, who was head of the Western Hemisphere Division of the CIA. And if this was a note to self, to discuss matters with J. C. King and George Hunter White, then by deduction, Charles is Charles Siragusa of the FBN, whose record as liaison with the Mafia has already been established. In this context, mob boss Santo Trafficante's arrival in New Orleans on August 13 is all the more intriguing.

J. C. KING AND AMWORLD

AMWORLD was among the most tightly held secrets of the Kennedy administration, and one that would evade five Congressional investigations following his assassination, until documents were finally revealed in 1990. According to author Lamar Waldron with Thom Hartmann in *Ultimate Sacrifice: John and Robert Kennedy, the Plan for a Coup in Cuba, and the Murder of JFK*, the first AMWORLD document was a SECRET, EYES ONLY five-page memo prepared on June 26, 1963. The authors reveal, "The memo is sent by J. C. King, Chief [of the CIA's] Western Hemisphere Division, to the 'Chiefs of Certain [CIA] Stations.' The memo is titled: 'AMWORLD Background of Program, Operational Support Requirements and Procedural Rules'. It begins: 'this will serve to alert you to the inception of AMWORLD, a new CIA program targeted against Cuba. Some manifestations of activity resulting from this program may come to your notice before long.'" Author Waldron continues to provide in-depth analysis of the highly classified operation, highlighting in particular that secrecy was so paramount, normal lines of communication were not adhered to.

Among CIA records that were finally released, a memorandum titled "AMWORLD MEETING IN MIAMI, 28-29 June 1964" includes the following: "AMBIDDY-1 [Cuban exile leader Manuel Artime Buesa] claims to have been contacted in the past by the Mafia for the sale of arms." (Note: The memo also states that the Dominican Republic is often mentioned within AMWORLD as a possible source of support, the significance of which is pursued further in Chapter 8.) In light of Lafitte's entry to indicate that Santo Trafficante arrived in New Orleans to meet with William King Harvey on August 13, the possibility exists that the meeting at Antoine's on August 16, and subsequent communication between Lafitte and Joannides and discussions with J. C. King, George Hunter White, and Charles Siragusa, may have surpassed plans for Lee Harvey Oswald's involvement in the forthcoming assassination of the president (plans that were weeks away from being solidified and sanctioned) but were equally, if not more, focused on deliberations at the highest level of AMWORLD, an operation that had been in play for months.

CIA Officer Henry Hecksher, a native of Hamburg, Germany, who joined the OSS and later contributed to the evolution of the CIA, was the case officer of Manuel Artime. As such, Hecksher became involved in AMWORLD in 1963. In 1964, he and Artime traveled to Madrid, Spain, to meet with Rolando Cubela, the Cuban revolutionary and founding member of the DRE whose agency contact officer was George Joannides. At the time, Madrid was still a base of operation for Otto Skorzeny and arms dealer Victor Oswald. Author Ralph

Ganis stresses the significance of the friendship Otto had maintained with the Berlin Operations Base, including chief of base William King Harvey in the early 1950s. Henry Hecksher, Artime's minder and directly involved in AMWORLD, had served under Bill Harvey in Berlin.

* * *

It is important to note that FBI Director Hoover's Special Agent in Florida, Stephen Labadie, appears again in the datebook a month after the August meetings in New Orleans, on September 24, when Lafitte writes, "Oswald D/T (Labadie / Florida) W. J." This is two days before Oswald departs for Mexico City. If there are doors to be unlocked between J. Edgar Hoover and Oswald's role as an effective the patsy after the fact, we're led by Pierre Lafitte to suspect that Stephen Labadie holds a key.

* * *

During this same period, Pierre's datebook indicates that Chief of Counterintelligence James Angleton's fingerprints were also all over another intrigue in play, known to many as "The Ellen Rometsch Affair."

CHAPTER 4
SUICIDES AND CALL GIRLS

George/OS talk to Stockdale about P. Graham
(George says Chestnut Lodge - Dupe.
—Lafitte Datebook, July 28, 1963

It is also alleged that the President and Attorney General
had availed themselves of services of playgirls.

—ALEX ROSEN, ASST. DIR. FBI
OCTOBER 21, 1963

It is an open Washington secret that when the "sex angle" was
introduced into the Baker case by revelations that a beautiful
German model had been sent home after reported (and denied)
affairs with Washington politicians, it scared almost as many
people in Washington as when the Russian missiles in Cuba
pushed the U.S. to the brink of nuclear war.

"SECRET RULES OF INQUIRY"
NEW YORK HERALD TRIBUNE
NOV 10, 1963

The whole world has just gone mad.

—MARY RUTH HAUSER
SEC. TO FORMER AMB. GRANT STOCKDALE
DEC. 3, 1963

On the morning of December 2, 1963, ten days after the assassination of President John F. Kennedy, Edward Grant Stockdale, a ruggedly handsome, forty-eight-year-old businessman and cohort of both Jack and

Robert Kennedy, fell to his death from the thirteenth floor of the Alfred I. duPont Building in downtown Miami.

Stockdale tumbled eight floors from his business office window before his body struck and landed on a fifth-floor ledge. He was wearing a white dress shirt and gray suit pants. Miami police investigators determined Stockdale's death to be an "apparent suicide." Stockdale left no suicide note or letter, according to investigators, and despite their determination, it remains unclear as to how Stockdale went out the window of his office. It is uncertain whether the window Stockdale went out of was open or closed. Scant newspaper reports seem to indicate it was open. Requests from these authors, and others, for a copy of the police investigative file brought the response that the file was no longer available. One official, who declined to be named for this book, said he thought the file "had been either lost or misplaced years ago."

The facts preceding his so-called "suicide" only serve to compound the difficulty of believing the investigator's conclusion. Stockdale, as usual, arrived at his office at about 10:00 a.m. on the morning of Monday, December 2, 1963. His office was on the thirteenth floor of the office building in downtown Miami. Stockdale was unable to get into his office because it was locked, and he didn't have a key with him. His administrative assistant, who usually opened the office each day, was at a dental appointment. She would arrive at about 10:30 a.m., ten minutes after Stockdale's death.

Finding his office door locked, Stockdale had gone across the hall to a law office and asked Mary Ruth Hauser if anyone had a key to his office. Hauser told Stockdale that she would call the building's manager to come with a key. Stockdale waited while Hauser made the call.

She recounted the next day: "He followed me into my office and stood there while I called down for a key. He stood there very calmly. He didn't seem at all agitated. . . . Somehow the subject of the President's death came up. . . . He told me he was in his office when his wife called to tell him the President had been shot. He said he just got down on his knees and prayed."

After this, a person with a key arrived, and Stockdale and Hauser went across the hall, still talking. As Stockdale entered his now-opened office, Hauser's desk phone started ringing, and she excused herself to answer it.

Hauser told police that about "five minutes later" there "was this terrible thud." It was the sound of Stockdale's body striking the roof ledge of the top floor of the Florida National Bank and Trust, about seventy-five feet below his office.

Hauser said: "I just wondered if I had gone right behind him. . . . I don't know, I guess it wouldn't have made any difference. The whole world has just gone mad."

Only minutes after Stockdale struck the fifth-story ledge, Dr. Sheffel H. Wright, who had an office in the duPont Building, rushed to the scene and pronounced Stockdale dead. A priest from a nearby Catholic church also arrived and administered the Last Rites. Newspaper accounts of Stockdale's death featured interviews with a number of people who had seen Stockdale before he arrived at his office that fateful morning. All said he seemed to be in "good spirits." Indeed, Stockdale even got a shoeshine just before coming to his office.

An article in the *Miami Herald Reporter*, however, by political reporter John B. McDermott revealed that Stockdale had attempted to talk to McDermott on Sunday, December 1. McDermott stated that Stockdale "wanted to tell me something—to talk things over." Unfortunately, McDermott didn't talk to Stockdale and seemed to have no clue as to what he had to say. McDermott's article also stated that on Saturday, November 23, the day after the JFK assassination, Stockdale flew to Washington, D.C., after he received a telephone call from Attorney General Bobby Kennedy. McDermott apparently had no idea why Kennedy had summoned Stockdale. Stockdale returned from Washington late the same day and then returned to Washington on November 26. On that day, he met with Bobby Kennedy and Edward Kennedy and then flew back to Miami the same day. The next day, Edward Kennedy called Stockdale's wife and told her he was concerned about her husband's "mental health." Again, McDermott provides no information about why Stockdale met with the Kennedys.

Interviewed in June 2004, Grant's daughter, Ann Stockdale—apparently acutely aware of the dangers of speaking candidly about her father's alleged suicide even four decades later—made no reference to revelations that rocked D.C. politics in the fall of 1963, including the Bobby Baker scandal that had forced her family to leave Dublin and the Ellen Rometsch Affair. Perhaps for Grant's daughter, the safer explanation was the Military-Industrial Complex:

[President] Kennedy asked Daddy to go to the Air Force Base south of Miami to see if (against Kennedy's orders) bombs were being loaded on the planes. Bombs were being loaded on the planes! I believe one of the reasons Daddy was killed was because he knew that the Government was being run by the Military Complex. The Military Complex didn't want the American people to realize (and still don't) that they were calling the shots. Daddy knew he was being followed . . . and he told Mom that they were going to get him . . . and they did. There was an attempt on my life also several days after Daddy's funeral. I realize now that this was a scare tactic to silence my Mother, i.e., if you speak about anything, your kids are dead. It worked!

Author and publisher David Talbot writes that Stockdale "flew to Washington and talked with Robert and Edward Kennedy about the assassination of their brother. On his return [to Miami] Stockdale told several of his friends that 'the world was closing in.' On December 1, he spoke to his attorney, William Frates, who later recalled: 'He started talking. It didn't make much sense. He said something about "those guys" trying to get him. Then about the assassination.'"

As intriguing as Ann Stockdale's and David Talbot's revelations are, few were aware at the time of Stockdale's acquaintanceship with Otto and Ilse Skorzeny in Ireland, and the possible impact that may have had on his untimely death.

WOLVES ON THE PROWL

Stockdale was a well-known and respected businessman in Miami, as well as in St. Petersburg, Florida, where he and his brother Julian owned and operated a real estate investment and sales firm, Grant Stockdale and Associates. Stockdale, a former US Marine during World War II, serving in the Pacific, was also a very close friend of John F. Kennedy, having become so in 1949 when Kennedy was a young Congressman from Massachusetts. Stockdale's friendship with JFK frequently involved visits by Kennedy to Stockdale's Coral Gables home that he shared with his wife and five children. Kennedy, Stockdale, and Stockdale's children often played touch football on Stockdale's expansive lawn, and then afterward everyone would swim in the warm Florida ocean waters.

As a Democrat, Stockdale was also a close friend to George Armistead Smathers, who, with Stockdale's strong support, was elected to represent Florida in Congress in 1946. Stockdale served briefly as Smathers's congressional aide and then served in the Florida Legislature from 1948 to 1950. In 1951, Smathers won one of Florida's US Senate seats. Stockdale joined Senator Smathers in 1960 in efforts to nominate JFK for the presidency. As a member of the National Democratic Party Finance Committee, Stockdale campaigned hard and widely for Kennedy's election. Both Stockdale and Smathers were close to Philip Graham, publisher of the *Washington Post*, who also worked diligently for JFK's and LBJ's election and whom Smathers had known since early childhood in Florida.

Apparently, George Smathers shared JFK's exuberant fondness for members of the opposite sex. CBS reporter and journalist Roger Mudd recalls Smathers spending time on the presidential yacht in the early 1960s. "Smathers was probably John Kennedy's best friend in the US Senate," said Mudd. "Together or singly, they were wolves on the prowl, always able to find or attract gorgeous prey. . . . It was a joke, our pretending to be covering the president, bobbing around in the ocean, squinting through binoculars to find out who was coming and going but always having our view blocked by a Secret Service boat just as another long-legged Palm Beach beauty climbed aboard."

Despite their close friendship, Smathers often acted as a right-wing Democrat, frequently disagreeing with Kennedy on policy and legislation, including his opposition to early civil rights efforts and JFK's backing of Medicaid. A virulent anticommunist, he proposed an embargo against Cuban tobacco and legislative bar against travel and trade with Castro's Cuba. The senator had the president's ear to a degree. Of note, Smathers also served as a covert CIA channel for a number of CIA assets in Florida, including wealthy Miami businessman William Pawley, who was close to Allen Dulles and financed a number of covert paramilitary actions against Castro.

In 1975, former Sen. Smathers testified before the congressionally created Church Committee investigating the CIA's covert and assassinations programs. Smathers told the committee:

[President Kennedy] asked me what reaction I thought there would be throughout South America were Castro to be assassinated * * * I told the President that even as much as I disliked Fidel Castro that I did not think it would be a good idea for there to be even consideration of assassination of Fidel Castro, and the President of the United States completely agreed with me, that it would be a very unwise thing to do, the reason obviously being that no matter who did it and no matter how it was done and no matter what, the United States would receive full credit for it, and it would work to his great disadvantage with all of the other countries in Central and South America * * * I disapproved of it, and he completely disapproved of the idea. [Asterisks in original document.]

The Church Committee report concerning Smathers continues, "Smathers testified that he had the 'impression' that the President raised the subject of assassination with him because someone 'had apparently discussed this and other possibilities with respect to Cuba' with the President. Smathers had no direct knowledge of any such discussion, nor did he know who might have been involved. Moreover, the President did not indicate directly that assassination had been proposed to him. Thereafter, Smathers said he tried to raise the subject of Cuba with President Kennedy and the President told him in no uncertain terms that he should not raise the subject with him again. Smathers particularly recalled one incident, which occurred after the above-quoted conversation, which stuck in his memory.

He recalled that one evening he was at the President's home and during conversation: 'I just happened to mention something about Cuba, and the President took his fork and cracked the plate and says, for God's sake, quit talking about Cuba.'"

Senator Smathers shared a close personal friendship, which included business dealings, with fellow Floridian Grant Stockdale. In 1962, the two were involved with Eugene A. Hancock in a venture, Automatic Vending Services, which provided services to government institutions. Hancock also served as president of the newly established Serve-U-Corporation founded in early '62 by Democratic insider Robert G. "Bobby" Baker, whose official role in Washington, D.C., was that of assistant secretary to the Majority Leader of the House of Representatives.

Baker had set up Serve-U along with his friend Fred Black. Joining them in the corporation were two notorious Chicago criminals, Benny Sigelbaum and Ed Levenson. A secret, silent partner in the corporation was Chicago Mafia boss Sam Giancana, whose own company manufactured the vending machines used by companies that were subcontractors of federally funded programs. Compounding this history are the claims that John Kennedy had at one time shared the amorous attention of Sam Giancana's favorite girlfriend, Judith Exner. Also involved with Automatic Vending Services was Florida banker Earl E. T. Smith, whose wife, Florence, is listed among John Kennedy's favorite former paramours. Florence, a trained journalist, would die of a cerebral hemorrhage within twenty-four hours of the suspicious death of *New York Journal-American* reporter Dorothy Kilgallen in November 1965. Kilgallen is best known in assassination research as having interviewed Lee Oswald's murderer, Jack Ruby, and insisting that she would soon break the Kennedy assassination wide open.

In February 1961, newly elected President John Kennedy had nominated Stockdale to be the US Ambassador to Ireland. On March 28, 1961, the US Senate confirmed the nomination. Stockdale and his family enjoyed their time at the ambassador's residence, Phoenix Park in Dublin, Ireland, where as ambassador, he often hosted formal gatherings and events for dignitaries.

Among the Stockdales' guests, in the spirit of céad míle fáilte (a hundred thousand welcomes), were Otto and Ilse Skorzeny. The Skorzenys had purchased a 155-acre estate named Martinstown House, in Curragh, County Kildare, in June 1959. Stockdale was acutely familiar with the former Nazi SS officer who often visited with various American businessmen in meetings held in the American Embassy in Ballsbridge, Co. Dublin, including military officers and intelligence officials, as well as various embassy staff members throughout 1960, 1961, and 1962. Former embassy personnel vividly recall Skorzeny coming to the embassy on a nearly "weekly basis." Evidence also reveals that the Skorzenys were occasional dinner guests joining the ambassador and his wife, and that Ilse Skorzeny was a frequent visitor to Miami, Florida. As we learn in a later chapter in pursuit of the Skorzenys' time in Ireland, the SS officer had been an active participant in aiding arms trafficking to the Irish Republican Army (IRA).

When the Serve-U Corporation scandal involving Democratic operative Bobby Baker finally exploded, under pressure from his close friend President Kennedy, Grant Stockdale reluctantly resigned his post in Ireland in July 1962.

STOCKDALE'S FRIENDS, PHIL GRAHAM AND FRANK WISNER

Just three weeks before the first clear reference to Ellen Rometsch in his diary, Lafitte writes on May 26:

> L.O. – Wisner
> Vosjoli   DC   JA

Then on June 16, Lafitte first acknowledges Ella by name in an entry that reads, "Ella acting classes – who?"

Four days later, on June 20, Lafitte makes a note to cable OS (Otto Skorzeny), preceded by the name Wisner. The note reads in full:

> Wisner - cable / OS
> NYC / Wash D C

On July 28, 1963, the project manager of the assassination of President Kennedy makes a note that George [Hunter-White] and/or Otto Skorzeny would talk to [Grant] Stockdale about P. [Phil] Graham and the prospects that Graham would end up at Chestnut Lodge, in a duplicate fashion of Frank Olson's journey toward death some ten years earlier:

> George / OS talk
> to Stockdale about P. Graham
> (George says Chestnut Lodge) - dupe –

OPERATION MOCKINGBIRD

Philip Graham, a wartime graduate of the US Army's Intelligence School at Harrisburg, Pennsylvania, served as an intel officer in the US Air Force in the Pacific theater during the war. In 1940, he married Katherine Meyer, the daughter of

Eugene Meyer, who owned the *Washington Post*. After the war, and following graduation from Harvard Law School, Graham replaced his father-in-law as publisher at WaPo and eventually became coowner of the newspaper, serving as president and chief executive officer as well as chairman of the board of directors of *Newsweek* magazine.

Over time, in his capacity as a rising star in print media, Graham developed a close friendship with Senator Lyndon Johnson of Texas and a young senator from Massachusetts, John Kennedy. In fact, it is said that he was instrumental in shaping the Kennedy-Johnson 1960 Democratic ticket. He was also known to be close with a good many other senators, especially his high school chum George Smathers, as well as representatives and federal officials. Among them were division heads at the CIA, including Frank Wisner of the Office of Policy Coordination. By the 1960s, any upheaval in Phil Graham's life, personal or professional, would become the business of Frank Wisner.

MORE ON WISNER

In the late 1940s, following his stint in the OSS, Wisner had moved to Washington to work for the State Department's Office of Occupied Territories. Wisner quickly became close to a large group of media and government officials in the nation's capital, of which Phil Graham was one of the first. Others followed: banker and Rockefeller consigliere John McCloy, James Jesus Angleton, Tracy Barnes of the CIA, future ambassador David Bruce, George Kennan of the State Department, and young CIA official Richard Helms. This group, as John Simkin underscores in his excellent Spartacus historical accounts online, became known as the Georgetown Set, with a women's branch called the Georgetown Ladies' Social Club, of which Katharine (Phil) Graham was a member along with Mary Pinchot (Cord) Meyer, Polly (Frank) Wisner, Janet (Tracy) Barnes, and Cynthia (Richard) Helms.

The same year the Georgetown Set took shape, Wisner organized Operation Mockingbird, a covert program designed to widely influence and manipulate the media in America. Simkin writes: "Wisner recruited Philip Graham to run the [program] within the American media," and that "Graham himself recruited others who had worked for military intelligence during the war." Simkin quotes Deborah Davis: "By the early 1950s, Wisner 'owned' respected members of the *New York Times, Newsweek*, CBS and other communications vehicles." And then adds, "Other journalists willing to promote the views of the CIA included Ben Bradlee (*Newsweek*), James Reston (*New York Times*), Charles Douglas (C. D.) Jackson (*Time*

Magazine), Walter Pincus (*Washington Post*), William C. Baggs (*Miami News*), Herb Gold (*Miami News*), and Charles Bartlett (*Chattanooga Times*)."

According to writer Nina Burleigh, whose book about the murder of Mary Pinchot Meyer—wife of CIA officer Cord Meyer—exposed secrets of Georgetown society, ". . . these journalists sometimes wrote articles that were commissioned by Frank Wisner. The CIA also provided them with classified information to help them with their work." This symbiosis between US intelligence and the Fourth Estate would come to haunt the nation for decades.

NEWSMAN PHIL GRAHAM'S DEATH

Earlier in 1963, Graham, said to be in the process of "an ugly divorce," flew to Phoenix, Arizona, with his mistress. In a striking display of extreme mental distress, Graham "crashed" the newspaper convention in progress. Author Nellie Bly in her book *The Kennedy Men*, picks up the story: ". . . there was a journalists' convention going on in Phoenix. Phil Graham had not been invited, but when he learned about it, he showed up in the banquet room during a speech, grabbed the microphone, and drunkenly announced to the crowd, many of whom knew and admired him, that he was going to tell them exactly who in Washington was sleeping with whom, beginning with President Kennedy. 'His favorite,' screamed Phil, 'was now Mary Meyer . . . '"

Bly goes on, citing a very controversial book by Deborah Davis, *Katharine the Great*, that Katharine Graham, and some say the CIA, had quite literally destroyed sales by buying and burning all available copies. As Phil ranted, Davis reports,

> . . . one of the newsmen called [President] Kennedy, who immediately called Katharine, wanting to know if, as a friend, there was anything he could do to bring Phil under control. The call came as Katharine was meeting with the *Post* executives in her home, planning to bring Phil back forcibly and commit him to a psychiatric hospital. She declined the President's offer, Kennedy had done enough. Phil's assistant James Truitt took the phone and asked the President to send Phil's psychiatrist, Leslie Farber, to Phoenix on a military jet. Phil was brought back to [his Phoenix] motel, where he was injected with a heavy sedative, and he was then taken to the airport in an ambulance. A sedated Graham, in a straitjacket, was taken back to Washington and committed to Chestnut Lodge, one of the most expensive psychiatric hospitals in the country.

Four months before the suspicious death of Graham's close friend Grant Stock-dale, Phil Graham's own lifeless body was found by his wife Katharine Meyer Graham at their Marshall, Virginia, farmhouse. Up until twenty-four hours before his death, ruled by the local sheriff and county coroner as suicide by shot-gun to the head, Graham had been a patient at Chestnut Lodge in Rockville, Maryland. He had been granted a one-day leave to spend time with Katherine at the family estate, Glen Welby.

Chestnut Lodge was an exclusive mental institution used extensively by the CIA for high-level officials. Some readers will recall that very shortly before his murder, CIA research scientist Frank Olson had allegedly agreed to check into Chestnut Lodge on the medical advice of Dr. Harold Abramson, a CIA contractor specializing in mind-altering drugs.

Some two years after his suicide. Graham's close friend at the CIA, Frank Wisner, died from a "self-inflicted" shotgun blast to his head on October 29, 1965.

WISNER AND PIERRE LAFITTE

Before we delve deep into the scandal that began to rock the Kennedy administration in the summer of '63, there are several Lafitte datebook entries critical to understanding the context of the breaking story with this investigation.

On April 21, Lafitte notes, "Carole T. Dallas G. D." Nancy Carole Tyler was the girlfriend of lobbyist and Senate staffer, Bobby Baker. As manager of the Quorum Club, he was also Carole's boss. Among Baker's clients were Texas oil-man Clint Murchison and military contractor General Dynamics. The "G. D." in the April 21 entry is almost certainly a reference to the aerospace and defense manufacturer that would soon be named in an exposé alleging that Baker had bribed congressmen to grant a $7 billion contract to the General Dynamics plant located in Fort Worth for production of the F-111 fighter jet. So, not only was Baker under scrutiny for the vending machine contracts, it was his role in the F-111 bribery scandal that would eventually bring him down.

Carole, a beauty in her own right, is known to have traveled with Baker to New Orleans along with the seductive young German woman from the Quorum Club, Ellen Rometsch. On May 14, Lafitte notes, *Carole – (airport) Paul Aguirre Others?*" Aguirre was a mortgage banker in Puerto Rico involved with Baker in a proposed housing deal that, once again, involved government funds.

Author G. R. Schreiber, in a book published in 1964 by ultraconservative Regnery Press, *The Bobby Baker Affair: How to Make Millions in Washington*, confirms

Lafitte's entries when he writes that East German-born Ellen Rometsch, on at least one occasion, "went along with Bobby and Nancy Carole [Tyler] and Paul Aguirre, a friend from Puerto Rico, on a jaunt to New Orleans."

Continues Schreiber, "The chief counsel for the Senate Rules Committee said that Bobby's Puerto Rican friend told committee investigators that if he were 'asked anything about what took place [on the trip to New Orleans] he would take all the amendments, from 1 to 28.'" We see from Pierre Lafitte entries that later in the year a shipment of LSD from New Orleans to Dallas was on the cards. Schreiber goes on, "The Rules Committee did not call Paul Aguirre, but Senator Hugh Scott reported on some of what the Puerto Rican told the committee's investigators. 'Mr. Aguirre admitted that Baker brought Carole Tyler and Ellen Rometsch with him from Washington to New Orleans on the May, 1963, trip.'" This claim coincides with Lafitte's record of May 14.

It should be noted that in 1964, as presidential candidate Barry Goldwater marched toward the nomination to challenge VP Johnson, who was destined to fill Kennedy's shoes, Regnery Press published three pro-Goldwater campaign-focused books, including Schreiber's, which they believed would make the biggest splash. Regnery was the creation of descendants of William H. Regnery, a founder of the "America First Committee" that was formed in the 1930s in opposition to US involvement in matters it believed were strictly between Europeans and Hitler's Nazis. More will be said about Regnery as this book comes to a close, but for now it is important to grasp that the Ellen Rometsch story was pivotal to the erosion of confidence in the Democratic administration of Kennedy in the summer and fall of 1963 as the president prepared to run again.

WISNER'S PROPAGANDA

Prior to direct reference to "Ella" Rometsch in the datebook, Pierre notes the name Wisner, conjurer of the agency's Cold War propaganda machine under his Operation Mockingbird, along with the letters *L.O.*, then *Vosjoli*, and then the letters *DC* and *JA* - presumably the District of Columbia and James Angleton of the CIA.

Three weeks later, Lafitte provides the first clue that he was at the very least aware of Rometsch:

Ella acting classes - who?

—Lafitte datebook, June 16, 1963

Four days following Lafitte's interest in acting classes for Ella, he again notes Frank Wisner, the mastermind behind the CIA program to manipulate the media, Operation Mockingbird:

Wisner - Cable/OS
—Pierre Lafitte datebook, June 20, 1963

Indeed, at the center of the scandal was a beautiful woman in her late twenties who had arrived from East Germany to the US in 1961, Ellen "Elly" Rometsch. "Ella," as she was known to the project manager, Lafitte, is referenced thirteen times between June 16 and October 18 in his 1963 datebook. If an operation designed to compromise President Kennedy for purposes other than simple blackmail was afoot, indications are that Wisner may have been in the shadows. If Ellen was indeed an East German spy, acting on behalf of Soviet Communists desperate to know, for instance, whether plans were in play for another attempted invasion of Cuba, she may have been recruited as a counterintelligence agent for interests outside the official channels of the CIA.

ELLEN FIMMEL ROMETSCH

(Ella R.—Q)
—Lafitte datebook, July 2, 1963

"She would come and go at all hours of the day and night," says Constance Larsson, a former neighbor. "There were private cars, taxis, limousines . . . toward the end the black limos were constant."

Larsson goes on, "We'd been living in the neighborhood for about three years before she arrived. Sometimes the cars had diplomatic plates, or those yellow government plates . . . everyone knew the government cars."

Larsson recalls, "She always left the house alone and came home alone. She would go straight from the house to the car or from the car to the house. If someone, a neighbor was nearby, or walking by, she'd give a curt little wave but keep moving, saying nothing . . . a woman with a purpose, but a woman of mystery . . . we didn't even know her name or her husband's until they had been living there a few weeks. I think I only spoke to her twice in all the time they were there and neither of those times came close to any kind of conversation."

"She was very attractive," says Larsson, "Not really beautiful, but close. There was a subtle hard edge to her . . . she wore too much make-up on one side of her face because of a ruddy complexion, but men were crazy about her looks . . . there was a sensual aura about her. Neighborhood men were taken with her. They'd find any kind of excuse to walk by the brick house Elly and Rolf lived in."

Her name was Ellen Rometsch. Friends called her "Elly." In 1963, Ellen was twenty-seven years old. She was born in 1936 in Kleinitz, East Germany. A November 7, 1963, secret FBI cable from Bern, Switzerland, reveals her birth name as "Elly Bertha Hildegarde, nee Fimmel, AKA, Espionage-East Germany."

Apparently, Ellen was a vivacious, very attractive young woman who many people remarked resembled Elizabeth Taylor. Others would comment that she resembled a buxom, more-rounded Brigitte Bardot. With no known exceptions, men who had enjoyed her company remarked that her sexual prowess was remarkable.

Ellen's husband's name—if in fact she was actually married to him—was Rolf Rometsch. He was a twenty-eight-year-old German Air Force sergeant stationed at the West German Embassy in Washington, D.C. A July 1963 FBI airtel from the Bureau's office in Germany to FBI director J. Edgar Hoover reads that Ellen may have been married once before in East Germany and that her married name was Grunwald. Hoover wrote on the airtel copy: "Return to me or destroy." Many FBI documents concerning both Ellen and Rolf have long ago been destroyed, according to the FBI, but not all.

FBI and CIA documents on Rolf are scant and consistently state only: "The subject [Ellen] has been identified as the wife of Rolf Rometsch, a German Air Force enlisted man who arrived in the United States on January 5, 1961, and the subject [Ellen] arrived on April 6, 1961." A memorandum from Director Hoover to the director of the US State Department's Bureau of Intelligence and Research states: "The exact status of [Ellen's] relationship with her husband at the present time is unknown."

Exactly how Ellen and Rolf happened to come to the United States and Washington, D.C., remains somewhat a mystery. The German Embassy maintains it has no records regarding Rolf and Ellen. An unnamed embassy administrative assistant, attempting to be helpful, told this author, "There may have been files at one time, but there are none now."

THE ROMETSCH CASE: "AN EXTREMELY SENSITIVE AND DANGEROUS MATTER"

On October 26, 1963, FBI assistant Director of General Investigation Division Alex Rosen wrote to Bureau Assistant Director Alan H. Belmont. The memorandum, still heavily redacted as of 2019, states: "Information in [the Rometsch case] has been developed that pertains to possible questionable activities on the part of high Government officials. It was also alleged that the President and Attorney General had availed themselves of services of playgirls."

The bulk of Rosen's seven-paragraph memorandum is redacted after this, but we are at least able to confirm from these documents that Ellen Rometsch "was interviewed by the Washington Field Office Agents on July 12, 1963" and that the Bureau "is being pressed vigorously to locate and reinterview Ellen Rometsch."

As noted, a month prior to this FBI interview, on June 16, Pierre Lafitte notes: "Ella acting classes - who?" That entry was followed on July 2 with the note in parentheses, "(Ella R. –Q)." And again on July 6 and July 7, Pierre writes simply, "Ella." Is it possible that in anticipation of interviews with the FBI, Mrs. Rolf Rometsch was being prepped?

FBI official Alex Rosen wrote again to Belmont on October 27, to alert Belmont that "at approximately 5:00 p.m. on 10/26/63, Kenneth P. O'Donnell called from the White House and asked to be briefed on the information developed by the FBI in our investigation last Summer concerning Ellen Rometsch and whether there was any information to the effect that she had been involved with anyone at the White House." (Kenneth "Kenny" O'Donnell was a special assistant to and best friend of President Kennedy.)

Rosen went on to explain to Belmont that about fifteen minutes after O'Donnell's telephone call, Attorney General Robert Kennedy had called him and "referred to the newspaper [*Des Moines Register*] article written by Clark Mollenhoff, reporter for Cowles Publications. He said that he was contacting Mollenhoff because there was no substance to the allegation about the involvement of White House personnel. At this time the Attorney General asked if we would conduct further investigation to resolve this particular allegation. As a result of this request and the Director's subsequent conversation with the President, we instituted investigation to locate and reinterview subject Ellen Rometsch who is believed to be in Germany, and—"

With this, the section of the memorandum ends due the redaction of its next six lines. The document's last paragraph reads: "With reference to the location of Ellen Rometsch in Germany, P. Kenneth [*sic*] O'Donnell called from the White House on Saturday at 9:00 p.m., and supplied an address for her in the suburbs of Cologne. He said that he got this address from [name redacted]. This was furnished to the Legal Attaché by telephone so that he could arrange an immediate interview."

Attached to this document was a typed page, headed: "Leads to be Covered by WFO." It reads: "Telephonic contact with Legat, Bonn, Germany concerning current address of [names redacted]. From a review of information in the case file concerning previous investigation and the current inquiry as set forth in this airtel reveals that the following individuals may have information concerning ROMETSCH" [the next 20 typed lines are redacted], then: "WFO does not contemplate, UACB [unless advice to the contrary of the Bureau] interviewing the other named individuals inasmuch as it is felt that to do so would go beyond the intent of this inquiry and may cause unnecessary damaging rumors which would be picked up by the interested press."

Two days later, on October 28, a German defense ministry spokesman stated that Ellen Rometsch "had been expelled from the US" but that she had "had no contacts in the US with East German Communists." The ministry spokesman also stated that Ellen's husband had "separated from his wife and asked for a divorce." However, *The Blade,* a respected Toledo, Ohio, newspaper reported that same day that Ellen's mother-in-law, Erika Rometsch, said that was news to her. "It's the first time I've heard of this," she said, adding that she had just seen her son the day before when he was on his way to "see his wife and child."

The Blade article ominously reported that US Sen. John Williams, a Republican from Delaware, "has obtained a nearly complete rundown on [Rometsch's] life in Washington for two years before she was expelled." The article, ". . . U.S. Capitol May Be Rocked by Story of Exotic Mystery Woman," then quoted reporter Clark Mollenhoff as saying: "If the investigation brings out all of the information reported to Williams and to federal investigative agencies, the testimony could rock Washington in much the same way the Profumo scandals rocked London last summer." (The Profumo affair closes out this chapter.) According to the article, Senator Williams declined to comment saying only that the entire affair "is an extremely sensitive and dangerous matter."

Also on October 28, Attorney General Robert Kennedy called J. Edgar Hoover to "discuss the Bobby Baker case and its various ramifications." Hoover told Kennedy that the FBI had "given this particular matter top priority." Hoover and Kennedy then discussed "the Ellen Rometsch case." Hoover wrote in a subsequent report on the call: "I outlined to the Attorney General the details of the situation and the ramifications of it."

Director Hoover also wrote that he told the attorney general about a conversation he had had "with the President on the preceding Sunday by phone in which the President expressed concern about the possible involvement of personnel at the White House" with Rometsch. Apparently, President Kennedy said nothing to Hoover about his own affair with Rometsch. Hoover told JFK that the FBI "had immediately interviewed the Rometsch woman," but the paragraph that follows this statement is nearly completely redacted except to read that Hoover advised AG Robert Kennedy of the results of the Bureau's interview with Rometsch. That same day, October 28, FBI official C. D. DeLoach wrote to the FBI's John P. Mohr, alerting him that:

> . . . the men in my office received a considerable number of telephone calls over the weekend regarding captioned matter [Ellen Rometsch-East Germany]. The calls arose as a result of the article in the Cowles Publications by Clark Mollenhoff. In his article, Mollenhoff pointed out that [Ellen Rometsch] was involved with a number of Administration officials, including White House personnel. We, of course, have maintained a strict "no comment" throughout the weekend. We will continue to say nothing.

The DeLoach memo continued,

> As an example of phone calls received [Edwin O. Guthman, Attorney General Bobby Kennedy's press secretary] of the Department called me five times on Saturday, 10-26-63. The first call concerned a request from him to kill Mollenhoff's story in the New York Daily News. I told Guthman we could not ask the Daily News to do this. The second, third, fourth and fifth calls from Guthman concerned a request to kill the story with Associated Press. In all instances Guthman claimed that he did not have sufficient personal contacts to kill the story himself.
>
> On the fifth occasion, Guthman told me that the President [Kennedy] was personally interested in having the story killed. I explained to Guthman on each occasion that it was not within the province of the FBI to kill the story. I told him also that we had interviewed the captioned female [Rometsch] and that the results of our interview had been furnished to the Attorney General. I told Guthman he should make his own statements to the press without dragging the FBI into the matter.

Making certain that he covered all of the issues, DeLoach concluded,

> Following Guthman's statement that the President was personally interested in the matter, I advised the Director [Hoover] telephonically of Guthman's calls and of the fact that we were making "no comment" whatsoever despite the pressure that Guthman was attempting to bring.

Reporter Clark Mollenhoff, by then at the center of the matter of deepest concern to the administration, was a tenacious journalist with impeccable sources in Washington, D.C., that eventually landed him a Pulitzer Prize. At 6 feet 4 inches tall and 250 pounds, he was also an imposing presence. He was widely respected throughout his long career as an investigative writer, which was only interrupted by two years in the US Navy, following his completion of law school.

Author Seymour Hersh, an equally respected investigative writer and newsman, broke ground in 1997 when he ventured into the implications of President Kennedy's history with Ellen Rometsch in what has been to date perhaps the most controversial exposé among JFK afficionados, not because his reporting was inaccurate—it wasn't, and indeed it was quite factual—but because it shattered many of the mythical features of Kennedy's supposed finer qualities. Hersh, renowned for a slew of CIA exposés, delivered a devastating account of Rometsch's Washington activities in his book *The Dark Side of Camelot.*

Some reaction to Hersh's deep and thorough digging into the Rometsch case has been fiercely oppositional, yet nobody has been able to prove that his evidence and accounts are wrong or fabricated in any way. Oddly, it is not his evidence that is called into question, but instead the fact that he had the audacity to publish it that is faulted. It is important for the authors of this book to repeat here that they take no pleasure or delight in writing about JFK's sexual exploits. We believe strongly that despite JFK's private life, he remains one of this nation's finest presidents.

HERSH ON MOLLENHOFF

Sy Hersh notes that Clark Mollenhoff's reporting included reference to Delaware Senator Williams's access to an account of Rometsch's life in D.C. over a period of more than two years, and that having been born in East Germany, she still had relatives on "the other side of the iron curtain." Mollenhoff had added, either parenthetically or based on information provided him by his sources within the government, "The possibility that her activity might be connected with espionage is of some concern for security investigators because of the high rank of her male companions." Thus, Mollenhoff revealed to the public that in July, the FBI had started investigating the possibility that *Ellen was a Soviet spy,* and that "with less than a week's notice, she and her husband were sent back to Germany . . . at the request of the State Department."

Hersh observes that Mollenhoff, who had covered labor corruption during the 1950s, had been an enthusiastic supporter of Bobby Kennedy's work as general counsel of the Senate Rackets Committee. Writes Hersh, "The two men had grown apart—the specifics of their dispute could not be learned for this book—and *the increasingly conservative* [emphasis added] Mollenhoff begun to write extensively, and critically, of the Kennedy administration's decision in late 1962 to bypass Boeing and award the TFX contract to General Dynamics. Writes Hersh, Mollenhoff's reporting "was taken most seriously by Bobby Kennedy."

Indeed, reporter Mollenhoff's conservative leaning was apparent in public settings when in October of 1962 he participated on a panel, "Washington Cover-Up," at Georgetown University alongside the president of the Ukraine Congress Committee of America (UCCA) and Georgetown economics professor Lev Dobriansky, evidenced in a photo in *The Ukraine Weekly*, and in ensuing years, Mollenhoff was not shy about his commitment to anticommunismm. A brief mention in an article dated Saturday, April 20, 1974, in *The Ukraine Weekly*, under the headline "Anti-communist League Holds 7th Conference In Washington," provides a window into his public support of the World Anti-communist League (WACL).

Hosted in D.C. by the American Council for World Freedom (ACWF), the conference boasted some twenty-five speakers, representing both free nations and countries under Communist suppression, including autocrat General Anastazio Somoza of Nicaragua and the Hon. Yaroslav Stetzko, former prime minister of Ukraine and head of the Anti-Bolshevik Bloc of Nations (ABN) since its inception as well as leader of the Organization of Ukranian Nationalists (OUN). The US affiliate of the Stetzko's ABN, The American Friends of Anti-Bolshevik Bloc of Nations is infamous among Kennedy researchers for its leading member, Spas Raikin, who traveled from Ohio to Hoboken, NJ, to meet Lee Harvey Oswald and his Russian wife, Marina, as they arrived from the USSR.

Among the US speakers at the 1974 WACL conference were prominent Republicans including future congressman John McCain, conservative journalist William F. Buckley, and Prof. Dobriansky. The lengthy article in the *Ukraine Weekly* continues to describe the events: "The first reception, hosted by three members of the American press, John Chamberlain, King Features Syndicate columnist, Robert Hurleigh, Mutual Broadcasting System columnist, and Clark Mollenhoff, Pulitzer Prize winning columnist and Washington Bureau Chief of the 'Des Moines Register and Star,' was held at the National Press Club."

Of interest to researchers in pursuit of significant domestic and foreign intrigues in the decades following the assassination implicating yet another web of ideologically aligned forces: at the time of the 1974 WACL conference, the Cowles Communication / *Des Moines Register* board included Ret. General George Olmsted, close friend to Rear Admiral Arleigh Burke, who resigned from the Navy before President Kennedy had served a full year as president. Olmsted was the force behind the financial empire that within the decade would be caught up in the Bank of Credit and Commerce International (BCCI) scandal. Later in this investigation, the network of WACL and Stetzko's ABN, tied to the assassination of Ukranian Stepan Bandera—who led the OUN said to be most closely aligned with Mussolini's fascism before his assassination, and their affiliation with General Charles Willoughby who is named frequently by Lafitte—will assume greater significance.

For now, in light of the Ellen Rometsch scandal, which was first widely exposed by Mollenhoff, who was first to compare the pending scandal to the Profumo Affair and the possibility that more than blackmail was in play, it is important to draw attention to several Lafitte entries:

> NYC Rest guide ad.
> Talk of Ella R. photographs
> . . . in NY at Previews
> —Lafitte datebook, September 17, 1963

> Meet with Willoughby at
> (Ella R) others at
> 49 East 53rd St.
> NYC
> —Lafitte datebook, October 15, 1963

As the reader will learn in a later chapter, Manhattan-based real estate firm Previews Inc. provided Ilse Skorzeny "employment," whether as an independent contractor, a salaried agent, or perhaps nothing but a cover for her travel in and out of the US. Among the founders of Previews were those behind the popular weekly magazine *CUE,* which at the time covered theater and arts and New York's social scene. It is yet to be determined if Ellen Rometsch's photos were being sought for a future edition of *CUE* magazine, but three days later, weeks after Ella had been allegedly shunted out of the US, Lafitte was noting that Otto Skorzeny needed to be consulted regarding "Ella":

> Ask OS
> Re Ella
> Cable Madrid
> —Lafitte datebook, October 18, 1963

Eight days later, on October 26, the Cowles's *Des Moines Register* broke the Ellen Rometsch story, and on October 28, according to Laffite, comprehensive planning for the assassination ensued.

* * *

To underscore his understanding of just how concerned the Kennedy administration was over possibility that Ellen Rometsch might have been given a visa to return to the US to testify before Senate Republicans, Sy Hersh writes: "With Lyndon Johnson on his way out, Jack Kennedy had every reason to look forward to the 1964 campaign and his reelection. There was some talk from inside the family of having a Kennedy-Kennedy ticket in 1964. . . . The only trouble spot, besides the growing difficulties in South Vietnam, was *Ellen Rometsch* [emphasis added] and her desire—as [FBI Director] Hoover told Kennedy over lunch . . . of returning to the United States to marry Senate investigator [LaVern Duffy]. The initial Kennedy payments to Rometsch hadn't done the trick, and now a way had to be found to keep her in West Germany—and happy to keep quiet."

Whether Hersh was interjecting his own subjective assessment or not cannot be determined by these authors, but his further revelations related to an incident involving hard cash and Grant Stockdale lead us to seriously consider that Hersh remained an objective reporter of these events.

In an interview with the son of Grant Stockdale, named after his father, Grant Jr. shared that his mother Adie had told him, "Kennedy said, 'I need you to raise some dough—fifty thousand dollars' 'Why me?' 'Because I need it and I can count on you to keep it quiet.' 'What's it for?' 'It's for personal use.'" According to Hersh, Grant Jr. said that the request made his father very uneasy. Writes Hersh, "His father had asked Kennedy how he would acknowledge this money [to donors], and Kennedy responded that 'it's never going to be acknowledged.'" The story continues that Stockdale Sr. did what Kennedy asked and raised $50,000 cash, telling the contributors that the money was for Jack Kennedy. The story gets even more complex because Stockdale had made it very clear—especially to his friends—that he was in dire straits financially, and in fact, his son's version of why the family left Ireland was that his father told his friend Jack Kennedy that he was going broke. He said that he had been personally financing some of the lavish entertaining at Phoenix Park in Dublin as ambassador and that he needed to resign the post to return to Miami to earn a living. This is in direct contradiction to the rumor that Kennedy forced Stockdale to resign over the brewing Bobby Baker scandal.

Grant Jr. continued his version of events in his conversation with Hersh, explaining that ". . . a family friend had gone with his father to the Kennedy compound to deliver the money. Kennedy said, 'Thank you,' opened a nearby closet door, and threw the briefcase in there. As reported, Stockdale was devastated by the assassination. By then, he had told everyone that the money he was collecting was for his friend Kennedy, but he no longer had proof." Hersh then asserts that Edward Grant Stockdale committed suicide.

FBI DIRECTOR J. EDGAR HOOVER AND THE ROMETSCH CASE

In gambling, the term "holdout" refers to numerous accessories used by cheats to help them "hold-out" a card or cards during a card game, but the the word can also refer to a person who delays signing a contract in hopes of gaining more favorable terms.

For reasons yet to be determined with certainty, instead of identifying a specific individual by surname or first name, Lafitte opted to apply the term *holdout* on five dates in 1963. Whether holdout is a code name, or an alias, it's clear that Lafitte was loath to identify this individual. As will be made clear later, in only two other instances does he substitute a code word for a name —"T" and "Caretaker"— entities the reader will encounter in future chapters.

The first reference to "holdout" was on August 16, when Lafitte makes notes of a meeting held at Antoine's. He reminds himself, or notes that someone else will, "call holdout." Guests at the table on the 16th with CIA officer George Joannides included two of FBI Director Hoover's Special Agents, Stephen Labadie from Tampa and New Orleans-based John Quigley. Labadie appears again in the datebook a month after the August meetings in New Orleans, on September 24, when Lafitte writes, "Oswald D/T (Labadie / Florida) W. J." This is two days before Oswald departs for Mexico City. If there are doors to be unlocked between J. Edgar Hoover and Oswald's role as an effective patsy after the fact, we're led by Pierre Lafitte to suspect that Stephen Labadie, in particular, may hold a key.

* * *

On October 20, Lafitte makes a note referring to "holdout" again, in the context of someone or something he referred to as Raven. A glossary of terms used by intelligence agencies reveals that *raven* is an agent employed to seduce people for intelligence purposes. A further search suggested that Raven could refer to a Sigint (Signals Intelligence) unit of the military/national security apparatus. And a third possibility is one of the nation's top cryptanalysts of his time, Francis Raven of the National Security Agency. Before drawing any conclusions, however, it is essential to determine the identify of "holdout."

We don't encounter the code word/term/alias *holdout* again until November 29, a week after the assassination of FBI Dir. Hoover's commander in chief, President Kennedy. Lafitte simply writes, "Holdout."

The day before, on Thanksgiving day, of all the traffic that caught the attention of the Johnson White House and Director Hoover, a classified message about Santos Trafficante from CIA headquarters to McGeorge Bundy, President Johnson's special assistant for national security affairs, and Hoover at the FBI stood out. On November 26, British journalist John Wilson had given information, entirely unsolicited, to the American Embassy in London that indicated an "American gangster-type named Ruby" visited Cuba around 1959. Wilson told the embassy official that while Santos Trafficante was in the Cuban prison, he was visited frequently by a guy named Ruby. On the 29th, the FBI came up with a preliminary report that Wilson was likely a psychopath, and yet the seed that the mob was somehow involved had been firmly planted. The significance of John Wilson-Hudson (for as records revealed later, that was his full name), who was known to Pierre Lafitte, will be made clear in the following chapters.

By November 29, Hoover had, with all of his characteristic hubris, already assured President Johnson that the investigation into the assassination was *almost* concluded.

The final entry of any significance made by Lafitte in 1963 was Thursday, December 12, which reads, "Holdout – here today." The entries surrounding the 12th indicate that Pierre and his wife are in New Orleans, including a scheduled dinner with friends. There can be little doubt that whoever holdout may have been, he was en route to New Orleans.

FBI Director Hoover's appointment calendar for that Thursday indicates he had only one meeting scheduled, at 3:30 with US Court of Appeals for the District of Columbia Judge Warren Burger. There is nothing on Director Hoover's calendar the remainder of that weekend. On Monday, December 16, Hoover was scheduled to have "lunch with the President at the White House."

The previous morning, Wednesday, December 11, Hoover met with the Deputy Chief of Staff for Military Intelligence, Army Major General Edgar Doleman, and the Chief of the Security Division of the ACSI (Assistant Chief of Staff for Intelligence). The name of the colonel had been redacted. ACSI is recognized by assassination authorities as the division of the Army that Dorothe Matlack, assistant director of the Office of Intelligence for the Army, reported to. It was Matlack who, at the insistence of Col. Sam Kail, a military intelligence officer who had been assigned to work with the CIA, made arrangements for George de Mohrenschildt and French-born Haitian banker Clémard Joseph Charles during their visit to D.C. prior to their departure for Haiti.

With much gratitude to researchers Paul Brancato and Lawrence Haapanen, the colonel who met with FBI Director Hoover on December 11 has been identified as Col. Graham E. Schmidt. Schmidt had been a member of the Nuremberg Military Community in the late 1950s while Operation Paperclip was in full throttle. Schmidt is mentioned by author Linda Hunt, who is responsible for a 1991 groundbreaking exposé of the operation in her book *Secret Agenda*. Hunt drew extensively from the administrative files, the "Top Secret" files, and the dossiers of the ACSI's Paperclip records stored at the Washington National Records Center. Hoover's guest on December 11, Col. Schmidt, was also named in documents related to shutting down Operation MKULTRA in September 1963. He is mentioned in transcripts of the 1977 Senate Hearing on Intelligence, which was holding the Army's feet to the fire for those experiments. The Senate hearing, chaired by Senator Daniel Inouye of Hawaii and Arizona Senator Barry Goldwater, opened with the history of two deaths: Frank Olson, the CIA scientist assigned to the Technical Services Staff in 1953 when he was thrown through a window of the NY Statler Hilton by Pierre Lafitte and company; and tennis star Harold Blauer, who died after the fifth dose of a mescaline derivative at the hands of Army Chemical Corps doctors conducting experiments at the NY Psychiatric Hospital. Involved in the initial financial settlement with the Blauer family was President Eisenhower's Assistant Attorney General Warren Burger, who is alleged to have buried the Army's role in the tragedy. Just three months after the MKULTRA operation was alleged to have been closed down, with Col. Schmidt dead center in the effort, Warren Burger was sitting in Dir. Hoover's office a day after Schmidt had been.

ACSI's Dorothe Matlack, in 1963, was working closely with Col. Sam Kail, who is prominent in Lafitte's datebook in the last half of 1963. An excerpt from coauthor Alan Kent's essay titled "A Well-Concealed 'T'" gives us a glimpse into the potential significance: "As George de Mohrenschildt prepared to venture into Haiti in the spring of 1963, he and his Haitian business partner Clémard Charles were being closely monitored for possible use by both CIA and military intelligence. Dorothe Matlack, Army Intelligence's chief liaison with CIA, was on top of this effort, and she leaned heavily on the 'smooth operator,' Sam Kail. CIA's Domestic Operation Division, headed by Tracy Barnes, was also involved in the de Mohrenschildt-Charles matter."

WHO HAD THE POWER TO COVER IT UP?

Thus asked the composite character, "X," played by actor Donald Sutherland in Oliver Stone's depiction of DA Jim Garrison's investigation into the assassination, *JFK* (the movie).

Much deliberation ensued between the authors of this book following the analysis of the "holdout" entries. A pertinent question surfaced as the pursuit of holdout grew more aggressive: "Who within the domestic intelligence agencies would have the most influence over the investigation on the ground in Dallas?" Would Hoover have been a "holdout" in the final phase of the operation—someone who *delayed signing a contract in hopes of gaining more favorable terms*—not that it wasn't widely known that Hoover wanted to see the Kennedys taken down, but that any criminal operation on US soil was his turf, meaning that the buck would stop at his desk? Was he hedging all bets? Was he asking for something in return? He also knew that any successful conspiracy operation would require cooperation of elements under his control to assure that everything went smoothly and that the assassination would remain unsolved or unprosecuted, or a patsy would carry the blame. Even the most skilled tactician, for instance SS Otto Skorzeny, would not be able to orchestrate a successful operation of this magnitude without the involvement of pivotal domestic forces (FBI) including those on the ground in New Orleans and Dallas; nor could the CIA's James Angleton, at least not in the most practical of terms. Despite all the power Angleton could exert, he still could not intervene in an on-the-ground investigation on American soil, and Dulles could only do so from a distance, under very specific protocol. The US military would have influence from behind the scenes, but they too would liaise with Hoover's FBI.

Those au fait with the culture will know that the Dallas contingency, responsible for the investigation in the aftermath of November 22, would preferably take their cue from "one of their own," someone who had for more than a decade enjoyed the largesse of Texas powerbrokers with the financial bravado to buck the East Coast elites, including Allen Dulles and James Angleton at the CIA. Director Hoover, with his close personal friendships with Texas oilmen, and Clint Murchison in particular, could tilt the balance. Murchison, who is alleged to have ended up with one of the three copies of the Zapruder film produced by Jamieson Labs, was a long-standing client of Bobby Baker, who had traveled to New Orleans earlier in the year in the company of the lovely Carol Tyler, and Kennedy's recent object of desire, East German Ellen Rometsch. Murchison had over the years paid for Hoover's annual retreats to the Hotel del Charro near La Jolla, California. According to Hoover's appointment calendar, August of 1963 was no exception. Known to host some of Dallas's finest card games in a condo located at 3535 Turtle Creek Blvd., an invitation to Murchison's del Charro games was equally coveted. Had Hoover, long alleged to have been a heavy gambler, been known as "Holdout," and was the term refined by Lafitte to fit the context of Project Lancelot?

ELLA IS DISPATCHED OUT OF THE US

In the midst of all that was going on for Lafitte in New Orleans beginning the second week of August, on August 23, he indicates that Angleton has given him an update regarding "Ella." He notes, "JA says Ella R sent back to Germany — Harvey [illegible] done [illegible] with [illegible]." The date coincides with official records indicating that indeed, Ellen Rometsch departed the US on that date, presumably never to return, and we learn that Wiliam King Harvey was still on his mind, as well.

On October 29, FBI Supervisor R. W. Smith wrote to Bureau Assistant Director William C. Sullivan a memorandum that informed him that the FBI had referred the Ellen Rometsch case to the CIA and that Rometsch had "left the United States in August 1963 to return to Germany."

The memo from Smith to Asst. Dir. Sullivan also reveals that pursuing certain details concerning Rometsch's presence in Germany had been turned over to the CIA. Documents make it amply clear that FBI information regarding Rometsch was being shared with the CIA and Defense Intelligence Agency [DIA]; however, Hoover and Bureau officials consistently lied to the Kennedy White House and Attorney General, saying, "all of the information developed has been made available to both [the White House and Attorney General], [and] our dissemination of information has not been made to anyone other than the Attorney General and the White House."

On October 30, FBI official C. D. DeLoach wrote to Bureau official John P. Mohr concerning an attempt that had been made to interview a "female" in regard to the Rometsch case that US Senator John J. Williams of Delaware had offered the Bureau "assistance in arranging." DeLoach's memo explains that he "told the Senator that in view of [redacted lines on Rometsch case] he might desire to delay before issuing any statement [about Rometsch] however, this again was a decision that only he himself could make." Wrote DeLoach: "Senator Williams told me he thought this was good advice and that he would withhold any statement for the present. He stated he did not wish to seek any information from us but that he would appreciate calling from time to time and letting us know of things he had uncovered himself. I told him that the Director would appreciate his calling us in this regard, however, he should definitely understand that in view of the pending nature of our investigations we, of course, could not divulge any information from FBI files. He stated he understood this and would not ask for any information."

On October 31, FBI official Alex Rosen communicated with Alan Belmont by memorandum about "a thumbnail resume concerning pertinent individuals who have been interviewed in connection with this [Rometsch] investigation to date." The résumé was attached to Rosen's memo. Rosen noted in his memo: "Our Legal Attaché at Bonn, Germany is currently checking with [name redacted] of the US Army intelligence with respect to any information in their possession concerning Rometsch. The investigation has not yet been completed."

The attached page reads: "As a direct result of a request by the Attorney General on October 26, 1963, investigation was initiated into certain aspects of the activities of Ellen Rometsch, the wife of an enlisted man in the German Air Force, formerly attached to the German military group in this country. The Attorney General made reference to an article written by Clark Mollenhoff of Cowles Publications wherein it was indicated that playgirl Rometsch had been attending parties and associating with Congressional leaders and 'prominent new frontiersmen.' The Attorney General asked that the FBI conduct further inquiry into the allegation that White House personnel may have been involved with Rometsch. . . . During the course of our inquiries information was developed with respect to the following individuals—" [The next and last six lines on the sheet are redacted.]

On November 8, Hoover received an "urgent" teletype from the FBI's SAC in its Baltimore, Maryland, office. The brief teletype alerted Hoover that the Baltimore SAC had reviewed US Army files at Fort Holabird, Maryland, with respect to locating Army intelligence records regarding an individual connected to the Rometsch case who "may have used a cover name in 1951." The individual's name and possible alias are redacted.

Also on November 8, Belmont wrote to Rosen, stating: "We have determined that several women, most of whom are of German background, have offered their services as 'play girls' to various individuals in and out of Government, several of whom have been prominent and in the public eye. Our inquiry has also disclosed information not necessarily connected with the original objective involving personal escapades, prostitution, parting, sex orgies, and so forth. Some of the prostitution activities indicate potential criminal violations of the White Slave Traffic Act . . ."

Throughout the second week of November, Hoover received at least five tele-types from the Bureau's Chicago, Philadelphia, New York, Los Angeles, and Washington, D.C., field offices concerning a Hoover request to each for assistance with the Rometsch investigation. All of these teletypes are heavily redacted, revealing nothing about those specific requests. Additionally, at the same time, Hoover received several airtels from the Bureau's various Germany offices. These airtels are so heavily redacted that one can make no sense about what is being communicated to Hoover.

On November 19, just three days before JFK's assassination, the FBI's Bonn, Germany, office notified Director Hoover that it was changing its Rometsch communications to reflect her name, "Elly Bertha Hildegarde Rometsch nee Fimmel," and that her a.k.a. [also-known-as] included "Ellen Rometsch; Mrs. Joachim Grunwald; Mrs. Rolf Rometsch." The Bonn office also alerted Hoover to the fact that Ellen's "first husband was a captain in the West German Army. He is now deceased." Details concerning Ellen's first husband and her life in Germany were completely redacted.

Two additional "urgent" cablegrams, dated November 14, to Hoover from the Bonn office reveal that, according to the FBI's George A. Van Noy, the Bonn office "inquiries [about Rometsch] in Munich [were] being pressed as strongly as possible," and that "exhaustive investigation to date fails to locate [name redacted]." Subsequent urgent cablegrams to Hoover from Bonn are all completely redacted.

ROMETSCH CASE EXTENDS INTO 1964

On January 16, 17, 18, 1964, the FBI's C. D. DeLoach wrote to FBI official Mohr memorandums, which, as of 2019, remain near completely redacted but do appear to detail several telephone calls regarding the Rometsch case in regard to "a new subject's name [redacted] who the FBI was most interested in interviewing regarding Rometsch and her contacts with Kennedy White House officials."

A few weeks later, on February 13, D. J. Brennan Jr. wrote to Assistant Director W. C. Sullivan advising that the FBI's investigation into the Rometsch case had involved several new interviews the results of which are heavily redacted but shared with the CIA and "Mr. Jenkins at the White House on January 18, 1964 by Mr. DeLoach." And on February 21, the FBI was alerted that President Johnson wanted a summary memorandum concerning the Ellen Rometsch case.

Surviving is a heavily redacted copy of the 22-page memorandum headed "Ellen Rometsch" and dated February 20, 1964 containing following the passages with the majority of its pages completely redacted:

A security-type investigation of Ellen Rometsch was conducted in July, 1963, which did not reflect that she was engaged in intelligence activities in the United States. During this investigation she was interviewed on July 12, 1963 at her residence in Arlington, Virginia.

The memorandum continues:

On October 26, 1963, The Des Moines Register, a Des Moines, Iowa newspaper, published an article by Clark Mollenhoff captioned, "United States Expels Girl Linked to Officials; Sent to Germany After FBI Probe." This article refers to a current Senate inquiry involving allegations regarding conduct of Senate employees and states that Senator John Williams of Delaware obtained an account of a German girl who was expelled from the United States in August, 1963, and who was a friend of several governmental figures. The article identifies the German girl's husband as a German Army sergeant and states that the FBI began an investigation concerning her in the Summer of 1963. After publication of Clark Mollenhoff's column, FBI investigation summarized hereinafter was conducted at the request of the Attorney General to ascertain if White House personnel were involved.

The memorandum remains *completely* redacted except for several handwritten margin notations that mark places in the document where it "Referred to another government agency."

On December 8, 1964, Director Hoover sent a cablegram to the FBI's Legat in Bonn, Germany, stating: "You are instructed through appropriate [redacted] source to make discrete inquiry in an effort to establish current whereabouts of Rometsch [redacted] . . . The possibility exists that based on current investigation being conducted and/or at the request of the White House we may desire to immediately interview Rometsch [other names redacted] who were last known to be in Germany. It is for this reason that Legat Bonn is being instructed to discreetly determine the whereabouts of these individuals in the event such interviews should be necessary."

At the same time, November–December 1964, officials at the FBI, CIA, and DIA were privately expressing serious concerns that Ellen Rometsch may have crossed over from West to East Germany and become lost in a maze of intrigue and Soviet intelligence sources. We don't know if the FBI was ever able to reinterview Rometsch, but it is certain that by early January 1965, the CIA had issued a series of orders to covert assets and operatives throughout East Germany to be on the lookout for Rometsch and any evidence of her exact location. Later still, German publications would claim that Rometsch was living in West Germany in a remote mountain area, but American intelligence was unable to confirm this, and apparently a gradual feeling settled on US officials that so long as Rometsch remained well away from America, things would be just fine.

A TAWDRY SUMMARY

In his 1967 book on the Baker scandal, *Washington Wheeler Dealers Broads, Booze and Bobby Baker*, author and former National Republican Committee media relations director Edward K. Nellor fills in some of the blanks on Ellen Rometsch. Writes Nellor:

> A case in point, one where the fix reached the top levels of government, and involved the Senate, the State Department, the Immigration Service, Military Intelligence, the FBI and the CIA, centered on the bedroom antics of an alien German beauty, 27-year-old Ellen Rometsch. Whatever Ellen did, and only a master key to all the security closets in Washington, D.C., will ever unlock the secrets, she got herself involved in the hottest, high-level Capitol scandal of the generation.

Nellor, who observed Ellen firsthand in Washington, goes on with his garish account of Rometsch's doings.

> Ellen, as ripe and pink as a German peach, traipsed around Washington in Dior-like gowns, rubbing elbows and apparently everything else with contract hustlers wheeling and dealing in high Congressional and Executive branch circles. . . . Sexually aggressive, inclined to loud laughter, swivel-hipped and with a quick wit that ran to bawdiness, Ellen was capable of arousing passions in a rock. Put together in a kind of loose-jointed way, she lacked the outstanding features of a beauty queen, but made up in availability what she had been denied in structure. Wiggling her way past the bar stools, her long, blond pigtails bobbing from side to side, she managed to make every male perched there feel like the whole show was for him. Touching each one in turn, talking constantly and, hips thrust forward and ever on the move, she was never denied attention. For her it was always front and center, full-stage and the role she played was as ancient as Rome

. . . she had a hard, clean Nordic air about her despite a comment from one admirer that she always looked like an unmade bed. It may have been wishful thinking or the fact that he'd seen her in one more often than in public, and was unaccustomed to seeing her in the glare of daylight.

(Note: Photographs of Rometsch that have been widely circulated on the Internet for decades indicate that the "long blond pigtails" described by Nellor may well have been an aspect of her act as an innocent seductress. She was a natural brunette.)

Nellor is hardly finished with his burlesque portrayal of Rometsch. He goes on:

Capitol Hill bistros knew Ellen well. So did Baker's staff employees and numerous others who call the U.S. Senate their home. She had senatorial limousines at her disposal, senatorial friendships and senatorial access to the right places in Washington. . . . However, she didn't quite take the pomp and circumstance seriously. Her mind was on other things. Like all the chummy types, she had an unerring instinct for the fattest pocketbook and the most aggressive male in the crowd. Ever ready to be entertained or comforted, she operated around the clock and in the highest priced booze dens. Never complaining, ever gay and eager, Ellen had one fault. She bragged too much about her money and what her clothes cost; where she was going and where she had been—Miami, the Dominican Republic, Las Vegas and Puerto Rico—and she talked a lot about who she knew in Washington, and sometimes what she knew about them. Never home, never husband-bound, she lived it up and laughed at those she played with. Her circle of girlfriends, besides Carol [Tyler], were in the same business.

Nellor also writes that Rometsch "vanished from the Washington scene," apparently having no clue that Bobby Kennedy had Ellen deported. According to Nellor, US Senator Carl Curtis of Nebraska tried as hard as he could to discover "where Ellen came from, how she got into the country, whether or not she was part of the 'entertainment facilities' provided for businessmen seeking government contracts, or even whether or not she flew to New Orleans on Eastern Airlines on January 19, 1962 with Bobby Baker and Carol Tyler [Baker's girlfriend], for a stop that included a meeting with a Puerto Rican businessman, before continuing on to Dallas and Miami." [See Endnote for clarification of dates.]

Curtis speculated with fellow congressmen that surely Rometsch, through the wily dispensing of her amorous charms, was able to seduce any government official into preventing any adverse action directed at her.

Writes Nellor: "Everybody knew about her—the FBI, CIA, Immigration Service and the State Department—had known about her for a long time, in fact—but then somebody pushed the button and Ellen was kaput." He continues to share another rumor "that Ellen was in a global network of German-born sexpots, shipped to Washington and elsewhere for limited service in the cause of good international relations."

MEANWHILE, ACROSS THE BIG POND: THE PROFUMO AFFAIR AND JFK

During the Summer of 1963, when JFK's sporadic affair with Ellen Rometsch was taking root in the president's active extracurricular activities, yet another sex scandal of epic proportions was unfolding in London, England. That the FBI and American intelligence community—primarily through the CIA, Defense Intelligence Agency [DIA], and Office of Naval Intelligence [ONI], as well as several obscure intel sections of the Pentagon—were closely monitoring each and every development of this scandal is most revealing regarding the roles JFK, and a number of his aides, played in what soon became known worldwide as the Profumo Affair.

According to author Anthony Summers in his Hoover exposé, "Britain's Minister for War, John Profumo, had confessed to having slept with a woman simultaneously involved with the Soviet Naval attaché in London, Yevgeny Ivanov. He resigned, but the crisis continued. The government of Prime Minister Macmillan, who had backed Profumo to the end, was shaken to its foundations. The press, meanwhile, fueled the controversy with daily revelations about the orgies and adulteries of the British establishment."

The FBI's record of the Profumo Affair is extensive and not surprisingly still heavily redacted (at least as of 2019), and again it reveals failings on the part of JFK and others in his administration. That President Kennedy had dalliances with at least two of the women at the center of the Profumo Affair is well documented by the investigative record. The record reveals that these two women, according to law enforcement authorities in the United States and Europe, were considered "*serious national security risks.*"

According to Seymour Hersh, "The president's interest was far from academic. Maria Novotny and Suzy Chang worked as high-class prostitutes in New York as well as London, and, as Novotny would tell reporters later, she and Chang had serviced Jack Kennedy before and after the 1960 presidential election." Chang, alleged to have been a Chinese Communist spy, acknowledged that, while senator, Kennedy had taken her to dinner at the 21 Club, the very public grande dame of the New York restaurant scene.

Fearless and dogged reporter Dorothy Kilgallen picked up on the Profumo scandal and published an article in the *New York Journal-American* on June 23, 1963: "One of the biggest names in American politics—a man who holds a very high elective office—has been injected into Britain's vice-security scandal." Kilgallen went on to describe one of the girls as "a beautiful Chinese-American girl now in London." She added that the "highest authorities" had "identified her as Suzy Chang." The fate of Kilgallen, referred to earlier, suggests that it wasn't only her interview with Jack Ruby that fueled animus toward her, but coverage of the Profumo affair, which was still on the minds of national and international powerbrokers in 1965. Perhaps serendipitously, Kilgallen had, in 1957, penned a short piece in her "gossip" column related to Pierre Lafitte.

* * *

The Rometsch story has never been fully resolved. According to BACM Research, the online paperless archives, "Files show that the FBI at least initially did not make files concerning Rometsch available to Robert Kennedy's replacement as attorney general, Nicholas Katzenbach. A memo summarizes a 1965 FBI interview of Robert Kennedy concerning Ellen Rometsch, John F. Kennedy *and former publisher of The Washington Post Philip Graham.* [Italics added for emphasis.] Files show that the FBI failed to develop any information connecting Rometsch with intelligence activities in the United States. Specific results of the FBI investigation were withheld. The memos however show the dissemination of whatever that information was and the interest of others to see it. A memo indicates that some FBI files on Rometsch have been intentionally destroyed by the FBI. Materials show the date and number of pages in the files which are currently heavily redacted or withheld in their entirety, which researchers may want to pursue in the future."

* * *

Before proceeding to the profile and history of Thomas Eli Davis, Jr., one of the most enigmatic characters in this investigation, the significance of the women caught in the call girl scandal, and the suspicious suicides surrounding them, continues to evade interpretation, let alone full understanding. But as reporter Sy Hersh reminds us, it was a paramount concern of Jack and Robert Kennedy. That Frank Wisner, the master of the CIA's propaganda machine, is identified in the same time frame that Ella Rometsch is on the radar of Lafitte and Otto Skorzeny; that James Angleton is also named, along with William King Harvey; that acting classes and passports are being procured for Rometsch; that Bobby Baker's girlfriend is named as having arrived in New Orleans the same time Rometsch is known to have traveled to the Crescent City; and that Otto Skorzeny's wife, Ilse, was in NYC and likely in communication with General Charles Willoughby related somehow to Ella—there is every reason to argue that the tactical operation to assassinate Kennedy employed in some fashion a beautiful East German call girl.

* * *

As postscript, Bobby Baker's own words sum up his control over the women who worked at the Quorum Club in D.C., including Ella Rometsch. Sy Hersh's expanded version of how President Kennedy stumbled upon Rometsch in the first place provides critical insight. Writes Hersh, Ellen was introduced to Kennedy "in the usual way, through one of his many procurers in Washington, this time Bill Thompson, the railroad executive . . ." Hersh reveals that "Baker told him he had been approached by Thompson in the Quorum Club and asked, 'who is that good-looking girl? That woman looks like Elizabeth Taylor.' Baker responded, 'She's a German, and her husband is a sergeant who works for the German Embassy. And she's a real pro as far as I'm concerned. I mean, everybody who has had a date with her has really enjoyed her company.' So Thompson asked, 'Bakes, do you think that if I invited her to the White House that she would go with me to meet President Kennedy?' Baker responded [incorporating a reference to Nazis that seems incongruous if she was an East German spy for the Soviet Union], 'Gee, she's a Nazi. She'll do anything I tell her.'"

CHAPTER 5
JACKS-OF-ALL-TRADES

I've seen Oswald. . . . This is first Sunday AK [after Kennedy].
                    —Thomas Eli Davis, Jr., December 1963

*Tom knew [Victor] Oswald . . . I mean, it was obvious to me. I don't know
where they had met before, but Tom told me he'd been there [Madrid] twice
before. . . . The other man there, in Madrid, at the meeting, was a German,
who had a long, ugly scar that cut down one side of his face. I don't remember
if I heard his name. He didn't say much, but I sensed Tommy knew him also.
We were there for a while. I went out for something, but came back just as
they were finishing up. The other Oswald, the man they said that killed the
President . . . I had no idea who he was until his name was in the newspapers. But when I saw his picture, I remembered him right away from being in
Mexico at a hotel thing with Tommy. He and Tom had been together for a
few days. That frightened me a lot, but Tommy said to forget about it.*
                    —Carolyn Hawley Davis, March 2004

*At the time [September 1963], I don't think I knew what his name was; only
that he was an American. He was easy to remember. Tall, lanky, blond hair,
that lethargic, drawling manner, easy going cowboy-like. In Mexico, he stood
out like a lone orchid among thorny cacti . . . I saw him at the Hotel Luma
before Elena spotted him at the Duran's party, but I knew who she was
talking about right away. He and Oswald made quite the pair, I would
imagine.*
                    —Viola June Cobb, November 2015

Shortly after JFK's assassination, on December 9, 1963, the US State
Department's consulate in Tangier, Morocco, sent a "Priority" cable to
Secretary of State Dean Rusk concerning an American named Thomas Eli
Davis, Jr. The next day, copies of the cable were forwarded by Secretary Rusk's
office to top-ranking officials at the CIA, including DCI John McCone,

Counterintelligence chief James Jesus Angleton and Deputy Director of Plans Richard Helms. Additional copies were sent to the Office of Naval Intelligence and the National Security Agency. A handwritten list on the CIA's cable copy indicates that it was distributed to eight additional top-ranking officers at the CIA.

(Note: Young Thomas Eli Davis was referred to as both Jr. and III in various government documents, newspaper accounts, and family records. Experienced national reporter Seth Kantor explained, "Davis preferred to put 'Jr.' at the end of his name, even on legal documents," but that as Davis's name was identical to his father (living at the time) and his grandfather, III would be more accurate. The reader will encounter both Jr. and III, depending on the respective source material.)

The cable stated that Thomas Eli Davis, Jr., carrying US passport number D236764 issued in New Orleans on January 31, 1963, had been arrested in Tangier the day before, December 8, for "trying to sell two Walther pistols." At the time of his arrest, Davis was accompanied by his second wife, Carolyn Hawley Davis, twenty-six years old, who informed arresting officers that the couple's home was in Chico, Texas. The cable does not mention it, but Davis was twenty-eight years old at the time.

Thomas Eli Davis was born on August 27, 1936, in McKinney, Texas. Next to nothing is known about his early years growing up in the Beaumont area of southeast Texas, one of two children of a well-established, hard-working, and highly respected ranching family. Tom's mother, Marciea Scott Davis was related to the respected Eubanks banking family associated with the Republic National Bank of McKinney, a rapidly growing town located thirty minutes north of Dallas. Young Tom Davis spoke fluent Spanish, as might be expected growing up around Beaumont, but he was said to be a "poor student," disinterested in, and unchallenged by, standard learning. Following high school, at the age of eighteen, Davis enlisted in the US Army. There are unconfirmed reports that he served in an intelligence-related military unit. Several FBI reports contain unconfirmed statements made by others that Davis was stationed in Korea during the war there and that he was a POW there for about 8 to 12 months. The details of Davis's military service cannot be confirmed. According to U. S. Army officials, Davis's records "have been destroyed." The authors were informed by the Army's central records depot that Davis was honorably discharged from the US Army in February 1957, having enlisted in early January 1955, thus seemingly making it impossible that he could have served during the Korean War (1950–1953) or that he was a POW. However, writer Dick Russell was informed years earlier: "Davis was discharged from a five-year Army stint in February 1958," and that he [Davis] later told the FBI that "he had served in an Army Ranger battalion in Korea."

Respected newsman and former White House correspondent for *Scripps-Howard* Newspapers Seth Kantor wrote in 1977 that although Davis grew up on a large ranch, he "never went near the ranch country." Kantor also stated several times that the CIA was very familiar with Davis's work and activities. Kantor also attempted to learn why Davis was issued a US passport in New Orleans so quickly after application, despite the fact that he was a convicted felon. Kantor wrote: "U.S. passport authorities refused for more than two months in 1976 to even admit that Davis had been issued a passport. Their intransigence was overruled by officials of the State Department's Bureau of Security and Consular Affairs on November 23, 1976. These officials, however, continued to refuse to confirm or deny that Davis' passport was revoked after the Algerian episode."

Moroccan National Security officers, after arresting Thomas Davis, contacted the US Embassy in Tangier by cable, stating that while the "sale of pistols" charge was "minor," they had decided to still detain Davis "on the basis of a rambling, somewhat cryptic, unsigned letter in Davis' handwriting which refers in passing to 'Oswald' and the 'Kennedy assassination.'"

The security officer's cable also stated that the "intended addressee" of the Davis letter was attorney Thomas G. Proctor, "a political contributor" to President Lyndon B. Johnson. According to the cable, Thomas Proctor was the "legal agent for Morocco's World Fair exhibit in New York," and his address was "the Hotel Iroquois in New York City," a favorite haunt of CIA and Federal Narcotics Bureau officials in the 1950s and 1960s. Worth noting here is that subsequent State Department cables stated that attorney Thomas Proctor had been "advised" by Davis in the letter "to contribute to Lyndon Johnson's campaign."

WHO WAS THOMAS PROCTOR?

Thomas Grattan Proctor was born September 7, 1913, in Indiana, where he grew up and was boyhood friends with his eventual law partner, Paul Vories McNutt. Proctor attended Notre Dame Law School, class of 1938. He married Audre Jane Yoder in 1939 in Vermont. While he built a career in law, Audre was employed by American Heritage Publishing. City property and telephone records reveal that he and his family maintained an upscale apartment in the city at 139 East 94th Street. They had lived there for about twenty years during which time Audre worked for American Heritage Publishing. Nonetheless, US State Department investigators attempting to follow up on Davis's letter reported that they "were unable to locate Proctor," although he was a well-established attorney in New York City at the time of Davis's arrest. Proctor, who shares qualities with Davis—albeit on a higher professional scale—as a "jack of all trades," had been named in a lengthy lawsuit that made its way to the NY Supreme Court in 1959. The suit, filed against the estate of his law partner and friend, Paul McNutt (High Commissioner to the Philippines under both Roosevelt and Truman), involved alleged steel contracts between McNutt and French-born US citizen Pierre Bourgeois valued at $20,000,000 in today's dollars. According to affidavits in the case, it was Proctor who had introduced Bourgeois to McNutt and allowed Bourgeois to use the firm's offices as a base against his partner's wishes.

Had any investigators found Proctor's New York address at East 94th, they may also have discovered that Lee Harvey Oswald's good friend, George de Mohrenschildt, had once lived at the same address. Oddly, fifteen years after State Department officials failed to locate Proctor, investigators for the House Select Committee on Assassinations (HSCA), which had reopened the investigation into JFK's murder in 1978, also "were unable to locate" Thomas Proctor. This, even though Proctor's family was still publicly listed at the New York City address. Proctor passed away in 1967, of cirrhosis of the liver, one year before his son Philip Proctor's Firesign Theatre was designated by *Rolling Stone* magazine as "the funniest team in America today." Phil Proctor, who is today a well-respected actor, all-round likeable fellow, and author of, among other works, *Where's My Fortune Cookie*, graciously shared with these authors some personal family photos, including one that captured his father in a bold Nazi salute. (Seen in photo section of this book.)

Apparently, the Committee, and the State Department, made no inquiry about Proctor (or Davis) to the CIA. Had they done so, and assuming the CIA would have fully cooperated, the fact that Proctor was also associated with CIA assets June Cobb and Warren Broglie, manager of Mexico City's Hotel Luma, might have come to light. Investigators also might have consulted *Martindale-Hubbell Directory of Attorneys* to track Proctor's legal career and current location, but apparently no one thought of this, in spite of the fact that Proctor's firm had once carried the name of Paul V. McNutt, a former government servant and elected official. Proctor was in fact McNutt's intended running mate in his presidential bid had FDR not chosen to seek another term.

Thomas G. Proctor, according to former colleagues—who declined to be identified in this book because of what they claimed could be "possible legal complications"—reported to the authors that Proctor had known both Cobb and

Broglie "since at least around 1959 . . . in New York City . . . maybe having met Cobb at the Hotel Iroquois, when she had lived there briefly before going to Cuba." The same former colleagues also state that Proctor, during the "early 1960s," traveled several times to Mexico City, "reportedly for work related to the [United States] Embassy there, and something to do with that country's Olympics bid." Mexico City won the bid and hosted the Summer Olympics in 1968. In an interview with this author [Albarelli], former CIA Mexico City asset June Cobb recalled that New York City politician Paul O'Dwyer, brother of former New York City mayor William O'Dwyer, accompanied Proctor to Mexico several times. In 1950, President Harry Truman had appointed the former mayor as Ambassador to Mexico. William O'Dwyer resigned as ambassador in 1952 but stayed on in Mexico until 1960.

Proctor practiced law in New York with Paul McNutt, both men having grown up in Indiana, where they were boyhood friends. While Proctor maintained a lifelong low profile, McNutt was, as mentioned, constantly in the political limelight. During the Great Depression, McNutt was President Roosevelt's director of the Federal Security Agency (FSA). Through the war years, the FSA acted as "a cover agency" for the War Research Service, a top-secret program with the objective of developing chemical and biological weapons. Head of WRS was George Merck, who would continue to advance research at Fort Detrick, MD, elaborated on in this author's previous work, *A Terrible Mistake*. McNutt failed in his effort to become FDR's third-term vice presidential mate but was appointed by Roosevelt as chairman of the War Manpower Commission, and as such he was in frequent communication with the National Industrial Conference Board comprised of industry titans concerned primarily about mounting labor unrest. McNutt's commission included representatives from the Department of War, the Department of Navy, the Department of Agriculture, the Department of Labor, and the War Production Board; the latter included representatives from Du Pont Corporation's Remington Arms and the Bullard Corporation. Both Remington and Bullard were military contractors based in Bridgeport, Connecticut, which was known as "America's Arsenal." Former members of the WPB were also serving on the board of Connecticut National Bank of Bridgeport in 1963, which housed Remington Arms headquarters, the relevance of which will be made clear later in this chapter.

According to Phil Proctor, during the war, his father served in the Selective Service, a department heavily influenced by Proctor's childhood friend, Chairman McNutt of the War Manpower Commission. McNutt caused a bit of a stir in this role when he proposed the "extermination of the Japanese in toto." Asked by the press what he meant by "in toto," McNutt said: "The Japanese people as a whole."

A decade later, Proctor surfaced in the Horn of Africa, perhaps for the first time, when he attended a military parade with Haile Selassie, emperor of Ethiopia. Phil, who cannot explain why his father might have been invited to Ethiopia, still has the sword of the "blue people" gifted his father by the emperor. Phil was not aware that his father was known to Pierre Lafitte, who, on February 5, 1963, made the note: "WerBell guns – in desert with Proctor in Eritrea." Certain words in the entry are nearly indecipherable, but once it was confirmed that Proctor spent time in Ethiopia, the location in the desert of Eritrea made sense. And when told the entry seemed related to a notorious gun trafficker, Phil seemed satisfied that it "all made sense." (Additional analysis of this and other datebook entries that name Mitchell Livingston WerBell are presented in Chapter 8.)

Proctor appears again on Pierre's radar on May 20:

Vosjoli with Davis
(Carolyn — Proctor) ask OS (Ilse)

With this entry, Lafitte names Thomas Proctor in context with the Davis couple, and prompted by mention of Vosjoli (Philippe Thierry de Vosjoli, the head of French intelligence at the time), we revisited the illegible words in the February 5 WerBell / Proctor entry. The word *mission* is clear although spelled with only one *s*; the letters preceding mission may well be a rough notation "Vosjoli."

As this investigation progresses, we encounter more and more clues of Tom and Carolyn Davis's connections to weapons manufacturers, global arms dealers, and gunrunners. We also pursue the role Philippe de Vosjoli may have had, witting or not, in the plans for Dallas. For now, a preview of Vosjoli should suffice: "In light of the harrowing story that he tells, it is well to note that de Vosjoli had close relationships with multiple people who are quite germane to this story, including Jim Angleton (de Vosjoli functioned as a CIA double-agent, working inside French intelligence) and Frank Brandstetter, who was a member of Jack Crichton's 488th Intelligence Reserve unit. When de Vosjoli declined to return to France in the immediate aftermath of the assassination of President Kennedy, he fled to Mexico, where he spent several months with Brandstetter at the Las Brisas resort in Acapulco. Intriguingly, Pierre Lafitte, engaged in a pivotal meeting at an iconic Dallas hotel on November 20, 1963, jotted in his notebook: "'Frank B. here . . .'"

* * *

In early 1960s, Thomas Proctor found himself engaged in formal business dealings with a Madrid resident named Victor Oswald, when, under the umbrella of NY law firm MacDonald and Douglas, he provided legal counsel to film projects in Spain invested in by Oswald.

Proctor's services were focused on the film *John Paul Jones*, produced and directed by Samuel Bronston and heavily backed by the CIA's propagandist, C. D. Jackson, and the CIA itself. As identified earlier, Jackson was responsible for propaganda under Donovan's OSS. To underscore the influence of American propaganda over film projects, including many of Bronston's movies, the roster of primary investors included US powerbrokers Nelson and Lawrence Rockefeller, Pierre S. du Pont III, Rear Admiral W. F. Boone, and Admiral Chester Nimitz, along with Jose Maria de Arieliza, a well-known Falangist and Spain's ambassador to the US. At the time, both Lawrence Rockefeller and Pierre du Pont represented their family dynasties on the exclusive board of a small financial concern, Pallas Bank, founded by the French banking family Neuflize Schlumberger. As the reader will learn, the Schlumberger family's oil well surveying service, headed by Jean de Menil of Houston, TX, who contributed significant funds to the OAS, looms large in our story.

According to historian Kenneth A. Osgood, investor Victor Oswald worked very closely with Bronston to secure overall funding for the film. When the project collapsed, Proctor filed a $1,000,000 claim against parties involved, including MacDonald and Lewis, Samuel Bronston and Oswald, but the suit was settled under undisclosed terms, and, as is apparent, Proctor remained in the good graces of global arms dealer and close associate of Otto Skorzeny Viktor Oswald.

* * *

With this as backdrop to the Davis couple's presence in Morocco just weeks after Tom was seen with Lee Harvey Oswald in Mexico City, the US consulate in Tangier, according to the December 9 cable, promptly dispatched an official to interview Carolyn Davis. Mrs. Davis, called "Kitty" by her friends, told the official who is not identified in State Department files, that her husband was "a soldier of fortune," having served "with US forces in Korea, where he spent a year as a POW." Mrs. Davis also stated that her husband had worked in "Indochina, Indonesia, Algeria and Cuba, always on the Western side, if there was one." She also informed the official that she and her husband had lived in Mexico City since 1962, and that Thomas traveled often to New Orleans. The reader is left to wonder if her initial claim made to the Algerian arresting officer that the couple's home was in Chico, TX, was meant to establish the couple's rights as American citizens; yet she later tells the US consulate official they've been living in Mexico City, perhaps establishing Tom's bona fides with a State Department official. After all, the couple had been at Hotel Luma just six weeks prior.

Apparently, Carolyn Davis felt so comfortable with the embassy official that she inquired if he "could arrange" for her husband to "get a similar job in Angola." Mrs. Davis also told an officer for the Consulate General for the US Embassy in Morocco that she and her husband had "come to Morocco at the urging of Abbes Elmandjra, New York agent for the Moroccan National Tourist Office to investigate the possibility of raising Moroccan commercial cattle." It should be noted that her husband, Tom, had never shown interest in his family's South Texas cattle ranch. Carolyn also told the embassy officer that she and Thomas "departed the US via Icelandic Airlines [Loftleiðir] about November 2, and arrived in Tangier via London, Paris, and Madrid on November 28." There is no indication in FBI files that the Bureau made any attempts to verify Mrs. Davis's remarks about Mr. Elmandjra or the air flights the Davises had taken to Europe and North Africa.

Abbes Elmandjra's full name was Omar Saadi Elmandjra. His title in 1964 was Economic Counselor Embassy of Morocco and Chairman of Moroccan Exhibit New York World's Fair. With an MBA from Columbia University, he also served at the time in a coveted role as representative member of the International Bank for Reconstruction and Development, under World Bank president Eugene R. Black. An executive with Chase Bank since before the war, Black's career had crisscrossed that of John Jay McCloy, president of World Bank and the Rockefeller's Chase Bank. Black would have been familiar with, if not directly involved in, the placement of global arms trafficker (and host to Thomas Eli Davis, Jr., that fateful November) Victor Oswald, as Chase's representative in Spain.

THE DAVISES IN MOROCCO

The December 9 State Department cable also notes that Moroccan authorities questioned the Davises and US Embassy officials about any knowledge they could have on an American named Howard Loeb Schulman, "who was allegedly in Tangier and peddling pro-communist propaganda." Stated the cable, neither the Davises, nor anyone in the embassy, knew anything about Schulman. The cable concluded: "Request department advice if Davis or any associate has police or other record in the U.S.; if information may be supplied local authorities it may facilitate release."

On December 20, 1963, FBI director J. Edgar Hoover sent a special courier to the State Department, hand-carrying a memorandum to the deputy assistant secretary of Security bearing the subject: "Lee Harvey Oswald, Internal Security." The two-page document made scant mention of Oswald and focused almost exclusively on Thomas Eli Davis and one other American citizen, Howard Schulman.

Director Hoover was writing in reply to a telegram he had received from the State Department ten days earlier. The telegram had advised that "Thomas Eli Davis, Jr. was being held by the Moroccan National Security Police [in a Tangier jail] because of a letter in his handwriting which referred in passing to 'Oswald' and to the 'Kennedy assassination.'" Hoover additionally was writing in reply to another telegram the State Department had sent to him on December 16, 1963, advising, "Howard Loeb Schulman was arrested by the Moroccan Sûreté [police] after having reportedly stated that he was wanted by the United States authorities in connection with the assassination of President Kennedy."

In his reply, Hoover explained to the State Department that in May, June, and July 1963, he had furnished State with several memorandums concerning Thomas Eli Davis, Jr., and his attempts during those months at "recruiting men for an invasion of Haiti." Oddly, Hoover, and without any details, claimed that this was actually a "scheme" on Davis's part "to become acquainted with the 'soldier of fortune' type of individual so that he might acquire background information for an article he planned to write." Hoover didn't mention that Davis had never written an article of any type and was not known anywhere as a writer or journalist.

As to Howard Schulman, Hoover explained that, since 1961, he had furnished the State Department with a good many reports concerning Schulman, "who has in the past expressed pro-Castro sympathies and made an unauthorized trip to Cuba." Added Hoover, "It has been revealed in these reports that this person possesses suicidal tendencies." Hoover concluded his memorandum by stating:

> It is requested that you expeditiously secure, if at all possible, the exact nature of [Thomas] Davis' reference to Oswald and the President's assassination. It is further requested that this Bureau be completely apprised of any oral statements he may have made concerning this matter to the Moroccan National Security Police or representatives of your Department in Tangier.

Here we should alert the reader to reports that Lee Harvey Oswald had been seen in Morocco at about the same time that Howard Schulman was there. These reports, which were deemed erroneous by the FBI, are detailed later in this chapter.

THOMAS ELI DAVIS AS BANK ROBBER

A few days after Christmas 1963, a little over thirty days after JFK's assassination, FBI Director Hoover would become aware that the story of Thomas Eli Davis, Jr., was far from over as it took a strange turn. An unnamed clerk in the Bureau's criminal files division informed Hoover that FBI records from June 1958 showed that Thomas Davis had been a bank robber.

Files revealed that in Detroit, Michigan, on June 18, 1958, at around noon, Thomas Davis, dressed in olive drab coveralls and an army fatigue cap, got into his 1957 Ford sedan with a loaded .38 automatic in his pocket and drove to a branch of the National Bank of Detroit. In the bank, Davis handed a teller a note that instructed, "Put the money on the counter. If you make one move other than for the money, I'll shoot you on the spot." Davis then curtly instructed, "I want a big pile of money, say about $2,000 will do it." The frightened teller pushed a pile of about $1,000 in twenties toward Davis, who started to pick up the cash. He then hesitated and pushed the bills back at the teller and said, "I just can't do it. I just don't have the heart."

Davis turned and ran out of the bank but was followed by another teller, who had pressed the alarm. This teller followed David down the street to an alley, where he observed Davis beginning to remove his coveralls. The teller ran back to the bank and directed a nearby squad car to the alley, where Davis was arrested without incident. When police officers searched Davis's car, they discovered several boxes of ammunition, two German-made rifles, and a handgun. Initial arrest reports describe Davis as having light blond hair, blue eyes, standing 5 feet 11 inches tall, and weighing 150 pounds. Officers also found his threatening note to the bank teller in the pocket of his discarded overalls.

Davis told police detectives at the Wayne County jail that he had never been in any trouble, had never been arrested before, and had just completed his first semester of college, flunking all his courses at the University of Michigan, where his wife Cora had just graduated. "It's been a rough few months for me," Davis said sheepishly, in his youthful, laconic style. He claimed that he had decided a year earlier, after realizing college did not suit him, to become a dealer in antique guns. To start his business venture, he had borrowed $500 from a Texas bank on the strength of his father's cosignature but was now late on his payments. This, he insisted, had prompted him to make a spur-of-the-moment decision to rob the branch bank.

Davis pled guilty in US District Court on July 10, 1958, after failing to make a bond of $50,000. The trial judge declared him guilty of attempted bank robbery but suspended his sentence and placed him on probation for five years. But, as a condition of his probation, Davis was asked to agree to undergo psychiatric treatment at a Michigan facility to be chosen by his probation officer in consultation with the judge. His probation officer and judge quickly chose Detroit's Lafayette Clinic. Perhaps not by coincidence, the clinic, at the time, was a site for top-secret behavior modification experiments being conducted by the CIA.

DAVIS AND PROJECT MK/ULTRA

According to FBI reports and State of Michigan probation records, dated June 1963, Thomas Davis was admitted for psychiatric treatment to Detroit's Lafayette Clinic, operated by the State of Michigan, beginning on July 16, 1958, and was formally discharged on October 1, 1958. One FBI report states that Davis's physicians believed that he "displayed tendencies and symptoms of a 'schizophrenic' [sic] mental condition." Other psychologists on the clinic's staff, according to Davis's medical records, disagreed and felt that the young Texan was "suffering for a long time from a basic character disorder evidenced by severe emotional upsets." However, "it was generally agreed that this condition was related to the family situation wherein [Davis's] mother, who has many fine qualities and traits, is on the domineering side. [His] father is characterized as a passive, rather weak type of individual, who at times has been a heavy drinker." (The reports reflect a degree of similarity to those filed on young Lee Harvey Oswald.)

Psychiatric speculation and babble aside, here the reader should be aware that, beginning in 1954, several psychiatric facilities in Detroit, including the Lafayette Clinic, were covertly used and funded by the CIA under the cover of the Human Ecology Fund as part of the agency's now-notorious MK/ULTRA mind-control program. Perhaps Davis's confinement to the Detroit clinic, like Lee Harvey Oswald's proximity to the CIA-funded Bordentown Reformatory in New Jersey, was mere coincidence, but this seems to us to be a real stretch of serendipity.

Human experiments on unwitting patients were conducted at the Lafayette Clinic, as well as at Michigan's Ionia State Hospital for the Criminally Insane. Ionia State Hospital was particularly abusive and cruel to African American inmates confined there, who were considered mere human fodder for any behavior-modification quackery that the CIA and US Army thought might yield domination over the minds of others. As is well established, the clear majority of CIA files on the Lafayette Clinic project have been destroyed, but a few Agency documents reveal that covert work conducted at the clinic included electrical brain stimulation, induced psychosis through psychotropic drugs, narcohypnosis, and "behavior modification techniques" [read: psychological torture].

Interviews with former CIA Chemical Branch and Technical Services Section staff, as well as legal depositions and files from the Agency's Artichoke Project, an operational program, reveal that several MK/ULTRA contractors made visits to the clinic. These visits included Dr. Jolyon West (who would later treat Oswald assassin Jack Ruby) and Dr. Amedeo Marrazzi, chief of clinical research for the US Army Chemical Corps. Visitors to the clinic also included CIA officials Robert Vern Lashbrook, psychologist John Gittinger, and chemist Henry Bortner. At the time, these three CIA officials were working under the direction of the CIA's Technical Services Division chief, Dr. Sidney Gottlieb. Among highly respected medical institutions, the Lafayette Clinic has long been considered a place of dubious practices. One such practice was recommended by the clinic's neurologist, Dr. Ernst Rodin, who achieved wide notoriety with his recommendation that individuals who took part in Detroit's race riots in the 1960s be physically castrated. Dr. Rodin, who treated Thomas Davis, came to the United States from Vienna in the early 1950s. According to Rodin's autobiography, *War and Mayhem*, he had been a member of the Hitler Youth movement and then served a short stint as a Nazi soldier before leaving Europe. Dr. Joly West was a protégé of Rodin.

Following his discharge from the clinic, Davis was transferred from federal probation oversight in Michigan to supervision in Fort Worth, Texas, and then to the federal probation office in Beaumont, Texas. While in Beaumont, between numerous trips to New Orleans, New York, and Mexico City, Davis, according to CIA files and confidential interviews with former Davis associates, was trained in deep-sea diving and learned how to operate seaworthy boats in preparation for forthcoming gunrunning activities.

A June 1963 FBI document concerning Davis, copies of which were routed to the CIA, State Department, and Office of Naval Intelligence, reveals that on June 20, 1963, in follow-up to an alleged renewed interest in Davis because of "his recruitment of soldiers of fortune in Los Angeles," FBI field agents visited the Lafayette Clinic for undisclosed reasons, but apparently, they meant to gather more information on Davis. The brief report filed by two special agents with the Bureau states that they met with clinic physician Dr. Elliot D. Luby, a toxicologist who carried out extensive experiments with sensory deprivation and LSD and other mind-altering drugs with Dr. Jacques Gottlieb (no relation to Dr. Sidney Gottlieb) and Dr. Rodin. Dr. Luby was able to provide the FBI with the needed information but, according to the report, "advised that he did not want his identity revealed in view of the fact that he or anyone else connected to the Lafayette Clinic are not authorized to divulge information concerning former or present patients without written consent of the former patient or present patient or by special authorization from a duly authorized court."

Readers may be wondering at this point about how Davis, a convicted bank robber on probation, could obtain a US passport in one day that would allow him to travel to Algeria and Morocco, a feat highly unlikely without government intervention. And what of several reports that he regularly used "Oswald" as an alias during his travels? And what of the "Oswald" letter in Tangier? Who was attorney Thomas G. Proctor, and how did Davis know him? Why was he carrying a letter in his pocket written to Proctor that referenced "Oswald," President Johnson, and the JFK assassination? What were Davis and his wife doing in Morocco? Also, how did Davis accomplish his release from the Tangier jail—not revealed in any FBI, CIA, or State Department files—and what did he do after his release? Taking up these questions moves Davis's convoluted saga into areas that are provocative, deeply intriguing, and that point to answers that are intricately tied to the mechanics of the JFK assassination.

In his 1977 pursuit of enigma Thomas Eli Davis, newsman Seth Kantor also revealed that the Texas native was released from his Tangier jail cell in early December 1963, through the intervention and assistance from "the mysterious CIA contract assassin known only by his CIA cryptonym QJ/WIN." Kantor provides no source for his information on QJ/WIN, and Kantor is now dead. Readers of this book now know that a leading figure of the QJ/WIN program was former Nazi SS officer Otto Skorzeny, and it is this fact that makes Davis's saga even more intriguing.

Well before Kantor wrote about Thomas Davis, *Dallas Morning News* reporter Earl Golz gained knowledge of Davis's links to another major player in the assassination story, Jack Ruby, Oswald's assassin, and to several other unsavory Texas gunrunners. Taken together, these links advance the mystery of Thomas Davis into "the stratosphere of serpentine connections." [See sociogram by that title.]

On July 10, 1976, Golz wrote a greatly overlooked *Morning News* account concerning Jack Ruby's role in running guns to anti-Castro forces in Cuba. Golz writes that after Ruby's arrest for murdering Lee Harvey Oswald, Ruby "was concerned that the name of a gunrunner for anti-Castro Cubans might come up during his 1964 trial [in Dallas]." The name was Thomas Eli Davis, Jr.

Golz further revealed, "Both Davis and Ruby said they had met several times before the assassination and discussed gunrunning as a lucrative business, but each of them denied ever engaging in the business together." This seems unlikely and depends largely on their definition of "together." According to Golz, who relied heavily on information from *Dallas Times Herald* police reporter George Carter, it was Ruby's attorney, Tom Howard, who said that when he had asked Ruby "if any surprise names might come up during the trial," the only name Ruby gave in reply was Thomas Davis.

Police beat writer Carter, who interviewed Davis on two separate occasions, said that Davis was an admitted gun runner and that he first met Ruby in 1958 at a party. Carter later had talked in depth with DMN reporter Golz, who eventually shared the typewritten notes from those revealing conversations with the highly respected assassination researcher, Gary Shaw, who has generously shared the detail with these authors. According to the notes, Carter saw Davis after the Warren Commission was out of session, and that at the time, Davis told him that he was still worried about being dragged into the assassination. Golz recorded that "Carter saw Davis twice and [the] second time he said he was going to leave [the] country. . . ." Golz notes continue, "Hardy Eubanks, McKinney banker, knew Davis, and Eubanks' wife was related to Davis through marriage. Eubanks said right away, 'You must be working on a book about the Kennedy assassination. I think you are on the right trail if that's what you are doing.' And that's when he [Eubanks] told me [Carter] that he [Davis] was a gun runner. About early '65 or so." According to Carter, he didn't get in touch with Davis directly, but about three or four days went by, and "I got a call in the police press room and the voice on the other end of the line said, 'This is Tom E. Davis, Jr. I heard you been looking for me.'"

Davis told Carter that he had been arrested in Algiers on the day of the assassination. And he said *"what made it look so bad for me was that I was using the name of 'Oswald.'"* In light of what we now know, Davis's use of the name "Oswald" may be entirely unrelated to Lee Harvey Oswald, but rather a code to associate himself with a global arms dealer, whom, according to his wife, he had met twice before the fateful encounter in mid-November 1963.

A year after the Golz article appeared in the *Morning News*, Seth Kantor wrote a similar article that appeared in the *Detroit News*, November 1977. The story echoed Golz's account but contained additional details about Davis, whom Kantor dubbed "a criminal and CIA operative." Kantor wrote that after Davis moved to Beaumont, Texas, he began running guns to CIA units training in Florida and Central America, adding that Davis's trip to Morocco was undertaken for the purposes of running guns to "secret army terrorists," who were attempting to kill French President Charles de Gaulle, and that after Davis was arrested, QJ/WIN "sprung him from jail." The reader will recall the significance of "secret army terrorists" intent on removing de Gaulle, many of whom operated in and out of Algeria and Morocco. As stated, Kantor provided no source or evidence for his statement about QJ/WIN, but people who knew Kantor well consistently stated that he maintained impeccable sources at the CIA.

Kantor's article went on to state that Davis (contrary to notes from George Carter insisting Davis said he met Ruby at a party in 1958) first met Jack Ruby "when he walked into Ruby's downtown Dallas club with a plan to film a stag movie using Ruby's strippers" as performers. Kantor also claimed that Ruby and Davis together shipped arms to Cuba and that Warren Commission investigators knew all about it, but that they only had Davis's last name and could not fully identify him. Kantor quoted a Commission memorandum dated March 19, 1964:

> Ruby has acknowledged independently that . . . he contacted a man in Beaumont, Texas, whose name he recalled was Davis. The FBI has been unable to identify anyone engaged in the sale of arms to Cuba who might be identical with the person named Davis.

An enigmatic character by the name of Robert Ray McKeown seems to have held a key to understanding, or perhaps concealing, more about Jack Ruby's history with Thomas Eli Davis.

When questioned under oath before the Warren Commission, convicted gunrunner McKeown vehemently insisted he did not know "a Davis from Beaumont." According to commission records, "McKEOWN stated that he 'knew of no one by the name of "Davis" who was convicted for gun running activity with Cuba.'" A resident of Bay Cliff, McKeown had a history of "business transactions" in Cuba that had landed him with indictments in the late 1950s. With that history in mind as Castro tightened his grip on Cuba, in 1963, a top Harris County Republican Party leader called McKeown to his office in the Continental Oil Building in downtown Houston, to pursue him to facilitate an introduction to Fidel for "purely commercial business reasons." The connections between CONOCO (Continental Oil) and the military-industrial complex are too numerous to identify here, except to highlight that CONOCO's board included former Secretary of Army Frank Pace, who was then chairman of General Dynamics involved directly in the bidding for the highly lucrative F-111 fighter jet contract being manipulated by lobbyist Bobby Baker. Pace had served as a board member for over a decade of the investment firm Nation-Wide Securities, alongside (intermittently) Gen. Max Taylor and Allen Dulles.

* * *

According to author and researcher Lisa Pease, "Texas gunrunner Robert McKeown said Ruby 'had a whole lot of jeeps he wanted to get to Castro.' Ruby wanted McKeown to write a personal letter of introduction to Castro for Ruby so he could talk to Castro about releasing some unnamed friends detained in Havana. At that time, Santo Trafficante was being held at the Trescornia detention center in Cuba. Was Ruby instrumental in winning Trafficante's release at that time? John Wilson Hudson (a.k.a. John Wilson), an English journalist supposedly detained with Trafficante in the camp, indicated that Ruby came to see Trafficante in Trescornia. After Ruby shot Oswald, according to CIA cables, Wilson contacted the American Embassy and reported that "an American gangster called Santo . . . was visited by an American gangster type named Ruby." If Ruby was trying to sell jeeps to *Castro*, as McKeown said, was this an arms-for-hostages type deal? Get Castro the jeeps and get Trafficante out of jail? Recent events remind us this certainly wouldn't have been the only such effort in history. Trafficante was released from the detention center in August,1959, possibly just after Ruby's appearance there."

The reader has met Santos Trafficante as having been known personally to Pierre Lafitte. He is identified by name in Pierre's datebook on a critical date, August 13, as noted previously. His man in Havana, Lewis McWillie, a known gunrunner who ran Trafficante's operations in Havana, is also named in Lafitte's records. On Tuesday, March 26, Lafitte writes (horizontal on the page) "McWillie – Tues with Davis – Oswald,"

The man most responsible for identifying Jack Ruby in the Trescornia scenario is this mysterious John Wilson-Hudson, whose wife was from the Weinstein-Bronfman family, originally from Canada. Available records do not establish with certainty that Mrs. Wilson-Hudson was related to the Bronfman dynasty of Canada. In a later chapter, Wilson-Hudson is identified in concert with someone Lafitte knows as "Bowen." The name Ruby also appears alongside Wilson-Hudson's in Lafitte's records.

"When Ruby was questioned on June 7, 1964, by two Commission members, then-Rep. Gerald Ford of Michigan and Chief Justice Earl Warren, he was not asked about any connection with Davis or with gunrunning. The FBI pursued the subject but interviewed the wrong Davis and got nowhere. Meanwhile, the

CIA kept the identity of the real Davis a secret," reported Seth Kantor, a scenario reminiscent of the Commission's alleged inability to identify attorney Thomas G. Proctor.

Because they were not declassified and were not available to newsmen or the public until 1996, Kantor did not have the added benefit of having read the Government's secret files on Davis. Had they been available to Kantor, and other journalists, the entire Davis affair most likely would have received far greater scrutiny.

The Davis letter to Proctor ostensibly appears reasonably explained and demystified in a December 30, 1963, State Department telegram from the US Embassy in Madrid, Spain, which had been requested to follow up on the department's investigation of Davis and his provocative letter to the NY attorney. Readers may be noting that Madrid was the home and headquarters for Otto Skorzeny's myriad operations, including anything to do with QJ/WIN. Madrid was also the city where Thomas Davis and his wife, Carolyn, attended a mysterious meeting before heading to Morocco—a meeting not mentioned in the initial State Department cables.

Contrary to numerous published accounts over the past twenty-five years, Davis's draft letter referred only to "Oswald" and not necessarily to "Lee Harvey Oswald." Indeed, as it turned out, explained the State Department cable, the supposed coincidental "Oswald" referred to in Davis's letter was Swiss-born Victor Oswald, a former OSS operative and now an extremely wealthy international weapons trafficker, who often brokered multimillion-dollar deals behind the scenes for the armed services of many countries, including the United States.

The December 30, 1963, State Department "priority" cable regarding Davis and his wife, authored by the Madrid-based American ambassador to Spain, Robert Forbes Woodward, also reveals that a Moroccan Security officer, identified only as "Hussein," informed the US Embassy in Tangier that the Davis letter in question was "three or four pages" long and had indeed been addressed to attorney Thomas Proctor. We note that at the time of this arrest, Carolyn Davis told the officer that the couple's home was in Chico, Texas.

As we know, the letter contained a short sentence that read, "I've seen Oswald," and the later phrase, "This is first Sunday AK [after Kennedy]." According to the cable, the "Oswald" was Victor Oswald (sometimes referred to as Viktor Oswald), with whom both the Tangier and Madrid authorities were amply familiar. The Woodward cable reads:

Until today had no idea Davis oral comments either to police or others. Upon receipt reference telegram I asked him. He said Oswald refers to

Victor Oswald of Madrid [emphasis added] to whom he had Proctor's introduction. Reference to "after Kennedy" was for dating letter as he had
forgotten date, and that he had told this to Police. He offers to repeat full
story to FBI when he returns to U.S.

Ambassador Woodward concluded with: "My opinion is Davis somewhat unstable and entire matter given disproportionate importance by local authorities who
fear any and all arms traffic in view local recent political events." This, in spite of
the fact that strategies for the assassination of his commander in chief had been
deliberated right under his nose.

What prompted the career diplomat's role in minimizing Davis's presence in
Tangier? Had he been even slightly curious, Woodward might have discovered,
through his diplomatic channels in the volatile region, that Davis had been
arrested on almost the exact charges in Algiers several weeks earlier, on November 22, the day of Kennedy's assassination in Dallas. This first arrest, deliberate
or not, provided Tom Davis with a rock-solid alibi in the event his relationship to
Lee Harvey Oswald in Mexico City (and possibly New Orleans) weeks earlier
might surface publicly over the ensuing months of the investigation. He might
also have come across the report of the consulate official who questioned Carolyn
Davis and was told by her that the couple had been living in Mexico City since
1962, rather than emphasizing their permanent home was in Chico, Texas, as she
had insisted with the Moroccan police. Might Woodward have sent a cable to his
colleague in Mexico City, Ambassador Thomas Mann, to confer?

Had Woodward followed the Warren Commission report published the following November, might he have noticed the name Davis, and come forward,
and would he have known the name Thomas Proctor, who was invested with
members of the du Pont and Rockefeller families in a high-profile film project in
Spain? A follow-up cable from Madrid to Secretary of State Rusk, sent hours
later, on December 30, 1963, reads in its entirety:

Victor Oswald, a businessman of Madrid, contacted this date, stated that
Davis came to Madrid approximately six weeks ago, with a letter of business introduction to Oswald from a friend of Oswald's, a New York lawyer
named Thomas Proctor. Oswald said that he only talked with Davis 5–10
minutes since Davis was only interested in cattle and was headed for
Morocco. Oswald stated that this was the extent of his contact with Davis?

And apparently, that was that for Ambassador Woodward, who had replaced
Andrew Biddle, a director of the World Commerce Corporation, in spite of the

role he filled in the single most influential American post in Madrid—with heavy responsibilities relating to North Africa, including Algeria and Morocco—at the same time that arms dealer Victor Oswald had been engaged with Otto Skorzeny and other Nazis in Spain's capital. Woodward's memo to State gave Victor Oswald—who had invested alongside Jackson, du Pont, and Rockefeller—a virtual pass, if not a seal of approval, and misled any who might be curious about Davis when he reported at face value Victor Oswald's version of the five-minute meeting in Madrid. We know from Carolyn Davis that the meeting lasted close to an hour. (See Endnote on Robert Woodward.)

But first, as readers may now suspect, there was far more to Tom Davis's allegedly brief meeting with Victor Oswald. Who exactly was Victor Oswald?

VICTOR OSWALD, ARMS DEALER EXTRAORDINAIRE

Victor Moritz Oswald was born on November 15, 1909, in Lucerne, Switzerland, although throughout his life he used several different birth dates. He was the youngest of three boys in his family. Little is known about his early life, but, during World War II, he served as a member of Bill Donovan's OSS. He moved to Spain in about 1948 and established several small businesses, including branch offices for his brother's chemical concerns, which were based in Germany. During the war, he became close friends with Alfred Barth, the vice president for Middle European Affairs for the Chase National Bank in New York, owned by the Rockefeller family. Barth was a close friend of John McCloy, who was also with the Chase National Bank and who in 1964 would become a member of the Warren Commission. In 1950, Barth traveled to Madrid to meet with Generalissimo Franco, and it was Victor Oswald who accompanied him to the private meeting. Not long afterward, Oswald became the official representative for the Chase Manhattan Bank in Spain, having been appointed by his friend Lawrence Rockefeller. Oswald was also a close friend and business partner with Pierre S. du Pont III.

Oswald was well-liked in Madrid's business community. He was a reserved and low-key person, always keen to talk business. He was also a low-profile member of Madrid's large coterie of former Nazis, some of whom joined him in his various business ventures, including Arno Richard Buettner, who, according to the Federal Register of 1942, was on the list of "obnoxious Germans proposed for repatriation from Spain," and who used Oswald's home address for several years on his personal letterhead. It is yet to be determined if Arno was related to Dr. Konrad J.K. Buettner, bioclimatologist who arrived at Brooke Army Medical Center in San Antonio, Texas, in 1947 under the umbrella of Project Paperclip.

As revealed in *A Secret Order*, by author Albarelli, Dr. Buettner's focus was on the effects of extreme heat and burns and was known to have consulted with Dr. Jose Rivera, known to many assassination researchers for his association with Adele Edison. Buettner and Rivera encountered each other on occasion at meetings held by the American Association of Clinical Chemistry held at Parkland Hospital in Dallas. The vital support provided Parkland by Dallas bankers, particularly those executives with Republic National Bank of Dallas—including director Algur Meadows, who had been Otto Skorzeny's business partner since 1952—will be studied in another chapter.

Similar to the steady influx of Nazi medical experts into Texas, historian and professor David A. Messenger writes on the steady influx of former Nazis into Spain: "It was acknowledged that most returnees [returning Nazis] were not intent on continuing pro-Nazi activities. As R. A. Burroughs, of the German Department in the British Foreign Office, indicated, 'Nothing could be reported from Germany sufficiently useful to induce Germans to return from Spain.' For most of these Germans, who had been active in business in Spain before the war or even before the Spanish Civil War, their contacts were there, not in Germany; their families were there, not in Germany; and thus, their prospects for rebuilding an apolitical life were better in Spain than in Germany. That said, the increasing rate of formerly repatriated Germans illegally entering Spain by 1947 was enough of a concern for Phillip Crosthwaite, of the British Foreign Office, to declare repatriation a failure and raise the fear that 'Germans in Spain are just as dangerous to us as Russians would be.' A subsequent report from Madrid indicated that 96 former repatriates had returned to Spain over the course of 1947. In 1948 there was a veritable flood. One report by Titus stated that 'almost the whole German colony, pre-war, is back in Valencia.' By June 1948 the German colony was estimated to number nearly 15,000, up from the 12,000 or so estimated in mid-1947. One of the sources within the colony told Titus that the increased numbers were 'stimulating the growth of an already active Nazi mentality here.'"

As noted, Oswald, headquartered in Madrid, was a very prominent arms dealer who did business worldwide. Some writers have aptly compared him to notorious arms trafficker Adnan Khashoggi—most infamous for his involvement with Lockheed Aircraft and the Iran-Contra scandal—with whom he frequently did business.

Significantly, Victor Oswald was also a longtime business partner with fellow Madrid resident Otto Skorzeny, who, more importantly and to the point here, was present for Davis's meeting with Victor Oswald. It is worth repeating precisely what Davis's wife revealed to the authors:

Tom knew [Victor] Oswald . . . I mean, it was obvious to me. I don't know where they had met before, but Tom told me he'd been there [Madrid] twice before. . . . The other man there [in Madrid], at the meeting, was a German, who had a long, ugly scar that cut down one side of his face. I don't remember if I heard his name. He didn't say much, but I sensed Tom knew him also. We were there for a while. I went out for something, but came back just as they were finishing up.

Clearly the German with the long ugly scar was Otto Skorzeny. Skorzeny's office was only about two blocks away from Oswald's. That Skorzeny was a participant in the meeting, which Davis's wife said, "lasted about forty-five minutes to an hour," throws new light on the gathering. Additionally, here we should consider a 1958 CIA memorandum that reads: "Grand master of arms traffic for Algeria is former Nazi officer of the SS, Subject [Otto Skorzeny], who is installed in Madrid. Principal military advisor to NASSER in Egypt."

Skorzeny and Victor Oswald had known each other since at least 1951. This was the point during which Skorzeny was establishing an independent engineering office in Madrid. Introductions between the two appear to have come through Johannes Bernhardt, the former senior SS intelligence officer who headed SOFINDUS, the corporate network used by the Nazis in Spain. Readers may recall that SOFINDUS assets were acquired by the Allies after the war. Victor Oswald, as a lead British intelligence operative, in addition to his OSS duties, was involved in the postwar acquisition of SOFINDUS, placing him in close contact with Bernhardt. Bernhardt had contacted the Allies even before the war ended, attempting to transfer millions of dollars of SOFINDUS assets in return for favorable treatment. That offer was graciously accepted. In 1951, Victor Oswald and Johannes Bernhardt were joined by Otto Skorzeny, who had been transferred to Spain by US intelligence. This new business relationship with the revamped SOFINDUS was the intended cover for much of the intelligence and covert activity carried out by Skorzeny.

One contract alone provided great legitimacy to Skorzeny's work with Victor Oswald. This was the Otto Wolff steel company out of Germany in which Ilse, Otto's wife, also played a prominent role. Although not all the business between Skorzeny and Oswald is known, according to author Ralph Ganis, who owns a significant collection of the private papers of Otto Skorzeny, there are numerous references to business matters between the two men. Ganis suggests that the tone with which Skorzeny describes these dealings with Oswald makes it amply clear that Oswald was a major partner. These ventures included arms sales, aircraft and aircraft parts, machine parts, and other industrial items, many of which were shipped to various Middle East countries, including Egypt, Israel, Syria, and Jordan, as well as numerous countries in Latin America, Western and Eastern Europe, and several countries in Africa.

Davis's wife's statement to the author in 2004 continues verbatim:

> The other Oswald, the man they said that killed the President . . . I had no idea who he was until his name was in the newspapers. But when I saw his picture, I remembered him right away from being in Mexico at a hotel thing with Tom. He and Tom had been together for a few days. That frightened me a lot, but Tom said to forget about it.

* * *

That Thomas Davis was in Mexico City "at a hotel thing" with Lee Harvey Oswald in September 1963 is a stunning and dramatic revelation. It is fully supported by jottings in the datebook of Pierre Lafitte for the dates September 29 and September 30, 1963. Lafitte's entries make it quite clear that he had advance knowledge about Lee Harvey Oswald's trip to Mexico City. The datebook for September 22, 1963, reads: "Oswald-Mexico." On the same day, Lafitte entered the name "Gaudet" into his datebook, and then, on September 26, he writes, "O traveling." On September 27, after Lee Oswald had arrived in Mexico City, Lafitte entered the words: "Oswald—Comercio hotel- to meet with Tom D. at Luma." About half an inch below this, Lafitte writes: "Meet with Broglie-Luma re O." And on September 29, he wrote: "Tom at embassy—done." On Oswald's last day in Mexico, Lafitte writes: "Cable to Madrid- all ok- tell Tom D. O says come to Madrid." That entry in particular looms large as we pursue Davis's further role in the assassination.

In 2015, Viola June Cobb, CIA asset in Mexico City, told the authors that, in September 1963, she became aware of Davis's presence in Mexico City with Lee Harvey Oswald but was not aware of the tall Texan's name at the time. Said Cobb:

> At the time [September 1963], I don't think I knew what his name was; only that he was an American. He was easy to remember. Tall, lanky, blond hair, that lethargic, drawling manner, easy going cowboy-like. In Mexico, he stood out like a lone orchid among thorny cacti. . . . I saw him at the Hotel Luma before Elena spotted him at the Duran's party, but I

knew who she was talking about right away. He and Oswald made quite the pair, I would imagine.

The coincidental timing of June Cobb spotting Davis at the Hotel Luma—managed by her good friend Warren Broglie—may be explained by Tom's wife, Carolyn's, simple comment that she recognized Lee Harvey Oswald as having been "at a hotel thing" with her husband. But it also begs the question whether or not June saw Carolyn that evening, and vice versa. Asked if she passed her sightings of Thomas Davis on to her CIA superiors in the American Embassy in Mexico City, including agency chief of station Winston Scott, Cobb said:

> I did what I always did with all such new information. I wrote it up, with all the details, on a small index card and passed it on to my handler. It's my understanding that those cards were quickly read and prioritized and then put before Scott or another appropriate person. I asked after the President's assassination if that card's information turned out to be helpful, but I never got a reply, which was not at all unusual. Scott was much less than a fan of mine. . . . I know the Davis presence in Mexico City was known to Charles Thomas, an agency man in the embassy under State Department cover. He was going to mention it in his letter to the Secretary of State but was talked out of it. There was a tremendous amount of game playing around Oswald in Mexico and at the party with Elena and her daughter. He was there, no doubt about it, but I think that Davis being with him caused a lot of consternation and agony in the embassy.

Days following the interview with Cobb, author Albarelli mailed copies of two photos of Thomas Eli Davis, Jr., and several books to her in New Rochelle, New York. During a conversation a few days later, June said, "It's the same man—same face, same hair, same nose, same hooded eyes. So, what does all this mean?" (In the interest of full disclosure: This author interviewed Viola June Cobb at least twice a week for over two years. She and I became good friends, as did a few members of my family, especially my grandson, Dylan, with whom June loved speaking. After about sixteen months of interviews, June became Dylan's proud godmother.)

Contact was also made with the CIA officer who recruited and handled June Cobb during the early 1960s. Working under the Agency pseudonym "Bill Mannix," the officer held the position of Chief of Cuban Operations in CIA's Mexico City Station, reporting to station head Win Scott. "Mannix" spoke guardedly but clearly with the author when asked about Cobb's identification of Oswald and Davis in Mexico City in 1963. He confirmed that "she" (Cobb) had reported seeing a man "who turned out to be Davis." He said that Station Chief Scott told him not to discuss Davis anywhere, or "commit it to any sort of writing, official or unofficial." The remainder of the author's conversation with "Mannix" follows:

"Why?"

"It's obvious, isn't it?"

"So you believe that June saw Davis in MC at the Luma with Oswald?"

"Yes."

No doubts? Why?"

"Because she wasn't the only person who reported him being there."

"Who else?"

"No. No comment on that. I've said too much. And with the understanding you won't use my name."

"But, 'Bill'? I can use that?"

"I can't stop you."

Win Scott's directive that Davis was not to be pursued shines intense light on Scott's role, witting or not, in the cover-up. And as we learned, the US Ambassador in Madrid, a close friend of Ambassador Thomas Mann, whom Scott knew well, followed suit, advising the State Department, and all those inquiring, that the entire Davis matter in North Africa had been given "disproportionate importance by local authorities who fear any and all arms traffic in view local recent political events."

CHARLES WILLIAM THOMAS REVELATIONS

Charles Thomas, another individual of intrigue mentioned by June Cobb, was also completely aware of Davis's presence in Mexico City at the same time as Lee Harvey Oswald's visit in September 1963. In a December 25, 1965, memorandum, attached to a "CONFIDENTIAL" letter he sent to US Secretary of State William P. Rogers in which he explained that he had thoroughly investigated the events that transpired during Oswald's stay in Mexico, Thomas wrote:

During this latter conversation [of January 9, 1966], Sra. De Paz [Elena Garro] admitted that she had to the [United States] Embassy [in Mexico City] on an earlier occasion with her daughter and mother-in-law and had talked to two embassy officers (presumably from the Legal Attaché's

Office) about the matter [of seeing Lee Harvey Oswald at a party]. She said since the embassy's officers did not give much credence to anything they said, they did not bother to give a very complete story.

Charles Thomas then launches into a very detailed accounting of the Garro's encounter with Oswald. The party, Elena told Thomas, was held at the house of Ruben Duran, who was a cousin to Elena Garro. Elena explained, "Lydia, Horacio, and Ruben Duran are all cousins . . . [and] Silvia Duran [who worked in the Cuban Embassy in Mexico City and who spoke with Oswald when he visited that embassy in September 1963] is married to Horacio, who is a rather weak man . . . Sra. De Paz [Garro] had never had anything to do with Silvia, who [Garro] considers a Communist and a whore. Ruben [Duran] was born in the United States and served in the US Army during the war. He still goes to the US from time to time but had no relatives or particular connections there. . . . The party in question was held at the home of Ruben Duran."

Thomas explained that Elena Garro was unsure of the date of the party. She said that it had been held sometime in September 1963 and recalled that "it was on a Monday or Tuesday because it was an odd night to have a party." Thomas's report then goes into his Lee Oswald and Thomas Eli Davis section:

At the party, the man she assumes was Oswald wore a black sweater [perhaps the same black sweater he wore in Dallas when he was murdered by Jack Ruby]. He tended to be silent and stared a lot at the floor. Of his two young American companions, one was very tall and slender and had long blond hair which hung across his forehead. He had a gaunt face and a rather long protruding chin. [A perfect description of Thomas Eli Davis, Jr., in the estimation of the authors.] The other was also rather tall and had short, light brown hair, but he had no real distinguishing characteristics. All three were obviously Americans and did not dance or mix with the other people. The three were evidently friends, because she [Elena] saw them by chance the next day walking down the street together.

Described by those who knew him as tall and handsome with dark hair, Charles Thomas was a US State Department employee who served as the department's Political Officer in the US Embassy in Mexico City from 1964 to 1967. Before that, from January 1961 to August 1963, he had been stationed in the US Embassy in Port-au-Prince, Haiti. Thomas was also a covert employee with the CIA's Branch 4, Covert Action Staff. He had been hired by the CIA in early

1952, following his service in the US Navy as an ensign assigned to still-secret intelligence matters. Thomas, before going to Haiti and Mexico City, had covertly served the CIA, under State Department cover, at several additional posts, including Monrovia, Liberia; Sierra Leone; Accra, Ghana; and Tangier, Morocco. Endnotes in this chapter provide more on Thomas's status with the State Department and CIA.

Interestingly, early on in his stint in Haiti, Thomas inadvertently ran slightly afoul of a team of three physicians working under contract with the CIA's ultra-secret MK/NAOMI project, according to former Army biochemist Gerald Yonetz, who was interviewed by the author in March 2002. Beginning sometime around 1954, both the CIA's Security Research Service and the US Army's bio-chemical research center at Fort Detrick, Maryland, sometimes working in tandem, favored using Haiti—due primarily to its complete lack of governmental regulatory authorities, but also the ease with which any supposedly concerned authorities could be bought to turn a blind eye toward questionable and unethical activities—for risky human experiments with psychochemicals and other more lethal drugs.

Charles Thomas, according to former Detrick researcher Yonetz, who made several trips to Haiti as well as to Africa, "was surprised at the conduct of the experiments, as well as their nature, and expressed innocent surprise and perhaps dismay" upon first learning about them. As is underscored in one of this author's [Albarelli's] books, *A Terrible Mistake*, and in several excellent articles by investigative journalists Dr. Jeffery Kaye and Jason Leopold (available on the Truthout. org website), the US Army and the CIA, under projects MK/ULTRA, MK/NAOMI, and MK/DELTA, conducted extensive covert experiments with many "incapacitating agents" beginning in the 1950s and continuing until about 1970, Haiti being one of the favored locations for certain experiments. Dr. Kaye reveals that the military and CIA were especially interested in antimalarial drugs derived from cinchona bark. The curative and medicinal powers of cinchona bark have been known for hundreds of years in Haiti. During the 1977 Congressional hearings on the CIA's stockpiling of lethal and incapacitating drugs, it was revealed that the CIA and army were interested in antimalarial drugs for "devious reasons."

Writes Dr. Kaye: "CIA-linked researcher, Dr. Charles F. Geschickter told Sen. Edward Kennedy in 1977 that the CIA was interested in anti-malarial drugs that 'had some, shall I say, disturbing effects on the nervous system of the patients.'"

Even more intriguing to this book's central subjects, Charles Thomas made quick amends for his comments about the experiments he had witnessed, and, before departing Haiti for his new assignment in Mexico City, he was invited to make some personal investments in private ventures being conducted in Haiti by a then obscure businessman, George de Mohrenschildt, a high-level source of mystery after the JFK assassination. Adding significantly more intrigue and mystery to Thomas's experience in Haiti is the fact that de Mohrenschildt's dealings there, involving Charles Thomas, also included Charles Norberg, covert CIA operative and Harvard educated, high-profile Washington, D.C., attorney apparently admired by Allen Dulles and Adolf Berle.

Shedding additional light onto the overall nature of Charles Thomas's private business affairs in Haiti is Bruce Adamson's essential book, *Oswald's Closest Friend: The George de Mohrenschildt Story*. Adamson reveals: "After de Mohrenschildt's suicide on March 29, 1977 [former CIA director] George H.W. Bush acknowledged he knew the man [George de Mohrenschildt] as a relative of his Andover pre-school roommate, but had not 'heard from him in many years.'" Adamson, however, goes on to say: "A recently declassified State Department document shows that Bush had heard from de Mohrenschildt in 1971. The document is a June 24, 1971 letter from Chief of Haitian Affairs, David R. Ross to Bush, who was the US Ambassador to the United Nations at the time."

The Ross letter to Bush reveals that de Mohrenschildt's "private attorney" for his Haitian affairs was Charles R. Norberg. In 1993, Norberg told Adamson he could not find his work files on his de Mohrenschildt's dealings, nor could he remember "the precise nature of his legal work on behalf of his former client." In his book, Adamson also reproduces, in its entirety, a letter dated May 20, 1971, that de Mohrenschildt wrote to US Congressman Earle Cabell, who was the mayor of Dallas when JFK was assassinated, as well as brother to Charles Cabell, who had been deputy director of the CIA until right after the failed Bay of Pigs invasion and JFK's subsequent firing of Cabell and Dulles. The letter, which requests help on Haitian issues, also identifies Norberg as his then-attorney.

AN UNTIMELY, SUSPICIOUS DEATH

In April 1971, Charles William Thomas, according to *Time* magazine, "took up a gun and shot himself to death." Thomas was 45 years old, had a wife and two children, and had served both the State Department and CIA for nearly 20 years. A November 15, 1971, *Time* follow-up article on Thomas's death referred to him as "a desperate man." Thomas, the article explained, "had been '*selected out*' of the Foreign Service" because "he had not been promoted from Class 4 level to Class 3 within the mandatory eight years." In State Department parlance, "selected out" essentially means "fired." The department gave Thomas one-year's salary, a $323 monthly retirement payment, which came out of money he had paid into a departmental fund, and said good-bye to its former employee. The CIA did nothing and said nothing about Thomas's death.

Before committing "suicide," Thomas spent nearly three years sending out résumés in hopes of gaining a new job. In total, according to the *Time* article, he "endured 2,000 job rejection letters; he was told 'too old' or 'too qualified,' and anyway, he had been fired by the State Department." Friends of Thomas's at the time of his death said that he was depressed, but not suicidal, and that he "deeply loved his children and wife" and "would not do that to them."

THE VERSATILE CHARLES ROBERT NORBERG

During World War II, Charles Norberg served in the US Army Air Force as an intelligence officer, and, like many of the characters that appear in this book, he encountered not only Otto Skorzeny and Pierre Lafitte, but also the ubiquitous George Hunter White in both Burma and India. Following the war, Norberg worked for both the CIA and in the public affairs division of the State Department and then joined the prestigious international law firm of Morgon, Lewis & Bockius. In 1965, he went into private practice.

We know now that Norberg was more than simply a CIA operative and well-connected attorney. Norberg was George de Mohrenschildt's personal attorney, representing him in a series of complex Haiti-based oil and geological ventures, some of which involved the "technical, in-country [Haiti] services of Thomas Eli Davis, [as well as] two or three other American soldier-of-fortune types who were in and out of Haiti, Guatemala, Panama and the Dominican Republic on a regular basis . . . wearing enough hats to stock a tony haberdashery shop," said a former State Department employee who declined to have his name appear in this book. He added, "There were also the seemingly mandatory former Nazis who were retained as shadows by the CIA . . . they were everywhere plus Florida." Some of these "technical" service soldiers of fortune and contractors were also occasionally employed by the Schlumberger Wireline and Testing corporation, founded in Houston, Texas, in 1935. They also worked in Latin America, the Belgian Congo, Haiti, South Africa, Serbia, Romania, and several other locations across the globe.

Beginning in June 1951, Charles Norberg had also been an initial and key member of the United States Psychological Strategy Board, which was created in 1951 by President Harry Truman through an executive order issued to the directors and agency heads of the CIA, State Department, and Department of Defense. Working closely with the PSB during the mid-1950s was propagandist C. D. Jackson, chief executive of Time-Life who also served as Eisenhower's liaison between the CIA and the Pentagon and member of the Operations Coordinating Board, and as the reader will recall, a primary investor in *John Paul Jones*, filmed on location in Franco's Spain.

Norberg served for about five years in the White House as the Psychological Strategy Board's assistant director. In the mid-1950s, when CIA director Allen Dulles and his close associate, senior statesman, Adolph Berle huddled with Cornell University physicians Harold G. Wolff and Lawrence Hinkle to create the Foundation for the Study of Human Ecology, Charles Norberg's name was at the top of their list of individuals they would potentially want to serve as members of the board of directors. Dr. Wolff especially admired Norberg's expertise in the burgeoning fields of enhanced interrogation and covert psychological operations. Dulles was continually impressed with Norberg's proposal to establish, within every US Embassy, a psychological operations officer working undercover as a State Department political officer. For over a decade, Norberg also served as legal advisor for the CIA-created front companies, Morwede Associates and Mankind Research Unlimited. Through his legal representation of de Mohrenschildt's oil and related ventures in Haiti, we have every reason to assert that Charles Norberg knew Thomas Eli Davis, a young man who was once an object of study at an HEF facility in Detroit, Michigan.

Author Albarelli's monograph, published in December 2010 (voltairenet.org), titled "CIA's Denial of Protecting Nazis is Blatant Lie," reveals that Morwede Associates worked closely with the CIA-created HEF (Human Ecology Fund) in the late 1950s and 1960s and focused some of its activities on matters that clearly fall into the esoteric realm. Under the umbrella of the CIA's Security Research Services, Morwede was among the front organizations protecting Nazi chemists transported to the US, including Dr. Freidrich "Fritz" Hoffman, a major beneficiary of the largesse of the Paperclip pipeline.

In the late '50s, Hoffmann's work for the CIA and Fort Detrick included development of lethal chemical agents to be used as weapons in Vietnam, proof that the dishonorable war was just over the horizon when John Kennedy took office. One of these weapons, the horrific and now-infamous Agent Orange, was authorized for use in Vietnam in November 1961 (implemented in '62 under Operation Ranch Hand), with the stated objective of "improving road and waterway visibility and clear camp perimeters" so that "greater numbers of enemy troops could be killed." A year earlier, two of the nation's leading corporations,

Schlumberger Ltd. of Houston, TX, and Dow Chemical of Midland, MI, combined forces to form a shared division named Dowell Schlumberger, to provide expertise and pumping services for the US oil industry, which would, of course, thrive during (the impending) all-out war in Southeast Asia. By 1962, Dowell's parent, Dow Chemical, was mass-producing Agent Orange under specifications perfected by Hoffmann and his team at Fort Detrick. Again, as counsel to Morwede Associates, it would be difficult to argue that Charles Norberg never encountered Nazi scientist Dr. Fritz Hoffmann.

Norberg—who does not surface in the Lafitte datebook—did, however, share a client, George de Mohrenschildt, with another D.C. attorney who does appear in Pierre Lafitte's notes. In back-to-back entries, Lafitte writes:

HERBERT ITKIN UNCOVERED

W team E. Johnson's
(Itkin)
—Lafitte datebook, October 26, 1963

Gali Sherbatov - L.O.
(Orlov)
(Itkin)
-Harvey-
—Lafitte datebook, October 27, 1963

In pursuit of analysis of these entries, author Albarelli wrote: *The name (Herbert) Itkin is found in new DB and related financial pages—Itkin's name is important on a number of levels. Fortunately, we have a fair amount of info on him . . . More to follow. Also, there is more on H. L. Hunt. That also will follow.*

Herbert Itkin and Charles Norberg shared other traits outside the legal profession including the ability to master the wearing of a number masks. According to researcher and assassination author Bill Simpich, "by May 1963, Itkin became the attorney for the Haitian government-in-exile. CIA documents show that Itkin's handler in 1963 was Mario Brod, who was recruited in Italy by James Angleton during World War II and had operational involvements in Haiti. Before his brother was killed, Bobby Kennedy himself was relying on mob tips from Itkin. In 1966, Itkin was reportedly researching under his code name 'Portio,' while Angleton held onto his private 'Mike/Portio/Haiti' file. In 1968,

CIRA (CI research and analysis chief) Ray Rocca swore that the 'CI Staff definitely never was in contact' with Itkin. By 1971, CIRA's bird-dog investigator Paul Hartman was asking to review Itkin's CIA file, no doubt to educate himself on some fine points."

According to government documents (not released until 1998), in 1963, Itkin, a partner in a NY law firm, was the registered agent for the "Haitian Government in Exile" representing Louis Dejoie and other Haitian exile groups in 1963. He reportedly furnished money to a group invading Haiti in August 1963. In 1972, in the midst of a scandal involving Itkin, his father-in-law called the CIA office in New York to say that "subject was closely tied to BKCROWN [CIA], giving it much assistance in Haiti and elsewhere, implying Itkin was a trusted informant or agent, not a staff employee."

Another news article of the period states that in September 1963, Itkin registered as a foreign agent of the Dominican Republic. By 1973, following a widely covered case, involving Itkin, the NYC water commissioner, mortgage applications, the Teamsters Union, and kickbacks, the Agency stated categorically that Itkin was "never employed by BKCROWN [CIA]. Either in Staff or Contract/Career Agent status." Itkin was, by then, an Agency ghost. However, in 1954, as a young oil lawyer, Itkin had wrangled a meeting in Philadelphia with Allen Dulles.

Author Nancy Welford, in "The Faux Baron: George de Mohrenschildt," reveals that Dulles set Itkin up with a meeting with George de Mohrenschildt, who told Itkin he was "from that man in Philadelphia [Dulles] and that his name was Philip Harbin." William Gaudet, in his HSCA deposition, confirmed that he knew George de Mohrenschildt as Harbin, from China. Before pursuing Gaudet, it is important to know that de Mohrenschildt, working under this alias, pursued oil matters with Herbert Itkin, serving as a nonpaid, voluntary agent between 1954 to 1960. By early '63, while Itkin was the registered attorney for the Haitian government-in-exile, George de Mohrenschildt and his wife, Jeanne, had left Dallas and established residence in Haiti in order to "pursue interests" on the island.

According to Martin Arnold of the *New York Times*, December 1968, Itkin was a Government informer. "Slight, hollow-eyed and sallow, living in fear of his life in protective custody at an undisclosed military installation base here, Mr. Itkin has emerged from the double-dealing world of the informer insisting that he worked for the Central Intelligence Agency. This is True. He has sworn that he was an informer for the Federal Bureau of Investigation, and this, too, is true." According to Arnold, "the obscure, money-grabbing forty-three-year-old lawyer, was known by the CIA code name 'Portio' and by the FBI as 'Mr. Jerry.'" At the time, Arnold had been covering Itkin's role as a principal witness in a pension fund kickback case, which, according to authorities, could also produce dozens of cases involving labor racketeering, gambling bribery, income tax evasion, and a wide range of other felonies. "However, his bragging 'has embarrassed the CIA,'" writes Arnold. "His [Itkin's] theatrical attempts to force the agency to help straighten out his domestic problems almost blew the cover of one of the CIA's most important operatives in New York City, the lawyer who was Itkin's CIA 'control.'"

We also learn from Bill Simpich's Kennedy assassination research into Herbert Itkin that James Angleton of the CIA had both an Itkin file and a "Mike/Portio/Haiti" file. (Itkin's code name was Portio.) Simpich reports that CIA general counsel Larry Houston claimed he could not find any Itkin files prior to 1964, most likely due to the fact that Angleton's personal Itkin and Portio files were kept apart from the CIA records system and were only discovered after Angleton was fired in 1974. According to Simpich, by the early 1970s, Itkin's skills as an informant for both the Central Intelligence Agency and the FBI prompted a member of the staff of US Attorney Bob Morgenthau to describe him as ". . . the most important informer the FBI ever had outside the espionage field. He never lied to us. His information was always accurate."

According to Jim Drinkhall, the *Wall Street Journal*, January 11, 1980, soon after the highly publicized kickback scandal and resulting arrests of Mafia and Teamster figures, Itkin and his family entered FBI witness protection, in Los Angeles, where they began a new life with a different name. Operating as a private investigator, allegedly under the name International Investigations, Inc., Itkin had a five-year business relationship with Dr. Armand Hammer, chairman and CEO of Occidental Petroleum. Drinkhall reported that the FBI was looking into payments totaling $120,000 made while Occidental was attempting to gain city approval for oil drilling in Pacific Palisades section of Los Angeles. "The FBI is checking reports that $80,000 was paid on Occidental's behalf to Herbert Itkin, a private detective who for more than five years in the early 1960s was an informant for both the FBI and the Central Intelligence Agency. It is believed that more than $60,000 of the payment never went into the detective agency's account and remains unaccounted for. Another $60,000 . . . was given to another company that converted the checks to cash and passed it on to Mr. Itkin." (Students of high strangeness and synchronicity might be interested to know that by the end of that year, Armand Hammer was ensconced in Claridge's in London, consummating his purchase of *The DaVinci Code*.)

* * *

Lafitte's "Orlov" noted in the October 27 entry, along with both Itkin and Harvey, is a clear reference to Fort Worth oilman Col. Lawrence Orlov. According to Prof. Peter Dale Scott in "Oswald and the Hunt for Popov's Mole," published in the *Fourth Decade*, Volume 3, Number 3, March 1996, "Col. Orlov, like Max Clark, was a veteran of the Air Force as well as a good friend of J. Walton Moore." In fact, they were handball partners. It should also be noted that the Colonel had been drilling for oil in Texas prior to the war and in 1963 was still engaged in the industry. Orlov's Dallas office was located in a relatively unassuming building only a one-minute walk from the more imposing Reserve Loan and Life Insurance Building—across the street from the First Baptist Church of Dallas—where both George de Mohrenschildt who was a client of Herbert Itkin, and their mutual friend, CIA station chief J. Walton Moore, leased office space. We pursue Russian-born Gali Sherbatov Clark, and her husband Max Clark, in Chapter 9 of this book.

Our assessment of the Itkin datebook entries is wrapped up by surmising that "Harvey"—October 26 and 27—is William King "Bill" Harvey. Lafitte's mention of Harvey in context of Gali Sherbatov, Herbert Itkin, and Lawrence Orlov is not entirely clear, but it should be remembered that Harvey was known from his earliest days with the FBI as a "Red-Hunter."

The complex histories of attorneys and agents provocateurs Charles Norberg and Herbert Itkin, in the context of de Mohrenschildt's presence in Haiti in 1963 and his ties to this strange cast of characters, are all the more intriguing in light of the tragic demise of Charles William Thomas, who could possibly have unmasked them both.

ANGLETON PUTS AN END TO CHARLES THOMAS

In August 1993, the CIA released a memorandum sent to the deputy assistant secretary for Security at the US Department of State bearing the Subject: *Charles William Thomas*. The brief memorandum states: "Reference is made to your memorandum of 28 August 1969. We have examined the attachments, and see no need for further action. A copy of this reply has been sent to the Federal Bureau of Investigation and the United States Secret Service." It was signed by the CIA's James J. Angleton.

We return now to North Africa and IDEN D.

LEE HARVEY OSWALD IN MOROCCO?

In June 1964, alarm bells went off at the CIA after detailed reports came in from Tangier reporting that a subject identified only as "IDEN D" had been seen in

Tangier in 1962 and 1963 in the company of Marc David Schleifer and several of his associates. "IDEN D," according to declassified CIA documents, was Lee Harvey Oswald. Marc David Schleifer was an activist deeply involved in the Fair Play for Cuba (FPCC) organization and is described in CIA documents as "an American Marxist and journalist" who had traveled in support of FPCC and other causes to Cuba, Mexico, France, Algiers, Algeria, and Tangier, Morocco.

In February and March 1963, a US State Department memorandum to the CIA and FBI noted that Schleifer was the editor of a new radical Algerian-based magazine, *Revolutionary Africa*. Earlier in August 1961, and then later in September 1963, Schleifer, according to CIA officials, traveled to both Cuba and Mexico, causing considerable alarm and attention from both the Agency and the FBI for his associations with the then-notorious American black militants and countercultural figures. In 1965, prior to moving to the Middle East, where he eventually went to work for NBC News, Schleifer converted to Islam from Judaism, changing his name to Sulayman Abdallah Schleifer. Suffice it to say, as some readers may already be thinking, Schleifer is suspected to have been with Lee Harvey Oswald and Thomas Eli Davis in Mexico City in 1963.

In June 1964, based on accounts from several CIA sources and assets, the CIA Chief of Station in Rabat, Morocco, reported that Lee Oswald had attended several gatherings and parties at the Tangier home of a man named Narayan Kamalaker. An Indian by origin and sometime-accountant for Coca Cola in Tangier, Kamalaker was married to a Russian woman named Sonya Dragadge, whose son reportedly worked for *Time* magazine in Rome. The CIA also claimed that another Tangier resident named George Greaves had told one of their British sources—identified as Paul Gill—that he knew people who knew Lee Oswald, but they were not in Tangier. CIA internal files stated that Gill had been a smuggler and gunrunner whose boat had been blown up by French frogmen. In Chapter 5, the reader will encounter another smuggling group based in the region that worked closely with Lt. Col. William A. Eddy, a close friend of American businessman Winthrop Buckingham.

According to one report, Paul Gill was associated with several Americans in Tangier, one of whom was Buckingham. At the time, Buckingham, who had for years been an associate of June Cobb's friend and CIA asset, Hotel Luma manager Warren Broglie, was managing a hotel in Tangier. Buckingham was also a long-time CIA operative who had played strong supportive roles with the OSS in North Africa. Over the years, Buckingham and Broglie had developed a close friendship, often socializing at hotel business gatherings around the world. Paul Gill was also closely connected to the American soldier of fortune Thomas Eli Davis, Jr., who often roomed with Buckingham and his wife, Ellen, when in Tangier. Ellen was born in Turkey, where her father served as a reverend in Smyrna.

Davis, according to the CIA, often used the alias "Oswald." This claim is supported by the interview notes of George Carter, "that he [Davis] used the name Oswald in his anti-Castro activities in the period 1959–1962 while the real Lee Harvey Oswald was in the USSR. . . . Carter's lead to Davis came from Jack Ruby's attorney, Tom Howard."

Last, the Rabat report mentions another American, Rev. Carl Ray Jackson, in relationship to Oswald as having allegedly attended a social gathering in Tangier with Schleifer. Additionally, Rev. Jackson's daughter, described as being a little "flitty," allegedly had seen Oswald several times in a Tangier "beatnik hangout." The astute reader, however, might ask why the thirteen-year-old daughter of a minister would feel compelled to make up such a story?

The CIA Station Chief in Rabat, Charles Cogan, was skeptical about these reports of Oswald sightings, stating somewhat humorously: "[It] would appear that the whole affair is a product of highly vivid imaginations brought to a simmer in a pot of kif, booze, beatnik poetry and stirred by the Tangier sea breeze."

However, CIA officials in Washington, D.C., remained concerned about the sightings and about Schleifer's activities. According to one former Agency official, once extensive follow-up investigation had been conducted, some analysts eventually concluded that there "was a strong possibility" that "some of the Tangier reports had some validity," while others may have been "mixed up with other reports that came from Mexico City regarding Oswald's activities there with counterculture types." A pattern emerged for any sincerely questioning Oswald's presence in Tangier.

PIERRE AND HIS VERY OWN JACK-OF-ALL-TRADES

The headline read, "Thomas Eli Davis, Jr. Recruits Mercenaries in Los Angeles." In early June 1963, prior to the portentous trip to Mexico City in September followed by their ominous journey to Madrid in early November, an FBI special agent interviewed Carolyn at her place of employment with Underwood Typewriters in Ventura, California, where the couple had apparently relocated. The special agent, John J. Schmitz, wanted to know why Carolyn's husband had placed an advertisement in the *Los Angeles Times* recruiting former Army paratroopers and rangers for "military-type work."

Carolyn Davis told Schmitz she had no idea why her husband had placed the ad. "I am only interested in my job and did not question him about it," she replied. Schmitz pressed her, asking why, if she knew nothing, did she attend a subsequent meeting at a motel where men who responded to the advertisement were present. Carolyn said, "I spent the entire time in my own room [in the motel] washing my hair and bathing. . . . The only reason I made the trip to Los Angeles was [so] that Tom could charge the expenses for the meetings on my American Express charge account." Asked Agent Schmitz, "You're sure of that?" Carolyn Davis was quiet for a moment and then said, "I can't be compelled to give testimony against my husband anyway."

During his interview with SA Schmidt some three hours earlier, Tom Davis appears to have been fully prepared that the FBI would show up on his doorstep with this confabulation: "I got an idea to write an article for possible sale. The article was to deal with soldiers of fortune and the methods used in organizing an army and the type of men employed in such an army, as well as the attitude of the US Government concerning the type of laws violated and possible punishment for any such violations." Davis went on to explain that he had placed the ad in the *Los Angeles Times* on May 12, 1963, requesting that any former paratroopers and rangers interested in military type employment write to a blind box at the newspaper. Davis said he received twenty-eight replies in response to the ad, and he then arranged a meeting with the selected men to be held on May 18 at the Tahitian Village Motel in Downey, California. (See Endnote for a thorough examination of this incident.)

Two days later, as noted earlier in this chapter, Lafitte makes a note that French spy turned confidant of CIA CI James Angleton, Philippe de Vosjoli met with Tom Davis and the same note refers to Tom's wife by name (with the correct spelling to indicate he was familiar with Carolyn), and in the same breath as "Proctor," followed by "ask OS/Ilse."

Within the week, it appears that Vosjoli was in DC with Frank Wisner and James Angleton.

* * *

Here it should be strongly noted that Jean Pierre Lafitte was previously connected to Thomas Eli Davis, prior to the notations in his 1963 datebook. This connection appears to have begun in New Orleans in 1961, about two years before Davis was issued a passport there. And, the Lafitte diary of 1962 also indicates that global arms dealer Victor Oswald had a hand in arms shipments to CIA training camps outside of New Orleans, Louisiana, an association that aligns with the ease of a Davis and Victor Oswald meeting the following year in

Madrid. In '61, Lafitte was working covertly for the CIA and sometimes the FBI, often traveling to Spain, France, the Middle East, and Africa, where he performed duties that fell under the "executive action" (assassination) category, although there is no indication within any of the numerous documents, letters, and files copiously reviewed by the authors that Lafitte ever acted as a killer. He appears to have only played supportive roles in "wet work" (murder) operations.

Apparently, Tom Davis first encountered Lafitte through his (Davis's) previously unknown activities as a confidential informer for the Federal Bureau of Narcotics, during which Davis sometimes surreptitiously met with narcotics agents George Gaffney, George Hunter White (known to Charles Norberg), and Charles Siragusa. Davis, according to a 1962 letter from Siragusa to George White, once met with French drug traffickers in Algeria, including Frenchman Jean Souetre. Siragusa referred to Davis in the letter as *"a galloping clod whose testicles are larger than his home state of Texas, but who lacks the adjoining brains . . . however, he's more loyal and trustworthy than a blind sheep dog, and he does bring in some damn decent information."* [Italics added.]

This establishes that Davis would have recognized Jean Souetre in person, regardless of any alias the skilled assassin might have been using at the time. We know also that Tom Davis's history with the Narcotics Bureau, and the inherent connections to Otto Skorzeny - QJ/WIN, also brought the gangly Texan into a still somewhat mysterious relationship with two men very much tied up in the illicit narcotics trade, Hanna Yazbeck and Edward Lawton Smith. On January 24, 1963, Lafitte makes a note, "Harvey" [William King Harvey] "White" [George Hunter White] "Smith" [most likely Edward Lawton Smith] followed underneath by "Canada." The number 848 precedes the three names. The possibility that this entry is the first of several that year related to nickel—known as "the only true war metal"—will be pursued in another chapter. Yazbeck often teamed up with CIA-QJ/WIN program participants for lucrative extortion schemes and prostitution and white slavery activities, frequently traveling to Algiers, Morocco, and America's West Coast.

As revealed, in his pursuit of Thomas Eli Davis, newsman Seth Kantor exposed that the Texas native was released from his Tangier jail cell in early December 1963, through the intervention and assistance from "the mysterious CIA contract assassin known only by his CIA cryptonym QJ/WIN." Readers of this book can now be assured that a leading figure of the QJ/WIN program was former Nazi SS officer Otto Skorzeny. An official intercession on behalf of Davis with Tangier officials, considered in light of an analysis of Lafitte datebook entries for late October and early November 1963, indicates the seriousness of the role played by Tom Davis.

* * *

As attested to by Carolyn Davis, she and Tom flew to London, Paris, and Madrid before arriving in Tangier, Morocco around November 28. Carolyn failed to mention to the authorities, or to author Albarelli some forty years later, that, according to statements her husband made in 1964/65, their intriguing journey included a stop in Algeria. Again, Tom had told police reporter George Carter that he was extremely concerned he might be dragged into the assassination investigation because he had chosen to use the name "Oswald" during his travels, in spite of his having the perfect alibi for November 22 when (as he insisted several times) he had been arrested in Algiers on the very day. That first arrest (on the same charges as the arrest in Tangier some sixteen days later) must have slipped Carolyn Davis's mind when interviewed over the years, an arrest that clearly provided proof that her husband was not in Dallas on the day of the assassination.

We know from Carolyn's official statement in December 1963 that she and Tom had spent time in London and Paris before making their way to Madrid for the mid-November meeting with global arms dealer, Chase bank representative, and avowed Nazi, Victor Oswald and his business associate, SS Otto Skorzeny.

We now consider another, far more deliberate and essential reason for the elaborate and obviously costly trip of the young, recently married couple in their midtwenties—one of whom had only recently completed parole for armed robbery. The likelihood that the Davises had an assignment beyond the ostensibly credible cover for their trip—for which a letter of introduction from New York attorney Thomas Proctor provided legitimacy when passing through customs—is supported by Lafitte's records.

The reader will recall the datebook entries of October 28 (Monday), and October 29 (Tuesday) that read simply and succinctly:

Lancelot Planning

This would indicate that during the forty-eight-hour period—less than a month before the assassination in Dallas—very definitive plans had been drawn up. Of likely interest to many readers, the former director of the CIA, Allen Dulles, happened to have been in Dallas on those dates, a detail pursued in a later chapter.

One week later, Tuesday, November 5, Pierre writes in his datebook,
O. says Lancelot + Go

As chief tactician for the assassination, renowned for his ability to devise blueprints for highly sophisticated military operations, Otto [O.] Skorzeny would insist on reviewing the schematics and detail that resulted from the "Lancelot Planning" sessions of the 28th and 29th. How might O. have accessed those physical documents? Lafitte provides us with two essential clues. The first, on November 2, reads:

'Runner Runner' w/T. 4 P.M.

"Runner Runner" is a term used by the FBI to refer to an informant. As we learned earlier, Thomas Eli Davis first encountered Pierre Lafitte through his (Davis's) previously unknown activities as a "confidential informer" for the Federal Bureau of Narcotics. Both Hoover's FBI and the FBN, which had enjoyed the services of Lafitte for over a decade, reported to and received funding through the US Department of the Treasury, headed by C. Douglas Dillon in 1963. It was Dillon, along with Allen Dulles, who encouraged Eisenhower to consider the assassination of the prime minister of the independent Democratic Republic of Congo, Patrice Lumumba.

With what appears to have been a crucial encounter on November 2nd, involving the FBI and T.—who served as Lafitte's liaison to his good friend James Angleton—we must revisit a datebook entry made shortly after Thomas Eli Davis and Lee Harvey Oswald were seen together in Mexico City. On October 30, Lafitte writes,

. . . tell Tom D.
O says come to Madrid

Keeping this clear directive in mind, according to Carolyn Davis, the couple departed on their sojourn to Europe and North Africa *about November 2*. Could the Davises have been carrying with them documents and schematics for Otto Skorzeny's perusal?

The November 4 datebook entry is our second clue in support of the hypothesis that the Davises were in fact couriers of vital drawings and written plans for the assassination. Lafitte writes on the 4th:

Roux-Leroy/time
Nov 5

Roux, as identified earlier, was an alias frequently used by expert marksman/ assassin Jean R. Souetre. Leroy refers to Robert Leroy, who, as the reader will recall, was associated with the notoriously lethal Aginter Press (which many argue was tied closely to Permindex), the brutal La Cagoule and OSARN, and, most relevant to the creative strategy required for a broad daylight assassination, Leroy had been one of Otto's lead commando instructors for years. Souetre, with the most to gain by being the direct recipient of the schematics and logistics in Dallas, together with Leroy, another of O's trusted commandos, are likely candidates for the Davises' handoff of the documents sometime between November 2 and November 5.

Further circumstantial evidence that indicates Otto Skorzeny was in possession of Dealey Plaza schematics appears in a November 15 datebook entry that includes:

> Building- phone booth/bridge
> O says turn them

THOMAS ELI DAVIS, JR., IN THE AFTERMATH

Little is known about the life led by Thomas Davis over the ensuing decade. A brief society mention in the Bridgeport, CT, local press in 1965 indicates that Carolyn's parents traveled to San Juan, Puerto Rico, for a visit, after which, Carolyn and two-year-old Thomas returned to Connecticut, where they would begin a new chapter, without Thomas Eli Davis, Jr.

On September 6, 1973, Davis died during what has been described as a "strange and suspicious accident." His badly burned body was found at an abandoned gravel pit in Wise County, north of Fort Worth, Texas. The local sheriff claimed that Davis had been electrocuted by about 7,000 volts carried by a power line. Thinking the line was dead, Davis had tried to cut it during an attempt to steal a large amount of copper wire, a mistake many close to Davis thought not possible. Reportedly, no autopsy was performed on Davis's body, even though this is required by law, but family members have stated that Davis's fingers and head were so badly burned and damaged that identification through fingerprints and dental records was impossible. At the time, said Davis's wife, "I could hardly look at his body, it was just so horribly burned. I relied on other members of his family then."

In 2009, assassination writer Mark Bridger interviewed Davis's nephew, Willie Palm. Said Palm: "None of us that knew him think his death was accidental. He was too smart to pull a dumb stunt like that and the water was muddied very nicely after his death. I worked with him in the late '60s doing some salvage work at the very same location he was later found dead." Palm continued: "He [Davis], in my opinion knew a lot more about the assassination deal than he ever alluded to. I tried to quiz his ex-wife about their dealings in Morocco back in 2000 before her death. We had both had a goodly amount of alcohol and when I brought up the subject, she turned completely cold and damn near sober and said, 'I don't know anything about what you're asking.' Whoever scared her into not talking did a damn good job. Neither of his sons were around him enough to have known him. The daughter that is attributed to him was adopted we think. None of my family has ever met her that I know of. I think she was his last wife's child and his stepchild.

"I was eleven years old when Kennedy was killed. My family had moved away from Texas in 1958 and we returned in '62. I didn't see much of my uncle except on an occasional 'drive by.' I got to know him later in the 60s [sic] but I was still a kid. He didn't talk a lot about his exploits to me. I know he hated Kennedy and wasn't the least upset that he'd been killed. [Thomas] told me that he was involved in the Bay of Pigs invasion and related that they were up to their armpits in the water and getting the shit shot out of them when they found out that Kennedy had withheld the promised air support. He also related stories of parachuting into Cuba, robbing a bank, then stealing a boat to 'high tail' it back to Florida with the loot that was then exchanged for US dollars to pay for fun and finance the next operation." Attempts by these authors in 2019 to discuss with Palm his uncle's history were met with immediate dismissal. Palm's online social presence reflects an extreme far right perspective of US politics.

Attempts to discuss Tom Davis with his son, living in Connecticut, were politely, but firmly rejected: ". . . they divorced when I was two. I never got to know him." When pressed to share what he might have learned from his mother, Carolyn, he said that he had nothing else to say.

Following Thomas Eli Davis's death in 1973, his former wife, Carolyn, was extremely reluctant, and often totally refused, to talk to anyone about him. However, about eighteen months after he died, Carolyn did mention a few people she thought her husband did know well. One she described as "a wealthy guy Tom did some work for in Texas." She later added, "The rich Texan had been a geologist, something that really fascinated [Tom]." Carolyn Davis also mentioned a "Cuban guy, I think, named Lauren, that Tom met in LA." It seems safe to assume that "Lauren" is Loran Eugene Hall, who, like Davis, was a soldier of fortune, and who was in California at the same time that Davis was recruiting for the Haiti invasion.

The rich Texan most likely was Lester L. Logue, who, according to FBI documents, was a Dallas-based petroleum geologist who became a multimillionaire in the oil business. Logue, mentioned in *The Skorzeny Papers*, whose offices were in the Meadows Building off Central Expressway located just minutes from downtown Dallas, is perhaps best known to serious assassination researchers as the Texas oilman and archconservative, who, in a meeting prior to the assassination with several wealthy Texas businessmen, reacted angrily when of one the men proposed, "Here's $50,000 and if the rest of you will match it we'll give it to this man to blow Kennedy's ass off." It has been alleged that a primary source of those proposed funds was Dallas oilman H. L. Hunt. Author Albarelli writes in *A Terrible Mistake* that Hunt had employed Carolyn Hawley Davis as an accountant for a brief period.

Lester Logue was a political associate of US Representative John Rousselot, an ardent member of the John Birch Society which received significant funding from, among others, H. L. Hunt. In 1975, a man named Harry Dean, who claimed to have been a former undercover agent for the FBI and the CIA, reported that in 1963, he had covertly infiltrated the John Birch Society where he learned that Rousselot, in partnership with fellow archconservative and Dallas resident US Army General Edwin Walker, had hired soldier of fortune Loran Hall, and Trafficante associate and gun-for-hire Eladio del Valle, who had been a young legislator in Batista's government, to kill President Kennedy in Dallas, Texas. Dean had no evidence to back up this bold claim, but credible reports that Hall and del Valle had been in Dallas on the fateful day made easy dismissal difficult. Lee Harvey Oswald, it may be recalled, allegedly had attempted to murder General Walker. Walker will be dealt with in depth in a later chapter.

As mentioned previously, Loran Hall intimated that he initially met Tom Davis through Carolyn Hawley Davis, who had briefly worked in Texas "doing accounting chores" for H. L. Hunt.

In 2015 and 2016, the authors filed several FOIAs [Freedom of Information requests] to the CIA for information and files on Thomas Eli Davis, Jr., and Thomas Eli Davis III, and Davis's wife, Carolyn Hawley Davis, who passed away on January 23, 2006. Our initial requests were turned down because of "reasons of national security." Meanwhile, these authors continued to conduct research into Carolyn Hawley Davis to offer a tapestry of the influences on Carolyn's life that led to her role in the events of 1963.

CAROLYN HAWLEY DAVIS

Carolyn Davis (née Hawley), the second wife of Thomas Eli Davis, could trace her Hawley ancestors of Connecticut to Joseph Hawley, 1603–1690. Early

Hawley family wealth derived from involvement in trade with the West Indies, including slavery. Carolyn's father, Samuel Waller Hawley, Sr., was one of the many namesakes of Joseph's first son, Samuel, who married the daughter of Connecticut Governor Thomas Wells, and in the late 1600s, the couple amassed large landholdings around Stratford, Connecticut.

Two centuries later, in 1847, following success in gold mining in the Western United States, another Hawley descendant, Edmund Summers Hawley, cofounded the Bridgeport Savings Bank in Bridgeport, Connecticut. Over the next century, the Hawley name became synonymous with banking and finance in the state and region.

Edmund Hawley's Bridgeport Savings Bank evolved over the next decade and a half, and by 1963, it had been merged into People's Savings Bank Bridgeport with Carolyn's father, S. W. Hawley Sr., president. People's Savings's board had interlocking board members with Connecticut National Bank of Bridgeport, where S. W. and Alexander, his brother (and Carolyn's uncle), were board members and executive vice president, respectively. This lineage, personal and professional, would have been the mainstay of Carolyn ("Kitty") Hawley's life at the time she met and married Thomas Eli Davis, Jr., from Texas, yet coverage of their wedding is virtually nonexistent. The exact circumstance of their first meeting also remains a mystery.

Once the couple divorced in the mid-1960s, Carolyn appears to have assumed a respectable role in her community. According to a news article,

> [Carolyn Hawley Davis] was appointed director of the Bridgeport chapter of Planned Parenthood League of Connecticut (PPL). Mrs. Davis, of Fairfield, formerly was director of special events for the University of Bridgeport. She replaces Royal J. Trew as director; he was killed in a motorcycle accident in July. Mrs. Davis will be responsible for the administration of the voluntary, non-profit agency's program in the Bridgeport area. . . . As UB's [University of Bridgeport, closely association with Columbia University] director of special events since 1972, Mrs. Davis organized and promoted university events, including lectures, concerts, convocations, commencements, dedication ceremonies, fundraising events, and university-community affairs programs; she acted as co chairman of the 1973 and 1974 Puerto Rican Arts festivals. [Bridgeport boasts the largest Puerto Rican community per capita in the US.] She formerly was assistant to the UB director of special events and Business of Columbia University. She is a member of the Planning, Budgeting and Allocations

Council of the United Way of the Eastern Fairfield county, a member of the Advisory Council, Voluntary Action Center of Bridgeport and an advisor of the Spanish and Puerto Rican Organization of Students at UB. [aviation inventor, Igor Sikorsky was a frequent lecturer at the University of Bridgeport.] She is a member of the board of directors of the Connecticut Zoological Society and is a member of the Concerned Woman Colleagues in Bridgeport. Davis was educated at Dana Hall in Wellesley, Massachusetts and at Connecticut College for Women in New London, where she majored in English.

In her midforties when interviewed in New York by Kennedy assassination research expert J. Gary Shaw, Carolyn was a very small, very thin woman, and not "curvy" in any respect. Shaw describes her further: "She was dark-haired, well dressed in dark colored attire neither flashy or classy. There was nothing really striking about her at all. She seemed extremely nervous and upset."

THE BROTHER AND THE SCHLUMBERGER DYNASTY

Carolyn's brother, Bruce Benson Hawley, had entered the family banking and investment business following graduation from Columbia University. While at Columbia, he met a young student from Paris, Josephine Schlumberger, daughter of the late Dr. P. Marc Schlumberger and Lady Diana Barry of London and the Dordogne, who had immigrated to the States to live with close relatives, Sylvie Schlumberger Boissonnas and husband Eric Boissonnas. Sylvie was one of three daughters of the late geophysicist and petroleum engineer, Conrad François Schlumberger. Conrad and his brother Marcel, two of six children of a prominent Protestant Alsatian banking family, received their degrees in engineering in Paris in the early 1900s and founded the oil field exploration company Schlumberger Well Surveying Corporation, which relocated to Houston, Texas, before the onset of WWII.

A son-in-law, Jean de Menil, took the reins and moved with his wife, Dominique Schlumberger de Menil, to Houston. The de Menil name is a recognizable one, particularly significant as he was a board member of Permindex, funded Jacques Soustelle and the OAS, and was an occasional business partner of George de Mohrenschildt. His testimony before the Warren Commission looms in the shadows of this particular area of the investigation with interesting ties to de Mohrenschildt, whose good friend Sam Ballen purchased a division of Schlumberger located in the Texas Panhandle. Sam and George played doubles tennis in early 1963 with Magnolia Labs chemist Everett Glover, who is named in Pierre's records, all of whom are pursued in detail in the "Lay of the Land" chapter of this book.

Another Schlumberger brother, Maurice, launched the Neuflize Schlumberger Bank, which would merge with French Protestant concern Mallet Bank in the 1960s. The Mallet family were French ancestors of a founding partner of the prestigious NY law firm, Curtis Mallet-Prevost (Prevost being a French family as well), alleged to have been involved in the plans to remove Franklin Roosevelt from office—an act that would have ensured the candidacy of Paul V. McNutt for president, with Thomas G. Proctor as his running mate.

* * *

We pause briefly to identify the significant history the Schlumberger family shared with the banking community in Europe and North Africa. In the 1920s, Yvonne Mirabaud, of the Mirabaud financial dynasty based in Geneva, married Jean Godefroy Schlumberger. Another Mirabaud, Nicolas, married into the Doll family, whose relative later married into the Schlumberger. In 1953, mining expert by training and influential banker by choice Henri LaFond, as head of the Mirabaud Group, arranged a merger between his bank and the powerful Bank of the Parisian Union (BUP). He became the chief executive of BUP. As the former chief engineer of the Corps de Mines and Secretary General for Energy for the Vichy, Henri was politically adept when he assumed one of the more powerful and prestigious positions within the global banking community. In his position, Lafond also spent extended periods of time in both Algeria and Morocco. Known as The Pope of the Lafond Group, a loose-knit collection of atomic energy, petroleum, electrometallurgy, heavy chemistry, mining and steel industry executives, he hosted at monthly lunches, a tradition that spanned more than twenty years.

On the morning of March 6, 1963, Lafond was gunned down in his car outside his home in Neuilly, an unsolved murder attributed to the OAS because Lafond purportedly failed to back the maintenance of French Algeria. Other reports suggest that it was either a question of mistaken identity—that the target, another resident of Neuilly who also drove a black Rover, was the editor-in-chief of *L'Echo d'Oran*, which advocated the reconciliation between Algerian and French nationalists—or it was retaliation for Lafond's anticipated intervention with de Gaulle for the pardon of Bastien-Thiry, the man charged with the Petit-Clamart attack. Lafond's assassination occurred the day that the conspirators were condemned to death. Of the network of bankers that the young couple—from either Chico, TX or Mexico City—brushed up against on that trip, it is entirely possible that the grieving Lafond family was among them in November 1963.

Eric and Sylvie Boissonnas, Sylvie's hosts responsible for her introduction to Carolyn's brother, Bruce Hawley, had lived in Connecticut since the late 1940s. A geophysicist by training, Eric served as director of Schlumberger's research laboratory based in Connecticut from 1946 until 1959. He also served on the family-controlled board of directors of Schlumberger Ltd. until dissent with a senior family member resulted in his removal from the board. Soon after, Boissonnas brought his passion for skiing into a joint venture with his brother Rémi when they developed the ambitious resort Flaine station in the Haute Savoie region of the French Alps. As we learned, Rémi and Eric's mother, Yvonne Mirabaud, were from one of the oldest French Protestant Parisian banking families, the Mirabaud Group. The group would eventually merge with the Neuflize, Schlumberger banking concern. Rémi Boissonnas served as a partner at Mirabaud, and following the merger, he was director of Henri Lafond's Bank of The Parisian Union (BUP).

Further indication of just how closely held the Schlumberger family operations were, Anne, the third daughter of the Conrad Schlumberger, married Henri-Georges Doll (a family name associated with another Mirabaud), who for decades was responsible for the company's research and development division and Boissonnas's boss.

* * *

It is difficult to conclude that Bruce Hawley, and by extension his parents and siblings, including Carolyn Davis, were not drawn into the Schlumberger dynamics through his marriage to Josephine. But beyond this familial connection to one of the more prestigious French immigrant families of the twentieth century—already destined to be a global concern essential to the oil industry—we were led even deeper into Carolyn's personal history and the details of her family's bank. Carolyn's father and uncle were board member and executive vice president, respectively, but more germane to this discovery, Connecticut National boasted corporate executives from the Military-Industrial Complex on its board.

The Chairman of the Board of CNB was Charles Krum Davis, who began his career with E. I. du Pont de Nemours & Co., another concern with deep roots in France, which fed America's war machine during both world wars. During WWII, C. K. Davis had served as the vice chairman of the American Ordnance

Association, whose members included at least six present and future board members of Connecticut National Bank who served the US Ordnance Department during the war. These men were executives of ancillary armament companies in Southern Connecticut, including the Bullard Company, whose products were essential to Du Pont. After the war, C. K. Davis had advanced through the ranks of du Pont to be named in 1954 the chairman of the board of the company's Remington Arms, US manufacturer of firearms and ammunition. This would not have been an easy feat within a tightly held French family business similar to Schlumberger Ltd. Board members of the Remington Arms Co. in 1963 included Henry Belin du Pont and William A. Rockefeller, as well as F. B. Silliman, who served on the board of the Connecticut National Bank and its affiliated financial institution in Bridgeport.

The official address of the Remington Arms Co. was the Hawley's Connecticut National Bank building, 888 Main St., Bridgeport, CT. A similar pattern of interlocking interests emerged in Houston. Schlumberger Ltd., and the Bank of the Southwest, along with the oil firm's counsel, Leon Jaworski, shared the bank's office building in the posh area of Post Oak. It will be remembered, Jaworski (also on the bank board) was a member of the legal team at the Nuremberg Trials alongside fellow Texan and good friend Robert G. Storey, both of whom feature in the Dallas chapter of this book. As will be revealed, Pierre Lafitte was familiar enough to reference Storey in his datebook at a critical juncture in the lead-up to the assassination.

Of potential relevance to the broader investigation, Remington Arms was a sister of the Remington Rand Corporation, which evolved into Sperry-Rand Corporation, whose chairman emeritus in 1963 was General Douglas MacArthur; his president was Harry Franklin Vickers. MacArthur was a long-term resident of the Waldorf Astoria in NYC, which had been managed by CIA operative Warren Broglie before his move to Mexico City and the Hotel Luma. MacArthur, who received pressure (and funding) from Dallas oilmen H. L. Hunt and Clint Murchison to run for president, famously referred to General Charles Willoughby as his "little fascist." Willoughby dominates the pursuit of who killed JFK.

The MacArthur/Vickers Sperry-Rand board included J. H. Rand, who is known to have been involved with sending, and later "retrieving" from Russia, Robert Edward Webster, whose modus operandi closely resembles that of accused assassin Lee Harvey Oswald.

Du Pont corporation's Remington Arms, headquartered in the Hawley bank building in Bridgeport, occupied a sales and supply office in Dallas in 1963. The location they chose was the Meadows Building, headquarters of Algur Meadows's

General American Oil Co., a firm that participated in Otto Skorzeny's 1952 scheme in Spain, along with other Texas independent oilmen, and Generalissimo Franco. In 1963, Meadows and Skorzeny reunited and launched a petroleum chemical operation in East Texas.

A little-known fact is that Dallas real estate magnate Mattie Caruth Byrd married David Harold Byrd, who owned 411 Elm that housed the Texas School Book Depository, officed next door to Remington Arms in the Meadows Building. Mattie was the daughter of W. W. Caruth, Sr., whose homestead provided the land for Southern Methodist University, where Nuremberg trial attorney Robert G. Storey built his reputation as a legal expert for the oil and gas industry. Other names ceremoniously inscribed on the buildings at SMU include oilmen Algur Meadows, Buddy Fogelson, and Jake Hamon (president of the National Petroleum Institute in '63), each with their own stake in Skorzeny's scheme in Spain. Caruth, Sr., was on the small board of Ralph Rogers's Texas Industries, a cement and gravel business with operations in Chico, Texas, where Thomas Eli Davis died.

* * *

Returning to Connecticut and the Hawley family, Remington Arms's parent company and C. K. Davis's first employer, E. I. du Pont de Nemours and Company, built an empire on the production and sale of gunpowder. During the Great Depression, it purchased Remington Arms, and in 1940 when the US Army became worried about its ammunition capacity, it asked Remington to collaborate in a plan for national expansion. With significant financing by du Pont, Remington built the Lake City Army Ammunition Plant (originally named the Lake City Arsenal) in Missouri, and Denver Ordnance ammunition plants, later adding three more plants, including the Lowell Ordnance Plant. Though the plants belonged to the US government, Remington was asked to oversee their operation, a reflection of the burgeoning symbiosis between the US military and industry.

Du Pont, which currently employs over 60,000 people around the globe, created its own financial concern, Delaware-based Christian Securities; however, Remington Arms clearly considered the Hawley's Connecticut National Bank a financial arm of its company—with representatives from the WWII US Ordnance Board as active board members the following decades. There can be no doubt that those executives in charge of operations of the bank received high-level security clearance, possibly stirring additional interest of the reader in Carolyn's marriage to Thomas Eli Davis, Jr.

Carolyn's father was elected the chairman of the National Association of Mutual Savings Banks in the early '60s. In that role, Samuel Waller Hawley had been called to testify before the US Senate in the spring of 1963, drawing sufficient publicity that by the late fall, it would have been easy for the State Department to trace Carolyn Hawley, once the report of the Davis couple's escapade in Tangier crossed the desk of the secretary.

Relevant to Sam Hawley's notable business profile is a review of the namesake of the progenitor of the Hawley banking dynasty, Edmund Summers Hawley. Edmund was an attorney for AT&T for three-and-a-half decades before becoming a director and administrator for the Institute of World Affairs. By 1963, he was the executive in charge of the IWA, an organization inspired by humanist, psychic researcher, and vice president of the League of Nations Gilbert Murray. The institute, meant to foster international relations with a focus on university students around the world, was funded by Alexander Hadden and his wife, Maude.

Originally based in Geneva, at the outbreak of the war, the Haddens opened an office in NYC. Over the years, the philanthropists created the Palm Beach Round Table—a series of small, elite political symposiums, not unlike those developed by the president of military contractor Dresser Industries, H. Neil Mallon, under auspices of the Dallas World Affairs Council. Allen Dulles was a sought-after speaker at both the IWA and the DWAC. In 1960, DCIA Dulles, in spite of concerted influence from his investment partner, Hugh Bullock of the firm Calvin Bullock and Nation-Wide Securities, was compelled to postpone an invitation to Maude's Round Table due to the workload of the incoming administration but promised to consider a future date. In 1958, Under Secretary Robert Murphy—whom readers will recall from earlier chapters—was the featured speaker at the 35th anniversary of IWA. NYC headquarters of the institute, then directed by Carolyn Hawley's close relative Edmund Hawley, were located at 527 Madison Ave., which, at the height of US conflict with Castro, housed the Cuban Families Committee for the Liberation of Prisoners of War.

The Hawleys' banking operation in Connecticut attracted to the board, founded by their common ancestor in the mid-1800s, the famed aviation pioneer Igor Sikorsky, a native of Kiev [now the capital of Ukraine]. Of significance to our inquiry into Tom and Carolyn Hawley Davis, in 1963, Igor was the honorary chairman of the Tolstoy Foundation, an aid organization that he helped found in 1939. On the board of the foundation in '63 was Herschel V. Williams, a Sr. VP of Previews, Inc., where Ilse Skorzeny enjoyed cover, as well as Paul Raigorodsky, the Russian-born oil geologist based in Dallas, known as the

"Czar of the White Russian community." Raigorodsky had served as head of the Office of Petroleum Coordination for War during the war, reporting to Donald Nelson (a corporate alumni of Sears & Roebuck), who was chief of the WPB; Nelson in turn, reported to Roosevelt's Secretary of the Interior, Harold Ickes, who was succeeded by Thomas Proctor's good friend and future law partner, Paul McNutt, as High Commissioner of the Philippines. At the time, Raig-orodsky's father-in-law was the vice chairman of the Dallas branch of the Federal Reserve Board in the 1920s.

Raigorodsky and H. V. Williams have already been mentioned, but for the purpose of understanding the significance of the petroleum geologist as a pivotal character in Dallas in the lead-up to the assassination as well as Williams's role in real estate venture Previews, Inc., it is important to first absorb the context of these Connecticut connections, including those with the Hawleys' bank. It was Raigorodsky who testified before the Warren Commission that Jean de Menil of Schlumberger, Ltd., was in direct discussions with George de Mohrenschildt related to operations in Haiti the summer of 1963—around the time that the Hawleys' daughter Carolyn was living with her husband, Tom Davis, in Southern California as he staged a recruitment for the invasion of the island.

When interviewed by authorities, Carolyn explained that she and Tom were traveling on her credit card; she also stated that she was employed by a "type writer firm." Bridgeport-based Underwood Typewriter (a military contractor during WWII) had a plant in Van Nuys, CA, just thirty minutes from Ventura, where the Davises said they resided when questioned by authorities at the Tahiti Village motel in Downey, CA. Carolyn's family bank board in Bridgeport included Dennis. S. Sammis, senior vice president of Underwood Corp. (See additional implications of the aforementioned detail in Endnotes to this chapter.)

Thus exemplifies the milieu and events surrounding the twenty-six-year-old bride, Carolyn Hawley Davis—steeped in three centuries of New England banking and social standing—as she stepped off that plane in Madrid with her new husband, twenty-seven-year-old jack-of-all-trades, a convicted felon and soldier of fortune from Texas, Thomas Eli Davis.

* * *

While Tom and Carolyn Davis were preparing for their September 1963 jaunt to Mexico City, where they had lived periodically, Lee Harvey Oswald was standing in line with William Gaudet. Both men were there to secure a visitor's visa allowing them into Mexico. Many familiar with assassination research will be familiar with the name Gaudet as the man who boarded the same bus in the Crescent City as Oswald on September 26 en route to Mexico City. As we learned, Lafitte entered the name Gaudet in his datebook following the words "Oswald – Mex City."

Gaudet, recognized by many assassination researchers as having worked for the CIA, is identified by Lafitte on September 22. Six days later, on the 28th of September, Lafitte's note reads, *Bowen & Hudson- Mex School cover- wife Spain -Rene to see her in [illegible],* leading to the next phase of the investigation.

CHAPTER 6
LONG SHADOWS

Bowen & Hudson- mx city
school cover- wife Spain-
Rene to see her in [illegible].
—Lafitte datebook, September 28, 1963

Hudson—Canada—
w/wife in British
Embassy.
—Lafitte datebook, October 10, 1963

—QRTS—
Day 1- Ruby- Wilson-H -
Bond . . .
— call Ilse NYC
—Lafitte datebook, October 30, 1963

Shadow: a dark (real image) area where light
from a light source is blocked by an opaque object.

Like a cancer, the assassination of President Kennedy cast a long shadow. A few weeks after he had been appointed director of Central Intelligence in January 1976, George Herbert Walker Bush asked his deputy director, former Agency analyst E. Henry Knoche, if he was familiar with information about Lee Oswald's assassin Jack Ruby visiting Santo Trafficante in a jail in Cuba before JFK's death in Dallas. DDCI Knoche said that he would check his files, but he failed to get back to Bush.

On September 15, 1976, DCI Bush sent a brief, typed note to Knoche asking: "A recent Jack Anderson story referred to a November 1963 (?) CIA cable, the subject matter of which had some [redacted] journalist observing Jack Ruby visiting Trafficante in jail. Is there such a cable? If so, I would like to see it."

The memo goes on to state and conclude: "This is the same cable that Mike Madigan, Minority Counsel for the SSC, has asked for."

A handwritten note, dated the next day, at the bottom of the page reads: "[Redacted name] gave me this, advising that at the time he was passing this [undistinguishable] to the IG, as DDCI was out of town." (See Endnotes.)

TRESCORNIA DETENTION CAMP, CUBA, AUGUST 8, 1959

Jack Ruby was over two hours late.

> *"Where the hell is he?" Santo Trafficante Jr. asked Dino Cellini in a low voice.*
> *"Don't worry, boss. He's coming. It isn't exactly easy to get here," Cellini said.*
> *Jake Lansky laughed and held out a glass of lemonade to Trafficante.*
> *"He's always late," Lansky said.*

Jack Ruby, Lee Oswald's assassin, was always late, but this time he had a good excuse. Ruby had used a fake passport under a different name to enter Cuba. A Cuban immigration officer (a Cuban soldier acting in this capacity) had thought he recognized Ruby at the entry gate as having visited before under a different name. Ruby talked his way out of a possible bad situation but was nearly three hours late in arriving at Trescornia Camp.

Trafficante had been picked up by the Cuban police on about June 9, 1959. He was then confined to the Trescornia camp. The reason for his detention has never been adequately explained by the Cuban or American governments. Writer Scott M. Deitche states that the camp "was a plain white one-story structure that was known as the Ellis Island of Cuba. It was where immigrants were held after disembarking in Havana Bay and before they were cleared to emerge on the island: 'Santo had a deep and wide cell to himself, and it was comfortably furnished. The cell to the left was designed for 4–6 inmates—but was crammed with about 17 to 20 on a regular basis. Included in that cell were Leslie Bradley, Hudson, Loran Hall, et al.' Narcotics figure Lucien Rivard was also detained at Trescornia, as were other gambling figures."

Of those named by Trafficante, readers are already familiar with Loran Eugene Hall, understood to have known alleged assassination bagman John Martino; Lucien Rivard, whose 1965 daring escape from prison in Canada would make headline news in the US as a known narcotics smuggler operating out of

Havana; and Leslie Bradley, trained pilot and self-described soldier of fortune who had been arrested for plotting and participating in an invasion of Nicaragua meant to embarrass Fidel Castro. According to FBI documents, "Cuban authorities charged that the [Nicaragua] plot was hatched on orders from the United States (CIA) to discredit the Castro regime." The lesser-known individual identified by Trafficante as "Hudson" was also involved in that failed plot. Deitsch writes that Hudson was an alleged "British Journalist," sometimes called Carlos Juan Wilson-Hudson, who "reportedly worked for Batista." We know with certainty that he was known to Pierre Lafitte as J. Wilson-Hudson, a.k.a. JW-H. Before delving into this obscure character identified by Trafficante as being present in Trescornia when Ruby visited the prison, it is important to place that imprisonment in context.

As revealed by author Albarelli in *A Secret Order*, over the years Leslie Bradley had dealt with a number of known mercenaries before advancing the Managua scheme, including Nicaraguan Chester Lacayo, Cuban army officer Maj. Jesus Carreras, legendary American soldier of fortune William Alexander Morgan, Loran Hall (both of whom have been discussed previously), David Morales (well known to students of the Kennedy assassination), and would-be journalist/soldier of fortune, Robert E. Johnson, whose significance will be made evident later in the chapter.

On November 14, 1977, Trafficante provided immunized testimony before the House Select Committee on Assassinations. The committee report on his testimony reads in part:

> Trafficante testified that there were two sections of Trescornia. In his section, there were never more than six or seven people. He stated that most of the time he was there the same people were incarcerated with him. There was a fellow named Civello, another named Gisseppi de George, and a man named Charles del Monico. There was also a man named Merola and a "young kid that came from the Johannson fight." Trafficante also stated there was "another guy which I read in the paper was supposedly a journalist [Hudson]. . . . I remember him vaguely. I didn't even know he was a . . . they used to come and go. It was not a matter that they would stay." Trafficante described the man as "a kook, a funny guy. For me he was a mental case." Trafficante admitted speaking to him and stated "when he came in there they made him look like a joke, he was supposed to fill out his food for the next day, the night before, like . . . Like breakfast and dinner and supper and he had to order it the day before. And that was

all in fun, he never would get . . . until we finally had to give him some of
our food.

This composed the entirety of Trafficante's less than articulate, and illuminat-
ing, comments on John Wilson-Hudson, a.k.a. John Carlos Wilson-Hudson/
Carl John Wilson-Hudson.

According to some authoritative writers, Jack Ruby had gone to Cuba to try
to arrange to get Trafficante released from detention, but there is no certainty
about this. Dallas reporter and writer Seth Kantor wrote in 1978: "There are no
U.S. Immigration and Naturalization Service records to show the dates of [the
Ruby visit involving Trafficante] that Ruby visit of several days to Havana—
although INS records do show that Ruby did fly from Miami to Havana on
Saturday, September 12, 1959, and then from Havana to New Orleans on September 13. Ruby never was asked for an explanation of that second trip—a yoyo
trip in which he bounced down to Cuba and back in a twenty-four-hour-span,
after having just visited Cuba for several days."

Kantor also writes: "Ruby told the Warren Commission that he found the trip
to Cuba somewhat of a bore, with little to do while McWillie was at work.
[McWillie was Lewis J. McWillie who allegedly traveled to Havana with Ruby.
McWillie had been an employee of Trafficante when the Mafia chief ran several
hotel and gambling properties in Havana. McWillie was also a known
gunrunner.]"

Continues Kantor: "*But a highly classified CIA message—kept from the Warren
Commission staff—indicated Ruby had found someone special to talk with during
the Havana trip; an American racketeer associated with McWillie, who did use an
assumed name. He was known, when he wanted to be, by the name of Louis Santos.
The classified message about Santos [actually Santo Trafficante Jr.] was sent Thanksgiving Day, November 28, 1963 (four days after Ruby shot Oswald), from CIA
headquarters to: McGeorge Bundy, President Johnson's special assistant for national
security affairs; U. Alexis Johnson, deputy undersecretary of State; and the FBI.*" [Ital-
ics added.]

The CIA's message reads:

On 26 November 1963, a British journalist named John Wilson, and also
known as John Wilson-Hudson, gave information to the American
Embassy in London which indicated that an "American gangster-type
named Ruby visited Cuba around 1959." Wilson himself was working in
Cuba at the time and was jailed by Castro before he was deported.

Assassination researcher Mike Sylvester, in a thorough analysis focused on mob connections and the assassination, published in *JFK Lancer* in 1993, asserts that at the end of June 1959, Wilson and three Americans were arrested in a suburb of Havana as they planned to carry out a sneak bomb raid on Nicaragua, using three airplanes and a small volunteer attack force. Fidel Castro had nothing to do with the attack plans and ordered Wilson and the other ringleaders arrested; thus, John Wilson was in jail at the time of the Ruby visit.

The message continues . . .

> In prison in Cuba, Wilson says he met an American gangster gambler named Santos who could not return to the USA because there were several indictments outstanding against him. [This is false. There were no indictments.] Instead, he preferred to live in relative luxury in a Cuban prison. While Santos was in prison, Wilson says, Santos was visited frequently by an American gangster type named Ruby. His story is being followed up. Wilson says he had once testified before the Eastland committee of the U.S. Senate sometime in 1959 or 1960.

Writes Kantor on this message: "The next day, according to a heavily doctored memorandum in CIA files, the FBI came up with a preliminary report that the Englishman John Wilson 'likely be psychopath [*sic*] We gather he gave this impression when testifying before Eastland Committee in 1959. Both the message on Wilson and the following day's memorandum were kept secret until mid-1976, when Washington attorney Bernard Fensterwald Jr. flushed it out through the Freedom of Information Act, along with hundreds of other CIA documents relating to the Kennedy assassination dating as far back as 1963. A check of the files of the Senate Judiciary Subcommittee on Internal Security, headed by Senator James O. Eastland of Mississippi, shows that while the Eastland panel explored a long list of hot political areas of Latin America in 1959 and 1960, Wilson does not appear on the witness list under any of the names he used . . ."

-see J. Dallas
T. says L.O. is 'idiot'
But w be used regardless
Set-up complete
JW-H
—Lafitte datebook, September 19, 1963

Considering this entry, it is provocative to underscore that the heavily "doctored" section of the memorandum that Kantor points out (now declassified) deals with Lee Harvey Oswald and his trip through London, England. The once-classified message reads: "No traces on OSWALD in Criminal Records Office. However, traffic index shows that OSWALD arrived in Southampton 9 October 1959 claiming in his landing card he had no fixed address but planned to remain in the U.K. for one week for vacation before going on to 'some school in Suisse.' However, he left London the next day 10 October by air for Helsinki. There are no records on return from USSR to US He passed through U.K. However, if moving thru in transit only it not necessary fill out landing card and therefore traffic index would not have record." The remainder of the message deals only with John (Wilson) Hudson. Was there some sort of link being pursued concerning Oswald and Hudson? Or was this simply a routine message dealing with U.K.-related information?

Kantor goes on: "U.S. Embassy records in London referred to Wilson only as a self-described 'free-lance journalist,' residing in Chile during most of the 1940s and 1950s. Wilson told American Embassy officials that he actually had been working for Cuban dictator Batista in the late 1950s and was deported by Castro after a term of imprisonment in 1959 . . . But a confidential November 28, 1963, memorandum from the office of Richard M. Helms, at that time CIA deputy director for plans, reveals much more about Wilson. The CIA file on him went back to 1951."

The confidential November 28, 1963, memorandum by Helms was sent to Sam Papich at the FBI. The file, wrote Kantor, "shows that Wilson [was] well educated at Oxford University [England], had been born in Liverpool, December 29, 1916, had reached Chile on January 28, 1939, from Buenos Aires, and 'was a contact of one Bert Sucharov, a suspected Soviet agent in Santiago, Chile.'"

THE MYSTIFYING JOHN WILSON-HUDSON

Who exactly was John Wilson-Hudson, and why does he appear in Pierre Lafitte's 1963 datebook? The short answer is that we now know Hudson was involved with the World Commerce Corporation (WCC) and had direct dealings with Otto Skorzeny.

The authors have unearthed information on Wilson-Hudson that is no less than intriguing and germane to our story. Described in government documents as having brown hair, blue-green eyes, a ruddy complexion, a small mustache, and wearing glasses, the official observed him as being very intelligent, astute, and well informed on current events. He carried with him a UN press pass (his wife, Eliana Gabriela, was active with the UN) issued in Santiago, as well as a document authorizing him to enter at will the Los Cerrillos airport in the country's capital at any time, issued by the International Police Section of the Chilean Investigation Service.

Gleaned from a number of CIA documents, we learned the following:

(1) Wilson-Hudson was a Spanish citizen of British descent who resided sometimes in Madrid and sometimes in Chile. He first arrived in Chile on 28 January 1939 bearing a Spanish passport. He was born in Liverpool, England, on 29 December 1916 or 1917. He studied at Oxford University in England and left his studies there in July 1936 "to enlist as a volunteer in the Spanish Loyalist Forces, whereupon he acquired his Spanish citizenship." Wilson-Hudson was married to Eliana (Gabriella Sara) Bronfman-(Weinstein).

(2) Wilson-Hudson, while in Chile in the capacity as a journalist, "opened a one-man crusade against the British Government, in violation of restrictions placed on such activities by foreigners in Chile."

(3) Wilson-Hudson's businesses were described by the CIA as "consisting of trade in copper, lead, and Sulphur." In the late 1950s, he traded in illicit nickel.

(4) A CIA report read: "Another report dated 20 June 1959 from a usually reliable source stated that PAUL HUGHES, an American soldier of fortune, claimed to have at his disposal three aircraft, including one bomber, and planned to launch an attack on Puerto Cabanas, Nicaragua, during the weekend of 27–28 June 1959. Hughes said that Carl WILSON, a British journalist, and about 65 volunteers would join him in the attack. Source commented that HUGHES also vaguely spoke of possibly bombing Managua for the psychological effect. WILSON said that Castro had no knowledge of HUGHES' plan."

(5) United Press International carried the story datelined 1 July 1959 from Havana, Cuba, saying that Police had raided a private home in suburban Biltmore the day before and seized a large quantity of arms and arrested three Americans and a Briton. The Americans were identified as Paul HUGHES, an officer in Castro's rebel army; Efron R. PICHARDO, of Miami, Florida; and Joseph BARDOR, of Los Angeles, California. The Briton was listed as Carl John WILSON.

Assassination researcher Mike Sylvester, in a 1993 article for JFK Lancer focused on mob connections to the assassination, advances details of the charges: "At the end of June 1959, Wilson and three Americans were arrested in a suburb of Havana as they planned to carry out a sneak bomb raid on Nicaragua, using three airplanes and a small volunteer attack force. Fidel Castro had nothing to do with the attack plans and ordered Wilson and the other ringleaders arrested; thus John Wilson was in jail at the time of the Ruby visit."

A 1951 secret memorandum from the CIA director to the FBI's director warned that John Wilson Hudson "is suspected of having dealings" with Bert Sucharov (a.k.a. Zakharov), a Canadian and suspected Soviet "paymaster" and agent.

A member of the Royal Canadian Engineers involved in the Dieppe Raid of August 1942, and known as the "The Mad Major" for his recklessness under fire while commanding one of two main groups of the Beach Assault Party, Bert Sucharov trained as an engineer before joining the RCE. According to a distant relative, "Bert was from Winnipeg, Canada, and he was in the military and served overseas I believe." After offering to introduce this author to a closer relative, she added, "In the meantime I will say it sounds like the same Bert Sucharov, *given that he did end up in SA.* Can't say whether he was a paymaster or not; I have absolutely no knowledge of anything to do with that. Will keep you posted if I hear back from his family." When contacted, the closer relative, writing from Rio de Janeiro, Brazil, was adamant: "I clarify to you that Mr. Bert Sucharov never had any dealings in Chile, and in 1951 he was not a major. I have never heard of the other names mentioned in your attachment. The soviet paymaster story is absolute nonsense."

At least two of the enterprises that Wilson-Hudson engaged in with the World Commerce involved the participation of "former" Nazi SS officer and Madrid resident Otto Skorzeny. In light of their previous history, a letter from Otto to his wife, Ilse, dated 14 April 1962, must be highlighted. Otto tells Ilse that he's expecting the arrival of Encio [suspected to be reference to former Cuban dictator Fulgencio Batista] coming from LUXEMBERG [*sic*] and is curious as to "what news he brings," adding the words "Nothing good." Twelve days later, on 26 April 1962, a message from the CIA Station Chief in LUXEMBERG is sent to the Director concerning QJ/WIN and a nickel smuggling case from 1954.

In fact, in 1954, Skorzeny had indeed been involved in nickel smuggling, confirmed in a US government document:

Skorzeny 201 File Document Control No. 6004 15 July 1954. According to overt information H. S. LUCHT COMPANY maintains business connections with a firm which is "known to engage in illegal trade with the Soviet Zone." The Madrid representative of LUCHT COMPANY is Otto Skorzeny, who appears to be involved in *the smuggling of nickel out of Spain for eventual Bloc destination.* [Italics added.]

The Lucht company was owned by Herbert S. Lucht, former head of the External Abteilung für Wehrmachtpropaganda (German Army Propaganda) in Paris. According to investigative journalist Joachim Joesten, Herbert's wife, Lea "Sissy" Lucht, was a niece of Belgian Rexist léader Leon Degrelle. As will be pursued in a later chapter, Degrelle had joined forces with Otto Skorzeny; Werner Naumann, who was the former undersecretary of the Nazi Propaganda Ministry; and the Luchts to form the Naumann Circle, dedicated to the restoration of the Reich.

Datebook entries show Wilson-Hudson was in and out of Canada during1963, and, combined with his shared past with Winnipeg native Bert Sucharov, the role of Canada as a nickel supplier to the US looms large. That role had been swiftly elevated when Fidel Castro nationalized the mining of nickel on the island of Cuba. The hard silvery-white metal whose "strength, ductility and resistance to heat and corrosion make it extremely useful for the development of a wide variety of materials—from wires to coins to *military equipment*" was far more than purely symbolic on the list of grievances the US military-industrial complex had against Fidel.

To place Wilson-Hudson in further context, we pause to consider the long shadow cast by beneficiaries of global trade in nickel.

A TRUE WAR METAL

Nickel is "the closest to being a true 'war metal.'"
—U.S. Department of Defense report, 1954

"Given the chance, Hitler would willingly have traded the whole Silesian basin, and thrown in Hermann Goering and Dr. Goebbels to boot, for a year's possession of the Sudbury Basin," journalist James H. Gray aptly wrote in an October 1947 article for *Maclean's* (Canada's weekly news magazine) about Sudbury Nickel Irruptive, a major geological structure in Ontario, Canada, and one of the world's largest suppliers of nickel and copper ores. Three decades later, Toronto-based communications consultant Stan Sudol, with an expertise in mining, reveals in his four-part series titled *The Republic of Nickel*, "the metallic 'Achilles heel' for any military and naval production has always been nickel . . . There has always been a largely ignored umbilical cord link between Sudbury's strategic nickel mines and the US military-industrial complex. Originally, it was American money and entrepreneurs who built the Sudbury mines and smelters."

According to Sudol, after WWII there was a small decline in nickel use, but the expanding North American economy, the rebuilding of war-shattered Europe, the Korean War, and the start of the Cold War continued to put pressure on this vital commodity. Prior to 1956 and significant finds elsewhere in Canada, "the only other major reserves of this metal outside of the Sudbury Basin were in the Soviet Union and Cuba. Fidel Castro nationalized previously owned American nickel mines during the Cuban Revolution of 1959. It is worth noting that in some circles, a full-blown war in Vietnam was a distinct possibility on the not too distant horizon."

In his speech before the United Nations, September 26, 1960, Fidel Castro explained, "But in our country the land was not the only thing in the hands of the US monopolies. The principal mines were also in the hands of the monopolies. For example, Cuba produces large amounts of nickel, and all the nickel was controlled by US interests. Under the Batista dictatorship, a US company called Moa Bay had obtained such a juicy concession that in a mere five years—mark my words, in a mere five years—it sought to amortize an investment of $120 million. A $120 million investment amortized in five years! So the revolutionary government passed a mining law that obliged these monopolies to pay a 25 percent tax on the export of minerals."

The shockwave of Castro nationalizing the Nicaro and Moa Bay facilities owned by the US government's General Services Administration and operated by privately held Freeport Sulphur Co. under its subsidiaries reverberated through the military-industrial complex. With a similar level of concern related to recent alarms that Cuba's sugar industry would be nationalized, DCI Allen Dulles turned his attention to nickel.

Buried in very bland government reports, DCI Allen Dulles had reported that the USSR was interested in buying Cuban nickel. "It was estimated that Soviet production met the nickel needs of the USSR but not the needs of the entire Communist bloc . . . The Soviet Five-Year Plan showed that the Sino Soviet Bloc as a whole was short of nickel. President Eisenhower said, 'it might be necessary to blockade Cuba yet.'" Within the year, America's nickel requirements had shifted fully to her neighbors to the north. However, the animosity of the agency's upper echelon, along with the corporate boards of a myriad of American companies with enormous investments in Cuba, similar to that of Freeport Sulphur, continued to smolder. Fidel was in their crosshairs.

These men would have also been keenly aware of the essential role that nickel played in the driving force of America's economy (as well as that of the economies of its perceived enemies), the petroleum industry. Technology had made possible the quantum leaps in oil field equipment design during the '50s and '60s, so nickel alloys that could sustain exposure to intense heat were in high demand for oil and gas exploration, drilling, and production worldwide. Also important to understand, those same qualities had quickly become critical to the evolution of nuclear power in all its forms based on the durability and resistance to corrosion and degradation at hot temperatures. The race for nuclear power and dominance was in full throttle.

Adding insult to injury, while reeling from its losses over Castro's appropriation of the nickel plants, following Kennedy's election Freeport Sulphur found itself under attack from a new quarter: a Senate investigation into stockpiling surpluses, requested by the president himself. In author Lisa Pease's thorough investigation into Freeport Sulphur, under the subheading "Freeport versus Kennedy: The Stockpiling Investigation . . ." in 1962, "President Kennedy asked Congress to look into the war-emergency stockpiling program, stating it was, a potential source of excessive and unconscionable profits., He said he was, astonished, to discover that the program had accumulated $7.7 billion worth of stockpiled material, exceeding projected needs by $3.4 billion. Kennedy also pledged full executive cooperation with the investigation, mentioning specifically $103 million in surplus nickel. The Senate pursued an investigation into stockpiling surpluses. Special attention was paid to three companies in which the Rockefeller brothers had substantial holdings: Hannah Mining, International Nickel, and Freeport Sulphur. A December 18, 1962 headline in the *New York Times* read 'U.S. Was Pushed into Buying Nickel, Senators Are Told.' The controversy spilled over into 1963, and Press Secretary Pierre Salinger stated that the Kennedy administration planned to make stockpiling an issue in the 1964 campaign."

On the heels of Kennedy's aggressive attack on US steel and oil monopolies, and his court challenge of the state of Texas's rights to tidelands for oil exploration, the question of stockpiling critical defense/war material, including nickel—"the only true war metal"—further highlights the threat posed to corporate interests by a Kennedy second term in office.

As noted in an earlier chapter, Lafitte had been indicted in 1962 in Boston on fifteen counts of mail fraud and transportation of stolen property after he allegedly swindled an investor, Ralph L. Loomis of Kittery Point, Maine, out of $350,000 through an alleged scheme aimed at financing mineral mining rights and diamond mines in Africa, *as well as nickel mining rights*, and fraudulent stock transfers involving Canadian Javelin Ltd. As we read, Lafitte had also talked his business associate, Harold Meltzer, into investing in both. Meltzer, the reader will recall, wasn't just a friend of mob boss Meyer Lansky, but a leading candidate for Siragusa's assassination team at the behest of the CIA.

* * *

Further to this alleged swindle of Ralph Loomis, we learn from court documents relating to an SEC case, "On December 23, 1958, we filed a complaint for an injunction in the United States District Court for the District of MA which alleged, among other things, that registrant and one Ralph L. Loomis were offering for sale unregistered stock of Canadian Javelin, Ltd., were circulating articles and communications describing such stock for a consideration received and to be received from the issuer and from underwriters without fully disclosing the receipt of such consideration and the amount thereof and were engaging in transactions, practices and a course of business which operated as a fraud and deceit on purchasers."

In discussing this case, the agent opined, "John Doyle, [the founder of Canadian Javelin, Ltd.] is not a fugitive from justice. He is, however, a genuine financial wizard, a skilled organist and a native of the US who may not return to that country because, as John Diefenbaker once inelegantly put it, 'he will end up in the coop for three years if he does.' He is also Chairman of the Executive Committee of Canadian Javelin Limited, a Newfoundland corporation described to me by a US government lawyer who has studied it for years as 'the most mysterious company known to man.' Canadian Javelin, through a network of subsidiaries, controls huge quantities of iron ore and timber in Labrador, oil and potash in Saskatchewan, silver in El Salvador, and other minerals from northern Quebec to Arizona." Lafitte's indictment for defrauding Ralph Loomis would have been ancillary to the SEC cases against Loomis and Payton.

"The most mysterious company known to man" harkens back to the World Commerce Corporation, described similarly by those searching the history of WCC. Wilson-Hudson was known to deal in nickel, to have been involved in at least two transactions with WCC, and to have had deep connections in Canada. It should be noted that John Doyle, founder of "the most mysterious company known to man," also spent much of his time on Nassau Island in the Bahamas along with a number of our persons of interest who were also involved with the World Commerce Corporation, including Sir Stafford Sands and Otto and Ilse Skorzeny. And it is further noted that Thomas Eli Davis listed as a recent employer *New Netherlands Mining*. While it is doubtful he worked for what was a long-defunct company by that name, it is worth contemplating that he meant Javelin's concern, *Newfoundland Mining*.

According to accounts, during that year, the Securities and Exchange Commission brought ten civil actions and instituted three criminal actions in which the illegal sale of Canadian securities in the United States was involved. Details concerning these actions include SEC v. Ralph L. Loomis and F. Payson Todd, SEC v. Canadian Javelin Limited, et al.: "On December 23, 1958, we [SEC] filed a complaint for an injunction in the United States District Court for the District of MA which alleged, among other things, that registrant and one Ralph L. Loomis were offering for sale unregistered stock of Canadian Javelin, Ltd., (a crime that a number of soldiers of fortune were accused of in the same time frame) were circulating articles and communications describing such stock for a consideration received and to be received from the issuer and from underwriters without fully disclosing the receipt of such consideration and the amount thereof and were engaging in transactions, practices and a course of business which operated as a fraud and deceit on purchasers."

A NICKEL DEAL IN THE MIDST OF AN ASSASSINATION PLOT

Analysis of a string of Lafitte datebook entries supports the hypothesis that Pierre was at least privy to, if not the orchestrator of, yet another nickel transaction that was underway in the summer and fall of 1963, and that John Wilson-Hudson was involved.

June 7, 1963
Else [*sic*] and W's wife= shipment $
-John 'Wilson-H'—Ruby

June 18, 1963
(Willoughby meet 8:000 pm)

June 19, 1963
ILSE 8:00 PM

June 25, 1963
nickel deposits $ Skorzeny – talk Ilse

September 16, 1963
-see J. Dallas
T. says L.O. is 'idiot'
But w be used regardless

Set-up complete
JW-H

September 28, 1963
Bowen & Hudson- mx city
School cover- wife Spain
Rene to meet her in [indistinguishable]

October 10, 1963
-Hudson- Canada
wife British Embassy

October 30, 1963
-QRTS-
Day 1- Ruby - <u>Wilson</u>-H -
Bond . . .
Call <u>Ilse NYC</u>

On June 7, Lafitte indicates a significant transaction involving the essential metal was underway; however, with the appearance of the name (Jack) Ruby, a character who we know with certainty would play one of the most significant roles in events that weekend in Dallas.

Lafitte also writes: *Ilse and W's wife = shipment $* and on the second line, *John Wilson-H – Ruby.* A little over two weeks later, he records, *nickel deposits $ Skorzeny – Talk Ilse NY*, telling us that Ilse was persistently involved in financial transactions. As representative of the couple's business interests who was permitted to come and go when Otto was not, she was logically omnipresent in Pierre's 1963 datebook.

Three months later, on September 16, he writes that Oswald '*will be used regardless, set up complete,*' and on the fifth line, *JW-H* (John Wilson-Hudson). Within days of that entry, Oswald is on the same bus to Mexico City as Albert Osborne, a.k.a. John Howard Bowen, both of whom boarded in New Orleans.

What do these entries suggest? We can deduce a relationship between a nickel deal and the overall assassination operation, either specific to the upcoming murder of Kennedy or related to the eventual murder of Lee Harvey Oswald, the plot's designated patsy who fell at the hand of Jack Ruby. It is also possible that the transaction was entirely distinct. Proceeding on the likelihood that it was related—that Otto and Ilse would not have accepted a suitcase full of cash for their troubles but would be satisfied with a lucrative and untraceable nickel deal—the reader is encouraged to adjust the lens from specific threads to a wide setting to view the tapestry in full, and recognize long and sometimes disparate shadows of the plot to assassinate John Kennedy.

Germane to the hypothesis, his September 22nd, note reads, '*Oswald - mex city Gaudet?*' William George Gaudet is known to many researchers as having been standing directly in front of Oswald to apply for a travel visa on the 17th. Gaudet's version of events fluctuated over the years, culminating with an adjustment to his initial story that he had flown directly to Merida from New Orleans, to admitting that he had stopped off—for only a day—in Mexico City en route. Like so many in this saga, Gaudet was vehemently anticommunist, establishing the *Latin America Report* in 1948, which he claimed was essential to Nelson Rockefeller's "Inter-American Affairs," a government organization we have encountered before in the context of Ambassadors Woodward and Mann (Spain and Mexico, respectively, in 1963).

By his own admission, under the banner of anticommunism, Gaudet was among private citizens that freely and routinely provided oral reporting on civil and military activities for the CIA. Among the names most often suspected of being Gaudet's liaisons was New Orleans attorney Stephen B. Lemann. With offices in the Whitney building in downtown New Orleans, Lemann was legal counsel for station WDSU owned by the Rosenstein family with wealth derived from Sears Roebuck, whose chairman, Gen. Robert Wood, was a cofounder of the American Security Council. Monroe & Lemann law firm handled the regional interests of the Whitney dynasty.

As such, Lemann would have been familiar with the machinations of one of the Whitney family's primary revenue streams, Freeport Sulphur, which had recently invested in a nickel processing plant, Port Nickel, to service the product shipped in from the mines in Cuba. During his high-profile investigation into the assassination, District Attorney Jim Garrison filed away a memo that suggested Stephen B. Lemann was involved with the CIA on a local level, specifically "paymaster," but this allegation has never been subjected to serious scrutiny. It is worth noting that skilled and discriminating researcher Tom Scully established beyond doubt that Stephen Lemann and Garrison were closely related by marriage through the DA's wife.

As Lemann's informant (assuming those allegations are well founded), Gaudet proved even more intriguing when obscure details began to fall into place. Author Albarelli was told in confidence that Jack Ruby had purchased artwork in New Orleans on behalf of Dallas oilman and coinvestor with Otto Skorzeny, Algur H. Meadows. FBI Special Agent Miller of New Orleans stated in a report of

November 27, 1963, unequivocally, that William G. Gaudet had phoned to tell him that he had knowledge Jack Ruby purchased paintings from E. Lorenz Borenstein in the Crescent City sometime in late 1959. Borenstein had developed a market for Pre-Columbian art in the US, having smuggled it from Mexico.

While it is doubtful the alleged Meadows acquisition facilitated by Ruby is directly related to this incident—by then, Al Meadows was paying thousands if not tens of thousands as he amassed his collection and the price of the paintings mentioned in Gaudet's call did not exceed $50—we can be confident that Jack Ruby was under occasional contract to procure art, including on behalf of Al Meadows, and that Gaudet was familiar with Ruby, the buyer, or both. Gaudet's phone call to the FBI coincided conveniently with John Wilson-Hudson's contact with authorities to announce, unsolicited, that he recognized Jack Ruby as having been in Cuba with Trafficante in '59. The two calls are significant given Gaudet's proximity to Oswald, his presence in Mexico City, and Wilson-Hudson being summoned along with "Bowen" to MC during the crucial episode.

Reading Lafitte's datebook, it is apparent that Mexico City, always a hub of intrigue, was certainly so in the second half of September. Not only are major players in the plot spotted on numerous occasions, but Pierre also pauses to make note of characters some might argue at first glance as being minor players: on the 27th, he indicates that "Algur" was either *in* Mexico City, *en route* to the city, or *involved with interests* there, followed on the next line with the name "Ilya." It is reasonable to assume, given his business history with Otto Skorzeny and by extension Pierre Lafitte, that Algur in Lafitte's entry is Dallas oilman/art collector Algur H. Meadows. It is equally reasonable to argue that *Ilya* is Philadelphia Pew family employee, Sun Oil petroleum geologist Ilya Mamantov, whom Jack Crichton—another "friend of Otto" who as we will read was essential to the plot's success on the ground in Dallas—would beckon to translate for Marina Oswald on the heels of, if not minutes before, the assassination on Elm. Six days following Lafitte's reference to Algur and Ilya, he implies a direct association between John Wilson-Hudson and Bowen. The entry bears repeating: *Bowen & Hudson- mex) School cover- wife Spain.*

By October 10, Hudson is either in Canada, or dealing with matters related to Canada. As noted, it is safe to conclude that "wife" at the British Embassy refers to Hudson's wife. Five days later, Lafitte is in New York with Charles Willoughby at the offices of Ilse's "US sponsor," Previews, Inc. We begin to see a pattern that suggests Gen. Willoughby may have also been involved in the financial aspect of a plot. It is reported that Willoughby was in Madrid shortly after this meeting, discussed in a future chapter.

Several weeks later, Lafitte leaves behind the second of two clues to indicate an association between John Wilson-Hudson (and by extension as reflected in datebook entries, John Howard Bowen) and Jack Ruby. The first, on June 7, which reads, *Else and W's wife= shipment $ — John Wilson-H'— Ruby,* provides the clue that the two were somehow connected; but on October 30th, Lafitte lets us know that they were involved in either a transaction that required a *bond,* or they were playing a critical role in positioning Ruby, who would eventually silence Oswald.

The significance of the October 30th entry, made just one day after Lafitte tells us about the "Lancelot Planning," is volatile because there is an inexplicable similarity between it and an entry in one of Jack Ruby's notebooks, which Dallas police located on the day Oswald was shot. It reads: *"October 29, 1963 – John Wilson – bond."* The FBI checked Dallas police and sheriff's records to determine if a "John Wilson" had made bond. They also consulted two different private attorneys whose names were John Wilson, both of whom indicated they had not dealt with Ruby. The FBI concluded there was no reason for the notebook entry. We now know otherwise.

LONG SHADOWS SHARED WITH TRAFFICANTE

Beginning in the mid-1950s, Santo Trafficante, who by then was well acquainted with Pierre Lafitte, spent much of his time looking after his investments in Cuba, including the Havana Hilton and the Capri. To grasp the breadth of his reach related to those behind the plot to kill Kennedy, we briefly widen this analysis by pointing out that Trafficante had contracted Conrad Hilton to brand and manage one of his hotels in Havana. It was Conrad who employed Warren Broglie for years before he ended up at the Hotel Luma, and it was Conrad who sent Frank "Brandy" Brandstetter to run their flagship Havana for Santo. It was Brandy who welcomed Fidel to the Hilton the night of his triumphal arrival in Havana. Some three years later, at the behest of Jack Crichton and under the auspices of the 488th Intelligence Division, Brandstetter was in Dallas the day Kennedy was murdered.

Following WWII, the Hilton Hotel brand was one of the most prestigious hospitality flags money could buy. Founded in 1919 with the purchase of a hotel in the small west Texas town of Cisco, within a half dozen years, Conrad Hilton built the Dallas Hilton, and by 1943, he was operating hotels coast to coast. In 1946 he began to sell stock in the company, and within the year, Hilton Hotels Corp, was listed on the NY Stock Exchange. Hilton was soon under contract to operate what he referred to as "the greatest of them all," the Waldorf Astoria on Park Ave., and in 1953, he chose to enter the European market in 1953 with The Castellana Hilton, Madrid, Spain. Conrad Hilton is named in a financial ledger kept by Pierre Lafitte.

Among the Waldorf's permanent residents in the early 1960s was military icon General Douglas MacArthur, indicating there would have been frequent presence of his admirers including Dallas oilman and archconservative H. L. Hunt and MacArthur's "little fascist" Charles Willoughby, who was on Hunt's payroll. Other suites were occupied by persons significant to our story including war profiteer J. Russell Maguire, publisher of the *American Mercury*. Informed pundits have dubbed the Waldorf the de facto "White House."

In the early '60s, Canadian John Doyle of Javelin Ltd. took ownership of the luxurious Hilton flag hotel in Panama. It was Hilton's Havana hotel that hosted Fidel Castro the afternoon he arrived with his troops in the capital. There to greet him was Conrad Hilton's protégé and managing director of the Havana property, Brandy Brandstetter of the 488th Intel. Another among Hilton's stable of managers, Warren Broglie has a significant role in the Mexico City leg of this investigation.

Trafficante had also brought into his Cuban fold the ruggedly handsome actor George Raft, who quickly invested in and became the public front for the Capri Hotel and Casino. Raft provides us yet another incident of strange synchronicity when he testified that during a flight to London, he sat beside Charles White (a.k.a. Charles Tourine), one of the operators of the Capri and the son of a ruthless NY gun dealer who had been caught dealing in illicit Canadian securities, a crime identified earlier in this chapter. That particular trip, Raft was on his way to London to work on a film project. His former producer of "The George Raft Show" at Hal Roach Studios, Robert Bradford, had formed his own company, Franco London Films. By coincidence, prior to launching out on his own, "Bob" Bradford (who married prolific author Mary Taylor Bradford) was executive producer of filmmaker Sam Bronston's projects, including *John Paul Jones*, a film listed on Thomas Proctor's résumé. As such, Bradford engaged with investors, including Victor Oswald, the arms dealer whom soldier of fortune Thomas Eli Davis was intent on meeting in Spain in November 1963.

Raft's "boss," Santo Trafficante, had ended up in Fidel's prison system in Cuba, in living conditions that, by all accounts, were hardly unpleasant. In fact, as noted earlier, one could argue that he was ensconced in Trescornia in relative luxury and permitted to "hold court." The claim that he feared returning to the States because the Feds meant to indict him continues to be unsubstantiated.

According to journalist George Crile III, Washington editor of Harper's magazine and an expert on the CIA's Cuban operations at the time, there were unconfirmed rumors in the Cuban refugee population in Miami that when Fidel Castro ran the American racketeers out of Cuba and seized the casinos, he kept Santo Trafficante Jr. in jail to make it appear that he had a personal dislike for Trafficante, when in fact, Trafficante was allegedly Castro's outlet for illegal contraband in the country. Measured conclusions to those rumors are warranted, but another Bureau of Narcotics report established a more definite link between Castro and Trafficante. It said Castro had operatives in Tampa and Miami making heavy bets with Santo's organization, and that Cuban operatives stateside communicated with Cuba and advised which bolita numbers were getting heaviest play before the winning draw, thus rigging the drawings.

A TIMELY PHONE CALL

Thanks to John Wilson-Hudson's phone call of November 23, 1963, the Warren Commission eventually was advised with an apparent high degree of certainty that while Santo was in Castro's prison, the Mafia boss had been visited by Dallas club owner Jack Ruby, thus reinforcing a developing theory that the "mob" was responsible for the assassination. For some inexplicable reason, many researchers argue that back in 1959 while visiting Cuba, Ruby had the power and influence to arrange for Trafficante's release from Castro's prison. It is an absurd proposition on its face; however, Ruby's role as bagman for the mob is a well-documented fact. For another inexplicable reason, in the immediate aftermath of Ruby shooting Oswald, a British-born citizen of Chile, Wilson-Hudson felt compelled to contact US officials to advise them of Ruby's apparent mob affiliation because he had seen Ruby with Trafficante. He was able to attest to the fact because in 1959 he too was in prison with a handful of his fellow adventurers, alongside Trafficante, and he just happened to notice a strange little guy from Dallas sufficient enough to identify him from photos some four years later.

* * *

As noted, five months before that call, in an entry made on June 7, 1963, Lafitte identifies John "Wilson-H" with Ruby and vice versa. Does that suggest that JW-H had an extended relationship with Trafficante and/or Lafitte beyond his timely imprisonment in 1959? The entry also refers to a shipment, and to $ [dollars]. While we can't be certain of the product in question, it is safe to consider that the two men were involved in a significant transfer, either of weapons, drugs, or precious commodities. And it still cannot be ignored that among those pointing Warren Commission investigators to Ruby's Mafia connections within days of his murder of Oswald was Hudson's unsolicited call with his rendition of the Ruby-Trafficante history in Cuba, prying open the Pandora's box of mob involvement. Nor can the near mirror image of Lafitte's October 30th entry compared with Ruby's notebook on October 29th be discarded as inconsequential.

Another piece of this particular puzzle captures our attention: back in March 1963, Lafitte included a note written horizontally on the page, *"McWillie – Tue with Davis – Oswald.* According to extensive testimony, Lewis McWillie, who served as what amounted to Trafficante's consigliere in Havana, played host to Jack Ruby in 1959 during the now-infamous trip that was reported to authorities, strictly by chance, by Wilson-Hudson. Mention of McWillie in the entry in the spring of 1963 adds further credence to the argument that his boss, Trafficante, continued interacting with Pierre Lafitte well into the early '60s.

FURTHER SIGNIFICANCE OF CLAY SHAW

In 1991, director Oliver Stone reignited the country's quest for full disclosure of the truth behind the assassination in Dallas by bringing to the screen *JFK*, based on the investigation by New Orleans District Attorney Jim Garrison that was launched in 1966. DA Garrison's pursuit of those responsible for the murder of Kennedy culminated with his conclusion that among them was Clay Shaw. The flamboyant Shaw had retired in 1965 as managing director of the International Trade Mart, which he had chartered in 1945 after completing his service in Donovan's OSS. Arrested in 1967, he was charged with involvement in the plot to kill the president. Shaw was placed on trial in Jan-Feb 1969. DA Garrison presented his case, the jury received their instructions, and Shaw was acquitted within hours. In the meantime, Shaw's beloved ITM had moved into its new, purpose-built tower on Canal Street in 1968, and among the tenants was its very own, exclusive "members only" Plimsoll club.

Being significantly distracted by his indictment and trial, Shaw would have only been on the periphery of the planning for the new headquarters, but as a gastronome himself, he most likely weighed in on the development of Plimsoll, including the choice of head chef. Candidates included Pierre Lafitte, noted for his culinary expertise in New Orleans since the early '60s, leaving the country to pursue his craft in Europe. Upon his return to Louisiana, having spent the mid-1960s in Europe, allegedly to pursue his craft, Lafitte applied at the club and was hired, where he awed the members with recipes recently acquired in Monaco. From a prestigious perch at the Plimsoll, he was quickly initiated into the distinguished Chaîne des Rôtisseurs. And then one day, as the readers have already learned, he was arrested.

Is there documented evidence that Clay Shaw was in Lafitte's world much earlier than 1967? At least by 1963? Yes, as defined in a previous chapter. On May 9, Lafitte notes, *Souetre and David[s] in April here*, and then asks, *Shaw where?* Later, on September 17, Lafitte asks, *Willoughby – Shaw?* This last Shaw entry is just one day after Pierre pens the initials *JW-H* (a.k.a. John Wilson-Hudson), known for nickel transactions in the past, as well as mercenary activities that landed him in a Cuban prison where he encountered Santo. As noted, Willoughby is named in the same string of entries as those regarding nickel and $, along with John Wilson-Hudson, who is known to have been involved in nickel transactions. We're now on solid ground to consider why Lafitte might have mentioned Wilson-Hudson, Willoughby, and Shaw in the same context.

Volumes have been written about Shaw, whose role in Permindex was explored in Chapter 2 of this book. But Lafitte's entries beg a question that has either slipped between the cracks, been overlooked, or dismissed out of hand. A memo to DA Garrison from Sal Scalia, 6/27/67 reads: "... *as an example that Shaw and two other persons either purchased or attempted to purchase a nickel ore plant in Braithwaite, Louisiana [Port Nickel] after the company was closed because of broken trade relations with Cuba. At this time, David Ferrie flew Shaw and his two partners to Canada in an attempt to receive the ore from Cuba but through Canada.*" Assassination researchers familiar with the "Winnipeg Incident" may wish to pursue the implications, particularly in light of Surcharov's deep roots in Winnipeg, of Wilson-Hudson's history with both Donovan and Otto Skorzeny, allegations that Ferrie knew Jack Ruby, and Ruby's name appearing in critical entries of the project manager's datebook.

A PRELIMINARY INTRODUCTION TO THE GENERALS

The Rev. John Howard Bowen shared membership in radical evangelical organizations with Billy Hargis, and Generals Edwin Walker and Charles Willoughby. Walker had recently participated in the purchase of the *American Mercury,* previously controlled by arms manufacturer J. Russell Maguire, and served as military editor of the publication.

General Willoughby, who published his own propaganda sheet, *Foreign Intelligence Digest,* was, as noted by CIA press officer Stanley Grogan, on Ulius Ammos's team of trustees for International Services of Information Foundation

(ISI) and provided commentary for INFORM, the publication of ISI. In a June 1961 internal routing slip from then-CI Deputy Director Grogan in charge of Press Relations to DCI Allen Dulles: "Willoughby bent my ear for over an hour yesterday trying to get CIA to pay $150 for each issue of the *Weekly Crusader*, they want to furnish us with one thousand copies for distribution. *Willoughby is a trustee on Amoss's staff . . .*" [Italics added.]

As we read in the next chapter, among the suspects that fell under command of Charles Willoughby in plans for Dallas was Robert Emmett Johnson. A skilled sniper, Johnson was also a fairly decent writer, and Ulius Amoss had brought him on board under the cover of "journalist."

JOHNSON'S BOSSES HIDING IN THE SHADOWS

Ulius L. "Pete" Amoss had served as a division chief in Bill Donovan's OSS, assigned to Greece and then Cairo, before he fell from Donovan's graces for alleged "administrative improprieties." According to a declassified document, during this period he "recruited, trained and launched numerous teams of assassins that carried out hits in North Africa, So. Europe, Switzerland, Spain and Portugal." His skill set also included setting up gambling operations as fronts for spying. As noted, while in North Africa, he served with Col. Carleton Coon and William Eddy, both of whom feature in Chapters 1 and 2 of this book.

Apparently Amoss's missteps in the OSS were not sufficient to prevent him from signing on with Frank Wisner, Deputy Director of Plans of the new iteration of American intelligence after the war, the CIA, and interested in retaining the services of Pierre Lafitte for "special projects" as far back as 1952.

In 1992, white nationalist Louis Beam, Jr., drew attention to Amoss's theory of "leaderless resistance," which is described, as an alternative to the "leadership" structure in "underground" groups. In this alternative, activity is autonomous, organized around ideology rather than leaders. It is explained as a system for keeping secret the plans of terrorist assaults against the Government, known only to a few individuals in small leaderless cells in order to prevent leaks or infiltration.

Author Albarelli had picked up on Ulius Amoss while pursuing the death of Frank Olson, writing, "According to a 1943 letter by [George Hunter] White to another FBN agent, [Harold] Abrahamson and [Frank] Olson had attended the session because they were interested in pursuing "aerosol delivery possibilities with Lowe's acetate." Also observing the effectiveness of these interrogation-drug sessions were OSS officers Charles Siragusa and Ulias [*sic*] C. Amoss . . . Siragusa and Amoss had come to New York for a meeting regarding what White referred to as the "Mafia Plan," an OSS assassination program. White had applied the less than crafty code name to the assassination program run jointly by CIA and FBN that was just then coming into existence.

Siragusa, who was familiar enough with Thomas Eli Davis, Jr., to remark on his loyalty to the cause, and Amoss had both traveled to NY for a meeting regarding what Hunter White referred to as the Mafia Plan. Amoss's involvement in the truth drug experiments is notable in the context of his later concept for leaderless resistance whereby a small, tight-knit group of individuals could operate without any deemed central control. It is not a stretch to assert that active participants in Dealey Plaza fit a specific profile including the ability to "operate without any deemed central control." Today, the model is favored worldwide by countless terrorist cells, as well as extremists groups in the United States.

AMOSS'S SPIDER'S WEB

Prior to America's active involvement in WWII, according to Amoss, the government seized control of his private businesses. He had invested in a number of companies that fed into the military contracting apparatus, including Shirgun Corp., a.k.a. Schirgun. The company's primary product was a gun bolt lock invented by Henry Schirokauer. Another investment was Boston Metals Processing Corp., in the business of heavy scrap metal. A third, GramTrade International, was an export-import business. The three companies share a similar profile of corporations that eventually came under the umbrella of the World Commerce Corporation, cofounded by Amoss's boss, Bill Donovan, and British spy William Stephenson. According to prolific researcher/author John Bevilaqua, who provided author Albarelli with invaluable context, a vice president of Boston Metals, Harold B. Chait, transported money from the company and also the Baldt Anchor and Chain Company using trust accounts at The Bank of Maryland to the South Florida Soldiers of Fortune, who put the funds into the hands of a ragtag army. "Both companies were CIA fronts for laundering money," asserts Bevilaqua.

The allegation makes a good deal of sense of the remarks made by Chait's wife on October 18, 1962. As President of the Baltimore Women's Committee for Cuban Freedom during a speech before the members, Phyllis Chait casually revealed that "one of the more fascinating aspects of CIA operations in Cuba is its method of supplying arms and ammunitions to Cuban liberation groups. Time and again, CIA cutters make their dash to Cuba and deliver such items as .45-caliber Thompson machines guns and .30-caliber ammunition . . .," explaining that there was a method in the agency's madness of delivering unmatched weapons and ammunition.

Mrs. Chait would have been familiar with those Thompson machine guns because her husband and his investor, Ulius Amoss, who, before passing away in November 1961, had enjoyed significant funding for his private intelligence operation from financier Clendenin J. Ryan, Sr., were invested heavily in Thompson Machine Guns corporation, Russell Maguire's partner in the military contractor. "I have heard former Castro gunrunners laughingly describe how they were sometimes given official escort when they wheeled Castro's munitions through the streets of Miami. . . ." the committed anticommunist told her mutually aligned friends, adding that "long before Castro launched his revolution in Mexico, Robert C. Hill, our ambassador to that country warned bluntly, that Castro had surrounded himself with Communists and that Communist aid and direction was paramount in his movement." As mentioned in the foreword of this book, Ambassador Hill was a close friend to the family of author Albarelli, and responsible for a seminal moment leading to key evidence that exposes the conspiracy.

From Doug Valentine's *Strength of the Wolf*, we learn that Col. Amoss and George Hunter White—who featured significantly in the clandestine life of Pierre Lafitte—first met in February 1942 while working on the "Eliopoulos case" with White's protégés, FBN Agent Charlie Siragusa and Charlie Dyar. Elias Eliopoulos was a Greek known as the "top-hat overlord of dope," described as having given definitive shape to the modern underworld of drugs. Valentine tells us that by March 1943, White and Amoss were investigating "the frequent tie-up" between smuggling and spying, personified by Eliopoulos, until Bill Donovan fired Amoss for importing *"an ex-convict from the United States for the purposes of expert assassination."* (Credible sources insist that Amoss never left Donovan's fold.)

While in Greece, Amoss had orchestrated various casino operations in order to facilitate spying, at the same time his Nazi counterpart, Otto Begus, was pursuing similar activities. This is important because Begus features significantly in the papers of Otto Skorzeny, as does Merwin K. Hart, whose National Economic Council also enjoyed the financial largesse of the Ryan family, the same Bridgeport, CT,-based arms manufacturers that backed Ulius Amoss's ISI after the war.

TIMELY DETOUR TO MERWIN K. HART

In the private papers of Otto Skorzeny, Hart is revealed as an associate of Baron Konstantine Maydell, the uncle of George de Mohrenschildt known to have befriended Lee and Marina Oswald. Hart and Maydell embarked on the promotion of yet another film project sympathetic to dictator Francisco Franco called *Spain in Arms*. A well-known anti-Semite, Hart was the founder of the National Economic Council, which supported Franco's fascist regime and opposed Franklin D. Roosevelt's economic policies.

The NEC's laissez-faire economic policies turned ugly when around 1947 Hart's anti-Semitism, which had previously expressed itself chiefly in the listing of Jewish names in an unfavorable context, became somewhat more explicit. According to a commentary by James Rorty, described in his obituary as a "poet, radical editor, journalist and author" who wrote at length against that tactics of Joseph McCarthy and "McCarthyism," ". . . the NEC's publication, *Economic Council Letter*, began attacking 'Zionists' and 'Zionist Jews' as supporters of Soviet Russia, conspirators, marplots, and fomenters of war. A year later the NEC sponsored the radio broadcasts of Upton Close, whose newsletter, advertised over the program, specialized in attacking prominent Jews. Additional clues to Hart's attitudes and associations are provided by his one-time employment of [Allen] Zoll to help the NEC's drive for contributions. . . ." It was Zoll who also founded a private intelligence agency, similar to Ulius Amoss's ISI. Zoll's American Intelligence Agency received funding from H. L. Hunt, scion of the Hunt oil dynasty. H. L., known as a significant financial backer of far-right traveling preacher Billy Hargis, also funded Merwin Hart.

Author Ralph Ganis writes that Hart's association with de Mohrenschildt through his uncle, Baron Maydell, "takes on great importance after the war, when Otto Skorzeny became close business partner with Merwin K. Hart. In fact, Hart and his NEC were a major part of Skorzeny's international commercial network and are found throughout the Skorzeny papers."

Journalist James Rorty expands on both Zoll and Hart, writing that they ". . . have been supported and aided by reputable businessmen who do not share their anti-Semitic attitudes. Because of this support, both of these bigots have been enabled to move in respectable conservative circles that would otherwise be closed to them . . . A few months ago Zoll tipped his hand by recommending to his readers a book by Professor John O. Beaty, one of the vice presidents of the National Council on Economic Education, entitled *Iron Curtain Over America*. The book is now in its ninth printing; one of those who encouraged its distribution is Russell Maguire, financial angel and publisher of the *American Mercury*, who is also a supporter of Zoll and Hart." The *American Mercury* was eventually acquired by anti-Semite, Holocaust Denier Willis Carto. Carto was among the first Americans to propagate the theory spawned by Waffen-SS Nazi Minister of the Interior and organizer of the mass murder of Jews, Heinrich Himmler. When it became obvious that Hitler's war was not going well, Himmler ordered camp commandants to destroy all records of the murder of millions of Jews in concentration camps across the Reich. Carto picked up the mantle and is accountable for over six decades of denial of what went on in those camps.

General Willoughby closes one particularly lengthy diatribe he shared with his good friend, DCI Allen Dulles, with a quote of fascist philosopher Oswald Spengler with, "Untergand de Abendlandes" in reference to Spengler's "Decline of the West." Without notes, (Francis Parker) Yockey wrote his first book, *Imperium: The Philosophy of History and Politics*, in Brittas Bay, Ireland, over the winter and early spring of 1948. Clearly, he shared Willoughby's admiration of Spengler in *Imperium,* a Spenglerian critique of 19th-century materialism and rationalism dedicated to "the hero of the twentieth century." It is believed that he meant Adolf Hitler. Holocaust Denier Carto of the Liberty Lobby, and later owner of the *American Mercury* as well as the *American Free Press*, took on the task of publishing Yockey's *Imperium* when Britain's infamous fascist, Sir Oswald Mosley, failed to do so because of personality clashes with Yockey. The reader is reminded that adman, propagandist H. Keith Thompson, long-time protégé of Yockey, handled public relations for Lee Oswald's mother, Marguerite Claverie Oswald, in 1964. It has been reported that Willis Carto was Yockey's last visitor in jail before he bit down on the cyanide pill he had tucked away rather than be interrogated by American authorities.

FURTHER TO ULIUS AMOSS

ISI, the private intelligence agency founded by "leaderless resistance" mastermind Amoss, was also funded by Russell Maguire. Of note, in addition to Charles Willoughby, trustees who carried the torch of ISI following the death of Amoss in November 1961 included Chairman of Baltimore Savings and Loan Henry P. Irr, who as head of the National Savings and Loan Association would cochair a senate subcommittee with banker Samuel W. Hawley of Bridgeport, CT, the father-in-law of soldier of fortune Thomas Eli Davis, Jr., in 1963. And as noted, the vice chair of ISI Trustees was Richard F. Cleveland who in his capacity during the Alger Hiss scandal would have encountered Robert L. Morris, the future president of the Dallas branch of the John Birch Society.

The ISI mirrored somewhat the profile of an organization known to American and British intelligence as "Nightingale," identified in Dick Russell's *The Man Who Knew Too Much*. This murky group further described by Miles Copeland, former CIA official, was made up of "aging emigres from Czarist Russia, joined by a smaller number of disillusioned Soviet Communists" that formed a near-fanatical secret organization. Their cohesiveness was greatly enhanced by the financial support they got from a multimillionaire American who was involved in a one-man crusade against "the evils of Communism." As we read in the next chapter, Nightingale was the notorious unit of Ukrainian soldier/mercenaries devoted to the founders of the Organization of Ukrainian Nationalists, Yaroslav Stetzko and Stepan Bandera.

Amoss had amassed an eclectic cadre of informers committed to wiping out communism. As we will read in a later chapter, the multimillionaire American was most likely H. L. Hunt, although he was far more often referred to as "that Texas multimillionaire" instead of "an American multimillionaire"; however, as we will read, two other US candidates of great wealth who launched private, rabid anticommunist intelligence gathering apparatuses surface in the investigation.

During the war, Amoss teamed up with the enigmatic George Hunter White when White's circle of powerful cohorts was wide, particularly for a man in his early 30s. Among them was Major Hugh Angleton, described by a friend as a red-faced farm boy from Boise, Idaho, who had gained infamy for having joined in the chase of Pancho Villa. When Hugh Angleton's son, James Jesus, was drafted directly out of college into Donovan's OSS, the ethics-challenged White befriended him based solely on the high esteem he held the major. Max Corvo, the head of OSS intelligence in Italy from 1943 through May 1945, said of Hugh Angleton, "he was ultra conservative, a sympathizer with Fascist officials. He was certainly not unfriendly with the Fascists." No doubt influenced by his father, as mentioned in Jeff Morley's *The Ghost*, James Angleton preferred collaborating with fascists to enabling Communists, the same as his boss Allen Dulles.

THE DOMINICAN REPUBLIC ASSUMES CENTER STAGE

Under questioning by Warren Commission counsel, Albert Jenner, who was an attorney for military contractor General Dynamics (the military contractor lobbied for in Congress by Bobby Baker, written about at length in Chapter 4), lurched from what seemed to be an unrelated line of questioning to inquire of witness George de Mohrenschildt very specifically: "Did you have any contact with the Dominican Embassy in 1958? In a somewhat elusive response, de Mohrenschildt said, "I think I was invited to—Dominican Embassy. Yes . . . Yes. I was trying to work up some kind of concession, I think. I was working on some kind of oil deal, and tried to contact the Dominican Ambassador—purely for business reasons—some kind of an oil project which had to do with the Dominican Republic." DeMoya had served as Trujillo's ambassador to DC at the time.

Also active in the affairs of Trujillo was professional mercenary Mitch Wer-Bell in the same timeframe as Johnson's presence in and out of the country alongside his brother, William, who worked for an anticommunist publication in the DR. Contributing to this hypothesis that Lafitte's "E. Johnson's" is Robert Emmett Johnson is mention of oil attorney Herbert Itkin, the double agent for the FBI and CIA, active in both Haiti and the Dominican Republic, in the same entry. As revealed, not only was Itkin involved with business interests of George de Mohrenschildt, who was alleged to have been in Haiti from the spring of 1963 until after the assassination, but, as a DC-based petroleum attorney with interests in the Dominican Republic, Itkin crossed paths with loyalists to Trujillo, including Trujillo's ambassador to the US, Manual de Moya Alonzo, and J. Russell Maguire.

According to a memo for J. Edgar Hoover dated Oct 29, 1959, from the Army Asst. Chief of Staff for Intelligence, Industrial and Personnel Security Group, as follow-up to Maguire's request for a high-level security clearance, Maguire and de Moya had mutual investments and oil interests. As noted in the report, Maguire's 1957 correspondence containing allegations of "vital nature to national security" made its way to the top, to Secretary of Defense Neil McElroy. Army intel then advised the FBI director that "in 1958, a check in the amount of $24,950 was deposited into the account of a publication owned by Maguire. The check drawn on the account of then Ambassador DeMoya, gave rise to the whether or not there was an obligation to register as a foreign agent." The report further states, "through our coverage of Dominican activities, we learned DeMoya had made substantial payments to Maguire who is known to be sympathetic toward Dominican regime" . . . and that Maguire had carried articles favorable to Trujillo in his magazine, the *American Mercury*.

In light of industrialist Russell Maguire's significant financial support of Merwin K. Hart's National Economic Council, juxtaposed with Merwin Hart's extensive business dealings with Otto and Ilse Skorzeny, war profiteer Maguire warrants additional scrutiny.

THE SHADOW OF GUNS AND PROPAGANDA

As early as 1941, J. (John) Russell Maguire was forced to dissolve his initial investment firm after an SEC investigation found that two companies under his control were guilty of stock manipulation. In spite of these illegal activities, he was able to purchase large shares in military contractor Auto Ordnance Corporation of Bridgeport, CT, which had been sold to Thompson Automatic Arms Corp. in 1939. By 1944, Thompson had secured $130,000,000 in contracts, including the US military and the Soviet Union, which earned a profit of $14 million, close to $200 million in today's money. The Thompson Automatic Arms Corp., a significant investment of Thomas Fortune Ryan since the 1920s, was inherited by his son, Clendenin J. Ryan, Jr., owner of the *American Mercury*, who in the early '50s contributed $50,000 (equivalent to half million today) to Ulius Amoss to advance his private intelligence service, ISI, whose subscribers were made up of America's most virulent anticommunist corporatists and which, by chance, employed Robert Emmett Johnson.

The reader will recognize Bridgeport, Connecticut, from the previous chapter as the hometown of Mrs. Thomas Eli Davis, Jr., whose family, the Hawleys, were fifth-generation bankers in service to the military-industrial complex and corporate headquarters DuPont's Remington Arms. Known as *"The Arsenal of Democracy,"* Bridgeport was also headquarters of Russell Maguire's Auto-Ordnance and Thompson machine guns.

Maguire, who established offices in Wichita Falls and the First National Bank of Dallas from which he directed his oil investments, had managed to keep his political views private until 1951, when he openly provided financial support of John Beaty's *Iron Curtain Over America*, once described as the most extensive piece of racist propaganda in the history of the anti-Semitic movement in America. A professor of English at Southern Methodist University in Dallas until his retirement as department chair in 1957, Beaty worked in close physical proximity at the university to Professor Ilya Mamantov and expert in petroleum law, the esteemed Robert G. Storey, both of whom feature in this investigation into the assassination. Maguire's magazine, the *American Mercury,* was by then headquartered outside Dallas, convenient to Maguire's oil operations.

Praised by retired admirals and generals, one review in particular of Beaty's *Iron Curtain* jumps out in relation to this investigation: Lt. General P. A. del Valle, USMC (ret.), said of the book, "I am impelled to write to you to express my admiration of your great service to the Nation in writing this truly magnificent book. No American who has taken the oath of allegiance can afford to miss it, and I heartily recommend it as an honest and courageous dispeller of the fog of propaganda in which most minds seem to dwell." As we learn in a later chapter, this is the same Lt. Gen. named in Pierre Lafitte's datebook, along with Gen. Charles Willoughby, in the context of New Orleans, Madrid, and a "church group meeting." For now, it is important to identify del Valle as a staunch anticommunist in alignment with ideology promulgated as early as 1952, by Clendenin Ryan and Maguire. Del Valle was also a close colleague with Wickliffe Vennard of Houston, who spearheaded the Constitution Party (also known as the Christian Nationalist Party) in Texas. (See Endnotes.)

A year after funding Beaty, Maguire leapt headlong into the extreme right-wing movement by purchasing the *American Mercury* magazine, hiring, among others, Allen Zoll, founder of the American Patriots, Inc., which made it to the US attorney general's list of subversive (fascist) organizations, and George Lincoln Rockwell, the founder of the American Nazi Party. Before an acrimonious split with Maguire over the latter's resistance to full-fledged financial backing of Rockwell's agenda, Rockwell had contributed an article about US follies in Iceland and met with Maguire in person to discuss "the movement." Rockwell's familiarity with Iceland stemmed from his second marriage to a member of Iceland's most prominent business and political families. Rockwell writes that during that momentous meeting with Maguire, the two agreed that what was needed was what Maguire called a "hard core." Rockwell took it a step further. He advised Maguire that he thought eventually they would need a Nazi Party. Rockwell later claimed that Maguire agreed but said it would have to be done *"with extreme secrecy."*

Throughout the early '50s, the *American Mercury* supported Sen. Joseph McCarthy and earned a reputation as overtly anti-Semitic and hard right. During the same time frame, Ulius Amoss was also embedded within the McCarthy apparatus through his FBI contacts.

By 1954, William F. Buckley, America's up-and-coming voice of establishment conservatism by comparison to both Ryan and Maguire's extreme views, was editing the magazine. During this period, Maguire also befriended the young Southern Baptist evangelist Billy Graham, and, according to authors Yeadon and Hawkins, "Nazi Hydra in America," Maguire gave $75,000 (three-quarters of a million dollars in 2020) to produce the film *Oiltown, USA*, praising the virtues of free enterprise development of God-given natural resources through the fictional Texas oilman and his religious conversion that manages to blend his born-again evangelism with unrestrained capitalism. The movie was promoted through Billy Graham's mesmerizing influence over a vast network of Southern Baptists, thousands of whom adored Benito Mussolini, to be discussed further in Chapter 9. Graham, a member of the First Baptist Church of Dallas when Rev. William Criswell reached his zenith, continued his friendship with Maguire after producing *Oiltown*. Graham provided several articles for his magazine and appeared on the cover in 1957. From 1954 to 1958, the magazine was managed by Natasha Maguire, Maguire's daughter with Susan Saroukhanoff Maguire, who was born in Tbilisi, Russia. After fleeing the Bolshevik revolution via the Ukraine, members of the Saroukhanoff family established roots in South America. Susan's sister later befriended the Grand Duchess Maria Pavlova, and the two women launched a branch of Elizabeth Arden in Argentina. The cosmetics firm has long been suspected of providing shelter for Nazi activity.

Dramatically in 1961, Russell Maguire made an abrupt decision and sold the archconservative magazine to the Defenders of Christian Freedom, spearheaded by rabid anti-Semitic evangelist Gerald Burton Winrod, who had been accused of being one of Hitler's first channels for spreading Nazi-approved propaganda in the US. His magazine, *The Defender,* was included on the recommended list of World Service, Hitler's official propaganda agency in Germany. According to Gerald L.K. Smith, the founder of the Christian Nationalist Crusade was ideologically aligned with Winrod. Smith met with Maguire in his Waldorf Astoria suite, and within weeks, Maguire had sold the magazine to Winrod. Maguire then disappeared from the American scene. Smith insists that he fled the country after being threatened by a potential blackmailer [unnamed by Smith]. According to Smith, Maguire moved to a Caribbean island. Sadly, two decades later, Maguire's oldest son was charged with kidnapping and molestation of a child. He was eventually found innocent by reason of insanity. A daughter, being treated for heroin addiction while in jail, fell from her bunk and died at age twenty-seven. One of his sons assumed control of the oil business and founded the Maguire Energy Institute on the campus of SMU in Dallas.

ALBERT OSBORNE POSING AS REV. JOHN HOWARD BOWEN

Referred to by author and assassination research expert Dick Russell as "the old preacher on the bus," Albert Alexander Osborne first told the FBI when they tracked him down in 1964 that he was John Howard Bowen. The Bureau was keenly interested in the man seen by two Australian girls sitting beside Lee Harvey Oswald en route from Laredo, Texas, to Mexico City. Described as an Englishman in his late sixties, Osborne told the girls that Oswald appeared to have been in Mexico before. A couple on the bus recalled that Osborne told them he was a retired schoolteacher who had taught in Arabia, as well as India. He said that he was writing a book about the Lisbon earthquake of 1775. Things got interesting as Russell revealed that he was "in fact, an itinerant preacher who traveled widely, without any apparent source of income other than sporadic donations to his mission in Oaxaca, Mexico. Supposedly, *he ran a school* there for several dozen impoverished Mexican youths."

Intrepid researcher Mae Brussell, long overdue for recognition by the wider community of assassination research, confirms, and takes it a bit further: "Bowen-Osborne had been running a school for highly professional marksmen in Oaxaca, Mexico, since 1934. The cover for the place was his particular mission, and he was the missionary. The FBI records on Bowen go back to June 4, 1942, in Henderson Springs, Tennessee. He operated a camp for boys known as 'Campfire Council.' Neighbors complained it was for pro-Nazi activities with young fascists. Bowen vehemently opposed the US going to war with Nazi Germany. They stomped on the American flag. Before that, Bowen worked for the Tennessee Valley Authority since 1933. His dual citizenship between Great Britain and the US took him over the entire globe. So did his use of multiple aliases. After the Warren Commission published their report in September 1964, several attorneys in the Southwest recognized the name of Osborne. September 8, 1952, Jake Floyd was murdered. The target was meant to be his father, District Judge Floyd. Two suspects were caught, one got away. Their testimony was about being hired by Osborne and how he ran the school for assassins. Later investigation revealed Osborne's connections to Division V of the FBI, and to Clay Shaw's Centro Mondiale Commerciale, with funding coming from New Orleans for the CIA, Anti-Castro Cubans, and others. . ." Brussell continues to expose that J. Edgar Hoover's Division V, Domestic Intelligence, working with the American Council of Christian Churches, had used this group from the Bowen-Osborne academy of assassins.

Russell confirms, "there was an actual John Howard Bowen, also a missionary with whom Osborne was acquainted. They were about the same age and looked very much alike. Seemingly around 1958, when Mexican authorities were considering deporting Osborne for having improper papers, he ended up with all of Bowen's ID." A woman who contributed to both Osborne's and Bowen's missions told Russell that Bowen had died probably in 1958, but that the two had a history of working together.

On September 26, 1963, Albert Osborne produced a counterfeit birth certificate to obtain a Mexico tourist card in the name of John Howard Bowen. Returning from Mexico on October 2, he continued on to New Orleans, where on October 10, he produced his true birth certificate to obtain a new passport in his own name, explaining that he was en route to Mexico City for a vacation. However, instead, he set off for a cross-country trip through the South, "visiting churches and collecting religious books." The *Knoxville Journal* published a short article on November 14 that "John Howard Bowen, organizer of Boys' Club here and missionary to the Mixtec Indians in Mexico for the past 20 years, left New York yesterday for a speaking tour in England, Spain, Portugal and

Italy . . . Bowen was invited by evangelical groups of each country." There the story gets muddled. Whether or not he traveled first to Scotland, and traveled some three hundred miles to stay with his sister in Grimsby, England, visiting family he had not seen in 40 years, is in question. But according to his sister, he left shortly before the assassination, saying he was on his way to London. We pick up with Russell's coverage here: "On November 22, 1963, from an English town a short distance from Grimsby, a mysterious phone call was made to a newspaper in Cambridge about twenty-five minutes before the president was shot. 'The caller said only that the reporter should call the American Embassy in London for some big news and then rang off,' a CIA cable released in 1976 reports."

Osborne/Bowen's modus operandi closely resembles the phone call made by John Wilson-Hudson after Ruby murdered Oswald, who was surrounded by a phalanx of Dallas authorities responsible for his safety, to alert the embassy that Jack Ruby knew Santo Trafficante. Wilson-Hudson's call, measured against Ruby's notorious history with the Dallas mob, fueled the intense investigation that may or may not have served as deflection. The significance of this coincidence is emphasized by Pierre Lafitte's note *"Bowen & Hudson- mx city."* Could they have traveled to MC to attend a major meeting where they would receive respective assignments?

Following the assassination, the FBI spoke to a Reverend Walter Hluchlan about Osborne's European speaking tour. Osborne was known to be a leader in the American Council of Christian Churches, the Fundamentalist multidenominational organization committed to preserving Christian heritage. Its sister organization, the International Council of Christian Churches, also founded by radio broadcaster and Fundamentalist Carl McIntire, boasted among its membership Generals Willoughby and Walker.

Rev. Hluchlan told the FBI that he received an undated letter from Osborne that stated that he had been on a preaching tour of England, Northern France, Spain, and North Africa. Researchers Peter Mellon and John Kowalski, who provide invaluable updated information in their essay, "The Dual Life of Albert Osborne," note that ". . . the letter does not exactly match the newspaper report cited above, as Northern France and North Africa replaced Portugal and Italy. The problem with the letter is that the return address is Mexico and not Europe, so there is no European postal stamp to confirm that he had visited any of these four countries. Mrs. Lola Loving, who knew both Osborne and Bowen, told the FBI that she had received a letter from him in Spain anywhere from a few weeks to two months ago. Her interview with the FBI however did not indicate that she showed them a copy of the letter with a Spanish postal stamp on it."

The essayists continue, "We know that was in England because his brother Walter and his sister Mrs. Featherstone confirmed that he had visited them in Grimsby. But this is where the truth ends and fiction begins. Walter Osborne told the FBI that his brother flew to Prestwick, Scotland with scientists who were traveling to Iceland to photograph a volcano. But it was not confirmed if Osborne got off the plane in Prestwick or went with them to Iceland. According to the FBI he arrived at his sister's home by train from Prestwick. The FBI was able to determine that he arrived at New York City on December 5, 1963 aboard an Icelandic Airlines aircraft that he boarded in Luxembourg, Belgium." Of interest to note, in early November '63, Thomas Eli Davis and wife Carolyn flew to Europe via Icelandic Air.

This investigation further benefits from Dick Russell's original study of Osborne, whom we believe was known to Pierre Lafitte as "Bowen." Russell argues that as an "itinerant preacher, there is no ruling out that he rode a similar circuit as Billy James Hargis . . . As most researchers know, oilman H. L. Hunt was a primary funding source for Hargis's Christian Crusade. Hargis had as a frequent traveling companion Gen. Edwin A. Walker, the target of shots allegedly fired by Lee Harvey Oswald in Dallas in April 1963. During World War II, Osborne was discovered by the FBI to have been a near-fanatical supporter of Nazi Germany.

When questioned by the FBI, Albert Osborne advised that he was an ordained Baptist Minister, and that he had not seen John Bowen since October 1963, contravening claims that Bowen had died in the late 1950s, but he believed that Bowen could be located at the Hotel Jung in New Orleans. According to a Louisiana State Police document, on November 20, 1963, General Edwin Walker met with some thirty-five conservative business leaders at the Hotel Jung, and again on the 21st, he was meeting with another ninety people at the Jung. Two years prior to these meetings, President John Kennedy had encouraged Walker to resign from his leadership role when, in 1961, he violated his military oath by distributing political literature produced by the John Birch Society. That literature promoted accusations that his commander in chief was a traitor.

Pierre Lafitte rarely writes the name "Walker" without including the name "Willoughby." It is with that knowledge that we proceed to profiles of "The Generals" and their significance to this investigation.

CHAPTER 7

THE GENERALS, THE TEAMS, AND THE KILL SQUADS

Congress meet- Willoughby- "soldiers kill squad"—
—Lafitte datebook, April 12, 1963

Willoughby & d. Valle
NO re Madrid
Church group meet.
check with Hunt & Vickers
—Lafitte datebook, June 5, 1963

Meet with Willoughby –
(Ella R) —others – at
49 East 53rd St. NYC
—Lafitte datebook, October 15, 1963

I n his indispensable book, *The Man Who Knew Too Much*, writer Dick Russell reveals that in April 1952, US Army Major General Charles A. Willoughby had "accompanied an American military mission to Spain whose ostensible purpose was to discuss with dictator Franco the question of establishing US air and naval bases there."

An August 19, 1952 article for *The Reporter* magazine by Frank Kluckhohn, discovered in CIA files released in January 2003, read:

Prominent Americans have, while traveling in foreign countries, often succeeded in embarrassing the men charged with carrying out the U.S. government's policies in those countries. The most recent and striking example of this was provided by Major General Charles A. Willoughby, U.S. Army, retired, who last January turned up in Spain, where he was an honored guest of Generalissimo Francisco Franco. Willoughby had served as General of the Army, Douglas MacArthur's chief of intelligence from 1941 . . . until MacArthur's removal in April 1951. He had retired from the Army in August 1951, and since then had played no important part in MacArthur's New York headquarters. Early in April of this year [1952] an American military mission arrived in Spain to discuss with Franco and his Ministers the question of establishing U.S. air and naval bases there. Before the negotiations started, the members of the mission knew how delicate their job would be made by the touchiness of the Spaniards. But the Americans had little warning of the way their task would be complicated by Willoughby. The latter, by casting himself as a sort of unofficial spokesman and go-between with Franco, succeeded in building up considerably the *Caudillo's* [military dictator's] confidence at the bargaining table.

While Kluckhohn is careful to insist that Charles Willoughby was not actively involved with his former commander's NY headquarters, and there is absolutely no indication in Lafitte records that Douglas MacArthur was even privy to the plot to assassinate the sitting president, Willoughby is seldom mentioned without MacArthur in the same breath. For that reason, it is essential to speak to the legendary military strategist before further study of his "favorite Nazi," General Willoughby.

"AMERICAN CAESAR" GEN. DOUGLAS MACARTHUR

A decade after publication of *Death of a President: November 20–November 25, 1963*—the only book commissioned by Jacqueline Kennedy in an effort to present a closely managed version of intimate family history—esteemed historian and biographer William Manchester published his biography of MacArthur. He chose for his title *American Caesar*, intended in the most flattering terms, but reflective of MacArthur's predominant worldview.

In contrast, military historian and author Trumbull Higgins, who in his final book, *The Perfect Failure*, astutely concluded that President John Kennedy "inherited a half-baked plan for invasion of Cuba which was prepared by the CIA under President Eisenhower," had in 1955 summed up both Willoughby's and MacArthur's attitudes toward elected government: "It was of course, MacArthur's incomprehension of the supremacy of civilian and Presidential authority in our country that led to his abrupt dismissal by President Truman. General Willoughby refuses to consider the implications of a soldier's defiance of civilian authority. He does not see why it was left to President Truman rather than to

MacArthur to decide whether or not to use the atom bomb in Korea. And he sees nothing wrong in his chief's having carried on public discussions with the Republican opposition at home while commanding a United Nations army in the field."

MacArthur's ultimate overreach occurred when he provided assurances to the Japanese embassies in both Spain and Portugal that he could expand the Korean War, in contradiction to President Truman's stated policy that he would avoid full-scale conflict with the Chinese Communists. His former intelligence officer, Willoughby, was at the time in hot pursuit of an agenda in Spain.

President Truman was livid when secret intercepts in diplomatic dispatches disclosed that MacArthur had defied his directive. The incident got him fired. By April 10, 1952, the five-star general was ousted from his role in the official military, but he was quickly appointed president of Remington Rand, a corporation fully equipped to rapidly adapt as a military contractor during wartime. Remington Rand's headquarters were in Rowayton, Connecticut, just thirty minutes from Bridgeport, where the company originated under Remington Arms Company.

In 1955, under MacArthur's leadership (which included Ret. Lt. Gen. Leslie Groves, who directed the Manhattan Project), Remington Rand merged with Sperry Gyroscope Corp, another military contractor providing maritime and aircraft equipment. Two decades prior, Sperry had acquired Vickers Inc., a manufacturer of control devices for powering hydraulic systems. At the time of his death, the founder of Vickers held 95 patents in the field. As WWII approached, both Sperry and Vickers were vital suppliers to the builders of virtually every type of weapon and support system, from aircraft and ships to tanks and transport equipment for the war effort.

The final merger in the spring of '55 resulted in Sperry Rand Corporation, best known for having been on the ground floor of computer manufacturing. A *New York Times* financial headline read, "MacArthur and Vickers Slated for Top frosts in 'Sperry Rand.'" While MacArthur served as chairman, the diversified company's chief executive officer was MacArthur's close friend and founder of Vickers, Inc., Harry Franklin Vickers.

As a side note, the founder of Rand Corp, J. H. Rand, who remained a dominant force in all companies that bore the family name, is somewhat infamous among assassination researchers as the employer of Robert Edward Webster, who is alleged to have defected to the Soviet Union in 1959. It was Rand who flew to Moscow to rescue Webster, a plastics chemist he hired in 1957, from the clutches of communism. Webster was attending an international products fair under the banner of the American Exhibition when he is alleged to have fallen in love with a KGB agent and subsequently sought to remain in the Soviet Union indefinitely. The product he had promoted at the trade fair was Rand's latest, a spray gun for *industrial use.* Along for the ride with Rand on his quixotic journey to retrieve Webster was one of the CIA's best spies, and a buddy of Rand's, retired agent Dan Tyler Moore of Cleveland, Ohio.

In 1952, Douglas MacArthur had feigned reticence at the prospect of pursuing the Republican nomination for president, but when Texas oilman H. L. Hunt launched a "MacArthur for President" campaign and poured the equivalent in today's money some $1.5 million dollars into the effort, MacArthur acquiesced. In spite of being a registered Democrat, Hunt recognized in the general all the qualities he required to promote his extreme conservative agenda. MacArthur eventually garnered ten delegates at the Republican Convention. Some might argue it was then the Texas oilman began to take stock of his political investments.

On retirement, the General and his wife chose for their permanent residence in New York City a suite in the Towers of the Waldorf Astoria Hotel complex that had been under management contract with Texas hotelier Conrad Hilton since 1949. As such, over the years MacArthur's needs would have been indulged by the Waldorf's Managing Director Warren Broglie, whose Hotel Luma in Mexico City was identified early on in assassination research. As we learned, Broglie was known to have close friends within the US intelligence apparatus, including June Cobb and Winthrop Buckingham, as mentioned previously.

MACARTHUR'S "LITTLE FASCIST," CHARLES A. WILLOUGHBY

Whether his exact words were "pet," "lovable," or "little" fascist, MacArthur recognized that Charles Willoughby was a devotee of the political ideology that swept Europe and Latin America. In fact, it would be the driving force behind Willoughby's professional life in decades to come. Journalist Frank Kluckhohn's fairly obscure coverage of the retired general in 1952 continued, "Although Willoughby described his stay in Spain as being 'without official character,' his initial audience with [Fascist Dictator] Franco lasted an hour and three quarters— extremely long for Franco audiences. During Willoughby's stay at the Velasquez Hotel, the Generalissimo was at great pains to provide him with government limousines and similar official amenities. During a lecture, in the course of which Willoughby described Spain as 'a cradle of superman,' he said, 'I have come to Spain because I feel safer in Spain behind the Pyrenees than in Paris behind the Rhine.' He neglected to explain why he wouldn't have felt even safer staying in New York behind the Atlantic, but the slur on NATO was obvious enough."

After his departure from Spain in July, Willoughby remained in constant contact with Franco's Ministers and Franco himself. (As a brief aside, author Albarelli tells us that in the Lafitte records "there's a page that goes into some bizarre Nazi related rants to JJA—James Jesus Angleton about Spain etc. that he, Lafitte, says he will keep only to himself . . . the record includes the name of avowed Nazi sympathizer H. Keith Thompson who assumed a role in the life of Lee Oswald's mother after the assassination and his murder." The episode has been discussed in a previous chapter.) Kluckhohn continued: "Those who knew something of Willoughby's background were not greatly surprised at his paying sudden attention to Generalissimo Franco. John Gunther has reported that while he was gathering material for his book *The Riddle of MacArthur*, he was at dinner one evening with Willoughby when the general suddenly proposed a toast to 'The second greatest military commander in the world, Francisco Franco' (MacArthur obviously being the greatest). Willoughby told one Madrid audience that at the US Army Command and General Staff School he had lectured in favor of Franco as early as 1936. After he had given an impassioned account of his pro-Franco sentiments at a Falangist luncheon in Madrid, Willoughby was toasted by Fernandez Cuesta, Secretary General of the Falangist Party, in these words: 'I am happy to know a fellow Falangist and reactionary.'"

Who was Major General Charles A. Willoughby, and why is his name found in CIA assassination files and in a dozen entries in the records of Pierre Lafitte?

Charles Willoughby's birth aptly begins with mystery. In his own biographical information given to the US Army, Willoughby stated that he had been born in Heidelberg, Germany, on March 8, 1892. He later passed this information on to *Who's Who in America*, stating that he had been the son of Frieherr (Baron) T. von Tscheppe-Weidenbach and of Emma von Tscheppe-Weidenbach, née Emma von Willoughby of Baltimore, Maryland. The Baron and Emma reportedly named their son Adolf August Weidenbach, sometimes, without explanation, reported as Adolf Karl Weidenbach.

Journalist Kluckhohn, writing on the name confusion in *The Reporter*, states: "*The Gothaisches Genealogisches Taschenbuch der Briefadeligen*, a standard catalogue of the German gentry, does nothing to help clear up the confusion about Willoughby's origin. According to it, General Franz Erich Theodor Tülff von Tschepe (with one 'p') und Weidenbach not only lacked the title '*Freiherr*' but did not receive letters patent from Wilhelm II entitling him to use the surname 'von Tschepe und Weidenbach' until 1913. He had five children, none of them born in 1892. One of Willoughby's friends from his early days in the US has stated that both the General's parents were German and that the name Willoughby was a rough translation of Weidenbach, which means 'willow brook.' When queried by the writer of this article [Kluckhohn] about his birth, Willoughby said he was an orphan and had never known his father, and finally said the *Who's Who* version of his biography was correct as far as he was concerned."

Adding high intrigue to the name confusion in February 1993 when he wrote an article about his book in the *LA Times*. The article recounted how Russell's former wife, Susan, sometimes accompanied him in doing research on the JFK assassination. Writes Russell:

> One afternoon Susan was studying an article by the late Mae Brussell—a researcher I had always considered a bit "fringy"—about the so-called "Nazi connection." Susan kept insisting I reread it and, secretly smug that she was off on a tangent, I put her off as long as I could.
>
> "Read carefully on the section on General Willoughby," she instructed. Reluctantly, I did. *Charles Willoughby, the onetime chief of intelligence for Gen. Douglas MacArthur (1941–1951), turned out to have been born in Heidelberg, Germany, as Adolf Tscheppe-Weidenbach.*
>
> "Hmmm," I said, "that sounds familiar." Scavenging through my files, I retrieved an anonymous letter, received in response to my first published piece on the assassination back in 1975. The letter-writer, who called himself "the Brooklyn waiter," pointed to an acquaintance named "Tscheppe-Weidenbach" as the possible "mastermind" of the JFK conspiracy. The name had seemed like gobbledygook to me at the time. "Honey," I said, 17 years later, holding aloft the letter, "I think we're onto something." We? Her eyes said. OK, we.

* * *

By 1952, Willoughby was widely known throughout the world as a war hero but also a staunch racist and anti-Semite. In spite of that, according to Prof. Scott in *Dallas '63*, he enjoyed the respect of military brass including General Maxwell Taylor, who would eventually serve as chairman of the Joint Chiefs of Staff. Willoughby claimed to have immigrated to the United States from Germany in 1910 when he was eighteen years old and joined the US Army at the lowly rank of private. He was promoted to sergeant in 1913, with Company O of the Fifth US

Infantry, and honorable discharged not long after. Upon leaving the Army, Willoughby attended Gettysburg College and graduated with a Bachelor of Arts degree after only one year, having allegedly attended the University of Heidelberg and the Sorbonne in Paris. His university attendance in Europe has been seriously challenged.

Giving new meaning to "fast track," in 1916, Willoughby, under the name Adolf Charles Weidenbach, was commissioned and promptly promoted as both a second lieutenant and first lieutenant. He was promoted to captain in June 1917, serving with the 16th Infantry, First Division. During that year, Willoughby was closely involved with Elyse Raimonde De Roche, who was executed by the French Army for espionage. (Not to be confused with the renowned French female pilot and first woman to hold a flying license, Elise Raymonde Deroche.) Shortly after the De Roche affair, Willoughby was ordered to Washington, D.C. as part of an Army Criminal Investigation Division investigation of American Army officers who were suspected of pro-German sentiments and actions.

During World War II, through the Korean War, Willoughby served as General MacArthur's chief of intelligence. MacArthur is quoted as jokingly referring to Willoughby as "My little fascist." He is also quoted as saying: "There have been three great intelligence officers in history: mine is not one of them." Many respected historians have stated that MacArthur's judgment was gross understatement. Following the end of the war, Willoughby shocked many military officers when he personally arranged for the exoneration of notorious and ultrabrutal Japanese army Lt. General Shiro Ishii, who ran the greatly feared Unit 731, which conducted some of the most terrible human subject experiments in history. Willoughby allegedly defended his actions by saying that the US wanted and very much needed the information Ishii had on biological warfare. Indeed, it has been reported that Ishii secretly traveled to Fort Detrick, Maryland, where he taught his horrific practices.

Historian Noel Twyman, whose assassination research has seldom if ever been successfully challenged, writes: "Willoughby has been described as a bull of a man (6 feet 3 inches tall and 220 pounds) who spoke with a German accent and affected a monocle. He was fluent in four languages. He had a reputation for being autocratic and arrogant. . . . Willoughby had received decorations from Benito Mussolini while serving as a military attaché in Ecuador. He had been toasted in Spain by the secretary general of the Falangist Party (fascists) as a 'fellow Falangist and Reactionary.' In a final gesture to Spain's fascism in 1952, Willoughby lobbied Congress to authorize $100 million for Spain's dictator, Francisco Franco."

According to Bruce Cumings, another historian who focused on Willoughby in his monumental work, *The Origins of the Korean War, Volume II*, "Willoughby was a profound racist and anti-Semite who saw the Soviet Bloc as 'the historical continuity of Mongoloid-Pan-Slavism.' He once wrote that 'when the teeming millions of the Orient and the tropics got their hands-on magazine rifles, Kipling's white man was on the way out. . . .'" Cumings continues, "During the Occupation of Japan and the Korean War, Willoughby maintained clandestine ties to Japanese militarists, including the bacteriological warfare criminal General Ishii; in the 1950s and 1960s he claimed to have close ties to Reinhard Gehlen and other former Nazi officers then being used by United States intelligence in the Cold War. . . . After MacArthur's sacking, Willoughby frequently visited Spain, and claimed to have been involved in the American military base negotiations with Franco. He set up a kind of right-wing international called the 'international comite,' using money from the Hunt brothers in Texas, linking Spain and Portugal together with German right-wingers, the Hargis Crusade, and others. He was an agent for Hunt Oil in seeking offshore oil rights in the Portuguese colony of Mozambique."

In an even less flattering characterization of Willoughby in the early 1950s, the *Toledo Blade* wrote that General Willoughby, one of MacArthur's chief advisors, was "pretty generally regarded as an overbearing sycophant vastly overstuffed with the reflected glory of his chief."

Many researchers have insisted that Willoughby's April 1952 visit to Spain was limited to only about two weeks, but Frank Kluckhohn insists that it lasted about sixteen weeks, far exceeding the times of others among his "military missions." Author Dick Russell, in 1992, pointed out another highly significant feature of Willoughby's Spain visit that seemingly Kluckhohn was unmindful about: in '52 Otto Skorzeny had already "set up shop in Madrid."

As we now know, Willoughby and Skorzeny met at least a half dozen times in Spain. Russell, unaware of these meetings while finalizing his book, speculated (correctly) that the two former military men had met and that Willoughby's 1952 trip was followed by several additional trips to Madrid throughout the following years, trips during which we are again certain that he met Skorzeny. (See Endnote.) There can be little doubt that during such sojourns, Charles Willoughby also met Otto Skorzeny's wife, Ilse, proving the October 15, 1963, Lafitte datebook entry - *Meet with Willoughby –49 East 53rd St. NYC* - all the more intriguing. The address on East 53rd was the headquarters of Previews, Inc., the global real estate firm that provided cover for the business and intelligence activities of Otto's wife, Ilse.

THE GENERAL AND THE DIRECTOR

Charles Willoughby was in frequent correspondence with the DIA's rising star, Allen Dulles, from the early 1950s. Writes Dick Russell:

> In 1955 . . . Willoughby's "German connections" were the subject of an exchange of correspondence with CIA director Allen Dulles and Dulles's then-deputy Frank Wisner, who was in charge of relations with the Gehlen network as well as the American resettlement of several hundred ex-Nazi scientists under "Operation Paperclip." By now Willoughby was living on Park Avenue in New York. I obtained the correspondence from among Willoughby's personal papers. . . .
>
> Dulles to Willoughby, January 17, 1955: I appreciate your letter of 5 January and its interesting enclosures, which I have sent to some of my people for study. Also many thanks for the interesting books which arrived separately. . . . Regarding your idea of a trip to a certain country for the purpose of writing a book, I find this matter interesting and I shall be in touch with you further about it.
>
> Willoughby to Dulles, March 17, 1955: I believe in "centralization" of intelligence. In a covert outfit, the command leadership is most important . . . I would be entirely satisfied to serve with or under you and have every conviction that CIA could not be in better or more responsible hands. . . .
>
> On the "book" idea, I take the liberty of making certain suggestions: i.) I am more interested in Europe or So. America than in the Far East, at this time. ii) It is true that I have an exceptional entrée in Spain. iii) However, I can develop the same thing in Germany. My father's family (though a divorce took place) is unimpeachable in Wilhelminian society. I am in touch with very high-level people. As you know, I have a Fluent command of French, German and Spanish. iv) I think "rapprochement" with Germany is becoming frightfully important. It can only be done on a personal basis, in the end. v) . . . I will develop for you a weekly report. . . .

The correspondence between Dulles and Willoughby continued. Among Willoughby's myriad of associations, OSS officer Ulius Amoss—architect of leaderless resistance—is reflected in memos that crossed Dulles's desk. In October 1955, Willoughby offered the director aid in setting up "promising . . . social contacts" between young American servicemen stationed in Germany and their counterparts, perhaps implementing Amoss's theories.

"The new generation has less to remember—and to resent," Willoughby wrote to Dulles, suggesting that "In American garrison towns, in Germany, this approach can become the first step in developing [sic] a literary youth-movement, by utilizing existing Karl May clubs." (Adolf Hitler, from his teenage years onward, was a devotee of the Wild West novels of Karl May, the German imitator of James Fennimore Cooper.) "From the viewpoint of social relations and youth indoctrination," Willoughby continued, "it fits neatly, as you know, into one of the many facets of 'psychological warfare.' It could become the medium by which we can gain young adherents and partisans. Anyway, I am going to try it . . . . However, I do not want to stand alone (though the Germans will take it up) and I suggest that you examine it, from the viewpoint of a 'discrete' penetration and the 'making of friends.'"

WILLOUGHBY, THE ABN, AND UKRAINE'S OUN

Prof. Peter Dale Scott, poet, assassination expert, and author cited previously, was among the first to recognize the potential significance of an obscure figure in the saga of Lee and Marina Oswald named Spas T. Raikin. Raikin holds the dubious distinction of having been one of the very first "officials" to have met Lee and Marina Oswald after they had left the Soviet Union, where Lee had allegedly defected in 1959, and arrived by steamship in the harbor at Hoboken, New Jersey. Raikin told the Oswalds that he was a representative for the Travelers Aid Society and that he was there to assist them any way he could.

Interviewed twice by author Albarelli, Raikin said that he didn't tell the Oswalds that he held a high-ranking position with the American Friends of the Anti-Bolshevik Bloc of Nations. The ABN was strongly supported by Willoughby since its formation in Munich, Germany, in 1946.

Confirming that SS Otto Skorzeny and General Charles Willoughby were at the very least aware of each other prior to Willoughby's trips to Spain that began in the early 1950s was their mutual associations with radical far-right Ukrainians. During WWII, leaders of the Organization of Ukrainian Nationalists (OUN), Yaroslav Stetzko and Stepan Bandera, had been held in the central Berlin prison at Spandau from September 15, 1941, to January 1942. In June 1941, Stetzko had announced the formation of a Ukrainian state, which was intended to align itself closely with the Nazis. Said Stetzko: "We will closely cooperate with the National-Socialist Greater Germany, under the leadership of its leader Adolf Hitler, which is forming a new order in Europe and the world." By April 1944, Otto Skorzeny had sought out both Stetzko and Bandera "to discuss plans for diversions and sabotage against the Soviet Army." The two were released by the German authorities in September and, as planned with Skorzeny, began organizing the native populace to fight the advancing Soviet Army.

According to historian Stephen Dorril, by 1946, the OUN-B's secret police was conducting an assassination campaign in western Germany. Ultimately, the OUN comprised the largest contingent within the Anti-Bolshevik Bloc of Nations (ABN), which enjoyed significant support of General Charles Willoughby from its founding in 1946 in Munich.

As may be suspected by some readers, the ABN was also strongly supported by the CIA, whose files are extensive on the group, as is correspondence between Allen Dulles and ABN leaders. In fact, according to CIA documents dated 1957, Raikin was a contract agent for the CIA, having been cleared for hire by the Office of Security. The initial use of Raikin was in service of a project utilizing unwitting agents, but by 1960 Raikin was fully aware of his attachment to the Agency.

In the minds of fascist-leaning politicians and power brokers in the US, Ukraine was the geographical bulwark against renewed Soviet aggression. Ultraright Ukrainians Bandera and Stetzko were the human face of that rabid anti-Communism.

On October 15, 1959, which coincidentally was the day Lee Oswald boarded a train from Helsinki to Moscow on the final leg of his defection, a twenty-eight-year-old KGB assassin, Bohdan Stashynsky, is alleged to have assassinated Ukraine Nationalist Stepan Bandera in Munich. On trial in Munich in 1962, prosecutors presented the most persuasive version of the murder: Stashynsky had used a *spray gun* to dispense a lethal but undetectable poison that induced symptoms that mimicked heart attack. On Tuesday, September 12, Pierre makes a note *SPRAY-GUN 2 WILLOUGHBY-SHAW?* The sheets from a ledger that author Albarelli gained access to further indicate the significance of "spray guns" in Pierre Lafitte's world in 1963. As mentioned previously, in one ledger entry, Lafitte notes, "*Walker team - spray guns - at least 5 . . .*" Another reads, "*. . . Rothermel says no on gas [strike through] guns but T says ok (Stash) . . . Walker says yes spray guns. Willoughby?*"

According to a recent book by Professor of Ukrainian History Serhii Plokhy, *The Man with the Poison Gun: A Cold War Spy Story*, Stashynsky's career as a triggerman for the KGB played out against the backdrop of the fight for Ukrainian independence after the Second World War. ". . . Bohdan was a member of the underground resistance against the Soviet occupation, but was forced to become an informer for the secret police after his family was threatened. After he betrayed a resistance cell . . . [he] was ostracized by his family and was offered the choice of continuing his higher education, which he could no longer afford, or joining the secret police."

Bohdan said later, "It was [only] a proposal, but I had no alternative to accepting it and continuing to work for the NKVD. By now, there was no way back for me." Stashynsky received advanced training in Kyiv and Moscow for clandestine work in the West and became one of Moscow's most prized assets.

Professor P. D. Scott was also the first to draw attention to the significance of the death of OUN's Stepan Bandera in the context of the assassination of President Kennedy. Bandera died at the hands of Soviet agent Bohdan Stashynsky. Scott notes that the assassination of Bandera was exploited by Ukrainian Nationalists and ABN spokesmen to demonstrate the importance of the opposition of the OUN and the ABN to any rapprochement between the American and Soviet governments, which was being advanced during the Kennedy administration, especially the president's perceived conciliatory policies following the Cuban Missile Crisis.

Just two weeks before the assassination of President Kennedy, one of those American pro-Ukrainian spokesmen, former Representative Charles Kersten of Wisconsin, who had served as a member of the Steering Committee of the World Anti-communist League (WACL), "began to develop the picture of a Soviet assassin conspiracy." Kersten had been researcher and assistant in the office of Senator Joseph R. McCarthy during the hearings.

Scott also tells us that "while in New Orleans in [the late spring and summer of] 1963, Oswald was linked to Americans who were in touch with the Latin American elements of Kersten's Steering Committee of the WACL, including Maurice B. Gatlin, who was involved with a right-wing group at the address used by Oswald for his 'Fair Play for Cuba Committee.'" Gatlin, in 1958, had attended a Congress that included the chairman of the American Friends of the ABN, Nestor Procyk. Two years later, Dr. Procyk, a physician practicing in Buffalo, New York, was in direct communication with (Ret.) General Charles Willoughby. In his September 2, 1960, letter, Dr. Procyk tells Willoughby that he and ". . . Mr. Stetzko [Ukrainian rightist leader of the ABN and OUN] fully appreciated the retired general's noble efforts . . ." A month later, Stezko writes to Willoughby directly under the letterhead of the Central Committee of the ABN, Süddeutsche Bank, A.G. Branch Munich.

* * *

On March 18, 1963, "retired" director of the CIA Allen Dulles wrote to Maj. Gen. Charles A. Willoughby, on the letterhead of his Q Street address in D.C.

rather than his New York office at 600 Fifth Ave. The International Building in Rockefeller Plaza was shared by an impressive roster of American giants of industry as well as small companies with interchangeable economic interests. Among them was Petroleum Resources Inc., an entity with deep history in supplying the US military during wartime. Petroleum Resources' board included both J. H. Rand and Joe Zeppa of Delta Drilling, the East Texas oil company on the ground floor of Skorzeny's scheme in Spain.

In the Spring of '63, following his ouster from the agency after the fiasco at the Bay of Pigs, and apparently feeling more relaxed in his communiqués to General Willoughby, Dulles wrote, "Enclosed is an advance proof of my Encyclopedia Britannica article on 'The Craft of Intelligence' . . . I am planning to expand this and bring it out as a book sometime in the fall. Hence any comments and criticism you might have would be sincerely appreciated. *Faithfully yours* [emphasis added], Allen W. Dulles"

Dulles adds a P.S.: Let's discuss some concrete collaboration. Your information work was superb. We tried to get hold of you, repeatedly, including Beetle Smith.

The familiarity with which Dulles addresses Willoughby in the March 18 note dispels any claim that his association with the general had always been at arm's length. Willoughby responds with equal effusiveness on July 15, 1963. By this time, Lafitte, who was embroiled in tracking the progress of what appears to be preliminary plans to assassinate Kennedy, had already mentioned Willoughby in his datebook on six dates. In the letter to Dulles, Willoughby apologizes for the delay in responding and suggests to Dulles a "thorough review in his own diminutive paper, the *Foreign Intel Digest*." He further recommends that "a preface to Dulles's book be authored by an outsider and vet of the intelligence fraternity . . ." followed by, "In general terms, I speculate on the possibility of collaboration in some related fields." Willoughby closes with emphasis on his language skills and history of having lived and worked "in these countries for years."

Willoughby's travel itinerary indicates that on or about October 10, 1963, he departed the US for specific destinations in Europe before attending the annual meeting of the International Committee for the Defense of Christian Culture (ICDCC) in Lucerne, Switzerland, on the 14th and 15th. In April of the previous year, the general had secured a membership in the ICDCC's international directorate, as well as a membership for his friend and founder of the Crusade for Freedom, Tulsa-based Billy James Hargis. The ICDCC was described by Willoughby as "Pan European"—transcending national boundaries. It has strong affiliates in Scandinavia . . . Spain, Austria, the Netherlands, and Italy. It recently moved into Latin America negotiating for a branch in Montevideo and seeking

similar cooperation in Argentina as well as consideration for an African potential. Assassination researchers will recall that it was Hargis who organized
"Operation Midnight Ride," a six-week cross tour designed to warn America that
its Christian ideals were under immediate threat of Communist forces on American soil. Joining Hargis in the operation, launched in February 1963, was (Ret.)
General Edwin A. Walker.

Although he was not a scheduled speaker, it is clear from Willoughby's notes
about his trip to Lucerne that he used the annual congress as an occasion to
advance whatever was on his mind. Present in Lucerne was Theodor Oberlander,
who featured prominently on the list of ICDCC speakers. Oberlander was coordinator of the Ukrainian Waffen SS units during the war and directly responsible
for crimes committed by the Nachtigall Unit (also known as the Ukrainian
Nightingale Battalion Group), working in support of Stetzko's OUN execution
"squads." Despite being an avowed Nazi, Oberlander had the support of Konrad
Adenauer, the first Chancellor of the Federal Republic of Germany, who said of
him, "he never did anything dishournable [sic]." In later years, Willoughby
would speak fondly of his frequent visits with Oberlander.

According to Prof Scott: "Fifteen days before he was shot down, President
Kennedy was warned directly that assassins were being trained in Russia to commit murders in the U.S. and England . . ." The notice originated with conservative
Charles Kersten of Wisconsin. Critical to the success of the assassination plot was
infecting the country with wild speculation about an immediate Communist
threat, driven home even within the administration weeks before Dallas, ensur-
ing that many within the D.C. establishment would immediately conclude that
the president had been taken out by "some silly little Communist."

Scott concludes this area of study by saying, "Three or four days after the
Kennedy assassination, a Munich right-wing newspaper linked to the ABN—the
Deutsche National-Zeitung und Soldaten-Zeitung—was able to publish the hith-
erto unrevealed story that Oswald shot at General Walker . . ." The legend of
LHO was complete.

UKRAINE POSTSCRIPT

In 1976, April 22 to be exact, at the behest of the Inspector General, the CIA
committed to file a Memorandum For The Record, "Subject: Assassination of
Stefan [sic] Bandera." This memo for the record was under the aegis of IG John
Waller. That year was Bush's initial access to agency documents, including the
assassination of President Kennedy. As referenced previously, during his tenure,

Director Bush also asked for the files on Jack Ruby's 1959 visit with Santo Trafficante in Trecornia Prison in Cuba.

The four-page memo to file regarding the assassination of the head of the ABN, Stepan Bandera, requisitioned by Waller goes to extreme lengths speculating about the circumstances of the murder of Bandera. Reads the memorandum: "[this] has been written in an attempt to determine whether there is sufficient information to support the KGB agent . . . claim that he assassinated Ukrainian emigre leader Stefan [*sic*] Bandera in Munich in October 1959 . . ." One observation states, "Results of the autopsy on Bandera's body showed traces of potassium cyanide positioning, but it was never established that the cyanide was the cause of death." The delivery system of the cyanide was a custom-built spray gun.

As is so often the case in the intelligence community, a close relative of John Waller, Martha Waller Moore, had coauthored *Cypher and Code* with former spy and relative by marriage Dan Moore. The reader is reminded that Dan Moore accompanied J. H. Rand to Moscow to ensure that Robert Webster—the chemist behind the *industrial use* "spray gun"—was returned to the US,

In September/October 1963, a notice was floated in D.C. news outlets that the OUN was planning to relocate their headquarters from Munich, Germany, to the US capital. There is no indication that the move actually transpired.

MARINE CORPS LT. GENERAL PEDRO DEL VALLE

"The hand of God . . ." So read an FBI informant's perception of a small luncheon gathering in 1964 attended by retired General Pedro del Valle.

Although del Valle appears but once in the 1963 records of Lafitte, it is a provocative mention when juxtaposed with information derived from an examination of del Valle's papers by assassination author Jeffrey Caufield in his highly regarded "General Walker and the Murder of President Kennedy."

To understand the informant in context, in late May 1963, fundamentalist preacher Billy James Hargis, closely aligned with General Willoughby and together with General Edwin Walker, was in New Orleans to conclude the evangelist's "Operation Alert" speaking tour. His traveling companion, Walker, alerted a receptive Crescent City audience, "It's harder every day to tell the difference between Kennedyism and Communism."

On the other side of Lafitte's chronology that refers to "d. Valle," Pedro wrote to Wickliffe Vennard, the leader of the Constitution Party living in South Texas on July 2nd. Further pursued in an Endnote to Chapter 6 of this book, Vennard was involved with the transfer of ownership of Russell Maguire's *American*

Mercury magazine to Nazi Willis Carto with General Walker retaining influence over content of the publication. In July '63, del Valle advises Vennard that he has had been in touch with a *worldwide Christian movement headquartered in Madrid, Spain,* "whose objectives are in accord with yours."

Caufield reveals that the Madrid group was to meet Vennard—author of *Federal Reserve Hoax: The Age of Deception,* published in January 1963 and promoted vigorously with the phrases "It's Your Money" and "the Age of Deception Exposed!" Del Valle tells Vennard that the Madrid contingency would be connected up with his representatives, who were to pose as tourists. The meeting was to take place at "a quiet hotel." Del Valle assured Vennard that his Madrid contacts would offer "collaboration and a scheme of action." As Caufield writes, "the letter is filled with cryptic references suggesting a secret operation that may have been related to an assassination plot." With hindsight, it is equally, if not more, plausible that rather than active involvement of this wide cast of characters in New Orleans and or Madrid, it was the blessing or imprimatur of the "church group" that was being sought.

While the above does not precisely coalesce, it is quite suggestive. A two-page letter, sent fourteen months later from French representative Henry Bandier of "Accion Cristiana Ecumenica: Movimiento International Anticommuniste" in Madrid to Monsieur le General C. A. Willoughby, John Birch Society, Belmont, Massachusetts, proposed organization of a Foreign Legion (Legion Extranjera) or Legion of Liberty (Legion de la Libertad), united in the fight against communism, perhaps a follow-up to the proposed "collaboration and a scheme of action."

Puerto Rican-born Pedro del Valle advanced through the ranks of the Marine Corps to achieve Lt. General. En route, he compiled a sterling record of military service, having worked in the US Marine Corp headquarters as an Executive Officer in the Division of Plans and Policies prior to the Second World War, leading the 11th Marine Regiment of the First Marine Division in the defense of Guadalcanal and, as Commanding General of the First Marine Division, playing a vital role in the capture of Okinawa in 1945. For that episode, he was awarded the Distinguished Service Medal. After the war, he returned to Washington, D.C., to take the post of USMC Inspector General, and he finished out his military career as Director of Personnel for the Marines. Del Valle's insidious anti-Semitism and fanatical racism had prompted three separate investigations: by the FBI, the ONI, and the war department's Military Intelligence Department. Another fervent admirer of fascist dictators, particularly Benito Mussolini, del Valle retired from the military in 1948, at which time he began his long descent into hell.

Allying himself with radical right wingers who were often several steps further down that road than the McCarthyites of the time, del Valle agitated that a Communist takeover of the US, absent some timely action, was pending. "Treason is everywhere about us, and I do not believe that we have any chance unless some strong military person is able to seize power by means of a coup d'état and take the Communist bull by the horns right at home . . . ," he thundered in a 1950 letter. Since the war, del Valle had been a featured speaker at countless far right gatherings that included representatives from the KKK, Christian Identity, the Minutemen, the Sons of Confederate Veterans, and innumerable other far right splinter groups. He also developed his own information network to keep him abreast of developments inside the radical right."

Among his correspondents was American Nazi Party leader George Lincoln Rockwell, mentioned in a previous chapter in context with J. Russell Maguire and the *American Mercury* magazine, which was sold eventually to a group including Wicliffe Vennard and General Edwin Walker. In a 1963 letter to Rockwell, who had been living in Reykjavik, Iceland, del Valle says, "Your kind invitation to come speak to your young patriots is an honor . . ."

Throughout his misshapen life, de Valle was constantly networking and constructing plots to save the Republic from schemes hatched by U.N. commies and Jews who were apparently willing to use American blacks and immigrants of color in order to achieve their ends.

As such, he was a lightning rod for controversy like his good friend Edwin Walker, both of whom were in complete agreement that the Kennedy administration was a dire threat to the United States.

In 1961, del Valle prevailed upon his still-respectful brethren in the US military establishment to allow Guido Giannettini, a brilliant strategist who was a long-term operative in Italian military intelligence circles, as well as having significant connections among "Western" military and intelligence services, to present a three-day course at Annapolis titled "Opportunities and Techniques for Coups d' Etat in Europe." As a thorough student of right-wing European figures, Jeffrey Bale, wrote of him: "he never made any secret of his pro-fascist and pro-Nazi views." Indeed, he "admitted having fascist associates and friends all over Europe, including (Otto) Skorzeny and many other ex-Nazis."

Giannettini, perhaps more than any rightist theorist, can be said to have codified the principles of what has been called the "strategy of tension," described as "a method of social control involving a series of covert attacks upon a population, intended to promote stress and fear among them." in such a way as to implicate their opponents, utilizing "false flag terrorism." Giannettini did not merely theorize. It would later come to pass that he was one of the planners of the bombing of Milan's Piazza Fontana in 1969. That act of terrorism, which killed 16 people and wounded many more, was—as later demonstrated in Italian court proceedings—part of the same "strategy of tension" Giannettini had advocated several years before. Leftists and anarchists were set up to take the blame, but the act had been executed by Italian military intelligence.

As Prof. Scott pointed out, the Giannettini course was given a very short time before the creation of the now-infamous Northwoods documents. The ideas that are prominent in those papers—involving innocent people being shot on American streets, boats fleeing Cuba to be sunk on the high seas, and a wave of terrorism to be launched in multiple American cities, to be blamed on Castro's Cuba and American leftists—were, as Scott writes, "pure Giannettini." We do not know who may have attended the Giannettini course, but the rapid spread of innovative concepts among like-minded officers would not be unlikely. As the American conservative Richard Weaver reminded us long ago, "ideas have consequences."

Giannettini's sponsor in Annapolis in '61, Pedro del Valle had always consorted with a vile collection of people, and none more so than those participating in the April 1963 "Congress of Freedom" meeting—mentioned by Pierre Lafitte in an ominous context of *"Willby [sic] soldier kill squads"*—in which, according to information furnished to the Miami Police Dept. Intelligence Unit (derived from an informant in attendance), the assassination of numerous well-known figures was seriously discussed. Later in the year and somewhere beyond the bounds of the suggestive, del Valle was the lead speaker at the Constitution Party convention in Indianapolis, Indiana, held from October 18–20, 1963, an event during which "the plot to assassinate a large number of individuals which had been discussed at the Congress of Freedom [in April] had narrowed to talk of killing President Kennedy . . . ," wrote Caufield. An all-star collection of radical right-wing talent, the convention featured, among others, Georgia racist Joseph Milteer, a member of the Congress of Freedom.

Conspiracies promoted by del Valle and this cadre of far-right extremists had over the decade included the takeover of America by the United Nations, which would then split the country into four zones, complete with the rule of the South by "a Mau Mau chief as Commissar," while the states between the Atlantic and the Rockies "quite likely would be under the dictatorship of Huk Filipinos," and the Pacific Coast states would resign themselves to rule by the Red Chinese, bolstered by hordes of "Red Chinese coolies." The "American branch of the white race" would be doomed. These same themes would dominate US politics in the 21st century culminating in the reactionary election of Donald J. Trump.

While a good deal of bizarre scenarios fueled by frantic anticommunists seem to veer into bad satire, Gen. del Valle really believed in the propaganda he advanced. And much like Trump, he had supporters in the swamps of the American far right who believed much of it, as well.

At the height of the Cold War, radical right-wing doctrine was more pervasive among top military and intelligence operatives than one would gather from a casual look at the history of the times that has been handed down to us. Of course, the paranoia and militarism was not uniformly shared among high-ranking US officers. A bond existed between certain staunch military men that often allowed for the acceptance of dangerous and volatile characters by more "establishment" figures including Army Chief of Staff Gen. Maxwell Taylor in 1955. As mentioned, Taylor, well aware of the essence of Willoughby, referred to him in a letter as "a distinguished alumnus of the Army" and enlisted his help "in interpreting the Army to the American people." On the subject of the assassination in Dallas on November 22, Pedro del Valle proclaimed, *"The hand of God directed the bullet that killed President Kennedy."*

MAJOR GENERAL EDWIN A. "TED" WALKER

Walker & Souetre in
New Orleans/ arms
(Davis? – where?)
Cable to O
—Lafitte datebook, April 30, 1963

*Paris murder
Willoughby—Walker
—Lafitte datebook, June 12, 1963

The action taken regarding Major General Edwin Walker is amazing. Is it a crime nowadays to be a patriot? Is it a crime to teach Americanism to our troops? Must a general be "relieved of command" when he is giving his troops something to fight for? Who is relieving of command those in government who are responsible for the Communist foothold in this hemisphere? Who is being "relieved of command" for other Communists favoring actions in our State Department?

—FRANK T. RYAN, PRESIDENT
WORLD COMMERCE CORPORATION
JUNE 25, 1961

This somewhat rousing endorsement by the president of the World Commerce may have gone unnoticed by the average American, but as reported in Chapter 2, the global power structure would recognize the WCC created by the director of the OSS, Bill Donovan, and his counterpart in Britain, William Stephenson. As reported, the WCC had over the previous decade acted as an umbrella front for several hundred companies whose primary aim was self-serving information gathering and espionage, sprinkled heavily with sometimes deadly counterintelligence operations, while extracting profits from global markets. Frank Ryan, a former OSS officer under Donovan, had worked closely with Otto Skorzeny for years. For that reason alone, his remarks in support of Gen. Walker are revelatory.

Several months after Ryan's vociferous support, a telling piece written by syndicated newspaper columnist Drew Pearson, and published in the November 24, 1961, edition of the *Washington Post*, tackled the cluster of extremists General Walker had attracted. Referring to the "increasing turn to the far right by high-ranking US military men," Pearson singled out Walker, still head of the Army's 24th Infantry Division in Germany, for politicizing his troops with right-wing propaganda. Pearson highlighted a letter to one of Walker's military supporters, Arch Roberts, from the American-born French rightist sympathizer Hilaire "Hal" du Berrier, who compared the Kennedy administration's crackdown on Walker to de Gaulle's attack on the rebel French generals who led the OAS. Du Berrier's history germane to the assassination is pursued momentarily.

Pearson's article had also cited del Valle as having come close "to urging armed insurrection" when he made statements calling for the "organization of a powerful armed resistance force to defeat the aims of the Usurpers and bring about a return to constitutional government."

Before Kennedy's Secretary of Defense Robert McNamara finally made his dismissal official, General Walker had established an anticommunist indoctrination training course for his troops called the Pro-Blue program. Largely designed by his aide, Major Archibald Roberts, the program's purpose was to indoctrinate Walker's troops in far-right, anticommunist ideology. At the height of the very public dispute between Walker and the Kennedy administration, ultraconservative publisher Kent Courtney and General Willoughby were planning to travel to Germany to visit Walker, and to offer him a paid position as the public face of right-wing resistance to Kennedy liberalism.

In early 1961, Soviet Premier Nikita Khrushchev boldly declared: "Communism will gain control of the world one day without resorting to bayonets or rockets." Said Khrushchev: "We do not need a war to achieve domination of our ideals, the most progressive Marxist-Leninist ideals." Khrushchev's declaration sparked a flurry of anticommunist verbal reactions from high-ranking US military officers. Not surprisingly, US Army Major General Walker was chief among these officers, speaking out loudly and frequently.

By April '61, Walker was relieved of his command in Europe by the newly elected president. As expected, this provoked deep animosity toward JFK, not only in Walker, but among officers who thought Kennedy was attempting to suppress anticommunism in the military. Walker became an avid member of the John Birch Society and signed up with Billy James Hargis's ultraconservative Christian Crusade with which Charles Willoughby was under contract. Together, Willoughby and Walker were also military advisors to the ultraright Council for Statehood and the Congress of Freedom, as was Pedro del Valle.

When contemplating the circumstances surrounding the Walker incident in April 1963, perhaps the only things most students of the event agree on is that the general resigned in 1959 and President Eisenhower refused his resignation, and that in 1961 Walker "resigned" again and President Kennedy "accepted the resignation." In dispute are the circumstances of April 10. Based on Walker's subsequent claim, a shot was fired into his home on Turtle Creek Blvd. in Dallas while he was sitting at his study desk. The shot missed. Within hours of the assassination, an FBI report presumed Lee Harvey Oswald was the Walker shooter. Very little else about the incident could be immediately verified, yet three days after the assassination, a Munich right-wing newspaper linked to the Anti-Bolshevik Bloc of Nations somehow determined that publishing the hitherto unrevealed story that Oswald shot at General Walker in April would meet standards of credible reporting, some seven months later and thousands of miles from the scene of the crime.

With access to his records, we now know that by April 7, Lafitte was, at the very least, aware of an upcoming incident when he wrote, "Walker - Lee and pictures. Planned soon—can he do it? Won't."

(Note: due to challenges in deciphering Lafitte's handwriting, it is possible that "won't" is actually "wait." Lafitte's first mention of the surname Oswald was twelve days earlier, on March 26, when he writes "McWillie – Tues with

Davis-Oswald." He does not refer to LHO as Lee in that instance. We know that weapons dealer Victor Oswald was in and out of New Orleans, but Lafitte never mentions him by his full name, so we conclude that "Oswald" is a reference to the future patsy. In that context, while it impossible to know precisely why Lafitte used Lee and Oswald interchangeably, it is logical to conclude that when he mentions "Lee" just three days before the alleged shooting on Turtle Creek, he means Lee Harvey Oswald. We also note that Walker's home was quite close to Lee Park on Turtle Creek Blvd. Dallas.)

In support of the hypothesis, Oswald had taken four photos of Walker's residence. The shots failed to strike Walker, even though he was sitting in clear view just a bit over 100 feet away from the shooter. Author Jeffrey Caufield views the shooting attempt as being "phony," as a piece of directed résumé-building for Oswald. Even J. Edgar Hoover, in his Warren Commission testimony, raised the possibility that individuals who were "associates of General Walker" could have been involved. Regardless, by late November, the backstory of Oswald as a commie was bolstered significantly by Walker's claim.

That Major General Walker was at or near the center of a tightly woven collection of militant right-wing plotters during the early 1960s is the thesis of Jeffrey Caufield's book, *General Walker and the Murder of President Kennedy: The Extensive New Evidence of a Radical Right Conspiracy*, a deeply researched study of Edwin Walker. Indeed, Gen. Walker, who was revered in right-wing circles as a martyr of the Kennedy administration's crackdown on military indoctrination of troops, seems to be ever-present in the communicative loop of men including General Willoughby, General del Valle, and oilman H. L. Hunt.

FBI HQ File 157-758, captioned "Council for Statehood; aka Congress of Freedom" [whose advisors included Generals Walker and Willoughby], relates to a right-wing group determined "to eliminate by force if necessary all Jewish people in government." Extremist Joseph Adams Milteer, whose threat against JFK is widely known to assassination researchers and discussed in depth in the report of the House Select Committee on Assassinations, told the FBI he had attended the Congress of Freedom convention in New Orleans in April 1963. Among the attendees was Walker's attorney, Oklahoma native and fellow graduate of the New Mexico Military Institute, (Ret.) Gen. Clyde J. Watts.

In retirement, Edwin Walker had recruited the brother of Larry Schmidt from a cadre of loyalists in Germany to serve as his driver in Dallas. Little has been researched into the brother, but his role at Walker's house gave Larry Schmidt direct access on a day-to-day basis. Larry had arrived from Germany with an agenda, "Conservatism USA" (CUSA). Exercising deference to America's conservative elite, his strategy was to first inveigle his way into the Young Americans for Freedom, founded by William F. Buckley. Gen. Willoughby served on the board. Regardless of Buckley's relatively moderate conservatism by comparison, in hindsight we realize the significance. As we read later, by the time the plot to kill the president was set in motion, Larry Schmidt was pushing a far more extreme agenda.

In another stunning piece of evidence, on April 30, 1963, Lafitte was aware of a connection between General Walker and OAS officer and trained assassin Jean Rene Souetre. He writes: "Walker = Souetre in New Orleans/Arms," confirmation of author Peter Kross's source, who contended that the two had met. This entry is all the more intriguing with mention of Thomas Eli Davis.

Above all, and it bears repeating throughout this investigation, Lafitte made a detailed note on October 9 that further implicates General Walker. It reads in full:

> OSARN--OSARN--OSARN--
> OSARN- get Willoughby-Litt-
> plus Souetre, others (Hungarians)
> Lancelot pro.- kill squads Dallas,
> New York –Tampa-(loaded .E) -T says
> called Oswald to purpose- weapons-
> Walker. Davis in N.O. with
> swamp groups Florida (Decker,
> Bender, Vickers, K of M)---

Two weeks and two days later, Lafitte indicates that the plans were ramping up and reaffirms that Walker was a key component. The date, October 25, appears to be particularly pivotal because Lafitte has been advised that *O says done - Oswald set in place*, and he makes a note - *call Walker & others*. By November 5th, a meeting was scheduled with the plot's designated man on the ground in Dallas, Jack Crichton. Lafitte writes tech *building*, then, *Walker*. The entry ends with *O. says Lancelot = Go. phone booth*.

Before pursuing the teams and squads and groups named in the October 9 entry, it is essential to consider the identities of Decker, Bender, and Vickers. Note: KofM refers to the Knights of Malta, and more specifically, the Shickshinny Knights of Malta, directly affiliated with the Russian Orthodox Church.

The primary candidate for "Decker" turns out to be General George H. Decker, whose military career ended in September 1962 as the Army Chief of

Staff. Interviewed for the John F. Kennedy Library Oral History Program, Decker was asked by Larry Hackman: "Can you recall the discussions on how to handle General Walker when this came up first in 1961, I believe? Were those decisions yours, or did McNamara and Stahr get involved in this to any degree?" Decker's response: "Well the decision [*sic*] were made in the Army and, eventually led up to General Walker's resignation. But this was an action that he himself took. He was relieved of his command of the division and returned to the United States. I talked to him at the time and told him that it seemed in the best interests of all concerned to remove him [but that] I still had confidence in his ability as an officer and that I hoped he'd go ahead and do the kind of a job that he was capable of doing. But he chose to resign, and it was accepted. He was not fired, in any sense of the word, from the Army. But he was a rather strong-willed person, too." Hackman pressed, "Did you have any strong feelings in this area of troop orientation and changes that should be made?" Decker hedged, "Well, of course, I'm a very strong advocate of troop orientation, to tell the troops what the facts of life are, but I thought that General Walker went too far in what he was attempting to teach in the Fifth Division, particularly in particularly in regard to communism, which was his principal subject. And it led to, as you know, quite a bit of trouble."

Army Gen. Decker had served as deputy commander of American forces in Europe in 1956, stationed in Rocquencourt outside Paris. He assumed command of the United Nations forces in Korea in 1957 before being named Vice Chief of Staff in 1959. In October 1960, just before leaving office, Eisenhower promoted him to Chief of Staff of the US Army.

In 1961, Decker awarded Ret. General Douglas MacArthur an honorary Combat Infantryman Badge, without doubt a personal privilege since during WWII Decker had served as chief of staff of the Sixth United States Army, which was a major element under MacArthur's command. Barring conflicts in his itinerary, we can assume that Gen. Charles Willoughby, MacArthur's pet fascist, would have been in attendance at the ceremony.

On the question of Cuba, specifically the Bay of Pigs, Army Chief Decker's views aligned with JCS Chief Lyman Lemnitzer: the ultimate success of the operation required air support. Post-Bay of Pigs, Lemnitzer wrote that the JCS bore no responsibility for the cancellation of the D-Day air strike. As Lemnitzer put it, Kennedy made this decision *"without ever telling the Joint Chiefs of Staff or ever asking about it."* During his testimony before the Taylor Committee responsible for evaluating the failure, Decker took it a step further: "The advantages of pre-D-Day strikes would be that Castro's aircraft would be knocked out prior to the landing. I was in favor of pre-D-Day strikes two or three days in advance." Decker summarized, *"It never occurred to me that we could disown supporting this operation."*

In the context of the strong possibility that Lafitte was referring to General Decker on October 9, a particularly intriguing claim made by Gen. Earle Wheeler reveals a good deal more. During a 1964 interview, Wheeler, who had been the director of the Joint Staff in 1961, claimed that *"we had a tremendous difficulty in getting information out of the agency [CIA]."* This complaint, however, was not made by any of the military officers who testified to the Taylor Committee and *conflicts explicitly* with the recollection of General George Decker. General Decker, who was the Chief of Staff of the Army in 1961, has stated that *"we were in pretty close touch with them [CIA]"*; when asked, *"Were there problems because they [CIA] were holding things too close?"* he replied: *"Oh, no. Oh, no. We had no problems with communication at all."* (JFK Library Oral History)

On the issue of Vietnam, and perhaps the death knell of his military career, several vignettes suffice to underscore that Kennedy's Army Chief of Staff was not in lockstep with the administration's strategic thinking related to military activity in Southeast Asia. According to Andrew J. Birtie, historian at the US Army Center of Military History, Kennedy "wanted to transform the entire US Army, both mentally and structurally, into the type of politically astute, socially conscious, and guerrilla-savvy force that he believed was necessary to combat Maoist-style revolutions—*and General Decker did not.*" (Italics added.) In fact, Decker was at the opposite end of the spectrum on the preferred way forward in Vietnam and Laos, once even raising the question of nuclear weaponry: "[The US] cannot win a conventional war in Southeast Asia; if we go in, we should go in to win, and that means bombing Hanoi, China, and maybe even using nuclear bombs."

According to Harry G. Summers, Jr., "President Kennedy's special military adviser and for a time chairman of the Joint Chiefs of Staff [Maxwell Taylor] would later tell the Senate that the United States was not trying to 'defeat' the North Vietnamese, only 'to cause them to mend their ways.' He scoffed at the concept of defeating the enemy as being like 'Appomattox or something of that sort.' Those who resisted, such as Army chief of staff General George Decker, a World War II combat veteran, were eased out of office." Summers, Jr., considered by many inside and outside the Pentagon as an undisputed expert on military affairs, went further in an article for the *Baltimore Sun*, writing, "We know that in June 1956, then-Senator Kennedy said, 'Vietnam represents the cornerstone of the Free World in Southeast Asia, the keystone in the arch, the finger in the dike.'

We know he almost single-handedly forced counterinsurgency on the military. He fired Army Chief of Staff General George Decker for opposing his ideas, made it known that future military promotions would hinge on support for a counterinsurgency doctrine, and recalled Gen. Maxwell D. Taylor from retirement to oversee conversion of the military to his views."

Was Decker more disgruntled with Kennedy than has been reported? Does he fall into a camp alongside Allen W. Dulles and Gen. Charles Cabell in the wake of the Bay of Pigs? Did he have direct access to the CIA as he suggests, including James Angleton, who was navigating the Lancelot project through Pierre Lafitte in 1963? Are there possible ties between Decker and individuals named Bender and/or Vickers?

* * *

Gerard "Gerry" Droller, a.k.a. Frank Bender, born in Germany in 1909 and considered by the agency as a "German specialist," was described by CIA's Jake Esterline as "insanely ambitious." Recruited into the CIA after the war, Droller was stationed in Switzerland before being sent to Germany where it is alleged by some that he was "responsible for reorganization of West Germany and the consequent strengthening of German-American relations." Perhaps, and most likely given Esterline's cryptic assessment, this smacks of self-promotion not to mention grandiosity by Droller, but his presence in Germany on behalf of the CIA is not in dispute. From there, he was transferred to the island of Formosa, and in another larger-than-life claim, he helped reorganize Chiang Kai-Shek's government and army. Regardless of his specific role, his intelligence history places him in the path of not only Gen. MacArthur and Gen. Willoughby, but that of Gen. Decker. In 1954, Droller took part in the successful operation to overthrow Jakobo Arbenz in Guatemala, along with Wisner, Hunt, and Tracy Barnes.

Fabian Escalante, head of Castro's Intelligence Directorate for decades and a controversial figure among assassination researchers, asserts that toward the end of February 1959, CIA representative Frank Bender met with Trujillo and his chief of intelligence, Colonel Johnny Abbes Garcia, to analyze the plans that they were preparing against Cuba. [The timing may not exactly coincide, but, as we learned in the previous chapter, Gen. Trujillo's lucrative business endeavors involved a character known to Pierre Lafitte in 1963, attorney Herbert Itkin, as well as Charles Norbert, both of whom provided legal services to George de Mohrenschildt.] Bender considered that the Caribbean Legion— as the mercenary expedition was to be called—could be converted into a kind of police force to be used whenever necessary.

Writes Escalante, "In actual fact, the plans were already well under way and the United States didn't even have to give its public consent. It only had to look the other way and then, once the deed was done, pretend that it had just heard about it. In other words, once again the United States could plausibly deny any involvement. Bender's only recommendation was to send emissaries to Cuba to recruit renegades and enhance the idea that in Cuba there was opposition among the revolutionary forces themselves. But he failed to mention that he already had agents in place doing just that, among them William Morgan." The reader will recall the significance of mercenary soldier of fortune William Morgan from Chapter 4. Escalante was also among the first to identify Jack Crichton as a financial backer of the infamous CIA hit squad, Operation 40. By 1960, Droller, under the alias Bender, was steeped in the intrigue of the immediate aftermath of Castro's revolution. According to the head of the Arbenz operation, Esterline, who was another "old China Hand," Bender and Hunt were teamed up to handle the political aspects of the attempts to get rid of Castro. The agency officer who made that decision was Tracy Barnes, a figure who looms large in this investigation.

Apparently very skilled at rallying enthusiasm of the Cuban exiles, Pulitzer Prize winning journalist Haynes Johnson describes one performance in the lead-up to the invasion:

> Then it was Frank Bender's turn to speak. They were to hold the beach for seventy-two hours, he said. And what were they supposed to do after that? "We will be there with you for the next step," Frank said. "But you will be so strong, you will be getting so many people to your side, that you won't want to wait for us. You will go straight ahead. You will put your hands out, turn left, and go straight into Havana." Frank made a sweeping gesture with his arm that no man present that day will ever forget. There was a great shout from the Cubans. Some had tears in their eyes.
>
> When it came to support, Frank was equally emphatic: *"there was no question they would have air superiority."*

Bender's assurance aligns directly with Decker's incredulity regarding the failure to provide air support: *"It never occurred to me that we could disown supporting this operation."*

VICKERS

As noted, the name Vickers surfaces in the datebook on two dates, June 5 and October 9, in what appear on the surface to be separate contexts. While it is possible that on June 5 Lafitte was making a note of funding requests or approval from H. L. Hunt and Harry Vickers (close friend and business associate of Gen. MacArthur)—both of whom were quite capable of financing international extreme right movements alluded to in the June 5 entry, "check with Hunt and Vickers"—there are stronger arguments that he means to check with CIA's E. Howard Hunt and a seasoned gunrunner by the name of Jesse Vickers.

Hunt has long been considered a primary suspect in the assassination. Contributing to the conclusion is the October 9 entry that names Vickers with Decker (Army Chief George H.) and Bender (a.k.a. Gerry Droller of the CIA). For more than a decade, Miami-based arms dealer Jesse Vickers had been active in the West Indies, a volatile region that consumed US military and intelligence resources. Vickers was arrested in 1953 for gunrunning, along with Efron Pichardo, who is named earlier in this book as having been imprisoned in 1959 with Capt. Paul Hughes, John Wilson-Hudson, and R. Emmett Johnson in Trescornia while Santo Trafficante held court. Meanwhile, Jesse Vickers had hooked up with Catherine (Mrs. W. Randall) Taaffe, self-described as "the only woman arms dealer registered in Washington, D.C."

Records suggest that Mrs. Taaffe had been an active participant in rather spectacular operations since the early '50s. She is named in progress reports related to PBSUCCESS, which culminated in the overthrow of President Arbenz of Guatemala, as having written a letter to her husband in NY, "instructing him to purchase aircraft from Sweden for a dissident group of Guatemalan Army leaders" who were planning to overthrow the government and eliminate the Communists. Described by author Joan Mellen in *The Great Game in Cuba*, Catherine was a "pint-size, brown-haired, brown eyed woman, five feet in height, and a self-styled Mata Hari" who acted as an informant for both the FBI and CIA as well as the Cuban National Revolutionary Police and the anti-Castro Acción Democrática Cristiana. There are indications that she was a friend of June Cobb, as well. By 1959, her business efforts were intermingled with not only Batista, but Generalissimo Trujillo of the Dominican Republic. We have learned previously that figures who were of primary interest to the project manager were also active in the DR, including DC attorney Herbert Itkin and skilled sniper R. Emmett Johnson.

According to a 1959 FBI document, "JESSE VICKERS . . . became associated with CATHERINE TAAFFE to utilize her contacts as wife of Colonel W. RANDALL TAAFFE. Since the departure of VICKERS and CATHERINE TAAFFE for Washington D.C. Colonel TAAFFE has been advising the Miami Office of their activities and reported that they were working on a large arms order, for which they had already secured State Department export licenses and complied with other Government requirements."

Another bureau document reads, "Taaffe is said to have been an American citizen interested in Cuban political and revolutionary activities and claims to have numerous connections among Cuban exiles in the United States and Cuban government officials in Cuba." The next entry, a report of another informant relying on a representative within *another US government agency,* advised that a case involving a C-74 airplane that was confiscated on May 22, 1959, by US Customs agents in Miami resulted in the arrest of the Dominican Consul.

Any mention of C-74s captures our attention. In an undated document found in the ledger maintained by Pierre Lafitte, he writes, "C-74 Globemaster. Walker yes on spray guns. Willoughby?" followed with an odd "note to self," *I have no idea where we will put these.* No doubt there were dozens of C-74s flying around the region during the early 1960s, but hearing the mention of that particular equipment by a man who was writing about Vickers in the context of Willoughby and Walker, one is persuaded to contemplate the implications.

Contributing to the curiosity is a related (undated) ledger sheet entry that reads in part, *Walker team - spray guns at least 5 – talk to Hunt $ - Hughes.* If Hunt is the CIA's E. Howard Hunt, might the Hughes in question be Captain Paul Hughes, who, along with John Wilson-Hudson (see Chapter 6) and Efron Pichardo—a gun dealer associated with Jesse Vickers—had attempted to discredit the Castro regime by organizing an invasion of Nicaragua, the operation that landed them in Trescornia?

As intimated earlier, was the assassination of President Kennedy, set for late November, wrapped up in an ongoing, broad-reaching—possibly international in scope—active operation? We leave that question with the next generation of committed researchers.

HIRED GUNS

Askins?
—Lafitte datebook, September 12, 1963

Askins - Willoughby OK
—Lafitte datebook, October 2, 1963

Canon-- S + V?
—Lafitte datebook, September 14 1963

Willoughby team – Canon (Z org) D.
—Lafitte datebook, November 21, 1963

"CACTUS JACK" CANON

The November 21 entry in the 1963 records of Pierre Lafitte constitutes an "end-game" in his running chronicle of plans to assassinate the president. These authors are convinced that *Z Org* is the unit long controlled by Col. Joseph (Jack) Young Canon.

Described as a taciturn, gun-loving Texan, Canon served under Gen. Charles Willoughby during the US Army occupation of Japan, running a Gestapo-like institution called the "Z Unit." Canon and his subordinates engaged in some of the same kinds of torturous practices that would later be seen during the United States's occupation of Iraq. He and Willoughby were busily fighting the Cold War in Southeast Asia at an early stage, and doing so with very little supervision because their commanding officer, General Douglas MacArthur, was also slavishly devoted to the anticommunist cause. Although Unit Z was formally dissolved in 1952, with Canon moving on to assignments in the Middle East, including Cairo, "many of its operations continued thereafter, and Canon continued to visit Japan at least until the mid-1950s," writes historian Teresa Morris-Suzuki.

In fact, according to Canon's deputy, Yeon Jeong, moves were underway to create a centralized national intelligence agency. Jeong stated that sometime shortly before Canon's departure from Japan in 1952, he and Canon were taken by Charles Willoughby to a meeting with Prime Minister Yoshida. The prime minister asked them to make a call on a government official already planning the creation of a new Japanese intelligence agency. Canon, head of the Z Unit, met with the official and briefed him about the workings of the US intelligence establishment. Of note, this is within the time frame when MacArthur's career-ending contact with the Japanese through their embassy in Spain took place. Soon after, Canon's military superior, Gen. Willoughby, was making inroads with Spain's fascist dictator, Francisco Franco.

Willoughby team— Canon (Z org) D.

That men of the egocentric character and intemperance of Gen. Willoughby and Jack Canon would be involved in an operation as spectacular as November 22, 1963, should probably not shock us. Among researchers into the assassination, in addition to chipping away at Charles Willoughby, Dick Russell was the first to glance Canon. In reference to the 1951 kidnapping and subsequent torture of a suspected Soviet spy, Japanese writer Kaji Wataru, Russell wrote: "A mysterious intelligence outfit, based in Okinawa and run by Colonel Jack Y. Canon, was accused of involvement, but hard evidence was lacking."

According to Richard Case Nagell, the double agent at the center of Russell's book, the Army Counter Intelligence Corps' (CIC) intelligence files stated that Canon's "ZED group" [perhaps an acronym, but more likely the pronunciation of the letter "z" in many cultures] was indeed behind the kidnapping; further, "the CIC was advised to stay clear of the project because it was considered to be an 'indiscreet' CIA operation."

When Nagell brought up Canon's name to an investigator for New Orleans district attorney, the investigator's notes read: "Jack Canon: rub-out man for the CIA." Russell noted, as would Morris-Suzuki many years later, that Canon had affiliations with projects of Gen. Willoughby, including the "International Committee for the Defense of Christian Culture," and Willoughby's *Foreign Intelligence Digest*, for which Canon became an associate editor.

Russell also noted that a 1977 article based on a book that had been recently released by a Soviet journalist, Michael Lebedev, featured Lebedev's claim that the assassination of Kennedy had been carried out by "an international fascist cabal," and that the fatal head shot had been fired by an agent with the alias of "Zed."

Described as quite unstable in later life, members of his unit in Japan considered Canon to be "unsuitable" as a commander of a military intelligence unit and better suited to active, preferably solo, engagement. He was known to have arranged the beating and killing of student leaders, liberals, leftists, socialists, labor union organizers, scholars, journalists, and anyone else who got in the way. A Nisei interpreter, who once helped Canon blow open a safe, recalled that the Colonel always behaved like "a movie-style gangster." In effect, Canon's legend in Asia became something that "would have chilled the blood of most America."

Known as "Texas Jack" and "Cactus Jack" interchangeably, Canon was stationed at Ft. Hood, Texas, in the late 1950s as a provost marshal. In 1958, he was sent up for court-martial, accused of "misappropriation of goods, threatening behavior, and shooting local livestock." After the court was presented with Canon's voluminous Army file (examined in camera), Canon was acquitted. During the 1960s, he was closely associated with multiple far-right groups established by his former boss, Gen. Willoughby.

According to a report titled "Belief, Decisiveness and Unity are the Prerequisites for the Maintenance of Freedom," from the September 7, 1964 Annual

Congress of the International Committee for the Defense of Christian Culture, ". . . Dr. [Billy James] Hargis [*sic*] speech about the Communist danger in the USA made it clear that large circles of people living in the Free World are very poorly informed about the Communist practices in the USA. His arguments also confirm the worries expressed by General Charles A. Willoughby, President of the American Section of the Committee, on the occasion of our Congress held in Lucerne in October 1963. *In Vienna Colonel [Jack] Canon of Illinois conveyed the greetings of General Willoughby.*" [Italics added.]

Canon retired from the military in his home state, very near the Mexican border in South Texas, where he reportedly engaged in weapons trade and experimented with the design of explosives and ammunition. On March 8, 1981, he was found dead in his home in Edinburg. He was 66 years old. Authorities recorded that he had been shot in the abdomen, but it was unclear whether the lethal injury was an accident or suicide.

COL. CHARLES "BOOTS" ASKINS, JR.

Boots Askins was a storied gunman in Texas since the early 1930s and had moved within far-right circles all his life. Author Jeffrey Caufield, in his study of the assassination of JFK, features a letter from Joseph Milteer (himself a racist and far-right associate of Willoughby and Walker) to Charles Askins pertaining to a forthcoming meeting of one of the myriad clandestine organizations that the radical right was running during the '60s, indicating very "hush-hush" stuff.

Born in October 1907, the son of a prominent hunter and writer, Askins, Jr., followed in his father's footsteps and, according to legend, "left some marks deeper than his dad." Prior to enlisting in the US Army, Askins had served in the US Forest Service and Border Patrol in the American Southwest.

During WWII, he served as a battlefield recovery officer, making landings in North Africa, Italy, and D-Day. Following the war, he was posted in Spain as an attaché to the American Embassy, assisting Franco's administration in rebuilding the arms and ammunition factories after the war. This is but one clue that Askins was well known to General Willoughby, and through that connection, he knew fellow Texan "Cactus Jack" Canon. In his role at the embassy in Madrid, Askins undoubtedly encountered Johannes Bernhardt of SOFINDUS, Otto Skorzeny, and Victor Oswald, all of whom need no further introduction to our reader. As attaché, Askins would also have been familiar with US Embassy officials including CIA agent Al Ulmer and fellow attaché Jere Wittington, Otto and Ilse's close friend and minder.

After several years in Madrid, enjoying the company of his family and bird hunting in the Spanish countryside, Askins was sent to Vietnam to join the select number of Eisenhower "advisors" training South Vietnamese soldiers in shooting and paratrooping. During those years, the colonel managed to earn his airborne qualification with both countries, amassing 132 jumps before calling it quits. While posted on the Vietnamese front, Askins would have encountered Jack Canon and Lucien Conein, among a number of other legends in that ill-fated endeavor.

Throughout his military career, Askins also indulged in big game hunting at every chance and continued to do so the remainder of his life. He retired to San Antonio, Texas, having been stationed at Fort Sam Houston when he returned stateside. He died there in March 1999. In a carefully worded statement, repeated by all who write about the legendary "Boots" Askins, "He retired from government service in 1963."

Author and expert on the topic of the use of lethal force, Massad Ayoob has been editor of *GUNS* magazine and the law enforcement columnist for *American Handgunner* since the 1970s. In a Nov–Dec 1999 article directed to rifle aficionados, particularly those fans of Remington Model 911, Ayoob draws the reader's attention to the legendary Charles Askins, Jr., summarizing him as "A controversial modern legend." During his career, as lawman and in the military, the colonel had aggressively sought out maximum action. The writer suggests that Askins's lack of hesitation to kill had also led to questionable shootings.

Ayoob, who knew Col. Askins personally, explained that for those who knew him, there was no other way to describe him other than a "stone-cold killer," indicating that facets of "Boots" Askins were not suited to law enforcement, including racism and a killer instinct that could sometimes "slip its leash." By the colonel's own count, he had killed twenty-seven, not including [racial slur] and Mexicans. In a separate account by an avid gun historian, we learned that Askins did not hesitate to shoot opponents regardless of race or nationality but didn't consider those of minority status worth counting in his tally. Askins himself said that he hunted animals so avidly because he wasn't allowed to hunt men anymore.

* * *

Thus are the profiles of at least two men selected by Charles Willoughby, with likely approval of Edwin Walker, to show up in Dealey Plaza. Whether the men considered themselves "hired killers" or just anxious and willing participants, we can suspect they had personal reasons that prompted them to be "in on the kill" in Dallas—a shared hatred of Kennedy and the policies he was advancing. It is clear from the datebook that by mid-September, both Askins and Canon were on the mind of the project manager for the assassination plot. Lafitte later writes that by December 4, Canon had "gone home."

A third name can be added to likely candidates of the W. team roster.

ROBERT EMMETT JOHNSON

In the early '60s, Robert Emmett Johnson, would-be journalist and skilled assassin, attested that he had been employed by Information Services International to support the agenda of dictator Rafael Trujillo of the Dominican Republic. ISI, founded and presided over by former OSS officer Ulius Amoss, dealt with extensively in the previous chapter, boasted as a trusted advisor General Charles Willoughby. The day following the critical note, "O says done,– Oswald in place," Pierre leaves a clue that the W. team included *E. Johnson*.

W team E. Johnson's
(Itkin)

Said to be fiercely independent and opinionated, Johnson advised Special Agents of the FBI in Miami on September 19, 1961, that he had been employed as Foreign Affairs Analyst for Dominican Republic leader Generalissimo Trujillo, who had been assassinated in May of that spring. Johnson held the "analyst" position from 1956–1960. At the time of his visit from the FBI (9/61), Johnson stated he was then employed by ISI, which he described as "an independent intelligence-gathering organization" founded by Amoss, a former Chief of Staff in the US Air Force. On the ISI board of Trustees was Charles Willoughby.

As mentioned in a previous chapter, inside Trafficante's world at Trescornia in 1959, among those he said he recognized—all of whom had a shared history— was mercenary sharpshooter Emmett Johnson. Factoring in Johnson's employment by the master of leaderless resistance, Ulius Amoss, and ISI trustee Charles Willoughby, there is sufficient reason to suspect that Johnson was on, or involved with, "W's" team.

According to the meticulous research presented by historian John Simkin, a declassified document says that in 1962, Emmett Johnson was a member of "Interpen" (International Penetration Force), established in 1961 by former US Marine Sgt. Gerry P. Hemming. With funding from Santo Trafficante and several wealthy associates, and organized (among other things) to train members of anti-Castro groups, Interpen set up a training camp in New Orleans in 1962.

Before he died, Emmett Johnson managed to publish several books under the imprint Paladin Books (publisher of Col. Charles Askins's books) under the name "Paul Balor." The cover of the second edition of his book, *Manual of the Mercenary Soldier*, published in 1993, features a clear image of Mitchell Livingston WerBell, notorious arms equipment manufacturer and dealer who had served in Donovan's OSS during the war.

"MITCH" WERBELL

No investigation into the long shadows cast while the conspiracy to assassination Kennedy took shape is complete without naming Mitchell Livingston WerBell, soldier of fortune and successful arms merchant. After WWII, and following a brief stint in public relations, "Mitch" pursued his skills as mercenary for hire and paramilitary trainer before establishing his armaments engineering firm outside Atlanta, Georgia.

Named in the Lafitte datebook on five dates during the first quarter of 1963, WerBell certainly warrants the concentrated study his life story has been afforded over the years, but for the purpose of this investigation, a brief excerpt from *American War Machine* by the revered assassination author, Prof. Scott, best encapsulates those aspects of his notorious career that are of specific interest:

> [Paul Helliwell ran] the OSS Detachment 202 in Kunming, China, a station that had made payments to its agents in opium. By 1949 if not earlier, Helliwell was engaged in purchasing Gen. Claire Chennault's airline Civil Air Transport for the OPC (Office of Policy Coordination, later merged with CIA), and he later became counsel to a bank laundering money for Meyer Lansky and the American underworld. . . . The members of Helliwell's small OSS detachment in Kunming (Helliwell, (Howard) Hunt, Ray Cline, Lucien Conein, and Mitchell Werbell [*sic*] cast a long shadow over both postwar intelligence-drug triarchies and the WACL's (World Anti-communist League) history. . . . Mitchell Werbell [*sic*], who went on to develop small arms for intelligence services like the DFS [Mexico's intelligence and security forces], was also involved with WACL [World Anti-communist League] death squad patrons like Mario Sandoval Alarcon . . . and was eventually indicted himself on drug charges.

While it is possible WerBell was engaged in some phase of the assassination given these affiliations—some in fact may speculate that he at least provided the gunmen with the expert silencers he was famous for—Lafitte does not name him beyond February 28, 1963. However, it's indisputable that in early 1963, Lafitte was privy to (and perhaps directly involved with) certain of WerBell's activities.

Lafitte's February 27 mention of "Austin," in the context of WerBell prompted the review of businessman Frank Austin and attempts to raise funds and political support throughout the region for a de facto Cuban government in exile. Following Austin's name, Lafitte makes a note of a phone number that traces to DC attorney Marshall Diggs. In early March, Lafitte makes a note "Diggs" and "Kohly." Diggs is alleged to have been a CIA contract operative, and Mario Garcia Kohly, a known associate of Frank Austin, was a Cuban investment banker whom they considered to be the leader in exile. The fundraising efforts fell under close FBI scrutiny, particularly a check in the amount of twelve million dollars, which may or may not have come from a *certain Texas oilman*. It has been speculated that because Diggs was known to have direct access to oilman H. L. Hunt of Dallas, the check came from the archconservative known for funding private, clandestine operations. While the episode is intriguing, for this investigation we're led to hypothesize that the WerBell, Austin, Diggs, Kohly operation, whatever its purpose, was ancillary to the plot to assassinate the president.

These FBI records of late 1962 and early 1963 confirm that WerBell had been working in the Southern Hemisphere, and it's clear he was committed to the eventual removal of Castro, but an earlier entry dated February 5 indicates that he was far afield: "WerBell guns – in desert with Proctor in Eritrea" with none other than the illusive Thomas Proctor. Covered previously in Chapter 5, it is worth repeating that it was Proctor who (eight months later) would provide the introduction of gunrunner Thomas Eli Davis to Madrid-based global arms merchant and close associate of Otto Skorzeny, Viktor Oswald. Some ninety days after Lafitte's entry referring to WerBell and Proctor in Eritrea, Lafitte names Tom Davis and his wife, Carolyn, alongside the name Vosjoli, the head of French intelligence Philippe Thiery de Vosjoli, whom James Angleton had been courting for months. The May 20 entry also refers to OS (Otto Skorzeny), Ilse (Skorzeny), and, once again, Proctor. We remind the reader that during an interview with Proctor's son, it was confirmed that his father had indeed been involved in supplying Emperor Haile Selassie of Ethiopia with guns in the early 1960s, which poses the possibility of deliberate exploitation of the territorial conflicts with neighboring Eritrea. When told that his father was apparently in Eritrea as well, Proctor's son remarked, "makes sense."

Was this particular arms mission involving WerBell, and perhaps French intelligence, just one more transaction Pierre Lafitte was tied to in 1963? Within two weeks, Lafitte's focus was turned to a cast of characters that included "The Generals," drawing ever closer to Otto Skorzeny's strategic plan to murder the president.

CHAPTER 8

THE SKORZENYS

Ilse 8:00 PM
—Lafitte datebook, June 19, 1963

Cable to Madrid – all – ok – tell Tom D.
O says come to Madrid
—Lafitte datebook, October 1, 1963

A COUPLE OF CHARMING NAZIS

Otto Skorzeny has come to be regarded, in some quarters, as the premier designer
and executor of German special operations during the Second World War based
on numerous factors, some borne of substance, and some a reflection of Skorzeny's
deft hand at delegating planning authority combined with an equally deft sense
of public relations. In the course of accomplishing his most high-profile mission,
the September 1943 glider-borne mountain top rescue of Benito Mussolini,
Skorzeny displayed great daring, but his subsequent claims to have planned the
operation were a substantial stretch.

Skorzeny biographer Stuart Smith, in *Otto Skorzeny: The Devil's Disciple*,
plausibly suggests that Major Harold Mors, who headed an elite airborne battalion near Rome at the time and had a tremendous amount of experience in
conducting airborne assaults, was the actual author of the operation at Italy's
Gran Sasso mountain that liberated Mussolini. Military historian Lt. Col. Flo-
rian Berberich would comment that "Actually, Skorzeny pretty much went along
for the ride—as a passenger . . ." Still, Skorzeny had been responsible for a great
deal of the intelligence collection that pointed the German paratroopers to Mussolini's location, and decisions he made on the ground played a large part in the
success of the operation, which had been formally handed to Skorzeny by Adolf
Hitler. Admiral William McRaven, arguably the world's foremost authority on
military special operations, concluded: "Whether Skorzeny was a straphanger or the

mastermind of the operation is inconsequential. Ultimately, success resulted from Skorzeny's action at Gran Sasso, and not from Mors'"

Subsequent to the rescue of Mussolini, Skorzeny was warmly congratulated and promoted in rank by Hitler and, at the behest of German Reich Minister of Propaganda Joseph Goebbels, appeared on "Deutschlander" radio, claiming that he was the man who liberated Mussolini, and embellishing the story with the tale of a nonexistent gun battle. Further special operations tasks given to Skorzeny in the waning days of the Third Reich had mixed results, but his legend had been made. Winston Churchill pronounced the operation as being of "great daring," and Western intelligence services took note of Skorzeny, foreshadowing postwar relationships. As Smith writes, another result of the Mussolini rescue was that "Skorzeny began to attract high-caliber military personnel of the type he had previously lacked . . ."

A military contemporary of Skorzeny's would note that while Otto was "intelligent," he was not "intellectual," and one of the keys to Skorzeny's future success—and his value to planners of political violence—would be his reliance on others for detailed operational planning. Early in his career, Karl Radl, a friend of Skorzeny's second wife, fulfilled that role. Radl, a lawyer and a brilliant "detail man," is described by Stuart Smith as "Skorzeny's Sancho Panza . . . While Skorzeny enthused over big ideas, Radl found practical ways of achieving them."

Otto's experiences at Gymnasium in Munich, briefly touched upon in Chapter 2, shaped what would become a lifelong worldview. A chilling prediction some three decades later (Cairo, Jan 30. 1953), published in Paris newspaper *Le Monde* and titled *Les Condamnations de Nuremberg seront responsables de l'horreur de la prochaine guerre*, reveals Skorzeny's core philosophy:

War is inevitable, and this time, it will be truly worldwide. It will unravel everywhere and there will be no limit to its battlefields. The condemnations of Nuremberg will be one of the main reasons, which will cause this was to be a conflict whose horror will be unparalleled. These condemnations gave birth, in fact, to a new conception which makes the victor a hero and the vanquished an odious criminal. By this fact, each leader will wage war like a demon in order not to be the loser and become, consequently, a criminal. All the atrocities that can be imagined by man, will be committed during this next war, in order to prevent the enemy from acquiring victory. What I have just said, I have repeated to the American representatives and I have warned them that all of the mothers of the entire world will one day curse America. —SS Otto Skorzeny

By then, he was comfortably ensconced in the congenial environs of Madrid, along with his wife, Ilse Luthje, a woman he had met and fallen in love with in 1949. Ilse claimed to be a countess, and to be the niece of former German Reichsbank head Hjalmar Schacht. Neither of these claims was quite accurate. Suggestion that she was directly related to "Hitler's Banker," Schacht, stems primarily from the affectionate term "Uncle Hjalmar" used both by Ilse and Otto, but there is a possibility she was directly related to Hjalmar in some way. "Countess" could have been a "borrowed" title. However, Ilse was, by all accounts, a brilliant operator who had worked for German intelligence during the war and had affiliations with French intelligence during the postwar period, as noted previously. Smith writes that, in an intellectual sense, ". . . Ilse would take over in Skorzeny's life where Karl Radl had left off."

Otto Skorzeny's recruitment by elements of US intelligence, beginning with an intense vetting by Arnold Silver of Army Counterintelligence (soon to enter CIA at a high level) at the multipurpose POW facility Camp King, has been well covered by historian Ralph Ganis in *The Skorzeny Papers*. Efforts to utilize Nazi elements in the ongoing Cold War with Soviet Russia, initially handled under the auspices of Army Counterintelligence, were gradually shifted to the Office of Policy Coordination (OPC), created by the National Security Council in 1948. OPC, a dangerously bifurcated agency that was supposed to take direction from the US State Department but was administratively tied with the newly created CIA, was a creation "principally of four men associated with the Council on Foreign Relations: the career diplomat George Kennan, and the three-man committee in 1948 chaired by CFR president (Allen) Dulles. Dulles and his allies also arranged for the OPC chief to be Frank Wisner . . ." Wisner, a brilliant, intense, and very odd man, took hold of OPC and quickly turned it into an unaccountable power base, with Allen Dulles as a behind-the-scenes partner.

OPC-run covert operations ranged widely and included assassinations of suspected double agents and the use of the kind of people who were adept at such violence. "We knew what we were doing," recalled CIA officer Harry Rositzke, a Soviet expert who had once worked with Wisner. "It was a visceral business of using any bastard as long as he was anti-communist." Colonel James Critchfield, a CIA liaison officer working with former Nazi Reinhard Gehlen at the time, knew Wisner and his operations well. "Some of the people Frank brought in were terrible guys," Critchfield recalled, "but he didn't focus on it." Those curious about characters who seem to have danced between the raindrops in the immediate aftermath of the war and the ensuing Cold War may find that Critchfield is among the most worthy of close scrutiny, particularly his role with Louisville-based Tetra Tech after the war.

In an interview Otto Skorzeny gave to CIA officer Daniel Wright in 1959, he recounted what appears to be his first formal contact with Wisner's Office of Policy Coordination (OPC). Shortly after his release from captivity in 1949, he was approached by a "Mr. Martin," Skorzeny told Wright. Martin claimed to be from the US State Department and requested Skorzeny's presence at a meeting. Martin appears to have been David Martin, then-Director of the International Relief Organization. Martin's IRO, which would shortly become the International Rescue Committee, was formally concerned with postwar refugee issues and aligned with OPC on matters concerning Soviet bloc refugees and would be utilized by CIA in multiple Cold War roles, particularly as a means to move technically sophisticated refugees from Soviet bloc countries.

During the latter part of the Second World War, Martin had served as an intelligence agent for the Yugoslav forces, led by royalist General Draža Mihailović, who were fighting against the rise to power of Josip Tito, and he proved to be very amenable to Cold War-era U. S. intelligence agencies. "David Martin had a talent for generating project proposals of interest to the intelligence community," wrote the leading chronicler of the IRC, Eric Chester. The meeting Skorzeny attended, in January 1949, involved Martin and numerous other significant individuals, including Boris Pash, an Army officer who had been detailed to OPC in 1948. Wisner assigned Pash to head a planning division of OPC (PB-7), which, among other tasks, dealt with "covert operations not tasked to the other planning branches." It would later be clear during testimony presented before the Church Committee, the 1975 Senate investigation into abuses by the CIA, the NSA (National Security Agency), and the FBI that the unspecified "wet affairs" included kidnappings and assassinations.

The meeting went on through the night and lasted fourteen hours, Otto claimed, covering topics that included plans for the return of Western pilots shot down while conducting covert operations inside Soviet bloc countries, sabotage inside Communist countries, and PB-7 plans. During Church Committee testimony, Pash recalled that at the meeting, there was a discussion regarding a potential Soviet invasion of Western Europe, what operations should be carried out to deny the Soviets access to key industries in the event of invasion, and what actions could be taken to prevent the capture of certain technically accomplished assets whose skills would be very valuable to Soviet military and scientific research.

At this point in the meeting, Pash recalled "a woman" sitting at the table who spoke up and said: "Why don't we murder them?" Pash claimed that the bluntness of the woman's comment caught many at the meeting off guard. "Who she was, I don't remember," Pash testified. "I don't know whether I knew her name then. She was in the group sitting around a table." Ganis strongly suggests that the woman was Ilse Luthje, working in concert with SS Otto Skorzeny. Otto would continue to be of interest to Wisner and to other hard-core factions of CIA even after becoming of use to French intelligence.

Indeed, the well-connected Ilse Luthje played a large part in facilitating Otto's late 1940s affiliation with the French *Service d' Ordre*, an organization that was open to the recruitment of former Nazi SS officers as assets, and was also involved in setting up French "stay-behind" teams as part of the storied "Operation Gladio." A postwar CIA report scrutinizing Ilse noted that ". . . the Countess maintains operational connections with the *Sûreté* [French security forces]. Her headquarters in Paris is at the Cabaret de Lido on the Champs-Elysées. She has regular contacts with Pierre Bertaux, the former chief of the *Sûreté* in Paris, and Colonel Remy, General de Gaulle's former G-2." In fact, Bertaux had allowed Otto and Ilse to live at his residence for a time in 1949. The address was a stone's throw from French Fascist agents operating under "Group Robert" who were embroiled in Project Jeanne.

According to author Ralph Ganis, the Skorzenys had been involved with Roger Wybot's SEMIC, the "Society for the Study of Industrial and Commercial Markets," which was essentially a detective agency within his counterintelligence apparatus. By the mid-1950s, Otto had taken great pains to distance Ilse from exposure of her role as an agent for the network. If indeed her expertise was in business, and this organization was an intel operation in service to corporate intrigue around the globe, Otto would have been intent on protecting the long-term value of her position.

Both Wybot and Bertaux would become close personally and professionally with the CIA's James J. Angleton, whose recruitment of a leading member of the French intelligence service, Phillipe de Vosjoli (named in the Lafitte datebook, twice), as a double agent is "one for the records" in the history of US counterintelligence. Referenced in an earlier chapter, it was a disgruntled agent within SEMIC who named Wybot as involved in the jewel heist of the Aga Khan and his Begum outside their villa, *Yakymour*, located in Le Cannet, Côte d'Azur. Pierre Lafitte is said to be one of the other thieves in that operation, along with notorious Corsican drug runner, Paul Mondoloni, a name that was on his mind well into 1963.

That Ilse greased the wheels for Otto here, and that she brazenly recommended murder as a tactic in a top-secret meeting, foreshadows her role in years to come.

During the early 1950s, Otto and Ilse would continue to cultivate high-level covert contacts as they operated from their base in Madrid. Of interest to the intelligence services of Western governments, not only due to his reputation as a planner and practitioner of special forces operations, Otto was of value for his increasingly large stable of special forces operatives. One likely Skorzeny involvement will be especially of interest to students of the assassination of President Kennedy. A CIA document cited by Ganis reveals that Skorzeny was in Berlin in March 1951, involved with "preparations for the establishment of sabotage and resistance groups, presumably with the KgU . . ." KgU (a German acronym for "Fighting League against Inhumanity") was a CIA-funded program, run under Wisner's OPC. KgU was created in 1948 and was part of the numerous cut-and-thrust operations that were being run against the Soviet zone of Germany as the Cold War heated up. Skorzeny was very likely a paramilitary adviser to KgU. The same memo reports that Skorzeny has "settled down officially in Madrid and opened an engineering office . . . *this is obviously a cover.*" (Emphasis added.)

AMERICA'S JAMES BOND

William King Harvey, dubbed as America's James Bond by USAF Maj. General and pioneer in clandestine operations and psychological warfare Edward Lansdale, arrived in Berlin at the close of 1952 to take control of KgU and another OPC project, the Investigative Committee of Free Jurists. Harvey's initial tasks were a prelude to his assuming control of the largest CIA operation in the world at that time, the Berlin Operating Base (BOB). Correspondence between Otto and Ilse, sourced by Major Ganis from the Skorzeny archive, reveals that Otto was involved with either Harvey or the preceding head of BOB, Henry Hecksher, in 1953. Otto cannily wrote that he had a visit from "BOB" and that he showed BOB a letter he had received from Egyptian president Gamal Nasser, among other topics of conversation. Regardless of whether Skorzeny was referring to Hecksher or Harvey, the visit he described has implications of note. And if Otto was in contact with Harvey this early, that contact, when paired with the efforts to assess Skorzeny at Camp King by Arnold Silver, comes back around in force when Silver becomes Harvey's chief aide in Project ZRRIFLE a few years hence, and the pair were involved in recruiting experts in "executive action" under CIA's QJ/WIN program.

Without a shadow of doubt, Bill Harvey was among those most prominent on the mind of the project manager for the assassination throughout 1963, as evidenced by notes made on twelve dates. As with a number of characters named by

Lafitte in this record, the notes are cryptic, but studied in full, they leave clear indication that Harvey was critical to whatever Pierre was working on. Some may challenge the fact that William King Harvey does not dominate these pages; however, it is the opinion of these authors that a voluminous record now in the public domain in support of his role in the assassination stands on its own. The notes of Lafitte merely serve as confirmation, and for that reason, we choose to provide the dates and text of all twelve entries in the Endnotes and let the reader and researcher take it from there.

Involved in the OPC's "Free Jurist" program, overseen by Harvey, was Colonel Robert Storey, who at the very least was already "acquainted" with Skorzeny from his stint as head of the Nuremberg Trials documents division. Storey, along with his close friend, Houston attorney and lead counsel for Schlumberger Oil Services, Leon Jaworski, would play an important part in the investigation of the assassination of President Kennedy, heading up an independent Texas investigation. Both Storey and Jaworski subsequently played a role authorized by Earl Warren in investigating Texas aspects of the assassination. The two men also had a Texas attorney present during all Warren Commission sessions to monitor the proceedings. Banker and oil industry expert Robert Storey was among the contacts whom Pierre Lafitte made note to call as planning for the assassination of President Kennedy neared the final stages. Storey is considered at length in the chapter "Lay of the Land."

Skorzeny, along with his future wife, Ilse, had become involved in a dizzying array of affiliations with economic entities as well as continuing to be of clandestine interest to US military and intelligence agencies, operating from a safe perch in Francisco Franco's Madrid. Their business relationships encompassed "steel, scrap metal, cement, electronics, arms and ammunition, aircraft and aircraft parts, financial lending, real estate, construction, energy development, automobiles, meat products, and even snake skins," moving toward the accumulation of a fortune that would total $3 million (the equivalent of over $13 million today) at the time of his death. Otto also represented a company—H. S. Lucht—which the CIA suspected was illegally trafficking Spanish nickel to the Soviet bloc. The Skorzeny's interest in nickel would apparently continue into the 1960s. (See Chapter 6.)

And then there was oil. How much Skorzeny made from oil-related investments is uncertain, but one such investment that he and Hjalmar Schacht partnered with Texas investors on is significant far beyond its economic impact. Known as the Meadows-Skorzeny venture, in 1952 an American syndicate led by oil exploration giant DeGolyer & McNaughton arrived in Madrid to put together an oil-drilling deal. A number of the participants in this venture—who were entertained by Skorzeny and Schacht—are individuals and entities that would come to be of interest to researchers focused on the murder of President Kennedy. Jack Crichton, representing DeGolyer & McNaughton, Algur Meadows and Judge Gordon Simpson of General American Oil Company, and Republic National Bank's mysterious Howard Corporation were all involved in the syndicate, covered in depth in the next chapter.

We learned in Chapter 2 that Otto had been invited into the tangled wide web of former OSS head William Donovan's World Commerce Corporation and forged multiple business operations with Johannes Bernhardt, head of the Nazi financial/investment vehicle SOFINDUS during the Second World War. All of these entities functioned not only as economic investments, but as vehicles for the clandestine moving of both "human capital" and funds, leading to the conclusion that the Texas contingency either participated in WCC or benefited from its activities in some manner.

Through the mid-to-late 1950s, Otto also found time to run special forces training camps outside of Madrid, camps which were apparently utilized—via circuitous arrangements—by US special forces personnel for training purposes. He also became even more involved in areas of strategic interest to the U. S. government and US allies, including Algeria and the Congo. One of his trainers at a Spanish camp was Jean Rene Souetre, introduced to the reader in Chapter 2, both in Algeria and in the US in 1963.

ILSE ARRIVES STATESIDE

By March 1954, Otto had finally married Ilse Luthje, his third and final marriage. A CIA analyst would remark that the Skorzenys formed a dangerous team. "He is extremely active, possessed of tremendous vitality, and willing to try almost anything . . . She is apparently a clever and intelligent woman who will not stop until she has reached the financial and social position which she believes is her due." Prophetically, the analyst remarked that together, "they were capable of considerable mischief."

Three years later, according to an interagency memo from CIA Counterintelligence to the State Department and FBI, Ilse Skorzeny managed what would become a historically significant feat, arriving in New York for the purpose of "assisting her husband in promoting some business deals." Major Ganis's evaluation, that her purpose was to "establish a headquarters, of sorts, for their overt and covert operations," is a more complete description of the circumstances. As we learn, it most likely was not by chance that Ilse joined New York-based Previews, Inc. to advance those interests.

Not only did the real estate firm, which specialized in putting together high-dollar international deals, provide an ideal cover for a woman intent on progressing their businesses across Europe, Latin America, and North Africa, but its cofounder was the former Director of Security for Wild Bill Donovan's OSS. The East 53rd address of Previews is identified in Lafitte records as the location for key meetings during 1963. What compelled a high-profile, international firm to place the name of a former Nazi, who was married to an infamous Nazi officer, on their roster? There are a number of clues to consider.

ANOTHER COLONEL

Ilse's nominal superior at Previews, also reporting to the board that included Donovan's former director of security, would be Col. Herschel V. Williams, who also led a fascinating life, laced with high-level contacts seemingly above his pay grade, and entrée into hard right-wing circles. A graduate of Yale with a Bachelor of Philosophy and Fine Arts in 1931, Williams had been an adman and playwright before the war. When America joined the Allies, he served with the Army Air Force in North Africa working as an intelligence officer under Texas native Col. Robert Storey. He left military service after the war with the rank of colonel, but in 1948, apparently having made a significant impression, USAF Col. Williams was recalled for "special duty" at the Pentagon to serve as a member of the Joint Intelligence Staff. He soon threw himself into the swirl of Washington, D.C., political society with such force that he would be discussed by men who sat at the pinnacle of the United States policy-planning network. By the time Ilse Skorzeny was added to the Previews roster in 1957—a move that defies coincidence—Col. Williams was an executive vice president of the company.

During 1953 and 1954, some fifteen seminar sessions were held at the Institute for Advanced Study in Princeton, New Jersey. Hosted by J. Robert Oppenheimer, "to discuss the foreign policy of the Truman years," these sessions brought together the men who played the largest roles in the creation and execution of policy during the Truman years: Dean Acheson, Averill Harriman, Paul Nitze, George Kennan, and a handful of their colleagues, in an atmosphere that was conducive to rare honest discussion by power brokers. Former head of Truman's Policy Planning Staff Nitze, when discussing voices around Washington, D.C., during the early 1950s who favored "preventive war" against the Soviet Union, said: ". . . well, what I was saying was that my recollection was that there was a group which used to meet with (James) Burnham from time to time which included Colonel Herschel Williams of the Air Force who was working in air intelligence under (Secretary of the Air Force Stuart) Symington—these people were wholly convinced of the validity of Burnham's point of view that this was the beginning of World War Three, that war was inevitable, and that we ought to get cracking at it."

A 1951 State Department Policy Planning memo, directed from PP staffer Robert Joyce to Nitze, expressed horror at the virulence of the "first strike" advocates in Washington at that time. Joyce honed in on a prominent advocate of war: "A Lt. Col. Herschel Williams I have long thought has played an important role in what might be called Air Force thinking in the 'drop it now' school." Williams "now considers himself somewhat of a geopolitician. He has a new and rich wife, [the daughter of a prominent Missouri Senator], and I understand entertains lavishly in Washington along the lines which he and his wife regard as a political salon. He does not disguise his extreme hostility to the Department of State and what he regards to be the Department's soft policy with regard to the Soviet Union. I have been advised he is listened to with attention and respect by some of his superiors in A-2. I am also advised that he is a close personal friend of Mr. Stuart Symington, who apparently has a high regard for Williams' views on the world situation. From my short meetings with Williams, I consider him to be an ignorant, conceited, and wrong-headed man."

Joyce continued: "I know for a fact that Herschel Williams is a close friend and more or less constant companion of Mr. James Burnham, the author of *The Struggle for the World, The Coming Defeat of Communism*, and other books. I am also advised that Mr. Burnham sees quite frequently Isaac Don Levine [sic]. As you know, Messrs. Burnham and Levine are former Marxists who are now among the leading and more extreme of the hate-Stalin-and-do-something-about-it-at-once school. In short, I believe there is a great deal of evidence that there is a James Burnham-Herschel Williams-Air Force-Symington nexus . . ."

The following day, Nitze sent an internal State Department memo in which he quoted a contact of his, Professor George Taylor, who had recently attended a dinner party held at the home of Freda Utley, a right-wing writer who was also a business associate of Otto Skorzeny. Taylor described the guests at the party as being a group of militant ex-communists who were "united by a sense of righteous urgency for immediate war with the Soviet Union." Another guest at the Utley party was identified by Taylor as "an Air Force Lt. Col. named Williams." Taylor told Nitze that "great adulation was paid to Williams by the ex-communists present. They listened to his words as authoritative. They praised him as the one man within the circles of government who understood the situation." Professor Taylor described Williams as "a very articulate man of about 40, endowed with a college sophomore comprehension of communism and a set of blood-curdling clichés."

Williams was also appointed to the board of the Tolstoy Foundation, alongside numerous intelligence-connected ultraconservatives including the kingpin of the Dallas White Russian community, oil industry expert Paul Raigorodsky, Jean de Menil of Schlumberger, and Igor Sikorsky, all of whom are pursued in Chapters 9 and 10. The Tolstoy Foundation was known as one of the most far-right postwar refugee organizations devoted to cultivating a particular kind of Russian émigré. Tolstoy board member Vadim Makaroff had even led a campaign of vilification in 1951 against the extremely conservative David Martin of IRC, whom we met previously, accusing him of being a "hidden Communist" due to Martin's policy of reaching out to certain *left-wing* assets. In addition to his legitimate reason for dealing closely with Ilse Skorzeny at Previews, Col. Williams was apparently in frequent communication with Otto.

On the go throughout her marriage to Otto, Ilse's passports indicate that among her primary destinations beginning in the late 1950s was Ireland. All indications are she was donning her real estate cap during her travels. According to author Stuart Smith, at a certain point, a few within the Irish government became uneasy with signs that Ilse's scheme of "encouraging wealthy foreigners to settle in Ireland" was paying off. The *Daily Express* reported that a friend of Otto and Isle's, cosmetics *impresaria* Madame Ingrid Marbert of Düsseldorf was planning to buy an estate in County Kildare. Stuart also writes, "Later that year, the Sunday Independent revealed that wealthy German filmmaker Kurt Linnebach had acquired a mansion [in the adjoining] County Clare. Were these isolated individuals or outriders of a trend? And if the latter, who else might be visiting, or even applying to join the colony? Rudel, Degrelle, Mosley?"

At the same time, the unconfirmed reports from a confidential source that Hans Ulrich Rudel and Léon Degrelle in league with Irish "farmer" Otto Skorzeny had their eyes on Ireland as a new base had surfaced.

OTTO AND ILSE IN IRELAND

Léon Degrelle funded a small part of the JFK hit . . . only because he despised Kennedy so much.

—AS TOLD TO AUTHOR H. P. ALBARELLI JR. BY PHEN LAFITTE

The leader of the far-right Catholic Rexist Party in Belgium, Léon Degrelle, served together with Otto Skorzeny during WWII when he was in command of the Belgian SS division. Having been "denazified," and subsequently recruited by US intelligence, Skorzeny set up shop in Madrid, where his party comrade Degrelle had been in hiding since crash-landing, literally, in Spain at the end of the war. In the early '50s, financing was made available for the two loyal fascists to organize a building firm that immediately secured lucrative Spanish government contracts, in addition to access to US government and Pentagon funds designated for construction of military airfields throughout Spain.

A decade later, according to historian Dennis Eisenberg in his thorough exposé, *Re-Emergence of Fascism*, "The early spring of 1961 saw one of the most important changes in plans for the fascist international's future activities. The scene was Madrid, the exact meeting place highly secret. Gathered around the table were such men as "Scarface" Skorzeny, [Rexist party leader Léon Degrelle, Waffen ace Hans Ulrich] Rudel and several other high-ranking Nazis [among them was the son of Klaus Barbie]. It was decided at this meeting to try and make Ireland the future home for their activities in the same way as the Argentine had been used in the days immediately after the war. . . . The methods used were the same as those which had been directed against Peron; the country will be flooded with capital in such a way that the Government would become dependent on the men who control the money purses. Now Ireland was to become a kind of 'refuge' on the door-step of Europe for fascist-minded extremists."

The cultural and political soil in Ireland had been tilled for just such an ambitious endeavor since the early 1930s.

Eisenberg continues, "But why Ireland? Why should the fascists try and make Dublin their new base? For one thing Ireland is much nearer to Europe and the country has never been at war with Germany. Secondly there are strong German sympathies among sections of Irish society mainly because of historic bitterness towards the British. Skorzeny and two representatives of a German and a Swiss bank had protracted talks with members of the Irish Government and they promised to transfer considerable sums of capital to aid its economic development. The Irish in turn promised to give permission for the Germans to use large tracts of Government owned land to afford them tax reliefs. The Irish insisted that the new industries should be scattered widely over the country so as to get the maximum benefit from the influx of capital."

As a model for this specific scheme, years earlier the renowned German aircraft designer and manufacturer, Wilhelm Emil "Willy" Messerschmitt, sought to bring fifty technicians with him to Madrid to develop the aircraft industry in

Spain. Drawing on reports from other US intelligence agencies, the FBI noted that Otto Skorzeny was allied with Messerschmitt in physically transplanting German industry to Spain. We can surmise that those handling the details of these projects included Col. Charles Askins, Jr.

While Skorzeny was ostensibly working on the Messerschmitt project on behalf of the Spanish government, an FBI agent charged with monitoring the progress cautioned, "it seems entirely logical we will be having the German air industry recreated under our very noses." Apparently, the powers that be in Dublin did not share the Americans' concern as they readily pursued similar opportunities with German industry a mere fifteen years after the purported fall of the Reich.

The politics of Ireland had concerned the US since the war. Tens of millions of immigrants and descendants of immigrants of voting age from Ireland helped influence American policy. A US government secret report from April 1949—amid the paranoia of Cold War politics—gave details on political parties, the power of the Roman Catholic church, and the negligible influence of Communists—with one "Dublin bookseller" considered the only Communist of note in the entire country. "Denial of Ireland to an enemy is an inescapable principle of United States security," it said, followed by, "Irish neutrality would 'probably be tolerable' but 'it could become necessary to utilize Ireland,'" it warned before cozily concluding that because Ireland was already ideologically aligned with the West and "strongly Catholic and anti-communist," it would "probably not remain neutral in an East-West war."—official statement, CIA.

Had Ilse and Otto Skorzeny opted to purchase property in the late '50s in any country other than Ireland, and were they not seemingly entrenched in Co. Kildare by 1959, where they sometimes contemplated and executed their next moves, the history presented in this chapter would belong to another book entirely. But for reasons we shall explore, they favored Ireland. It is critical to first understand that the essential scaffolding for their welcome, as well as the fulfillment of dreams of another base for the Reich, had been constructed as early as the 1930s.

When speaking of the "lay of the land," Rene Lafitte was clearly referring to Dallas and the scene of the crime, as will be studied in full in our next chapter. For now, we will consider *the lay of the land that was Ireland* in the lead-up to the assassination, made all the more poignant considering Jack Kennedy had been in his ancestral home just four months before he died that violent death in Texas. As president, he had insisted that he could take a side trip en route from Rome to the States in late June if he so wished. When his close friend and confidant

Kenny O'Donnell challenged, *"Ireland? There's no reason for you to go to Ireland. If you go to Ireland, people will say it's a pleasure trip,"* Kennedy responded in his inimitable fashion, *"That's exactly what I want. When I say I want to go to Ireland, it means that I'm going to Ireland. Make the arrangements."* Said to have loved every minute of the extended stopover, the president's last words as he boarded Air Force One were, "I'll be back in the springtime."

We now consider the practical circumstances that afforded Otto and Ilse entrée to Ireland in 1957, in spite of, or perhaps because of, his notoriety as Hitler's favorite commando.

THE SKORZENYS CHOOSE ÉIREANN

According to Otto's personal papers acquired by collector Ralph Ganis, one of his first contacts upon his arrival in Spain in late 1950 was Irish innkeeper Philip Mooney. Ganis only speculates that Mooney may have been an intelligence operative or part of Wild Bill Donovan's Secret Paramilitary Group. We will identify several further clues to lead one to guess that at the very least, Mooney, along with several other persons of interest in Ireland, knew Bill Donovan. Skorzeny remained in contact with Mooney until he died sometime before spring of 1957.

It was Mooney who, sometime in the early '50s, introduced Skorzeny to fellow Irishman William Hynes, an engineer who moved easily within Madrid social circles. Hynes in turn introduced Otto to yet another engineer, American Edgar H. Smith from Bristol, Pennsylvania. Smith's travel records provided by the Bristol library indicate that he was age forty-one in 1945, lived in Washington, D.C., and was employed by the US Army. His itinerary in the late '40s included four-month stints in Paris as well as flights from Lisbon, through Spain, en route home to DC. His obituary indicates that he served a brief time with the Civil Aeronautics Board, and that he founded a NY-based company, Intercontinental Engineering Corp, although records for Intercontinental suggest that Smith may have purchased an existing firm.

In the early 1900s, Intercontinental advertised in the *New York Times* that they provided "engineering services around the globe." For certain his father, engineer Edgar Albion Smith, was involved in laying Brazil's Madeira-Mamoré (Devil's Railroad) to provide access to Bolivia's rubber resources at the close of the 19th century.

It was through US Army staff officer Ed Smith that Skorzeny, under the alias Rolf Steinbauer, then met US Army Captain Jere Wittington, the military attaché assigned to the US Embassy in Madrid. We have no evidence that Smith continued to socialize with Skorzeny, but during the course of the friendship with Wittington—courtesy of Smith, Skorzeny told the attaché that he sincerely believed a showdown with the Soviets was coming soon, and that he had a plan to counter this Soviet threat. Although Skorzeny had alluded to the same with the engineer Edgar Smith, he failed to go into any great detail. Wittington would pass the information he gleaned from Skorzeny to the Central Intelligence agent in charge, Al Ulmer, a person of keen interest to many assassination researchers.

The introduction to Wittington, which originated with Irish inn-keeper Phil Mooney and advanced through Irish engineer Wm. Hynes and Army officer Ed Smith, would become the basis for a long-standing CIA contact cover program for Skorzeny. Over the ensuing years, the mechanism relied on utilization and manipulation of attachés from the Army as well as various other military branches.

Phil Mooney died before Ilse and Otto Skorzeny secured visas to enter Ireland in 1957, so it was left to his wife, Gladys, with whom he owned the prestigious Portmarnock Golf Club in North Dublin, to manage the red tape, and eventually arrange for a formal, newsworthy "coming out party" for the Nazi couple in the Nation's capital. Records indicate that Otto first applied for visas in March 1957. Within three months, Gladys, who claimed that she and Phil met Otto in Gibraltar in the early '50s, pulled out the stops, and one evening in early June, the Skorzenys were introduced to what the media defined as "the cream of Dublin society." As author Stuart Smith quotes the Evening Press, "the ballroom was packed with representatives of various societies, professional men . . . and, of course several Teachtaí Dála . . ." Smith continues, "there was much clicking of cameras and popping of flashbulbs as the great man, signing autographs all the while, foregrounded the land of a helicopter—still an extreme rarity in those days—that had been brought in from an airshow near Dublin to fete the occasion . . . Skorzeny and his stylish 'honey-blonde, blue-eyed' Prussian wife attracted favorable comment in the Irish and British media. . . ."

Portmarnock was one of Ireland's oldest and most revered links courses, located ten minutes north of Dublin City Centre and fifteen minutes from Dublin Airport. The clubhouse was situated on 160 acres immediately adjacent to Dublin's Velvet Strand, where aviation history was written in 1930 when Charles Kingford Smith, pilot of the Southern Cross, took off from Portmarnock beach for the first Atlantic Crossing from east to west. Since opening, the links golf club has hosted eighteen Irish Open championships and, according to the promotion, "remains one of the most respected venues in world golf. No other Irish course has been graced by so many distinguished players in a rich history encompassing a broad sweep of significant events." One of those events involving a famed Nazi SS officer and his intriguing wife, the former Countess Finckel-stein, would be directly tied to a controversial period in contemporary history of the young nation.

THE GUESTS

Gladys Mooney's guest list was the who's who of Dublin's political, legal, business, and social glitterati. Representative of the star quality in attendance that evening was famed aviator John Cecil (Jack) Kelly-Rogers, who lived in Portmarnock, "just up the road" from the Mooney's Portmarnock Golf Club. At the time, Kelly-Rogers was the chief pilot and chief operating officer for Aer Lingus, the Irish national airline that he had joined shortly after the end of the war. Aer Lingus, the semi-state airline established under the Ministry for Industry and Commerce, was, by his own account, the greatest single personal achievement of Sean Lemass, then-minister of the department. As we will read, Lemass would later serve as Deputy PM and then PM while Otto Skorzeny and his Nazi associates jockeyed for position with the Irish government.

Prior to signing on with Aer Lingus, Kelley-Rogers had been present at the creation of the British Overseas Airways Corporation, which was formed just as the Second World War began. He was soon appointed Winston Churchill's personal transatlantic pilot for the duration of the war. In 1940, Kelley-Rogers navigated the darkly painted camouflaged Short S.30 flying boats, including the G-AFCZ Clare, making six return crossings of the Atlantic with passengers. One of the three passengers on the first trip of the "Clare," designated NA W9, was Colonel William "Wild Bill" Donovan, special advisor to President Franklin Roosevelt and head of the Office of Strategic Services, whom we met in Chapter 1. According to author Peter Kross, "Bill Donovan left England on August 3, 1940, aboard the BOAC flying boat *Clare*. There were only two other passengers aboard, and upon his return Donovan would say that the trip was "boring." Donovan arrived in New York the next evening and the following day had a meeting with Secretary Knox. Over the next few days, Donovan met with every important military and political representative of the president, including members of Congress who had been briefed on his clandestine trip." Nearly two decades later, might pilot Kelley-Rogers have been particularly curious to encounter one of Bill Donovan's greatest assets, Otto Skorzeny, in Dublin?

Kelly-Rogers also maintained the flying-boat shuttle from Poole to Foynes on the Shannon estuary. When mileage range was increased for trans-Atlantic aircraft, making flying boats obsolete, Shannon Airport was constructed. It is believed that Otto Skorzeny participated in the engineering for Shannon over the decade. The regional airport proved essential to connections between the US, Europe, and, most significant, the Middle East. In recent years, it has been the focus of activists protesting its use by US military transports in spite of the nation's long-standing position of neutrality. Shannon's significance to geopolitical concerns, especially during the 1950s and 60s, cannot be overstated. The flying range of airplanes of the 1960s required that trips across the Atlantic be done piecemeal. The northern route from Britain to the US involved stops in Ireland, Greenland, Canada, and NY. The southern route followed a flight path over the Caribbean, access to The Bahamas, and on to Miami.

Between 1954 and 1957, tourist visa regulations in Ireland were liberalized for certain applicants, with Germans seen as potential tourists. Labor Minister Norton introduced legislation in 1955 that created the Irish tourist board, Bord Fáilte, which became fully operational in 1957. The Irish-German Air Transport Agreement had been established in 1956. This allowed Aer Lingus to fly to Frankfurt and Düsseldorf by 1957, cities also used by the Irish airline as hubs for travel to other parts of Europe. Lufthansa also introduced direct flights to Dublin and began to operate to North America via Shannon. The United States military currently relies on Shannon for hundreds of weekly US military flights to and from combat zones.

ILSE THE REAL ESTATE AGENT

As we know from *The Skorzeny Papers*, ". . . almost all the correspondence from Otto to Ilse describing business opportunities, meetings with key individuals, status of negotiations and contracts, banking issues, financial arrangements, and business ventures, evaluations of potential partners and potential partners and possible difficulties, and cost of profit estimattions [sic]. Categories: banking, financial opportunities, import-export, construction, steel manufacturing, raw materials (lumber) mining, surplus aircraft sales and parts and a variety of other financial pursuits."

Although there is no specific reference to "real estate transactions," we know that by 1957, Ilse Skorzeny was operating under the umbrella of international real estate firm, Previews, Inc. In that role, her interest in an elaborate and exclusive collection of private residential homes near Cannes, France, captures our attention.

According to Irish historian Fin Dwyer, whose extensive research into circumstances surrounding the Skorzenys' arrival in Ireland has proven invaluable to understanding the dramatic period, another guest that summer evening in Port-marnock was a mysterious, monocled Parisian identified as Mr. Beckhardt. He had flown into Dublin the day of the reception, especially for the Skorzeny event, only to depart the following day. At the time, he was described as a banker "*having had connections to French intelligence.*" In light of both Otto and Ilse's association with French Intelligence officers Pierre Bertaux, Director of the Sûreté Nationale, and Roger Wybot, head of the DST, both of whom were introduced earlier, it is not surprising they might want a "Mr. Beckhardt from Paris" to be included in the evening, and vice versa. A French intel agent (former or not) adds further to the implications of the welcome that the Skorzenys were afforded in Ireland.

We know from the military record of "Pierre" Beckhardt that he was born January, 16, 1913, in Strasbourg, that he achieved the rank of lieutenant during WWII, and that he served in the Central Bureau of Intelligence and Operations, or BCRA, an organization the reader is already familiar with. The commander of the BCRA, Major Andre DeWavrin, under the nom de guerre "Colonel Passy," was responsible for what was to be the forerunner of the SDECE, or French intelligence service. As elaborated on in a previous chapter, the Americans considered DeWavrin to be unpredictable, if not completely untrustworthy, and after the assassination of Admiral Darlan, and following the scandal of the Duke Street Murder, even the most hardened (including Bill Donovan), thought twice about associating with DeWavrin, whom some referred to as *nothing but a "Sicherheitsdienst thug."*

As mentioned, Donovan realized that the BCRA had secretly set up what he termed "an inquisitorial chamber," and that the French secret service was using "black methods" of interrogation. Whether or not our Lt. Beckhardt was a party to these "black arts" is not known. Neither is it known if he rejected them, regardless of how distanced he might have been from Duke Street. We do know he served in North Africa during the war, and that he felt comfortable flying into Dublin in 1957 to catch up with Otto and Ilse, old friends of Roger Wybot who ran Col. Passy's counterespionage service of the BCRA.

According to French historian Olivier Wieviorke, recruits into the service included distinguished men, but shortage of manpower from 1940 to 1944 was a recurrent problem. During the first half of 1942, more than two volunteers were judged unfit for underground action and sent back to their original units. As a result, for example, the R-Section, which was the intelligence division of BCRA, could send only five agents into the field monthly prior to early 1943. Wieviorke writes, "In all, scarcely more than four hundred men—a tiny number—were dispatched to the metropolis prior to the Normandy landing on June 6, 1944."

This places BCRA Lt. Pierre Beckhardt serving among a heady company of highly trained spies during the war.

The posh French residential enclave that captured Ilse Skorzeny's interest was situated a little over ten kilometers from Cannes on the Côte d'Azur. The modern story of "Castellaras Le Vieux" begins in the early 1920s with Jacques Couelle, a budding Parisian architect who had been sent by US mining industrialist Evander Schley, whose El Potosi lead and silver mine in Northern Mexico was the foundation of a vast empire. Schley had told Couelle to "pick a spot in the warm ochre earth of Provence and construct a replica of a French château." The mining magnate had been heavily invested in Rockefeller's Chase Bank since the turn of the century, placing him in contact with those doing business with weapons dealer Victor Oswald and Otto Skorzeny in Madrid.

Ten years later, the decades-long dream financed by Parisian banker Pierre Beckhardt finds its way into our story. According to the same *New York Times* story, *"Backed by Pierre Beckhardt, a soft- spoken Paris banker* [emphasis added], Couelle was hard at work by the end of the decade, and Castellaras Le Vieux, as the village is formally called, came into existence." Coulle's Château Castellaras occupied the landscape in the hills above Cannes for two decades before the wife (Begum) of the Aga Khan III designed Villa *Yakymour* outside Le Cannet, which sat between Castellaras and Cannes. The irony cannot be overlooked that the Aga Khan and Begum had been robbed in 1949 of all the jewels they had with them, outside the gates of Yakymour, just ten kilometers from Schley's empty Château, allegedly by Roger Wybot, Pierre Lafitte, and others.

Coincidentally, Ilse's Irish estate in 1959 was located within ten kilometers of two of the Aga Khan's Irish studs in the Curragh. It should be emphasized here that had the Aga Khan not become enthralled with the potential that Ireland offered his thoroughbreds, his investments in bloodstock, Irish racing and betting, which was heavily influenced by the founders of the Irish Hospital Sweepstakes, and by politician Charlie Haughey et al., Ireland's position in international racing may have never achieved the fiscal success that it did.

A committed Nazir Ismailli Shia Muslim whom some students of the religion regard as the original "assassins," a sect that in contemporary times has attracted the elite in business and diplomacy, the Aga Khan III was born into his position. Since a young man, he had been enamored with Egypt, spending extended periods of time during the winters in a villa near Aswan. It is likely he was aware of Skorzeny's presence in Egypt in the 1950s, if for no other reason than Nasser's contentious Aswan Dam project on the Nile River. Following his death in 1957, Aga Khan was entombed in an exquisite mausoleum on the banks of the Nile.

Concerns expressed by some within the Irish government suggest that Ilse was very effective in convincing Europeans to purchase property in Ireland, including the Princess Marbert from Düsseldorf, whose travel was made much easier by the Shannon-to-Düsseldorf flights launched in the mid-1950s. Conversely, Ilse would have a "built-in" market in Ireland for property acquisitions on the Continent, including those financed by "Mr. Beckhardt," among the horse set and those with newly acquired wealth in Ireland resulting from the economic strategies coming out of Bonn and New York.

THE IRISH "MAFIA"

Among those representing the Irish government at the reception for the Skorzenys was Mayo "Mafia" and backbench Teachta Dála (TD) Paddy "The Bishop" Burke, known as such for his diligent attendance at constituents' funerals. Decades later, his son Ray would be identified in the press as among the most corrupt politicians the country had ever known. Bishop Burke was joined at the Skorzeny reception by up-and-coming member of Dáil Éireann, TD Charles J. Haughey, anxious to welcome the glamorous couple just in from Madrid. In a little over a dozen years from that first public outing with Otto and Ilse, Charlie Haughey would play a central role in the "Arms crisis of 1970." The scandal, and the preceding border campaign of 1956–1962, dubbed "Operation Harvest"—a guerilla warfare action carried out by the IRA aimed at overthrowing British rule in The North—are backdrop to the prime years spent in Ireland by guerilla warfare expert and alleged arms dealer Otto Skorzeny and wife Ilse.

Another significant civil servant official who joined the throng at the Portmarnock, one who loomed in the shadows of the Skorzenys' eventual purchase of Irish property, was assistant secretary of the Department of Justice Peter Berry. In 1936, assigned to Ireland's justice ministry, Berry compiled volumes of research on the IRA and a dossier in manuscript form on Communist groups in the country, earning himself the powerful position as head of the intelligence division of the Department of Justice in 1941. He would hang on to this post, under numerous titles, for the next three decades until his retirement in January 1971. In other words, while at the Portmarnock reception, Berry was the man most responsible for foreign and domestic intelligence. Not dissimilar to America's FBI Director J. Edgar Hoover, Berry came to be recognized as the department's éminence grise, given his encyclopedic knowledge of subversive individuals and organizations.

According to the *Dictionary of Irish Biography*, Cambridge University Press (upon which we have relied heavily for detailed biographical information on a number of those named in this chapter), Berry—much like Hoover in the US—"competed vigorously with military intelligence for control of internal security, and after 1945, succeeded in reasserting the primacy of the Department of Justice while the military were reduced to peripheral status." The heads of Garda Special Branch and the Garda Security Unit S3 reported directly to Berry, well known for his fondness of electronic devices such as telephone scramblers. All this history and experience as he hobnobbed with Hitler's most valued SS commando, Otto Skorzeny, in June 1957.

In stark contrast to Ireland's welcome of known Nazis, including the Skorzenys, it was Peter Berry who opposed asylum in 1953 to ten Jewish families from the Soviet Bloc, stating that "Jewish immigrants were recognized as posing a 'special problem' by the departments of Justice, Industry and Commerce, and External Affairs." Berry asserted that Jews in Ireland, "by refusing to assimilate and by acquiring disproportionate wealth and influence, had created widespread anti-Semitic feeling among the Irish people." He also suggested that, "international Jewry" was using financial influence to secure preferential treatment for Jewish refugees who were no more deserving than millions of other displaced people.

In some cases he adopted what he described as a "go-slow policy" in handling such applications, even when they had been approved by the cabinet. Yet Berry found no difficulty in turning a blind eye to, if not offering outward support of, the continued presence of a significant number of German Nazis in Ireland who had been responsible for the tragic plight of those several hundred Jews, and millions more. Neither could Berry have been oblivious to persistent rumors that predominately Catholic Ireland had been a critical route for Nazis fleeing Europe via the Vatican "ratlines."

By March 1957, Berry had advanced to the post of assistant secretary of the Department of Justice; he would be regularly deputized during long periods of the official Secretary's illness, which afforded him significant power and placed him in direct contact with his ultimate boss, the Minister for Justice. Oscar Traynor was in charge of the Dublin Brigade in 1916, a unit that included the aforementioned Seán Lemass, who was serving as deputy prime minister on March 20, 1957 as Otto Skorzeny applied for a visa in Madrid.

No doubt Gladys Mooney's sister-in-law, Mae Mooney, a well-known civil servant in her own right, attended the June "meet and greet," as well. Conveniently, in her professional capacity within the Department of External Affairs, and in spite of the Republic's extremely restrictive emigration policies in the summer of '57, Mae contacted the Madrid Embassy to facilitate a three-month visa for Otto and Ilse Skorzeny to enter Ireland, perhaps drawing on influence from Peter Berry and Oscar Traynor.

When the Skorzenys again applied for visas the following year, their applications were supported once again by Gladys Mooney; but this time, Dublin businessman Richard "Dick" Duggan, infamous for having created the Irish Hospital Sweepstakes, joined Mrs. Mooney in vouching for the charming German couple.

In the months following the reception, which appears to have been designed to test the political, social, and commercial waters of Ireland for the Skorzenys, the couple embarked on a search for suitable property, ultimately settling on Martinstown House in the Curragh, Co. Kildare. Described by some as a castle, others call it a "rambling 19th-century shooting lodge and farm," the more apt description of illustrious architect Decimus Burton's design would be "a strawberry Gothic-style manor." Martinstown was situated on 165 acres of farmland abutting the edge of The Curragh (*the place of the running ho*rse), home of world-renowned flat racing.

SIR OSWALD AND LADY DIANA MOSLEY

A detour is fitting: As mentioned in Chapter 1, historian Robert Skildesky revealed that Oswald Mosley, founder of the British Union of Fascists, "hung around such characters as Otto Skorzeny *a top Nazi incorporated into Western intelligence work.*" That "hanging around" was made easier in Ireland in 1959, where the Mosleys were comfortably installed only a pleasant morning's drive south of Martinstown.

In the early 1950s, Mosley and his wife, Diana Mitford, had purchased Clonfert Palace, Co. Galway, Ireland—rumored to have been prompted by tax issues in the UK—where they resided until a fire in December 1954 gutted their home. Early in 1955, the Mosleys purchased the elegant Georgian house, Ileclash, built on an elevation over the Blackwater outside Fermoy, Co. Cork, on the southeast coast.

Mosley married his second wife. Diana Mitford—one of six Mitford sisters who captured the maelstrom of British and American press in their day—in 1936 in the Berlin home of Nazi propaganda chief Joseph Goebbels with Adolf Hitler as one of the guests. Mosley, who would become a lifelong friend of Nazi Ulrich Rudel, endorsed Hitler's policies following the outbreak of World War II, which led to his internment, after which he was shunned by the British establishment. In a note of irony, Diana's sister, Deborah, married into the Cavendish family and eventually earned the rank of Dowager Duchess of Devonshire. Her brother-in-law, the

Marquess of Hartington, married Kathleen Kennedy, the older sister of John F. Kennedy. Lismore Castle, the seat of the Duke in Ireland, played host to the young Senator Kennedy, a trip he frequently recalled with deep fondness.

Mosley and his wife, both unrepentant fascists to their deaths, were entrenched in the Republic of Ireland by the time Otto and Ilse Skorzeny began visiting the country.

From his base in Ileclash, in the late '50s, Sir Oswald was spending increasing amounts of time mixing with aspirant neofascists in Europe and with the theorists of apartheid in South Africa. In Britain, meanwhile, a new issue was developing that offered him a route back into proper politics: West Indian immigration. In August 1958, race riots erupted in Notting Hill, an area where a growing number of West Indians—many of them recruited to work as nurses or on the London Underground—were settling alongside other immigrants, including a large Irish population. Mosley's Union movement immediately saw the potential for capitalizing on popular resentment and came to the defense of the gangs of Teddy Boys who had been prosecuted for "nigger-bashing."

In April 1959, commuting to London from Fermoy, Co. Cork more and more frequently, Mosley announced that he would stand in the general election to be held the following September. In August, he appeared in court alongside two brothers accused of assaulting and shooting a black medical student.

It was probably the renewed publicity Mosley was attracting that summer of '59 that provoked Noel Browne, former Irish minister of health to describe Mosley in the Dáil as an "undesirable" who might use his residence in the Republic of Ireland as a "funk hole" to allow him to engage in racist activities elsewhere.

A similar concern continued to plague the Mosleys' neighbors to the north despite attempts to portray the Skorzenys as ideal implants into polite society. According to Martin Lee, in *The Beast Reawakens*, while in Ireland, "Skorzeny bred horses and spent summer months relaxing with Ilse." Author Stuart Smith relates that Otto told interested inquirers, "Horses . . . would be joining the livestock, as they were 'part of my wife's childhood," This in contrast to the fact that few credible stud farms would boast that their thoroughbreds had "joined the other livestock" as a feature. Of all the locales in the country for serious horse breeding, there would be no better setting than one in the midst of the 5,000 acres of flat open plain of the Curragh; however, the Skorzenys' desire to raise a few horses as a hobby left over from Ilse's childhood could have been amply served by a wide range of affordable farms away from the heady wine of the Curragh.

In Skorzeny's own words: *"From 1957 to 1960 I simultaneously organized an army in India and another in the Congo, supplied and advised both the Algerian*

FLN and the French OAS, and thanks to my Irish sheep I was also able to take an interest in the activities in the IRA." We will venture that Otto's occasional suggestions that he and Ilse meant to engage in raising thoroughbred horses was a cover, and that their choice of the Curragh, influenced from the shadows, provided the penultimate cachet and access to some of Ireland's most influential businessmen, politicians, and global thoroughbred racing's most wealthy, not to mention close proximity to military training facilities.

Supporting the Skorzenys' controversial bid for the right to permanent Irish residency, along with Justice Peter Berry, who we know from news reports was present at the June '57 reception, was Berry's boss, Minister Oscar Traynor, who played a role in the foundation of the Republic when he served as leader of the IRA's Dublin Brigade under Gen. Michael Collins during the 1916 uprising. That brigade included Seán Lemass, who as mentioned was responsible for the creation of Aer Lingus in the mid-1930s. Lemass, a career politician, went on to serve in primary cabinet positions of the government for decades, culminating in his election as Taoiseach in June 1959. Another IRA comrade of Lemass and Oscar Traynor was James Joseph (Joe) McGrath, who over the ensuing decades would become the scion of a family dynasty the equivalent of America's Rockefellers. McGrath was one of the founding triad of the Irish Sweeps, along with Richard Duggan, who joined the soiree for the Skorzenys and ultimately assured their permanent residence status in Ireland.

Traynor had risen through the ranks of the movement toward independence and during WWII served as Ireland's Minister for Defence, a portfolio he would fill again from 1951 to 1954. As defense minister, he had been responsible for all military training and activities of the Curragh Camp. In March 1957, he was appointed to the prestigious post of Minister for Justice, by chance just in time to influence entry visas for the Skorzenys. As justice minister, he was serving under his old comrade, Deputy Prime Minister Sean Lemass.

Three years later, Traynor was replaced by Charlie Haughey, a member of the Irish Parliament who would be embroiled in scandal his entire political career. Haughey assumed the role of attentive "unofficial" host and frequent visitor of Otto and Ilse Skorzeny while they were in residence in the Curragh. It is noteworthy that The Curragh Camp, the largest British Army base on the island before the founding of the Irish Free State in 1922, when it was recovered by the new government, was located ten minutes from the Skorzeny's new residence.

Given rumors that Otto Skorzeny was operating a training camp while in Ireland, and due to the layout and limited facilities at Martinstown House, the Curragh Camp would be a logical option for training; but the possibility that he preferred Baldonnel military base, less than a half-hour away, with its airfield should also be considered. Perhaps he took advantage of both, or all three. According to the area's local historian Reginald Darling, "Irish army officers even planned to ask Hitler's former henchman to give a talk at the Curragh Camp but it was cancelled when senior officials got wind of it because of the obvious diplomatic sensitivities."

THE NEIGHBORHOOD

Follow the money. I know I don't have to remind you of that, but I know it's not always easy to carry out.
                              —H. P. ALBARELLI JR. TO COAUTHORS SHARP AND KENT

The man who vouched for Otto and Ilse's visa applications in 1958, Richard "Dick" Duggan, was a solicitor and one of Ireland's best-known businessmen for having advanced his father's scheme, the Irish Hospital Sweepstakes, which by the '50s had reached a worldwide market. With a passion for horseracing that led to his becoming one of the principal racehorse owners in Ireland, Duggan and partner Joe McGrath brought in another horse racing enthusiast from South Africa, Captain T. Spencer Freeman, and the triad was granted the exclusive franchise to run a sweeps on behalf of (and many allege *on the back of*) Ireland's healthcare system.

Welsh-born T. Spencer Freeman was another trained engineer who had finished his schooling in Johannesburg. He brought to the scheme the operational and promotional skills honed during WWI when he organized the entire mechanical transport salvage operation in France. Further inquiry could produce a number of common denominators with persons of interest to the investigation.

In 1939, at the outbreak of WWII, Spencer took leave at the Sweeps and placed his services at the disposal of the British government. His reputation for organizational skills and perhaps his service in WWI must have caught the attention of Lord Beaverbrook's Ministry of Aircraft Production because he was soon named principal director of the ministry's Emergency Services Organization—responsible for restoring production in all munitions factories and frequently commandeering commercial factories' facilities—and director at the Ministry of Aircraft Production under Beaverbrook.

Known to his friends as Max (Aitken), Beaverbrook had served as head of the British Ministry of Information at the end of WWI and later became a close confidant of Prime Minister Winston Churchill. Beaverbrook's staff member, Spencer Freeman, also served on the radio board committee under the control of the British war cabinet, a position he attained through the influence of his mentor. He shared this stint with a captain in the British Army from Co. Tyrone, No. Ireland, Captain Peter Montgomery of the board of BBC Northern Ireland. Students of DA Jim Garrison's investigation into the assassination of John Kennedy might well recognize Peter Montgomery as having been a lover of New Orleans businessman, board member of Permindex, and defendant, Clay LaVerne Shaw, who flew to Ireland a few short months after the assassination.

Following the war, Spencer Freeman returned to Ireland, bringing with him connections to powerful men he had encountered under Beaverbrook's command. He resumed his role with partners Duggan and McGrath, and being as avid a promoter of horse racing as his partners, Freeman purchased the Ardenode Stud in County Kildare, located only minutes from The Curragh flat-racing course and the Skorzeny's future manor, Martinstown House.

Freeman and Duggan's partner, Joseph Joe McGrath, shared a passion for horse racing to the extent that he, among the three, became Ireland's best-known racehorse owner and breeder, winning The Derby in 1951. Brownstone's, McGrath's stud farm, which catered to world-class racehorse breeders including the Aga Khan III, who was the leader of over thirteen million Naziri Ismailli Muslims, was located minutes from Spencer Freeman's Ardenode Stud, and what would be the Skorzeny couple's choice of residence in 1959. McGrath had in 1944, in spite of "The Emergency," Ireland's term for the world war, engaged in significant horse trading, including the purchase of *Nasrullah* from the Aga Khan.

TILLING THE SOIL

Prior to attaining the bragging rights of "richest man in Ireland," Joe McGrath had been a member of the Irish Republican Brotherhood. His coworker in an accountancy firm at the time was famed Irish revolutionary leader Michael Collins. McGrath joined Collins' guerilla army of the Irish Republic, and the two revolutionaries established a close bond. McGrath also earned notoriety for organizing numerous bank robberies to fund the cause where a small percentage of the proceeds was retained as a reward by him and his fellow soldiers. According to Paul McMahon, in *British Spies and Irish Rebels: British Intelligence and Ireland, 1916–1945*, "McGrath maintained a private army of a number of the worst thugs and gunmen produced by the IRA in the troubled times, and had used his Sweepstakes organization on behalf of the 'new IRA' to move men, money and documents between Ireland, Britain and the US."

According to McMahon, at the outbreak of WWII, the British intelligence service believed that there was a nest of potential quislings within Fianna Fail party circles, and perhaps the most sinister member of the group was Joe McGrath. Indeed, among Joe McGrath's closest friends during that period was Dan Breen, who in 1943 sent a congratulatory note to Hitler that read, *"May he live long to lead Europe on the road to peace, security and happiness,"* and days before his death, Breen had asked the German minister to forward his birthday wishes to the Führer. In May 1947, Breen attended the funeral of Nazi spy Hermann Görtz, instrumental in "Plan Kathleen," another code name for the IRA invasion of Northern Ireland with the support of Nazi military.

After eighteen months on the run, Görtz was captured and interred for four years. Following the prime minister's amnesty granted to German soldiers and spies, Görtz remained in Ireland for almost two years during which time he pleaded for permanent residence. To establish a bona fides, he took on the role of secretary for the Save the German Children Society (which, it must be highlighted, excluded children of Jewish extraction). IRA member and committed fascist Dan Breen served as treasurer. The Co. Wicklow-based society would have been familiar if not indirectly associated with Stille Hilfe für Kriegsgefangene und Internierte ("Silent assistance for prisoners of war and interned persons").

Like Görtz's "Save the German Children Society," Stille Hilfe also provided support for children of Nazi servicemen, in particular those of prominent SS officers including Otto Skorzeny's daughter Waltraut, and the son of Otto's good friend and future business colleague, Werner Naumann. It was Naumann whom Hitler designated as his nominal replacement in the event of his own demise, and Naumann who engaged with Otto Skorzeny and Victor Oswald through the corporate front, H.S. Lucht Co. Stille Hilfe—"Silent Help"—later boasted as its honorary chairman Albert Schweitzer, founder of the Swiss-based college that a decade later would capture the interest of Lee Harvey Oswald.

THE BLUESHIRTS

When McGrath and Freeman and Duggan ran the inaugural Irish Hospitals Sweepstakes in 1930, the supervisor was General Eoin O'Duffy, Chief Commissioner of the Garda Siochana (under the CID), a devout Roman Catholic, rabid devotee of "corporatism," and a primary instigator of Ireland's earliest public dalliance with fascism. Without doubt, Peter Berry (named previously) and O'Duffy brushed shoulders at the CID.

Eoin O'Duffy supervised the Manchester Handicap inaugural Irish Hospital Sweepstakes for Richard Duggan, Spencer Freeman, and comrade Joe McGrath.

A Roman Catholic from Co. Monaghan in The North, O'Duffy trained as an engineer before joining the Republican cause. Another of Michael Collins's foremost supporters, he served alongside Joe McGrath under the command of General Collins, who in 1922 promoted him to Chief of Staff of the Irish Republican Army. He was later appointed chief commissioner of the newly named Garda Siochana, the equivalent of the chief of police of the Irish Free State. O'Duffy's Garda was then merged with Joe McGrath's police intel service, the CID. O'Duffy also founded the security organization for what is now the right-leaning Fine Gael political party. Named The Army Comrades Association, then the National Guard, it became known colloquially as the "S," whose members adopted many of the symbols of fascism including the notorious outstretched arm salute.

When Taoiseach Eamon de Valera banned the movement for what appears to have been internal, politically practical reasons, O'Duffy reconstituted it under the banner "League of Youth."

Long a supporter of fascism's corporate state ideal, popularized by the papal encyclical Quadragesimo Anno, O'Duffy became more and more involved in international fascism, attending the German Nazi-sponsored International Action of Nationalism's conference in Zurich in December 1934. Inspired to found the National Corporate Party of Ireland in June 1935, he then attended the Italian-sponsored Comitati d'azione per l'Universalità di Roma convention at Montreux, Switzerland, in September of that year, where he was appointed to the secretariat of the Fascist International. Further exemplifying O'Duffy's exploitation of the allegiances shared by countries dominated by the Vatican, and the support afforded Franco's Spain by many Irish Catholics, in 1936 Gen. O'Duffy led 700 of his followers to Spain to help General Franco in his war against the republican government. They formed part of the XV Bandera Irelandesa del Terico, a part of the Spanish Foreign Legion, and although they saw little if any action, an ideological bond with Franco and his Spain was sealed.

The Attorney General of Ireland with oversight of O'Duffy and the Garda in the early '30s was one John A. Costello, who would serve as Taoiseach of Ireland from 1948 to 1951 and again from 1954 to 1957, leaving office the same month that unrepentant racist Peter Berry assumed a position of increased influence in the Department of Justice, and just ninety days before Otto and Ilse "came to town." In 1934, at the height of Gen. O'Duffy's efforts to promote a corporate and vocational state that closely resembled the regimes of Mussolini and Franco, Costello stood before the Dáil in defense of the wearing of uniforms (other than those worn by official government sanction) and in opposition to a bill designed specifically to curtail O'Duffy's Blueshirts. Costello declared, "*The Minister gave extracts from various laws on the continent, but he carefully refrained from drawing attention to the fact that the [Mussolini's] Blackshirts were victorious in Italy and that the Hitler shirts were victorious in Germany, as, assuredly, in spite of this Bill . . . the Blueshirts will be victorious in the Irish Free State."*

Both Costello and O'Duffy were noted for their fealty to the Vatican over and above their allegiance to the young Irish State. Costello once declared, "I am an Irishman second, I am a Catholic first, and I accept without qualification in all respects the teaching of the hierarchy and the church to which I belong." Similarly, O'Duffy, whose fervent Roman Catholicism was greatly reflected in the ethos of the Garda and of course the Blueshirts, whose policies were based on the ideological adherence to and eventual adoption of a corporate and vocational state subordinate to the Vatican. Historians debate whether these policies prove O'Duffy was more loyal to the Vatican or more inspired by Fascist Italy; regardless, his version of Catholicism and devotion to the Vatican had vestiges of fascist ideology.

Just over a decade later (O'Duffy died an alcoholic), an even bolder effort to destroy the infant Irish democracy and replace it with a one-party totalitarian state was initiated by Belfast-born Roman Catholic Gearoid Ó Cuinneagáin, a young pro-Axis activist. His aim was even more ambitious: the fusion of totalitarianism and Christianity that would make Ireland a "missionary-ideological state" wielding global influence in the postwar era. In 1937, he published his first call for an alliance between Ireland and Mussolini's Italy against their common enemy, Great Britain.

However, according to author R. M. Douglas, "although he [Ó Cuinneagáin] respected what Germany and Italy had achieved, he had no wish to become the local Irish representative of 'the Hitler fan club.' On the contrary, he genuinely believed that a fascist Ireland could become more influential than its Continental counterparts—not militarily but ideologically. By narrowly basing their respective versions of fascism on 'blood and soil' and imperial conquest, Hitler and Mussolini could never hope to spread their systems to countries other than those they directly controlled. Ó Cuinneagáin maintained that Ireland's twentieth-century destiny was instead to become a model of the politics of the future for others to follow. By combining totalitarian efficiency with the universal values of Christianity, Ireland would be a laboratory for a wholly new ideology: a fascism designed for export. As a 'missionary-ideological state,' spreading its doctrines overseas, Ireland could look forward to becoming 'mistress of the Atlantic as it is the wish of Japan to become mistress of the Pacific. With the difference that we shall be masters in the Pacific Ocean also. . . . Should we play our cards carefully and cleverly it will be possible for us from the capital of Ireland to dictate to the dictators themselves."

To that end, Ó Cuinneagáin organized Ailtirí na hAiséirghe, the "Architects of the Resurrection," which further cast an uncomfortable light on the popularity of antidemocratic, anti-Semitic, and extremist ideas in wartime Ireland. According to Douglas, "in 1945, the party gained one seat in the Dáil 'the precise moment when newsreel footage of mass graves, including that in Bergen-Belsen which had been liberated in April were being displayed on cinema screens across Ireland.'"

In July, Aiseirghe's film critic described such footage as "hate-mongering" fabrication, foreshadowing the propaganda of holocaust denial by Nazis British Citizen David Irving, Americans George Lincoln Rockwell (who himself visited Ireland in 1962) and ardent adherent and promoter of the writings of Francis Parker Yockey, Willis Carto, over the ensuing decades. Carto, as the reader will recall, first promoted Holocaust denial in the US, and by the mid-1960s owned a publication whose military editor was General Edwin A. Walker.

Not long after, the Irish Friends of Germany and Cumann Naisiunta (National Association) formed by O'Cuinneagain and several former Blueshirt members including Ernest Blythe—who as Minister for Finance had approved funding for Siemen's hydroelectric scheme—began to organize and assist in planning for German invasion of Ireland known as Plan Kathleen under the cover of Irish-language classes. The plot was discovered, and principal members were taken into custody. However, O'Cuinneagain was not caught and went on to organize the "Branch of the Resurrection," a "Hitler Youth Movement under the guise of an Irish class."

The cultural, ideological soil in Ireland had been tilled by the likes of O'Duffy, Costello, and Ó Cuinneagáin when at the end of WWII, Nazis began to avail of Vatican ratlines conceived of by Catholics Bishops, Nazi organizers, and US intelligence expert James Angleton and cohorts. At least a dozen noted Nazis settled in Ireland with little opposition, and while some within the Irish government expressed deep concern when Otto and Ilse Skorzeny arrived on the scene in 1957, they could very well be meaning to not only advance a revived Nazism in the country, but to use Ireland as a base for propagating the ideology on a global scale, it was not until the turn of the 21st century that the veil was lifted sufficiently to grasp the full meaning of the disturbing history.

NAZI PARTY IN IRELAND

In 1927, Austrian native Adolf Mahr arrived in Ireland to take up a position as Keeper of Irish Antiquities at the National Museum of Ireland. Six years later, he joined the Nazi party and became the head of the *Auslandsorganisation*, an organization for Germans living abroad, described as *"useful for propaganda and espionage activities."* It has been said that Mahr was Germany's top diplomatic representative in prewar Ireland, representing the Irish branch of the Nazi Party at the May 1937 coronation of George VI in London. At least twenty-three Germans were recruited to the party during Mahr's 1934–39 term (roughly a quarter of all adult German males in the twenty-six counties). Mahr's efforts on behalf of the Nazi Party were not restricted to German citizens. According to Irish military intelligence files, he made many efforts to convert Irish graduates and other persons with whom he had associations to Nazi doctrines and beliefs, an indication that the Republic was on the radar of Hitler and his global fascist movement for many years prior to his push into Poland.

Many suspected that not only was Mahr a member of the party, he was a spy for the Nazis, "handily placed" in the National Museum of Ireland. Irish government official Frederick Boland from the Department of External Affairs said of Mahr, "[he is] the most active and fanatical national socialist in the German colony here."

The "No. 1 Nazi in Ireland" was assisted in his party duties by Oswald Müller Dubrow, Dublin-based director of Siemens Schuckert, whose labor advisor in 1925 had been the first Irish Minister of Industry and Commerce, Joe McGrath. Oswald Dubrow operated as Mahr's deputy in the Nazi party's Auslandsorganisation, which kept an eye on Germans living abroad, enforcing discipline among party members and producing regular reports for Berlin. In July 1939, the museum director left Dublin for a holiday in Austria with plans to attend the sixth international congress of archaeology in Berlin in August. Not long after he departed Ireland, Mahr had received a letter from an SS war maps office in Prague thanking him for his "efforts" It is rumored that during that official trip, Mahr also meant to attend the Nazis' annual rally at Nuremberg in September; however, Hitler invaded Poland on September 1, and the event was canceled.

According to those military intelligence records, Adolf Mahr and Otto Reinhard, former director of forestry in Ireland's Department of Lands, were employed during the war in "one of the German intelligence sections which dealt with matters concerning a landing in Ireland." There can be no doubt he was in receipt of reconnaissance procured under "Operation Green" incorporated into the detailed documents for an invasion of Ireland to coincide with the invasion of England in 1940, "Operation Sea Lion," for which Hermann Görtz planned to recruit members of the IRA was a key component. These operations would have been of intense interest to Hans Ulrich Rudel and leading Nazi collaborator, Léon Degrelle.

In fact, Hans Ulrich Rudel, a reconnaissance pilot before training as a Stuka pilot in the Luftwaffe commanded by Reich Aviation Minister Hermann Göring, reflected with pride on the potential for the Fall Grün (Operation Green), a 1940 plan to invade Ireland. The operation had been a critical component of Hitler's bolder goal of invasion of Britain once he had weakened British forces in France. Ireland was of huge strategic significance to the operation code-named Operation Sea Lion: ". . . weather reports were crucial, meaning Ireland once again became of significance to the Fuhrer who placed two of his most trusted lieutenants in charge, Grand Admiral Erich Raeder of the German Navy and Reichsmarschall Hermann Goring of the Luftwaffe. To underscore the significance of Ireland, Operation Green was compiled into five separate volumes which looked at the island from every conceivable military viewpoint including industry, transport, infrastructure, climate, and weather. When Mahr was called to Germany at the outset of the war, he was assigned to the head of Goebbels' propaganda organ, Redaktion-Irland, coordinating broadcasts to neutral Ireland. Mahr decided to focus efforts on an anti-imperial, anti-partition and pro-neutrality campaign as well as efforts to use Irish-America as a tool to promote isolationism in the US which proved invaluable to Reich Minister Joseph Goebbels' propaganda organization. Most likely Goebbels' #2, Werner Naumann was closest to the specialized propaganda machine that involved Mahr. As noted, Nauman was integral to the operations of H. L. Lucht, tying him directly to Skorzeny and arms merchant Victor Oswald during the Cold War."

Prior to leaving Ireland to serve the cause more directly in Germany, Adolph Mahr provided lists that included "Jude" in brackets after the names of known Jews in Ireland, in effect signing a series of postdated death warrants. He was later responsible for handling the foreign anti-Jewish action on the radio, and in that role, in early 1944, he attended a joint SS, Foreign Service Office, and Propaganda Office meeting on the subject of the "Jewish Question."

Mahr advocated for a greater German impact on the airwaves of other countries, suggested that lists be drawn up of Jewish freemasons, journalists, writers, and economists, and recommended that a publication of a diplomatic handbook of Jewish world politics be published in English and French. The minutes of this particular conference were circulated although some of the proposals were so secret that they could not be written down.

Author Mark Hull observes in *Irish Secrets: German Espionage in Ireland, 1939–1945*, "While it doesn't place Mahr as an architect of the Holocaust, it makes his sympathies clear. In law, abetting a crime often gets you the same penalty as those who actually carry it out." Mahr was the coordinator of the project responsible for identifying the "True Celt," alongside eugenicist Earnest Hooton, close friend of Carlton Coon who advocated assassination as a tool of statecraft with no hesitation. After the war, Mahr was interned by the Allies, and in spite of attempts to return to his job in the National Museum, he "never put foot in Ireland again." He had fulfilled his assignment.

A STATE WITHIN A STATE

Adolf Mahr was not the only member of the Nazi party living in Ireland at the same time their Führer, Adolph Hitler, was implementing his appalling scheme to round up "undesirables" into concentration camps, the first of which was the infamous Dachau Prison—and it stretches logic to believe that German expats living and working in Ireland were not receiving news from the fatherland. Among them were other high-ranking Germans and Austrians brought in to fill roles in the development of the Irish Republic including Colonel Fritz Brase, head of the Irish Army's School of Music. In that role, Brase rearranged many traditional Irish jigs and reels to sound like thundering Prussian martial pieces.

By the early '30s, he got into hot water when he requested of the Irish Army's chief of staff to set up a branch of the Nazi Party in Dublin. Nevertheless, he succeeded and kept his party membership a secret until 1934; Otto Reinhard, as mentioned, appointed the Forestry Director with the Department of Lands, beat out sixty-five other candidates for the job. Before leaving for Germany at the outbreak of the war, Reinhard lived on Silchester Road in Glenageary, a village southwest of Dublin and one of the areas where Nazi spy Hermann Görtz had been provided safe haven; Heinz Mecking, chief advisor with the Irish Turf Development Board 9 precursor to Bord na Mona, which controls Ireland's supply of peat for electricity generation, took over as NSDAP chief in Dublin when Adolf Mahr left for that working holiday in Berlin in July 1939.

When war broke out in full force, Mecking joined the German army and later oversaw turf production for the Russian winter campaigns of 1941 and 1942. Todd Andrews, who served under Mecking, recalled in his 1982 memoir that: "As German triumph followed German triumph in Europe, he [Heinz Mecking] became increasingly uninvolved in his assignment [for the TDB]. He set himself up as a Nazi intelligence agent photographing railway stations, river bridges, signposts and reservoirs . . . When war broke out he had to return to Germany, with reluctance. He thought that he would be more useful to his country acting as an intelligence agent in Ireland."

These men became the nucleus of the Nazi party in Ireland in the 1930s while news of Hitler's diabolical policies trickled into mainstream media. Civil Servant rules at the time prohibited staff from becoming members of Irish political parties, but there was no rule against membership of a German political party. To emphasize the deep history between Ireland and Germany, from its beginnings in 1933 until its demise in 1939, the Nazi Party in Ireland was led by members of the Irish Civil Service—at taxpayers' expense.

Other Nazi party members in Ireland in the lead-up to the war included Friedrich Weckler, chief accountant at the ESB (the semi-state Electric Supply Board) in 1930, having worked previously on the Shannon hydroelectric scheme for the giant German engineering company Siemens. In that capacity, he would have known Mahr's deputy of the Nazi party, Otto Durbow of Siemens, and most likely was in frequent contact with Joe McGrath, labor advisor to Siemens. ESB accountant Weckler resided in Dalkey, the upscale village of south Dublin. It was in Dalkey that Nazi spy Hermann Görtz availed of hospitality of someone living on Nerano Road just blocks from the library who would welcome Otto Skorzeny ten years later, which prompts a reasonable assumption: Nazi party members Weckler of ESB and Heinz Mecking of the Turf Board, beyond being passive party members, had been among those working in league with Görtz.

Several more Nazi party members were living in Ireland before the war including Heinrich Greiner of the Solus lightbulb factory in Bray, Co. Wicklow; Hans Hartmann, a student of Irish language and folklore at University College Dublin who would broadcast Nazi propaganda in Irish from Luxembourg under the direction of Adolf Mahr; Hilde Poepping, exchange student at University College Galway, also working with Mahr at the German Foreign Office and the Irish section of German Radio in Berlin during the war; Karl Kuenstler, a Siemens engineer; and Robert Stumpf, a Baggot Street Hospital radiologist who in 1939, invited a group of Irish doctors and wives to tour the Third Reich.

It was this Nazi milieu that established the foothold for what would later become a desirable environment for Rudel, Degrelle, and Skorzeny's plot to further "the cause of Nazism" from a base in Ireland.

CLISSMANN

When Hitler invaded Poland in the first week of September 1939, and German exchange students in Ireland Helmut Clissmann and Jüpp Hoven answered the call, it was only logical that they join the Admiral Canaris' Brandenburger Regiment of German intelligence. Renowned as Germany's elite warrior spies, the

Brandenburger Special Forces operated in almost all fronts during the war, including infiltration in India, Afghanistan, Middle East countries, and South Africa. They also trained for Operation Felix (the planned seizure of Gibraltar) and Operation Sea Lion (the planned invasion of Great Britain) and, of course, Operation Sea Eagle, the planned invasion and subjugation of Ireland. Historian Ian Adamson writes, ". . . every Brandenburg recruit had to be fluent in at least one foreign language . . . [they] were also schooled in the customs and traditions of their specific region. Knowing every habit and mannerism in their area of operations would enable the men to blend in and operate as effective saboteurs." In Brandenburger circles, Jüpp Hoven was a well-informed expert on matters concerning the IRA, and at the secret headquarters of Admiral Canaris on the Berlin Tirpitzufer, it eventually fell to Dr. Hoven to play an important part in the Abwehr's Irish operation and the destruction of Belfast.

The Brandenburgers' commando operations against Allied supply lines in North Africa were by way of clandestine missions in Egypt, Libya, and Tunisia. Helmut Clissmann's military résumé during the war included a post in Tunis, and it is fair to suspect that he encountered a number of our persons of interest during these operations. After Canaris fell under close scrutiny as a threat to Hitler, 1,800 Brandenburgers were transferred to the Waffen SS under the command of one Sturmbannführer Otto Skorzeny.

In 1930, nineteen-year-old Helmut Clissmann, a proud member of the Young Prussian League, made his first trip to Dublin. Over the ensuing three years, he traveled back and forth, and by 1933, he was able to resume his studies permanently as an exchange student at Trinity College in what he considered his "land of opportunity." Among his fellow Germans studying at Trinity was Nona Keitel, daughter of Hitler's army chief of staff, General Wilhelm Keitel. The general was in the early days of the war in frequent communication with Admiral Wilhelm Canaris, the head of Adolf Hitler's Abwher, which Clissmann would join at the outbreak. Whether or not Nona was a conduit for Clissmann or merely a fellow student in Dublin oblivious to what was happening in Poland may be irrelevant, but a number of questions are posed.

In May 1940, her father, chief of staff of the High Command of the German armed forces, wrote to Admiral Canaris that the Brandenburgers had "fought outstandingly well," which was further validated when Hitler presented the Iron Cross. Among those Brandenburgers was Clissmann. Eventually, General Keitel was reviled even by some of his military colleagues as Hitler's habitual "yes-man." His defense at Nuremberg encapsulated that of so many others responsible for atrocities, "I was only following orders." Keitel was indicted at Nuremberg as one of the major war criminals and found guilty on all counts of crimes against humanity, criminal conspiracy, and war crimes, and executed in 1946.

In interviews before her death, Budge Clissmann (then Mulcahy) recalled meeting the General's daughter, Nona, through Helmut before she left Ireland for a year of study at the Sorbonne in Paris. While a student in France that year, she lived in the home of Irish envoy Leopold Kerney, who some years later would serve as Ireland's minister to Spain. This association proved significant as events unfolded involving both the Nazis and the IRA.

Budge's family, the Mulcahys in Co. Sligo, were ardent and active supporters of the Republican movement that continued to aggressively resist the Anglo-Irish Treaty of 1921. As such, their daughter was not only an avowed Republican, but by the time she enrolled in Trinity, she had become a strong proponent of the Nazis in Germany. To understand the depth of Helmut Clissmann's service to the Nazis, both ideological and practical, we look back at the years he served as a spy in Ireland at the same time that Hitler undertook the torturous experimentations that have been thoroughly documented worldwide over the past eight decades. Years later, Schering AG, the pharmaceutical firm that helped catapult Clissmann's Irish-based business concept to success, lurked in the shadows of diabolical experimentation.

According to Budge, in the mid-1930s, the Nazis sent Helmut back to Dublin to run the German Academic Exchange Service (DAAD)—a body that encouraged Irish students to study and/or teach in Germany for one academic year, while German students attended Irish universities. His official responsibility was to establish and run branches in Dublin, Cork, and Galway. However, not only did he operate what was essentially an Abwehr spy unit made up of these branches, but following directives of his superiors in Germany, he began developing ties with certain members of the IRA as well, facilitated by Budge Mulcahy. Over time, Clissmann became known as "the best-informed German in Ireland." His German exchange service was a valuable organ of the director of the National Museum of Ireland, Adolf Mahr (by then in the throes of searching to the Aryan race with Earnest Hooton) under his NSDAP from 1933 to 1945.

In 1938, when Budge Mulcahy and Helmut Clissmann, who was already a dedicated spy, married at University Church, St. Stephen's Green, the German military intelligence had long been fully committed to forging links with the IRA leadership in Dublin. The best man at this wedding was Clissmann's childhood friend, Joseph "Jüpp" Hoven. As presented in an article by the Ulster intellectual Emyr Estyn Evans titled "The Celtic Racialist and Nazi Spymaster in Dublin before the Second World War," cited by historian and former Lord

Mayor of Belfast, Dr. Ian Adamson OBE, in his article, "The Hidden History of Herr Hoven," Mahr wrote of another acquaintance, saying, "Suspicion fell too on another German, a certain Herr Hoven, then living in Belfast, though officially domiciled across the border. He [Hoven] often called to see me, and I once asked him when he hoped to return to Germany. His unguarded reply, 'Not until early September,' seems to have been prophetic, for war was declared on 3 September 1939." This is clear indication that Clissmann's friend and best man, Hoven, was in direct communication with Hitler's apparatus, and that his message to Mahr was to inform him of the Führer's launch of WWII. It is also an indication that Mahr, Hoven, and Clissmann would have been privy to Hitler's system of concentration camps and what was going on inside.

Jüpp Hoven and Helmut Clissmann were students at Trinity from the same neighborhood of Aachen, on the border of Germany and Belgium. Both young men knew Ireland through educational trips and longish stays in the country. Indeed, the two were ostensibly products of the Young Prussian League. Dr. Hoven, who was studying anthropology in Ireland, was tasked with become friendly with Frank Ryan, the former editor of the I.R.A. weekly paper *An Phoblacht*, who was a student of "Celtic" philology and archaeology. The timing and backdrop of both Hoven's and Clissmann's activities in Ireland would have been Harvard Professor Hooton's search for the True Celt in collaboration with Nazi Adolf Mahr, under whose authority, as head of the Irish NSDAP, Helmut Clissmann was being financed. Prof. Hooton's protégé, Carleton Coon, has been covered in depth earlier in this book.

As referenced previously, the Brandenburgers' commando operations in North Africa were by way of clandestine missions in Egypt, Libya, and Tunisia, but after Canaris fell out of favor and Brandenburgers had been transferred to the command of Skorzeny. Once the Abwehr had been relatively dissolved, the skeletal Streifkor were annexed by Skorzeny and formed into the four regional battalions of the SS-Jagdverband (Hunting Units). The embryonic unit was Nordwest, which covered Belgium, the Netherlands, and Denmark. Under SS Skorzeny, hundreds from these units were allowed to continue to conduct the kinds of missions they were originally trained for. We know from correspondence that Mrs. Helmut Clissmann had written to her father to say that Helmut was stationed in Belgium, and we further know that this was his unit. In fact, it was Copenhagen where Budge settled throughout the war, and Copenhagen is where our focus is drawn as we pursue Helmut and Otto.

The unit's first operational mission (Operation Osprey) was a proposed deployment to Ireland; however, the mission was scratched, and in early 1943, five members of the unit were parachuted into Iran to assist guerilla opposition to the Allied occupation. The Special Service Troop, which eventually numbered 100 volunteers, received its training at the Totenkamph (Death's Head) Barracks in Berlin, and Helmut Clissmann once again became part of the operation and placed in charge of training the troop in the use of British weapons and in sabotage operations. Clissmann's training was wasted again when it became apparent that no Anglo-American forces would invade Ireland, and the final proposal for Operation Osprey was discarded.

BRADY AND STRINGER

In *The Skorzeny Papers*, author Ganis reveals the names of two Irishmen—James Brady and Frank Stringer—that he found elusive, except that he knew with certainty that they served under SS Commando Otto Skorzeny. According to British journalist and author Adrian Weale, the two were operating under aliases Charles deLacy and Willy LePage, respectively: "In the spring of 1941, the Abwehr trawled through 'British' POWs that they held in the hope of finding Irish Republicans who would be prepared to act as the nucleus of an 'Irish Brigade' modelled on famed Irish revolutionary and gun-runner Roger Casement's concept from the First World War. In May 1941, about 50 Irishmen were concentrated at a special POW camp at Friesack where they were to be subjected to propaganda and persuasion."

According to Mark Hull, in "Irish Secrets. German Espionage in Wartime Ireland 1939–1945," it was Helmut Clissmann, along with several Irish Nationals including Frank Ryan, who did the trawling at that camp to recruit Irish prisoners. Among their recruits were Brady, a.k.a. deLacy and Stringer, a.k.a. LePage. Eventually, the services of Brady and Stringer were dispensed with, but rather than doing agricultural work as POWs, both opted to join the Waffen-SS. They reported to Senheim in October 1943 and were posted to "Jagdverband Mitte" in March 1944, under their aliases.

Hull continues, "By the end of 1942 no one, least of all SS Oberfuhrer Veesenmayer, believed that Operation Taube II would still materialize. He officially notified von Ribbentrop that about twelve men were nevertheless still standing by. This was an overstatement. Available were Ryan, Clissmann, Rieger, possibly Brady, O'Duffy, and Stringer. Veesenmayer added to these Jüpp Hoven, Lt. Hocker, and Christian Nissen, who could be made available." Further proof that Brady and Stringer were acquainted with Rieger and Clissmann, Terence O'Reilly adds, "At the end of April 1943, Brady and Stringer, still working on the farm at Klein Kiesow, received a visit from a man who introduced himself as 'Franz Richter.' This was in fact, none other than Brandenburger Obergefreiter Bruno Rieger, who had accompanied [Helmut] Clissmann in his abortive voyage to the Irish west coast in 1940." O'Reilly also reminds us that Rieger had participated in Clissmann's evaluation of the SS commandos at Oranienburg the previous November.

Clissmann, who lived in Eire before the war and was considered an expert on Irish matters, along with Rieger had found the three platoons of trainees in a feisty and arrogant mood, noting that their utter contempt for all things foreign would not make themselves popular in Ireland. The two platoon leaders issued their negative report while at the same time Hitler began to reconsider the invasion because of the changing strategic situation. In conversations with commander Helmut Dorner, it was decided with Oberführer Edmund Veesenmayer to make the SD unit available for other duties, and a number of the Irish nationals recruited by Dorner were released for alternate missions. Veesenmayer, who had worked directly with the head of Hitler's dreaded Gestapo Adolf Eichmann—the man responsible for implementation of the extermination of the Jews—was subordinated to Ernest Kaltenbrunner, chief of the Reich Main Security Office (RSHA). It was Kaltenbrunner who had advanced Otto Skorzeny's career by naming him head of the newly formed sabotage units following Admiral Canaris's fall from grace. Months after the Clissman/Rieger report, it was recorded that when SS Otto Skorzeny encountered the unit, he had been as unimpressed as they were.

* * *

Not all German Nazis failed to return to Ireland following the war. Among them, and most relevant to a spirit of welcome to neo-Nazis in the 1950s was Helmut Ewald Clissmann. Established in 1949 by him and his wife, the firm of HE Clissmann continues to offer a range of services to the pharmaceutical industry including storage and distribution. According to the Clissmann 2020 promotion, "Our principal client is Bayer Ltd., the Irish subsidiary of Bayer AG. Our relationship with Bayer grew from our relationship with Schering since 1950." As mentioned, records of the Holocaust prove that Schering pharmaceuticals lurked in the shadows of the diabolical experiments on victims of the Nazi regime.

To summarize, Clissmann was a close associate of Veesenmayer, who was subordinate to Kaltenbrunner, who was Otto Skorzeny's immediate superior. Can there be any question that Helmut Clissmann knew Otto Skorzeny, and that both knew Brady and Stringer, in the late 1950s when Otto and Ilse's intention to purchase property and spend extended time in Ireland was made public? While the entire guest list for their welcome party at Portmarnock is not readily found, nor is a complete record of the later comings and goings at Martinstown House, it can be deduced that if Helmut and Budge Clissmann were not among those in the milieu known publicly, there would have been a significant reason.

INDUSTRIOUS GERMANS IN IRELAND

German pencil manufacturer Faber-Castell invested in a major production plant in Fermoy, Co. Cork, not far from Ileclash purchased by the Mosleys. After the Second World War, Count Roland of the Faber-Castell dynasty set about reacquiring the foreign subsidiaries that had been confiscated and founded new sales organizations and factories in Ireland, Austria, Argentina, Peru, and Australia. With the exception of Australia, Count Roland appears to have been most comfortable operating within Fascist regimes.

As author Martin Lee tells us, Kluf [a Waffen SS veteran identified in a US State Department report only by the code name] disclosed "the existence of a secret international organization composed of former SS officers and partially funded by the Soviets [and who were] supposed to work with the Russians against the Western orbit." Kluf pegged Skorzeny as an important figure in this underground operation. . . . In addition, Kluf explained, this international neo-Nazi network received funds from German industry. He specifically identified Countess Faber-Castell as an important backer. An SRP supporter funding the party's brief heyday, Countess Faber-Castell hid Otto Ernst Remer in her Bavarian chalet before he fled to Egypt. Kluf told the State Department that Remer had "also been cooperating with the Russians."

Of note, Dan Burros of the American Nazi Party had in his possession evidence of direct correspondence with Otto Remer in the early 1960s, suggesting that Burros was supplying propaganda material to Remer while he was based in Oran, Algeria. At the same time, American fascist H. Keith Thompson, who would represent Marguerite Oswald in the months following her son's murder, lobbied for Remer's exoneration for years following the war. Dan Burros's contact information was found in Lee Oswald's address book.

Kluf then proceeded to spin what sounded like a fantastic yarn about a group of SS fanatics who were preparing to instigate an armed insurrection against Western oil companies in Iran . . . "We now know that during the war, a group of Irish recruits into the Brandenburgers were dropped into Iran on a very particular mission so this would be familiar territory. We also know that Shannon

Airport provided unfettered access via direct flights to the Middle East, another example of the geopolitical/geographical importance of Ireland."

* * *

Author Lee brings us full circle to the Skorzenys' involvement with the H. S. Lucht Company, the import-export firm named earlier in this book. According to Lee, the company owned by Frau Lea Lucht, believed to be a cousin of General Léon Degrelle, who, along with Otto and Hans Ulrich, had his sights on Ireland, maintained an office in Leipzig. Skorzeny had used H. S. Lucht to recruit technicians and military experts for special projects in the Middle East. In 1959, or perhaps early 1960 (records are somewhat obscured), the former assistant to Hitler's foreign minister, Baron Alexander von Dörnberg, who was a mountain of a man in comparison to Otto Skorzeny, bought a holiday home and twelve acres of land near Glengariff, Co. Cork. Under his official title during the war, SS-Oberfuhrer Chief of Protocol German Foreign Office from 1938 to 1945, he had reported directly to Nazi Foreign Minister Joachim von Ribbentrop.

There can be little doubt that von Dörnberg was also present in the infamous meeting in the "tea room" when von Ribbentrop, along with Hitler's top advisors and in the presence of SS Otto Skorzeny, teased out the specifics for the plan to extricate Benito Mussolini to safety.

Dörnberg, who had accompanied von Ribbentrop to Moscow to sign the Molotov-Ribbentrop Pact in 1939, may have also had an established relationship with Russians involved in that "secret international organization composed of former SS officers" engaged with Moscow to "work against the Western orbit" during the 1950s. Certainly, his geographic proximity to BUF Oswald Mosley and Skorzeny, and their easy access to the Countess Faber-Castell via her plant in Fermoy, begs another question: had the meeting between Skorzeny and Mosley in Ireland in 1956 as alleged by author Steven Doril, in *Blackshirts: Sir Oswald Mosley and British Fascism* been fortuitous or deliberate? We have no documentation that Skorzeny secured a visa for that earlier trip to Ireland, but we know that several years later, he met with Mosley and Léon Degrelle in Bonn. These were not social gatherings. By 1960–61, it was being alleged that a shipment of arms to North Africa out of Cork Harbor was planned.

A HAVEN FOR NAZIS ON THE RUN

At the time of these land purchases in Ireland by known Nazis, international newspapers began to claim that Ireland had become a "haven for Nazis on the run from war crimes." The flaw in Irish legislation that allowed nonnationals to purchase property while only possessing holiday visas became apparent, and British and Italian media wrote of a "German invasion" of Ireland and "Germans were retaining a 'foothold in Britain's backdoor.'" But a note from Conor Cruise O'Brien, then a senior official in the Department of External Affairs, in June 1957 refers to the visa application from Skorzeny, who is described as well known for his military exploits with "special" units of the German army in the Second World War including his rescue of Mussolini: "Skorzeny, who is now stateless, resides in Spain. He is on the UK Home Office Black List as an undesirable character. I think this means no more than that *he made their faces red in the matter of Mussolini. We are not aware of any specific war crimes charges against him.*"

Among the first German firms to establish a major presence in Ireland post-World War II had been crane manufacturer Liebherr. Founded by his family in a small town in southern Germany, 130 miles west of Munich, Hans Liebherr recognized the requirements to rebuild Germany after the war and set about providing the tools and machinery needed by the construction industry, including the first mobile tower crane. In the 1950s, Liebherr determined that to gain a foothold in the British and North American markets, he would build a production site in Ireland. He chose the southwest, outside Killarney, Co. Kerry. By the early '60s he had expanded outside of Europe and built a plant in South Africa. Whether or not he made contacts in the SA apartheid government thru his German Nazi contacts is not known, but among the names in the contact book of Hans Ulrich Rudel—the member of the triad with Skorzeny and Degrelle that was intent on moving the base of operations for the neo-Nazi movement from Argentina to Ireland—was Hans Liebherr.

Despite a degree of internal opposition, Germany became a chief focus for Costello's government with Minister Norton making numerous promotional visits to West Germany in 1955, and the Industrial Development Authority (IDA, formed in 1949) producing promotional material in conjunction with Norton's Department of Industry and Commerce. As one government official opined at the time, "The guilty honeymoon that Éire had with Hitler's Germany during the war is now being evolved into a peace-time trade relationship."

Having established that the social, political, business, and ideological climate in Ireland could well have been attractive to the Skorzenys, steps are necessary before drawing an educated conclusion as to what motivated the couple to invest in a significant property in the Curragh, ship furniture and a Mercedes-Benz, and leave the sunny climes of Spain, where they lived and did business in virtual solidarity with those surrounding them, to spend as much time as their visas allowed in cold, damp, conflicted Ireland.

It is first important to understand the stall in the Skorzenys' purchase of property between June 1957 and 1959. The delay is best explained by Stuart Smith, who writes in the aforementioned biography of Skorzeny, "In fact, in 1958, the remaining war crimes charge hanging over Skorzeny—concerning atrocities in Czechoslovakia—had been rescinded by Austria. As a token of its good faith, his home country at last issued him a passport . . . That left the Irish government grappling with the nebulous rumors including Skorzeny's alleged involvement in arms-trafficking with the National Liberation Front (FLN)."

Smith suggests there were rumors that had to be discarded, one linking Skorzeny to the flight of Adolf Eichmann to Egypt, but other rumors that Ireland's intelligence service (Peter Berry included) missed: "One was a proposed 1958 mission to kill Fidel Castro on behalf of Fulgencio Batista . . . and the other was allegations that Skorzeny assisted in Moise Tshombe's 1961 secession from the newly independent Democratic Republic of Congo by training some thirty Katangan rebels in Spain." This effort was endorsed by Americans, perhaps only nominally, but in some instances, we have reason to believe they provided more than passive support. For instance, we know that Dallas oilman and executive for Empire Trust John A. "Jack" Crichton, who was Lafitte's man on the ground in Dallas on November 22, 1963, was a signatory of the American Committee for Aid to Katanga Freedom Fighters.

It is also clear that Smith was determined to expose the justification of the Skorzenys' right of purchase property in Ireland. He observes, "Denying Skorzeny residency, absent any evidence against him, would go against the grain of Ireland's neutrality in international affairs," and he continues by calling attention to Éamon de Valera's perhaps ill-conceived note of commiseration on the death of Adolf Hitler as well as a failure to hand over suspected Nazi war criminals to the Allies. This begs the question whether or not the Irish public writ large was fully aware of the extent to which Nazi criminals lived in their midst, and might that naïveté been appealing in light of the apparent heat being applied to Skorzeny as a high-profile resident of Madrid, Spain.

By 1959, matters had evolved, and Otto made his way toward Ireland. Despite having been asked specifically by Michael Andrew Lysaght Rynne to take an alternate route, Skorzeny was refused permission to enter Britain on landing in London. Rynne was then Irish ambassador in Madrid, appointed by John A. Costello, who once claimed that "the fascist Blueshirts will be victorious in the Irish Free State." During his tenure, Rynne's role as ambassador had required keeping fellow ambassadors informed of the Irish government's line on such matters as the 1956 Suez Canal crisis, a topic no doubt with which Otto Skorzeny was most familiar.

Ambassador Rynne's admonitions may well have been informed by sympathies shared between outgoing Prime Minister Costello; Éamon de Valera, who retained Rynne when he regained the post of Prime Minister; and any Nazi officer living in Ireland. However, and to underscore the complexities of this period in Irish history, Rynne was reporting to Frank Aiken, then-Minster of External Affairs, who in spite of purportedly supporting the right of countries such as Algeria to self-determination and speaking against South Africa's system of apartheid, had a history of Nazi sympathies himself but was among the very few who openly opposed Skorzeny's entry and right of property ownership. Perhaps his opposition was an indication of infighting among the contemporary fascists. Regardless, Aiken did not prevail because Mae Mooney, a civil servant within his own department, managed to secure the first visas for the Skorzenys.

As feared by Ambassador Rynne, Otto was detained in London and cross-examined, but he was soon escorted to his connecting flight.

THE NEW IRISH ECONOMY AND THE ELUSIVE FRANÇOIS GENOUD

As revealed earlier, the US philanthropic arm of the global petroleum behemoth Rockefeller Foundation provided the equivalent of $1.5 million in today's dollars in search of the pure Aryan in Ireland. By 1960, Rockefeller consigliere John Jay McCloy was also representing American industrialist and avowed anti-Semite Henry Ford in Ireland. The implications become even more relevant to Otto Skorzeny and his cabal's proposal for Ireland's economic strategy in the 1960s: *"Skorzeny and two representatives of a German and a Swiss bank had protracted talks with members of the Irish Government and they promised to transfer considerable sums of capital to aid its economic development."*

We also know from author Martin Lee that "rumors of Skorzeny's presence in Germany or of his influence being felt in Nazi circles are intermittently heard," McCloy wrote in a cable to President Kennedy's Secretary of State, Dean Acheson.

"There is a British Intelligence document dated 20 Nov 53, entitled 'François GENOUD' [sic] which contains some background on this mysterious Swiss. It notes that he is the literary executor for both Hitler and Bormann and 'possesses many Nazi documents.' He is described as being in contact with British Fascist Sir Oswald Mosley at the time, as well as with Paul Dickopf (who would eventually become head of West Germany's equivalent of the FBI), the BKA, despite his impeccable Nazi resume; indeed, he was even for a while a head of Interpol like his predecessor [and Skorzeny's boss], Ernst Kaltenbrunner. Genoud worked for Dickopf in the Abwehr, and his credentials as an Abwehr agent are referenced in the British document, as well as his connection with Naumann Circle and with one Frau Lucht of Düsseldorf, which indicates the H.S. Lucht firm of Düsseldorf managed by Werner Naumann."

Designated by Hitler as his titular heir, Naumann never relented from his commitment to resume the Reich in Germany, to the extent that he was arrested in 1953 and charged with attempting to infiltrate political parties. After his release, Naumann took charge of the H.S. Lucht Co. based in Düsseldorf, a firm that Otto would use as a front for years. The Lucht firm, along with Hjalmar Schacht's Lombard Odier banking concern based in Düsseldorf, was a cornerstone for advancing schemes coming out of Bonn. No doubt it was through these business opportunities that Ilse Skorzeny had access to Princess Marbert, whom she pursued to purchase property near Martinstown House. Also, critical during this time frame, were the tightly held negotiations between Chancellor Konrad Adenauer, Otto Skorzeny, and Dr. Wilhelm Voss, who was then in Egypt pursuing efforts to collaborate with the Muslim brotherhood. Dealing with the Muslims was a feature for all of these players during the mid-1950s. By the late '50s, the Republic of Germany and the US both were planning to flood the Irish economy.

US AMBASSADORS

Within months of taking office, President Kennedy terminated the mission of America's ambassador to Ireland under Eisenhower, R. W. Scott McLeod, and replaced him with his good friend from Florida, Grant Stockdale. Kennedy had been one of the only senators who voted against McLeod's nomination as ambassador in 1957.

Prior to the appointment by Eisenhower, McLeod had served as head of the State Department's Bureau for Security and Consular Affairs. A notorious homophobe and rabid anticommunist whose photo held a space on the desk of Senator Joseph McCarthy had worked closely with the senator's red-baiting hearings, placing him in immediate proximity to mob lawyer Roy Cohn as well as Robert Morris, two of American's staunchest anticommunists. We read about Robert Morris and his cohorts in Dallas in our next chapter. Scott McLeod presented his credentials in Dublin on July 17, 1957, just weeks after the Skorzenys were feted at Portmarnock. During his four-year tenure in Ireland, he had ample time to become acquainted with Otto and Ilse and their newfound friends in Ireland.

John Kennedy's good friend Grant Stockdale presented his credentials in Dublin on May 17, 1961, just weeks after McLeod left the post. As ambassador, both McLeod's and Stockdale's duties included hosting formal and informal events for dignitaries and Ireland's elite. At this juncture, it is worth repeating the history between Stockdale and Otto Skorzeny as revealed in Chapter 4: "Frequently attending these gatherings in all their splendor were Otto and Else Skorzeny. . . . Without doubt, Stockdale was amply familiar with former Nazi SS officer Otto Skorzeny, who often visited the embassy for meetings with various American businessmen, military officers, and intelligence officials, as well as various embassy staff members throughout 1960, 1961, and 1962. Former embassy personnel vividly recall Skorzeny coming to the embassy on a near 'weekly basis.' Evidence also reveals that the Skorzenys were occasional dinner guests joining the ambassador and his wife. . . ."

The ruggedly handsome forty-eight-year-old Florida businessman "fell to his death" from the 13th floor of the DuPont Building in Miami, just ten days after his close friend John Kennedy was brutally taken down in Dallas. As noted previously, no author until now has identified Stockdale's connections to Otto and Ilse Skorzeny and the possible impact of those connections on his untimely death.

With few exceptions, up until the 1990s, all US ambassadors to Ireland had backgrounds in either the military or intelligence (and often both), and/or served on the boards of military contractors.

OTTO UNDER SCRUTINY

Skorzeny's interview with CIA officer Daniel Wright in 1959 no doubt covered his activities in Ireland. Would he have filled the CIA in on any of the rumors that had been circulating, several of which culminated with a January 1961 article in the Madrid newspaper *Pueblo*, which featured a brief interview of Otto Skorzeny catching the attention of the Department of External Affairs in Dublin?

"That's a fact. It has been said that I am living in Ireland, and all my friends greet me with great surprise on meeting me in Madrid. I continue to live in Spain. What has happened, actually, is that I have bought a property in Ireland, in order to spend the summers there. I have now also bought a property in (Majorca)," said Skorzeny. When asked how he had come to buy the property in Ireland, Skorzeny replied: "My wife had capital there. And I also. My book, *Secret Missions*, translated into English, had a good sale in Ireland. As well, money was owed to me for my journalistic contributions to the press in Ireland. We decided to invest the money in a property. Do you know, [sic] that to take capital out of Ireland taxes of almost fifty percent have to be paid?" Skorzeny said that he enjoyed his stays in Ireland, observing that "up until two years ago it was very cheap." The Embassy official noted that "it is obvious that Skorzeny is at pains to make himself agreeable in both Spain and Ireland, thus keeping a foot in either door." However, a secret G2 memorandum in February 1961 noted that:

> Information—unconfirmed at this state—from a delicate but very reliable source indicates that international arms dealers have been in touch with Otto Skorzeny with a view to setting up an arms dump in this country to later transshipment to Africa for sale to dissident elements in that continent.

By July 1961, G2 further noted:

> "Since then we have had no further information connecting" [Skorzeny] with trafficking in arms, but we have recently received a report from a source whose reliability we cannot judge containing the following information. Skorzeny is reported to have had in the last few months meetings with: (a) Ex-Colonel Hans Ulrich Rudel, believed to be the well-known wartime German air force Officer, and close associate with Sir Oswald Mosley. The English edition of Rudel's book *Stuka Pilot* was published by Euphorion Books, Dublin in 1952. (b) Sir Oswald Mosley. (c) Leon Degrelle—may be identical with a person of that name who was active in the German interests in Belgium during the last war. (d) One of Eichmann's sons, and others named in Spain and Germany. The subject of their deliberations is reported to have been plans to liberate, or failing this, to kill Eichmann in Israel. In this connection it might not be without significance that we have information which suggests that Skorzeny had visited Egypt several times since June 1960.

The author of the memo closes by acknowledging that while the reliability of the information is difficult to assess, he or she felt there might be some substance to it. We know with certainty that Otto's five-year passport issued in 1959 includes entry stamps to Ireland and to Cairo. Did the CIA "ask the question"?

Historian Terence O'Reilly emphasizes that there is no evidence that Eichmann or his sons were in Europe at the time, or that Ilse knew Mrs. Eichmann, or that Skorzeny ever met Mosley, the leader of the BUF. However, other authors insist that Skorzeny did meet with Mosley as early as 1956, and as we have emphasized, the two couples, all four of whom were avowed Nazis, lived within two hours' drive from 1959 until the mid-1960s, after which the presence of the two couples began to be more limited. We also know that Diana and Oswald

Mosley published a book by Skorzeny's good friend SS Hans Ulrich Rudel under their Euphorion Books imprint in 1952.

Those forces tracking Otto Skorzeny did not relent, and by February 4, 1963, the New York-based 'Jewish Telegraph Agency' under the headline "Austria Seeks Extradition of Skorzeny: Tested Poison on Jews" reported that "A warrant accusing Otto Skorzeny, formerly a high official in the Nazi SS, of having committed war crimes, was issued here this weekend by the Austrian Ministry of Justice . . . According to the charges, Skorzeny had invented *a poison-loaded piston* [Emphasis added], which under his supervision was tested on Jewish inmates at the Sachsenhausen concentration camp. He was also accused of part responsibility for the demolition of two synagogues in this city during the Nazi regime."

A warrant was issued for him in Spain, but the government refused to recognize the extradition; it is possible that Irish authorities were under no duress to consider the same, as he was only a temporary resident in the Curragh. Skorzeny had traveled to Ireland in January 1963 (his 1959 passport was still valid and indicates travel to Dublin), which suggests he might have fled the heat of extradition in Spain for an even safer political climate in Ireland, where the press was less likely to pursue the scandal. The chances of his being extradited from neutral Ireland were virtually nil. We do know that a visit to the Curragh in January belies Skorzeny's insistence that they purchased their Irish home for "summer holidays." As Otto suffered the close scrutiny of Nazi-hunters on the Continent, it is indisputable that Ilse was in a better position, including a cover purpose to travel to Madrid, NYC, Dublin, and Dallas with very little notice, fulfilling the critical component of not only the planning, but the execution of those plans in Dallas.

OTTO, THE CHIEF TACTICIAN

Lafitte first makes specific note of Otto Skorzeny in his 1963 datebook on April 30, *Walker + Souetre in New Orleans/Arms (Davis?) – where? Cable to O.* As detailed previously, Skorzeny ran special forces training camps outside of Madrid, and among his chief trainers in the arts of sabotage and assassinations was Jean Rene Souetre, the extreme-right OAS officer known for his expert marksmanship. Another close associate of both Lafitte and of Skorzeny was a French terrorist who had served in La Cagoule, Jean Filliol. Filliol and his mistress, Alice Renee Lamy, who was also an expert shot, were infamous for the interrogation and torture of over one hundred people in one day in occupied Paris. Decades later, Lamy and Filliol found their way to Dallas in late 1963, checking into a hotel, likely Lafitte's favorite, The Stoneleigh on Maple Ave. in Oak Lawn, as we read in our closing chapter.

Three weeks later, Pierre writes simply, *"ask OS/Ilse."* Between those entries he continues to name Souetre, adding [Thomas Eli] Davis and [Clay LaVerne] Shaw. On June 20, Lafitte indicates that he has cabled, or he plans to cable, Otto Skorzeny. On this date, Pierre also has Frank Wisner, former head of the agency's OPC, on his mind.

We don't see Otto again until the 28th of July, when Pierre writes, *"George" [Hunter-White] / Otto talk to Stockdale about P. Graham."* This suggests that Hunter-White, aware of Otto's history with Ambassador Grant Stockdale, is asking about Phil Graham, or he's asking Otto to phone Stockdale to discuss Graham. (See Chapter 4.)

Otto and his valued trainer, Jean Souetre, are named in the same entry again on August 11th when Pierre notes that he has sent a cable to O in Madrid, followed by Souetre's name. The first week of September, in a chilling note, Pierre writes, *O.S. gas guns - 6,* followed by *Garland here - A* [in a circle]. Garland is no doubt a reference to a close associate of George Hunter-White, Garland Williams. The familiarity of using his Christian name in the entry represents a decade-long association between Lafitte, Williams, and "George" Hunter-White.

Author Albarelli was in contact with the Williams family in search of additional Lafitte correspondence but met a wall when the subject of money in exchange proved problematic on a number of levels. Williams was former head of the NY branch of the FNB and officer with the Army's Central Intelligence Corps. He had also worked directly for Joseph Caldwell King, as identified in author Albarelli's *A Terrible Mistake*, assisting the former chief of the CIA's Western Hemisphere as he oversaw the agency's Amazon Natural Drug Co. The intriguing entries presented previously about an August gathering in Antoine's Room in New Orleans that included George Joannides are all the more so if indeed the "King" named in that entry was actually Joseph Caldwell King.

Lafitte says that he sent a cable to Madrid that all was *ok,* and to tell Tom D. (Davis), *O. says come to Madrid.* Eight days later, the most incriminating statement written by Lafitte to date reveals a recap of Otto's strategy, worth repeating once again now that we have Otto's role as tactician in context:

OSARN_OSARN_OSARN_
OSARN-get Willoughby-Litt-

> plus Souetre, others (Hungarians)
> Lancelot proj - kill squads Dallas,
> New York, Tampa-(Labadie) -T says
> called Oswald to purpose- weapons-
> Walker. Davis in N.O. with
> swamp groups Florida (Decker,
> Bender, Vickers, K of M)---

To underscore the ideology driving Otto's choice for involvement in the plot to kill Kennedy, one that unites all those named on October 9 including Lafitte, the history of the Secret Organization of National Revolutionary Action (OSARN) as presented in Chapter 1 warrants repeating, as well:

> OSARN was closely aligned with Benito Mussolini and Hitler. OSARN's purpose was stated: "We want to build a new Europe in cooperation with national socialist German and all other European nations freed from liberal capitalism, Judaism, Bolshevism and French Masons . . . to regenerate France and the French race . . . to ensure that Jews who stay in France are subject to harsh laws, preventing them from infesting our race. . . . OSARN was also closely associated with Reinhardt Heydrich, head of the dreaded Nazi Gestapo."

By November 5th, within a day or two of Tom and Carolyn Davis's arrival in Madrid, Otto had told Pierre that Lancelot is a "go," adding a reference to a "phone booth." This is particularly telling if the Davis couple had just delivered detailed schematics of Dealey Plaza and the kill zone. By November 15th, Otto seems to have reconsidered the tech building—phone booth/bridge, telling Lafitte to "turn them." That is the last mention of Otto or Ilse Skorzeny until the 28th, when Pierre makes a note to "call Madrid." On December 1st, he is sending cables to New York and Madrid.

THE WOMAN BEHIND THE MAN

The year 1963 was a difficult one for Otto as he evaded Nazi-hunters, navigated lawsuits, and encountered challenges to his passing through customs in and out of Europe. Allegedly, entering the US of A was out of the question, although there may remain top-secret documents yet to be released to the contrary. But his wife Ilse seems to have been permitted to globetrot at will. As such, she would be the eyes and ears and legs on the ground representing the couple's private interests and advancing their broader goals. After all, she was reputed to have been involved in intelligence work for Hitler's Germany, and by spring of 1957, she was employed in an intelligence-drenched real estate company, a firm that would open a Dallas branch in the spring of 1963.

As such, Ilse was a subject of Lafitte's attention in 1963, beginning in May, when she's mentioned in the entry "ask Otto and Ilse" on the 20th. By June 7, she is named in the context of a "shipment," and by June 19 she is at a meeting that Pierre is also interested in. On June 25th, Pierre is aware of nickel deposits involving Otto while Ilse is in New York. It can be reasonably argued that she was critical to a major nickel transaction. It would not be unusual for the couple to take payment for services rendered, not in a suitcase full of cash, but in lucrative deals involving materials critical to global conflict that they themselves helped foment.

Ilse remains "dormant" in Pierre's world until October 15, when another meeting is held in New York at the offices of Previews Inc., 49 East 53rd, involving General Charles Willoughby. On the 24th, Ilse meets with "T," and on the 30th, one day following the forty-eight-hour planning session for Lancelot, Pierre makes a note to call Ilse.

Seven days later, on November 7th, Ilse is in Dallas dining with Hitler's Banker, "Uncle" Hjalmar Schacht, at the *Warsaw*, a popular Oak Lawn restaurant, the Old Warsaw best known for its old-world European ambiance. Joining Ilse and Hjalmar at the Old Warsaw, during which money was a topic of conversation, was the baffling character "T," whose identity thus far in this book has evaded scrutiny beyond basic recognition of the critical link he provided among James Angleton, Otto Skorzeny, and Pierre Lafitte. Lafitte went to extremes to avoid revealing the name of "T," at least in these records, and for that reason, these authors relied on a body of research amassed over decades to piece together a list of candidates. The most reasonable candidate for "T" is presented in Alan Kent's essay found in the appendix.

Following this lunch, Ilse disappeared from the project manager's records.

FROM THE CURRAGH TO DALLAS

Certain historians argue the Skorzenys didn't spend all that much time in Ireland; however, there is every reason to argue that they intended Martinstown to be as permanent a residence as the government would allow. Reports insist that they became familiar figures in the Curragh, including frequent sightings in and

around the Curragh of their daughter Waultraut, by then a teenager. Major
Turner, former owner of Martinstown, introduced them around to the locals, an
indication that the former British Army officer and handicapper with the Curragh Turf Club held his '"former enemy" in a certain regard. We note that Joe
McGrath, who almost single-handedly built Irish horse racing into an international venue, founded the Irish Racing Board, and from 1956 to 1962 served as
chairman. There can be very little doubt that he, at the very least, was aware of
the Skorzenys living in the Curragh.

Major Turner's father had constructed the first corporate slum housing in
Dublin, a reflection of disdain for the working poor that might have been a foundation for their comradery. Eventually, other Irish citizens would not be deterred
from hosting Otto and Ilse. On August 31, 1960, Skorzeny spoke of his exploits
before the Dalkey Literary Historical Debating Society at the Cliff Castle Hotel
on Coliemore Rd., another headlining event in the exclusive enclave of South
Dublin. Perhaps those Dalkey natives who provided safe haven to Nazi spy Hermann Görtz while he was on the run a decade plus earlier were in attendance.
When asked, Otto said, "there should not be talk of inferior or superior race. It
is clear however, that some races are without proof of culture." Whether or not he
did so that evening in Dalkey, or on other occasions when asked about the war,
Skorzeny frequently exonerated the Hitler regime by blaming death-camp atrocities "on a handful of wayward fanatics."

Photos and film footage of the couple at Martinstown House convey an
almost bucolic existence. Ilse, in particular, appears refined yet very relaxed, surrounded by the wealth that only bloodstock breeding and flat racing can conjure.
It is disturbing to think that underneath her civility was a continuous stream of
plots and schemes, one in particular culminating with the violent coup in
Dallas.

The Irish media applied numerous public descriptions of the Nazi couple
while they were in residence in the Curragh. The tone in most articles was generally one of admiration, not repulsion; for instance, Skorzeny was portrayed in
the local press as sort of a cloak-and-dagger figure, the Third Reich's Scarlet
Pimpernel, while the petite, blonde-haired, blue-eyed German "Countess" was
portrayed as adding a certain je ne sais quoi to horse country. Behind those eyes,
as we now know, was a soul as comfortable with assassination and murder as that
of Scarface. It is entirely possible that the plot—in part—to assassinate Kennedy
was advanced from Martinstown House.

As mentioned, just three months before the reception in Dublin, and at a peak
moment in Otto's involvement with Abdul Nasser in Egypt, Ilse arrived in New

York City to establish what would prove a significant expansion of the couple's operations. Jane Roman, the ubiquitous CIA staff member reporting directly to James Angleton, in an interagency memo to State and Hoover's FBI, noted Ilse's arrival in America. Roman described Ilse's purpose for entering the States as related to "promoting some business deals." State shot back that they were "fully aware of Mrs. Skorzeny's presence" in the US, no doubt including her cover at Previews, Inc. By the spring of 1963 when the real estate firm set up shop in Dallas, Texas, Ilse's ties to intel and crime organizations that frequently involved assassination, with a real estate firm as a cover, assume deadly connotations.

IRELAND POSTSCRIPT

Six months after the murder of his brother in Dallas, Senator Edward Kennedy, the youngest of Joe and Rose Kennedy's sons, flew to Ireland. He had recently announced his campaign to run for a six-year Senate term in Massachusetts, so perhaps the nostalgia and poignancy of following his brother to Ireland, a year following the president's demonstrably successful visit, was too much to resist. Perhaps coincidentally, Ted Kennedy was in their Irish ancestral home county, Wexford, on May 30, Jack's forty-seventh birthday. At the time, the possibility he might be in Ireland for any reason other than to commemorate his beloved brother, and to bolster confidence in the Irish-American voters in Massachusetts, was never discussed in the popular media. He returned to the States, and less than three weeks later, on June 19, 1964, he was a passenger in a fatal plane crash that killed the pilot, Edward Zimny of Lawrence, MA.

This was the third of four air tragedies that would devastate the Kennedy political dynasty. Pulled to safety by fellow passenger Senator Birch Bayh, Ted was hospitalized with severe back injuries for the following six months. Toward the end of 1964, his brother, Attorney General Robert F. Kennedy, made a trip to Mexico City, ostensibly to observe the young radical movement in the country. Coverage of the mysterious trip was tightly controlled, and it was only years later that researchers began to speculate on the real purpose of that trip.

Some historians argue he was pursuing links between the assassination of his brother and a network operating in Mexico. Considering the highly suspicious death of former Ambassador to Ireland Grant Stockdale and his uncharacteristic display of alarm the week following the assassination in Dallas, it is possible that Ted had been seconded to Ireland in May '64 on a similar mission.

CHAPTER 9

DALLAS . . . LAY OF THE LAND

Dallas . . . Dallas, ah goodness, I'm not sure what to say . . .
I wasn't there anywhere near as often as Pierre . . . not at
all. But Pierre would say it was . . . Dallas was like the arms
and legs of the American secret service, your CIA. . . .
—Rene Lafitte

Rene says oil smooths the way to silent,
and sometimes deadly, change.
—Lafitte notes

The lay of the land . . . lay of the land, Dallas
—Lafitte datebook, November 19, 1963

The 1963 records of Pierre Lafitte provide indisputable evidence that Dallas was always the designated scene of the crime to overthrow the US government as President Kennedy prepared to run for reelection.

The rationale for selecting Dallas may seem complex and even controversial, in particular to those who believe the Chicago, Miami, or Tampa plots were meant to succeed. Lafitte's entry on November 1, *"Trial runs . . . mistakes aplenty – Not Good"* sets that record straight.

This chapter will explain that of all American cities, including Miami, Tampa, or Chicago, Dallas had "everything going for it": a right-wing Republican climate that considered Kennedy an anathema to its political goals; a social and religious community that embraced segregation and recoiled at the suggestion that a Roman Catholic could navigate the delicate balance between church and state; a law enforcement apparatus with allegiance to the city's ultraconservative political agenda; a crime syndicate that manipulated both sides of that law; and a thriving corporate and financial cabal operating in symbiosis with the oil industry and military contractors, all of whom aligned far more with the ideologies of fascist regimes than with democracies. Adding to the assertion is a Lafitte note, "Rene says oil smooths the way to silent, and sometimes deadly, change." Above all, as Renee told the author, Dallas was the *"arms and legs of the CIA,"* a truth borne out.

* * *

Some of the best and brightest investigators and authors in the decades following the assassination have wrestled with an effective structure to employ when disseminating the fruits of their research. The challenge with this chapter was to present the matrix of dates, players, locations, and events directly relating to Dallas in a fashion that a less knowledgeable reader could readily follow, while holding the attention of the experts—some of whom will be cynical, some not.

At the heart of every story there's this idea of collage . . . in fact perhaps at the heart of every detective story, there's the idea of collage . . . in effect the detective is trying to put the world together in a way that makes sense of events . . . bits and pieces of the world glued, stitched, stapled together in a way that hopefully forms a picture of what's out there in reality.

—Errol Morris, documentary filmmaker

Morris is referring to his 2017 documentary, *Wormwood,* which had benefited from the generosity of H. P. Albarelli Jr., who provided the director with exclusive details from his own investigation into the murder of CIA scientist Frank Olson that had implicated Pierre Lafitte. The director explains the methods he employed to tell the Olson story, including his use of ten cameras to capture multiple angles from which he would choose the final cut. The result was a collage. Similarly, this chapter focused on Dallas has been recorded from multiple vantage points to determine which "camera angles" capture the clearest resolution of the crime that took place there. The resulting collage consists of key individuals and their networks—overt as well as clandestine—set in specific locations and intertwined in service to ideologically driven motives, all of which were essential to the success and subsequent cover-up of the plot to kill Kennedy.

The datebook kept by SS Otto Skorzeny operative Pierre Lafitte, whose decade-long association with James Jesus Angleton has been established, provided the authors several options for organizing the information critical to this chapter. It was determined that physical locations in Dallas, five specifically, would provide the best scaffolding: the Republic National Bank building; the Meadows Building; 3707 Rawlins St. in Oak Lawn; the University of Dallas; and the Texas School Book Depository at 411 Elm.

The organization of the chapter also required frequent reference to members of the boards of directors of pertinent corporations and financial concerns. On the surface, the excruciating detail may seem to lack relevance; however, when considered in context, it reveals what the conservative-dominated media of the day chose not to reveal—that capitalism at its most toxic in Dallas was controlled by a tight-knit, interwoven cabal acting on mutual self-interests and, in their view, by osmosis, the best interests of America.

HOW IT ALL BEGAN

On Monday, December 18, 1950, David Martin, executive director of the International Rescue Committee (IRC), and his special assistant, Dr. Richard Salzman, spoke before a large group of prominent Dallas, Texas, businessmen at a special luncheon at the eighteen-story Baker Hotel, a popular venue for leading conservatives of Dallas. The event was underwritten by the just-forming Dallas Council on World Affairs, a group that would soon form a tight bond with CIA director Allen Dulles.

Martin and Salzman, who had traveled to Dallas from their home office at 62 West Forty-Fifth Street in New York City, told the assembled businessmen of their plans for bringing over "2,000 top men of science and letters from Europe to the United States and settling them into jobs where their know-how is needed." In his capacity as director of the original International Rescue Organization (IRO) in late January 1949, Martin had met secretly with Col. Boris Pash and Otto and Ilse Skorzeny, bringing them into the intelligence network assembled by the CIA that included the IRO and World Commerce Corporation. By the time of the Martin-Salzman Dallas visit in 1950, the board of the IRC had included several leading Soviet social democrats, a fact that drew criticism from their rival for CIA funding, the Tolstoy Foundation made up of many Monarchists and right-wing Russian exiles who refused to cooperate with even moderate socialists. Vying for contributions in Dallas, Martin told the audience, "These 2,000 plus displaced scholars and scientists are the cream of a crop of 25,000 exiled professionals abroad who have fled from Communist countries. These scholars and professionals include engineers, medical doctors, journalists, veterinarians, artists, dentists, geologists, chemists, political scholars, legal experts, architects, and professors of the technical sciences, the humanities and the arts."

Added Dr. Salzman, "They are people Russia would pay heavily to import. They are men who would not only enrich our American culture but could be of infinite value to our war and defense efforts."

Explained Martin, "IRC's goal is to resettle these 2,000 gifted refugees before the revised displaced persons act expires in June 1951, but so far there has been a barrier against brains in the resettling of displaced persons because Americans and Canadians are much more willing to sponsor a farm hand sight unseen than to assure a job to an unknown scientist or engineer." Martin paused and said, "This is where we need the vision and intellect of businessmen like all of you."

Martin continued, "Each displaced person must have a sponsor in his new homeland to guarantee his housing and a job before he can be admitted. The IRC has already processed 750 of the 2,000 professionals, and some are already arriving in the country. Each one is thoroughly screened politically before he is invited to this country."

According to Martin, "Each person is screened by the United States Army Counter Intelligence Corps. We work very closely with the government and the military. Each person is also screened by the Displaced Person Commission. And perhaps the most important screening is that given by his fellow refugees."

Said Dr. Salzman, "It is in our national self-interest to get all 2,000 professionals screened and processed. Never has this country prepared for a war in which so little was known about the enemy. These 2,000 are the men who know the chemistry, the geology, the geography, the politics, the roads and bridges behind the Iron curtain." Explained Martin, "To finance this very worthy and crucial project the IRC last month launched a $1,600,000 fund campaign entitled the Resettlement Campaign for Exiled Professionals. Much of this fund will be spent in this country to prepare the newcomers to fit the requirements of American industries, universities, hospitals, and other employers." Added Dr. Salzman, "The IRC not only needs more money but also is carefully hunting for job opportunities for the skilled refugees."

At a question-and-answer session following their presentation, Martin and Dr. Salzman referred several times to an earlier column by Victor Riesel that had appeared in the Saturday, March 25, 1950, edition of the *Dallas Morning News*. Riesel's column, extremely supportive of the IRC's efforts and its Iron Curtain Refugee Campaign, acted to pave the way for the Martin and Dr. Salzman visit and presentation. Wrote Riesel: "That's why the IRC is frankly the savior of political and intellectual leaders. That's why it tries to keep alive a handful of creative minds such as Ivan Duvynec."

Duvynec had been "a top-ranking Soviet graphite geologist, who prepared master geological and hydrogeological maps for the Soviet government before he "slipped from behind the Iron Curtain and wandered into this end of the Cold War," but not before "his sister had been shot by the Soviet secret police" and his "three brothers, scientists all," were placed in "prison camps somewhere beyond the Arctic Circle" and his parents had died." Out of Ivan Duvynec's pain, and the thousands like him, Riesel wrote, "can come power for freedom across the globe."

Even before the 1950 IRC visit to Dallas and Riesel's column, other concerted efforts had been made to gain the support of the Dallas business community in refugee activities including that of Faye Green, a former Dallas schoolteacher who went to Europe in 1944 and became section chief of the Department of Care and Maintenance for displaced persons (DPs) for the IRC in Geneva, Switzerland, and returned to Dallas several times, in including late 1949, to speak on issues involving DPs.

Earlier that year, Eugene M. Solow, head of the Dallas Jewish Welfare Federation who had been a member of a Dallas delegation to Rome, assisting in surveying the needs of displaced persons in Europe and Israel, began pushing hard for enhanced displaced persons support. And at another meeting, February 1949, held at the Baker Hotel, representatives from seven Catholic churches discussed the issues of dealing with bureaucratic "red tape" that they felt slowed the flow of displaced persons from Europe to the United States. Church officials complained that only 5,000 of over 60,000 displaced persons had arrived in the United States since January 1948.

Thus, one of America's most politically conservative cities, oil-rich Dallas, opened its arms to White Russian immigrants who had fled communism and began to make their mark on the community, foreshadowing the arrival of Kennedy's assassins in 1963.

The following is meant as a snapshot to convey an underlying attitude, not of the general population, but that of the power brokers who dominated the city and surrounding area. On the surface, Dallas was a shiny, stylish example of the best of capitalism in the South and Southwest in the early 1960s. However, the underworld of bookmaking, prostitution, and narcotics had reared its ugly head publicly in 1957 with a surprise event in a remote area of New York State that threatened to rock the city's inflated opinion of itself.

According to a reflective exposé in *"D" Magazine* by reporter Jim Atkinson in 1977, "For Dallas, the Apalachin affair [the November 14, 1957, mass arrest of some 100 of the highest-ranking bosses in the infamous Italian network, La Cosa Nostra] was its own kind of shock. After all, here was a young, vigorous city that prided itself on its safe streets and clean City Hall. But there was certainly no denying that one of its residents had turned up at the largest gathering of the Mafia in history . . . [respected] Dallas businessman Joe Civello's presence at

Apalachin in 1957 would turn out to be less significant than the absence of another key underworld figure: New Orleans Mafia boss Carlos Marcello. Marcello, one of the most powerful and sophisticated mob bosses in the nation, had wisely stayed away from Apalachin; strapped with a 1953 deportation order and other legal troubles, the forty-seven-year-old Sicilian feared such a foray from his Louisiana fortress would overexpose him to federal authorities.

"In the aftermath of Apalachin, it would become at least probable that Civello had attended as Marcello's surrogate. This suggested that the 55-year-old imported foods grocer was not only a member of the mob, but a member of some rank. And it suggested one more possibility, one which Dallas law enforcement officers had only guessed at before: that Dallas was an operating outpost for the varied illicit interests of the Marcello mob."

In spite of that spectacular arrest in November '57, and the ensuing national press coverage and indictments, on October 8, 1963, a *Dallas Morning News* headline read: "Officer Says Syndicated Crime is Doubtful in Dallas." Reporter John Geddie had recently interviewed head of the Special Operations Division of the Dallas Police Department: "Captain W. P. 'Pat.' Gannaway gave three reasons Monday for Dallas being a prime plum but forbidden fruit for Cosa Nostra-type syndicated crime.

"Captain Gannaway, head of the Dallas Police Department's vice, narcotics, and intelligence bureaus 'credited the police force, the district attorney's office, and good juries for keeping big time crime out of the city.' Gannaway insisted, ". . . the manner of survival proves it [the syndicate] is not well organized in Dallas . . . Walk down the street and try to place a bet . . . Most won't know where . . . there is no main heroin contact . . . and you don't see prostitutes walking down the streets of Dallas." Geddie concluded the report with a quote from the captain, "*There may be members of organized crime in Dallas practicing their trade elsewhere, but not in Dallas.*"

Captain Gannaway's observation was especially ironic considering how closely aligned his protestations were with the Director of the Federal Bureau of Investigation J. Edgard Hoover vs. the task force on organized crime headed by US Attorney General Robert F. Kennedy. RFK had already widened his investigation into Dallas mob connections by calling for federal grand jury hearings a month before Geddie's interview with Gannaway. According to investigative journalist Mark North, author of *Act of Treason: The Role of J. Edgar Hoover in the Assassination of President Kennedy* who uncovered a deeply buried case against a Dallas bookmaker by the name of John Eli Stone, "Robert Kennedy, knowing he could not get indictments in Dallas because of the pro-Mob mind-set, had chosen the smaller conservative city [Wichita Falls, Texas]."

North observed that ". . . reporters were there when Philip Bosco [a Joe Civello bookmaker] was called into the Grand Jury room. From Bosco, RFK had the opportunity to gain a detailed understanding of the Pearl Street Mafia. But true to omertà, Bosco took the Fifth against self-incrimination. He was brought before Judge Sarah [*sic*] Hughes, who 'exempted him from criminal prosecution . . .'" According to North, after Bosco again refused to answer, and again took the Fifth, a reluctant Judge Hughes scheduled a contempt of court hearing to, in North's words, *"placate RFK's prosecutors."* North's investigation into the deeply buried facts surrounding the 1963 case revealed that the prosecutor was meaning to also prosecute the Civello mob. (Note: Mark North chose to refer to the Civello crime family in Dallas as *Pearl Street Mafia* because it originated in the Pearl Street Market district.)

The records that North unearthed revealed that on October 21 the grand jury reconvened in Wichita Falls, and by the afternoon it had issued a sixteen-count indictment for violation of federal gaming statutes against Dallas bookmakers John Eli Stone and brother James, along with Isadore "Izzy" Miller, as well as Albert Meadows, who had been arrested for violation of federal gambling laws. Writes North, ". . . the Dallas media understood the lethal nature of the threat that the prosecution posed. Exposure and verification of the Joseph Civello mob's long-term criminal operation in Dallas was what city officials had long been denying. A major scandal was in the making . . . and RFK's assault was gaining momentum." North concluded, "Reporters were describing the trial as 'a full-scale investigation into gambling and racketeering in the North Texas area. It was lethal prosecution in the making.'"

Those indicted in Wichita Falls on October 21, including Isadore Miller along with his brother, and John, and Jim Stone, all bookmakers and gamblers for whom Jack Ruby "ran book" were, according to North, the closest to Ruby in the lead up to the assassination. He also reveals that following the indictments, Ruby understood that he would be next: "According to codefendant Izzy Miller, Ruby was prescribed a 'drug for nervousness.' Ruby was close to the breaking point. In addition to his criminal association with Stone and Bosco, he had been in regular communication with a key Marcello lieutenant in New Orleans . . ." North determined that with Joe Civello's arrest and prosecution, the frightening dimensions of the epidemic of crime created by him and his Mob associates had been revealed; in fact, national media interests had labeled Civello an anonymous officer of an invisible government.

McWillie - Tues
with Davis - Oswald
—Pierre Lafitte datebook, March 23, 1963

Crime syndicates across the country relied on certain elements within law enforcement to turn a blind eye, and Dallas was no exception, as evidenced by the remarks of Pat Gannaway, the head of the division that was purported to be dedicated to uncovering and impeding organized crime. It is well documented that for decades, a number of noted Dallas business and social elite enjoyed the pastime of gambling and the attendant vices. Of particular interest are the oilmen identified during inquiries of the House Select Committee on Assassinations when they learned from Jack Ruby's Havana gambling friend Lewis McWillie that Billy Byars, H. L. Hunt, and Sid Richardson all gambled at Benny Binion's legendary Top of the Hill Terrace located west of Dallas when it was managed by McWillie between 1940 and 1958. McWillie was also asked about Murchison and Toddie Wynne Sr. and their friendship with Civello capo Joe Campisi.

According to Scripps Howard investigative reporter Seth Kantor, who was one of the more skilled reporters of his day, "Ruby's special Las Vegas connection was Lewis McWillie, the syndicate gambler Ruby had visited in Cuba in 1959. Ruby had made a series of calls in 1963 to McWillie, who was closely associated with Meyer Lansky's hoodlum empire and was installed in Las Vegas as pit boss at the Thunderbird casino." Kantor continues, "On May 10, 1963, Ruby had a .38 caliber Smith and Wesson Centennial revolver shipped to McWillie, according to records of Dallas gun dealer, Ray Brantley." Brantley will be of particular interest to certain researchers who are aware Dallas police officer Joe Cody was reported to have been contacted immediately following Jack Ruby's murder of Lee Harvey Oswald because the gun used on Oswald was licensed to Cody. That gun's history traced directly to Ray Brantley, the same Dallas gun dealer whom Ruby had used to ship a revolver to Lewis McWillie.

Beyond, or perhaps because of, the underworld of the Dallas mafia that was subordinate to the mob in New Orleans and Chicago, there appears to have been a slow and steady transfer of Third Reich authority to Dallas.

A LOOK BEHIND THE CURTAINS

Fidelity Union Tower, a cornerstone of downtown Dallas architecture in the heady days of the 1950s when the city cemented its reputation as the center of oil and finance in the South and Southwest, was designed by up-and-coming Dallas architect T. E. Stanley, once identified by *Time* magazine as head of one of the largest firms in the country and perhaps best known for the design of what is now the Trump International Hotel and Tower.

Stanley's tower in Dallas, the new headquarters of Fidelity Union Life Insurance founded by Carr P. Collins, Sr., was at the time the tallest skyscraper west of the Mississippi. Among the first primary tenants of the skyscraper was Deli-Taylor Oil, the pillar of oilman Clinton W. "Clint" Murchison's empire. Murchison's numerous other enterprises were often represented by lobbyist and indispensable consigliere to Senator Lyndon Johnson, Bobby Baker, the man who promoted the talents of German-born seductress and suspected spy Ellen Rometsch, identified in Chapter 4 of this book.

Indicative of the influence of insurance magnate Carr P. Collins over the development of not only the Dallas skyline, but the religious ethos that dominated the politically conservative city for decades, was the role he played in the selection of W.A. Criswell, a young preacher from the Texas Panhandle, as pastor of the First Baptist Church of Dallas. In the early 1930s, Brother Criswell had attended Baylor University, one of the country's most conservative religious institutions of higher learning, the same period that an outpouring of affection and admiration of Italian dictator Benito Mussolini permeated the Baylor campus. (See Endnote.) The young Criswell, whose performance in the pulpit was described very early on as "a fiery exhibition, a roller coaster of whispers, bellows and shouts," was an early pioneer of the megachurch, growing First Baptist from 5,000 members to over 25,000.

His wider influence across America was exemplified by being twice elected head of the Southern Baptist Convention, the largest non-Catholic congregation in America. From those influential posts Criswell administered to what many of his critics claimed, a blindly loyal flock through a myopic and parochial lens. In the 1950s, he would serve as the spiritual mentor of a young Rev. Billy Graham, who would join him to advance the Southern Baptist, ultraconservative religious thought on a global scale for another fifty years. "The Southern Baptist conservative movement," said Barry Hankins, an historian at Baylor University and coauthor of *Baptists in America: A History*, ". . . in some ways comes straight out of First Baptist Dallas." An early opponent of forced integration, Rev. Criswell publicly criticized the Supreme Court decision in Brown v. Board of Education and in 1960 vehemently opposed the Democratic presidential candidacy of John F. Kennedy, the young, attractive, and relatively broad-minded Roman Catholic who represented Massachusetts in the US Senate. As *Dallas Morning News* reporter Alan Peppard wrote, "John F. Kennedy was just days from securing the 1960 Democratic nomination for president when Dr. W. A. Criswell strode, bible in hand, to the carved wooden altar of the mighty First Baptist Church in Dallas. Chopping the July air with disdain, he prophesied that the election of the Catholic Kennedy would "spell the death of a free church in a free state."

That same year, Criswell's sponsor Carr P. Collins was also the driving force behind the move of Bishop College, the all-negro institution of higher education located in the East Texas town of Marshall since 1881, to a parcel of land located in the racially segregated Dallas neighborhood of South Oak Cliff, land that had been donated by entertainment mogul Karl Hoblitzelle.

A native of St. Louis, Hoblitzelle moved to Texas and founded Interstate Circuit and Texas Consolidated Theaters. In the 1930s, his movie distribution companies were the subject of a Supreme Court case that became one of the Court's most known antitrust opinions, taught in every basic antitrust course in the United States and a leading precedent in the area of conspiracy inference. Regardless, Hoblitzelle continued to operate over 130 predominately segregated theaters in Texas and expanded his investments in Dallas real estate. In 1942, Hoblitzelle and his wife formed the Hoblitzelle Foundation initially as a trust held at Republic National Bank of Dallas, but later as a nonprofit corporation to be used for *"charitable, scientific, literary, or educational efforts."* That same year, he was appointed Chairman of the Board of Republic National, a post he occupied at the time of the assassination of President Kennedy in Dallas.

In 1967, the *New York Times* reported that the Hoblitzelle Foundation had long served as a conduit for the Central Intelligence Agency, funneling money to academic journals on behalf of the agency's Congress for Cultural Freedom, an endeavor overseen by the Office of Policy Coordination, which is a topic that will be pursued in due course in this chapter.

Earlier in the year, on April 17 to be precise, Princess Catherine Caradja, exiled from her beloved Romania since the war, visited Dallas, a city that had welcomed her in the past, to speak before the International Federated Women's Club gathered at the Stoneleigh Hotel about the danger of the spread of communism—a highly personal cause of hers, perhaps due to the confiscation of her family's oil fields during the war. Three years prior, a January 22, 1960, *Dallas Morning News* headline read, "Princess Continues Red Fight." The princess described "what life without birth and justice is like and how the Reds mean to take these away." Reporter Louise Falls noted that the princess had presented her warnings about the "Red Threat" across America's forty-eight states in forty-eight months. Princess Catherine Caradja returned in 1963 and began to spend long stretches of time in Texas, where she was welcomed across the state by archconservative groups, eventually purchasing land outside of San Antonio.

Of importance, prior to becoming the director of the Office of Policy Coordination, Frank Wisner had been posted in Romania by the OSS, where he set up intelligence networks to spy on the Soviets, and during which time he befriended aristocracy including King Michael of Romania. Official government documents reflect that Wisner, who oversaw Radio Free Europe, which was managed by covert action officer Cord Meyer, Jr., and broadcast in countries behind the Iron Curtain including Romania during the Cold War, was alleged to have had an affair with Princess Caradja. (See Endnote for Cord Meyer.)

In spite of having left the CIA in 1962, the princess's paramour, Frank Wisner, is apparent in the appointment calendar of his former boss, Allen Dulles. Wisner, whom Lafitte names several times, appears in Dulles's calendar three times—including one with Cord Meyer, Jr.—on dates that must be considered more than curious in the context of the planning for the assassination in Dallas. (See Alan Kent essay "Notes on the Appointment and Call Diaries of Allen Dulles 1962–1963" in the Appendix.)

A well-known, highly regarded oil "expert" by the name of Jack Crichton returned home to Dallas from a three-week, State-sponsored tour of Romania sometime between October 15th and October 19th, 1963, a span of time that appears highly relevant to our investigation according to entries in the Lafitte records:

October 17
JA call yest. Says High-level gathering in DC
Lancelot – Go-ok-Oswald-others.

October 28
Lancelot Planning

October 29
Lancelot Planning

But we get ahead of ourselves. John Alston "Jack" Crichton's partner in AMC Oil, James Aston, and his boss Karl Hoblitzelle each owed much of their good fortune in part to the astute lending calls made by banker Fred Florence, the head of Republic National the year that the Hoblitzelle Foundation was formed. Florence had cut his teeth in lending to what some financial experts considered risky wildcatters in the oil fields of East Texas, including H. L. Hunt and Algur Meadows. As the empires of both Hunt and Meadows expanded, so did Florence's beneficence, including the annual financing of the private vacations of H. L. Hunt's spiritual advisor, Pastor W. A. Criswell and his wife.

Many of the Criswell trips included shopping sprees, also financed by Florence, in pursuit of the Criswells' mortal passion of antique collecting and fine china in particular. During one such trip soon after the end of WWII and in spite of the reverend's avowed contempt for Adolf Hitler, Reverend and Mrs. Criswell purchased a fine set of Meissen porcelain alleged to have been commissioned by Hitler as a gift for one of his officers.

Returning now to Bishop College, it must be argued that the "negro college" was representative of the general attitude toward race that permeated Dallas establishment as forced desegregation loomed in the early '60s; generous funding for strictly segregated schools was far more palatable than having one's child sit next to a "negro." Businessmen Carr Collins and Karl Hoblitzelle were joined in their significant financial support of Bishop after its move from deep East Texas to the similarly black-dominated neighborhood of South Oak Cliff by Leo F. Corrigan, Jr., also a native of St. Louis.

Quietly—in the shadow of far more high-profile businessmen in Dallas—by 1957 Corrigan's various national and international real estate investments amassed a worth upward of $500 million, the equivalent of $4.5 billion today. His properties included the internationally recognized Adolphus Hotel, whose investors included the founder of SMU's International Oil & Gas Education Center, Robert G. Storey, Jr.; and The Stoneleigh Hotel, a preferred venue of right-wing organizations, home to Russian-born petroleum engineer Paul Raigorodsky, known affectionately as "The Czar" of the White Russian community in Dallas, and a favorite accommodation of Pierre Lafitte and his family when in Dallas. Corrigan also owned the Maple Terrace apartment building adjacent to The Stoneleigh, whose tenants included Raigorodsky's friends, Mr. and Mrs. George de Mohrenschildt.

In a somewhat moral contrast to his upstanding social position in the Dallas community, Leo Corrigan also leased space to Jack Ruby's Carousel Club and Vegas Club. Similar to Carr P. Collins, developer Leo Corrigan appreciated the talent of architect T. E. Stanley to the extent that Stanley became his architect of record, designing international projects including in the Bahamas, Hong Kong, and on the island of Malta. The significance of this will be made clear as Corrigan's seldom-studied interlocking investments begin to unfold, in particular those involving Dallas oilman Algur Meadows, Sir Stafford Sands, and John C. Tysen, the president of international real estate firm Previews, Inc., all of whom were involved in the Bahama Development Co. The reader will understand this more with the analysis of the third of our five locations, the Oak Plaza professional office building located at 3707 Rawlins in the Oak Lawn neighborhood of Dallas.

For now, Bishop College, the institution that inspired power wielders like Corrigan, Collins, and Hoblitzelle to pour money, time, and energy into its expansion based on what may or may not have been altruistic motives, must remain our focus for one final scene. It will be recalled that Russian-born George de Mohrenschildt (referred to by most Kennedy assassination researchers as "the handler" of accused assassin Lee Harvey Oswald)—in spite of a forty-year career in the oil industry during which time he developed hundreds of contacts as evidenced in his extensive phone diary—closed out his working life by returning to teaching at the predominately black college in South Oak Cliff, a source of income he had not pursued since the 1930s. While at Bishop, de Mohrenschildt experienced what was diagnosed as a mental breakdown. A year later he was dead. Tomes have been written about the man, but for all intents and purposes, he remains an enigma. However, we can reveal with certainty that he was on the mind of our chronicler, Pierre Lafitte, in the hours leading to the assassination of President Kennedy in Dealey Plaza as revealed in the November 20th entry that include *Call Storey. Duvall, De M.*

The aforementioned dot connecting is but a microcosm of the business, religious, political, and social climate that dominated the careful and deliberate selection of Dallas as the scene of the crime of the century. We close the circle with a unique vignette that captures decades of conspiracy continuity following the coup in Dallas.

Over a half-century after T. E. Stanley designed her father's skyscraper, socialite Ruth Collins (Sharp Altschuler) would help navigate the City of Dallas through an ostensibly public catharsis by chairing the 50th Memorial of the assassination of President Kennedy in Dealey Plaza. In an act of perhaps defiant irony, her public relations announcement of the details for the 50th commemoration was held in the posh Crescent Club atop the Hotel Crescent Court with an impressive view of the Dallas skyline including the well-recognized rocket atop the Republic National Bank building in the background.

Surrounded by upscale office buildings that immediately attracted international banks including Union Bank of Switzerland and BNP Paribas as well as NY investment firm Brown Brothers Harriman, and a retail complex designed to appeal to the highest end national and international clientele, the Hotel Crescent Court was the third in a string of five-star properties developed by Rosewood Hotels founded by Caroline Rose Hunt with funds inherited at her father's death. The Rosewood chain eventually boasted exclusive resorts in postwar Vietnam and the oil-saturated Middle East, where Caroline's father, the infamously eccentric, anti-integration, anticommunist, independent oilman Haroldson Lafayette Hunt first ventured in the 1940s.

The epitome of the "Dallas Oil Tycoon," H. L. Hunt—a major donor to conservative religious leaders including Rev. W. A. Criswell and his Southern Baptist

Church—opposed integration even more vehemently than his religious advisor. In fact, he had been so struck by Brother Criswell's warning about Kennedy in July 1960 that he had 200,000 copies of the sermon distributed to ministers across the country, and three years later, on the eve of President Kennedy's arrival in Dallas, his son, Nelson Bunker, followed suit and contributed to the notorious, inflammatory black border advertisement, "Welcome Mr. Kennedy to Dallas," that many argued was intended to incite extreme and negative reaction to the president's visit.

Haroldson Lafayette Hunt was the embodiment, and some might argue archetype, of the deadly mood in 1963 shared by the Dallas power structure on the day Kennedy was gunned down. Hunt's suspected involvement in the assassination stemmed from his fanatical anti-integration and virulent anticommunist politics and the fact that his wealth could and did finance any number of organizations, causes, and individuals that aligned with his extreme politics, including Generals Edwin A. Walker and Charles Willoughby. We've learned that both men figure significantly in the Lafitte datebook and in the ledger sheets, as does the name "Rothermel," a surname of H. L.'s confidential assistant, Paul Rothermel. According to Hunt's former attorney, John Curington, in his book "*H. L. Hunt: Motive and Opportunity,*" his boss had his own ideas about assassination teams that could be deployed at his will, designating them "kill squads," a term used by Lafitte.

While other events in the days and months prior to the assassination have propelled researchers to accuse Hunt of involvement, including the alleged visit to the Hunt Oil offices by Jack Ruby, the documented fact that Jack Crichton signed on as a director of the board of the H. L. Hunt Foundation in July of that year, and whether or not Marina Oswald went to the Hunt offices in the days after the death of her husband, few have paid sufficient attention to Hunt's true ire toward Kennedy—an ire shared in particular with oilman Clint Murchison—grounded in the new president's position on the Texas Tidelands Case and the oil depletion allowance that could have a permanent negative impact on the bottom line of their empires.

Any summary of the lay of the land that was Dallas at the time of the assassination is incomplete without mention of E. M. "Ted" Dealey, editor/owner of the *Dallas Morning News,* and Mayor Earle Cabell. First, the mayor. It has been confirmed that Cabell had a 201 file with the Central Intelligence Agency, making him an "asset" within his brother's intelligence apparatus. Some argue the file is meaningless, but considering his brother, Charles Pierre Cabell, had been Dulles's #3 at the agency prior to the Bay of Pigs fiasco, it is reasonable to assume the mayor was a likely candidate for recruitment.

Beyond that familial connection, Earle Cabell was an early supporter and participant in the Crusade for Freedom, an outgrowth of the National Committee for a Free Europe founded in 1949 that enjoyed the full support of General Ike Eisenhower. (See Endnote.) And, without acquiescence of the dominant newspaper of the day, Ted Dealey's *Dallas Morning News*, the initial cover-up, critical in the early hours of the successful plot to assassinate the president, would not have been possible. According to Stanley Marcus, retail magnate and doyen of international fashion, Ted Dealey's newspaper was *"opposed to social progress, the United Nations, the Democratic party, federal aid, welfare, and virtually anything except the Dallas Zoo."*

Dealey's record of publishing an unbiased account of the day's events is indeed abysmal, but more directly related to the assassination itself, his team had seen fit to approve the threatening black-border advertisement the morning Kennedy arrived in Dallas, speaking volumes. One well-publicized moment defines Ted Dealey's opinion of President Kennedy and his administration when in response to an invitation from the president to comment during a luncheon in D.C., Dealey stood and snarled: "The general opinion of the grassroots thinking in this country is that you and your administration are weak sisters. If we stand firm, there will be no war. The Russians will back down. We need a man on horseback to lead this nation, and many people in Texas and the Southwest think that you are riding Caroline's tricycle."

Archconservatives and spectacularly wealthy oilmen H. L. Hunt and Clint Murchison—one of whom deplored the government, the other manipulated it for personal gain—serve as archetypes of the independent oilmen in Texas, many of whom were headquartered in Dallas. Along with Jack Crichton, Robert G. Storey, Jr., and Algur Meadows, all of whom warrant intense scrutiny and whose names appear in Lafitte's records, Hunt and Murchison and dozens of similar ilk belong in any analysis of what Lafitte's wife meant when she opined,

". . . oil smoothes the way to silent, and sometimes deadly, change."

With the preceding as backdrop, we move now to five primary locations central to the assassination of President Kennedy.

300 NORTH ERVAY — REPUBLIC NATIONAL BANK AND HOWARD CORP

The following from The Handbook of Texas, compiled by the Texas State Historical Association and available online, offers an introduction to a little-known fact behind the phenomenal success of Republic National Bank of Dallas from the 1940s through the early 1970s: "In what some consider his most important management decision, [Fred] Florence [as head of Republic National Bank] organized a wholly-owned subsidiary, the Howard Corporation, in 1946 to receive the petroleum properties of Republic National in exchange for its authorized capital stock. The company, which took its name from Howard County, Texas, where some of the oil properties were located, acquired numerous shares of Teléfonos de México, invested in twenty Texas banks, Highland Park Village, and six other shopping centers, and undeveloped real estate, and paid huge dividends. By 1948 Republic was the largest bank in Texas. Howard's stock was transferred to a separate trust in 1955, but in 1973 the Federal Reserve Bank required Republic to divest itself of the Howard Corporation's non-banking assets in order to form a holding company known as the Republic of Texas Corporation."

> *The veil of secrecy was lifted from "The Howard Corp" et al. by officers of the*
> *Republic National Bank of Dallas.*
> —AL ALTWEGG, BUSINESS ED., DALLAS MORNING NEWS, FEB 1964

In the early '60s, Business Editor of the *Dallas Morning News* Al Altwegg began to delve into the shadowy Howard Corp. Under a March 10, 1963, headline, "The Howard Corp. Unique in Banking," Altwegg reported that as early as 1959 someone had raised the question of whether or not Republic National Bank was in violation of the National Bank Holding Act. The trustees of Howard Corp., which included the president of Republic, James W. Aston, reporting directly to Chairman Karl Hoblitzelle, managed to convince Texas banking authorities that there was no violation of the state's laws prohibiting branch banking. Republic's scheme was to purchase majority shares in various banks around the area under what seem to have been shell corporations within the Howard Corp, trust, thereby skirting scrutiny because each corporation held the controlling shares independent of Republic Bank. Those thirteen "nonbranch banks" included Lakewood State Bank, whose president at the time of the assassination, Robert G. Storey, Jr., was an alleged CIA asset after the war and looms large in our story.

Many authors interested in the machinations of the Central Intelligence Agency have over the years referenced *the Washington Post* article by staff writer Richard Harwood published February 18, 1967, as evidence that Republic National Bank was a conduit for the CIA:

> In Dallas, Texas, a charitable foundation intimately associated with the
> Republic National Bank and other major companies, apparently has served

as a conduit for at least $580,700 in CIA funds since 1958 . . . the Hoblitzelle foundation began making major grants to the International Development Funds, about which nothing is known, and the Congress for Cultural Freedom.

With this, Harwood revealed that the Hoblitzelle Foundation, referenced in the prelude to this chapter, was a conduit for the agency and argued that, by association, the Republic National Bank was a CIA conduit: "Business Leaders Are Tied to CIA's Covert Operations." The report read in part, "There was mounting evidence yesterday that leaders of the American business establishment have been deeply involved in the cover operations of the Central Intelligence Agency in the United States. In Dallas, Texas, a charitable foundation intimately associated with the Republic National Bank and other major companies, apparently has served as a conduit for at least $580,700 in CIA funds since 1958. One of the foundation trustees is Federal Judge Sahar [sic] T. Hughes, who administered the oath of office to President Lyndon Johnson following the assassination of President Kennedy."

The roots of the reality that Republic National was a conduit for the CIA may run far deeper than reporter Richard Harwood was able to discover or at least report at the time. The CIA's "Operation Mockingbird," the inspiration of Frank Wisner and spearheaded by Cord Meyer, Jr., was part of the agency's ongoing propaganda machine known as the "Mighty Wurlitzer."

We know, from earlier in the book, that in late July, 1963, Pierre Lafitte made a note regarding George [Hunter-White] and Otto Skorzeny and a discussion with [Grant] Stockdale pertaining to P. [Phil] Graham and the likelihood that he would end up in Chestnut Lodge as had CIA scientist Frank Olson a decade earlier.

As noted, editor Philip Graham had been a key recruit of the Wisner/Meyer propaganda operation—the scheme that convinced leading newspapers across the country to facilitate the agency's message. Although Graham committed suicide three months prior to the assassination in Dallas, there is no evidence that *the Washington Post* had cut ties with the agency that he had established in the ensuing decades. For that reason, we can't know with certainty that the newspaper encouraged Richard Harwood to dive as deeply into Republic National Bank of Dallas as he could have in 1967.

Karl Hoblitzelle, a man with no prior banking experience, took over the reins of chairman of the board of the bank from Fred Florence. However, there is no evidence that the foundation he and his wife founded in 1942, which became a significant force in the development of the city with particular emphasis on establishing Dallas as a medical Mecca, was a front for the CIA other than being used to "promote culture" as reported by The *Washington Post*. No doubt Hoblitzelle shared common financial interests with the bank he chaired, including the value of shares and aligned investments, but this guilt by association was founded in fact. There's the possibility that reporter Harwood was "on to something" that extended beyond Hoblitzelle the man and his foundation.

The *Washington Post* reporter went on to identify other foundations around the country that also served as conduits for the agency, including one based in Houston. Again, he drew attention to President Johnson by stating that the attorney who was also a trustee for the named Houston foundation, Leon Jaworski, was "a friend of President Johnson [and] rumored from time to time to be in line for appointment as Attorney General of the United States."

From there, Harwood might have considered Jaworski's law colleague and personal friend, Robert G. Storey, Jr., both of whom had served Judge Jackson during the Nuremberg Trials, and Storey's role with Republic National Bank. The threads might have led to discovery of more information about the mysterious Howard Corp, held in trust in secret by Republic National Corporation. Assets and profits of Howard Corp. were in essence being run off the books, a highly desirable mechanism for the CIA.

The parent company of the bank, Republic National Corporation headed by Fred Florence, who as mentioned earlier was the inspiration behind The Howard Corp just after the war, purchased controlling shares of Lakewood State Bank, a bank organized in 1941 by banker J. F. Parks, Sr. along with the Storey family of Greenville, Texas. Robert Jr. would be named to the board of RNB in 1949.

The Howard Corp., which held approximately $15 million in assets, generating millions in profits annually, represented a potential for channeling far more substantial funds for the CIA than the Hoblitzelle Foundation, far earlier, perhaps as early as the close of WWII, when agency asset Robert Storey returned to Dallas to resume his law practice and join the boards of Republic and Lakewood, a bank that he would soon preside over as president in spite of having no experience in banking.

As noted earlier, both Storey and Houston lawyer Leon Jaworski had served under Judge Robert Jackson during the war tribunals, which included the trial of SS Otto Skorzeny. The details of that trial have been elaborated on previously in this book.

Following the war, Robert Storey's colleague, Jaworski, returned to Houston and resumed the practice of law from his offices located in the Bank of the Southwest. He would soon be elected to the bank board and was retained as

Legal Counsel for Schlumberger, Ltd., whose headquarters were also located in the Bank of the Southwest building. The reader will recall details of Schlumberger in the chapter focused on jack-of-all-trades Thomas Eli Davis, Jr. Dallas offices of both Schlumberger, Ltd. and attorney Leon Jaworski were located in the Republic National Bank building.

In a 1973 article in the *New York Times* during that newspaper's pursuit of the role that Leon Jaworski was to assume in the Watergate investigation, headlined "Jaworski Reportedly Had Role in Setting Up C.I.A. Aid Conduit," the newspaper followed up on Richard Harwood's reporting in The *Washington Post* story six years earlier and identified the M. D. Anderson Foundation as the Houston conduit for the CIA providing similar services to the agency as had the Hoblitzelle Foundation of Dallas. At the same time, the *Houston Chronicle* also revealed Jaworski's acknowledged role in another alleged CIA conduit, the American Fund for Free Jurists, when he told the newspaper that he "possibly helped channel Central Intelligence Agency funds" to the lawyers' group.

Following the assassination in Dallas, Robert Storey and Leon Jaworski found themselves reunited at the formation of the Warren Commission investigation, Jaworski working directly with the federal commission's legal team on behalf of the interests of the State of Texas, and Storey as direct liaison between the authorities of the City of Dallas and Allen Dulles, recently "retired" director of the Central Intelligence Agency and de facto head of the commission.

ROBERT G. "BOB" STOREY, JR.

Career highlights of Robert Gerald Storey, Jr., known to close friends as "Bob," were achieved through the legal profession, but particularly significant to this saga was his role in the development of modern Dallas that included inspiration for an international merchandise mart, not unlike the New Orleans International Trade Mart envisioned by Clay LaVerne Shaw. Bob Storey's concept came to fruition when developer Trammell Crow built the Dallas Trade Mart, Kennedy's ultimate destination as the limo turned onto Elm. Crow is notorious as having been involved with Clint Murchison and attorney/real estate developer Angus Wynne in their Great Southwest Corporation and the Six Flags project where, in another masterful move, Marina and Marguerite Oswald were secreted away and interrogated in the days following the assassination.

Storey also established the Southwestern Legal Foundation on the campus of his beloved Southern Methodist University, where he served as the Dean of the Law School for many years. But it's Storey's position among the elite of the oil industry, both national and international, that confirms Rene Lafitte's astute observation that "oil soothes the way." His idea for an International Oil & Gas Education Center under the aegis of his Southwest Legal Foundation housed on the Campus of Southern Methodist University, placed him in the cat bird seat of the petroleum industry.

Identified by many as a "roving ambassador at large," promoting freedom and the American way of life, a 1957 *Dallas Morning News* piece titled "Dean Storey: World Affairs Expert" reported that his recent trip around the world marked his fourth such journey since the war. Storey, a member of Neil Mallon's Dallas World Affairs Council that most researchers agree functioned under the guidance of Allen Dulles and the CIA, was as anticommunist as any of those previously identified in this book. In a speech before the International Convention of Christian Churches in Kansas City, 1961, Storey spoke of the challenges that Christianity faced during the Cold War because of the power, growth, and dangers of the "Marxist virus." He noted that *"the Communists feel any means to reach their objectives are justified, a Christian is restricted by the teachings of Christ from committing certain acts which the Communist is free to commit"*; ironic, considering he is named in records of the plot to murder a man in the harsh light of day in "Christian-centered" Dallas.

Prior to assuming the mantle of his father, who was held in high esteem in Dallas business circles, Storey served in both World War I and II. One official record reads:

In World War II, the Air Force sent him to London as a combat intelligence officer. He was promoted to colonel for his work with the War Crimes Commission in the Balkans and later awarded the Bronze Star and the Legion of Merit. In 1945, Storey planned to return to Dallas and to the practice of law, but US Supreme Court Justice Robert Jackson had other thoughts. Justice Jackson had been appointed chief prosecutor at Nuremberg, and he wanted Storey by his side as special counsel. Storey was on the prosecution team that prosecuted Herman Goering, Rudolph Hess, and other high-ranking Nazi officials. Storey served as dean of the law school from 1947–1959. From 1952–53, he also served as president of the American Bar Association. During that time, he created the Southwestern Legal Foundation as a means of sponsoring the development of a major legal center and served as its director until 1972.

However, the November 20th datebook entry 'Call Storey' followed by the name 'Duvall,' and the initials 'DeM' penned by the project manager of the plot to murder Kennedy reveals a darker side to the esteemed jurist. There can be little doubt that the Duvall mentioned is Judge Jesse C. Duvall of Fort Worth, TX. Judge Duvall had served as prosecutor during the Dachau trials at the conclusion of WWII. Among the defendants was SS Otto Skorzeny.

Duvall, a US Army Major during WWII, was serving under Judge Robert H. Jackson at the same time Jackson had seconded Col. Robert G. Storey to search for evidence to support the charges against Nazi war criminals. Judge Jackson had known Storey through the American Bar Association before the war, and when he heard that Storey had uncovered valuable documents related to Russia, he tasked his friend with the search for evidence to be presented in the war crimes trials. That search resulted in the discovery of forty-seven crates of Nazi records.

Now we see Storey and Duvall named side by side in private records of the manager of a conspiracy, two days before the assassination, followed by a reference to DeM, which we can safely assume was George de Mohrenschildt. During an interview with the FBI, Judge Duvall revealed that he had met the de Mohrenschildts in January 1963 and several months later had dined with the couple in Dallas. He reported that over dinner, de Mohrenschildt had asked if he might assist his new friend, the recently repatriated defector to Russia, Lee Harvey Oswald, with his dishonorable discharge.

In one of the more odd twists of fate in this saga, Judge Duvall was also approached in the immediate aftermath of Jack Ruby's shooting of Oswald. It seems that the man, an acquaintance of Judge Duvall whi for over two decades had worked as a bookkeeper for Ruby in early 1963, alleged that he had seen Jack Ruby and Oswald together in Ruby's Carousel Club.

Bob Storey passed away in 1981. Judge Duvall followed him a year later.

JACK CRICHTON

In 1963, the president of Republic National Bank—parent company of Bob Storey's Lakewood Bank & Trust—and reporting directly to chairman Karl Hoblitzelle was James W. Aston, who was also engaged in a number of private pursuits including oil ventures with one John Alston "Jack" Crichton, the ultra-conservative oilman who has long been suspected of involvement in the assassination. This book lays to rest any doubt of Crichton's role in the COUP of November 22, 1963.

According to esteemed assassination researcher and author Prof. Peter D. Scott, Crichton signed on as director of the newly formed H. L. Hunt Foundation as evidenced in a document dated July 22, 1963, one day after Crichton's 488th Military Intelligence concluded annual training. In 1956, while engaged in machinations in Batista's Cuba, Crichton had time and inclination to organize the 488th, which he headquartered in Dallas, with himself ultimately responsible. The stated focus of the unit was *covert petrochemical intelligence studies at home and abroad, including in the Soviet Union.* In direct control of the unit was Lt. Col. George Whitmeyer, commander of all Army Reserve units in oil-rich East Texas, home of Delta Drilling. Delta had been integral to the 1952 Meadows-Skorzeny venture in Spain. It has been repeatedly estimated that at least 50 percent of the Dallas Police Department's officers and detectives were members of the 488th Intelligence Detachment. During an interview about the 488th, Crichton claimed there were *"about a hundred men in the unit and about forty or fifty of them were from the Dallas Police Department."*

The 488th annual training in '63 took place at The Pentagon, one of only two attachments from Texas to be in DC that summer.

Contributing to Crichton's joining the board of the Hunt Foundation that summer was his shared political views with H. L. Hunt, the eccentric oilman who but for his wealth might never have been taken seriously. Their rigid position on segregation was best exemplified during Crichton's 1964 run for Texas governor, when he argued against "the unjust, unconstitutional federally forced desegregation in the state of Texas." In light of datebook entries referring to meetings with Jack Crichton through the year, it is possible that he also served as conduit for funding from H. L. Hunt.

Crichton received a BS degree in Petroleum Engineering from Texas A&M University and a MS degree from MIT. By age twenty-six, he was a major in the Army, serving in Bill Donovan's OSS, precursor to the CIA. With his language and technological and engineering skills, Crichton was "more than a natural for the intelligence agency." The nature of his secretive work for Wild Bill's agency remains difficult to obtain, but we know from a diary he kept through 1965 that his assignments eventually covered *five theatres,* some of which clearly ignited his interests in oil production, and prepared him for one of his first major breakthroughs—a project on the southern tip of the Arabian Peninsula. As a soldier and officer, Crichton was awarded the Air Medal, five Battle Stars, and the Bronze Star. He returned as a Colonel in the US Army Reserve, a civilian to pursue a profession in energy, a Republican with undefined aspirations. His life would soon become a grab bag of intelligence and political activities.

"They honed my experience at finding oil and gas, and understanding intricate oil negotiations."

Crichton was referring to the firm of DeGolyer & MacNaughton, one of the country's most sought after oil and gas exploration and engineering firms.

In 1946, Everette Lee DeGolyer, while working for the wartime OSS, recruited the young and energetic trained intelligence officer to operate a network of key petroleum companies that within about fourteen months folded into the larger network of Donovan's World Commerce Corporation (WCC). As noted in Chapter 2, many of these WCC enterprises also served as fronts for covert activities, including commercial sabotage and assassination.

DeGolyer had first encountered Crichton while serving the war effort as director of the Petroleum Reserves Corporation mission to the Middle East. Prior to that, DeGolyer had served as director of conservation with the Office of the Coordinator for National Defense and then as assistant deputy director of the Petroleum Administration for War. The reader may recognize that DeGolyer would have worked in close proximity with Thomas Proctor's mentor, Paul McNutt—both identified in Chapter 5—in managing manpower and logistics for the war.

Following the merger of the Crichton-run network of companies on behalf of DeGolyer into WCC, Jack remained on as vice president of DeGolyer & McNaughton and its subsidiary, Core Laboratories, Inc. Before taking his own life in 1956, DeGolyer, who was born into a dirt-poor family in Kansas and suffered for years from aplastic anemia, organized a company called Isotopes, Inc. to provide radioactive isotopes for oilfield purposes. He had also enjoyed the friendship and priceless professional endorsement of Lord Cowdray, British engineer and heir to the Pearson family fortune including Mexican Eagle Petroleum Co., whose favored hotel in Dallas was The Stoneleigh.

By the mid '50s, Crichton was ensconced in a penthouse office suite of the Vaughn Tower, twelve stories above busy Commerce Street in downtown Dallas. Crichton felt very much at home in the office building named for Dallas businessman and ardent Republican Jack Vaughn, who also preferred T. E. Stanley's architectural designs. In fact, he commissioned Stanley to design a number of buildings in oil-rich areas of the state, including Midland and Amarillo, Texas, headquarters of Dorchester Gas, one of Crichton's most commercially successful domestic oil ventures.

Fellow students in his Texas A&M class included the future mayor of Dallas, Earl Cabell, also an alleged CIA asset. At the time, sources identified Crichton as being the president of a successful oil and gas company founded by a New York bank, The Pinnacle Trust Company, established in New York with Dean Matthey as chairman of the board and Dean's colleague, Harry Brurdydi. They set up under the direction of C. Leslie Roos. It was said that "Ross was connected." Jack was hired to serve as president. Prior to that, he had been vice president of Operations of San Juan Oil Company. His tenacity was key in his hiring.

The numerous deals Jack made during this period included purchase of East Texas Oil, followed by Old Ocean Field in South Texas. This in turn was followed by Karot properties in Louisiana, New Mexico and Texas, and the huge properties of Hagy, Harrington, and Marsh in the Panhandle and Hugoton Fields of Texas and Oklahoma. "Pinnacle holdings were huge and successful," wrote Crichton.

When Pinnacle needed to make a deal with the King of Yemen to look for oil in the desert, they first consulted with the US State Department, whose primary goal was to beat the Russians. Crichton suggested to his bosses that he go to Yemen to prepare a full report. His bosses then conferred with State and came back to Jack to order his group to Yemen within the week.

"And tell nobody," execs at Pinnacle told him.

"Where have I heard that before?" said Jack.

Before leaving, Crichton gave the second in charge at Pinnacle a cover story and met with a rep from the Navy Academy and Wharton School of Finance to get briefed. "Jack carefully tucked his .38 revolver into a bag" and packed the papers for a Yemen Development Corporation. He had negotiated a $100,000 salary and 50 percent of the net profit to the Yemen Development Corporation.

Soon after, the CIA sent Jack a secret cable that read: "We believe the King of Yemen is under the influence of an Italian doctor and is being given morphine shots repeatedly. Find out what you can regarding this and report back to us upon your return."

The CIA wrote upon the cable at the bottom of the message: "OS or IS may know the King." We safely assume this refers to Otto or his wife, Ilse Skorzeny.

During the trip, Jack had learned that the Russians were speeding up efforts to get a concession ASAP in Yemen. Later the same week, Pinnacle execs, including Dean Mathey, who would eventually head Empire Trust reported the oil concession term was for thirty years from the date of signing with an option to renew at the end of the period. Jack carefully read the English version and said all was fine. "We can live with this," he said. And with that success, Crichton advanced his value to a myriad of government and private interests.

THERE'S SO MUCH MORE TO JACK CRICHTON

*Jesus, let me tell you, let me . . . in so many ways Jack Crichton is critical . . .
is the critical linchpin to solving any mystery in the JFK assassination, but any
real investigator must have all the pieces to the Crichton puzzle. I mean it.*
—Col. Albert Haney, Florida, 1996

Crichton has been scrutinized by assassination researchers for decades, prompted primarily by his role with the 488th Intel Unit, yet oddly, most have failed to closely examine his early activities in Spain after the war. Had they done so, they most likely would have encountered details of his relationship with Otto Skorzeny. In Spain, in 1952, Crichton first met Skorzeny while he was working with Tyler, TX-based Delta Drilling on the Meadows-Skorzeny venture, led by Algur Meadows of Dallas. Crichton had heard the stories about the former Nazi's daring exploits; the saga of his Mussolini rescue was everywhere, unavoidable, as were dark rumors about Skorzeny that traipsed the truth spectrum. When Crichton shook Skorzeny's hand for the first time, his hand was gripped tightly, and he felt genuine friendship coming from the gregarious former SS officer.

Jack Crichton also felt friendship toward the man who would later befriend Lee Harvey Oswald and wife Marina. In late 1952, George de Mohrenschildt worked closely with Crichton on the Meadows-Skorzeny venture. Without doubt, George also consulted often with Skorzeny, advising on the need to finesse certain matters with the Spanish Government, providing him detailed explanations about problems the scheme would encounter. Crichton later said of him, "I liked George. He was a nice guy."

In August 1953, on the heels of the Spanish oil deal, Crichton was hired by NY-based investment firm Empire Trust Company, the investment bank identified in a previous chapter in the context of the Canadian-based Bronfman fortune and Permindex. Crichton was quickly named a vice president of the banking operation that could trace its roots to London. His boss at Pinnacle, Dean Mathey, would soon become chairman of the board of Empire and honorary chairman of the Bank of New York following the merger of the two financial empires. Decades later, BoNY would be purchased by Frankfurt-based multinational investment bank and financial services company Deutsche Bank, most recently infamous for lending massive funds to the future president of the US, Donald J. Trump. It should be noted that before the merger, Bank of New York had exchanged a major financial contribution for a seat on the board of the JFK Library at Columbia Point, MA.

Prior to the US declaring war on Germany in 1917, Empire Trust is reported to have been of keen interest to the German Secret Service developing a highly sophisticated wireless system to transmit critical information. The cipher code for the system employed innocuous personal names. Empire Trust was identified as "Albert Hardwood," a name impossible to locate in contemporary records, phone books, business directories, etc., of the period. According to revelations in *The German Secret Service in American* by John P. Jones and Merrick Hollister, published in 1918, the diplomatic code was a dictionary, its pages designated by serial letters, its words by serial numbers. Thus the message "12-B-15-C-7" signified the twelfth and fifteenth words on the second page, and the seventh word on the third page. This particular dictionary was one of a rare edition. It is interesting to note that Lafitte, who cabled Otto Skorzeny on numerous occasions, frequently reverted to code in his entries. Two examples, back to back, August 10 and 11:

A Z+16-2
(Ella R. check on)

and

A Z+18-2 (e)
-cables sent to O
Madrid (Souetre)

The authors' further research finds that by 1951, Empire Trust served as a proprietary for the CIA as well as part of a well-concealed network of small to large banks, many located in the Dallas, Texas, area. Among them was the Lakewood Trust, cofounded by the R. G. Storey family.

Further evidence of Crichton's mysterious usefulness on the global playing field, from 1954 through 1958, before Fidel Castro gained control of Cuba, he became deeply involved with negotiating with Cuban dictator Fulgencio Batista for oil drilling rights on the small island. At this same time, George de Mohrenschildt was working as a trusted consultant for the Cuban-Venezuelan Oil Voting Trust Company (CVOT).

As historian and assassination expert John Simkin has aptly explained, de Mohrenschildt was "a key figure" in assisting Crichton and other American oilmen involved with working things out with Batista. Crichton's and de Mohrenschildt's efforts paid off handsomely, and a signed agreement with the Cuban dictator was reached whereby over 10,000,000 acres of Cuban land were turned over for oil exploration. Within another year, this acreage had reached over 15,000,000 acres. However, on January 1, 1959, CVOT fortunes under the agreement with Batista began to take a drastic turn toward doom after Batista fled Cuba—with millions in US dollars from American oil companies and the many Mafia-run business enterprises in Cuba—and Fidel Castro seized the reins of power for the small island nation.

Pierre Lafitte tells us all we need to know to conclude once and for all that Jack Crichton was involved in plans for the assassination of President Kennedy on November 22, 1963.

Meet with Crichton at Tech building.
O says Lancelot go
phone booth
—Lafitte datebook. November 5, 1963

Terry says call+ [illegible]
7436 Kenshire, Dallas
J. Crichton
—Lafitte datebook, November 11, 1963

Crichton w T. (Caretaker)
—Lafitte datebook, November 14, 1963

Jack C.—grates and span.
—Lafitte datebook, November 17, 1963

Crichton's own November 1963 diary revealed "his unit's participation" and "concealed involvement" with the Dallas leg of President Kennedy's Texas trip.

A SEGUE TO BRANDY

An anointed member of Crichton's 488th Military Intel unit was the equally provocative character Frank "Brandy" Brandstetter, the Army intelligence agent and CIA operative who just happened to be in Dallas the day before President Kennedy was murdered. Said to be a tall, handsome, mustached man with an indefatigable bent for adventure, Brandstetter was born in Transylvania, Romania, in 1912 and journeyed to the United States as a teenager with less than a dollar in his pocket. His close friendship with Jack Crichton is frequently overlooked, yet we find his name in Lafitte records just two days before the assassination. The page reads: *"Frank B. here, others- Jack- four days- MC."*

Brandstetter volunteered for the US Army during World War II. His fluency in Hungarian, German, Austrian, and French caught the attention of Army intelligence officers, and he was quickly routed for training at Fort Ritchie, Maryland, and later at Fort Holabird, Baltimore, Maryland. During the early war years, he was also trained by British intelligence in England before he parachuted with the 506th Airborne Infantry Regiment on D-Day. Near the end of the war, Brandstetter led a POW interrogation team that spent several weeks at Camp King during the same time Otto Skorzeny was there. Besides Jack Crichton, Brandy is also known to have been a good friend of CIA official David Atlee

Philipps, who had risen through the ranks from part-time agent, intelligence officer, chief of stations, and eventually chief of Western Hemisphere operations.

Brandstetter and Phillips both spent long periods of time in the volatile political climate of Cuba and Mexico City. Also close to Brandstetter were George de Mohrenschildt, Dallas conservative radio entrepreneur and alleged agent and friend of Jack Ruby, Gordon Mc Lendon, Army Colonel Sam Kail, and Dorothe Matlack, described by scrupulous researcher and author Bill Simpich as a renowned figure for pioneering the Army's use of human intelligence and serving as the Pentagon's liaison to the CIA. As we learned earlier, Sam Kail, who was frequently on loan to the CIA, is identified in Lafitte records on several dates, most significantly Wednesday, November 6, when Pierre notes Meet with Kail (T). The significance of Kail in context of "T" is pursued in the appendix essay by author Kent, "A Well-Concealed 'T.'"

Brandstetter was at the helm of Conrad's Havana Hilton on the eve of the Cuban Revolution. In the spirit and purported apolitical views of a large percentage of hoteliers around the world, he welcomed revolutionary leader Fidel Castro with open arms. Brandy had for years been a close colleague of Warren Broglie, who managed the Hotel Luma in Mexico City. It was Broglie's hotel where the infamous, still ill-defined meetup with Lee Oswald took place.

On November 21, 1963, the day before the assassination, Brandstetter was in Dallas, Texas, reportedly conducting a seminar for Army intelligence personnel despite the that nearly every military intelligence officer in the area was tied up with preparations and activities related to JFK's visit. Weeks later, Brandy would be involved directly in the world of his friend Phillipe de Vosjoli, the former top agent at the SDECE and prized recruit of James Jesus Angleton named in three entries of the Lafitte's 1963 records. The official storyline is that de Vosjoli suddenly realized that attempts on the life of Charles de Gaulle were somehow related to the assassination in Dallas. His alleged awakening begs the question why Pierre Lafitte might have included his name in the same context as Thomas Davis, his wife Caroline, and the attorney for a film being made in Franco's Spain, Thomas Proctor, months before the assassination of Kennedy.

CRICHTON'S ITINERARY ON THE ROAD TO DEALEY PLAZA

On September 13, 1963, just weeks after he and Brandy (presumably the hotelier joined in) and their fellow members of the 488th Intel had completed training at the Pentagon, the *Dallas Morning News* published a brief notice, "Dallas Man

Joins Oil Group for Romanian Visit." Crichton had been invited to participate in a US State Department delegation in conjunction with the American Petroleum Institute on a fact-finding mission to Princess Caradja's beloved Romania and native land of his good friend Brandy Brandstetter. (Of note: Jake L. Hamon, Dallas oilman who in his capacity as president of the American Petroleum Institute traveled around the globe, had also been an active participant in the Meadows-Skorzeny venture in Spain where he met Ricardo Sicre, vice president of the World Commerce Corporation who is named throughout the Skorzeny papers.)

In spite of being locked behind the Iron Curtain at the time, the Americans were somehow allowed access to Romania's petroleum executives. The delegation that departed on September 23rd included a state department representative, two representatives of Rockefeller's Standard Oil and Socony Mobil interests, and one from Continental Oil. Rockefeller's Chase Manhattan Bank, whose president would become a driving force on the Warren Commission, used Republic National of Dallas as a correspondent bank in Texas; Continental Oil's board included former Sec. of the Army Frank Pace, who was outgoing president of General Dynamics—military contractor embroiled in the TFX scandal that exposed lobbyist Bobby Baker. A subsidiary of Continental, Jan Jacinto Petroleum has been identified as a CIA conduit. Pace was also a longtime board member of Nation-Wide Securities with former DCI Allen Dulles and Gen. Maxwell Taylor. Ten percent of Nation-Wide's investments were in the petroleum industry. (See Endnote.)

On October 17th—one day before James Angleton told Pierre Lafitte that there had been a high-level gathering in DC,—the *Dallas Morning News* published a brief announcement, "Former CIA Boss Sets Dallas Talk." The story read: "Allen W. Dulles, former director of the Central Intelligence Agency will address a meeting of the Dallas Council on World Affairs at noon on Monday, October 28, in the Baker Hotel . . ." Neil Mallon, a member of the board of Republic National Bank, had been a friend and confidant of Allen Dulles throughout Dulles's tenure as director of Central Intelligence. It was through Dulles's prompting that Mallon founded the Dallas chapter of the Council on World Affairs, an invaluable instrument for the agency since 1951 and the perfect venue on October 28, 1963, for Dulles to promote his book and speak on national security issues including reference to specific activity in hot spots around the world, suggesting he was being briefed in spite of his having left the agency in 1961. The Dallas chapter of the Independent Petroleum Association of America also held their monthly meeting on October 28th.

On October 27th, the *Dallas Morning News* followed up and announced that oil expert Jack Crichton, having recently returned from an oil tour of Romania, would present his report to the Petroleum Engineers on the following Friday, November 1st.

On October 29th, Kent Biffle of the *Dallas Morning News* published a summation of Allen Dulles's speech the night before under the headline *"Allen Dulles Looks Behind Red Moves"*: "Khrushchev announced he 'isn't going to the moon next week' to foil the Kennedy plan for a joint moon effort. Dulles said, 'Russians are arming Algerian troops in hopes of finally gaining a solid foothold in Africa . . . The Soviets have been trying for ten to fifteen years to find the foothold they want in Africa. They tried in Egypt, the Congo, Guinea and Ghana.'" Biffle continued, "Dulles said that in arming the Algerians against the Moroccans, the Reds are again trying to find a satisfactory foothold in Africa." We should underscore here that as DCI Allen Dulles had been a frequent visitor to the hotels and homes of numerous close friends in Dallas, Texas, including of course Mallon. Indeed, some people close to the CIA director would quietly remark that Dallas had become an important base of operations for the CIA, second only to headquarters in Langley, Virginia. (See Endnote.)

Dulles's October 28th talk before Mallon's Dallas Council on World Affairs further tilled the soil when he included reference to the Algerians' fight for independence—a subject close to the heart of this book. The speech was a companion piece to other recent impassioned anticommunist pleadings at various venues around the city including those of the woeful, anti-Red princess from Romania. Jack Crichton's report to Dallas petroleum executives—scheduled within days of Dulles's speech at the DCWA—recapped his Romanian oil tour, which most assuredly described the plight of that country under The Reds, planting propaganda and stoking the anticommunist fires in Dallas. Crichton's talk was just four days prior to Lafitte making a note, *Meet with Crichton at Tech building.*

* * *

When Dallas Police Captain Patrick Gannaway, a member of Jack Crichton's US Army Intelligence Attachment, falsely claimed that a roll call had taken place in the Texas School Book Depository, thus exposing only one missing employee—Lee Harvey Oswald—members of the conservative press corps were prepared. It was Gannaway who first hinted to them that Lee Harvey Oswald was a Communist.

'Police Capt. Pat Gannaway said the suspect was an employee in the building where a rifle was found. Gannaway said the suspect had visited Russia and was married to a Russian. This was not immediately confirmed.
—DALLAS, NOV. 22 (UNITED PRESS INTERNATIONAL)

That roll call never took place, but somehow the name and an addresses for the "commie lone nut" was shared with the authorities, who soon made their way to the Paine home in Irving, setting in motion events that culminated in Oswald's murder on Sunday, the 24th, by Jack Ruby. The *perfect patsy* would never tell his story, and the *Dallas Morning News* would promote an alternate tale.

* * *

It has been reported that Crichton met with oilman and influence buyer H. L. Hunt the day after that assassination. Crichton's failed attempt to secure nomination of the Republican Party in their effort to remove John Connolly as Governor of Texas in 1964 did not slow him down. Among his last major enterprises was Arabian Shield Development, a natural corporate name for a petroleum industry leader with decades of experience in the Middle East. His efforts were focused in Yemen, as were those of Hunt Oil. It should be noted that Arabian Shield also dealt in nickel. There can be little doubt that during his travels, Crichton had developed friendships with executives of some of the world's leading oil behemoths, including American geologist James Terry Duce, an executive of Arabian American Oil Company (ARAMCO), which is provocative in light of the familiarity Lafitte assigned to the November 5 entry, *"Terry says call . . ."* followed by Crichton's home address in North Dallas. Jack Crichton died on December 10, 2007 at the age of 91.

TENANTS OF REPUBLIC NATIONAL BANK BUILDING

Not only was 300 N. Ervay home to the financial institution that was Republic National Bank and Howard Corp. frequently operating in concert with Empire Trust of NY, but a significant number of other placeholders within the military/industrial/intelligence apparatus benefited from access and security provided within the building's environment.

We turn now to four of those major tenants that relate directly to, or were positioned closely to the periphery of, the plot to assassinate President John Kennedy: Schlumberger Oil Services; Lone Star Steel (which on the surface provided the essential commodity for the military during WWII, Korea, and Vietnam, but played a far more intriguing role); Ling Temco Vought (LTV, the aerospace concern that served as precursor to today's mega military contractor L3 Technologies); and Neil Mallon's Dresser Industries (which serviced the petroleum industry on an international scale). Each of these contractors was locked in a symbiosis with the military-intelligence apparatus, reliant on the military for profits and dependent on intelligence for security.

SCHLUMBERGER OIL WELL SERVICES

In Chapter 5, "Jacks-of-All-Trades," we learned that soldier of fortune Thomas Eli Davis, Jr., married into a family with direct personal and business ties to Schlumberger. We consider now further implications of the family-dominated worldwide oil services company whose headquarters had been relocated during the war from France to Houston, Texas. The move was made at the behest of Jean de Menil, the son-in-law of one of the two Schlumberger founders. As mentioned, when de Menil shopped for the ideal location of his Dallas office, he chose the Republic National Bank building. Counsel to Schlumberger, Leon Jaworski, followed close behind.

Schlumberger origins extend to the turn of the 20th century, when Conrad François and his brother Marcel, two of six Schlumberger children of an affluent Alsatian Protestant family, received their degrees in engineering in Paris. They soon founded the oil field exploration company, Schlumberger Well Surveying Corporation, which was relocated to Houston at the onset of WWII. Another Schlumberger brother, Maurice, launched the Neuflize Schlumberger Bank, which would merge with Mallet Bank, a French Protestant concern, in the early '60s.

The Mallet name may be familiar to some as a member of the Mallet-Prevost family who surfaced in the allegations that industrialists in league with certain military officers attempted to remove President Franklin D. Roosevelt in an overthrow of the US Government in 1933 in order to install a fascist-style regime. A student in Paris, Jean de Menil, descended from French barons from the time of Bonaparte, met and married Conrad's lovely daughter, Dominique, both now famous among America's most committed patrons of the arts, and for the extraordinary collection they amassed. Prior to assuming the helm of Schlumberger Overseas in the Middle and Far East, and Schlumberger Surenco S.A., de Menil was vice president of Banque Nationale pour le Commerce et l'Industrie in Paris. By 1963, the elegant couple had become a fixture in the American art world, but it is Jean's vast network of friends and colleagues in the world of oil and gas that interests us.

JEAN DE MENIL'S GOOD FRIEND PAUL RAIGORODSKY

In 1952, Raigorodsky, as president of Petroleum Engineering, Inc. and partner of the Clairborne Gasoline Co. was handpicked by the deputy to the United States Special Representative in Europe, (Ret.) Major General Fred L. Anderson, to be senior civilian director to oversee oil production for defense in Europe. "We use the word defense—not war," said Raigorodsky at the time of his appointment, shortly after he was given a top-secret office in Paris, France, at 32 Avenue d'Iena. Prior to going to Paris, Paul had lived in Texas "off and on" since 1921. Born in Russia in 1898, he arrived in the US from Kiev around 1920 and soon met and married a native of New Orleans, Ethel McCaleb, a student at the University of Texas and daughter of a San Antonio banker who served on the Federal Reserve. The couple had two children and divorced before the US entered the war.

Fast-forward to 1964: due to his vast network of friends within the White Russian community and the heady air he breathed in the petroleum world, Ragairodsky was called to testify before the Warren Commission. Raigorodsky identified one of Houston's most esteemed businessmen and philanthropists, Jean de Menil, as a "very close friend of mine, the financial head of Schlumberger Co." His testimony continued to reveal that another friendship, that of roving petroleum "expert" George de Mohrenschildt, led to discussions with Jean de Menil about a proposed scheme in Haiti.

Was Tom Davis's charade in July 1963 intended to disguise actual recruitment for planned invasion of Haiti, or elsewhere in the region? Was his wife, Caroline, a conduit between the Schlumberger family and Tom, her malleable husband from Texas?

Raigorodsky told WC lead counsel Albert Jenner, "When I wouldn't go with George in the deal, he asked me to give him any suggestion as to who may be interested, so I suggested John De Menil because the Schlumberger Co. is a worldwide organization and they deal with every country in the world—you know what I am trying to say?" Eventually de Menil decided to forgo the opportunity, citing the somewhat weak business pitch by de Mohrenschildt.

Raigorodsky's friend de Mohrenschildt would from time to time use the attorney services of one Herbert Itkin, a fact detailed in a previous chapter that described activities in both Haiti and the Dominican Republic.

Relevant to this investigation, the name *Itkin* appears in the Lafitte datebook on both October 26 and October 27, 1963. The entry of the 27th includes the name *Gali Sherbatov* in the October 27th entry, initials L. O. *'Orlov'* and *'Harvey.'*

The critical entries fall within the time period of Jack Crichton's resurfacing from Romania, Allen Dulles's presentation before the Dallas Council on World

Affairs, and the forthcoming "Lancelot Planning" of the 28th and 29th. It should also be recalled that CIA's assassination chief William King Harvey was known from his earliest days with the FBI as a "Red-hunter."

The previous Thursday, October 24, for a reason yet to be determined, two Dallas residents who were employees of Socony Mobil Oil Company, Everett Glover and Volkmar Schmidt, appear in Lafitte's datebook. The note reads simply, "*Glover Volkmar K.C. Stanley.*" Both Glover and Volkmar will be pursued in the fifth and final location, 411 Elm—Texas School Book Depository.

* * *

Author and assassination researcher Bill Simpich writes, "by May 1963, [Herbert] Itkin became the attorney for the Haitian government-in-exile. CIA documents show that Itkin's handler in 1963 was Mario Brod, who was recruited in Italy by James Angleton during World War II and had operational involvement in Haiti. Before his brother was killed, Bobby Kennedy himself was relying on mob tips from Itkin. In 1966, Itkin was reportedly researching under his code name 'Portio,' while Angleton held onto his private 'Mike/Portio/Haiti' file. In 1968, CIRA (CI research and analysis chief) Ray Rocca swore that the 'CI Staff definitely never was in contact' with Itkin. By 1971, CIRA's bird-dog investigator Paul Hartman was asking to review Itkin's CIA file, no doubt to educate himself on some fine points."

It is worth repeating the two entries:

October 26th
W team E Johnson's
(Itkin)

October 27th
Gali Sherbatov-L.O.
(Orlov)
(Itkin)
- Harvey-

Paul Raigorodsky told the Warren Commission: "Now, I don't know it for a fact, but except as I was told by Father Royster that the Oswalds came through Fort Worth originally. Now, this is hearsay—that I believe they got acquainted with the people by the name of Clark, in reference to Gali's married name."

Mr. JENNER. Max Clark?

Mr. RAIGORODSKY. I mean, that's all hearsay—I do not know it for a fact. While she is a Russian, in fact she is a first cousin of a very close friend of mine, Prince Scherbatoff, who lives in New York and lives in Jamaica. That's where I see him occasionally. Now, it is my understanding that the Clarks told some of their friends—again, this is hearsay, that "Here is a Russian married to an American and they don't even have milk for the babies."

Raigorodsky's good friend George de Mohrenschildt also named Gali Clark in his Warren Commission testimony:

Mr. JENNER. All right. Now, when did you first meet either Marina—I will put it this way: When did you first hear—

Mr. De MOHRENSCHILDT. The first time—

Mr. JENNER. Of either of these people—Marina Oswald or Lee Harvey Oswald?

Mr. De MOHRENSCHILDT. As far as I remember, George Bouhe, who is a close friend of mine, and a very curious individual, told me that there is an interesting couple in Fort Worth, and that the Clarks know them already—Max Clark and Gali—they know them already. Somebody read about them in the paper—I don't know exactly, I don't remember the exact wording anymore that somebody read about them in the paper, maybe Mr. Gregory, and discovered them, made a discovery.

According to her obituary, "Gali Clark was born in France in October 1922. She was the daughter of Prince and Princess Mikhail Mikhaïlovitch Scherbatoff, exiled from Russia after the 1917 Revolution. Her father's portrait hangs in the Hermitage Museum in St. Petersburg, Russia. She met her husband, Max E. Clark, in Nice, France, during World War II. He was a pilot in the US Army. They were married in 1945 at the Orthodox Russian church in Nice, France, and after the war, they came to live in Fort Worth, where Max E. Clark was a lawyer."

Clark's clients included military contractor General Dynamics with a primary plant located in Fort Worth overseen by the President of GD, Frank Pace. We remind the reader of the brewing scandal during the months leading to the assassination, involving government contracts for the TFX F-111 fighter plane produced by General Dynamics in Fort Worth, and Bobby Baker, who traveled with his girlfriend, Nancy Carol Tyler, as well as Ella Rometsch, from New Orleans to Dallas at the height of the scandal.

* * *

We conclude the assessment of the October 27th datebook entry by first surmising that *Harvey* can only mean William King "Bill" Harvey, who surfaces on numerous dates in the Lafitte material. Bill Harvey has been covered sufficiently in this book, so it is only necessary to highlight his presence in context of *Gali Sherbatov* and *Itkin* and *Orlov.*

As noted previously, *"Orlov"* is clear reference to fellow Fort Worth citizen, Col. Lawrence Orlov, a veteran of the Air Force as well as a good friend of J. Walton Moore.

Ragairodsky's testimony that confirmed his wide range of associations with intriguing characters, from Jean de Menil, to George de Mohrenschildt, to Gali Scherbatoff pulls us toward a deeper grasp of the milieu.

THE SIGNIFICANCE OF THE TOLSTOY FOUNDATION

Paul Raigorodsky counted among his close friends Col. Herschel V. Williams, an adman, Hollywood screenwriter, and real estate executive who worked alongside Mrs. Otto (Ilse) Skorzeny at the global real estate concern Previews Inc. After the war, while employed by Previews, Williams joined the board of the Tolstoy Foundation along with Russian-born Raigorodsky, and Schlumberger's Jean de Menil.

The Tolstoy Foundation, according to their official history, was established to respond to the needs of the Russian refugees of World War II who *for various reasons were handicapped in providing for themselves and to create a center for Russian culture in America to serve the American born generation of Russian descent.* Cofounded by Russian-American Igor Sikorsky, aviation pioneer and creator of the Sikorsky helicopter, the foundation was confronted with the serious issue of repatriation by early February 1945. They made the decision to take on the task of bringing these refugees to Canada and the US: "They arrived by boat or plane and their expenses were initially paid by the International Relief Organization (IRO). In 1946, the Tolstoy Foundation initiated a subcommittee of the American Council of Voluntary Agencies for Foreign Service under the name of the United Relief Committee in Aid to 'Displaced Persons of Central and East European Origin.'" It was through this subcommittee that Estonian-born Ilya Mamantov and his wife, Alexandria, entered the US only to find themselves two decades later as central characters in the drama that unfolded on the weekend of November 22, 1963, in Dallas.

Sikorsky served as chairman of Tolstoy when he was nominated to the board of the Connecticut National Bank, Bridgeport, founded by the in-laws of

Thomas Eli Davis, Jr. Bridgeport, "America's arsenal" was also home of de Menil's Schlumberger Research Center.

Col. Williams', and Paul Raigorodsky's mutual interest in the Tolstoy Foundation suggests a certain degree of commonality between Williams, his employer Previews Inc., and the staunch conservative, anticommunist movement in Dallas with Raigorodsky as its semiofficial representative; and certainly, there is a strong likelihood that Ilya Mamantov, who spoke openly and frequently against "The Reds," was at least familiar with Col. Williams. However, far more intriguing is the fact that while serving in military intelligence during the war, Col. Williams reported to Dallas's own, Col. Robert G. Storey, Jr., a man who needs no further introduction, but the significance of the history between these two men cannot be overstated.

LONE STAR STEEL

Lone Star Steel manufacturing operations were located in the small East Texas community sixty miles to the Northeast of Tyler called Daingerfield. Referred to as "A Secret Cold War Military Installation" in the *East Texas Journal* of October 21, 2017, the Daingerfield Project was a closely kept secret, secured within a compound behind the gates of a state-of-the-art government-funded steel plant built during WWII:

> With the opening of the Lone Star Steel Company and the United States Navy Bureau of Ordnance Aerophysics Laboratory, the population of the town tripled during and after WWII. Research involved wind tunnels creating airflow at supersonic speed and compressing air related through nozzles to create thrust. . . . The steel plant's blast furnace blower and steam generating plant provided nearly four times the capacity needed to build the biggest wind runner on earth . . . the guided missile business appears to be a coming thing . . . the first thing that was different than any other secure area on a military [installation] was being behind the gates of a publicly held company making steel . . . the thing that was really different was the first time I saw a fuel truck be back into a blacked out bay where we opened up the area under a false floor in the tanker and unloaded a rocket engine.

At its height, the Daingerfield Project employed 373 physicists, scientists, engineers, and technicians. The labs also tested prototypes developed by military contractors from Australia, Canada, and England as well as the Department of Commerce and NASA.

The heads of four Dallas banks and one from the oil-rich North Texas town of Wichita Falls held positions on the board of Lone Star Steel, signifying each institution's extensive investments in the success of the military contractor that would soon be ramping up for a full-blown war in Vietnam. In addition to: Nathan Adams, chairman of First National Bank of Dallas; R. L. Thornton, Jr., former Dallas mayor and chairman of Mercantile Bank; James Aston, president of Republic National Bank of Dallas; T. L. Bell, Robert Storey's representative from Lakewood State Bank; and Charles McGaha, president of City National Bank, Wichita Falls, the board of Lone Star included Tyler businessman Watson Wise, who was a business partner of Jack Ruby's banker Michael Nash, and Joe Zeppa, cofounder and president of Delta Drilling. Both Wise and Zeppa joined Republic National Bank board member Algur Meadows in the founding of Premier Petro Chemical Corp. located in nearby Longview, Texas, a scheme of apparent great interest to SS Otto Skorzeny as evidenced in his private papers.

Longview was also home of the heavy moving equipment company LeTourneau, Inc., another domestic and foreign contractor that benefited greatly when nations, including the United States, were at war. Lafitte in fact was knowledgeable of LeTourneau when he recorded *"DeLong meet"* in his datebook, a likely reference to engineer L. B. DeLong's corporation whose numerous patents were invaluable to LeTourneau. We encounter the name LeTourneau as the book closes with the revelations of assassin Jean Rene Souetre.

Before leaving the Tyler-Longview area, it is of interest that when it came time to sell a sizable ranch in East Texas, the family of founding partner of Delta Drilling, Ukrainian-born Sam Dorfman, chose the international real estate firm Previews, Inc. to handle the transaction. Sam's close relative, Louis Dorfman, Jr.'s Dallas office was located in R. L. Thornton's Mercantile National Bank, introducing another web of interlocking interests, both business and political. Thornton served on the board of Jack Crichton's Amarillo-based Dorchester Gas, along with D. H. Byrd, owner of the building located at 411 Elm. Mercantile National was housed in a pair of adjacent buildings: one was home of the bank, and the other, Mercantile Continental, served as headquarters of H. L. Hunt Oil in 1963, a fact that has long fueled speculation that Ruby's visit to the twin buildings was somehow related to his gunning down the accused assassin Oswald, then in custody of Dallas law enforcement.

Hunt is also alleged to have dispatched his head of security, Paul Rothermel, to secure a copy of Abraham Zapruder's film, which was alleged to have captured the disturbing images and incriminating detail of the assassination. A reminder to the reader that the name Rothermel appears in the financial ledger of Lafitte. First-edition copies of the Z film are said to be still in existence.

Another thread in this web of chance circumstances was Jamieson Labs, which produced those copies of the Zapruder film once Eastman Kodak's Dallas facility had developed the original. Hugh Jamieson, owner of the lab, was the next-door neighbor of Robert G. Storey—named in the Lafitte records—located in the prosperous but understated Lakewood neighborhood of Dallas.

An equally intriguing milieu housed in Thornton's Mercantile building provides an expanded look behind the curtain. In a well-documented episode, Jack Ruby had recently met Connie Trammell, a young University of Texas student who was on the brink of graduation and looking for opportunities. She told Ruby that she had contact information for Lamar Hunt and that he might be interested in her as an employee. Ruby jumped at the opportunity, explaining that he needed to take care of some business in the Mercantile, and that it was a simple enough act of kindness to drop her off to meet Lamar, the son of H. L. Hunt.

Ruby's business was most likely related to the leases on his establishments, the Carousel Club in downtown Dallas and the Vegas Club in Oaklawn. According to Ed Jordan, an officer at Mercantile National who would later join Lamar Hunt on the board of the city's prized Cowboys football team, he also managed Corrigan Properties for his father-in-law, which owned the buildings that housed Ruby's clubs. Jordan later reported that on the day in question, Ruby insisted that he wanted to "see to the boss," which Jordan knew to be his father-in-law, Leo Corrigan, Jr.

Jordan's colleague at Mercantile National was Jacques Villere, a dapper Frenchman from New Orleans who joined the Dallas bank in 1946, advancing to vice president of Mercantile's international department by 1968. When Jacques moved from New Orleans to Dallas, he left behind his brother, Pierre Blaise Villere, to continue in a public relations enterprise the brothers had launched together. Their clients in the Crescent City included Clay Shaw's International Trade Mart, and Permindex, the international front closely aligned with the World Commerce Corporation, which, as covered earlier, benefited from the business acumen of Jack Crichton. Jacques Villere became honorary consul of Belgium and is seen photographed with Dresser's Neil Mallon on the occasion of bestowing him with the Cross of the Chevalier de l'Ordre de la Couronne. According to Major Ganis in *The Skorzeny Papers*, the Villere brothers appear in the private papers of Otto Skorzeny.

LTV

TEMCO, acronym for "Texas Engineering and Manufacturing Company"—a precursor to LTV—was an aviation concern that began simply enough as a WWII era airplane manufacturer helped along by investments from Dallas oilman D. H. Byrd. In 1947, TEMCO was making B-25 bombers for South American countries, including Brazil and Mexico, and by the end of 1948, TEMCO would roll out its first "reconditioned" airplane for the Chinese Nationalist government, backed by the Office of Strategic Services (OSS) during the closing days of WWII.

By 1956, TEMCO had interlocking boards with Dresser Industries of Dallas when Neil Mallon, president of Dresser, joined D. H. Byrd's TEMCO board. Eventually, Byrd sought out electronics expert James "Jimmy" Ling to form Ling-Temco, and by 1962, Jimmy Ling had purchased the Chance Vought Company, founded in 1917 to take advantage of the growing military and civilian aviation after WWI. As researcher Linda Minor opines, "then Ling-Temco-Vought (LTV) 'sorta got outta control,' as we say in Texas." The board of LTV in 1963 included Clyde Skeen from Braniff Airlines; L. T. Potter, whom we should know from Lone Star Steel; and the owner of the building that housed the Texas School Book Depository, David Harold Byrd. An additional and equally important bridge between LTV and Dresser Industries, tenants in the Republic National building in 1963, was the editor of the *Los Angeles Times*, archconservative Norman Chandler, on the board of Braniff Airlines with Clyde Skeen of LTV. Former Governor of Texas Alan Shivers, who was elected to the board of Dresser Industries that year, also sat on the board of Braniff Airlines with Chandler and Skeen. At the time, Mallon's Dresser board also included Lewis MacNaughton of DeGolyer-MacNaughton. Lewis, and his partner Everett DeGolyer, were board members of Republic National Bank along with Mallon and Algur Meadows. As noted previously, their firm had profited significantly from the 1952 Meadows-Skorzeny oil scheme in Spain.

What might seem to some a benign maze of interdependent board relationships is highlighted here to emphasize what was, in fact, nothing short of a *hive* of military contractors with ties to intelligence, operating under the rocket symbol atop the RNB building, which had been placed there by architects Harrison & Abramovitz, designers of Allen Dulles's dream project, CIA headquarters at Langley.

In the official report published in the 1963 edition of Moody's Industrial Manual, Ling-Temco-Vought stated that the company and subsidiaries were engaged in "research, development, and production of space vehicles; aircraft missiles; surface vehicles; special purpose airborne electronic systems; radio, radar, sonar, and television communications equipment; aircraft missile, and space guidance systems . . . and also provides service . . . to government . . . for modification and overhaul of aircraft, missiles and ships; test range operations; electronic systems maintenance."

LTV's Vought F-8 Crusader entered fleet service in 1957 in a time of rapidly advancing technology. The aircraft enjoyed a long career by fighter standards, and following the adoption of a unified designation system, the reconnaissance aircraft flew a number of dangerous missions during the Cuban Missile Crisis. These began on October 23, 1962, with the newly designated RF-8s flying from Key West to Cuba and then back to Jacksonville. The intelligence collected during these flights, along with that produced from Lockheed's U-2 spy plane (nicknamed "Dragon Lady"), confirmed the presence of Soviet missiles on the island. Flights continued for six weeks and recorded over 160,000 photographs. Dallas graphics firm, Jaggars Chiles Stovall (JCS), processed many of those reconnaissance photographs for the federal government. In a stroke of coincidence, four months after leaving the Soviet Union, on October 11, 1962, the former defector Lee Oswald was referred to JCS by the Texas Employment Commission. He began work the following day. Four days later, President Kennedy held the first meeting with the Executive Committee of the National Security Council (EXCOMM), responsible for studying those photographs and determining the administration's course of action during the Missile Crisis. In another coincidence, or example of "small town Dallas," a senior vice president of Jaggars Chiles Stovall lived in the same block as Roy S. Truly, who a year later would play a role, witting or not, in positioning Oswald, the patsy, in the Texas School Book Depository.

By 1965, with the official US entry into the Vietnam War, LTV's F-8 became the first US Navy aircraft to routinely battle North Vietnamese MiGs. According to an online source, "The F-8 entered combat in April 1965, the F-8s from USS *Hancock* (CV-19) quickly established the aircraft as an agile dogfighter, though despite its 'last gunfighter' moniker, most of its kills came through the use of air-to-air missiles. . . . The US Marine Corps also operated the Crusader, flying from airfields in South Vietnam. Though primarily a fighter, F-8s also saw duty in ground attack roles during the conflict."

These military contracts were overseen under the roof of the Republic National Bank building, the home of LTV's corporate headquarters. At the time, LTV employed 20,000 Americans, the majority located at the plant in Greenville, Texas, forty miles north of Dallas. Greenville was the hometown of Col.

Robert G. Storey, Jr., and the town sheriff for over a decade happened to be the father-in-law of Officer J. D. Tippitt. Following a series of divestitures and spin-offs over the next four decades, remnants of LTV survive in Greenville through L-3 Technologies, contractor for the Department of Defense, selected US government intelligence agencies, aerospace companies, and commercial tele-communications and wireless customers.

A highly suspicious stock trade of Friday, November 22, the day of Kenne-dy's assassination, first researched by Prof. Peter D. Scott and presented in the third chapter of his 1973 unpublished manuscript *The Dallas Conspiracy*, revealed that directors of LTV, James Ling and D. H. Byrd, purchased 132,600 shares of LTV stock for around $2 million through an investment vehicle the Alpha-Omega Corp. that the two used for such speculation. (See chapter notes for additional detail of the stock trade.)

Ling and Byrd were to be rewarded handsomely when the first major prime defense contract postassassination went to LTV for the construction of the Navy A-7 Light Attack plane. That contract was let in February 1964. The *New York Times* estimated that the contract "could run into more than a billion dollars." In fact, the $2 million investment by Byrd/Ling was worth $26 million by 1967. Of even greater importance, the award led to the final ascendance of LTV into the top tier of US defense-related companies. During the 1960s, as the Vietnam War continually sucked an ever-greater amount of funding from the US economy, LTV would consistently be among the top-ten aerospace companies in dollar volume of prime contracts.

By 1967, as the Vietnam War began to extract in earnest the very life-force of America's future, embodied in the men who were drafted, the US Justice Depart-ment revealed in its suit against Ling-Temco-Vought (L-T-V) that the two hundred largest industrial firms in the country held almost 59 percent of all manufacturing assets (compared to 48 percent in 1948). Obviously, that suit did nothing to impede war profiteering, nor did it halt the war.

DRESSER INDUSTRIES

The history of Dresser Industries, rising from a simple Oklahoma-based pipeline business that serviced the oil industry to a conglomerate composed of long-estab-lished military contractors on a global scale, is complex. In the late 1920s, having survived as a solid but unexceptional business—except for the coveted patents they held—the Dresser family sold out to a fledgling private banking firm, Brown Brothers Harriman. In what is alleged to have been a purely serendipitous moment, Ohio native and Yale graduate Henry Neil Mallon ambled through the doors of BBH, only to have Roland Harriman, a founding partner, spot him and cry out, "Dresser!" In spite of having no specific training in the specialized pipeline industry, Mallon, who was a friend of banker and politician Prescott Bush, who had joined the Harriman banking firm, assumed the presidency of Dresser. During WWII, Mallon also mysteriously established a line of communication with NY lawyer and fellow OSS agent, Allen Dulles, who would eventually control the Central Intelligence Agency, suggesting that Mallon long had the backing of close friends in positions of power.

The roots of Mallon's benefactors extended to 19th-century England. BBH was the result of a merger of Alex, Brown & Sons and the old-line Harriman family interests in the US. One of the first American financial organizations to help finance postwar rehabilitation in Europe, the firm boasted some of the country's most notable executives and directors in the field of finance including George Herbert Walker of St. Louis and lawyer/statesman Robert A. Lovett of Texas, whose father was a founding member of BBH. It was Lovett junior whom a young President Kennedy would consult on how best to fill his first cabinet. Another propitious nepotistic hire at BBH was George Walker's son-in-law, Prescott Bush, the congressman who would spawn generations of politicians including US presidents George H. W. Bush and George W. Bush.

During the 1930s, the son of railroad tycoon E. Roland Harriman, W. Averell Harriman, and his banking firm BBH had turned a blind eye to the rise of fascism in Germany and continued to do business with both Communist Soviet Union and Germany long after Hitler's invasion of Poland. Particularly odious is that he did so from a unique post as US Ambassador to the Soviet Union beginning in 1943. The firms that BBH, and by extension Harriman, profited from during the war included: Union Banking Corporation—the American arm of German steel magnate and "Hitler's Angel" Fritz Thyssen, who helped fund the rise of the Nazis; Seamless Steel Equipment Corporation; Holland-American Trading Corporation, and Silesian-American Corporation whose records reveal that Harriman's partner, Prescott Bush of BBH, was board member; and Dresser Industries.

Eventually, Neil Mallon had gobbled up on behalf of BBH and Dresser a significant number of military-related industries to create one of the country's most important cogs in the "defense of freedom." According to his obituary, Mallon ". . . built Dresser from an obscure pipeline equipment concern to a world leader in energy related products. . . . Dresser currently employs 40,000 people in North America and reported earnings of $172.3 million in 1982 on revenues of $4.16 billion."

Mallon proved to be an enigma in early Kennedy assassination research. Little is reported about his birth and childhood, perhaps because it lacked luster, perhaps because his early life has been deliberately obscured, or perhaps because he was a tool of US intelligence in league with the military-industrial complex who benefited from decades of cover. However, Mallon may also be one of the more significant characters lurking behind the curtains, pulling strings. It has been credibly established that he was not only responsible for Prescott Bush's son, George H. W. Bush's move to Texas, but that he was an early investor in Bush's oil venture Zapata Oil with operations in the Gulf of Mexico made available to US intelligence as needed.

Although it is not the mandate of this book to debate whether Mallon's protégé, George H. W. Bush, was privy to information, let alone an active participant in the events in Dealey Plaza, no assessment of the "lay of the land" of the assassination or analysis of Dresser and Neil Mallon—with his entrenched friendship with James Angleton's boss, Allen Dulles—would be complete without considering Bush. The fact is, nowhere in the records of Pierre Lafitte, who was clearly possessed of specific and detailed information related to the planning and execution of the coup in Dallas, is there a direct reference to Bush.

It could be argued that given the aforementioned history, Neil Mallon, and those with whom he had fraternized within the petroleum industry and the intelligence community long before his young protégé (thirty years his junior), is as much a candidate for being privy to plans for the hit in Dallas as GHW Bush. According to freelance investigative journalist Anthony Kimery's monograph, "George Bush and the CIA: In the Company of Friends," available online at *CovertAction Magazine*, December 2018, "Mallon was a friend to numerous ranking Cold War era intelligence officials, including Allen Dulles—an OSS veteran and ground floor official of the CIA . . . Mallon steered prospective candidates for spy work to Dulles and often provided cover employment to CIA operatives . . . " According to Kimery, among them was George de Mohrenschildt, another particularly important operative with whom Mallon was well acquainted, who had been part of the spy network Dulles ran inside Hitler's intelligence organization. Mallon personally introduced the Count to a young twenty-four-year-old from Connecticut, George Bush, at about the same time he handed Bush the highly sensitive responsibility of negotiating Eastern-bloc deals. It soon became apparent that Bush was able to wheel and deal with the Communists' petroleum experts without the slightest grimace by US authorities. In fact, writes Kimery, "when a Yugoslavian oil industry official came to the US in 1948 to talk to Dresser Industries, the State Department barely flinched and he went straight to neophyte salesman George Bush in Midland, Texas." Bush and de

Mohrenschildt, whose mutual focus on Yugoslavia is well documented, joined a cadre of young men who served as Mallon's (and by extension Dulles's) eyes and ears, arms and legs in the petroleum industry during the Cold War.

From his perch in Dresser headquarters in the Republic National Bank building, Mallon, who served on the board of Republic National and was the ideal conduit for his friend Allen Dulles and his fellow board member at Republic National, Algur H. Meadows, leads us to the second location under scrutiny.

5646 MILTON — THE MEADOWS BUILDING

-Mexico C.-
Algur-Mex City
Ilya-
—Lafitte datebook, September 27, 1963

Dallas—Meadows B. w/ T.
—Lafitte datebook, November 10, 1963

Located on Milton Street across from Southern Methodist University between Greenville Ave. and North Central Expressway, the nine-story professional office building was the headquarters of its namesake, Algur H. Meadows, and his General American Oil Company of Texas. But before considering the alarming significance of Lafitte's entries . . .

ALGUR HURTLE MEADOWS

Algur Meadows, known to close associates as "Al," was the first Dallas businessman to join financial forces with Nazi SS Otto Skorzeny, who had managed to avoid severe punishment just five years earlier when he was among those Nazis tried at the Dachau Trials following the war.

Ten years prior to JFK's assassination, Al Meadows launched what would become a close, mutually rewarding friendship with Skorzeny when his company, General American Oil of Texas, entered into a highly lucrative Spanish oil venture with the blessing of Skorzeny's friend Francisco Franco. At the time, Meadows was emerging as one of the nation's most "successful independent oilmen."

Born in Vidalia, Georgia, in 1899, Meadows graduated from Centenary College Law School in 1926 and cut his teeth in the oil industry as an accountant for the Rockefeller's Standard Oil Company of Louisiana. In 1928, along with friend Ralph G. Trippett, Meadows created General Finance Company, and within the decade, the two had teamed up with an expert on oil wells, J. W. Gilliland, to form General American Oil of Texas. The headquarters were soon relocated to Dallas, and Meadows, the major stockholder of the company by 1941, was elected president. Some ten years later, just six months before joining Skorzeny in expansion efforts in Spain, he was named chairman. Over the next decade, General American acquired nearly 3,800 oil wells in fifteen American states and Canada and continued to drill aggressively in Spain. In 1958, Skorzeny and Meadows launched what was reported to be another very profitable oil venture, this time in Morocco. (Of interest perhaps to those who study the trajectory and symbiotic nature of the independent oil industry, two decades later, the chairman of Houston Natural Gas, Robert Herring, who along with his wife, Joanna, had partied frequently with the Meadowses over the years, wrangled an appointment for Joanna as honorary consul to Morocco.)

By the time Skorzeny entered the picture, General American was already reaping over $100 million a year in profits, a huge amount of money in 1952. These revenues were being reinvested in a well-concealed network of small community banks in Texas, mortgage companies, insurance companies, and commercial and residential real estate development companies, many in and around the Dallas-Fort Worth area. This conglomerate mirrors almost to the letter the description of Howard Corp., the shadowy trust held at Republic National Bank revealed earlier.

At the time of Meadows's highly touted Spanish oil venture with Skorzeny, which required the approval of Franco, the former Nazi SS officer had already endeared himself to the Spanish general, who had long sought the attention of Italian fascist dictator Mussolini.

In a letter from Mussolini addressed to Franco, dated August 25, 1940, Mussolini wrote,

I should like to say to you, dear Franco, that I, with these my practical considerations, do not wish to hasten you in the least in the decision that you have to make, for I am sure that in your decisions you will proceed on the basis of the protection of the vital interests of your people and am just as certain that you will not let this opportunity go by of giving Spain her African Lebensraum. . . .There is no doubt that after France, Great Britain will be defeated; the British regime exists only on one single element: the lie . . . I certainly do not need to tell you that you, in your aspirations, can count on the full solidarity of Fascist Italy. I beg you, dear Franco, to accept my most cordial and comradely greetings.

—MUSSOLINI, The Chief of Government and Duce of Fascism.

Among Mussolini's goals had been to create an Italian empire in North Africa. In 1935, the dictator provoked war with Ethiopia, conquering the country in eight months. (This history is a marker for events that unfolded in 1963, when as we know from Pierre Lafitte, global arms deals were very much alive and well in disputes between Eritrea and Ethiopia.) Following Mussolini's victory in Ethiopia, he sent 70,000 Italian troops to Spain to support Franco and defeat the republican government in the Spanish Civil War. Among Il Duce's mottos, "'Believe! Obey! Fight!" The camaraderie that developed between Spain's own fascist dictator and Benito Mussolini reminds us of the obsequious tone of Dr. Armstrong's memories of the Baylor "Browning Pilgrims'" when encountering Il Duce in 1931, covered in more detail in the chapter notes. It was, after all, Mussolini who extolled the virtues of fascism—in fact, many argue he invented the ideology—as an alternative to socialist radicalism and parliamentary inaction. "Fascism," he promised, "would end political corruption and labor strife while maintaining capitalism and private property. It would make trains run on time." Nothing could appeal more to the interests of archconservative business, civic, and religious leaders across Texas.

AN OIL DEAL IN SPAIN

From a 1952 article in the *Dallas Morning News*, "the Spanish government granted rights to begin oil exploration to several Dallas oilmen." In addition to Al Meadows's General American Oil of Texas, the report notes that other relevant members of the syndicate included the Howard Corp. (whose assets and profits went undisclosed in official filings of Republic National Bank), and Delta Drilling of Tyler, TX, the company that was slated to do the actual drilling in Spain. Jack Crichton was Delta's man on the ground.

According to correspondence with Ilse, Otto Skorzeny's financial banking partner, Hjalmar Schacht—widely referred to by historians as "Hitler's Banker" as head of the Reich's central bank—invited Otto to attend the initial meeting with the Texas oilmen. Information disclosed in Skorzeny's papers indicates that German banker Schacht arranged the finances for the venture and was actually on hand to greet the Dallas contingent of oilmen.

To date, the identity of the individual or individuals who served as liaison between the Dallas contingency and Schacht has yet to be determined, but considering that Howard Corp. (an off-the-books entity of Republic National Bank) was a member of the Texas syndicate in Spain, we can assume someone within the Howard Corp./Republic Bank cabal was directly involved. This places Nazi banker Hjalmar Schacht in the middle of the Dallas oil and finance community as early as 1952.

November 7, 1963

11:30 meet Warsaw

with T. Hjalmar / Ilse - Get $

The Spanish venture was actually the brainchild of the engineering/geological firm of DeGolyer & MacNaughton, discussed in depth early in this chapter. Both men would serve on the board of Republic National over the years. Also strongly investing in the scheme was Clint Murchison's Delhi Oil Corporation, a firm referenced in the prelude to this chapter. Recall that it was Delhi-Taylor Oil that occupied the Fidelity Union Tower along with insurance magnate Carr P. Collins, and designed by architect T. E. Stanley, who figures prominently as we approach 3707 Rawlins and our exposé on Ilse Skorzeny's front, Previews, Inc.

MEADOWS AND ART COLLECTING

Frequently accompanied by his wife, Al Meadows would travel to Spain often to huddle with Skorzeny over business interests, but also so that he and his wife could spend time socially with Otto and Ilse and pursue a keen interest in collecting art. On one of the earliest trips, the Meadowses were introduced to the Prado Museum in Madrid, and thus was launched a near obsession with the works of the old Spanish masters, including Goya and El Greco. Rumors have persisted in the art world that Meadows purchased a number of highly coveted paintings that had been stolen by the Nazis from Jewish owners during World War II, with the assistance of Skorzeny, who allegedly had been given about a half dozen of the paintings at the end of the war (along with a substantial amount of gold). These rumors have yet to be substantiated. Around the same time, the New York Times reported that the French police and investigators for INTERPOL arrested the principal members of a large art forgery ring, which reportedly had swindled Meadows out of a very large amount of money. The Times reported that the scheme involved an accomplished copier of masters, Hungarian Elmyr de Hory, and a French dealer, Fernand Legros. Legros claimed he was innocent of any wrongdoing and that he too had been duped by members of the forgery group. It has also been alleged that in the early 1960s, Jack Ruby picked up a mysterious painting from a New Orleans art dealer that appears to have been one well suited for the Meadows collection, again unsubstantiated.

Encouraged by his second wife, Meadows then began adding paintings by French Impressionists and post-Impressionists to the collection, including some four hundred pieces of original art from the family of French artist Jean Despujols, who died in 1965. Exemplary of the symbiosis between for-profit business and its impact on Dallas culture, many of these works were eventually donated to the Dallas Museum of Art after Meadows's death. In fact, it is estimated that the Meadows family and the Meadows Foundation, by the end of 2016, had donated well over $1 billion to charitable groups in Texas. But no institution benefited more from Meadows's largesse over the years than Southern Methodist University, a college built on land provided by Mattie Caruth Byrd's family. The Meadowses' collection of Spanish art at SMU is considered the finest collection in the world, outside of Spain.

In June 1978, Meadows was killed in what was described as a strange automobile accident involving two college students who fled the scene.

WHAT ABOUT ILYA

> Algur-Mex City
> Ilya- . . .
> —Lafitte datebook, September 27, 1963

It is not possible to say with certainty why Algur Meadows and Ilya Mamantov might have been in Mexico City as Lee Harvey and Tom Davis arrived at their respective hotels. Some records suggest that Oswald, or a person posing as Oswald, had requested the services of a Russian translator in his communication with the Russian Embassy; and Algur's close relationship to Otto Skorzeny raises alarms that he traveled, with Mamantov, to Mexico City in relation to events that were about to unfold. However, without documentation, beyond this single entry, we pursue the other potential significance of this entry: the close bond that developed between Algur Meadows and Jack Crichton, a central character in our investigation. A *Dallas Morning News* April 4, 1958, headline read, "West Texas Field Acquired by Local Company." Al Meadows had recently acquired interests in an oil field for a cash outlay of $16 million; 25 percent of that transaction involved New York investment group Empire Trust Company, represented in Dallas by Jack Crichton. The drilling would take place in the Dora Roberts Field, named after the rancher who owned the land, which was one of the largest and most abundant oil fields at the time. It spanned several counties including Howard County, the namesake for the Howard Corp. held in trust and under a veil of secrecy by the Republic National Bank of Dallas, where Al Meadows served as a senior board member. In 1967 Meadows's General American Oil merged its affiliate *Premier Petrochemical* [sic] in a joint venture that later worked with Exxon Corporation—whose roots lay in Rockefeller's Standard Oil of New York, a.k.a. Socony Mobil—to explore and develop 10,235 acres in Alaska. Premier Petrochemical was a joint concern with Otto Skorzeny.

It was Meadows' partner in oil schemes spanning from West Texas to Spain, Jack Crichton, who orchestrated introductions between the Dallas Police Department and Ilya Mamantov.

Mamantov was born in Tartu, Russia, in 1914 and fled with his family to Latvia in 1920. Fleeting once again in 1944 to Germany, the Mamantov family was among Latvians selected to take refuge in one of 300 refugee camps maintained by the United Nation Relief and Rehabilitation Administration, founded in November 1943, in what is referred to as the Displaced Persons Camps. By 1949, new reasons arose for reorganization of the camps in relation to the increasing number of emigrating people and gradual transfer of refugees under German administration.

In 1949 implementation of the International Refugee Organization's plan whereby camps were established for special categories of refugees depending on the options to settle them in immigration countries was initiated. Most likely, the Mamantovs encountered the Tolstoy crowd during this ordeal. Eventually, Ilya and his wife Alexandria (Sondra to her friends) arrived in NY in 1949, and following a brief period in the city, he landed work in southern New Mexico and West Texas in his chosen field of geophysics specific to the oil industry. Sources indicate he worked for Atlantic Richfield, a company that grew from independent oilman Robert O. Anderson's Hondo Oil Co. based in Roswell, NM. It was Anderson who provided petroleum for the practical needs of the town of Los Alamos and the National Lab during the Manhattan Project.

In 1955, the year Ilya was hired by Jack Pew's Sun Oil Co., he coincidentally secured his prized US citizenship, and the Mamantov couple moved to Dallas, where Sun Oil headquarters had transferred from Pennsylvania. Ilya applied his education as a petroleum geologist and was later employed as a Russian language professor at Southern Methodist University, a position secured for him by Pew who, as Prof. Scott indicates, was "a spiritual heir of his relative, Sun Oil president J. Howard Pew, a leading supporter of Rightists causes in the United States who at one point was on the Executive Advisory Board of the John Birch Society."

Prof. Scott argues that it was Mamantov's mistranslation of Marina's Russian that was later used to bolster what Scott calls "Phase-One" . . . the story that Russia and/or Cuba were behind the assassination. On the heels of Ilya's misinterpretation, Chief of the Intelligence Section of the Dallas Police Department Don Stringfellow, according to Scott a member of Crichton's 488th, notified the 112th Army Intelligence Group, which in turn cabled the US Strike Common at Fort MacDill Friday for a possible retaliatory attack against Cuba. It was Stringfellow who accompanied Captain Pat Gannaway of the Special Services Bureau to 411 Elm allegedly to conduct a roll call that culminated in identifying Lee Harvey Oswald as having left the building when all others remained. The roll call appears to have been bogus, yet Gannaway without hesitation advised the media that Lee Harvey Oswald, presumably absent from an employee roll call, had been in the Soviet Union and brought his young Russian wife with him back to America. Statements made by Gannaway in the early hours following the assassination fed the fear that a Third World War was conceivable because a "commie" killed Kennedy. Some argue that Ilya Mamantov merely and unwittingly contributed to the chaos and confusion, but considering that he was known to Pierre Lafitte, we ask if Ilya was a critical pawn in the earliest hours to establish the myth of *the patsy*.

As noted, Ilya was a trained geophysicist. During his testimony before the Warren Commission, he explained that he had done a good deal of translating over the years for the American Geophysical Union. His employer at the time, Sun Oil, had been an early beneficiary of drilling in Spain and owned a significant percentage of certain of Al Meadows's General American Oil operations in the venture spawned in 1952 along with Otto Skorzeny with the financial expertise of Nazi banker Hjalmar Schacht.

A brief note on Jack and Roberta Pew of Sun Oil Company—best known for funding the Pew Charitable Trust: after arriving in Dallas, the couple assumed a low-key social life compared to their economic peers, preferring a behind-the-scenes role in pursuit of their very conservative politics. Nonetheless, they were privy to data disseminated judiciously by a number of national security agencies intent on keeping certain wealthy Americans apprised of national and global security issues. To reiterate, Pew employee Ilya Mamantov was seconded by Jack Crichton to serve as translator for the young Russian-born mother of two in the hours after her husband, Lee Harvey, had been arrested for the murder of Dallas Police Patrolman J. D. Tippit.

> Rene t merde merde fuck fuck
> -O Tippett [*sic*] (Why?)
> -ask JA who is Tippet? [*sic*]
> —Lafitte datebook, November 22, 1963

In 1964, Pew protégé Jack Crichton, as president of the Dallas Chapter of Alumni of Texas A&M University, was responsible for securing scholarships to his alma mater, Texas A&M, for the sons of Officer J.D. Tippit.

ANOTHER VENTURE

Underscoring the significance of the aforementioned history shared by Algur Meadows, Jack Crichton and Otto Skorzeny, and viewed in context of the early stage of planning for the assassination in Dallas, Meadows announced yet another major venture in early January 1963. The press release read, "The formation of Premier Petro Chemical Corp with Dallas headquarters to build a $4,000,000 plus plant on the Houston Ship Channel." The release highlighted that Meadows would serve as chairman, and twenty-five percent of the firm's stock would be held by General American. According to Ralph Ganis, the private papers of Otto Skorzeny confirm his keen interest in this latest scheme launched by his good friends in Texas.

Other Premiere Petro stockholders included Meadows' fellow board member at Republic National Bank, Lewis W. MacNaughton, senior chairman of DeGolyer & McNaughton and the driving force of the 1952 Meadows-Skorzeny venture in Spain; David Harold Byrd, president of Byrd Enterprises whose portfolio included the Texas School Book Depository building at 411 Elm, and whose wife's real estate offices were located in the Meadows Building; Joe Zeppa, board member of Lone Star Steel and president of Delta Drilling Company (cofounded with Ukrainian born Sam Dorfman) which had been a critical component of the Spanish venture; Frederick R. Mayer, president of Denver-based Exeter Drilling Co. and board member of H. L. Hunt Foundation; B. G. Byars, an independent oilman from Tyler who co-financed and managed Ike Eisenhower's Gettysburg Farm; Watson Wise, Tyler oilman involved in ventures with Michaux Nash—Jack Ruby's banker.

TENANTS OF THE MEADOWS BUILDING

To place the Meadows Building, headquarters of General American Oil, in a wider context, not only did independent oilman and far-right Republican Lester Logue occupy a suite on the 6th floor—a man whom Kennedy researchers will recognize as having (allegedly) attempted to hire trained sniper Loran Eugene Hall to shoot Kennedy—but far more intriguing are the offices on the floor above Logue.

As noted previously, Mattie Caruth Byrd, the wife of D. H. Byrd, who together owned the building that housed the Texas School Book Depository at 411 Elm, was a tenant of the Meadows Building. Mattie was the daughter of W. W. Caruth, the dynasty that owned hundreds of acres donated to the development and expansion of Southern Methodist University, soon to be surrounded by one of the most prized real estate developments in the city, Caruth's University Park. Mattie managed the Caruth real estate projects from her office on the 7th floor of the Meadows Building, including a major development in the early '60s that involved the next door neighbors of Jack Crichton. As such, Mattie was steeped in the importance of maintaining records of property purchases, including detailed descriptions of the buildings she and D. H. owned.

Mattie Byrd shared the 7th floor with the Dallas office of global chemical conglomerate DuPont Corp. and its subsidiaries, Remington Arms and Peters Cartridge, whose corporate headquarters were located in the Connecticut National Bank building, Bridgeport CT. (See Endnote.) We encountered Remington Arms in our pursuit of Carolyn Hawley Davis, wife of Thomas Eli Davis, Jr., whose name skirts on the edges of references to Loran Eugene Hall, Logue's choice to take a shot at the president. (Note: Hall was in California at the time Thomas Eli Davis, III, was running his alleged scam to recruit mercenaries for an invasion of Haiti. Hall corroborated the story and added that he believed that Davis's wife had worked briefly for H. L. Hunt in his Dallas accounting department. Whether or not this was Carolyn Hawley, Tom's second wife, has not been determined; if true, it establishes a direct tie between Hawley, Davis, and H. L. Hunt.)

3707 RAWLINS — OAK PLAZA

Leasing agents for professional office buildings, particularly smaller projects in unique locations around Dallas, were sensitive, perhaps to the extreme, when signing up tenants—particularly those that would be first to occupy new construction. Ideal tenants were those with sympathetic professions or similar socioeconomic profiles or both, and word of mouth among those interested in the property often influenced the leasing. The process could be thought of as the original model of a "gated community," and economic discrimination. We can be certain that whoever handled the leasing for architect T. E. Stanley's new professional building at 3707 Rawlins in the Oak Lawn neighborhood—a ten-minute drive from the center of downtown Dallas—applied high standards. Before considering the implications of each of the initial tenants—including Stanley's own architectural firm that moved immediately into the Rawlins Street project—we turn to the one tenant that we know to be of interest in the assassination of President Kennedy in Dallas on November 22, 1963.

PREVIEWS, INC.

Founded in the early 1930s, the name "Previews, Inc." was adopted in 1933 when Talbot Henderson, a real estate agent for the Douglas Elliman Co. in New York, got the idea of showing films of properties to potential buyers from the city before embarking on the time-consuming process of arranging on-site viewings. Henderson convinced two Rhodes scholars from his college years, two brothers with strong business and finance experience in NYC, a family relative—Oliver Keep, who was the publisher of *Cue,* Magazine along with Keep's brother, and a man who would not only replace Keep as publisher of *Cue* but twenty-five years later take over the helm as chairman of the board for the magazine.

Founded in 1932, *Cue* (the precursor to *New York* magazine) cemented itself almost overnight as the go-to theatre, arts, and entertainment magazine for New York society, from "Bohemia" to Park Ave. Reading between the lines, Talbot of Previews, Inc., along with Oliver Keep and Archbold van Beuren, both of whom were on the ground floor of *Cue* AND of Previews, saw the potential for a quid pro quo arrangement . . . use the slick magazine, *Cue* to promote exclusive real estate to the target markets of Previews, and in turn, *Cue* would benefit from the advertising revenue and the panache of being associated with those who could afford the unique national and international properties that Previews represented.

A portion of the van Beuren family fortune had been derived from land that was developed into Union Square in Manhattan in the 19th century. Archbold's biography, including his role in the founding of Previews and *Cue* before WWII, may not seem relevant to our story, that is, until one considers that at the close of WWII and before the OSS was circumvented by the Central Intelligence Agency, Archbold van Beuren had served as Chief of Security for William "Wild Bill" Donovan's Office of Strategic Services.

As has been reported extensively, it was only after months of wrestling for funding and jockeying for positioning that Donovan failed and his OSS was shut down, at least officially; however, as we learned in earlier chapters, this was not before he had set in place a vast intelligence apparatus deeply embedded in industry around the world via the World Commerce Corporation.

While there is no solid proof that van Beuren's Previews, Inc. was a component of that apparatus, we do know of several individuals involved with the international real estate organization that fit the profile of nonofficial intelligence agents trained to exploit their private, professional roles. Among them, US Army/Air Force Col. Herschel V. Williams.

AMERASIA

Before Donovan's concept of how an effective American intelligence should be run was thwarted, he and his security chief, Previews cofounder van Beure, featured in a sensational episode in the annals of domestic espionage. According to Harvey Klehr and Ronald Radosh, authors of *Amerasia Spy Case: the Precursor to McCarthyism,* "*Amerasia* was the first of the great spy cases of the postwar era. In June 1945, six people associated with the magazine *Amerasia* were arrested by the FBI and accused of espionage on behalf of the Chinese Communists . . . first public drama featuring charges that respectable American citizens had spied for the Communists, 'It provoked charges by conservatives of a cover-up of extensive Communist infiltration of the government and accusations by liberals of a witch-hunt designed to intimidate the press. And it played a significant role in the hearings held to examine Senator Joseph McCarthy's charge that the State Department had been infiltrated by a clique of 'card-carrying Communists.'"

Freda Utley, author of *The China Story*, first published in 1951, also found the *Amerasia* case of interest, reporting that "In February 1945, Archbold van Beuren, an OSS official, happening to glance through the pages of *Amerasia*, . . . was startled to find an article virtually identical with a secret OSS report sent to the State Department two months before. Being already worried about serious leaks of confidential information, Van Beuren went at once to Frank Brooks Bielaski, director of undercover investigations for OSS. Bielaski decided to raid the offices of *Amerasia*, an obscure but influential magazine devoted to propagating the Communist case. He did not apply for a search warrant for fear that the Amerasia staff might get wind of the investigation and destroy the evidence. When on the night of March 11, 1945, OSS representatives entered the *Amerasia* offices, after picking the lock, they found the place 'literally strewn with confidential Government documents. . . .'"

In June 1945, the Federal Bureau of Investigation arrested *Amerasia* editor Philip Jaffe and five others associated with the journal. The charge, espionage on behalf of Chinese Communists, did not hold. . . . Ultimately, there was no trial. Jaffe pleaded guilty and one other person pleaded no contest in 1945—on the relatively benign charge of unauthorized possession of government documents. Even the Justice Department admitted that all parties were merely guilty of "an excess of journalistic zeal."

390 Coup in Dallas

After the *Amerasia* case, Archbold van Beuren resumed his roles with *Cue* Magazine and Previews, Inc., and in 1958 he assumed control of the board of the magazine and remained as founding board member of Previews through 1959.

As previously identified, in March 1957, Ilse Skorzeny was in the US representing her business interests which were intertwined with those of her husband, Otto. According to government documents, not only was the CIA aware of Ilse's presence in the US—as evidenced by a secret interagency message from Jane Roman to her boss, James Angleton, that read, ". . . for the purpose of promoting some business deals."—but the US Department of State was as well, responding to the agency's notification that it was "fully aware of Mrs. Skorzeny's presence in the US."

Although the circumstances surrounding Ilse Skorzeny's association with Previews, Inc. have yet to be nailed down, we know from the Skorzeny Papers that they were initiated as early as 1957. It is not unreasonable to postulate that Archbold van Beuren would have been, at minimum, aware of Ilse's role with, or use of, Previews—the company he had been integrally involved with since its inception before the war. As mentioned, Ilse Skorzeny's close associate at Previews was company vice president, former Col. Williams, who was not only a relatively successful screenwriter, but an advertising executive for over a decade, which positioned him within the milieu of van Beuren, certainly through Previews, but also through *Cue* Magazine, or perhaps both from the early 1940s.

Advancing the in-depth review of the presence of Previews, Inc. in Dallas in November 1963, John Colquhoun Tysen, who joined Previews, Inc. in 1936, was no doubt hired directly by a young board that included Archbold van Beuren. By 1950, van Beuren and the Previews board elected Tysen as president of the real estate firm in 1950.

Born to American citizens living in Paris, where Tysen senior represented Morgan banking interests in France, John C. was educated at Downside School and later Trinity College Cambridge in the United Kingdom. Downside's alumni included noted spy novelist Nigel West (the pen name for British MP Rupert Allason) and Tom Bethell, whom many Kennedy assassination researchers recognize as having infiltrated the Garrison investigation. (Bethell befriended "the godmother" of Kennedy research, Mary Ferrell, with whom he shared a keen interest in New Orleans jazz.)

As president of Previews, Tysen successfully positioned the domestic and foreign inventory as "glamorous, exotic, without precedent," from Tangier to the Tyrol Mountains. By the early '60s, Tysen, who was elected chairman a year later, had been in and out of Dallas pursuing potential clientele among the city's social and business elite including bankers, wealthy oilmen and ranchers, their wives, and their lovers for years. During the same period, Tysen was also in and out of the Bahamas, having recently joined the board of Sir Stafford Sands's Bahama Development Co. along with Dallas developer Leo F. Corrigan, Jr.

Tysen's employee, Mrs. Otto (Ilse) Skorzenys is known to have used the Bahamas as one of several key international locations from which to conduct the business projects of "the Skorzenys."

Hitler's banker, Hjalmar Schacht—advisor to the Skorzenys—is known to have financed Sir Stafford Sands's various projects stemming from his connections in the Bahamas. It is logical to conclude that these introductions alone might prompt John Tysen to lease space for the Previews Dallas office in Oak Plaza professional building occupied by Corrigan's architect of choice, T. E. Stanley, who had recently designed the Emerald Beach Hotel in the Bahamas for Leo and his partner in the project, Algur Meadows, "a dear friend of Otto and Ilse Skorzeny since 1952."

11:30 meet Warsaw (+hotel)with T.

Hjalmar / Ilse - Get $

—Lafitte datebook, November 7, 1963

In 1963, the Stoneleigh Hotel was within walking distance of one of Dallas's most respected old-world European style restaurants, the Old Warsaw.

The reader is reminded that not only did Corrigan Properties own the buildings that housed Jack Ruby's clubs, it owned the Stoneleigh, described by Lafitte's daughter as the family's preferred accommodation in Dallas. It was also the home of Paul Raigorodsky, who opted to live there full-time.

Corrigan's father had also bought The Adolphus and maintained family ownership of the famed hotel under the banner of the Dallas Hotel Co. His board (and no doubt investors) included Robert G. Storey, Jr. and R. L. Thornton, Jr., of Lakewood State Bank and Mercantile National Bank, respectively.

In early 1963, John Tysen and the board of Previews apparently determined that The Adolphus Hotel in Dallas was no longer suitable to long-term goals of the company in the Dallas region, and the lease on Rawlins was negotiated with Corrigan's architect, Ted Stanley. During the spring, in spite of an ideal marketing opportunity to exploit the new building to potential tenants that would be attracted to the pastiche of a NY-based real estate firm, only a few small notices and obscure advertisements in the *Dallas Morning News* and the *Fort Worth Star Telegram* announced that Previews's office in Dallas would open on March 17. Up until then, the firm had been represented in central and north Texas for a number of years by realtor and former US Air Force officer John M. Park out of a small office in a strip mall area across from the entrance to Texas Christian University in Fort Worth, TX. It is yet to be determined if Park was known to USAF Col. Herschel Williams of Previews.

OTHER TENANTS AT 3707 RAWLINS

In the midst of critical planning taking place in Madrid for the assassination of President Kennedy, an intriguing alliance between Swiss-born arms dealer Viktor Oswald and American film director Sam Bronston was coming apart at the seams. Bronston had been in Spain since 1958 to take advantage of Franco's need for a stable economy. The proposed movie project was titled *John Paul Jones*. According to *The United States and Public Diplomacy: New Directions in Cultural and International History*, edited by Kenneth A. Osgood and published by BRILL, 2010, in a chapter titled: "Hollywood, Dictatorship and Propaganda," "Bronston also approached other distinguished and well-heeled private citizens of a patriotic bent . . . [his] efforts to secure adequate funding for the production waxed and waned during 1956 and 1957. During this time the producer made three contacts with profound ramifications for the rest of his career. First, a member of a second wave of blue-blood investors included Pierre S. du Pont III, an outspoken conservative patriot [who served on a very small board of an exclusive bank founded by the Schlumberger family, Pallas Bank, along with one of the Rockefeller brothers.] The second crucial contact was with Victor Oswald . . . who was a representative of the Chase Manhattan Bank in Spain [owned by the Rockefeller including Nelson and Laurence who both invested in the John Paul Jones project]."

We highlight again that Victor Oswald was a former American OSS/British Special Operations Executive operative, who, as early as 1952, entered into business deals with Otto Skorzeny and Hjalmar Schacht.

BARRON ULMER KIDD OIL COMPANIES

In what could be argued as a simple twist of fate, in May 1963, Bronston investor, in league with Victor Oswald, Pierre du Pont's daughter, Jane deDoliete "Leit" du Pont married Dallas independent oilman Barron Ulmer Kidd, Jr. Following three days of wedding festivities that extended from du Pont territory to Pierre III's residence in New York City, the couple was married in Christiana Hundred,

New Castle County, Delaware. Billed in Dallas society pages as one of the top social events of the season, a large contingent from Dallas joined the East Coast establishment to support one of their own, oilman Barron Kidd's son, as he married into the vast DuPont dynasty.

It was a busy spring for the Kidd family of Dallas. Barron Kidd Oil companies had just two months earlier moved into 3707 Rawlins, the same month that Previews, Inc. moved into the same location.

We know that over the previous decade Ilse had been in and out of Madrid and is known to have been in close contact with Victor Oswald, who, along with Barron Kidd's father-in-law, Pierre du Pont, was pivotal in the financing of Sam Bronston's film project in Spain.

It is from the Lafitte book that we also know Ilse was in Dallas in 1963, specifically on November 7, when she dined with Hjalmar Schacht at the Old Warsaw. With Previews's offices opening in March, an easy walk from the Old Warsaw and The Stoneleigh Hotel, there is no reason to argue this was Ilse's first visit to Dallas.

WESLIE G. ROGERS OIL COMPANIES

Oklahoma oilman Wesley G. Rogers was the other primary tenant at 3707 Rawlins when the professional office building opened its doors. Rogers listed six oil and gas-related businesses on the building marquis compared with Barron Kidd's seven. Although Rogers maintained a large spread near Holdenville, OK, the family spent most of its time in an exclusive residential enclave in North Dallas. Their close neighbors included: Buck Wynne Jr., of the Wynne family dynasty, whose real estate investments involved Clint Murchison, Trammel Crow, and Leo Corrigan, among others; Jack Ruby's banker, Michaux Nash, who did business with one of the principals in the Algur Meadows 1963 petrochemical scheme in Longview, TX, that caught Otto Skorzeny's keen interest; and Jake Hamon, the notorious independent oilman involved with the Skorzeny-Meadows scheme since 1952, president of the American Petroleum Institute and a close friend of—among others in the industry both national and international—Paul Raigorodsky and Clint Murchison.

In the spring of 1963, Wesley Rogers leased office space for six separate oil and gas entities in the Oak Plaza professional building at 3707 Rawlins. As noted, Rogers joined an exclusive roster of new tenants that included Barron Kidd Oil (under seven separate business names); Delhi Properties managed by J. Sowell, a former tenant of the Adolphus Tower, who stood as groomsman for Barron

Kidd, Jr., in the du Pont/Kidd wedding in Delaware; All World Travel agency, Tom Stanley's architectural firm; and John Tysen's Previews, Inc. Within the decade, Rogers would become the father-in-law of Donald A. Byrd, former Dallas Police officer who served in the narcotics division under Pat Gannaway at the time of the assassination of Kennedy. Byrd would eventually advance to the position of Dallas police chief, a powerful post he held until crashing his car into a tree in the Highland Park neighborhood on his way home from a party hosted by one of H. L. Hunt's sons. During his tenure, Byrd was in charge of approving release of department documents pertaining to events in Dealey Plaza on November 22, 1963.

* * *

Thus far, this chapter has revealed the conditions that were conducive to a successful attempt on the life of the elected president, John F. Kennedy. We conclude this analysis of the "lay of the land," so appropriately labeled by Rene Lafitte, with the University of Dallas and the Texas School Book Depository.

UNIVERSITY OF DALLAS AND THE HUNGARIAN CISTERCIANS

To place the University of Dallas in context, some might argue that its history parallels that of the all-black Bishop College that Dallas business luminaries (including insurance magnate Carr P. Collins, Republic National Bank chairman Karl Hoblitzelle, and international developer Leo F. Corrigan, Jr.) chose to relocate from East Texas to South Dallas with the intent of providing the city's "negro" community their very own exclusive (read segregated) environment of higher education.

Similarly, the newly established University of Dallas—located in Irving, between Dallas and Fort Worth—provided an exclusive environment appealing primarily to orthodox Roman Catholics. Most Kennedy researchers will recognize Irving as the home of Ruth and Michael Paine, the couple that minded the Oswald family, where they played out their roles in one of the most dramatic events of the century, and a line of inquiry as we close this chapter at the scene of the crime in Dealey Plaza.

For now, Thomas Gorman, only the fourth bishop to serve the Diocese of Dallas, immediately upon taking office in 1954, followed through with a decade-old desire of the Church by inviting a group of displaced Hungarian Cistercian monks from the Monastery of Zirc, Hungary, to come assist in the founding of the University of Dallas.

According to numerous histories, the Cistercian Order was founded in France in the 11th century as a reform of older forms of Benedictine life. Spreading rapidly across Europe, their monasteries became centers of learning. The French Revolution brought dissolution of many monasteries, but some were reestablished, and the crusade to spread the Roman Catholic faith around the globe continued.

Following World War II, the Communist authorities disbanded the Cistercian Abbey of Zirc, Hungary, among the first monasteries in the country, founded in 1182. At least thirty monks successfully fled Zirc and found refuge in other monasteries in Western Europe and the US, specifically Our Lady of Spring Bank Abbey, then located in Oconomowoc, Wisconsin.

When Thomas K. Gorman, Bishop of the Dallas Diocese, was in the process of establishing his beloved university, he solicited support from several local religious orders and then reached out to the refugee monks at Spring Bank; his good fortune was that the Wisconsin monastery was undergoing a schism of sorts when the prior laid down new expectations for his highly educated flock, most of whom had their doctorates in their chosen fields. The prior ordered that they pray and work the fields, literally, rather than bother with educating young adults. Without hesitation, the errant monks of Spring Bank took up Bishop Gorman's invitation and soon arrived in Dallas, receiving formal establishment by the Holy See of their monastery on February 19, 1955. Its canonical status was that of a dependency of Zirc Abbey in Hungary, reflecting the close ties and influence of a country soon to undergo a revolution that rocked the Western world.

The first Catholic school of higher learning in the area, the University of Dallas could be considered as representative of the more conservative movement within the Roman Catholic Church. The Eastern European-style orthodoxy, and clear anticommunist sentiments, may have contributed to the recruitment of Dr. Robert J. Morris as its president.

During the war, the New Jersey native commanded a counterintelligence and psychological warfare unit responsible for writing propaganda leaflets to be dropped over cities in Japan. Having secured a law degree from Fordham University, Morris was qualified and perfectly suited to twice serve as counsel on the Senate Judiciary Subcommittee on Internal Security, from 1951 to 1953 and again from 1956 to 1958. In 1951, the *New York Times* described the subcommittee as having a mandate that is practically "limitless in the whole field of security" and a role that "far overreaches the House Committee on Un-American Activities, as it far outreaches Senator Joseph R. McCarthy, Republican of Wisconsin" (future home of the Hungarian Cistercians). According to Whittaker Chambers,

"Bob Morris really accomplished much of what the Senator is credited with." Bishop Gorman brought Robert Morris on board as president of the Univ. of Dallas in 1960.

Dedicated assassination researcher Mae Brussell, whom some consider one of the most unsung heroes of the effort, began to pursue Robert Morris, along with Generals Willoughby and Walker, as early as 1984, when she recognized their deep ties to the Nazi movement that survived the war. She identified Robert Morris as having trained in US counterintelligence and psychological warfare as well as his early association with the publisher of the *National Review,* William F. Buckley, Jr., whose disdain for John Kennedy permeated his editorial magazine. It was Buckley who formed the Young Americans for Freedom that took hold on college campuses across the country with a pledge to root out the curse of communism.

After arriving in Dallas, Morris began cultivating associations with right-wing extremists including the generals and their acolytes, the Schmidt brothers, and the man with the financial means, H. L. Hunt. As a skilled counterintelligence propagandist, Morris was now in the perfect position to assist with furthering the legend of Lee Harvey Oswald. It behooves us to offer a verbatim account of Mae Brussell's assessment of the Walker "incident." One can clearly recognize the hand of a skilled propagandist like Morris:

November 23, 1963, one day after Kennedy's death, Gen. Edwin Walker called Munich, Germany, from Shreveport, La. Walker's important story, via transatlantic telephone, was to the Nazi newspaper *Deutsche National Zeitung un Soldaten-Zeitung.* Walker couldn't wait to tell them in Munich that Lee Harvey Oswald, the lone suspect in the Dallas murders, was the same person who shot through his window in April 1963 . . . There was never one shred of evidence, or a reliable witness, that could make this connection. Dallas police and FBI were taken by surprise . . . In order to cover this over-exuberance of trying to link a Marxist assassin to this alter-cation, it became necessary to have Ruth Paine deliver that ridiculous letter to Marina Oswald on December 3, 1964. The delayed letter was to have been written the night Lee was out shooting in Walker's home.

But General Walker, now home from military service in Munich, knew the importance of such propaganda. He was calling the same people who, under Hitler, published and controlled the newspapers. There were two motives for this call. First, it gave international attention to the fact that Oswald, the Marxist gunman, was shooting at Walker as well as the

President. General Walker knew too many people in the Defense Department and in the Dallas-Fort Worth area that could be part of this assassination. He made himself appear as a victim instead of a suspect.

The other reason, along with the expertise of Robert Morris's counter-intelligence and psychological warfare training, was to create a profile for Lee Harvey Oswald.

No possible motive could explain why Oswald would really want to kill President Kennedy. By having Oswald appear to shoot the right-wing General Walker with his John Birch connections, his militant anti-communist stance, then shoot John Kennedy, the same Commie-sympathizer Walker was accusing of treason, it would appear that Oswald was just nuts. He didn't know right from left . . . The Munich newspaper Walker called was linked to the World Movement for a Second Anti-Komintern, part of the Gehlen and US right. Some of Hitler's ex-Nazis and SS-men were on the Staff. The editor, Gerhard Frey, was a close friend with various Nazi members of the Witiko League. The Witiko League and the Sudetendeutch Landsmannscraft were organizations for displaced refugees. By the summer of 1948 they formed large organizations and by 1955 Dr. Walter Becher was elected to the executive board of the Witiko League. Becher was one of the kingpins of Nazi front organizations . . . Becher had been praised frequently by the "American Opinion" [the extreme right publication of the John Birch Society].

General Willoughby, identified extensively in previous chapters, was a virtual roving board member for ultraright-wing, rabid anticommunist organizations around the country, including Bill Buckley's Young Americans for Freedom (YAF)—a group that would soon be led in Dallas by former US Army enlistee Larrie Schmidt, who had been stationed in Munich, Germany, serving under General Edwin A. Walker. While in Munich, Schmidt organized CUSA (Conservative - USA) along with a handful of fellow soldiers intent on returning to the US to take charge of the conservative movement. His first act in Dallas, 1962, was to join the local chapter of the John Birch Society (JBS), whose first president was Robert J. Morris.

Not long after arriving in Dallas, where Gen. Walker had established headquarters, Schmidt found himself in the home of Robert Morris. Some have reported that it was Morris who served as the first president of the John Birch Society (JBS) in Dallas, while others believe it to have been Mayor Earl Cabell. Regardless, the JBS found very fertile ground in a city driven by far-right politics conjoined with the quest for global dominance of petroleum supply. JBS included both men on its roster of proud members.

Dr. Morris was so impressed with Schmidt's performance that evening that he appointed him to the position of director of YAF Southwest, which was tied directly to Morris's friend and fellow right-wing conservative, Gen. Willoughby. In the lead-up to President Kennedy's arrival in Dallas, Larrie Schmidt was instrumental in the preparation and publication of the infamous "Welcome Mr. President" advertisement critical of Kennedy that appeared in the *Dallas Morning News* that fateful Friday morning.

As has been widely reported, the ad was paid for by a number of Dallas anticommunists including oilman Joe Grinnan—who it should be noted shared an office address at the Adolphus Tower with Dr. Robert Morris—and, as noted earlier, Nelson Bunker Hunt. Bunker's father, H. L., had long been a primary financial backer of both Willoughby and Walker, to the extent that Willoughby ended up on Hunt's official company payroll not long after the assassination. Grinnan was identified by Paul Raigorodsky as a "good friend" in the same breath as Raigorodsky also identified oilman Barron Kidd (business neighbor of Previews, Inc. in Oak Lawn) as a close friend.

Of note, the address of Mrs. Frank Brandstetter in 1963 was listed as a condominium in the 3700 block of Turtle Creek, where we can assume Brandy stayed the week of November 18, 1963. That summer, the Brandstetter's building had a new tenant, an independent oilman who seems to have floated below the radar until now. Kidd's house in Oak Lawn had recently burned beyond salvage, necessitating the move to the Turtle Creek condo. Kidd, whose politics clearly aligned with the ultraconservative wing of the Republican Party, was a member of the Texas Crusade for Freedom and close friend to a number of his peers in the oil industry including Clint Murchison, Sr., Jake Hamon, and Paul Raigorodsky, about whom much has been considered in this chapter.

Larrie Schmidt was traveling in a car with Joe Grinnan, a coordinator for the Dallas chapter of the JBS, when they first heard the news of the assassination. Schmidt's brother Bob had followed him to Dallas, where he was soon added to the payroll of General Walker. (Note: It has never been established that Socony-Mobile oil geologist Volkmar Schmidt was related to the Schmidt brothers, but according to Warren Commission testimony, he too "came from Germany." According to assassination researcher Mae Brussell, Volkmar Schmidt was from Munich.) Investigative journalist Dick Russell, in his groundbreaking book, *The Man Who Knew Too Much*, asserts that according to a former employee of H. L. Hunt, the Schmidt brothers were with Lee Harvey Oswald when Walker was fired on while sitting in the library of his home on Turtle Creek Blvd. in Dallas. Another milestone in the legend of Oswald as patsy was achieved that evening.

After leaving the University of Dallas in 1962, having been pressured to resign due to his controversial views and activities that drew attention to the monks, Morris organized the Defenders of American Liberties, closely modeled after the American Civil Liberties Union, but with a very different political agenda. The group's first cause was to defend former Major General Edwin A. Walker, who was accused of inciting unrest on the campus of the University of Mississippi when James Meredith tried to enroll as the school's first black student. Over the years, Texans would come to view Morris as either passionate, crazy, conniving— or all three. Although he is alleged to have cut ties in Dallas, he joined the race for Republican senator of Texas in 1964 and again in 1970.

It is reasonable to suspect that Robert Morris encountered Wild Bill Donovan and Donovan's chief of security, Archbold van Beuren, while serving in psychological warfare during WWII. Respected historians argue that the Amerasia spy case as outlined previously was the genesis of the McCarthy Hearings. (See Endnote.)

Serving as consultant to the Senate Subcommittee while Morris was legal counsel was Dr. Anthony Kubek, who would be named as chairman of the Department of History and Political Science at the University of Dallas. Kubek, a devout Roman Catholic and staunch anticommunist, was a nationally prominent authority on American foreign policy, especially US policy in Asia. His published writings included *The Amerasian Papers*, a two-volume study issued by the US Senate Committee on the Judiciary. No doubt he too was familiar with the name Archbold van Beuren. Dr. Kubek was among those present at the first Larrie Schmidt presentation at the home of Dr. Morris. It was around this time that he penned a cordial letter to General C. A. Willoughby, advising that during a recent visit to the Hoover Institute, he had been asked to evaluate a copy of "MacArthur's Pacific Campaigns," and sending along best regards to the general from Dr. Robert Morris. By pure coincidence, Kubek lived less than a half mile from Ruth and Michael Paine, placing him in close proximity to Lee Harvey Oswald for a number of months. "Tony" Kubek, through his connections to the China Lobby, also knew Isaac Don Levine, who wrote for one of the lobby's extreme-right publications. Levine, designated in the datebook as "handler" for Marina Oswald, was assigned his role as early as November 28, three days after Jack Ruby shot her husband.

* * *

Around the time Bishop Gorman was cutting the ribbon at the University of Dallas in Irving while nine Cistercian monks exiled from their homeland of Hungary looked on, 5500 miles away outside Rome, Italy, the exiled Prime Minister of Hungary, Ferenc Nagy, was overseeing a very ambitious project outside the Italian capital. Nagy's role in the questionable real estate conglomerate, Permindex, was introduced in Chapter 2, but it is timely to revisit that history. According to a March 12, 1959, A.A.P.-Reuters headline. "A Market Place for All the Word," "A group of ambitious financiers are busy converting a 'phantom' city, built by Benito Mussolini near Rome, into a site for Europe's first international shopping centre for businessmen. The project, designed to compete with the international trade mart at New Orleans and other similar schemes in the United States, will give Europe a single show window where private businessmen can display, or order, goods manufactured in all parts of the world. The organizers, Permanent Industrial Exhibitions, 'Permindex,' have taken four large, abandoned palaces . . . that were part of a dream world of the Italian Fascist dictator who planned them as the focus point of a grandiose world far and monument to the external glory of Fascism. Dr. Ferenc Nagy, a former prime minister of Hungary and president of Permindex, described the working plan. . . ."

As mentioned, Permindex's president Ferenc Nagy had served as Prime Minister of Hungary from February 1946 to May 1947, having been elected in Hungary's first democratic election. He had fought on the side of Germany in World War II and suffered considerably, but in 1944 he was jailed by the Germans. At the end of the war, Mr. Nagy arrived in the United States penniless yet managed to buy a farm at Herndon, Va., where he developed a dairy herd and eventually relocated to Dallas where he was residing on November 22, 1963. Always active in the Presbyterian Church, Nagy assumed a prominent role working with exile groups, as did most émigrés in Dallas, to end not only Communist domination of Eastern Europe, but the spread of the scourge to America.

Through his associations with Jean de Menil of Schlumberger, there is the possibility that rumors alleging Nagy was involved in gunrunning on behalf of financial benefactors that included de Menil and his close friend Clint Murchison were based in fact.

Clearly, Ferenc Nagy found a welcome mat in the rabidly "anti-Red" climate of Dallas, Texas. But perhaps equally as enticing to Nagy was the particular brand of procapitalist culture and the city's self-defined mandate to spread its own version of democracy around the globe. It could be argued that Robert Storey's brainchild—the Dallas Trade Mart, Clay Shaw's International Trade Mart in New Orleans, Permindex, and CMC all seemed inspired by Benito

Mussolini's *dream world, the focus point of a grandiose world and monument to the external glory of Fascism.*

* * *

As we approach 411 Elm, the final destination of the plot to murder the sitting president of the United States, we employ an obscure character—one with no role in the assassination, but with a personal history and circumstantial encounters while a professor at the University of Dallas in Irving, Texas—to serve as backdrop.

According to his obituary, Fr. Ralph March was accepted as an oblate of the Cistercian Monastery of Zirc, Hungary, and could thus pursue his high school studies at the Cistercian school of Saint Imre in Budapest. Upon his graduation in 1940, he entered the novitiate of the Cistercian Order in Zirc, where he also studied philosophy and theology in preparation for ordination to the priesthood.

On the day World War II ended in Europe, May 8, 1945, he was ordained a priest in the Abbey of Zirc by Jozsef Mindszenty, later cardinal-archbishop of Esztergom. He returned to Budapest to continue his studies at the University of Budapest and at the Franz Liszt Music Conservatory there. . . In the same year, he emigrated to the United States because the Communist suppression of the Abbey of Zirc in 1950 had made it impossible for him to return to his homeland. He joined fellow Cistercians exiled from Hungary in the Cistercian monastery of Spring Bank in Wisconsin and taught at Marquette University until the founding of the University of Dallas, where he served on the first faculty in 1956, and, in the same year, was a founding member of the Cistercian Monastery Our Lady of Dallas. From 1960 to 1962, Fr. March, who had left Hungary before the Soviet Communists invaded in 1956, would have reason to engage directly with Robert Morris, the second president of the University of Dallas. As we have learned, Morris had been a lead investigator for bitterly hostile anticommunist Senator Joseph McCarthy and twice served as counsel on the Senate Judiciary Subcommittee on Internal Security, from 1951 to 1953 and again from 1956 to 1958. During his tenure at the University of Dallas, Morris was closely involved with General Edwin Walker and those within Walker's circle of far-right acolytes.

In addition to his professorship at the University of Dallas, and working at St. Bernard's Parish, Fr. March directed four choirs: The Dallas Catholic Choir, the Saint Bernard Chorus, the University Chorus, and the Madrigal Singers.

411 ELM — TEXAS SCHOOL BOOK DEPOSITORY BUILDING

It is well established that Harold D. and Mattie Caruth Byrd purchased the six-floor red brick building located in Dealey Plaza and in the early 1960s leased the entire property to an established business known as the Texas School Book Depository (TSBD), a primary distributor of schoolbooks for the state of Texas that drove curriculum around the country. Tenants at 411 Elm spanned the world of textbook publishing whose boards (with few exceptions) included at least one retired high-ranking military officer.

It has also been well established that D. H. Byrd was not in Dallas at the time President Kennedy was assassinated. The avid big-game hunter was on safari thousands of miles away in Tanzania, Africa. What is not widely known is that Byrd was on safari with a very good friend of Otto Skorzeny, Werner von Alvensleben, who was the director/guide for Safarilandia, a big-game hunting company in Portuguese East Africa. These connections are described in the private papers of Skorzeny, a significant portion of which was purchased by Major Ralph Ganis, whose book, *The Skorzeny Papers*, based on information found in the collection, is frequently cited in this work. Ganis also informs us that another patron of Safarilandia was Hassan Sayed Kamil, the Swiss-Egyptian engineer well connected to Oerlikon, manufacturer of automatic cannon, heavy machine guns, and ammunition. Also involved with Oerlikon was Wilhelm Mallet, identified in US military records from Operation Safehaven as a German living in Spain, September 1945. Safehaven was touted as the American government's project to ensure that Germany wouldn't start another war by rooting out and neutralizing its industrial and commercial power wherever it might be found. Wilhelm Mallet was an associate of Otto Skorzeny, as well as global weapons dealer Viktor Oswald, Otto's partner in a number of ventures.

Without doubt, as property owners of 411 Elm St, the Byrds held schematics not only of the building itself, but a detailed plan of Dealey Plaza and neighboring properties essential to any skilled tacticians and assassins involved in an assassination plot. Do references to the Meadows Bldg. in Pierre's records provide clues that before leaving for his final destination of Spain, Thomas Eli Davis was instructed to visit Mattie Byrd in her offices at the Meadows Building?

Very shortly after Kennedy's assassination, indeed only a matter of a few days, the Baron and Baroness von Alvensleben arrived in Dallas, Texas, as guests of Harold and Mattie Byrd. With that incredibly unique milieu in mind, contributing significantly to the known history of Byrd's role as a cofounder of Civil Air Patrol, which attracted a youthful Lee Harvey Oswald, we close this chapter with a focus on the dynamics that caused Lee Harvey Oswald to be at the scene of the crime, in the Texas School Book Depository at 411 Elm at 12:32 pm, Friday, November 22, 1963.

When Everett Glover, a chemist working with the geology group in the exploration section of Socony Mobil Oil Co., was called before the Warren Commission in March 1964, he was questioned by senior counsel Albert Jenner, described by acclaimed author Russ Baker as "a corporate lawyer whose principal work was defending large companies against government trust-busting. . . . Jenner's most important client was Chicago financier Henry Crown, who was the principal shareholder in General Dynamics, then the nation's largest defense contractor and a major employer in the Fort Worth area." Of interest, Gali Sherbatoff's husband, Max Clark, an attorney who provided industrial security, was also employed by General Dynamics.

Glover, who was separated from his wife in 1963, explained his living situation during the period that most interested Jenner: ". . . these are the people I just referred to. One man, Richard L. Pierce, who works with me in the same section of my laboratory, joined me December 1, of 1962, and the second man, Volkmar Schmidt, who came from Germany and worked with the company as a geologist, came to live with me approximately January 1. It was an arrangement we tried out to see if there would be mutual satisfaction."

Volkmar-- (Glover) +

(K.C. Stanley)

—Lafitte datebook, October 16, 1963

Volkmar is named again, alone, on October 24. The reader is reminded of the critical gathering in DC on or around October 17th, and the flurry of activity over the following five weeks in preparation for operation Lancelot.

Whatever reason Lafitte might have had for noting the name Glover alongside Volkmar in mid-October, we know from Glover's testimony that a critical event much earlier in the year set the stage for the crucial role Oswald would fill in the assassination plot.

Mr. GLOVER. One of my avocations is ice skating. I do not know the exact time, but sometime in the period, I would say 1956 to 1959, when I have been ice skating, I met Mrs. de Mohrenschildt on the ice rink skating by herself. She skated a considerable time, maybe, probably, part of a year, and then later she brought Mr. de Mohrenschildt there, and that is the first acquaintance I had with them. This was a casual acquaintance. . . .

Mr. JENNER. Maybe we can get at it this way. What is your present recollection as to the intervening span in which you had either little or no contact with the de Mohrenschildts? How long did that run?

Mr. GLOVER. Well, I know when I met them—I think I know when I met them again. This was in connection with playing tennis. And that must have been in the spring, I believe, of 1962, sometime in that period. . . .

Mr. JENNER. Would you say that the intervening period when you had a little or no contact with the de Mohrenschildts covered as much as a couple of years?

Mr. GLOVER. I would say that is what I think, but I could check this point if necessary.

Mr. JENNER. We will let you know as to whether we want you to do that. That acquaintance was then renewed under what circumstances?

Mr. GLOVER. I went to a party at a friend's house one night.

Mr. JENNER. Who is the friend?

Mr. GLOVER. The man's name is Lauriston C. Marshall.

Mr. JENNER. That is a new name to me.

Mr. GLOVER. Well, he is called Larry, but his name, I am quite sure, was—

Mr. JENNER. L-a-u-r-i-s-t-o-n C. M-a-r-s-h-a-l-l? [Marshall was the director of the Graduate Research Center of the Southwest, cofounded by executives of military contractor Texas Instruments. See Endnote and Essay in the Appendix.]

Mr. GLOVER. Yes.

Mr. JENNER. All right.

Mr. GLOVER. He lived in Garland here.

Mr. JENNER. Garland, Tex.?

Mr. GLOVER. Right. This is not where I met the de Mohrenschildts, but that is the connection. I was at his house and I met Sam Ballen. [See Endnote.] And something was said about playing tennis, and it turns out that he likes to play tennis and I also like to play tennis. I hadn't played very much since I had been in Dallas, but I always wanted to play more than I had a chance to, and he said, "How about tomorrow morning?" and I agreed, okay. So when I went to play tennis the next morning, it turned out that the other two people involved in this match of four people, doubles, was [sic] the de Mohrenschildts.

Mr. JENNER. You played doubles in tennis with him the next morning, Sunday morning?

Mr. GLOVER. This sounds right. I believe it was a Saturday night party, and I was playing Sunday morning. I believe that is what it was.

Mr. JENNER. And your friendship with the de Mohrenschildts blossomed?

Mr. GLOVER. Well, we played tennis an awful lot more. That was the basis.

Mr. JENNER. You say the double, the lady who played tennis with you on that initial occasion, was the same lady who had accompanied Mr. de Mohrenschildt earlier on the ice rink?

Mr. GLOVER. That's correct.

Jenner continued to quiz Glover for some time about George de Mohrenschildt, his wives, his notorious trip to Mexico, and his relationship with Lee Harvey Oswald, who from the outset had been the commission's sole suspect in the assassination. Soon after, de Mohrenschildt was positioned in popular vernacular as the "handler" of a pro-Castro, Russian defector-turned-Communist. Without doubt, George and his wife, Jeanne, befriended the young couple on their arrival in the Fort Worth area at the behest of J. Walton Moore.

It was George who first introduced Everett Glover to Marina Oswald. However, unless George slipped back into the US without leaving a paper trail—evidence that thus far escapes these authors—he had left Dallas in late May 1963 en route to Haiti—remaining in the region well into 1964—making it difficult to "control" the actions of Oswald following the alleged attempt on General Walker. Yet the legend has persisted for nearly six decades.

It is possible that upon George's departure from the US in late May, Lee was handed over to another "caretaker," or that Marina was assigned a "caretaker" as well, in the absence of the de Mohrenschildts. Lafitte's term implies a code word for an individual or individuals and appears more than a half dozen times in the datebook. It is one of very few instances that our scribe seems particularly compelled to protect an identity. He made no such effort when he wrote "DeM . . ." in the datebook, so it is unlikely that a code word, "caretaker" or handler, was used to protect George de Mohrenschildt. The likelihood that FBI Special Agent Bardwell DeWitt Odum filled that role, with the assistance of Ruth Paine and husband Michael, is pursued in the essay titled "'Caretaker' Analysis" found in the appendix of this book.

Senior counsel Jenner then proceeded to delve into circumstances that perhaps he didn't recognize as potentially significant, the introduction of Ruth Paine to Lee and Marina Oswald.

Mr. JENNER. When was the last occasion you saw the Oswalds?

Mr. GLOVER. This, as I said before, was a few days to a week I believe, after the time I saw them at the de Mohrenschildts.

Mr. JENNER. Was that at your home?

Mr. GLOVER. That was at my home.

Mr. JENNER. Was this a visit or an assembly that you organized?

Mr. GLOVER. Yes. I was the prime mover in organizing it.

Mr. JENNER. Tell us what motivated you and what you went about doing, and who was there.

Mr. GLOVER. Well, I didn't get a very good impression of Oswald this first time, because I didn't talk to him. But I talked with Volkmar Schmidt and we talked with Dick Pierce who was living with us, and we talked about it. . . .

Mr. JENNER. All right, okay, go ahead about your party now.

Mr. GLOVER. It so happened at this time that Ruth Paine, who is an acquaintance of mine.

Mr. JENNER. How did you become acquainted with Ruth Paine?

Mr. GLOVER. I became acquainted with Ruth Paine either through the Unitarian church here in Dallas, or through a singing group which had members in it, from the Unitarian Church. I am not sure which. As I remember, it may not be entirely correct, but sometime after '56 I think, '56 or '58 in there, I was more active . . . Sometime during that period Michael Paine came to sing with the Unitarian Church. It seems he had been trying out various choirs around the town . . .

Mr. JENNER. Was this kind of a Madrigal group?

Mr. GLOVER. Yes. This was what it was called, depending on the membership at any time. They sing all kinds of things.

Mr. JENNER. Go ahead about your party.

Mr. GLOVER. Okay, so I knew at this time I had seen Ruth Paine on a few occasions in the past 6 months or a year, and I must have been talking with her or seen her somewhere previous to this time of the party, at which time she mentioned that she was going, she thought she was going to teach a course in Russian at St. Mark School; and that she was trying to brush up on the Russian, on—-or maybe I am just thinking she said this latter. But she was interested, and I didn't really know—I think at that time I was aware of the fact she had majored in Russian in school, or knew Russian very well, and de Mohrenschildt's wife Jeanne, was trying to find someone who could converse with her, and I thought I would tell Ruth Paine about her, maybe she would be interested in talking with this woman. So I invited her, and she said she would be interested. That is the explanation of how she came.

Mr. JENNER. Did you tell Ruth Paine about the Oswalds, to the extent that you knew about them at that time?

Mr. GLOVER. I am sure I did.

Mr. JENNER. Did she indicate whether she had any acquaintance or knowledge of the Oswalds?

Mr. GLOVER. Well, it never occurred to me to question this until it was brought up by the FBI. As far as I know, this was completely new to her.

Mr. JENNER. Your reaction at that time, in any event, was, as far as Mrs. Paine is concerned, your knowledge of her, she knew nothing about the Oswalds?

Mr. GLOVER. That's right, completely new to her.

With this testimony, Everett Glover—named in Lafitte's datebook along with his housemate and colleague at Socony, Volkmar Schmidt from Germany—established himself as the conduit for introduction of the Oswald couple to his fellow Madrigal singers, Ruth and Michael Paine. It was Ruth who some nine months later would facilitate Oswald's hiring at the Texas School Book Depository, where he would fulfill his designated role as the "perfect patsy."

With Oswald "in place," as noted in the October 25 entry—"O says done–Oswald in place"—our attention is drawn to November 20, when the project manager for the assassination notes: "rifle into building-yes/ok/DPD". Without drawing conclusions, this Warren Commission testimony of the representative of the TSDB tenant, South West Publishing Co., has long been buried and warrants review:

Mr. CASTER. Yes; I was born in New Mexico, educated in New Mexico, received my college degrees at New Mexico Highlands University at Las Vegas, N. Mex. I taught school in New Mexico from 1939 until I started to work with Southwestern Publishing Co., in 1952. There was a period of about 2 years that I spent in the U.S. Navy.

Mr. BALL. And have you had your offices since 1952 in the Texas School Book Depository Building?

Mr. CASTER. The offices have been in the Texas School Book Depository Building, but not in this particular building here. We have occupied three places since I have been with the Southwestern Publishing Co.

Mr. BALL. Your office is on which floor?

Mr. CASTER. Second floor.

Mr. BALL. Did you ever bring any guns into the School Book Depository Building?

Mr. CASTER. Yes; I did.

Mr. BALL. When?

Mr. CASTER. I believe it was on Wednesday, November 20, during the noon hour.

Mr. BALL. Whose guns were they?

Mr. CASTER. They were my guns.

Mr. BALL. And what kind of guns were they?

Mr. CASTER. One gun was a Remington, single-shot, .22 rifle, and the other was a .30-06 sporterized Mauser.

Mr. BALL. Who owned them?

Mr. CASTER. I had just purchased them during the noon hour that day.

Mr. BALL. Well, tell us about it—what were the circumstances of the purchase?

Mr. CASTER. Well, I left the Depository during the noon hour and had lunch and, while out for the lunch hour, I stopped by Sanger-Harris sporting goods department to look for a rifle for my son's birthday—I beg your pardon, Christmas present—son's Christmas present, and while I was there I purchased the single-shot .22—single shot—and at the same time was looking at some deer rifles. I had, oh, for several years been thinking about buying a deer rifle and they happened to have one that I liked and I purchased the .30-06 while I was there.

Mr. BALL. And did they box them up?

Mr. CASTER. They were in cartons; yes.

Mr. BALL. And then you went back to work, I guess?

Mr. CASTER. Yes; I picked both rifles up in cartons just like they were, this was during the noon hour, and as I entered the Texas School Book Depository Building on my way up to the buying office, I stopped by Mr. Truly's office, and while I was there we examined the two rifles that I had purchased.

Mr. BALL. Did you take them out of the carton?

Mr. CASTER. Yes; I did.

Mr. BALL. Who was there besides you and Mr. Truly?

Mr. CASTER. Well, I'm not really sure who was there. I think you were there, Bill, and Mr. Shelley was there—and Mr. Roy Truly. The only people that I know about, in any event, were there; there were workers there at the time, but I'm not quite sure how many. I couldn't even tell you their names. I don't know the Texas School Book Depository workers there in the shipping department.

Roy Truly will testify before the commission: "It was during the lunch period or right at the end of the lunch period on November 20. Mr. Caster came in the door from the first floor and spoke to me and showed me two rifles that he had just purchased. I looked at these and picked up the larger one of the two and examined it and handed it back to Mr. Caster, with the remark that it was really a handsome rifle or words to that effect, at which time Mr. Caster explained to me that he had bought himself a rifle to go deer hunting with, and he hadn't had one and he had been intending to buy one for a long time, and that he had also bought a .22 rifle for his boy."

Truly had told the FBI on November 22, 1963, that one was a .22 Caster he said he had bought for his son, the other a larger rifle Caster said he had bought for deer hunting. He said that Caster showed them to him, and that he had sighted the larger rifle and then returned it to Caster. Truly said that Oswald may have seen him with the rifle "within the past few days."

Ball continued his questioning of Warren Caster:

Mr. BALL. In that office, though, Truly's office, how many were there?

Mr. CASTER. We weren't in Mr. Truly's immediate office, we were just there over the counter.

Mr. BALL. In the warehouse?

Mr. CASTER. We were there in the hall—just right there over the counter in front of the warehouse; that's right.

Mr. BALL. And did you take the guns out of the carton?

Mr. CASTER. Yes; I did. They were removed from the carton.

Mr. BALL. Did you handle them?

Mr. CASTER. Yes; I did.

Mr. BALL. Did anybody else handle the guns?

Mr. CASTER. Mr. Truly handled them and I'm not sure whether Mr. Shelley had the guns in his hands or not; I'm not positive.

Mr. BALL. How long a time were you there with the guns, and by time, just estimate it.

Mr. CASTER. Well, it couldn't have been more than ten minutes.

Mr. BALL. What did you do with the guns after that?

Mr. CASTER. I put them back in the carton and carried them up to my office.

Mr. BALL. And what did you do with them after that?

Mr. CASTER. I left at the end of the working day, oh, around 4 o'clock and took the guns in the cartons and carried them and put them in my car and carried them home.

Mr. BALL. Did you ever have them back in the Texas School Book Depository Building thereafter?

Mr. CASTER. They have never been back to the Texas School Book Depository Building since then.

Mr. BALL. Where were those guns on November 22, 1963?

Mr. CASTER. The guns were in my home, 3338 Merrell Road.

And with that, Warren Commission Counsel Joseph Ball failed to meet the lowest standard of rules of witness testimony by simply asking, "Can we be certain that the rifles were on Merrell Road on the 22nd?"

* * *

The assassins who escaped into oblivion while Dallas authorities and media, and the Warren Commission, deflected the eyes of the world from them to a *lone-nut Communist* serve as the focus of our closing chapter.

CHAPTER 10
D'AFFAIRE KENNEDY

DRAFT OF FRENCH ARTICLE

The French Government is prepressing records that might solve the *Affaire Kennedy*. Equally interesting, it appears to be hiding the documents at the behest of the American CIA, which has blunted all investigations—official and otherwise—for the past nineteen years.

It will be recalled that in 1978, a special investigating committee of the US Congress concluded that President Kennedy was probably killed as the result of a conspiracy, but they were totally unable to identify either the riflemen or those ultimately responsible for the killing. One brief CIA document now available to this newspaper may hold the key to the complex mystery.

In early March 1964, the American Government began an urgent investigation of three Frenchmen, one or more of whom may have been in Dallas on November 22, 1963, and who were expelled by the American Government . . . presumably to Mexico . . . the next day. At least two of the three Frenchmen were hard-core OAS veterans who were capable of all sorts of mayhem and who had no "legitimate business" in Dallas on the day of the murder.

The American investigation ended a few days later, as suddenly as it began—and without reaching any conclusions. Only very recently has the genesis of the investigation been discovered in some obscure French police files.

It seems that in late February 1964 a freelance French journalist attended a party in Montreal. Present was an OAS veteran who, in a drunken state of mind, confessed to having been present in Dallas on November 22, 1963. More important, he attempted to recruit the journalist, who had dual French-Mexican citizenship, to assist in an OAS plot to assassinate General de Gaulle when he was scheduled to visit Mexico in March. The journalist declined, but he did print his story in an obscure French newspaper, the *Côte Basque Soir* of Bayonne.

As a result, the French authorities began an urgent investigation and asked the American FBI and CIA to do likewise. However, as the time for de Gaulle's departure approached, French authorities had to decide what threat to his security was posed by the presence in North America of a group of dangerous OAS veterans who may or may not have been involved in the assassination of Kennedy.

They concluded that the threat was very real and very great. However, in true style, the General decided to make the trip anyway. He departed for Mexico on March 16, 1964. The investigation of the threat apparently stopped on both sides of the Atlantic at that time.

From 1964 to the late 1970s, the story remained buried. However, ultimately it came to the attention of an American lawyer (Bernard Fensterwald) who was a classmate of John Kennedy at Harvard and who has researched the President's murder for many years. He has made several trips to Paris in recent years, attempting to see the French investigation of this matter. He wants to see if one or more of the OAS veterans was *in fact* hired as a mercenary to kill the president.

So far, the French Government has "stonewalled" him, in exactly the same way as the US Government. Despite the fact that he has seen a few documents from the French file—and therefore known of its existence—the French Government continues to insist that the file no longer exists. Further, he is told that he could not see it, even if it did exist, because it would be an invasion of privacy, etc., etc.

—Undated Draft, sometime in 1981 as revealed by attorney Bernard Fensterwald:

Can the reader imagine what would have happened if before World War II a Nazi had assassinated Franklin D. Roosevelt—can the reader imagine the reaction and the excitement of the press and other communications media if Hitler had sent Goering to pose as a mourner at the casket and the grave of an assassinated Roosevelt?

—Gerald L. K. Smith, 1964

Oh, the way I fucked up this world, who would ever dream that the mother-fucker was a Nazi and found me the perfect setup for a frame . . . . I was used to silence Oswald. I walked into a trap the moment I walked down that ramp Sunday morning.

—Jack Ruby, c. 1965

Souetre—Mexico City-
—Lafitte datebook, November 12

On November 12, 1963, former French army commando and paratrooper Jean Rene Marie Souetre—and two associates, both Hungarians, Laslo Vango (Laszlo Varga) and Lajos LNU (Marton), who had fled their homeland's failed revolution and come to Spain, where they were trained in specialized sabotage and assassination techniques by Souetre at two of Otto Skorzeny's three training compounds outside of Madrid—landed on a commercial flight from Spain in Mexico City, Mexico. Each man carried several passports issued under various aliases, as well as their actual identities. Along with their passports, each man also carried about $1,000 in US currency.

* * *

As this investigation draws to a close, the implications of the arrival in Mexico City on the 12th of November of two Hungarians and the former OAS paratrooper and marksman Jean Rene Souetre, when considered in the context of the datebook entry of the same date, cement that Pierre Lafitte was kept apprised of the progress of Otto Skorzeny's logistics for the assassination, down to the cast of characters destined for Dealey Plaza. By October 9th, Lafitte already knew that Souetre and the Hungarians were on that list as evidenced: *OSARN-OSARN-OSARN-OSARN-get Willoughby-Litt- plus Souetre, others (Hungarians)* . . .

According to Rupert Allason, writing under the pen name Nigel West, the ambush of Charles de Gaulle's motorcade of two cars escorted by a pair of motorcycles on the evening of August 22, 1962, in the suburb of Petit-Clamart was probably the best organized effort to violently remove the president of France. Former Air Force officer Jean-Marie Bastien-Thiry led a dozen gunmen in that particular attempt on de Gaulle. Among them were three Hungarians: Lajos Marton, driver Lazlo Varga, and ex-legionnaire Sergeant Gyula Sari. Fifteen months later, just ten days before the assassination in Dealey Plaza, as evidenced in the aforementioned record, Marton and Varga arrived in Mexico City with Jean Souetre, leading the investigator to conclude that the two Hungarians then traveled on to Dallas with Souetre. Otherwise, who were "the Hungarians" referenced by Lafitte on October 9?

Although it's possible that not all those named in the October 9 entry were ultimately assigned to the Dealey Plaza plot—perhaps some were prepping for the March 1964 renewed effort to kill de Gaulle during his trip to Mexico

City—the fact is Lafitte notes *"Lancelot proj"* immediately following *"plus Soue-tre, others (Hungarians)."* When Souetre shows up with Varga and Marton in Mexico City five weeks later, it is only logical to seriously consider that they all ended up in Dallas although there are no records to suggest that a skilled sniper was among this group of Hungarians—on the contrary, according to Christopher Othen, author of *The Plot to Kill Charles de Gaulle,* "Sari and Marton bolted out of the side door and knelt by the front wheel, firing their submachine guns" that unseasonably cool evening in Petit-Clamart. More likely, it was their vehement resentment toward de Gaulle's plan to free Algeria and their flagrant bravado that instilled confidence in both Skorzeny and Souetre.

Also named on October 9 was Gerard Litt, a lethal character going back to WWII whom we met in Chapter 1. To recap, Litt's name surfaced when self-described amateur detective Paul Gluc, then living outside Paris, contacted J. Edgar Hoover to say, "This information concerns the holders of many of the missing cards, Jean Souetre, as well as Jean Paul Filiol, both known to have been in Dallas on 22 November 1963 . . . . Included in this knowledge are Mme. Lamy and M. Litt, all mentioned before, and extremely distasteful individuals . . . . I am anxious to spell this out for you by coming to Washington, D.C."

Assassin Gerard Litt has been described as a psychopath . . . something of a human toad . . . a coward, and a bloodthirsty anti-Semite, his personality as brutish as his physical composition. He and fellow psychopath Jean Filliol emerged from the ranks of the secret, radically right Catholic group, La Cagoule, written about in depth previously, and dealt directly with Skorzeny's *Groupe Serpent.* He eventually became one of Skorzeny's main allies . . . a black marketer who controlled a group of ex-Cagoulards and gangsters engaged in drug trafficking, pushing heroin processed in Marseilles to Allied troops. As noted, these were many of the same heroin processors with whom Pierre Lafitte would work when Litt later traveled to Montreal, Canada, and the United States. With Skorzeny, Litt had agreed to form anticommunist groups and organize stay-behind networks in France and elsewhere. Guerrilla members of these networks were to be trained at "a special school near The Hague under code name 'Jeanne,'" perhaps after Litt's wife's name, although the name was also meant to refer to "Jeanne d'Arc," the infamous French revolutionary of the fifteenth century. While we only have a glimpse of him in the Lafitte records, no doubt it was easy for the project manager to understand why Otto would choose to factor Litt into the plans for the brazen, broad-daylight attack in Dallas.

The reader also met Jean Paul Robert Filliol early in this investigation. Like Lee Harvey Oswald, Filliol failed to complete high school. He gravitated toward fierce patriotism, rejected his parents' Protestantism, and became an ardent Roman Catholic, attending Mass regularly. Like Oswald, he joined the military, serving in the French army on active duty for about two years. After similar lackluster attempts at earning a living, Filliol embarked on his radical, fascist activities. Along the way, he met a violence-prone French girl, Alice Renée Lamy, and together they proceeded down the trail of murder and mayhem, ending up in the Stoneleigh Hotel in Oak Lawn, Dallas, on the eve of the assassination of John Kennedy. Whether they were "along for the ride" or active participants is yet to be determined, but with certainty, Otto, Ilse, and the project manager were aware of the presence of the maniacal couple.

Before departing the Stoneleigh—and although the project manager for the Dallas operation makes no mention of him by name—there is reason to conclude that Enrique Ernesto Pugibet, a former member of the French Resistance and gunman for hire posing as a cattle rancher, checked into the same hotel at the same time, not by chance, but by design. According to attorney Bernard Fensterwald, whose investigations unearthed facts few had ever pursued in earnest, he had the opportunity to talk with then FBI informant Allen Wright and to document the essence of what Wright had tried to tell New Orleans DA Jim Garrison. Fensterwald's notes were summarized by researcher Mary Ferrell, whose collection served as the "mother ship" of assassination files for decades.

According to Wright, Ernesto Puijet [*sic*] checked into the Stoneleigh Hotel in Dallas on November 19, 1963. Wright further alleged that the hired gunman was still in Dallas on November 22, 1963. The individual in question was Enrique Ernesto Pugibet, who, according to FBI informant NY T-1, was a prized and protected FBI source at the time and involved directly in a political assassination. Wright says that Pugibet had killed Jose Almoina Mateos, former secretary to Trujillo, in Mexico, in May 1960, and upon his return to the Dominican Republic, Pugibet was given a new automobile with a driver, allowed to carry a pistol, provided a home in Ciudad Trujillo, and assumed a very high position in "Radio Caribe." NY T-1 said that this followed the pattern of Trujillo's methods of rewarding people who had done important jobs. Records also reveal that Pugibet was connected to (Norman) Rothman, a well-known operative of Santo Trafficante Jr. In the late '50s, Rothman had hired Lewis J. McWillie, well known in the Dallas area for his illegal gambling establishments, as pit boss for the Sans Souci in Havana, thus pulling McWillie further into the Trafficante orbit of this investigation. Both McWillie and Trafficante appear in the 1963 Lafitte records.

Enrique Pugibet as a likely suspect in Dallas is greatly enhanced when considered alongside the history of gunman/would-be author Robert Emmett Johnson, present in Trecornia Prison when Ruby is alleged to have visited the Mafia boss Trafficante, and active in Dominican Republic through the early 1960s as revealed in Chapter 7. Pugibet's history is explored in depth in the essay found in the appendix titled: "Enrique Ernesto Pugibet: A Timely Arrival in Dallas."

KOVACS, ORTIZ, AND JOLY

There is no clear evidence that any of these three men, or a combination of, were present in Dallas on November 22, 1963, so perhaps the reader might question why they end up in these pages. Simply put, they appear among the outstanding items for research left on the desk of author Albarelli.

A February 26, 1962, exposé "Neo-Nazis Linked to Algeria French" by correspondent Waverley Root, then living in Paris, published in the *Washington Post*, reveals that European extremists—known as Ultras—in Algeria were "now tied in with the worldwide clandestine neo-Nazi organization which has existed ever since the end of the war, built around a core of Hitlerites who escaped post war justice. The head of this international Nazi underground has always been believed to be Madrid's man of mystery, Otto Skorzeny, the SS trooper who rescued Mussolini from his captors." More chilling, Root continues, "Skorzeny is reported to maintain contacts with former Nazis scattered throughout the world, especially in Latin America and the Middle East. *They have not given up hope that Nazism may yet triumph throughout the world, and they seem prepared to lend their aid in any desperate venture of like political ideology which might achieve a Rightist authoritarian government anywhere.*" (Emphasis added.)

Root's informed sources said that "two of four defendants in the trial escaped and made their way to Spain." The trial he refers to was the result of the arrest of those involved in the 1957 bazooka attack on General Raoul Salan. The far-right extremists were convinced that the general wasn't fully on their side to halt the movement toward independence from France in Algeria. All charged with the attack had been found guilty. Among them was Doctor René Kovacs, who was sentenced to death in absentia following his escape. A physician by training, Kovacs was born in Algeria of (notably, for our purposes) Hungarian parents. Along with his aide, Joseph Ortiz, a restaurateur and fellow far-right extremist, the two fled to Spain.

Root contends that Algerian Europeans devoted to far-right politics had long been alleged to have international connections. "Thus gave birth to any imperfectly known organization called the Red Hand," writes Root, referring to a mysterious terror group organized to counter the National Liberation Front

(FLN) in Algeria. According to freelance journalist Joachim Joesten, among the earliest sleuths to arrive in Dallas in pursuit of the facts of the assassination of Kennedy, the creator of the Red Hand was none other than the head of France's DST—a man readers are now familiar with—Roger Wybot. Author Ralph Ganis, who pursued Joesten's findings in depth, tells us that the Red Hand operated in the manner of paramilitary groups that sprang up after WWI, in which Otto Skorzeny participated. Writes Ganis, "It was also very similar to the old Cagoule, the 'hooded ones.'"

Waverley Root also concluded that Kovacs and Ortiz, who both fled to Spain, were involved in *the Skorzeny ring.* Rounding out the triad with Kovacs and Ortiz, Root tells us that Belgian citizen Pierre Joly "turns up regularly in French extreme-right activities of a conspiratorial nature. Joly [whose duties appear to have included propagation of extremist ideology on the printed page] was among those who appeared in Madrid when the refugees from the revolt trial arrived there." Root then summarizes the significance of these figures ending up in Spain:

> The existence in Madrid, on territory where extreme Rightists of all countries can reasonably expect to find political refuge of the headquarters of an international neo-Nazi organization, helps to encourage a funneling of all revolutionary Rightists groups into the same conspiracy. But political kinship tends in any case to throw the like-minded of all countries together, so that even without formal organization there has been built up an intricate maze of cross-relationships among Right extremists of all countries.

From there, the correspondent highlights the current crisis in Katanga, a breakaway province from the Republic of Congo, which had contributed to the January 17, 1961, assassination of Congolese Prime Minister Patrice Lumumba. The success of the operation has been attributed to, among others, Otto Skorzeny.

Root draws attention to the likely role played by Algerian Ultras operating outside Toulouse—long a hotbed of French Algerian activity—in delivering three French jet planes from a factory outside Toulouse to Katanga. Of note, on September 25, 1963, Pierre Lafitte writes "LeCatet"; research strongly suggests this could be a location within the commune of Montbeton, north of Toulouse, where a number of airfields were located, perhaps related to training camps.

As we learned, the American Committee for Aid to Katanga Freedom Fighters included Jack Crichton, the Dallas oilman who had been in business with Otto Skorzeny since 1952 and served as his point man on the 22nd of November.

LEROY AND ROUX

Lafitte's notation for November 4th is as intriguing as any in the 1963 datebook. The names "Leroy" and "Roux" appear on either side of sketches that appear to be a representation of "crossfire," as if he were noting the position of the two men involved in an operation. Because the two names do not appear at any other time in the datebook, it is possible that the date provides us with a clue. On November 1, the manager seems perturbed: "trail run—mistakes a plenty. not good." The following day, November 2, he draws a smaller version of the sketch for November 4. Well known to many researchers are the alleged plots to assassinate Kennedy during the fall of '63 in Chicago or Tampa. It is not clear if *trial run* refers to the plot of November 18 in Florida and involved Leroy and Roux or if the two men were running practice drills for November 22 in Dallas. We can only speculate that Lafitte employed Souetre's cover for Dallas, "Roux," in his early November note-taking.

For that reason, we review the previously outlined facts regarding Robert Leroy. A prewar member of Action Française, the Far-Right political group, and then La Cagoule's terrorist underground, Leroy participated with the Requête Carlist militia forces during the Spanish Civil War and served as a French SS officer during WWII. Along with SS officer Otto Skorzeny, he served as the strategic leadership for Aginter Press, established to implement the Strategy of Tension, with support from the Portuguese security service PIDE and the CIA. He later joined Skorzeny's efforts to train Egyptian leader Abd al-Nasir's intelligence and security services. Especially intriguing, he recruited a hundred German advisers from Nazi soldiers serving during WWII, the SS underground, and from among technical experts with military industries: "The purpose was to train Arab guerrillas in commando tactics and in protecting the former Nazi technicians working for Nasir from Israeli 'hit' teams. The job was carried out at the CIA's bequest."

Leroy's significant role with Aginter Press insists that we repeat the following verbatim: "A portentous January 1968 affidavit sworn by Aginter Press assassin and Jean Rene Souetre associate Jacques Godard reveals the group's relationship with certain American persons and organizations: 'In the course of our services we had relations with certain persons and organizations like, for example, President Tshombe and with Biafra. We likewise were in charge of relations with the John Birch Society, which was an American political group financed especially by Texas oil producers whose activity is absolutely anti-communist. Everywhere where there is a struggle, either open or covert, with Communists, the John Birch Society lends its financial aid to the people who are struggling against international communism.'"

Assassination researchers, convinced that the Bay of Pigs was the single fuse that lit the flame of the Lancelot project, may be disappointed that there is no specific mention of the usual suspects in the Lafitte records. Instead, those named in Chapter 7—"Texas Jack" Canon, "Boots" Askins, and R. Emmett Johnson—acting in concert with the aforementioned Hungarians Varga and Marton, and known former Cagoule assassins Lamy, Filliol, and Litt along with Leroy and "Roux" (and possibly the French gunman, Pugibet, who booked into the Stoneleigh Hotel at the same time), can be confirmed as members of *teams and squads* in Dealey. Assuming that the Florida *swamp groups*, referred to by Lafitte in his infamous October 9 entry, were made up of anti-Castro exiles and hired mercenaries trained in Plantation Key and the Lake Pontchartrain site, the common denominator between *all* would be one of Otto's favorite commandos, serving as lead assassin in Dallas, Jean Rene Souetre.

WHO WAS JEAN RENE SOUETRE?

His birth name was Jean Rene Marie Souetre. He was born on October 15, 1930, in La Brède, in the Gironde Department of France. When he first came to the attention of the CIA and the US Department of Justice, just days after the assassination of President Kennedy, he was identified as having at least eleven aliases, including Michel Mertz, Jean Mertz, Michel Roux, Eugène [Commander] Constant, René Martin, Gremmont, and Mangin. Perhaps coincidentally, perhaps not, he shared several aliases with Pierre Lafitte. In 1963, Souetre would meet several times in the United States with Lafitte, but we are getting ahead of ourselves.

Described earlier, Jean Souetre stood about an inch over six feet tall and was thin, weighing about 180 pounds, but deceptively muscular in build. He was also fast, very fast. Former colleagues say, "He could move like a panther, and could be just as deadly." He was fluent in his native French, spoke near-perfect English and Spanish and German. He was handsome, had thick, dark, slightly curly hair and sparkling hazel-gray eyes that would alter in sunlight to green or sky blue. His smile was infectious but reserved for real moments of joy or humor. He loved women and married three times that we know of. His first wife divorced him after it became apparent that he was also wed to the OAS and soldiering.

It has been reported that he came from a family with a military tradition, so, in 1950, when he was twenty years of age, he enlisted into the French Air Force. In 1953, when he was a captain with the Security branch of the French 4th Air Force, he was stationed near Reims, France. There, he was often in professional and social contact with a US Army captain from Houston, Texas, named

Lawrence Alderson. (It should be noted, briefly, that Captain Alderson was replaced by a military officer named LeTourneau, who also developed enough familiarity with Jean Rene Souetre to end up in the records of Pierre Lafitte. The surname LeTourneau, a prominent East Texas family whose business continues to provide heavy equipment to the military, is considered later in this book.)

Alderson, as readers will learn, became a dentist after leaving the US Army, but he and Souetre remained friends and corresponded annually. By 1954, Souetre had received a commission as a junior officer and succeeded in becoming a master parachutist and airborne soldier, parallel in America to being an Airborne Ranger. He also volunteered for a new commando unit that was being formed by the Air Force, called the Fusilier Commando Parachutiste de l'Air. Souetre received the Chevalier de la Légion d'Honneur and the Croix de la Valeur Militaire while serving in Algiers in 1955–1959. Both medals were revoked after Souetre joined the OAS.

This unit put Souetre under Colonel François Coulet, a legendary officer, who had been given permission to create the air commandos for fighting on the mean streets and areas of Algeria. Combat in Algeria ranged from high-risk night drops, close-in hand-to-hand fighting, to sophisticated means to a wide range of ultraterrorist techniques. Col. Coulet had seen combat in the Second World War as a parachute captain and, after the war, served as a French diplomat but remained in the reserves. From 1950 to 1954, he served as French Ambassador to Iran and in 1955 was French Ambassador to Yugoslavia. Later, in 1956, he reentered the service to establish the air commandos.

The air commandos were a small unit, with less than two hundred men, who had been hand-chosen to then endure some of the most rigorous military training known. Coulet prided in providing his men the best training possible. Reportedly, Coulet favored Souetre because Jean reminded him so much of himself in soldiering ways. The Spartan-like select unit of two hundred was broken down into small detachments that were attached to Foreign Legion Parachute regiments and other airborne units. Souetre excelled in the commandos, serving in Algeria from 1955 to 1959, and was involved in intense combat operations. Souetre's air commando detachment, designated CPA 10, was attached to the Foreign Legion 1st REP. That unit would eventually be disbanded by Charles de Gaulle because of its leading role in the April 1961 General's Putsch. Like many of the paratroopers and commandos in Algeria, Souetre would become a rabid supporter of the *Ultras* and for keeping Algeria under French control.

In April 1960, Souetre was assigned to command the French air commando training battalion, a promotion that widely marked his own expertise in the techniques of warfare and his decided flair for leadership. This was the same time that American rangers from the 505th Airborne Infantry, out of Germany, under the leadership Lieutenant Anthony Herbert, arrived at Pau to conduct training with the French commandos. An account of Herbert's ranger's time at Pau, France, was described earlier but deserves repeating for its significance to Captain Jean Souetre.

As the French commander of the training area, Capt. Souetre would have worked with Lt. Herbert and the American rangers, who were there specifically to learn *unconventional* warfare tactics. It will be recalled, while conversing with French paratroopers, the subject of Otto Skorzeny came up between Lt. Herbert and a French commando one evening after duty hours in a local Pau café. The French soldier asked Herbert if he would like to meet Skorzeny, as he was aware of his training sites in Spain. This after-hours question led Lt. Herbert to pursue contact with Skorzeny toward arranging additional expert training for his rangers from a living legend in the field. Through his French contacts, Herbert made arrangements for the meeting, and by summer 1960 Herbert's men found themselves at Skorzeny's secret training sites in the Pyrenees Mountains of Spain, just across the border from France. Lafitte mentions Lecotet, on the other side of the Pyrenees, north of Toulouse.

Herbert's men made several trips to Skorzeny's camps, which Herbert referred to as "Skorzeny's School of Commando Tactics." These were the same sites used by US MAAG forces and the French military, hence their knowledge of them. It is interesting that Lt. Herbert, while at the sites, noted that Skorzeny was absent from the training frequently. This, of course, makes sense because this was the period when Skorzeny was wrapped up in Operation Tropical, Algeria, and the Congo.

Skorzeny's aide explained to Herbert that his superior was absent because he had "other things going on." The arrangements that were made for Herbert to meet with Skorzeny confirm Capt. Souetre's commandos were fully aware of the nature of Skorzeny's training schools, which they also attended.

By late 1960, Souetre was in trouble with French authorities, who had taken notice of his intense political views toward Algeria. Upon receiving orders for a garrison assignment in Nimes, France, Souetre failed to report to duty. Instead, he went AWOL and then deserted, taking with him a loyal group of highly trained soldiers.

Souetre next surfaces in Algiers, where he and André Brousse de Montpeyroux organized the First French Algerian Marquis in a rural area near Mostaganem, an ancient port city and province capital in northwest Algeria. The formation of the group was announced in one-page leaflets circulated throughout the city. A second leaflet, targeting French military officers and noncommissioned officers, urged readers to support the OAS cause. On February 22, 1961, Souetre and Brousse de Montpeyroux, now Second Marquis leader, three sergeants, and five civilians were arrested on the premises of a Moslem Brotherhood religious sanctuary in Bouguirat in Mostaganem, where they were suspected of attempting to assassinate several of its occupants and then blowing it up . . . and charged with "plotting to commit illegal acts, sedition, and illegally possessing military arms."

Following their arrest, Souetre and Brousse were transferred, first to the Prison de Maison Carrée in France, then back to Algeria, where they and the others arrested with them were tried before a military tribunal on December 17, 1961. The press referred to this group as Souetre's "First Algerian Marquis."

Four days later, they were sentenced to three-to-four years in a detention camp at Saint-Maurice l'Ardoise; however, the sentence was suspended and replaced with an administrative detention of indeterminate length. Apparently, the terms of confinement were somewhat generous because, in January 1962, Souetre was allowed to marry Josette Marcaihou of Aymeric. Indeed, the camp's commander, General Claude Clément, attended the ceremony. Souetre and his new wife enjoyed a confined honeymoon, but days later the newlywed soldier escaped the camp along with seventeen others. After his escape, Souetre quickly assumed a leading role in planning the OAS attack on General de Gaulle at Petit-Clamart. De Gaulle escaped unharmed. Very much involved in the August 22, 1962, attempt to kill de Gaulle were Souetre's close associates Laszlo Varga, Lajos Marton, along with Hungarian Gyula Sari, and Corsican-born François Duprat, identified as one of the lead architects of Holocaust denial in France.

About a month after escaping, Souetre emerged in Feb–March 1962 living in Spain, and from there he often traveled to Portugal. On several occasions at this time, Souetre approached CIA officials and tried to persuade them to provide the OAS with backing as the best and most "viable alternative to communism" in France. As we have seen, there are at least two declassified CIA documents that purport to outline these meetings. Meanwhile, his new bride, provided false identity papers, had joined him in Madrid, but because of his continued OAS activities, she soon left him, returning to France, where she filed for a divorce. Due to her use of false documents in Spain, her divorce was interrupted by her falsification of papers. Having paid the fine for the offense, she was released, the divorce was finalized, and Josette Marcaihou disappeared from history.

Phen Lafitte recalls, "Of course, I had no idea he had been held in a detention camp, but I remember he and papa talked some about it when [Souetre] was in New Orleans in mid-1963, months before the assassination . . . . It was one of those 'never-again' conversations . . . never again this, never again that . . . . Men like papa and Souetre can't be caged for any length of time. Their essence is freedom, it's elemental to them."

Souetre, still based in Spain, began traveling back and forth to Algeria, where he boldly picked right back up on his OAS violent activities. Little is known about these activities, as they blended in with a massive blur of such actions, but it is known that he worked closely with Jacques Achard, known to many as "the most dangerous OAS leader" and "the eyes and ears of General Salan," and Pierre Sergent, both of whom were very much part of Otto Skorzeny's ever-expanding network. Achard headed an OAS group called the "A-Commandos," which was notorious for its murderous brutality toward Muslims. Achard, also, was a very close friend of Skorzeny's business partner, Clifford Forster. Before advancing the investigation into Souetre:

LINEN, FORSTER, AND LEVINE

Clifford Forster, staff and counsel to the American Civil Liberties Union from 1940 to 1954, was, according to author and collector Ralph Ganis, named frequently in the private papers of SS Otto Skorzeny. Ganis explains that the ties between Skorzeny and Forster most likely extended to Viennese-born Karl Von Forster, Clifford's father, who raised his family in the same neighborhood as Otto Skorzeny's family before opening a highly successful linen company in Paris.

After the war, having immigrated to the US, Clifford Forster ran the American Friends of Paix et Liberté designed to counter the propaganda of the French Communist Party. He later formed several similarly aggressively anticommunist committees in the US focused exclusively on threats to French colonial dominance in Algeria. By 1960, he was chairman/cofounder of The American Committee for France and Algeria, launching a bulletin similar to Willoughby's *Foreign Intel Digest* called *Integration,* the preferred term of fascist sympathizers to define the resolution of the Algerian question. Forster wrote, ". . . [we] believe that, in the interests of humanity and Western civilization, American policy as well as that of our allies will be best served by an Algeria *integrated* with France." (Sept. 1960—emphasis added.)

By 1961, President John Kennedy was taking a different position that strongly favored Algerian independence from France.

Forster had argued, "The importance of Algeria and indeed all of North Africa to the defense of Western Europe cannot be underestimated . . . . These are the simple strategic facts involved in the global struggle between East and West . . . ."

424 Coup in Dallas

A close read of Forster's analysis of "the importance of Algeria . . ." exposes a far less noble motive. Referring to *Oil, Gas & Chemical Service*, June 8, 1959, Forster alerts his readers that the petroleum industry publication sounded the warning in these terms: "Recent exploratory successes in North Africa and the development of sizable oil reserves in Algeria have directed attention to the entire northern part of the continent of Africa. The vigorous exploration and development of oil reserves in the Sahara Desert areas of Algeria will bring France into the ranks of important oil producing nations . . . ." Intentional or not, Forster was transparent: rightful independence of Algerians hinged on dominance over the country's natural resources.

Reflecting on the 1952 "Meadows - Skorzeny" scheme launched in Franco's Spain compels researchers to wonder how the discovery of vast oil reserves in the Sahara factored into the long-range projections of Texas independent oilmen.

Among the far-right propaganda outlets touted by Forster's *Integration* were those published by Kent Courtney, an active member of the White Citizens Council and the John Birch Society (JBS). A critical aspect of what appears on the surface as a loosely knit network, which in retrospect surfaces as a powerful worldwide ideological movement, was the American Opinion Speakers Bureau, promoted by the JBS. That stable of speakers included Clifford Forster. Featured speaker at Billy James Hargis's annual "Christian Crusade" convention held in Dallas in 1964, just months after the assassination, was Otto Skorzeny's business friend Clifford Forster. As noted previously, Christian Crusade was wrapped up in the Congress of Freedom identified in the Lafitte datebook.

Apparently, Algeria was still on the mind of former director of the CIA Allen Dulles in October 1963. In so many words, Dulles agreed with Forster that in spite of Algerian independence secured in 1962, capitalism writ large was not served by that major political shift on the African continent. During his trip to Dallas, October 28/29—the forty-eight-hour period critical to "Lancelot Planning," according to Pierre Lafitte—the dynamics in Algeria dominated Dulles's speech before the Dallas Council on World Affairs.

In his December 1963 bulletin, *Integration*, Clifford Forster published a multipage reflection. Woven through his diatribe, Forster demanded that his readers believe Lee Harvey Oswald was a deranged and—and if that wasn't convincing—a highly manipulated figure central to a Communist Conspiracy to permanently remove the president of the United States to seize control of America.

The experienced propagandist, clearly still consumed by the threat that an independent Algeria posed to his worldview, then convoluted his arguments and cleverly manipulated his readers to also question President Kennedy's loyalty to America, writing, "Joseph Kennedy was determined to have one of his sons become president, and in the course of pursuing this goal, discovered that you had to play ball with the [Communist] Conspiracy to make it. The alliance with the [Communist] Conspiracy took place in 1957 and was formally consummated on July 2, 1957, with Kennedy's now-famous Senate speech on Algeria and Western colonialism. For the first time in his career, Kennedy had adopted the Communist line. From then on he developed a [Communist] Conspiracy-approved line on domestic and foreign issues."

The propaganda promoted by Forster and his ilk continues to date, most recently with the publication of *Operation Dragon*, by former CIA director R. James Woolsey and coauthor, former Romanian acting spy chief Lt. Gen. Ion Mihai Pacepa. Published by Encounter Books, provider of "Books for Smart Conservatives," the description claims the authors have ". . . finally and definitively put to rest the question of who killed President Kennedy on November 22, 1963. All evidence points to the fact that the assassination—carried out by Lee Harvey Oswald—was ordered by Soviet Premier Nikita Khrushchev, acting through what was essentially the Russian leader's personal army, the KGB (now known as the FSB) . . ."

Forster's December '63 contribution to the "clean-up operation," claiming that Oswald was as a lone nut and a former defector to Soviet Russia sent home to murder the president, coincided with the role assigned to Forster's fellow board member at Paix et Liberté, one Isaac Don Levine, who is central to the Epilogue of our saga. As we learn later, it was Levine who was assigned the task to "deal with" Marina Oswald in the aftermath of her husband's murder, as reflected in Lafitte's November 28 entry: *Levine will deal w/ Marina e.t. . . . JA . . . call Madrid.*

* * *

Underscoring the likely motivation for Otto's selection of Jean Souetre and his historic accomplices, is their shared conviction that Charles de Gaulle's liberation policies were anathema to their profascist agenda. After the failed 1961 French generals' putsch, the OAS was determined to halt de Gaulle's move toward Algerian independence at all costs. The price was not simply removal of the president, but deadly removal. The war between de Gaulle and the OAS had ramped up when de Gaulle's political changes continued to move forward in Algeria. In May 1961, the French government had started negotiations with the FLN. These talks did not have immediate success, and over the course of the next year, the level of extreme violence had escalated. Finally, in March 1962, a cease-fire was reached, setting the stage for the Evian negotiations that would eventually lead to independence for Algeria. Taking command of the "secret army" was General Raoul Salan, who, by the time Pierre Lafitte made note of him in his 1963 diary, was still in prison on orders of President de Gaulle on November 22. However, Hilaire du Berrier, the North Dakota native described as an ambitious soldier of fortune, pilot, and spy, identified by Lafitte on the same day as Salan, was not. Regardless, it appears that the former leader of the OAS and his sympathizers, including du Berrier and Jacques Soustelle, preferred as the next leader of France and Algeria by powerful Texas oilmen, were at the very least a rallying point for events in play in the spring of 1963.

Respected attorney and assassination researcher Bernard Fensterwald reports, "The whereabouts of Souetre from this point forward become much less clear. However, on April 27, 1962, it was announced in Algiers that Lt. Pierre Guillaume, OAS Chief in the South Zone of Algeria, had been arrested. And 'sources' reported that he had been replaced by ex-Captain Souetre. In June–July 1962, after the Declaration of Algerian Independence, all OAS members had to leave Algeria in a rush. In August, a large number of OAS groups and individuals in exile merged into the *Armée Nationale Secrète*, which had representatives in Canada, New Orleans, and Latin America; in other words, the OAS was continuing the war against de Gaulle wherever they could, inside and outside Metropolitan France."

May 1963 found Souetre still moving back and forth from Spain to Lisbon, where he had agreed to join and provide expert training to the terrorist group, Aginter Press referenced in Chapter 1. Aginter Press had become a reliable and very active depository for freelance, hired assassins and experienced contract mercenaries. Under the auspices of Aginter, Souetre actively recruited French and Belgian mercenaries for the war in Angola. During this period, as noted earlier, Otto Skorzeny was absent from training camps as he focused on Angola, among other global hotspots.

About mid-1963, according to a former member of SAC (de Gaulle's special anti-OAS police), who knew Souetre very well, Souetre did the following in April-May, 1963:

(a) met [the CIA's] Howard Hunt and Jean Claude Perez (Chief of ORO) in Madrid (b) went to the Caribbean with Laszlo Varga, Lajos Marton, and [a person with the last name] Buscia; (c) went to New Orleans and met with Carlos Bringuier [datebook entry, April 30: 'Walker – Souetre in New

Orleans']; (d) went to Dallas and met with General Edwin Walker [confirmed in the datebook]; (e) went to Lake Pontchartrain and helped train anti-Castro Cubans [May 9 entry: Souetre and Davis in April here]. It is known, in any event, that during this period he [Souetre] had many contacts with anti-Castro Cubans. It is also known that he visited Spain in July 1963.

Author Peter Kross wrote in 2012 that "it is believed that Souetre met with [the CIA's assassination program coordinator] William Harvey at Plantation Key in Florida to plot strategy." This "strategy" assumedly concerned Cuban anti-Castro matters or assassination. Kross further states that Souetre "was also said to have met with retired Army General Edwin Walker, who was fired by JFK for inciting his troops with right wing propaganda while he was on active duty." He adds to his Plantation Key claim by stating:

> According to researchers looking into the events at Plantation Key, Souetre told that ten Cuban exiles were to be sent to the Lake Pontchartrain camp from Miami in July 1963, where they were to receive further military training. At the time that the New Orleans training camps were in existence, David Ferrie, Guy Banister and the other anti-Castro crowd all showed up at one time or another in these camps, and it has been written that at one point, Souetre met Lee Oswald at one of these camps and may have introduced himself to Oswald as "Alfred from Cuba."

To date, we see no evidence from the Lafitte material to prove that Otto or Ilse Skorzeny had any dealings or contact with David Ferrie or Guy Banister, both of whom have been named by highly credible authors as having played direct roles in the assassination. The situation with General Edwin Walker, however, is decidedly different. Lafitte's datebook for 1963 clearly reveals that Souetre and Walker did meet on April 30, and that Souetre was by then deeply enmeshed in Otto's plan for Dallas, as revealed when Lafitte adds to that entry, *Cable to O.*

* * *

Expert assassination researchers are aware that the first widely publicized report that accused assassin Lee Harvey Oswald had also tried to assassinate Gen. Walker on April 10, 1963, seven months before he was indicted for the Kennedy shooting, appeared in German newspaper *Deutscle National-Zeitung und*

Soldaten-Zeitung, based in Munich. The weekly paper made no secret of the fact that it had about a half-dozen former Nazis and SS members on staff; however, that they were well acquainted with Otto and Ilse Skorzeny was never mentioned. The paper's owner, publisher, and chief editor, Gerhard Frey, who had known Otto Skorzeny for several decades, went on to found the ultraright Deutsche Volksunion party in 1971, which espouses a mix of extreme-right and racist views similar to those of the defunct Nazi Ahnenerbe group. Frey and his staff, as writer Peter Dale Scott has underscored, were close to a good many far-right American groups, including the John Birch Society, and JBS members including Gen. Walker and the Christian Crusade leader Billy James Hargis.

In January 1964, only weeks after Kennedy and Oswald had been laid to rest, Hargis published a book titled *The Far Left*, dedicated to Walker: "We dedicate this volume because he [General Edwin Walker] has been willing to pursue his sincere anti-Communist goals. Few Americans would be willing to make the sacrifice that he has made. Even in the face of death, he seemed resigned to give his life joyfully for the cause of Freedom, Liberty and Christian Americanism." This endorsement echoes the words of Otto Skorzeny's friend and business associate since the early 1950s, Frank Ryan, who had served as president of the World Commerce Corporation under Bill Donovan of the OSS. Those words, shared publicly on June 25, 1961, bear repeating: "The action taken regarding Major General Edwin Walker is amazing. Is it a crime nowadays to be a patriot? Is it a crime to teach Americanism to our troops? . . . "

Gen. Edwin Walker always maintained that the German newspaper was the first to alert him about Oswald having taken a shot at him, but jottings in Pierre Lafitte's datebook made a few days before the attempt on Walker occurred make this seem unlikely. As noted in a previous chapter, Lafitte wrote on April 7, 1963: *"Walker – Lee and pictures— planned soon- can he do it? Won't."* [It is possible the last word is *Wait.*] The following day, Lafitte made a note: *Hal du Berrier (Salan R.).*

Lesser known than the German newspaper's scoop positioning "the patsy" a hundred yards from the window of Walker's house on the night of April 10 are the remarks made in the aftermath of the assassination by "Hal" du Berrier, the correspondent who wrote primarily for the *American Mercury*, which was owned by J. Russell McGuire with General Edwin Walker as the magazine's military advisor. Du Berrier revealed that he was staying in Walker's home in Dallas on November 22. It should also be noted that du Berrier's history included a role in the Spanish Civil War, service in Bill Donovan's OSS, perhaps providing him introduction to Frank Ryan and Otto Skorzeny, and spying for Italian fascists.

By the late 1950s, he had begun publishing *H du B Reports, A Foreign Affairs Letter*, with particular focus on Saigon, Vietnam, a concern he shared with his close friend, French rightist General Raoul Salan.

Seizing the opportunity to capitalize on the assertion of conservative writer William F. Buckley (another featured political essayist for McGuire's *American Mercury* before a falling out) that *had an anti-communist been responsible for the assassination of President Kennedy, a bloodbath in the United States might well have occurred*, Hargis promoted a report from "French" correspondent Hilaire du Berrier, who had been staying in Walker's home when Kennedy was murdered. Hargis noted that while the report was frightening, it warranted consideration because it somehow verified the view of the highly esteemed conservative Bill Buckley, thus giving du Berrier's account greater stature and a wider audience than it might otherwise have been accorded. Although Buckley had for months been speaking out against the rapid growth of the fringe movement within the Republican Party, the John Birch Society of which Hargis and Walker were members, the leader of the Christian Crusade apparently recognized this brief window to advance the Oswald legend on Buckley's coattails.

Hargis quoted du Berrier directly: "Out of the Dallas crucible came facts which realistic America must face: for meanness, viciousness, dishonesty, and absence of all sense of honor, the groups referred to as the American Right are no match for the organized, entrenched, and internationally-supported Left lined up against them. Radio, TV, the press, government agencies, and militant politicians took a position against America's interests and for the Left. Your correspondent [Hilaire du Berrier] was in Dallas when it happened. The first announcement of the killing was still coming over the air when the first threatening telephone call reached the home of General Edwin A. Walker who also lives in Dallas . . . . General Walker was out of Texas at the time of the death of the President. Had he been in Dallas, he would have been assassinated by the Left that is shouting 'Hate Mongers! Bigots!' today." Du Berrier further bemoaned, "Though out in force, Dallas police never stopped or questioned a driver circling the home of the General who had been shot at on April 10, 1963 . . ." and then skillfully introduced the proscribed backstory of Oswald as the patsy by adding, ". . . by the same Communist assassin who would later take the life of the President of the United States. These threats continued despite the fact that Oswald, the pro-Communist, had already been charged with the crime." It was du Berrier, close confidant of General Salan of the OAS—both of whom are mentioned by Lafitte in April just forty-eight hours before a bullet lodged in the wall of Walker's study the night of April 10—who reinforced, if not helped initiate, the legend that Oswald was a Communist responsible for both April 10 and November 22.

* * *

Keeping Lafitte's exclusive confirmation in mind—that Souetre, Walker, du Berrier (alongside Gen. Salan of the OAS) and Otto Skorzeny comprised a powerful web in the plot and the cover-up of the assassination—we turn to author Peter Kross, who provides additional revelations about former OAS Capt. Souetre, writing that he took part in the clandestine operations at the New Orleans training camps with Gerry Patrick Hemming and Frank Sturgis. Hemming was an ex-Marine who at one time worked for the Castro regime before changing sides. He would later claim that he was in the home of Walker in April of 1963, not long after the shot was fired at the general.

Attorney Bernard Fensterwald, working closely with Texas based assassination researcher J. Gary Shaw, was astutely recognized by author Dick Russell when he published that Souetre, while living in Madrid, met there with the ubiquitous CIA operative E. Howard Hunt. Also attending the meeting was Jean Claude Perez, OAS intelligence chief. Fensterwald's report originated with a seeming credible source, a member of the French police and Charles de Gaulle ally Gilbert Le Cavelier.

Russell's widely published revelation comes in part from a conversation with assassination investigator Steve Rivele in 1992. Russell listened as Rivele recounted that Souetre had nefarious ties to the Corsican mob and said, "I spoke with an undercover officer narcotics agent in Marseille who had been following him (Souetre) for years, and there is no question he was on the Paris end of the drug traffic."

Of course, this brings up the subject of drug trafficking and Souetre's possible involvement. For over two decades now, there have been reports that Souetre was tied tightly to major drug trafficking, but many of those reports are merely redundant and not connected to any credible sources or evidence. Here we shall provide a portrait of Souetre and a history of drug operations based on credible reports—beginning with statements of high-ranking and credible sources within INTERPOL in France: "Souetre's dossier with us is fat with evidence," and it presents a portrait "tied to several well-known traffickers and networks," including "that of Florida Mafia boss, Santo Trafficante, Jr." The same sources said that Souetre's trafficking turned exclusively on "generating the needed funds for OAS and OAS-related operations . . . motivationally not unlike the American intelligence services."

As presented by INTERPOL sources, some of Souetre's drug operations were conducted under his alias, Michel Mertz, and at least one of these operations closely involved Pierre Lafitte.

In early 1964, Jean Rene Souetre rose to a notorious prominence after the SDECE sent an inquiry to the FBI about Souetre and his presence in Dallas, Texas, on the day President Kennedy was assassinated. The FBI had little in its files on Souetre, but the CIA notified the FBI that it had a large dossier on the Frenchman as well as photographs of him. The full content or extent of the CIA's files on the Frenchman have never been revealed despite numerous Freedom of Information filings, all of which have been denied to date. Readers will soon learn far more about the French and FBI inquiries, the CIA's position on information about Souetre, and the Agency's subsequent activities.

The one redacted page (see copy in this book), either from a secret memorandum or a cable dated April 1, 1964, on Souetre that was released by the CIA in 1977 reads:

8. Jean SOUETRE aka Michel ROUX aka Michel MERTZ—

On 5 March [1964], [Mr. Papich] of the FBI advised that the French had [hit] the Legal Attaché in Paris and also [the SDECE man] had queried the Bureau in New York City concerning subject stating that he had been Expelled from the U.S. at Fort Worth or Dallas 48 hours after the assassination. He was in Fort Worth on morning of 22 November and in Dallas in the afternoon. The French believe that he was expelled to either Mexico or Canada. In January he received mail from a dentist named Alderson living at 5803 Birmingham, Houston, Texas. Subject is believed to be identical with a Captain who is a deserter from the French Army and an activist in the OAS. The French are concerned because of de Gaulle's planned visit to Mexico. They would like to know the reason for his expulsion from the US and his destination. Bureau files are negative and they are checking in Texas and with INS. They would like a check of our files with indications of what may be passed to the French. [The FBI's Mr. Papich] was given a copy of CSCI-3/776, 742 previously furnished the Bureau and CSD3-3/655, 207 together with a photograph of Captain SOUETRE.

Bracketed words were initially redacted by the CIA. This page is but *a part of a page from a 14-page document*. Where are the other pages? What do they say? As of early 2019, our FOIA requests have not been fulfilled.

JEAN SOUETRE AND DR. ALDERSON: PRE-ASSASSINATION

The story has been consistently repeated that the FBI had no interest whatsoever in Lawrence Mason Alderson, a dentist in Houston, Texas, prior to the JFK assassination. As has been revealed by several authors, this is not true.

Nearly seven months before JFK's assassination, on April 8, 1963, The Special Agent in Charge of the FBI's New York office sent a brief memorandum to FBI director Hoover marked "Attention: Foreign Liaison Unit." The memo's subject was: "ALDERSONS, 5803 Burlinghall, Houston, Texas. [IS-FRANCE.]" The memorandum, still partially redacted to date, opens with the words: "For the information of the Bureau and Houston, on 4/3/63, CSNY [Confidential Source New York, name redacted] reliable [several lines redacted]." The memo's next and final section reads: "Houston is requested to identify the ALDERSONS, and when this information is forthcoming, the Bureau is requested to advise what, if any, information may be furnished to this source." The memorandum is stamped in bold letters: "EXP. PROC" [Expedited Processing].

About a month later, on May 3, 1963, the FBI office in Houston sent a memorandum to FBI director J. Edgar Hoover concerning Lawrence Mason Alderson and what was referred to as a "New York letter to the Bureau dated April 8, 1963 captioned 'Alderson, 5803 Burlinghall, Houston, Texas, IS-France.'" (The memorandum was also marked "ATTENTION: FOREIGN LIAISON.")

The April 8 letter (actually, a memorandum) was from the Special Agent in Charge, New York FBI office, to director Hoover subjected the same as the Houston memo: "ALDERSONS, 5803 Burlinghall, Houston, Texas, IS-FRANCE." The memorandum referred to a request the FBI received on April 3, 1963, from French intelligence asking for information on the "Aldersons of Houston, Texas." The document provides no explanation about why French intelligence were asking for information on Alderson.

The May 3, 1963, memorandum provided director Hoover with details about Lawrence M. Alderson and his wife, Beverly Alderson, who had been "employed by Humble Oil Company, Houston," with a termination date shown as July 31, 1957. Lawrence M. Alderson, stated the memorandum, "in 1955 was employed by the Harris County [Texas] Tax Collector's Office, County Courthouse, Houston." The document continues: "He graduated from the University of Texas Dental School June 1, 1959. Records of the Tax Collector's Department, Houston, [where Lawrence Alderson worked] contain the following information: In 1955 ALDERSON was employed as a temporary employee while attending the University of Houston. In 1956 and 1957 he had summer employment upon his return from the University of Texas at Austin, Texas. On a June 1957, personnel form ALDERSON listed himself as married. His 1955 and 1956 forms listed him as single. A check of marriage records, Harris County Courthouse, for 1956 through July 1957, did not reflect a marriage record for Lawrence Mason Alderson."

The document continues: "ALDERSON listed service in the US Army from September 1952, to August 1954. His father, James B. Alderson, is employed as a supervisor, City of Houston Treasury Department, and he resides at 8157 Grafton, Houston, Texas with his wife (subject's mother), Edith M. Alderson. Records of the Registrar's Office, University of Houston, reflect that Lawrence Mason Alderson was admitted as a student on September 20, 1948. He obtained a BS degree from the University of Houston on August 30, 1952. His address at that time was 8157 Grafton, Houston. His file indicates that in 1955 Alderson attended the University of Houston during the Spring quarter, 1955."

The document then states that the Houston FBI Office contains no references to Alderson, his wife, Beverly, or his parents, and that the Houston Police Department records "were negative on the subject." The document concludes: "New York is requested to keep Houston aware of any information that [three words redacted] may furnish regarding the subject. Verification of the subject's military service and also his educational records while at the University of Texas are being left to the discretion of the New York Office."

On May 20, 1963, the FBI's Special Agent in Charge sent a memorandum to director Hoover, subject: Lawrence Mason Alderson, but also bearing Jean Rene Souetre's CIA assigned 201 file number: 105-120510. The memorandum was also marked: "1-Mossburg," meaning a copy went to the FBI's E. Hyatt Mossburg, a Special Agent in the Washington, D.C., headquarters of the FBI. Copies also went to the Bureau's Foreign Liaison Unit and its Houston office.

A typed "NOTE" on the document made at least two references to the Confidential Source in New York [CSNY], but five lines were redacted, obscuring the paragraph.

The memorandum reads: "CSNY [name redacted] should be advised that the Aldersons, referred to in New York letter 4/8/63, may be identical with Dr. and Mrs. Lawrence M. Alderson, who reside at 5803 Burlinghall, Houston, Texas. *Dr. Alderson is a dentist in Houston, Texas. He reportedly served in the US Army from 1953–1954. Our files contain no information indicating that Dr. Alderson and his wife have been outside the US or have been engaged in any anti-France activity.* [Italics added.]

Despite the fact that the memorandum bore the 201-file number for Jean Souetre, it contained no reference to him.

SOUETRE AND ALDERSON

On March 4, 1964, an URGENT cablegram was sent to J. Edgar Hoover, FBI director from the Legat in Paris, concerning "Jean Souetre, aka Michel Roux, Michel Mertz, INFO CONCERNING." The contents of the three-paragraph cable remain entirely classified and redacted.

Following JFK's assassination, on March 5, 1964, the FBI Special Agent in Charge of the Bureau's Houston, Texas, office sent an airtel to FBI director J. Edgar Hoover, Washington, D.C., concerning "Jean Souetre, aka, Michel Roux, Michel Mertz, MISCELLANEOUS INFORMATION CONCERNING NATIONALITIES-INTELLIGENCE."

The airtel enclosed for director Hoover "five copies of a letterhead memorandum reflecting results of investigation in captioned matter [Jean Souetre] in this Division. Two copies of this memorandum are being furnished Dallas since that office has an interest in this case." The cover page concluded: "UACB [Unless Advised Contrary by Bureau] or Dallas, no further action being taken in connection with this matter and the case is being considered RUC [Referred Upon Completion to Office of Origin]."

The letterhead memorandum from the FBI's Houston, Texas, office, dated March 6, 1964, has as its centered subject: "Jean Souetre, also known as Michel Roux, Michel Mertz." It reads:

On March 5, 1964, Dr. Lawrence M. Alderson, Dentist, 639 West Forrest, Houston, Texas, advised that he met Jean Souetre in France in the summer of 1953. He stated at that time he was stationed as a First Lieutenant with the United States Army in Petette Malioun [sic] a small town near Rheims [sic], France, where a depot was being established. He stated that Souetre was connected with security in the French Fourth Air Force and in this capacity extended many courtesies to Dr. Alderson and the men serving under him.

Dr. Alderson stated that since leaving France he has occasionally corresponded with Souetre. This correspondence has usually been in the form of exchanging Christmas cards. He stated to the best of his recollection he has not, however, received any card from Souetre for over a year. He stated he has never tried to contact him telephonically or by cablegram.

Dr. Alderson advised that he knew little of Souetre's background but stated that sometime in approximately 1955 Souetre went to Algiers and remained there for three or four years. He stated in approximately 1959 or 1960 he received cards from him fron [sic] a city in southern France.

Dr. Alderson stated that Souetre is reported to have married a girl from a well-to-do family from Bordeaux, France. Dr. Alderson advised that he never knew Souetre to be in the United States.

Dr. Alderson stated that a Captain, first name unknown, Letourneau [sic] (phonetic) replaced him at the depot in Petette Malioun, France, and it is his understanding that Captain Letourneau became well acquainted with Souetre. He stated Letourneau was from Texas, but he does not know his address.

On March 5,1964, Mr. Horace C. Harris, Immigration and Naturalization Service, Houston, Texas, caused the records of that service to be checked and no record identifiable with Souetre under his name or known aliases was located.

The records of the Houston Police Department and the Harris County Sheriff's Office, both Houston, Texas, were also checked on March 5, 1964, and no record identifiable with Souetre was located.

Inquiry among airlines in Houston revealed that there is no direct air service between Houston and Canada. Persons flying from Houston to Canada must proceed to New York or other border cities and utilize Trans-Canada Airways.

On March 5, 1964, Mr. A. Crixell, Pan American World Airways, Houston, Texas, checked the records of that company for flights to Mexico City during the period November 22 through November 30, 1963, and no information was located regarding Souetre under his name or known aliases. The records of Pan American World Airways, however, did indicate that that Dominique P. Roux and Viviane H. Roux departed Houston, Texas, for Mexico City on November 22, 1963. The records also reflect that John P. Mertz, Irma Rio de Mertz and Sara Mertz departed Houston, Texas for Mexico City on November 23, 1963. These records contained no further identifying data regarding these individuals.

The FBI document provides no reason or explanation about why the FBI had questioned Dr. Alderson about his knowing Jean Souetre. It makes no mention whatsoever about the assassination of President Kennedy.

On March 13, 1964, a cablegram stamped "CONFIDENTIAL" was sent to director HOOVER from the LEGAT PARIS bearing the subject: JEAN SOUETRE, AKA, IS-FRANCE. Its brief content remains classified and redacted to date.

RUSSELL'S INTERVIEW WITH DR. ALDERSON

In January 1981, writer Dick Russell interviewed Dr. Alderson for his book *The Man Who Knew Too Much*. This appears to be the last published interview that Alderson did. Dr. Alderson told Russell that he and Souetre "had corresponded in a few subsequent letters" after Souetre "went off to Algiers—in 1955 or 1956 at the latest." Said Alderson: "The last letter I had was from Jean's wife, who said he was very upset because the French government was giving Algiers to the Communists. That was why he deserted, and went underground with the OAS."

Alderson told Russell that almost immediately after the Kennedy assassination, he received a visit from two FBI agents, "who were very vague about their purpose in seeing him." Following this visit, Alderson recounted that he "noticed he was under surveillance." He told Russell, "I could hear them on the telephone, see them out in the alley. It didn't really bother me—I did it for two years in France—but I didn't know what the heck it was about."

About a month after the FBI first visited him, Alderson said, "the FBI dropped by again." Writes Russell: "After considerable hedging, Alderson was told that they had traced him to Souetre 'through a Christmas card I'd sent that was undelivered a few years before that. They admitted they had been observing me, and taped my telephone, for nearly a month.'"

(Of course, as readers are now aware, the FBI had been digging into the Aldersons' lives and backgrounds for nearly ten months, seven of them before the assassination occurred.)

Russell continues: "The agents informed Alderson that they were investigating the Kennedy assassination. They told me that Souetre was in Dallas that day, *and was flown out that afternoon by a private pilot. As far as they were concerned, in a government plane.* They said Jean was a very questionable character, a freelance soldier of fortune. They had known he was in the United States, and had traced him as far as Dallas the day before the assassination. They kept saying, 'If he contacts you, we want to talk to him. And he can lay the ground rules. We don't care where he is, or what country it's in. You be a go-between.' In other words, they were not saying he killed Kennedy. Because at that point, everyone was totally convinced it was Oswald. But they sure wanted to talk [to] him, anywhere, anytime. I told them truthfully that I hadn't seen Jean in years, and that's where the matter ended."

As the FBI agents who spoke with Alderson remarked, this plane, part of a CIA proprietary, was technically a "government plane." According to Lafitte, the private plane that carried Souetre from Dallas was piloted by Joseph Silverthorne.

THE PILOT

/Nov 22/

Willoughby backup

team [the word team has a strike through] squad- tech

building-- phone booth/bridge

O says turn them.

Silverthorne-

Ft. Worth

-Airport

Mexico

—Lafitte datebook, November 15

Silverthorne, a long-mysterious name that also appears in William Harvey's infamous, handwritten QJ/WIN notes, is Joseph "Joe" Silverthorne, a former member of the OSS and a CIA asset who had the wide reputation of being an incredibly daring bush and cargo pilot, and an occasional and trusted assassin. Silverthorne flew over 250 flights for United Fruit Co. in the 1950s. He traveled "for a certain federal agency" to "countless countries" for "reasons best left unsaid." He said: "Bill Harvey was my friend; I never made fun of him. You don't do that with friends." (Albarelli's Florida interview with Silverthorne.)

* * *

On March 9, 1964, the FBI's S. J. Papich sent a memorandum to FBI official D.J. Brennan bearing the subject "JEAN SOUETRE, INFORMATION CONCERNING." The memo's first line states: "Reference is made to cable from Legat, Paris, dated March, 1964." (Legat, Paris is the FBI representative in the US Embassy in Paris.) The memo continues: "With regard to information in CIA files concerning the subject [Souetre], Mrs. Jane Roman, CIA, advised the Liaison Agent on March 6, 1964, that her agency furnished information to the Bureau by letter dated July 12, 1963, to the State Department captioned 'OAS Attempt to Enlist the Cooperation of the United States for its anti-de Gaulle Activities,' a copy of which was designated to the Bureau. In addition, Mrs. Roman furnished the following: (a) A photograph of Souetre (b) A copy of a CIA report dated June 25, 1963, captioned 'Alleged Plans of Secret Army Organization in Portugal for post-de Gaulle Takeover in France.' ACTION: The above information and enclosures are being directed to the attention of the Nationalities Intelligence Section."

The attached CIA report was marked "Secret" CIA Information Report marked: "No Foreign Dissemination, No Dissemination Abroad," and dated June 25, 1963. The report, initially generated in May 1963, bears the subject: "Alleged Plans of Secret Army Organisation in Portugal for post-de Gaulle Takeover in France."

The source for the report's information is described: "Competent American observer from a Western-European in close touch with Captain Jean Souetre, official of the OAS, from Souetre, who expected the information to reach officials of the US."

The information follows:

On 21 May 1963, Rene Souetre,* who claimed to act as external coordinator for the OAS organization based in Portugal, said that after de Gaulle, there would be only two choices in France: Communism or the OAS? Therefore, the OAS believed that it was important to allow de Gaulle to remain in power while the OAS strengthened its organization. Souetre pointed out, however, that the OAS must be prepared to counter a Communist plot at any time, as de Gaulle was an old man and also since he could easily meet with an accident. Souetre smiled as he made this last statement, but hastened to add that the Communists might see fit to assassinate de Gaulle in order to precipitate the revolution.

Souetre claimed that the OAS had a list of the Communist penetrations of the French Government and expressed the belief of the OAS that the de Gaulle government was siding with Communist takeover by seeking rapprochement with the USSR. Souetre particularly mentioned what he termed de Gaulle's "chief advisor," Jacques Foccart, as being a witting collaborator of the Communists.** The OAS, according to Souetre, was now trying to penetrate the French army and the Government in order to build a counter force to the Communists within the French Government.

Souetre explained that the OAS intended to prevent a Communist takeover at the Post-de Gaulle election by the expedient of preventing the election from taking place.

*Headquarters [CIA] Comment: Information from both press and official French sources indicates that Souetre is the name of a former French army captain who escaped from a detention camp in 1961. Subsequent to his escape he was alleged to have been involved in an assassination attempt against de Gaulle. Souetre was born 15 October 1930, in the Gironde Department of France.

** Headquarters Comment: Jacques Foccart is the Secretary General to the Presidency for African and Malagasy Affairs. He also has an undetermined role in intelligence matters probably derived from the fact that from 1958 to 1959 he was acting as technical advisor on security and intelligence matters to the President. One of his responsibilities is believed to concern political action in Black Africa, and another that of collating and digesting for the President the intelligence reports from the various French Services.

Some readers may be aware that in 1963, Jane Roman was the senior liaison officer with the CIA's Counterintelligence Staff at CIA headquarters in Washington, D.C. The Agency's Counterintelligence Staff was headed by James Jesus Angleton. Historian Jefferson Morley has written that Roman's CIA position as senior liaison officer "set her apart" from many CIA officials and that, because of her position, she was most likely a person who "might have information about the assassination story" that had never been shared with anyone. That she was the person at the CIA to disseminate information about Jean Souetre is certainly significant. She was also widely noted for having handled some of the CIA's early files on Lee Harvey Oswald. Jane Roman was married to Howard Edgar Roman, also a CIA official, former OSS officer, and a very close friend to Allen Dulles, CIA director. Howard Roman ostensibly resigned from his Agency position in 1962 so that he could work with DCI Dulles on his book, *The Craft of Intelligence*, published in 1963, elaborated on in the essay found in the appendix of this book. Morley and others have noted that Howard Roman, as Dulles's research assistant on the book, "was with Dulles at the moment" on November 22, 1963, "when Dulles heard of JFK's assassination." Prior to his resignation, Roman, a Harvard graduate, had been an expert on the Soviet Union. At Harvard, he received a doctorate in German. Jane Roman was his second wife.

(Readers may recall that it was the CIA's Jane Roman who also reported on Ilse Skorzeny's arrival in New York City, a fact that apparently went undisclosed to those who might grasp the implications.)

ENTER THE *NATIONAL ENQUIRER* WITH AN ACTUAL ACCOUNT

On April 13, 1977, David Duffy, a reporter for the tabloid *National Enquirer* based in Boca Raton, Florida, visited the Dallas FBI offices on the second floor of the Mercantile Continental building. Duffy introduced himself to James A. Abbott, the Bureau's Special Agent in Charge, as a British citizen and a foreign correspondent for the newspaper.

Duffy then moved straight to the point of his visit and asked, "What investigation, if any, has the Bureau conducted on a Frenchman named Jean Rene Souetre, also known as Michel Roux and Michel Mertz, who was in Dallas on November 22, 1963, the day President Kennedy was assassinated?"

When Special Agent in Charge Abbott hesitated to answer, Duffy added, "This Souetre was supposedly a former French Army captain, who deserted the army and then became a militant member of the OAS, a French terrorist group. Souetre was deported to Mexico or Canada shortly after the murder of President Kennedy."

Abbott, still uncertain how to reply to Duffy but wanting to learn all that the reporter knew about Souetre, asked Duffy what, if any, evidence he had about the Frenchman named Souetre. What Duffy said next surprised Special Agent James Abbott.

Duffy, a tenacious investigator who favored more realistic and hard-hitting stories than the *Enquirer* was generally known for, smiled impishly at Abbott and held out a single sheet of paper. "Here, it's a Xerox copy, but I think you can read it . . . it's from a Government agency, maybe even the Bureau."

"How do you know that?" Abbott asked.

"It came from a Freedom of Information request," Duffy replied. "My editor gave it to me . . . . We're quite interested in Souetre and why such a seemingly dangerous man was in Dallas that day . . . and whether or not Souetre was the assassin or somehow involved."

"Can I make a copy of this?" Abbott asked, holding up the single sheet.

"What's that?"

"On Oswald," Duffy said. "I'm working on a story that centers on his being an informant for the Bureau or CIA, and that Oswald and Ruby knew each other well."

David Duffy's *Enquirer* story concerning Jean Rene Souetre did not appear in print until about six years later, on November 22, 1983. Apparently, Duffy's investigation covered a half-dozen assassination-related subjects he did not share with Abbott. The *National Enquirer's* cover boldly proclaimed: "Special Section—10 Exclusive Stories: JFK, New Suspect in JFK Slaying—A French Terrorist." The bold letters were positioned beside a photo of JFK with his hands folded, as if praying.

Under the headline "Is This the Man who killed JFK?," Duffy's account on Souetre contained some remarkable reporting that at the least may have made an untold number of the large dailies feel a bit uncomfortable, if not envious.

Wrote Duffy, in a full-page article positioned around two previously unseen photographs of Jean Rene Souetre, whom Duffy tracked down in France and interviewed, the new suspect in JFK's death was Jean Souetre, "a notorious French terrorist" who was "in Dallas the day Kennedy was shot" and "was reportedly deported from the US under mysterious circumstances just 48 hours after the assassination."

Continued the article:

> Incredibly, in the 20 years since JFK's death, Souetre's name has never popped up in any report on the assassination, including the official Warren Commission report! Yet the *Inquirer* [*sic*] tracked down and questioned Souetre. And while he denied any involvement in the assassination, he admitted he believes there was a "French connection" in the case. Souetre said he has learned that a vicious French criminal named Michel Mertz was in Dallas the day JFK was shot and "may well have been involved."

The article then aptly states: "But incredibly, Michel Mertz is an alias Souetre himself had used, according to the FBI."

DUFFY TALKS TO DR. ALDERSON

Of special interest to us here is Duffy's writing about Dr. Lawrence Alderson. Duffy writes:

> The FBI apparently knew Souetre may have been involved in JFK's death. They tailed one of his former friends, Dr. Lawrence [*sic*] of Houston, "for a month" after the tragedy, Alderson told the *ENQUIRER*. "When the FBI finally came to interview me (about six weeks after the assassination), they told me they had traced Souetre to Dallas a day before the assassination and lost him," said Alderson, a dentist. "They told me they felt Souetre had either killed JFK or knew who had done it. And they wanted to know who in Washington had had him flown out of Dallas." Dr. Alderson said he met Souetre in 1953 in France while he was serving in the US Army and Souetre was a French Air Force officer.
>
> "But the last time I saw was in 1954," Alderson said. "Later he dropped out of sight and joined the OAS."
>
> Dr. Alderson said he volunteered in 1977 to tell the House Assassinations Committee "everything I knew about Souetre" but incredibly they never talked to him.

Duffy's article continues: "Yet that very same year [1977], Souetre's name popped up again in an FBI memo from the head of the Dallas FBI office [Abbott] to the

FBI director. The heavily censored memo—obtained by the *Enquirer*—says someone [name deleted] 'wanted to know what investigations, if any, the Bureau conducted on Jean Souetre . . . who was supposedly located in Dallas, Texas on 11/22/63, the day President Kennedy was assassinated.'"

THE *ENQUIRER* AND BERNARD FENSTERWALD

David Duffy's work on his article was thorough. Somewhere along the line of his research and interviews, he came across information about a Washington, D.C.-based attorney named Bernard Fensterwald. Wrote Duffy:

> The *Enquirer* working with top experts on the assassination and once clas-sified data obtained under the Freedom of Information Act, managed to penetrate the thick shield of silence surrounding Souetre. But the U.S. government has now blocked efforts to find out exactly how much intelligence agencies know about Souetre's role in the 1963 assassination.
>
> Prominent Washington attorney Bernard Fensterwald Jr. unsuccess-fully sued for release of all other U.S. intelligence documents mentioning Souetre. In his court papers Fensterwald cited evidence of a "French con-nection" he had turned up in released CIA and FBI documents plus information he'd personally obtained from French intelligence sources.
>
> "We may have found the actual killer—and that man is still alive and available for questioning," declared Fensterwald, executive director of the Committee to Investigate Assassinations and former counsel to various Senate sub-committees for 12 years.

Attorney Fensterwald told the *Enquirer* that court papers he had filed reflected that Dr. Alderson had told him that "he had been visited by the FBI" and that FBI agents had told him that they "felt Souetre had either killed JFK or knew who had done it."

Reads Duffy's article: "Souetre himself admitted to the Enquirer he was once a major suspect in a 1962 assassination attempt on de Gaulle. And according to [Fensterwald's] court papers, 'All indications are that Souetre was a trained and experienced terrorist and perfectly capable of murder.'"

The article continued and asked: "But why would Souetre want to kill JFK? 'Next to de Gaulle, the OAS despised Kennedy the most,' Fensterwald's court document points out. 'As a U.S. Senator he (Kennedy) made long and passionate speeches in favor of Algerian independence. He quashed every attempt by the

CIA and the U.S. military to aid the OAS in their fight to keep Algeria French . . . they (the OAS) hated him (Kennedy) with a passion.'"

Concluded the article: "Today Souetre runs a casino in the town of Divonne-les-Bains in France. When the *Enquirer* contacted him there, Souetre admitted he was once a suspect in the assassination attempt on de Gaulle but denied he had any part in the JFK assassination. Souetre insisted he wasn't in Dallas on the day of the killing—but he said he has learned that another French military officer who looks like him was there that day. To this day neither the Warren Commission nor any other official panel probing JFK's death has ever mentioned Souetre or a possible 'French connection' in the case."

The *Enquirer* ended its article with a somewhat sensational quote from Richard Sprague, the former director and chief counsel of the [House Select Committee on Assassinations], which had closed up shop in 1979. Said Sprague: "Neither the FBI nor CIA ever pointed out that [the French connection and Jean Souetre] was an area they had made any inquiry on or checked into. If I were still probing the assassination today, it's certainly something I'd want to investigate."

Following the Warren Commission by about fifteen years, The House Select Committee on Assassinations (HSCA) had been authorized by Congress to investigate the murders of President Kennedy and Martin Luther King. Richard Sprague was its first chief counsel, and after knocking heads with the CIA, he was forced to resign. Robert Blakey took over his job. The HSCA's final report of the JFK assassination found that Kennedy "was probably killed as a result of a conspiracy."

In 2003, Blakey said: "I now no longer believe anything the [CIA] told the committee any further than I can obtain substantial corroboration for it from outside the Agency for its veracity." The HSCA issued a report titled *Oswald, the CIA, and Mexico City,* also cited as the "Lopez report." The report raised a number of interesting issues concerning Oswald's second visit to Mexico but failed to mention the possibility of his first and made no mention of the French connection in any regard, including any attempt to assassinate de Gaulle in Mexico.

SHAW'S INTERVIEW WITH DR. ALDERSON, 1977

A highly respected member of the first generation of researchers, and considered by most as a leading authority on the assassination, J. Gary Shaw's pursuit of the trail left by newly released records of the arrests of men identified as *Jean Souetre,*

Michel Roux, Michael Mertz in the first forty-eight hours of the assassination led
him to Dr. Alderson. By October 1977, Shaw was on the phone interviewing the
Houston dentist about his friend since the 1950s, Jean Souetre. Pleasantries
aside, Shaw launched in:

GS: I won't take but a minute, but I'm an architect, as the girl has probably told
you, in Cleburne, Texas. But among the things that I do as a maybe hobby,
is looking into the events surrounding November 22, 1963, and the killing
of President Kennedy. One of the things I learned just recently is that a fellow by the name of Jean Souetre, who's a Frenchman, knew you or received
mail from you and he was in Dallas . . . in Ft. Worth on the morning, and
in Dallas that afternoon, and was later on expelled from the United States
for reasons as of yet unknown.

Dr: How did you find this out?

GS: From a CIA document that was recently declassified. You've probably been
reading somewhat about this. My interest lies in a photograph I have of Souetre and . . .

Dr: Swetra . . . [pronouncing]

GS: How is it?

Dr: Swetra . . .

GS: Swetra, okay . . . and see if I could identify it as it being he. Could you help
with that?

Dr: Sure. Be happy to.

GS: Okay. Maybe you could even give me a little information about his, I don't
know how well you knew him or anything.

Dr: Very well.

GS: Very well?

Dr: Your information is very correct, but there were a few more things involved
but all I'm getting is second and third hand because I have not seen him in
many, many years. As a matter of fact, I have not seen him in quite a bit
before that time but . . . he was flown out of Dallas and I don't know why
and don't know by whom.

GS: Do you not even know why he was there?

Dr: I don't have the vaguest idea, according to the CIA when they interviewed
me, he was on his way to see me. I don't know how they knew this or I don't
know whether they had even come in contact with him.

GS: What kind of individual was he?

Dr: I don't know, it's hard to explain. He's a career soldier. From what I can
gather he was in the French Underground Movement in Algiers. I do know
he did leave the French Air Force. When I knew him I was a Security

Officer with him in France and lived with him. So, I knew him quite well. He was very well educated. He was very outgoing, forward, dynamic. He was from a very poor family therefore, in France you don't have a thing if you're from a poor family unless you have a military career behind you.

GS: Right.

Dr: So, he was very interested in this and this was why I never did really understand why he left it. But he very definitely left, I presume, his wife . . . I have not heard from her in, well, many years. She was a very well-to-do, beautiful, Southern French wine-family type situation. And the last time I heard, I heard from her and she was the one that had told me that he had left the French Army and had gone into the underground trying to save Algiers. So evidently he was rather committed or felt committed to leave his career, which was the only career he had. *And the next time I heard from him, quite truthfully, was when the CIA, or the FBI rather, had me tailed for about two months following the investigation. And I knew I was being trailed and followed.* [Italics added.]

GS: And didn't know why?

Dr: And didn't know why. It got interesting after a while, and they finally called and made their show and came in and interviewed me and they were trying to find Jean under any circumstances under any conditions. They just wanted to talk and, you know, and I never heard from him.

GS: Right. What did he look like? Do you . . . can you give me just a . . .

Dr: He was good-looking, tall, rather angular, last time I saw him. He had kind-of curly hair, dark brown, good-looking guy, handsome guy.

GS: What did he do? Did he have any trade other than professional soldier?

Dr: Not at all, he was a professional soldier. That's why I say, in France, you know, either you're left a trade or left something in life or you have nothing. There's no happy-middle-class-in-between in France. And he was from the lower class, he didn't belong to the happy-middle in-between class which didn't exist, so that is why his whole life was French Air Force. And he was a very prominent upcoming French Security Officer. When I knew him, he was a lieutenant.

GS: Well, it's a strange set of circumstances. I'll read you the dispatch if you like.

Dr: I'd be interested in seeing it. If you want me to look at a picture, I'd be happy to identify a picture for you.

GS: Okay.

Dr: I'd be interested in seeing it. I've never heard from the investigation, except I contacted the, I guess, defunct Committee that doesn't exist anymore or, whether they do exist I really don't know, they've been through so much hassle the last year or so.

GS: Right.

Dr: *They felt that Jean knew who or he himself had assassinated Kennedy. And what they wanted to know was who in Washington [D.C.] had him flown out of Dallas.* [Italics added.]

GS: You don't know?

Dr: I don't have the vaguest idea.

GS: Well, it's a strange affair. When I saw your name and saw that you were still in Houston, I felt the best thing to do was call. Was it in a service connection that you knew him? Was it in Germany?

Dr: No, it was in France. Matter of fact, he was in the, I don't remember, Second French Air Force Headquarters, whatever it was, in which is uh, just outside of France.

GS: Well this thing reads like this: Jean Souetre, also known as Michal Roux, I guess that is the way you pronounce that, also known as Michal Mertz on 5 March 64, the FBI advised the French had the Legal Attaché in Paris and also the [redacted word] had questioned the Bureau in New York City concerning subject [Souetre] stating that he had been expelled from the U.S. at Ft. Worth or Dallas 18 hours after the assassination. He was expelled to either Mexico or Canada. In January he received mail from a dentist named Alderson living at 5803 Birmingham, Houston, Texas. Subject is believed to be identical with a captain who is a deserter from the French Army and is active in the OAS.

Dr: That's true.

GS: The French are concerned because of De Gaul's [*sic*] planned visit to Mexico. They would like to know the reason for the expulsion from the U.S. and his destination. Bureau files are negative and they are checking in Texas and with the INS. That's basically it.

Dr: *Well, you know you will find another report because that's not the one that was filed. You will find one in the FBI files which was my interview.* [Italics added.]

GS: Okay, I'm running your name down with the Archives. I doubt that I will find it in the National Archives. It is probably a withheld report, because we have not come across it yet.

Dr: *The last contact I had with the CIA was in France when I was working with them. So, the only contact I had in this country was with the FBI.* [Oddly, Shaw does not ask Dr. Alderson the nature of his CIA connections in France.]

GS: I see . . . . Well, you have been helpful. I think what I'd like to do if you don't mind is send you these photographs and let you look at them.

Dr: Are they fairly recent?

GS: No, they were taken in 1963.

Dr: Okay, the only one I had was taken long before that, but he could have aged.

GS: Do you have a photograph of him?

Dr: Yes.

GS: Well, I would be interested in seeing that too.

Dr: Yes, be happy to. Mail it down if you got it. 10600 Fondren, Suite 102.

Gary Shaw's dogged pursuit of records related to Jean Souetre, Michel Roux, Michael Mertz and Christian David, as well as Thomas Eli Davis, resulted in FOIA suits against the Dept. of State, the FBI, CIA, the DEA, and INS under the auspices of the DOJ. Essentially, plaintiff Shaw, who was represented by assassination investigator/attorney—and his good friend—Bud Fensterwald, (himself a plaintiff), took the government to task for failure to perform the search requests in good faith. In February 1983, Shaw v. US Dept. of State, 559 F. Supp. 1053 (D.D.C. 1983,) the court ruled:

> Having considered defendants' motions, plaintiffs' oppositions thereto, the supporting affidavits and the entire record herein, and based upon *in camera* review, it is, this 28th day of February 1983, hereby ORDERED, that defendants' motions shall be granted; and it is FURTHER ORDERED that judgment shall be entered in favor of defendants the Department of State, the Federal Bureau of Investigation, the Central Intelligence Agency, Immigration and Naturalization Service, and the Department of Justice and against the plaintiffs Gary Shaw and Bernard Fensterwald, Jr.

Both Shaw and Fensterwald, without benefit of the evidence revealed in the records of Pierre Lafitte, had astutely suspected that the failure of Texas officials to hold Souetre or possible accomplices for questioning revealed a potentially explosive breakthrough in the investigation into the assassination. Fensterwald wrote of the arrests: ". . . An INS Inspector named Virgil Bailey picked up a Frenchman at an apartment on either Gaston or Ross Street in Dallas. He believes the arrest was on Sunday, November 24, 1963, but can remember none of the details other than the person arrested was French, and that the matter was top priority . . . . Another INS Inspector named Hal Norwood received two urgent calls from INS Headquarters in Washington, stating that they wanted

Mr. X (named unrecalled by INS), a foreigner, picked up immediately. Norwood was very surprised to find that Mr. X was already in the hands of INS Dallas; he had been picked up on November 22nd or 23rd as the result of a call from the Dallas police, who had apprehended him."

Not only had authorities failed to pursue their own arrests made in the first forty-eight hours of the assassination—with one spectacular exception, the arrest of the patsy Lee Harvey Oswald—but for decades, the responsible agencies deflected investigations into Jean Souetre and the clues he left behind that would expose the hierarchy behind Project Lancelot.

In the immediate aftermath of the murder in Dealey Plaza, Pierre Lafitte, the project manager of Lancelot, recorded:

> Silverthorne to MX
> (Jean's gone out)
> Rene dit [says] coup de grâce
> Call J.V.
> (JJA)
> —Lafitte datebook, November 23, 1963

> Red Airport [sketch of a box with an X in the center]
> —Lafitte datebook, November 24, 1963

> Canon - Home
> Shells - Souetre
> (November 26)
> W Teams returned FK [FR?]
> (November 28)
> —Lafitte datebook, December 4, 1963

And with that, Jean Souetre and accomplices slipped out of the country. Those they served were never brought to trial, and the Coup in Dallas was a rousing success.

EPILOGUE

Levine will deal w/ Marina e.t.
[illegible writing] / ck
JA
(coded [illegible])
call Madrid
—Lafitte datebook, November 28, 1963

Levine A z-4 z
—Lafitte datebook, November 30, 1963

This fellow Levine is in contact with Marina to break the story up in a little more graphic manner and tie it into a Russian business, and it is with the thought and background of a Russian connection, conspiracy concept.

—John J. McCloy, Warren Commission Jan 21, 1964

After much deliberation over the significance of Isaac Don Levine having closed out the assassination project manager's 1963 datebook, Albarelli determined that, logically, Levine would also close out the investigation. Levine's anticommunist dogma, which would permeate his life's work, took shape prior to America's entry into WWII and thus serves as the symbolic bookend to the foundational chapters of this book. His writings, and in particular his networking—from the sensational Alger Hiss spy case, to the associations he developed during the reign of Senator Joseph McCarthy, and the services he provided the CIA—gave us a keener grasp of why Levine was selected by Warren Commission members Allen Dulles and John McCloy to influence the propaganda surrounding Lee Oswald as a "Commie Lone Nut." It is the political history of Levine and that of a young Manhattan attorney named Roy Marcus Cohn—Joe McCarthy's lead counsel who serves as our foothold on contemporary US politics—that capture the decades-long repercussions of the assassination of President Kennedy and the *Coup in Dallas*. But first . . .

* * *

Ten years after the 1952 launch of the Skorzeny-Meadows oil scheme in Spain, which has served as a significant backdrop to this investigation, geologist Declan Ford, who spent most of that decade in Madrid consulting on the project on behalf of Dallas-based DeGolyer & MacNaughton, was living in Dallas when he and his new wife were introduced to the Oswald couple recently returned from the Soviet Union. Katherine Declan, who also emigrated from Russia, had become an active member of the White Russian community in Dallas.

In the aftermath of Jack Ruby's murder of Lee Oswald, Katherine and Declan invited the young widow Marina Oswald to spend time in their home in the north Dallas suburb of Richardson. While at the Fords', Marina remained under US government surveillance, as reflected in reports for February 1964 that identified Isaac Don Levine of Baltimore, Maryland, as having been seen coming and going from the Ford address.

Numerous stories have circulated about how the conservative author, well known in particular among right-wing extreme anticommunist circles, was introduced to Marina with the intention of becoming the chronicler of choice to write her story. A persuasive argument is made that following the assassination, Declan's brother, Joseph Ford, a professor in California, had bumped into Levine at the home of a mutual colleague and mentioned to him that Declan was living in Dallas and might arrange an introduction to Marina. Another version stemming from the testimony of Marina's first "agent," who was the manager of the Six Flags Over Texas Motel where she was held virtual captive for several days, asserts that Meredith Press of Des Moines, Iowa, thought that because Levine was considered an expert on the USSR, having been born in Belarus, he would be most suited to the task of recording her story. (The reader is reminded that another well-regarded reporter of that era, Clark Mollenhof, was the first to break the story that President Kennedy had sexual relations with Ellen Rometsch, the woman suspected by many in Washington as an East German spy. Mollenhoff reported for the *Des Moines Register*.)

Established here for the first time is Levine's official assignment in the cover-up of *Project Lancelot*—the logistical plan to assassinate the president of the United States—rendering the various versions of his access to Marina Oswald irrelevant, except to implicate Declan Ford, whose professional history was tied directly to a Madrid scheme of the man who would eventually serve as chief tactician of the plot to kill Kennedy, Otto Skorzeny.

Lafitte writes on November 28, long before Levine was formally introduced to Marina Oswald, that Levine would "deal with Marina." He also indicates that he (Lafitte) is going to check with James Angleton, custodian of intelligence files on Lee Oswald. There is also the suggestion that Lafitte means to revert to encryption:

JA
(coded cryp)
call Madrid

Two days later, Lafitte does just that and pens what appears to be code, "Levine A z-4 z."

On December 1, Lafitte made another related note, "cable to NY & Madrid." For the record, in 1963 former DCI Allen Dulles, who would promote Levine as the ideal chronicler of the Communist conspiracy angle to the assassination, leased an office at 630 Fifth Avenue, the forty-story International Building in Rockefeller Plaza shared with British Intelligence as well as a small petroleum consortium that included East Texas oilman Joe Zeppa, an original member of the Skorzeny-Meadows scheme in Madrid.

* * *

Close scrutiny of the call diaries of the former DCI reveals that five days after *Lancelot* project manager Pierre Lafitte recorded that Levine would be seconded to "deal with Marina," Allen Dulles requested that multiple copies of Isaac Don Levine's book, *The Mind of an Assassin*, a study of the Kremlin-dispatched murderer of Leon Trotsky, be delivered to his office in anticipation of distributing the book to commission members.

Dulles's enthusiasm for Levine was shared by Warren Commission member John McCloy, who couched Levine's role as providing invaluable service to the new commission by promoting *the Russian connection, conspiracy concept.* McCloy and Dulles, who were both at the apex of the military-industrial-intelligence complex during the Cold War, served as "elders" of President Johnson's commission that had been charged with determining the truth behind the assassination of John Kennedy. McCloy's subtle imprimatur gave additional credence to Levine's role in perpetuating Oswald as a lone commie assassin, a.k.a. *the patsy*, a role reflected in the datebook of the assassination project manager.

Naive members of the commission, including many counsel and staff, could be assured that anything Levine wrote would have the blessing of the esteemed Mr. McCloy, former High Commissioner for Germany following the war, consigliere to the Rockefeller banking dynasty, and president of the Ford Foundation and Council on Foreign Relations.

Joseph Finding, writing for the *New York Times*, April 12, 1992, reports, "As High Commissioner for occupied German, McCloy granted clemency to dozens of Nazi war criminals. He freed, or reduced the sentences of, most of the 20 SS extermination squad leaders whose crimes he freely conceded were 'historic in their magnitude and horror.' Of the death sentences handed down at the Nuremberg trials, McCloy carried out a mere five. Of the remaining 74 war criminals who were sentenced at Nuremberg to prison terms, he let many go free . . ." The US military commander of Germany at the end of the war prior to McCloy stepping in as civilian commander, Gen. Lucius Clay, had also helped undermine the prosecution of SS Otto Skorzeny for war crimes.

Prior to America's entry into the war, the Dulles brothers, through the Sullivan Cromwell law firm, had represented numerous German corporations that benefited significantly as fascism and the Nazi regime took hold. As noted in the highly acclaimed *The Secret War Against the Jews* by Nazi research specialists John Loftus and Mark Aarons, after Hitler's defeat, Dulles and his accomplices in the OSS exerted a good deal of influence to ensure that US investments in Nazi Germany were not seized for reparations. In Switzerland, where Allen Dulles was serving under OSS chief Bill Donovan, the German SS was somehow able to buy up a large amount of stock in American corporations and launder the money through Rockefeller's Chase Bank. Senior staff at Chase Bank included John J. McCloy. Soon after the war, arms dealer Victor Oswald, who became a close associate of Otto Skorzeny throughout the Cold War, would be appointed the Chase Bank representative in Madrid. According to Loftus and Aarons, "The operations [in Switzerland] were the product of Dulles's money laundering for the Nazis." The mysterious Swiss banker, François Genoud, identified earlier in this book, was central to the effort.

Within a short time, large numbers of "former" Nazis were being allowed entry into the US via "Operation Paperclip" facilitated by the CIA working in tandem with Hitler's former head of intelligence Reinhard Gehlen and his favorite commando, Otto Skorzeny, in the shadows. As noted in *The Nazi Hydra in*

America by Glen Yeadon and John Hawkins, the primary sponsor of the Gehlen network was Allen Dulles.

DULLES'S VETERAN CIA PUBLICIST, LEVINE

Isaac Don Levine was born in 1892 in Mozyr, Belarus, into a Zionist family. Eventually regarded as one of the more outspoken foes of the Soviets, Levine had arrived in the United States in time to finish high school in Missouri. Following college, he worked as a writer for the *Kansas City Star* and the *New York Tribune*. Intent on exposing Soviet espionage activities in America and Europe, Levine collaborated with his close colleague, Soviet intelligence agency defector Walter Krivitsky, on a graphically revealing story of the horrors of the Stalin regime.

According to extensive research into Krivitsky, available at historian John Simkin's invaluable website, Spartacus Educational, when he was found dead in his Bellevue Hotel room in Washington, D.C. in February 1941, Asst. Sec. of State Adolf Berle wrote in his diary: "General Krivitsky was murdered in Washington today. This is an OGPU [Soviet secret police] job. It means that the murder squad which operated so handily in Paris and Berlin is now operating in New York and Washington." Krivitsky had told the *New York Times*: "If they ever try to prove that I took my own life, don't believe them."

Krivitsky's death haunted the halls of US intelligence for at least another fifteen years. In June 1956, James Jesus Angleton and Richard Helms, both of whom were functioning at the pinnacle of the post-war CIA, had a meeting to discuss the death of Krivitsky. Writer Gary Kern, in *A Death in Washington: Walter G. Krivitsky and the Stalin Terror*, underscores that their remarks about his death are withheld from the public because they are alleged to be covered by national security. Says Kern: "An appeal of this decision to the FBI brought the reply that the material in question was classified by the CIA and one should appeal to this agency. An appeal to the CIA brought the reply that the document was generated by the FBI and one should appeal to the agency. Thus, the memo falls between two chairs, and the nation remains safe and secure." The pursuit of the Krivitsky case seems to have stalled there.

With the end of WWII, a hefty amount of funding from the CIA was channeled to Isaac Levine and the American Committee for the Liberation of the Peoples of Russia during the early 1950s. The ambitiously bold propaganda objective was nothing less than the overthrow of the Soviet regime. Levine also joined the board of the American Friends of Paix et Liberté along with founder Clifford Forster, funded in part by the CIA. Forster, as the reader will recall, was a close business associate of Otto Skorzeny throughout the Cold War. Levine also played a part in QK/Active, which, according to the Mary Ferrell Foundation collection found under the title "CIA Cryptonyms," was "the political organiza-tion and activation of the Russian emigres to secure the cooperation of the peoples of Russia in the struggle of the Western democracies against the rulers of Russia in the postwar era." By 1951, Levine was responsible for developing "a secret program to exploit Russian and Ukranian émigré population that he poured into Germany and other parts of Western Europe," a program that included Otto and Ilse Skorzeny.

As underscored by historian Jerry D. Rose in an article for the *Fourth Decade*, Levine was an influential member of "a group of like-minded contributors that published a regular stream of alarmist analysis of the 'dangers' to the USA of the Soviet Union and of China after its 'fall' to the Reds in the late 1940s." Levine, who would later become a nationally syndicated columnist and editor of the monthly anticommunist magazine *Plain Talk*, was soon very much involved in the "China Lobby," as it became known. As such, he was the beneficiary of the financial activism of textile industrialist Arthur Kohlerg, who made his fortune in bogus Irish linen products being produced in China. Known as the "China Lobby man," Kohlberg, who died in 1960, was the primary financier of what was on the surface an ad hoc collaboration of anticommunist American business interests.

The purpose of the lobby was more defined, specifically to defend and advance the regime of Chinese leader Generalissimo Chiang Kai-shek, who members of the lobby believed was "the hope of a Christian and democratic China." Primar-ily, it was Chiang who could protect US corporate interests in the Republic of China under threat of falling to communism and the resulting nationalization of their investments. Kohlberg was also chairman of the American China Policy Association, with Levine and Claire Booth Luce, wife of magazine magnate Henry Luce, serving as prominent members of his board. Kohlberg and Levine were also the organizing members of the American Jewish League Against Com-munism (AJLAC), as was Roy Cohn, lawyer and counsel to Joseph McCarthy's Permanent Subcommittee on Investigations and Army-McCarthy hearings. Cohn, who figures significantly later in this epilogue, would serve alongside investigator Robert Morris, future attorney to General Edwin Walker and presi-dent of the Dallas Chapter of the John Birch Society.

By the time Wisconsin Senator McCarthy had launched his virulent cam-paign against domestic communism that many believe was deliberately triggered by the 1945 Amerasia Spy Case, he too had become a willing propagator of the

China Lobby rhetoric. As such, McCarthy was another recipient of funding and advice from Alfred Kohlberg. The reader is reminded that the Amerasia case had been pursued by OSS security chief Arthur van Beuren, whose real estate firm, Previews, Inc., would provide Otto Skorzeny's wife, Ilse, a business cover.

McCarthy's search for Communists was aided by Kohlberg's alliance with FBI director J. Edgar Hoover to compile the infamous *Red Channel* book that blacklisted individuals in television and radio. Germane to the arcane aspects of this analysis, an area Albarelli never shied from, Kohlberg was known for playing on the "dark side," planting innuendo and casting doubt on the loyalties of his targets. Blackmail of adversaries was not beneath any within his milieu, which included McCarthy's counsel, Roy Cohn. A close friend and advisor to Massachusetts businessman Robert Welch, cofounder of the John Birch Society, Kohlberg served on the original national council of the Birch Society, where, prior to his death in 1960, he would have interacted with Robert Morris and Generals Willoughby and Walker—all of whom were central to this investigation into the assassination of President Kennedy.

* * *

Once described by Rhodes Scholar and Princeton professor John V. Fleming as a "notorious reactionary if not an outright Fascist," Isaac Levine had evolved rapidly, both philosophically and politically, toward rabid anticommunism. It was Levine who had advised a young congressman, Richard Nixon, that Levine's colleague Whittaker Chambers, a writer and editor for Luce's *Time* magazine, had confirmed to Asst. Sec. of State Adolf Berle that his low-level State Department official was a Soviet spy. Alger Hiss, the official, was charged with espionage. His trial and conviction contributed to the lingering atmosphere of paranoia following the Amerasia scandal, the first major US spy case of the post-World War II era, and set the stage for what would descend into aggressive red-baiting of any who might harbor even the most innocuous Communist sympathies.

After the guilty verdict in the Hiss trial was announced, an exuberant Joe McCarthy officially launched his career in Wheeling, West Virginia, with an infamous speech titled "Enemies from Within." That day, he became the country's most vocal, visible anticommunist, but his personal notoriety barely disguised the wealthy corporatist forces behind him in a campaign to instill fear and distrust throughout the government and the population writ large. Eventually, this thin veneer of anticommunism would be exposed as Protofascism.

Inevitably the Cold War heated up, and Isaac Levine, who had sown the seeds for the Hiss trial with his friend and esteemed statesman Adolf Berle, became a major voice of anti-Soviet propaganda.

* * *

In another example of the far-right backing Senator Joe McCarthy enjoyed was fascist sympathizer J. Russell Maguire of Thompson Machine Guns, dealt with at length in an early chapter of this book. Maguire's *American Mercury* magazine had promoted American Nazi George Lincoln Rockwell, as well as providing an audience for a young Christian evangelical Rev. Billy Graham and FBI Director J. Edgar Hoover.

Maguire's magazine was eventually sold off to a shadow company of Willis Carto, with General Edwin Walker remaining on as military advisor and partial owner. It was Carto who single-handedly brought Holocaust Denial to the US around the same time that McCarthy and his team, including Roy Cohn, launched their red-baiting. It cannot be ignored that Carto's final propaganda sheet, *American Free Press*, provided a venue for a number of reporters and journalists who in the mid-2000s would infiltrate the Kennedy assassination research efforts under the guise of truth-seeking that they sold as being in alignment with John F. Kennedy's philosophy and policies had he lived to serve out his term. In fact, history insists that contributors to AFP are closely aligned with Carto's legacy, not that of John F. Kennedy.

FAST-FORWARD, "LEVINE WILL DEAL WITH MARINA" — NOVEMBER 28, 1963

Sometime in March 1964, after Jim Flahaty, CIA Officer, Mexico replaced Dave Philips, the [Mexico Chief of Station] wrote: "Suggest sending. There have been stories around town about all this, and [Charles] Thomas is not the only person she has talked to. [This was suspected to be Elena Garo]. Wigdail [possibly an unknown cover name] has a little folder which he is putting all the little scraps he can find relating to Oswald to the Cubans; when he gets enough of them I suppose he will try to do a dope piece. If memory serves me, didn't LICOOKIE [This was June Cobb] refer to Oswald and the local leftists & Cubans in one of her squibs?" The Chief of Station also wrote, "Isaac Don Levine is writing a book about the assassination; Wigdail says that the Cuban connection bothers him increasingly as he proceeds in his research. IDL [Isaac Don Levine] had long talk with Marina not long ago in Russian. IDL is Russian Jewish, and reputable scholar—and left convinced that she hiding information." Purportedly, Levine found Mrs. Oswald was a "Soviet patriot" and had "not told" of any contact with the Soviets.

Before advancing Levine's assessment of Marina, and relevant to the task he had been assigned, the reader is reminded of the role of H. Keith Thompson, avowed Nazi sympathizer, who was tapped as representative of the interests of Lee Oswald's mother, Marguerite Oswald. As presented in earlier chapters, Thompson was an acolyte of Francis Parker Yockey, author of *Imperium*, which became the "bible" for the worldwide fascist movement. Why the mother of an alleged Marxist would feel that Thompson was a suitable agent has never been fully explained, nor has the reason for his scheduling her appearance with Hitler's Banker, Ilse Skorzeny's "Uncle" Hjalmar Schacht, on a Chicago talk show in March 1964 been adequately explored.

Indeed, by early 1964, clearly under the direction of those identified in numerous Lafitte datebook entries, and with the endorsement of John McCloy and Allen Dulles, Isaac Levine was collecting material for a book that would concentrate the nation's focus on the patsy, Lee, and his widow, Marina Oswald. According to author Peter Dale Scott, who very early on identified the "arrangement" with Levine that is now confirmed in Lafitte's Nov. 28, 1963, datebook entry, it was Henry Luce's publisher and right-hand man, the seasoned propagandist C. D. Jackson, who followed Allen Dulles's recommendation that Levine ghost-write Marina's story for *Life* magazine. Most are familiar with the fact that Jackson was also instrumental in what was essentially the seizure of explosive evidence in the assassination investigation when he negotiated the private purchase of the Abraham Zapruder film. Scott also reminded us that years earlier, the Jackson-Dulles-Levine team had collaborated on the US-CIA psychological warfare response to the death of Joseph Stalin.

Allegedly, the CIA was gleaning information about the Oswald couple from Hede Massing, "who is known to the Bureau," as well as from Levine himself. Hede Massing (Hede Tune, Hede Eisler, "Redhead" Hede Gumperz) was an Austrian actress in Vienna and Berlin, a Communist and Soviet intelligence operative in Europe and the United States during the 1930s and 1940s. After World War II, she defected from the Soviet underground and came to the United States to work for the Americans.

Levine allegedly told Ms. Massing that he had secured "five letters written by Lee Harvey Oswald." Levine was given these letters by Ruth Paine, but she told the FBI that she had "six letters, four personal, written by Mrs. Oswald in New Orleans to Mrs. Paine and two to Mrs. Paine from Marina in Dallas." Mrs. Paine also had "a note which she intended to deliver to Marina but never did." All correspondence between Maria and Ruth Paine was in the Russian language. Paine had testified before the Warren Commission that she didn't want to make the letters available to them and reminded the commission that although she showed the letters to Levine, she did not want them made available to the public.

According to the Dallas SAC Gordon Shanklin, who reported to Director J. Edgar Hoover, "Mrs. Paine denied giving any letters to Isaac Don Levine." (Note: In the absence of legitimate jurisdiction, the CIA was compelled to relent to Hoover's FBI assuming control of the investigation in the public's mind, and in turn, Gordon Shanklin became Hoover's point man in Dallas. As reflected in an essay available in the appendix titled "Caretaker"—Lafitte's code word for someone he is communicating with and about—evidence points to the hands-on role, pre- and post-assassination, of a member of Shanklin's force on the ground in Dallas.)

The FBI memorandum sent to William Sullivan, third-ranking official in the bureau, from William A. Branigan, Russian intelligence specialist who joined the bureau the same year as SA Bardwell Odum, who had known Ruth and Michael Paine prior to the assassination, reads,

> According to Shanklin on 3-6-64, "Mrs. Paine was contacted concerning her effects as they might relate to the Oswald investigation. She stated that she had reviewed them and that they contained nothing of any significance regarding the investigation of Lee Harvey Oswald. One letter, written about June 5 at New Orleans by Marina, indicates that Lee Oswald wanted to send Marina back to Russia. She said she recalled sometime in the latter part of March 1963, Marina told her Lee wanted to send her back to Russia. She said the tone of conversation and the letter indicated to her that Lee did not intend to return to Russia himself. At that time she declined to make these letters available because they contained a great deal of personal talk regarding personal difficulties both in the marriage of Mr. and Mrs. Paine and in the marriage of Lee Harvey and Marina Oswald. She stated that she did not desire that the contents of these letters be made public and if she furnishes them to the Commission, it will be with the understanding that they are not to be made public."

The memorandum continued: "According to SAC Shanklin [Dallas SA Bardwell Odum's immediate superior], Marina Oswald was contacted 3-31-64 and she advised that she has not signed any contract with Levine to write a book nor has she authorized him to write about her. Marina stated that she has talked to Levine on several occasions about her own background and the background of Lee Harvey Oswald but she has entered into no agreement with Levine to write any articles."

The memorandum goes on: "On 3-31-64 [redacted name] was contacted by Agents of the New York office and she advised that the letters referred to by her were, according to her understanding, presently in the possession of the President's Commission but these letters had been exhibited to Isaac Don Levine by Mrs. Paine. According to [redacted name], it is her understanding that Levine is preparing an article for 'Reader's Digest.'" [It is thought that the redacted name is Ms. Hede Massing.]

The memorandum ends: "It will be noted that Isaac Don Levine appears in *Who's Who in America*. He is a writer, born in Russia in 1892. He collaborated with General Walter Krivitsky, a Soviet defector, who was later found mysteriously dead in a hotel room in Washington in the late 30's. Levine's most recent book *The Mind of the Assassin*, was published in 1959 and dealt with the murder of Leon Trotsky. We have had previous contact with Levine and he maintains a residence in Waldorf, Maryland."

During the commission hearings in May 1964, very rough notes confirm just how interested Allen Dulles was in Levine's assignment:

[I]n hearing Mr. Levine speak with someone on the Commission staff about his ideas concerning the assassination and in particular about what he had learned when he was working with Marina to write her story . . . . [Mr. Levine is no longer working with Marina for this purpose.] Mr. Rankin and I contemplated that the only record of it would be whatever notes I found appropriate to take. Mr. Dulles, however, felt that some sort of transcript would be advisable and therefore at the last minute Mrs. Welsh and later Mrs. Heckman were asked to take notes as best they could. (At the end of the conference Mr. Levine assured Mr. Rankin and me [that] he would be happy to return at any reasonable time to repeat any portions of this discussion which we wanted to put into the form of sworn testimony . . . .)

Also attached to a list of 33 "Fresh Clues to the Assassination." These were given to us about a week before the conference by Mr. Levine. There is frequent reference to them in the attached transcript. Also attached is a sort of biography of Mr. Herminio Portell-Villa. This was mailed to me by Mr. Levine shortly after the conference at my request. Mr. Portell-Villa is the Cuban historian mentioned in the latter part of the transcript . . . of special interest are the following: on page 14 through 18 discussion about the alleged attempt to shoot Nixon . . . about the "party line" page 19 through 20, which I know Oswald was reading to the effect that Oswald and Khrushchev were hatching some deal which would sell true communism down the river . . . At the very end of the transcript Levine says that when the Oswald's left Russia they smuggled "out a message to one of the relatives of the Ziger's who was living in the United States . . . .

The Chief of Station also wrote, "Isaac Don Levine is writing a book about the assassination; Wigdail says that the Cuban connection bothers him increasingly as he proceeds in his research. IDL [Isaac Don Levine] had long talk with Marina not long ago in Russian. IDL is Russian Jewish, and a reputable scholar—and left convinced that she [sic] hiding information."

* * *

Serious researchers of the assassination have long asserted that Allen Dulles, along with John Jay McCloy, led other Warren Commission members to conclude that there was no conspiracy behind the assassination of the elected president and that Lee Harvey Oswald acted of his own volition and was solely responsible for shots fired from the 6th Floor, including the magic bullet from his rifle that struck both Kennedy and his companion John Connally. We now know that Isaac Don Levine was tapped by the conspirators as early as November 28 to manipulate Marina's personal story to convince the world of Lee Oswald's Communist-driven motive.

COAUTHOR'S POSTSCRIPT
BY LESLIE SHARP

Following a lengthy work session in Florida, among the books that author Albarelli pulled from the shelves of his eclectic collection to send home with me was Yeadon and Hawkins's *The Nazi Hydra in America*. While he didn't necessarily consider the book to be a primary reference directly related to the assassination of President Kennedy, it was one of the most recent resources he had been perusing as we wrapped up the book. I was familiar with the material, but Albarelli insisted that it should be considered in specific context as we drew the investigation to a close. He was convinced that the fascism of Kennedy assassination tactician SS Otto Skorzeny, members of the Gehlen Organization, and the thousands of beneficiaries of Operation Paperclip—all of whom had been sheltered and nurtured by Bill Donovan, Allen Dulles, and James Angleton's network inside US intelligence—was once again on the rise. Albarelli had concluded that a metaphorical Fourth Reich was being revamped in real time.

Of the dozens of pages he flagged for me to study, two topics identified in the index of *Nazi Hydra* stood out: a single entry, *Cohn, Roy*; and twenty-plus entries related to the *America First Committee*. What might they share in common, and how might that commonality be relevant to contemporary US politics?

* * *

We knew from government records that the enigmatic John Wilson-Hudson, named on several key dates in the 1963 datebook kept by assassination project manager Pierre Lafitte, was the alleged journalist who conveniently named Dallas nightclub owner Jack Ruby as an associate of Mafia don Santo Trafficante. We further learned from the research of A. J. Weberman and Michael Canfield, authors of *Coup d'État in America*, that Wilson-Hudson had in 1939 formed a version of the US isolationist pressure group, the America First Committee, in Santiago, Chile, known there as The Universal Peace Movement. That long-buried aspect of Wilson-Hudson's history began to make sense of the web the enigmatic John Hudson found himself in two decades later when he was imprisoned by Cuban revolutionary Fidel Castro.

According to the authors of *Nazi Hydra*, the America First Committee was not originally created to help the Nazis; however, thanks to one of the original founders of the AFC, General Robert E. Wood, pro-Nazis from the Silver Shirts and the KKK—whose practice of wearing white hoods had been mimicked by the malicious band of terrorists, La Cagoule—were welcome. The AFC isolationist movement had, in the late 1930s, opted to ignore the diabolical threat that Nazi Party Führer Adolf Hitler posed to Jews, Romas, homosexuals, and "the other" throughout Europe, arguing that America should not engage in deeprooted "conflicts" outside her shores. Tragically, the undertow proved to be a subtle sympathy for—and for some, an endorsement of—the Nazis' anti-Semitism, racism, anti-immigration, and homophobia.

The founding members of AFC, many of whom genuinely believed that the US should not be dragged into a war in Europe, would soon find themselves standing alongside profascist groups wishing to see Hitler and dictators Mussolini and Franco succeed. Parallels of the effectiveness of General Wood's extreme arm within the AFC in creating an umbrella for a racist, anti-immigration, homophobic movement reemerged with a vengeance during the US presidential campaign of 2016.

* * *

Membership in the America First Committee grew quickly, attracting around 800,000 Americans, due in part to the wealth of the founders, who could subsidize the slick promotion for the movement, a phenomenon perfected over ensuing decades. Described by its detractors as *an isolationist pressure group whose original leaders included anti-Semitic and pro-fascists,* the AFC capitalized on the believability of famed aviator and Nazi apologist Charles Lindbergh to assuage skepticism and concern. Just weeks before the US entered WWII, at a rousing speech in Des Moines, Iowa, home of Cowles media company and *The Des Moines Register,* the famed aviator was joined by textile industrialist William Henry Regnery. One of the organizing members of the AFC, Regnery's parents had emigrated from Germany. His son Henry would later found one of the foremost Holocaust Denial and anti-Semitic publishing houses in the US following the war. Other prominent leaders of the original AFC included the Rev. Gerald L. K. Smith, who was perhaps the most prominent fascist clerical of the 20th century, and, of course, Gen. Wood, Chairman of Sears Roebuck and future founder of the American Security Council comprised of corporatists, some of whose international investments had been adversely impacted by President Roosevelt's stated policy against the rise of Hitler's Nazism.

Following the attack on Pearl Harbor, the AFC had no choice: either disband or be accused of un-American activities. However, there is substantive evidence that the fundamental ideology remained a dominant influence over the conservative movement in the US and would surface under numerous guises during the following half-century, the most prominent being the John Birch Society, whose leadership in the early 1960s included prime suspects in our investigation.

* * *

Three decades following the assassination of John Kennedy, the America First dogma was resurrected unabashedly by Patrick Joseph Buchanan, who at the time was considered an extreme-right Republican and who would run for US president three times. His 1992 presidential campaign platform centered on "Make America First Again." Included in Buchanan's defense of what had by then become a relatively controversial ideology promoted by the original America First Committee were the signatures of widely respected Americans on early recruitment posters for the original AFC including Quaker Oats's Bob Suart, future Supreme Court Justice Potter Stewart, and an asst. varsity coach at Yale and future Republican congressman, US president, and Warren Commission member, Gerald Ford.

While he is not a household name, the most significant signature on that poster was that of the chairman of the *Yale Daily News*, Kingman Brewster, who had strategized with Charles Lindbergh to create America First. Brewster would later be appointed president of Yale University. In a touch of tragic irony in the investigation into the assassination of John Kennedy, whose father Joe was a committed isolationist and had influenced John to sign on with the AFC, Brewster would later appoint James Angleton's protégé, Tracy Barnes, as special assistant for community relations at Yale when Barnes left the CIA.

In another run for US president, Buchanan began identifying as a paleoconservative and traditionalist. In his October 2004 essay for his monthly newsletter, *The American Cause*, titled "The Resurrection of America First," Buchanan reinvigorated the movement, stating that "the achievements of the organization [AFC] are monumental."

To his credit, in a piece for the *National Review* founded by William F. Buckley—whose own attempts to disenfranchise the dangerous fringe of his party, the

John Birch Society, had slowed their momentum—fellow conservative writer Windsor Mann summarized, "Buchanan's brand of populist-nationalism is no longer marginal on the right. It is ascendant. A year after National Review released its 'Against Trump' issue, it ran a cover story making the case for nationalism. [Fox News pundit] Tucker Carlson discarded his libertarianism in favor of right-wing nanny-statism. Bennett, who accused Buchanan of 'flirting with fascism,' supports Trump, who quoted Benito Mussolini, the founder of fascism, approvingly [stating, 'it's a very good quote']." According to Mann, Trump made this state of affairs possible, and Buchanan made Trump possible. He writes, "Just as Barry Goldwater's defeat in 1964 precipitated Ronald Reagan's victory in 1980, Buchanan's presidential campaigns in 1992, 1996, and 2000, laid the groundwork for Trump's presidency. His three candidacies exposed fissures on the right and showed Trump that there was an untapped market for nativism, protectionism, and isolationism."

Mann also called attention to a quote that Donald Trump had borrowed from an online account, @ildulce2016: "It is better to live one day as a lion than 100 years as a sheep." We know that it was Il Duce, the fascist dictator Benito Mussolini, who was rescued by Hitler's favorite commando, SS Otto Skorzeny; we also know that it was Skorzeny, captured in a cordial if not flagrantly warm photo with Benito's son Romano in 1960, who served as the tactician for the plot to assassinate John Kennedy in Dallas.

* * *

Although Buchanan's presidential campaign of 2000 was dwarfed by Republican moderate George W. Bush's, his ideology never lost traction among archconservatives and libertarians. So, by 2015, as candidate Donald Trump developed his campaign strategy, the soil had been tilled, and he was able to effectively resurrect the America First theme for his presidential campaign, tweaking the slogan to "Make American Great Again." In one of his first major speeches, which was promoted as a an unveiling of his foreign policy platform, Trump used the Center for the National Interest as backdrop. From the venue of CNI, whose leadership was, ironically, a virtual who's who of alleged "deep state" alumni—including President Richard Nixon's Secretary of State Henry Kissinger—Trump declared that "'America First' will be the major and overriding theme of my administration." According to a junior fellow at the think tank who was fired for publicly expressing his concerns that the real estate tycoon and reality TV show host had been invited to speak, "the speech was more that of a booster rally than a serious presentation." The America First theme of anti-immigration would also drive his domestic platform, appealing to passions of the extreme right with a vitriolic vow to construct a permanent wall between Mexico and the Southern border of the US.

* * *

In response to questions about the 2016 campaign and election, William "Bill" Regnery, grandson of one of the founders of the America First Committee and nephew of publisher Henry Regnery, seemingly appreciated the archetypal role filled by Donald Trump when he reached for a word to describe the effect: "I think Trump was a *legitimizer*," he argued. White nationalism "went from being a conversation you could hold in a bathroom, to the front parlor," said Regnery. His family publishing house, Regnery Publishing's first two titles had been critical of the Nuremberg Trials, and the third was a pro-Nazi book attacking the Allied air campaign of WWII. By 1954, Regnery was doing its part in advancing the Cold War with the publication of books for the John Birch Society. According to CIA agent E. Howard Hunt, who is cited in the Lafitte records, the agency had subsidized Regnery because of "its pro-Nazi stance." Hunt had been central to many CIA operations run by CIA officer Tracy Barnes.

It was Bill Regnery who philosophically and financially mentored what became known in the mid-2000s as the "alt-right." Avowed Neo-Nazi Richard Spencer served as his spokesman. While at Duke University, Spencer had brushed against a future advisor to the 45th president, Stephen Miller, who would later serve as aid to Senator and future Attorney General Jeff Sessions. Together, the two archconservatives formulated the idea of "nation-state populism," an economic nationalist movement modeled on the populism of Andrew Jackson, the senator from Tennessee before becoming the seventh president of the United States, whose harsh policies toward enslaved people and Native Americans are a blight on America's past. Nation-state populism would greatly influence the Trump anti-immigration campaign.

Ten years earlier, in 2005, Bill Regnery had formed the National Policy Institute. The first NPI chairman, Louis R. Andrews, explained that in the 2008 election, he had voted for Democratic presidential candidate Barack Obama because "I want to see the Republican Party destroyed so it can be reborn as a party representing the interests of white people, not entrenched corporate elites." In a July 2017 piece titled "The Moneyman Behind the Alt-Right," *BuzzFeed* reporters Aram Roston and Joel Anderson noted, "Suddenly, the seed money

Regnery had doled out—often in small grants under $25,000—started to show returns. The alt-right became a political force, trolling America with obscure philosophizing, pro-Trump messages, and outright racism, while Richard Spencer gave Regnery's movement of aging white nationalists a clean-shaven, camera-ready face. Since Trump's win, the movement has only gained prominence."

* * *

When Donald Trump was elected president, a number of leaders from the alt-right movement assumed important advisory positions, including those responsible for creating a platform for the "alt-right," the online publication Breitbart News. In a piece titled "An Establishment Conservatives' Guide to the Alt-Right" published in 2016, the Italian philosopher and occultist Julius Evola is touted as "one of the thinkers in whose writings the origins of the alternative right can be found." Evola, identified earlier in this book, was the intellectual and spiritual inspiration of leading Italian fascists, including "The Black Prince" Julius Borghese and Stefano delle Chiaie, who were inclined toward murder and blackmail as political solutions. As noted, Evola was also an early admirer of American fascist Francis Parker Yockey, whose fervent adherent, H. Keith Thompson, would serve a similar role to that of Isaac Don Levine when he became a publicist for Marguerite Oswald. Yockey's writings were advanced almost exclusively by American propagandist Willis Carto, philosophically aligned in 1963 with Rev. Gerald L K. Smith, a cofounder of the America First Committee. Carto would leave as his final legacy the *American Free Press*, where Patrick Buchanan found a well-primed audience.

Journalist and historian of extreme right-wing movements in the United States Chip Berlet noted that Trump's vision of America has been narrowed to focus on and to reflect the ideas of [Steve] Bannon and [Bill] Regnery. Bill Regnery's uncle, Henry, had also published *Human Events*, a journal alleged by historian James Ziegler in *Red Scare Racism and Cold War Black Radicalism* to have been used by the CIA for smear campaigns. *Human Events* rapidly evolved as one of the standard-bearers for American conservatism and continues to provide space to far-right provocateurs including Buchanan and Ann Coulter, who once dismissed child immigrants filmed crying under the stress of desperate conditions imposed during the Trump administration as whining actors, admonishing the president to "not fall for it." Steve Bannon, referred to by Berlet, who for eight months served as Chief Strategist and Senior Counsel to President

Trump, was executive chairman of the alt-right platform Breitbart News until 2018.

After the campaign, and the 2016 presidential election, it became clear that the vision of the original America First and "the destruction of the administrative state," a phrase *Washington Post* opinion columnist Greg Sargent suggests was shorthand for "national regulations and international commitments created by allegedly unaccountable bureaucrats who are supposedly disenfranchising U. S. workers and weakening American sovereignty," had once again seeped into the political psyche.

A FAR-RIGHT ECOSYSTEM SPANNING DECADES

This analysis began with the question: what might the America First Committee and a figure named Roy Cohn have in common, and how might that commonality relate to contemporary politics? In addition to pointing me in the direction of the history behind Roy Cohn's protégé Donald Trump's own version of *America First*, Albarelli's thinking before he passed was also influenced by our research into the history of rabid anticommunist Senator Joe McCarthy and the men surrounding him, including Robert Morris of the John Birch Society, who served as attorney to one of our prime suspects, General Edwin A. Walker. Morris worked alongside Senator McCarthy's legal counsel, Roy Marcus Cohn.

As backdrop to our evolving interest in Cohn, Yeadon and Hawkins had also covered a scandal that surfaced in the early 1980s involving political advisor Robert Keith Gray and his role at Hill and Knowlton public relations and advertising. Gray is now acknowledged as having served the national and international intelligence apparatus for years.

Gray's association with a Korean CIA agent named Tongsun Park, and the Rev. Sun Myung Moon, owner of the *Washington Times* newspaper and leader of the Unification Church (recognized by most as "The Moonies"), led reporters to the George Town Club, a honeypot for Washington's elite. A blackmail operation run by the CIA's Edwin Wilson and Frank Terpil that was being run out of the club operated by Park—not dissimilar to lobbyist Bobby Baker's Quorum Club of the 1960s, which provided a stage for the German seductress Ellen Rometsch—would shake D. C. once again.

As Yeadon and Hawkins point out, it was Nebraska Senator John DeCamp's investigation into leading figures in the George Town Club scandal that bled into what became known as the Franklin Credit Union child sex scandal of Omaha, Nebraska. In his exposé, *The Franklin Cover-up*, DeCamp explained that Ed Wilson's blackmailing was *an extension of Roy Cohn's oper-ation during the McCarthy era.* [Emphasis added.] DeCamp writes, "Gray's associate Wilson was apparently continuing the work of a reported collabora-tor of Gray from the 1950s—McCarthy committee counsel Roy Cohn, now dead of AIDS. According to the former head of the vice squad for one of America's biggest cities, *'Cohn's job was to run the little boys. Say you had an admiral, a general, a congressman, who did not want to go along with the pro-gram. Cohn's job was to set them up, then they would go along. Cohn told me that himself.'*" [Emphasis added.]

Ownership of Rev. Moon's *Washington Times*, which was responsible for breaking some of the more salacious reporting of the George Town Club and Franklin Credit scandals, was later transferred to Operations Holdings, an alleged front company of Rev. Moon's Unification Church. In partnership with the *Washington Times*, in 2013, the far-right media company Herring Networks, Inc. debuted *One America News Network (OANN).* During the Trump administration, as the hugely popular conservative media outlet *Fox News* came under pressure from the marketplace to provide a modicum of unbiased reporting, *OANN* became a clear favorite of Roy Cohn's protégé, President Donald Trump. As a result, and in anticipation of his reelection in 2020, a group of Trump allies contemplated a buyout of the cable channel, adding significantly to the perceived monetary worth of the collaboration between Operations Holdings and Herring Networks and its potential to pro-mote the alt-right agenda in the years to come.

SO HOW DOES IT ALL COME TOGETHER?

Roy Marcus Cohn, identified as one of the most powerful attorneys in Senator Joseph McCarthy's stable during the Senate Permanent Subcommittee on Inves-tigations and the ensuing Army-McCarthy hearings—and Robert Morris of the Senate Internal Security Subcommittee, who would later become a senior execu-tive of the John Birch Society—each epitomized the philosophical argument that the only bulwark against the scourge of the Earth, communism, was unregulated capitalism functioning in league with a fully sympathetic and compliant govern-ment apparatus, the generally accepted definition of *fascism.*

In the early 1950s, Cohn had caught the eye of FBI Director J. Edgar Hoover, who soon recommended the twenty-four-year-old attorney to his personal friend, Joe McCarthy, to fill the role of his chief counsel. For assistant counsel, McCar-thy fulfilled another request, that of his good friend Joseph P. Kennedy, who was looking for a spot for his young and restless son, Robert F. Kennedy. McCarthy designated RFK as assistant counsel to his committee, working alongside Hoover's professional protégé, Roy Cohn, who is alleged to have later served on the board of Permindex at the same time as Clay LaVerne Shaw, the target of the Jim Garrison investigation into the assassination of Bobby Kennedy's brother.

Perhaps concerned for his political future as a liberal Democrat, or perhaps out of genuine disgust, Kennedy began to object to the aggression with which the committee, especially Cohn, was pursuing intelligence on suspected Communists. He would eventually resign his duties as minority counsel, and although he managed to maintain a cordial relationship with McCarthy in deference to his father, a seismic rift developed between him and McCarthy's counsel, Roy Cohn, one that would fester for a decade. When Robert took over the reins at the Justice Department in 1961, Cohn's close association with FBI Director Hoover factored into the acrimony caused by Kennedy's shift of focus from domestic surveillance to organized crime. RFK's decision hampered Hoover's obsession with a young minister and Black activist, Martin Luther King, Jr. whom he had been spying on, and set the stage for what would become a virtual standoff between the attorney general and the director of domestic intelligence. After the assassination of Bobby Kennedy's brother, Hoover was free to pursue his fixation with King, and, brazenly, his bureau initiated attempts to blackmail the unflinching, charismatic leader of the civil rights movement.

In a stroke of synchronicity in September 1963, just weeks after suspected East German spy and seductress Ellen Rometsch was quietly shipped out of the US, Roy Cohn was indicted in the Southern District of New York with the blessing of Attorney General Robert Kennedy. US Attorney Robert Morgenthau, a good friend of the Kennedy family and an early appointee of President John Kennedy, had been aggressively investigating Cohn since taking office in 1961. That investigation culminated with the late 1963 indictments for perjury and obstruction of justice. According to Cohn's oral history taken by James Oesterle for the Robert F. Kennedy Oral History Program of the Kennedy Library, when Robert Kennedy received the fateful call that his brother had been assassinated in Dallas, he was at home in Virginia having lunch with Bobby Morgenthau to discuss the Roy Cohn case. History records that the call came from Cohn's old friend, Director Hoover.

THE FORESHADOWING FRIENDSHIP

It was Joe McCarthy's legal counsel Roy Cohn, a founding member of the American Jewish League Against Communism with Isaac Don Levine, who would later leave an ethical and philosophical imprint on a brash young man from

Queens, Donald J. Trump. By the time Cohn first met him in 1973, Trump was already in line to inherit control of his father's real estate empire, but it was Cohn, as much as Trump's father, who was a known Nazi sympathizer, who schooled the would-be real estate tycoon in the *art of war* in business, inculcating in Donald his own disdain for democratic government and its institutions. In the estimation of British historian Eric Hobsbawm, author of *Uncommon People: Resistance, Rebellion and Jazz*, Cohn made his legal and political career "in a milieu where money and power override rules and law—indeed where the ability to get, and get away with, what lesser citizens cannot, is what proves membership of an elite." In an interview for their July 1981 issue, Cohn told *Penthouse* magazine, "I decided long ago to make up my own rules."

When Trump's ambitious Manhattan project, Trump International Hotel and Tower located at 721 Fifth Ave.—rumored to have served to elevate what was a fairly sketchy reputation within the real estate community—was threatened by a city-wide concrete strike, Cohn exploited his associations with certain New York crime families to "maneuver around" the union that threatened the remake of the former headquarters of Gulf and Western Company. Until the relationship abruptly ended with a diagnosis of AIDS, Roy Cohn had, for thirteen years, nurtured a symbiosis with his protégé by helping make Donald richer than even Fred Trump had anticipated, at least on paper.

As a side note, the original Gulf and Western building had been designed by famed architect Philip Johnson and up-and-coming Dallas architect Thomas Stanley, who, as the reader will recall, moved into the anchor space of his new building in the Oak Lawn area of Dallas in the spring of 1963. As designer and landlord of Oak Lawn Plaza, Stanley had leased offices to Previews, Inc., the firm that provided cover to Ilse Skorzeny as she maneuvered into place Otto's primary players in the assassination. Existentially, and in what Albarelli refers to as "high strangeness and synchronicity," the core of the Trump Tower structure in Manhattan, which became a bastion of controversial global wheelers and dealers, can be traced to the core of Oak Lawn Plaza and the offices of Previews Inc. and at least one individual responsible for preparations for the November 22, 1963, assassination of John Kennedy.

PRELIMINARY CONCLUSIONS

During lengthy debates over the rise of the alternative right being led by Donald Trump, the possibility of authoritarianism similar to pre-World War II was a logical extension of our research into a similarly volatile period of the early 1960s. The question arose: why, unlike the 1960s, when leading conservatives like William Buckley disavowed fringe elements—especially the John Birch movement—had leaders of the GOP in 2016–2018 failed to intercede before another, stronger fringe element could split the country, perhaps irrevocably this time?

The question was perplexing, to say the least. The possibility of extreme pressure on key players was an obvious answer, and that possibility led naturally to the question of the ultimate pressure, blackmail. In light of the many national scandals that dominated the nation's news cycles during the campaign of 2016, in the context of political blackmail, one in particular warranted attention. A sensational child sex trafficking case had been exposed in Florida in 2005 with New York financial investor and sybarite, Jeffrey Epstein, at the center. Suspicion that the cameras and film equipment scattered throughout his various enclaves were focused as much on his high-powered guests, including political leaders and influencers, as his underage victims, the possibility of tried-and-true blackmail could not be easily set aside. Had Epstein perfected the playbook developed over the decades by fascist regimes and employed by Americans like Kohlberg, Hoover, Cohn, Gray, and GOP consultant and "dirty trickster" Roger Stone? And if so, on whose behalf? In future, researchers and reporters will discover, or disavow, this speculation in the months and years to come.

* * *

Other parallels of the Trump campaign and administration, juxtaposed with the rise of authoritarianism throughout history, included the rhetoric at campaign rallies and media events that persisted through the first three years of his administration, giving rise for additional concern. The dynamics in motion were reminiscent of the isolationist, nationalistic, anti-immigration America First Committee, the McCarthy era, the John Birch Society of the 1960s, whose platform of limited government was code for segregation and unregulated capitalism, and the Tea Party movement of the 2000s, which in retrospect was a harbinger for Qanon, a phenomenon yet to be fully understood.

But as we considered the possibility that key influencers within the GOP might have been blackmailed to silence genuine opposition to the Trump platform, and as we reviewed the turmoil that was unfolding across the country during 2017 and 2018 and stratagems that could lead to the reelection of President Trump, the pervading premise of Yeadon and Hawkins's *Nazi Hydra*—that Nazism with all the attendant dark arts, more than any other system of modern governing, would best serve unrestrained and unfettered capitalism and racial superiority—took on alarming significance.

EXTREME RIGHT ADVISORS AND EXECUTORS

With decades of Roy Cohn's business and political tutelage under his belt, NY business entrepreneur and would-be president Donald Trump had been able to attract a seasoned group of political campaign strategists, among them Roger Stone. As a young legislator, future president Richard Nixon had been a member of the House Un-American Activities Committee and had engaged directly with Roy Cohn, who would eventually introduce Nixon's "dirty trickster" Roger Stone to Donald Trump.

Stone, who not only readily adopted the ideology of Cohn, but improved upon his tactics to earn the sobriquet, achieved infamy when he was caricatured in the film "All the President's Men," the exposé of the Watergate investigation that led to Nixon's downfall. Stone has long acknowledged the influence that the 1964 Republican Party candidate Barry Goldwater, who was scheduled to challenge President John Kennedy's run for a second term, had on his early political development. It is that thin, seemingly innocuous thread, within an immense series of spiderwebs spanning almost six decades since the assassination of Kennedy, that captured our fascination.

Stone's inspiration, Barry Goldwater—acknowledged as having started the twentieth-century conservative revolution—had garnered the endorsement and support of what was referred to as a fringe element of the party. In fact, the John Birch Society had been hugely successful in recruiting followers and securing votes for Goldwater. JBS spokesmen had included Isaac Levine's mentor and AFC member Arthur Kohlberg. JBS leaders included McCarthy Hearings investigator Robert Morris and Generals Charles Willoughby and Edwin Walker, both of whom Pierre Lafitte identifies as having been directly involved in the assassination of John Kennedy.

* * *

After the fall of Nixon, Stone pursued a Rasputin-esque political career and formed a consultancy firm with Republican lobbyist Paul Manafort, whose credentials would later earn him a brief role as campaign chairman for presidential candidate Donald Trump, a stint that implicated him enough to be among the suspects of the Russian collusion allegations that roiled the 2016 US elections.

Manafort was indicted in October 2017 on charges of mortgage fraud, conspiracy, and falsifying bank records; he was tried, convicted, and sentenced to seven-plus years. Before leaving office, President Trump pardoned Paul Manafort.

In 1980, Stone and Manafort's firm had gotten behind the presidential candidacy of California Governor Ronald Reagan. When Stone was provided a Rolodex of New York supporters of the governor, the only name he considered of value was Roy Cohn. A decade later, Stone joined the presidential campaign of Arlen Specter, who is known by assassination researchers as having invented the "magic bullet" theory that persuaded the Warren Commission that Lee Oswald was the sole assassin of President Kennedy. Fast-forward to 2007, Stone was instrumental in bringing down New York Attorney General Eliot Spitzer, who was destined for a significant role in national Democratic Party politics. That particular dirty tricks operation, which included an strong element of Cohen-style blackmail, coincided with Stone's association with self-help guru Keith Raniere, the leader of a cult he dubbed NXIVM whose tactics included amassing the deeply private histories of his female adherents that left them vulnerable to coercion, if not blackmail. Raniere, who at one time carried Roger Stone on his payroll, relied on funding for his cult from the heirs of Edgar Bronfman of the Seagram's liquor empire, primary investors in both Empire Trust and Permindex, as discussed in early chapters in this book. Bronfman's daughters attained Raniere's highest ranks, and in 2006, one of them purchased a multimillion-dollar Manhattan apartment in Trump Tower.

Ten years later, Stone, who for our purposes represents an archetypal element of the far-right ecosystem that spans decades, surfaced at Trump Tower to ignite the presidential campaign of Roy Cohn's protégé, Donald Trump. He too was later indicted. His crimes were obstruction of an official proceeding, making false statements, and witness tampering. Stone was convicted and sentenced to forty months in prison, but days before he was scheduled to report to the prison facility, President Trump commuted his sentence.

* * *

Resurrecting America First ideology, Donald Trump initially attracted millions of moderate conservatives of the Republican party; but alongside them, not unlike the influence General Wood had over the America First Committee of the late 1930s, Trump galvanized nascent white supremacists, anti-Semites, staunch racist anti-immigrationists, Christian evangelicals harboring homophobic prejudice, and unrepentant cryptofascists and Neo-Nazis, all of whom found

474 Coup in Dallas

themselves welcome under his tent once he descended the escalator of his prize flagship property, Manhattan's Trump Tower, to announce his candidacy for Republican nominee for president of the United States.

Many argue that no candidacy or presidency has embodied what historian Hobsbawm described as *"the ability to get, and get away with, what lesser citizens cannot"* more than that of Donald Trump. Under his watch, the rise of hatred of *the other* and distrust of democratic government culminated on January 6, 2021, in a violent insurrection meant to interrupt the peaceful transfer of power following the 2020 election. Students of 20th-century history, during which the rise of Mussolini's fascism gave birth to the Nazis and Hitler's Third Reich, recognized the parallels between the Weimar Republic the fragile constitutional democracy that governed Germany before the rise of Adolf Hitler—and the threat that a weak administration of the President-elect would pose to stability and the critical repair of America's experiment in democracy.

* * *

Several weeks before Hank Albarelli suffered a health crisis that would soon take his life in June 2019, he summarized for this coauthor, *I think serious consideration should be given now to doing 3-4 end pages that speak generally to Fourth Reich. Rise of—revamped to these times but true Nazism—good way to end the book.*

AFTERWORD
BY CHARLES ROBERT DRAGO

Charles Drago, screenwriter and essayist, is the author of the Introduction to *A Certain Arrogance: The Sacrifice of Lee Harvey Oswald and the Wartime Manipulation of Religious Groups by U.S. Intelligence* by George Michael Evica.

The Jackboots of the Pharisees
Reflections on the Work of H. P. Albarelli Jr.

"I must, before I die, find some way to say the essential thing that is in me, that I have never said yet—a thing that is not love or hate or pity or scorn, but the very breath of life, fierce and coming from far away, bringing into human life the vastness and the fearful passionless force of non-human things."[1]

—BERTRAND RUSSELL

Two brothers are born into privilege. Innate patriotic impulse nurtured by cultural tradition, in tandem with an eager acceptance of *noblesse oblige* to act on behalf of the poorest among their fellow citizens, lead one to heroic military service and both to high political office.

The former's efforts to institute socio-political reforms elevate his popularity among the citizenry he champions to the degree that members of the ruling class come to view him as an existential threat to the maintenance of their long-entrenched secular and religious control systems. They facilitate his public assassination.

The latter accepts as inheritance and moral duty his leadership role in expanding upon the good works that brought about his brother's martyrdom. As a not-unforeseen consequence, the forces responsible for orchestrating the earlier assassination conspire against him and issue another death sentence—one that, successfully executed, achieves the desired effect of permanently nullifying the brothers' reforms.

I write, of course, of Tiberius and Gaius Sempronius Gracchus, tribunes of the plebs of the Roman republic between 163 and 133 BCE. And I take careful note of components of their assassination conspiracies' shared story elements, most notably their *dramatis personae*—certain Roman senators and their action officer, the counsel Lucius Opimius (Facilitators), who served the meta-force (Sponsors) ultimately responsible for the Gracchi's liquidation and described in their modern iterations millennia later by Thomas Merton simply and chillingly as the Unspeakable.

Let us seek clarification from Merton scholar and historian James W. Douglass, who, in his epochal *JFK and the Unspeakable*, so impactfully brought the concept to our attention.

> "'The Unspeakable' is a term Thomas Merton coined at the heart of the sixties after JFK's assassination—in the midst of the escalating Vietnam War, the nuclear arms race, and the further assassinations of Malcolm X, Martin Luther King, and Robert Kennedy. In each of those soul-shaking events Merton sensed an evil whose depth and deceit seemed to go beyond the capacity of words to describe. 'One of the awful facts of our age,' Merton wrote in 1965, 'is the evidence that [the world] is stricken indeed, stricken to the very core of its being by the presence of the Unspeakable.' The Vietnam War, the race to a global war, and the interlocking murders of John Kennedy, Malcolm X, Martin Luther King, and Robert Kennedy were all signs of the Unspeakable. It remains deeply present in our world. As Merton warned, 'Those who are at present so eager to be reconciled with the world at any price must take care not to be reconciled with it under this particular aspect: as the nest of the Unspeakable. This is what too few are willing to see.' When we become more deeply human, as Merton understood the process, the wellspring of our compassion moves us to confront the Unspeakable."[2]

Is it possible to personify the Unspeakable? Identify it by name and face at any point in time? Or is the Unspeakable by nature forever immaterial—as Carl Jung described "the shadow" in *Aion: Researches into the Phenomenology of Self*, a universal archetype common to the human psyche and, despite repression, not infrequently made manifest?

> "The shadow is a moral problem that challenges the whole ego-personality, for no one can become conscious of the shadow without considerable moral effort.

To become conscious of it involves recognizing the dark aspects of the personality as present and real. This act is the essential condition for any kind of self-knowledge."[3]

The moral efforts of Henry Patrick Albarelli Jr. are evidenced in part in his relentless search for and implicit courage to confront the Unspeakable. Hank's place within the diverse roll of researchers of the assassination of John Fitzgerald Kennedy is self-evident. He belongs among the 1 percent comprised of truly radical historians[4] who have refused to contribute to fifty-eight years (and counting) of competing, ego-gratifying, cover-up-enhancing regurgitations of long-established proofs of conspiracy. Instead, they seek to return the Dealey Plaza fire—to define and effect justice for JFK and the countless souls collaterally damaged by his assassins. Such goals, they seem to tell us, cannot be achieved with lasting positive consequences absent the to-date elusive acknowledgment of the Unspeakable in its most powerful human hosts.

* * *

Anyone with reasonable access to this case's legitimate evidence who does not conclude that JFK was killed by criminal conspirators is cognitively impaired and/or complicit in the crime. —CRD

Can the search for empirical truth via strictly observed applications of the scientific method co-exist with a quest for spiritual enlightenment that transcends the left-brain tyranny of weights and measures? Can these ostensibly disparate investigative approaches combine to inform and inspire and direct each other in their treks along a double helix of ascending pathways toward a commonly sought summit?

Hank's voice answers persuasively in the positive. My sense is that he understood this basic truth: absent the application of said symbiosis to our quests, the Unspeakable—and thus truth and justice—will remain beyond our understanding, let alone our reach. Accordingly, he did not avert his eyes when his dogged scholarly research led to confrontations with synchronicity and what has come to be labeled "high strangeness"—some of the scat of the Unspeakable that marks its trail through history.

Synchronicity—defined by Carl Jung as "acausal parallelism" or "meaningful coincidence"—should not be confused with the phenomenon of the doppelgänger—classically an unrelated human double and, in literature, often a harbinger of evil and even doom. What I have described within the context of the

JFK assassination (and, by extension, in intelligence operations in general) as the "Doppelgänger Gambit" finds two or more iterations of the same operation, individual, object, or occurrence that, upon examination, lead to irreconcilable conclusions among investigators that ultimately promote internecine, inquiry-stymying conflicts.

Note, as revealed in JFK assassination studies, the presence, with apologies to crows everywhere, of a double-murder of doppelgängers: two—and sometimes more—Oswalds, rifles, Zapruder films, Kennedy brains, autopsy films, moving images and still photographs, official US government investigations (one producing a lone-nut verdict, the other citing evidence of a probable conspiracy), identifications of Mechanics, Facilitators, Sponsors, et al. The Doppelgänger Gambit, then, is a tactic employed in service to cover-ups and, more broadly, disinformation campaigns. This is not to discount the appearance in our studies of "natural" doppelgängers, which may be appreciated as examples of high strangeness.[5]

Hank was well aware of the numerous assassination conspiracies identified throughout JFK's presidency—none, I submit, more suggestive of the storytelling genius of the Big Event's key Facilitators than the so-called Chicago plot. For sound reasons too numerous to detail here but earmarked for the in-progress collection of my JFK essays, I have concluded that that little drama, ostensibly set to be performed on November 2, 1963, was a designed doppelgänger—a blank-firing feint, crafted in its beyond-coincidence mirror images of Dallas-related components to function as a bodyguard of lies protecting the one true plot from inevitable internal security breaches.

In theory, controllers of the conspiracy's protection components could attribute inevitable leaks of Dallas plot details to the doppelgänger Chicago event that would be intentionally blown close to the target date of the all-too-real operation. The intended, and in fact attained, benefit to the conspirators would be a justifiable relaxation of heightened active threat security measures for the Texas trip.

For one of a score of parallel plot constructions, compare the backgrounds of Lee Harvey Oswald and the alleged Chicago would-be assassin, Thomas Arthur Vallee:

Both were former Marines.
Both had served at Marine bases in Japan that hosted the U-2 spy plane: Oswald at Atsugi, Vallee at Camp Otsu.

Both had been involved with anti-Castro Cubans: Oswald in New Orleans, Vallee at a training camp at Levittown on Long Island, New York. Both had recently started working at premises that overlooked the routes of presidential parades: Oswald at the Texas School Book Depository on Elm Street in Dallas, Vallee at IPP Litho–Plate at 625 West Jackson Boulevard in Chicago.[6]

Hank may have agreed with my hypothesis, given his revelation, on page 325 of his *A Secret Order.*[7] An intelligence official who declined to be named in the book told him, "It's a common ploy with the CIA. *Sometimes there can be three or four operations in play at one time but only one is actually fully planned and intended to go forward.*" [Emphasis added.]

* * *

A brief pause is in order to present a working model for political conspiracies—one that Hank appears to have applied felicitously to his study of deep events. The widely accepted Evica-Drago Model postulates a three-tiered pyramidal structure. At the base are the Mechanics who literally execute the targets. Above them are the Facilitators who, within multiple substrata, design, engage in, and otherwise support the development of the *plot* (in both the dramaturgical and jurisprudential senses) and who are responsible for the long-term maintenance of its security systems. All cast versions of Jung's "shadow."

At the apex, in the deepest shadows, are the Sponsors—the Unspeakable incarnate.

This structure is quite literally timeless. Witness how Facilitators of the Unspeakable's agenda litter the centuries: the Pharisees, whose woes were enumerated by Jesus on his long march to Golgotha; Hindu ideologue Vinayak Damodar Savarkar, who emboldened Mechanic Nathuram Godse to hasten the Mahatma's transcendence; the Anglo-American financial powers that conjured Hitler; the "boys in the woodwork" whose cooked intelligence product nourished the beasts of war in Southeast Asia and whose heirs today summon the dybbuks of terror and midwife the rebirth of the Cold War.

Each of the model's three levels is constructed to include decoys—*False* Mechanics, Facilitators, and Sponsors—designed as shiny, conflicting objects to attract, mislead, and preoccupy the vast majority of well-meaning investigators and ultimately to reduce them to squabbling, wholly unproductive, in some instances absurdly narcissistic[8] *de facto* accessories-after-the-fact to world historic crimes.

Hank had no time for Junior G-men poseurs, for the blandishments of self-anointed leaders of the pack. He was tireless, fearless, and incorruptible. His judgments, numerous and often profound, never were rushed. He named names not with arrogance, but with confidence.

* * *

Let us join Hank in affirming that, in the 20th and 21st centuries, the Unspeakable has manifested, if not uniquely, then arguably most melodramatically, in the vessel known as Nazism.[9]

We are not taken aback, then, as Hank thoroughly details the high-level Facilitator roles (my characterization) played by legendary Nazi commando and Fourth Reich plenipotentiary Otto Skorzeny in the conspiracies to publicly execute JFK and assassinate Patrice Lumumba and Salvador Allende. For starters.[10]

Skorzeny's foul breath drapes like a shroud over asymmetric warfare and terrorism, the strategy of tension, xenophobic/race-based nationalism, and weaponized religiosity as they have evolved over the past century and persist globally to this day.[11] His fervor may be described accurately as religious in nature. As author Peter Levenda has sagely observed:

> *What many fail to realize is that the ideology of the Nazi Party—particularly as refined by the SS—was essentially a spiritual ideology . . . a cult. To try to understand it as a purely political entity (in a modern, American context) is to make a grave mistake.*[12]

The Unspeakable nests parasitically (though not exclusively) in a spiritual landscape. Nazis, not unlike other religious zealots, are seldom if ever inclined to stray from their flock. Let it be noted, then, that those who would describe Skorzeny at any postwar point as an "ex-Nazi" would have better luck in discovering a species of ex-cockroaches.[13]

* * *

There is one sure way to grasp fully the reasons why conspirators allowed the dramaturgy of the prevailing American political system to be preserved even as

JFK was killed at noon beneath a flawless sky before hundreds of onlookers and scores of camera lenses. One must study the 1933 so-called "Wall Street Plot" to overthrow the United States democracy and replace it with a Fascist system in which President Franklin Delano Roosevelt would serve as puppet-in-chief.

What was designed as a bloodless coup was foiled by Smedley Darlington Butler, the widely beloved, then recently retired Marine Corps general and two-time winner of the Congressional Medal of Honor. Conspirators attempted unsuccessfully to recruit him as the figurehead leader of a veterans' "army" that would march on the White House and evict the duly elected president. Butler, who understood that war is a racket, played a flawless double game and ratted them out. A contemporaneous congressional body, the McCormack-Dickstein Committee, investigated Butler's charges and determined that they were based in fact.

You will find scant reference to these events in mainstream history texts. The committee's papers were not released until this century. Lessons were not learned.[14]

Thus history rhymed on January 6, 2021, when a contemporary insurrection-ist "march" on the Capitol got a couple of klicks closer to success before it too was blunted. To date, a contemporary Butler-like champion of democracy has not been identified, and the argument is made that the assault collapsed of its own unmanageable weight and the intervention of a handful of courageous uni-formed defenders. But studies of deep events lead one to suspect that the insurrectionists' masters (none of whom were named "Trump"—a Facilitator, but hardly a Sponsor) achieved multiple, stratified operational objectives, includ-ing a "perfect failure" scenario that serves the agendas of those who enjoy the spoils of a prolonged strategy of tension and significantly benefit from a wholly concocted "the system works" control mechanism.[15]

What the Wall Street-empowered, American Fascist plotters fatally ignored was the value and applicability to their mission of the principle of parsimony—or at least a variation on that theme. As I have expressed that failed coup's most important lesson as it was learned by the successful JFK assassination Facilita-tors, "Why bother to rewrite the play when you can simply recast the leads?"

It was my mentor, writing partner, spiritual guide, and now spirit guide George Michael Evica who first publicly described the JFK assassination conspir-acy as a dramatic construct. He appreciated the event in its constantly evolving parameters as a drama—brilliantly conceived, written, and performed, replete with all the elements of storytelling: settings, major and minor characters, plot, subplots, conflict, theme, and narrative arc.[16]

I am convinced that Hank had reached the same conclusion. How could he not have done so, given his clear, repeatedly shared allusions to the story form's hypnotic, behavior-modifying powers in the rise of Nazism in particular and the historical operations of the Unspeakable in general?

I do not know if Hank was familiar with Bertolt Brecht's *The Resistible Rise of Arturo Ui*. I am certain, though, that he would have appreciated the playwright's Hitler-referencing warning:

> *Don't yet rejoice in his defeat, you men!*
> *Although the world stood up and stopped the bastard,*
> *The bitch that bore him is in heat again.*

Concentration camps and *kinderlager* endure along America's southern border. Evangelicals are perverted and weaponized to become theosophists of a reimagined Vril Society. The White House has presented as the new Wewelsburg; current renovations are decorative. Eugenics, once broadly embraced—infamously in Nazi Germany—as a morally defensible science and valid social movement, recently resurfaced as a political tactic at the highest levels of the United States government. Indeed, eugenics has been a part of the American experience since the early days of the 20th century.[17]

* * *

> "we sang as best we could
> for the sake of those who are gone,
> and it does no good"
> – Richmond Lattimore, "Witness to Death"

After more than a half-century of futile efforts to penetrate the defenses erected around the JFK assassination plot's true Sponsors, I can think of no more fitting manner to honor Hank's living memory than to summon Albarelli-esque courage and offer my own identification of the Unspeakable.

I fear that we who comprise the choirs of complacent *castrati* endlessly reprising discordant songs of discovery and theory ostensibly for the sake of the martyred king have been looking for the Sponsors in all the wrong places. For suddenly, on a fine morning, while engaged in ritualistic ablutions, I saw one, faintly, with features distorted by steam and frothy lather. And I was immediately put in mind of Ray Bradbury and "The Million-Year Picnic," the short story that concludes his *The Martian Chronicles*.

A family of human colonizers is enjoying a lovely day along a Martian canal dug by the planet's long-vanished original inhabitants. Father and son engage in a colloquy as simply rendered and profoundly revealing of theme as any you might read:

> *"I've always wanted to see a Martian," said Michael. "Where are they, Dad? You promised."*
>
> *"There they are," said Dad, and he shifted Michael on his shoulder and pointed straight down.*
>
> *The Martians were there—in the canal—reflected in the water. Timothy and Michael and Robert and Mom and Dad.*
>
> *The Martians stared back up at them for a long, long silent time from the rippling water . . .*

I am obliged to note that, while my respect for Hank's heart and intellect is limitless, I do not always agree with his conclusions regarding certain important, case-related issues. This admission, I suspect, brings a smile to his face in the next realm. He never would dream of issuing jackboots and demanding that his peers and students march in lockstep with him.

I can state, proudly and for the record, that, in my estimation, Hank has brought us closer than ever to encompassing truth and lasting justice for John Fitzgerald Kennedy.

In this essay's epigraph, Bertrand Russell wrote of his quest to express, as it existed within himself, "the fearful passionless force of non-human things." In his fearless, passionate strength and moral purpose, H. P. Albarelli Jr., reaches out from beyond time to embrace us with his deep, fierce humanness.

NOTES FOR THE AFTERWORD

[1] Brixton Letter 33, to Constance Malleson, July 5, 1918.

[2] *JFK and the Unspeakable: Why He Died and Why it Matters*; Orbis Books, 2008; https://www.amazon.com/JFK-Unspeakable-Why-Died Matters/dp/1439193886 /ref=sr_1_1?keywords=jfk+and+the+unspeakable&qid=1566489873&s =gateway&sr=8-1.

[3] *Aion: Researches into the Phenomenology of Self*; https://www.amazon.com/ Aion-Researches-Phenomenology-Collected-Works/dp/069101826X/ref=sr_1_1?key- words=Aion%3A+Researches+into+the+Phenomenology+of+Self&qid =1566491421&s=gateway&sr=8-1.

484 Coup in Dallas

[4] A *partial* list of the small, currently active group of these rather heroic figures includes Professor Peter Dale Scott, Dr. John Newman, James W. Douglass, and the handful of their peers to whom I apologize for my failure to name them here. Among those deserving of posthumous recognition are Vincent J. Salandria, JD, Professor George Michael Evica, Sylvia Meagher, Shirley Martin, Harold Weisberg, Penn Jones, and others among the earliest researchers elegantly and thoughtfully identified by John Kelin in his book-length study, *Praise from a Future Generation: The Assassination of John F. Kennedy and the First Generation Critics of the Warren Report* (Wings Press, 2007).

I must add that I am not arguing for a cessation of disciplined research into the remaining dark corners of this case. Dr. Newman, for one, is all about such inquiries. But chief (my word) among his goals—to the degree that I am able to discern them—is identification of the proven crime's Sponsors

[5] The Doppelgänger Gambit is not unique to the JFK assassination, as the following example illustrates. Writing in *Conjuring Hitler: How Britain and America Made the Third Reich* (Pluto Press; 2005), his invaluable book-length "chronology of Germany's undoing," Guido Giacomo Preparata offers a double exposure of the mysterious May 10, 1941, flight to England by—allegedly—Rudolf Hess. "Where he vanished and how, and what happened to him afterwards, is not known. The [official] story . . . is a cheap myth. A fabrication which neither the Nazis nor the British, or their loyal archivists, ever endeavored to dispel. *In fact, there appear to be two Hesses, two planes leaving different locations, two uniforms, an alleged imposter in the prison of Spandau, and an amnesiac, stuporous defendant at Nuremberg*[.]" [Emphasis added.]

[6] http://22november1963.org.uk/jfk-assassination-plot-chicago For an indispensably broad (if not particularly deep) overview of the doppelganger plot, see Edwin Black, "The Plot to Kill JFK in Chicago, Nov. 2, 1963"; *Chicago Independent*, November 1975. Available at http://www.thechicagoplot.com/The%20Chicago%20Plot.pdf.

[7] TrineDay; 2013.

[8] I cannot help seeing them as a cadre of "Professor" Irwin Corey impersonators—self-proclaimed "World's Foremost Authorities." Jazz critic Leonard Feather celebrated the Beat-era comic Corey's "rambling pseudo-historical explanations to which there is usually some sort of crazy logic." "Did you realize," Corey told his audience at the Lighthouse [jazz club] in 1977, "that there are more Albanians in Hermosa Beach than there are in all of Ireland?" Abortion, Corey explained later in his "lecture," "has been part of the American system since its conception." Alas, his unintended JFK researcher impressions are hilarious but ultimately leave a bitter

taste. The video link here might have been filmed at any number of JFK assassination conferences. https://www.youtube.com/watch?v=-CsdRGbQPr0.

[9] Lest you fail to discern the presence of a Nazi-related iteration of the Unspeakable imbedded in JFK assassination research, I refer you to the recent appearance of an ostensibly deep politics-focused, truth-friendly print journal whose owner/publisher was once employed in an editorial capacity by the organization of the neo-Nazi, Holocaust-denying, anti-Semitic, racist propagandist Willis Carto. When I publicly called him on his Carto affiliation, the publisher first tried, via a ham-handed public relations flak, to buy me off by offering to dedicate an issue of the journal to me. When that offer was declined, and as the spotlight—reference intended—remained focused on him, the publisher scurried to bury his Carto ties by renaming and redesigning his journal and otherwise hiding behind the kill-the-messenger outpourings directed to me by some of his indignant contributors. All of those mouthpieces strenuously claimed that the Carto-related charges could be easily explained away. Said explanations have yet to appear after more than a year of waiting. Hank was well aware of this situation, and along with Leslie Sharp, he joined the small but insistent chorus demanding transparency from the publisher. Sadly, "you should live so long" is, in Hank's case, indeed more than just an expression.

[10] Hank's renewed, unrivaled attention to the JFK assassination-related roles played by Pierre Lafitte (especially) and, to a lesser degree, Jean Souetre and to the naming of additional Mechanics and Facilitators are of paramount interest as they challenge many of us to consider acts of valid revisionism of long-held conclusions. The ongoing, invaluable research and writing of Dr. John Newman are persuasively arguing for precisely such reevaluation.

(Question as case-in-point: Has the role in the JFK assassination conspiracy played by David Sanchez Morales been exaggerated [melo]dramatically by cover-up creators to deflect attention from Lafitte and, by unavoidable extension, his masters, the high level Facilitators not primarily within civilian and private intelligence agencies, but rather nested within the five-sided abomination in Arlington? Or are Morales and Lafitte cast members of the Doppelgänger Gambit road show?)

And while my references herein to Skorzeny may strike some as inappropriately passing, it is precisely because of the comprehensive focus Hank directed at him throughout *Coup in Dallas* that I refrain from further, redundant explication.

[11] As the inevitable defeat of Germany approached, Nazi preparation for postwar survival, influence, and, indeed, prosperity took at least three major tracks: political, military, and economic. Overlaps were anticipated and welcomed as opportunities for expansions of wealth and power. If Skorzeny can be identified as the key player

in military-related operations, Martin Bormann emerges as the controller—the avatar—of Nazi wealth. Paul Manning, author of the highly respected and sought-after *Martin Bormann: Nazi in Exile* (Lyle Stuart, 1981). notes: "In the final days of any war, grabbing and looting are commonplace. Martin Bormann, however, was wrapped up in the dispersal of several billion dollars in assets around the globe. He dwelled on control of 750 corporations; he had utilized every known legal device to disguise their ownership and their patterns of operation: use of nominees, option agreements, pledges, collateral loans, rights of first refusal, management contracts, service contracts, patent agreements, cartels, and withholding procedures."

The darkness, Manning courageously indicates, is all-enveloping: "Bormann is as protected from seizure as the money and investments he guards, for those he has benefited are grateful. Simon Wiesenthal, the famed hunter of Nazis, found this out when traveling to Buenos Aires in search of Bormann. He was told in no uncertain terms by the Jewish leadership there to cease stirring up trouble, and to leave the country, which he did. On a directive from Bormann, Jewish and gentile bankers and businessmen alike are represented in the management of German-Argentinian firms, as well as in other West German corporations."

[12] *The Hitler Legacy: The Nazi Cult in Diaspora*; Ibis, 2014; https://www.amazon .com/Hitler-Legacy-Diaspora-OrganizedTerrorism/dp/0892542101/ref=sr_1 _1?keywords=levenda+the+hitler+legacy&qid=1566486267&s=gateway&sr=8-1.

[13] How do we explain the likes of "good Nazis" Werner von Braun, Reinhard Gehlen, and their Project Paperclip *Kameraden*? you ask. Did they not carry America to the moon? Did they not best the Soviet foe on the pitches of the Great Game? Art, here in the form of an insight by Mort Sahl, informs. The sophisticated comedian and satirist noted that the 1960 von Braun biopic *I Aim at the Stars* should have been subtitled, *"But Sometimes I Hit London."*

And what of the quaint notion of Nazis reconstituted as American patriots? I give you the lines written by William Goldman for his Josef Mengele-inspired character Dr. Christian Szell—as played with reptilian coldness by Sir Laurence Olivier—in the film *Marathon Man*. Arriving in New York from a prolonged and involuntary South American exile for an emergency meeting with his U.S. intelligence officer controller, Szell walks through a crowded airport terminal and to his aging bodyguards venomously observes, "The land of plenty. They were always so confident God was on their side. Now I think they're not so sure."

[14] For details, see *The Plot to Seize the White House*, by Jules Archer. Recently reprinted and available here: https://www.amazon.com/Plot-Seize-White-House Conspiracy/dp/1510734694/ref=tmm_hrd_swatch_0?_encoding=UTF8&qid=&sr=.

[15] How many times have you heard pundits describe the JFK assassinatiion's immediate aftermath as evidence of "our system working flawlessly" and "a peaceful transition of power"? "Peaceful" as in the slaughter depicted in Zapruder film frame 313.

[16] Literati—storytellers—proliferate within the ranks of relatively high-level Facilitator (and False Facilitator) suspects in the JFK assassination. The most haunting example: While an undergraduate at Yale, James Jesus Angleton edited the literary magazine *Furioso*. He published and carried on correspondence with Ezra Pound, William Carlos Williams, e.e.cummings, and T. S. Eliot, among others. At the risk of committing criminal understatement, I note that by the time Angleton assumed the duties of CIA Chief of Counterintelligence, he had become capable of exhibiting at least seven types of ambiguity. Among other professional writers who, fairly or not, crowd the line-up are David Atlee Phillips, E. Howard Hunt, Edward Lansdale, and Clay Shaw.

[17] As scholars Teryn Bouche and Laura Rivard have noted, "Eugenics was not only the purview of academics, and it became a popular [American] social movement that peaked in the 1920s and 30s. During this period, the American Eugenics Society was founded, in addition to many local societies and groups around the country. Members competed in 'fitter family' and 'better baby' competitions at fairs and exhibitions. Movies and books promoting eugenic principles were popular. A film called *The Black Stork* (1917), based on a true story, depicted as heroic a doctor that [sic] allowed a syphilitic infant to die after convincing the child's parents that it was better to spare society one more outcast." https://www.nature.com/scitable/forums/genetics-generation/america-s-hidden-history-the-eugenics-movement-123919444/.

ESSAYS

A WELL-CONCEALED "T"
BY ALAN KENT

Since it became obvious—very early on—that the character whom Pierre Lafitte refers to as T in the notes he created in the course of acting as project manager for the assassination of President Kennedy was a crucial link in the plot, we have all (Hank Albarelli, Leslie Sharp, and myself) pursued the evidence that Lafitte presented to us as a guidepost to identifying this person. I have explored multiple possibilities over months, examining characters of varying degrees of plausibility, relative to the evidence we have to work with.

At one point, author and assassination expert Dick Russell suggested the possibility that T was the elite CIA legend Tracy Barnes. Subsequently, I have made lists of the characteristics of T as he appears in the datebook, and have overlaid this information with various potential "Ts," including Barnes. I have also utilized the valuable insights gleaned from extensive conversation among Albarelli, Sharp, and myself. What do we know—or can reasonably infer—about T as he moves through the pages of the datebook?

1.) There are only two people that Lafitte repeatedly refers to by a single initial. One is T. The other is Otto Skorzeny. Clearly, Skorzeny was both a key player in this story, and a long-time, highly respected affiliate of Lafitte's. It seems very likely that T was a similarly renowned figure in the circles that Pierre had moved in.

2.) As mentioned, T is acting as an intermediary between Angleton and Lafitte. He is also, at times, making decisions on various matters. "T says no," and "T says yes" are examples of these directives. Apparently, T was highly trusted by the ultimate author(s) of the project designed to eliminate JFK. Lafitte, who was a powerfully independent force, seems to take direction from T.

3.) That T acts as a conduit of instructions from Angleton—and is mentioned in the December 5 entry with Angleton ("JA – close out Lancelot – T")—indicates that this person is very close to Angleton; probably a long-time colleague of Angleton's.

4.) Assuming that T is a long-time colleague of Angleton's, and a "presence" in intelligence circles, the fact that he is actively involved in this project is a likely indication that he regarded JFK as did numerous CIA hard-liners: as a betrayer at the Bay of Pigs, and as a national security threat for multiple reasons, which have been thoroughly covered in the historical literature of the period.

5.) That T is available for multiple personal meetings during October and November 1963 in Dallas and New Orleans is indicative of T having some sort of plausible official business to attend to in these cities.

6.) If T was a high-level performer in intelligence circles, his participation in a plot to kill Kennedy certainly indicates a "rogue" personality. Very likely, there would be other indications of him acting independently of formal chains of command.

7.) T is engaging in a complex plot to assassinate a sitting president and is trusted by those who conceived this plot to operate at a high degree of competence. This is probably not the first time that he has been involved in the directing of subordinates who are preparing for a political assassination.

To summarize the picture of T as he emerges in the pages of the datebook, he seems to be a highly regarded, probably high-ranking, long-standing colleague of Jim Angleton, who (like JA, as depicted in several of Lafitte's entries) is confident that he can move outside the formal structure of command to engage in a plot that he regards as necessary to remove a "national security" threat from power, who has experience with the strategy and tactics of organizing political assassinations at a high level in the past, and, in 1963, was positioned such that he could engage with plotters in New Orleans and Dallas without drawing undue suspicion to himself. Of course, T would likely be someone whose first or last name begins with the letter T.

Without delving into the history of multiple speculative attempts to tie these characteristics to various people, I am going to focus on Tracy Barnes. Because a study of Barnes's lengthy career at CIA provides hits on every one of the seven points listed above. I'm not going to attempt a biography of Barnes—something that should certainly be executed by an enterprising historian—but I will cite material that seems relevant to a judgment about Barnes as T. In the interest of clarity, I will approach Barnes from the standpoint of the portrait of T that emerges from the Lafitte datebook entries, in an attempt to arrive at a reasonable position on the identity of T. Or rather,

I will attempt to reconstruct the path I traveled toward the conclusion that T was very likely Barnes.

The data that I choose to feature will be very plainly cherry-picked. I have no doubt that Barnes was capable of great charm. By all accounts, he was a fine husband and family man. In his final post-CIA stint, he apparently did excellent work in race relations for Yale in a role as a kind of ambassador to inner-city New Haven. But in his work at CIA, he was as hard and ruthless as many of his less genteel comrades. No less an operator than Richard Helms considered him to be reckless and irresponsible. His wife, Janet, said of Barnes that during his time as chief of staff at two Agency postings in the 1950s, "Every morning, Tracy got up and went to war." It is Barnes as risk-taking warrior that we are primarily interested in here.

BARNES

Was Barnes of the stature—within the intelligence community, and particularly within the realm of covert operations—that Pierre Lafitte would defer to him in a matter of such importance as the assassination of President Kennedy? I think so. A brief overview of Barnes's career follows . . . Barnes was among a small handful of Agency operatives who virtually defined the nature of covert operations, and of Agency-related political violence.

With an OSS background, and a well-deserved reputation for daring that was made during the Second World War, Barnes's path into CIA was cleared by the man who would mentor him and who would act as his patron as long as he was in power within CIA—Allen Dulles. Dulles met then-Captain C. Tracy Barnes in 1944 and was taken with him quickly, writing to his OSS superior David Bruce: "I have met Tracy Barnes here today and am anxious to get him to Switzerland as soon as possible . . . we can find useful work for him." As noted in the compilation of Dulles's reports from the time period (*From Hitler's Doorstep: The Wartime Intelligence Reports of Allen Dulles, 1942-1945*, 1996, Pennsylvania State University Press, p. 540), Barnes's code name during the time of his WW2 exploits was "Trick," which may be of interest to the reader noting the significance of Pierre Lafitte's many references to "T" in his 1963 datebook entries.

Barnes's first major postwar positions overlapped for a time. During 1950–1952, he served as counsel to the Undersecretary of the Army and held the position of Deputy Director of the Psychological Strategy Board. The PSB came to be in April 1951, as an Army project, designed to interface between the

Department of State, the Defense Department, and the National Security Council, in order to formulate national policy on matters that were very broadly categorized as "psychological operations." In 1953, it was placed under the control of the NSC and specialized in creating PSYOP plans for scenarios of battle against Communism but, as had the PSB, ranged widely in its interests.

The Board's name was changed to the "Operations Control Board," and it lived until 1961, when incoming President Kennedy elected to axe it. "It functioned primarily as a small, but carefully selected, staff operation helping to formulate policy in specific areas of the utmost sensitivity," wrote Eric Chester. The PSB "grew to be a monster, out of control . . . .," said Townsend Hoopes, then an aide to Secretary of Defense James Forrestal. Russ Baker, in *Family of Secrets*, wrote that the PSB "explored everything from the use of psychotropic drugs as truth serum to the possibility of engineering unwitting assassins, i.e., Manchurian candidates." Baker does not source this sentence, but a recently published study of PSB/CIA interaction during this period of time finds evidence that PSB liaised with the Agency in matters related to the 1950s CIA "mind control" projects Artichoke, Bluebird, and MKULTRA. The author of the study notes that available documentary evidence on these relations is scanty.

John Prados, who researched PSB through the resources at the Truman Library, explained the paucity of evidence: "In December 1988, after the author wrote about the PSB in a systematic way for the first time, the CIA sent a plane with a team of armed guards to Kansas City. The team went to the Truman Presidential Library in Independence, Mo., seized the PSB records, and returned them to Washington . . . . The CIA held onto the records for months, extracted several hundred documents from the set, and only then returned them to the Truman Library. It cannot have been the quality of the PSB's planning for psychological warfare that accounted for this degree of concern at Langley."

As is the case with subsequent career adventures, Barnes's work with this strange organization is less than clear. For the record, it will be noted that Barnes's stint with the PSB, which apparently interacted with CIA mind control experiments, corresponds with the time period that Pierre Lafitte was engaged with George Hunter White in the process of setting up scenarios in Greenwich Village in which unsuspecting victims were given frequently massive doses of LSD and related hallucinogenic drugs—activity that was being sponsored by CIA under the aegis of "Project Artichoke," and that Federal Bureau of Narcotics operative White and FBN "special employee" Lafitte had been vetted for this project by head of CIA Counterintelligence James J. Angleton.

Barnes formally entered the CIA in 1952, riding Dulles's recommendation to the Deputy Director of Plans Frank Wisner. Not that Wisner would have needed much prompting. Barnes had worked with Wisner during the 1930s at the Wall Street law firm Carter, Ledyard, and Milburn, following his legal training at Harvard Law School. When, in 1952, then-Deputy Director of CIA Dulles and Wisner placed him at the head of the newly created "PP" staff (Psychological and Paramilitary warfare), Barnes was being fast-tracked toward the top of the intelligence community. The formal title of the position he achieved in October '52 was: "Assistant Director of CIA for OPC," a heady accomplishment that bespoke deep connections with powerful men, people who would promote and protect Barnes as long as they enjoyed positions of power.

When a member of Barnes's PP staff, E. Howard Hunt, once requested advice from Barnes on the most efficient way to "dispose" of a suspected European double agent, Barnes sent him to PP staffer Boris Pash, who was supposed to be in charge of arranging such matters. Hunt later claimed that Pash showed little interest in his request. Evan Thomas wrote: "If Pash showed restraint, it was self-imposed. Barnes, his colleagues said, was willing to try just about anything." Let's keep that judgment in mind as we head toward Guatemala.

The effort by the Eisenhower administration to destabilize and topple the government of Guatemalan leader Jakobo Arbenz was the venture in which numerous CIA personnel gained the future trust of D.C. politicos. It was the time of Tracy Barnes's life. Barnes was placed in a formal position of command of PBSUCCESS by then CIA Director Allen Dulles. By this time, Barnes was a grade GS-18 employee, and he reported only to Dulles's Deputy Director of Plans Frank Wisner during the 1953–54 Guatemalan operation. The story of PBSUCCESS has been told often. Suffice to say that it was the operation that earned the CIA the gratitude and trust of Eisenhower and had the toxic effect of convincing Dulles and his most trusted men that they could accomplish just about anything.

Two aspects of PBSUCCESS that have to do with the development of Barnes are of interest here. In the process of creating the team that would manage to combine psychological, intelligence, and military tactics in the course of persuading Arbenz to flee his country, Barnes brought together an all-star bunch of past and future Agency talent. David Phillips, E. Howard Hunt, Rip Robertson, David Morales, Col. Al Haney, and Henry Hecksher all utilized their formidable skills for Barnes. Several of these characters would later be of interest to researchers of the assassination of JFK.

It should also be noted that the CIA Chief of Staff in Guatemala during this time was Birch O'Neal, a former FBI man. O'Neal would later be selected by James Angleton to head Angleton's darkest hole in CIA counterintelligence, CI/SIG, the "special investigative group," which would—belatedly—open a CIA 201 file on Lee Oswald a year after he had defected to the Soviet Union. If Oswald was being handled as a "vest pocket" operation by Angleton, as many of the deepest researchers into the JFK murder now believe, O'Neal would very likely have been the only Agency officer with whom Angleton would have shared details of that project. No question that Barnes would have closely liaised with O'Neal during the Guatemalan operation. Of note, O'Neal was from a family of respected Georgia politicians, and his Christian name, Birch, was in honor of close family relatives in the Birch family, whose son, John, was the namesake of the ultraconservative political movement, the John Birch Society.

And, regarding assassination, plans for the disposal of Guatemalan assets of Arbenz, as well—potentially—as Arbenz himself were on the table during the life of PBSUCCESS. In 1953, a CIA officer proposed the assassination of Arbenz in a manner that would suggest the culpability of Guatemalan Communists who had turned on Arbenz. Numerous plans to hit various members of the Guatemalan government floated in and around the anti-Arbenz effort. The beneficiary of the US coup against Arbenz, Castillo Armas, had at his disposal special "K" groups whose purpose was to kill leading political and military leaders within the Arbenz government. In the end, Arbenz was tricked into defeat, and—as far as is known—these plans were not put into action. But Barnes was deeply involved with them. In response to a request from Al Haney, CIA HQ sent a five-page roster of fifty-eight Guatemalans who were marked for assassination, including "high government and organizational leaders" suspected of Communist leanings. This targeted killing was approved by Frank Wisner, and by Barnes.

The mindset that Barnes brought to the Guatemalan operation—and a telling indication of his core views—was his response to the concerns expressed by a young David Attlee Phillips, whom Barnes recruited to run a "black" propaganda radio station. Purportedly, Phillips expressed some doubt about participating in the overthrow of a democratically elected government. The answer that he quotes Barnes as giving him (in his autobiographical *The Night Watch*) showed that Dulles's and Wisner's choice to head what they regarded as a vital Cold War mission had no doubts: "It's not a question of Arbenz. Nor of Guatemala. We have solid intelligence that the Soviets intended to throw substantial support to Arbenz . . . Guatemala is bordered by Honduras, British

Honduras, Salvador, and Mexico. It's unacceptable to have a Commie running Guatemala."

After Arbenz was defeated, in an operation that involved "Frank Bender," among others, Barnes and a handful of his top men were congratulated personally by President Eisenhower, and Barnes was rewarded with two stellar CIA Chief of Staff posts, in Frankfurt, Germany, and in London. In Germany, Barnes attempted to nurture and encourage a group of European émigrés who had volunteered to serve as a secret CIA paramilitary force. This was part of a mostly discarded vision of "rolling back" Communism, a plan that Dulles and Wisner at CIA and numerous hard-core Air Force and Navy men had played with for years. Jim Critchfield, a CIA officer who had served as a liaison to the Gehlen organization, told Thomas that, in the late 1950s, "he [Barnes] still believed in rollback. There was no gap between Tracy and Wiz. Tracy tried to keep the émigré force alive while he was in Germany."

He returned to the United States in 1960 to take the number two position (Assistant Director of Plans) under the DD/P, Richard Bissell, in the Cuban project designed to overthrow Cuba's Fidel Castro. Bissell left a great deal of the Cuba Project operational tasks to Barnes, including the myriad assassination plots that were developed during this time period. Barnes was hip-deep in the theory and practice of political assassinations during the early 1960s. David Wise, in *The American Police State . . .* describes Barnes's approval of a plan to eliminate an Iraqi colonel, a suspected Communist sympathizer, with a poisoned handkerchief.

In 1961, a senior CIA official approved the delivery of three carbine guns to Dominican Republic dissidents who were interested in eliminating Trujillo. Subsequently, one of the guns was found in the possession of one of Trujillo's reported assassins. In an interview given for a 1999 oral history-based study of CIA operatives, Richard Bissell stated that Barnes had authorized the transfer of the carbines, claiming that ". . . almost certainly, the State Department would have been consulted."

No evidence exists that anyone above or parallel to CIA's DD/P was notified of this contribution to the murder of Trujillo, an assassination that Col. William C. Bishop claimed—in a very detailed account—to have participated in. Deputy Chief of the CIA History Staff Michael Warner delineated an important aspect of Barnes's role at the time in his valuable study "The CIA's Internal Probe of the Bay of Pigs Affair": "Although he [Barnes] rarely imposed operational direction himself, he often reviewed and approved decisions in Bissell's name." In other words, Barnes was willing and able to step outside formal chains of command to set in motion plans that he believed were necessary—even, as in the Trujillo matter, when they involved the operational details of a political assassination.

It is widely accepted today that CIA's planning for the Bay of Pigs landing was premised on two eventualities that did not occur: 1.) That Castro and several of his key men would be assassinated prior to or during the invasion, and 2.) That if—or, more accurately, when—the invasion began to fail, President Kennedy would fully commit forces for an invasion of Cuba. CIA assassination planning against Castro at the time was being vetted from the offices of the DDP, allowing "deniability" to CIA head Dulles.

Larry Hancock writes: "Although Bissell denied any knowledge of Castro assassination projects to the CIA's own Inspector General, confirmation of his role is now available from numerous sources . . . This suggests that Bissell, and very likely Barnes, were at the center of virtually every CIA assassination project of the early 1960s, perhaps explaining Barnes' bland reassurances to Howard Hunt that everything was under control (a response given when Hunt kept proposing that Castro should be assassinated). It may also explain why Barnes was very much aware of *special circumstances* that would have found the Brigade arriving in a leaderless and chaotic Cuba. That would help make a great deal more sense out of the planned invasion . . ." The Bay of Pigs attack on Castro's Cuba was to have been a replica of the success had in Guatemala, and most of the Agency officers who had served under Barnes during that operation were reassembled for the Cuban venture.

Reportedly, the dramatic failure of the Bay of Pigs invasion had such an effect on Barnes that he became physically ill for several months. His wife, Janet, would say that Tracy was "sick at heart." "The phone rang, day and night, the families of the people killed. Tracy's only way to deal with it was to keep working. He was very bitter about how it happened—about the Kennedys." When CIA IG Lyman Kirkpatrick wrote up a scathing internal examination of CIA Bay of Pigs planning, directly pointing at the "delusions" of Barnes and Bissell, Barnes was tasked by Bissell to offer up a response. He drafted the DD/P rebuttal to Kirkpatrick, completing it in January 1962.

Barnes argued that the invasion had not been given a real chance to succeed and that Kirkpatrick had nitpicked alleged CIA mistakes, when the real fault lay in the failure by the Kennedy administration to remove Cuban T-33 jets with a devastating "D-Day" airstrike. "It is impossible to say how grave was [CIA's] error of appraisal, since the plan that was appraised was modified by the elimination of the D-Day airstrike. Had the Cuban Air Force been eliminated, all these estimates might have been accurate instead of underestimated . . . ," wrote

Barnes. The fast-and-loose game Barnes played with air strikes that had never been promised by Kennedy would buttress the prevailing view of CIA hard-liners that "one more airstrike would have saved the Brigade," as Michael Warner wrote.

Kennedy's disinclination to move toward an overt war-footing as the Cuban exile invaders were being slaughtered at Playa Giron would blacken his name for all time among those Cuban and American participants in the failed invasion. As far down the road as 1998, Grayston Lynch, one of the two CIA paramilitary officers who were directing the army faction that went to war in the Bay of Pigs invasion, would write a book titled *Decision For Disaster*, in which he railed at Kennedy administration cowardice, using the same arguments that Barnes had laid out in his response to the IG Report. The other CIA trainer who watched his men perish while waiting for JFK to act was Barnes's Guatemalan paramilitary expert, Rip Robertson. In 2001, British author Matthew Smith introduced an important story to American readers. Smith was told this story by a man whom he and many others regarded as a very reliable source.

In November 1963, Wayne January was a partner in an aviation company based at Dallas's Redbird Airfield. The company represented by January owned a small fleet of DC-3 planes, which they were attempting to sell off. The final plane was sold by phone in mid-November to an entity called the Houston Air Center. The buyer sent a man whom January described as an Air Force colonel to sign for the plane on November 18. The military man brought with him a Cuban pilot who would check the plane over prior to the completion of the deal.

Over the next few days, the pilot and January got to know each other and established a certain trust. On November 21, as final work on the plane was about done, the pilot told January that "They are going to kill your President." January—shocked—asked a simple question: "Why? Why would anyone want to do that?" The pilot told January that he had been a mercenary, hired by CIA for participation in the Bay of Pigs invasion. He described the horror of the final day of the invasion; the brutal "mopping up" that Castro's forces inflicted on the men who were sent on an impossible mission by the Agency. He emphasized that the people above him, the people that he believed to be involved in a plan to kill JFK, were animated by the "betrayal" of the president. January had kept the tail number of the Douglas DC-3 that was sold to the Houston Air Center, and subsequent research validated the history of the plane as January had remembered it.

The point of this story is not necessarily that the Air Force colonel, or the Houston Air Center, or the Cuban pilot, were involved in the assassination. But the pilot knew something. And he knew that hatred of Kennedy due to what many perceived as being criminal negligence at the time of the Bay of Pigs operation was one of the motives of those who were involved in the assassination.

There were other motives that moved those who became enmeshed in the plot that Pierre Lafitte inadvertently chronicled for future generations. Some were no doubt "economic," in a selfish sense. *Coup in Dallas* presents evidence that JFK's sexual dalliances with women who could have been seen as being Soviet agents played a part in the run-up to the assassination. But the full-on hatred of Kennedy by right-wing "national security" zealots began in early 1961. As Don DeLillo wrote in *Libra*, ". . . after the Bay of Pigs, nothing was the same." And it wasn't. Not for Kennedy. Not for the men at the helm of CIA whom Kennedy sent packing. Dulles, Cabell, and Bissell, and soon after their departure, Army Chief of Staff Gen. George H. Decker, who was eased out, as well. And not for the one high-level Bay of Pigs planner who walked between the raindrops without being drenched in the aftermath of the disaster: Tracy Barnes.

I will return to a survey of Barnes's post-Bay of Pigs career in a moment, focusing on the time period that is most relevant to our inquiry. But we should probably ask—and answer—a key question that was implicitly raised in my earlier portrait of T: Was Barnes close to the man who was one of the key planners of the assassination of President Kennedy, CIA Head of Counterintelligence James Angleton? T certainly was. And so too was Tracy Barnes. Barnes and Angleton were both Yale men, and both had attended Harvard Law School, although Angleton did not graduate. Barnes, a few years older than Angleton, did not attend these institutions at the same time as did Angleton, but both men were members of Yale's secret society "Scroll and Key," the major rival of the more famous "Skull and Bones" for the souls of young Yale men.

Purportedly, Scroll and Key possesses the silverware of Adolf Hitler in its archives. Be that as it may, membership in a blueblood society such as Scroll and Key is a life-long bonding experience. Angleton and Barnes—and their wives—also met with some regularity at the Washington, D.C., society gatherings that became known as the "Georgetown Set" during the 1950s. These meetings began in the late 1940s, organized by Frank Wisner, and featured the reminiscences of former OSS men, such as Angleton and Barnes. Barnes's secretary when he was Assistant DD/P, Alice McIlvaine, told long-time CIA operative George Holmes that "everyone in the clandestine service" at that time regularly attended meetings at the DD/P's office—except Angleton, who was notorious for going his own way. In contrast, McIlvaine said, "When Angleton called, Tracy ran to his office."

After the post-Bay of Pigs purge of the top echelon of CIA by President Kennedy, Barnes was still employed, but there is a great deal of murkiness about his work-related activities from late 1961 through the early part of 1963. There is reason to believe that Barnes was involved in the use of CIA proprietary companies as cover instruments, which foreshadowed his 1963 role as head of CIA's Domestic Operations Division. Joe Trento, in *The Secret History of the CIA*, relates the story of an August 1961 briefing that Barnes gave to top CIA officials regarding covert projects.

Barnes touted the purchase of a cigarette factory in Africa as cover for Agency operations. Justin O'Donnell, Bill Harvey's deputy at Division D—a man who had refused to be directly involved in CIA plans to assassinate Lumumba, and who was becoming increasingly wary of covert action—blew up at Barnes and exclaimed: "A cigarette factory in the middle of Africa? For Christ's sake! What in God's name are we going to do with it?" As Larry Hancock writes, he probably was "giving Barnes grief, since he knew that it was a cover for an assassination project." O'Donnell had been a top-notch Agency employee for years, but after he questioned Barnes dramatically, he was on the street within three weeks, attesting to Barnes's continued power and to his unwillingness to brook dissent.

One of Barnes's 1961–62 duties was coordinating payments to the families of National Guard volunteers killed during the Bay of Pigs invasion. In Victor Marchetti's *The CIA and the Cult of Intelligence*, the former executive assistant to Director of Central Intelligence Richard Helms revealed that these payments were being handled under Agency cover through Double-Chek Corporation. Barnes's involvement with CIA proprietaries was a signature feature of his career.

As a summation of Barnes's tendencies by a knowledgeable source who dealt with him frequently during the early 60s, Jake Esterline, Task Force Chief for the Bay of Pigs operation, told CIA historian Jack Pfeiffer that Gerry Droller ("Frank Bender") had been brought into the operation, along with E. Howard Hunt, to handle the "political aspects" related to the plan, and that he (Esterline) "sort of" ran Bender, but that he "never knew what Tracy was going to do next, when I turned my back . . ."

Thomas writes: "For a long time, he [Barnes] wanted to get the CIA involved in spying in the United States, just as MI-6 ran a London field station." Of course, CIA was specifically barred from such activity. Nonetheless, Barnes got his wish. CIA's Domestic Operations Division is shrouded in a great deal of mystery to this day. One will find start dates for the organization that range from 1962–1964 in published material. A part of this confusion probably lies in the fact that some of what DOD was involved in was ongoing informally before it had a proper home. However, according to a CIA IG report, DOD was officially inaugurated on February 2, 1963. Thomas quotes Howard Hunt, who was brought into DOD by Barnes as his Covert Operations chief, to the effect that DOD under Barnes was less than what Tracy had desired, that it was a "trash heap for ops that no one else wanted."

The specific actions that DOD was supposed to have been created for involved the conducting of clandestine operations within the US against "foreign targets," entities or individuals who were alleged to be operating in the US under the control of foreign powers; practically speaking, under Communist control. The word "foreign" provided a fig leaf of legitimacy for this division, but the designation of its responsibilities in the once-classified document that formalized DOD stated that the scope of its activities was to "exercise centralized responsibility for the direction, support, and coordination of clandestine operational activity within the United States." Far from being the "trash heap" Hunt described, the creation of this division of the CIA provided carte blanche for activities that were supposed to be beyond the pale for the Agency. DOD would later play a part in the massive rights violations that were part and parcel of CIA's "Operation Chaos."

Barnes continued to deal extensively with CIA proprietary companies during his stint as head of DOD, offering up opportunities for the clandestine moving of funds for "off the books" projects. Victor Marchetti spoke haltingly of DOD to researcher Bill Davy, after offering up the opinion that Clay Shaw's extant Agency documentary record suggested that Shaw was working for Barnes's mysterious unit: "It was one of the most secret divisions within the Clandestine Services. This was Tracy Barnes' old outfit. They were getting into things . . . uh . . . exactly what, I don't know. But they were getting into some pretty risky areas. And this is what E. Howard Hunt was working for at the time . . ." Malcolm Blunt, the premier source on the clandestine history of CIA as revealed in both documentary evidence and oral history, recently responded to my question about the activities of Barnes's DOD simply by shaking his head.

While the precise nature of what Barnes was doing as head of DOD in 1963 cannot be laid out with precision, Hancock offers a very plausible guess: "The full nature of Barnes's new Domestic Operations Division is undocumented; it seems likely that it included the responsibility for intelligence collection through the previously existing CIA Domestic Contact Service . . ." DCS, a long-standing CIA presence by 1963, was tasked with the exploitation of "foreign intelligence information" from sources within the United States who were suspected of having developed such information while visiting foreign countries of interest.

Certainly, that would have included a defector to a "denied" Communist country such as Lee Oswald. DCS operated field offices within the US "for purposes of intelligence collection, *operational support*, and other assigned missions." As in the internal description of the purposes of DOD, there is a great deal of slipperiness in this mission statement.

A BRIEF STOP: J. WALTON MOORE AND ASSOCIATES

A few days before his death, George de Mohrenschildt told author Edward Epstein that he had been contacted by the head of DCS in Dallas, J. Walton Moore, in 1961, several months prior to Lee Oswald's return from the Soviet Union, and briefed about Oswald. De Mohrenschildt was a frequently used source of Moore's, dating back into the late 1950s. Moore would later dissemble when testifying about his contacts with de Mohrenschildt, stating that he had seen George infrequently in the 1960s, but de Mohrenschildt's wife, Jeanne, called Moore up on this, claiming that she and George quite frequently dined with Moore and his wife. While it is often stated in the literature that Barnes was "Moore's boss" from his perch as head of DOD, this assertion cannot be proven. Still, the overlap between DOD and the DCS seems strong enough to suggest that as a likelihood.

Moore occupies a unique and very interesting position in the story of the Kennedy assassination. De Mohrenschildt told Epstein that he "would never have contacted Oswald in a million years if Moore had not sanctioned it." When de Mohrenschildt first made contact with Oswald, he arrived in the company of a CIA informant, Col. Laurence Orlov. Orlov, a long-time oilman and acquaintance of de Mohrenschildt's, was also an informant for Moore at DCS in Dallas, as well as being a social companion of Moore's. Joan Mellen writes: "It seems apparent that J. Walton Moore . . . had set up the meeting between de Mohrenschildt and Oswald." And, it could well be added, if what de Mohrenschildt told Epstein about a 1961 contact from Moore regarding Oswald is accurate, that Moore would seem to be on a short list of people who were involved very early on in maneuvering Lee Oswald.

Moore, an ex-FBI man, as well as an OSS agent during his service in the Second World War, had joined CIA in 1948, being assigned to Domestic Contacts at that time. By the 1960s, Moore was exceptionally well known and respected within CIA. A friendly and personal letter from then-Deputy Director of CIA Gen. Charles Cabell is in the record. Cabell, addressing Moore as "Walt," thanked him for his hospitality during a recent (1960) Cabell visit to Dallas. Late in Moore's career, a note in his personnel file shows that the Houston-based DCS office was upgraded in status—the New Orleans DCS office was placed under the Houston office in Agency command structure, and both offices were subordinate to the Dallas office, still headed by Moore.

After the assassination of Kennedy, Moore would pop up periodically during times of intense interest in the assassination. In 1976, with the HSCA investigation into Kennedy's death about to begin, Moore—still in the position in Dallas with DCS that he had occupied since 1948—wrote to the head of that division, asking for help in handling "the exposure of [Clay] Shaw's connections with CIA." When de Mohrenschildt died from gunshot wounding in 1977, Moore clipped the news stories reporting the death and sent them to the chief of CIA's Domestic Contact Division. On a cover sheet over a *Dallas Times-Herald* article that stated that the HSCA had uncovered "new, unproven evidence on Oswald's ties with CIA, FBI," Moore wrote "Nothing new, is there?"

Moore's Agency files also feature a detailed account of the story of Gilberto Policarpo Lopez (December 1963), a young man, whose late 1963 travels parallel those of Lee Oswald. Lopez moved suspiciously before and after the assassination of President Kennedy—attempting to get a visa to Cuba in Mexico City in the fall of 1963, and boarding a plane from Texas headed for Mexico City in the immediate aftermath of the assassination. A note from CIA DD/P Richard Helms to Win Scott at the Mexico City CIA station is also in Moore's files. The note is suggestive of Lopez being involved in a highly compartmentalized intelligence operation. Beyond the particulars of the Lopez story, the significance for our interest is that Moore is being entrusted with highly sensitive information pertaining to an investigation of the murder of President Kennedy, information that was not widely shared within CIA. J. Walton Moore was not "regular folks" in CIA by the 1960s; he was something out of the ordinary—particularly for an employee whose record reflects no obvious advancement for nearly thirty years.

As George de Mohrenschildt prepared to venture into Haiti in the spring of 1963, he and his Haitian business partner Clémard Charles were being closely monitored for possible use by both CIA and military intelligence. Dorothe Matlack, identified previously, was on top of this effort, and she leaned heavily on the "smooth operator," Sam Kail. CIA's Domestic Operation Division, headed by Tracy Barnes, was also involved in the de Mohrenschildt-Charles matter. On April 26, 1963, Gale Allen, a case officer from DOD, requested an "expedite check" on de Mohrenschildt from CIA's Office of Security. That request was not revealed in any of CIA's released records on de Mohrenschildt but was referred to in a December 1974 memorandum written by Jerry Brown of Office of Security Analysis. In a 2004 interview with historian David Kaiser, Allen claimed to have no recollection of de Mohrenschildt but suggested that he was probably acting on behalf of someone else who "had plans for de Mohrenschildt." Bill Simpich writes: "The man with the plans was apparently C. Frank Stone, also of DOD, who asked (CIA records-keeper) Anna Panor to request more information on de Mohrenschildt. Stone's name can take us down the path of a still-mysterious CIA operation known as WUBRINY. "WUBRINY" was apparently Thomas J. Devine, a long-time CIA staff employee who was well acquainted with George H. W. Bush.

If Tracy Barnes was T, I think that we can see—from a distance—the outlines of a nexus of men whom Barnes—as head of DOD—would have had "legitimate" operational interest in meeting in Dallas and New Orleans in 1963. People who centered around the Domestic Contact Service, including assets of J. Walton Moore, who seems to have been on the ground floor of CIA's active outreach to Lee Oswald in 1961, 1962, and 1963. While these people—de Mohrenschildt (whom Lafitte makes a note to "call" as late as November 20, 1963) and Col. Orlov, as well as Dallas resident and high-level intelligence agent Sam Kail—were no doubt involved in numerous schemes that Barnes could have had interest in, we know from the evidence of the Lafitte datebook that these people also had roles to play in the forthcoming murder of JFK, as the planning for that event rolled on through 1963. It is possible that Moore himself is being referred to in a key entry. On September 16, 1963, Lafitte wrote: "T says Oswald is idiot, but will be used regardless." Above that is a note to "see J. in Dallas."

BACK TO TRACY

Another "suggestion," about Barnes and DOD activity in 1963, presented as if it were known with some certainty, can be found in Donald Freed's *Death in Washington: The Murder of Orlando Letelier,* published in 1980. Freed, relying on the research of a formidable collection of investigative reporters and researchers, notes that Barnes—unlike his Agency superior, DD/P Richard Bissell, and his long-time patron Allen Dulles—came up standing after the Bay of Pigs fallout. Freed writes: "Barnes was put in charge of the new, most secret, and unconstitutional Domestic Operations Division, and Howard Hunt became his operations officer, running totally illegal domestic fronts, including one in New Orleans disguised as the Fair Play For Cuba Committee." The specific source of this assertion is not given in the book, so—much like some other claims about the

DOD—it cannot be substantiated. But Freed had great sources . . . We will leave that claim here, in the interest of a full perspective.

We do not know what Barnes was doing in October and November 1963, the period of time in which Lafitte's T arrives in New Orleans and Dallas (and possibly Madrid) for multiple meetings that were concerned with the final planning for the assassination of JFK. The Thomas book has nothing on Barnes's activities during this time period. The Assassination Records Review Board, very interested in any internal Agency documents that would pin Barnes down at critical times, requested "chronological files" on Barnes from 1959 to 1964. Of the handful of top-level CIA operatives whose personnel files were of particular interest to ARRB, Barnes was the only figure whose files the Records Board referred to in that manner. After a fair amount of uninformative communication with Agency contacts on the matter, CIA gave the ARRB a few scattered documents that pertained to Barnes. ARRB was not going to get information of this caliber.

During the Watergate scandal, a reporter filed a FOIA request for the records of Barnes's assistant, Howard Hunt, focusing on Hunt's travel during the time he was employed at DOD. "No travel records were found" was the official response. Agency Services Staff head Charles Briggs, the Agency respondent to FOIA requests at the time, allowed that Hunt's travel records could be had within the Office of Finance but denied further exploration on the basis that Hunt's personal privacy would be infringed, and on the more interesting grounds that, when all information relating to operational data was removed from Hunt's files at the time, the resulting documents would be "useless to the requestor."

As his old Agency nemesis, Richard Helms, moved toward the top of CIA, Barnes's power and influence waned. Barnes and Bissell had kept Helms at arm's length from decision-making positions during the 1950s and early 1960s. Even though Helms had occupied a position parallel to that of Barnes in the early 1960s (both men were assistants to the DD/P Bissell), Barnes was not only senior to Helms but, more important, enjoyed the protection of his patron, Allen Dulles, and subsequently the favor of John McCone, with whom Dulles was in close communication throughout McCone's reign. Barnes reportedly had gone straight to Dulles at one point in time in an effort to force Helms out of CIA. Helms, who would testify to his distaste for the "cowboy" operations of Barnes and Bissell, was promoted to DCI by Lyndon Johnson in 1966, and Barnes was gone from the Agency within weeks. Helms rubbed in his new power by forcing Barnes's old friend Des Fitzgerald, then DD/P, to fire Tracy.

Following the 1969 death of Allen Dulles, Barnes engaged in melancholy reminiscences with a very few close friends. When he was employed in his last worldly gig, at Yale, Barnes became close to Peter Almond, a graduate student who ran the Yale community relations program. "In long, if somewhat guarded conversations with Almond, he 'talked of having grown weary with the direction of the Agency. By the time he got to Yale, I think he was fed up with the CIA, in a profound way,' Almond would relate. 'He was sick about it. He did not speak directly, he was elliptical, but clearly he was talking about assassinations . . .'" His former colleague—and fellow Yale classmate—Richard Bissell would write about Barnes in his memoirs. Bissell, continually tied up in technical details, often ceded operational decisions to Barnes during his time as DD/P. He gently questioned Barnes's judgment and and implied that Tracy had "led him astray," as Thomas puts it. Barnes suffered a series of small strokes in 1969, and a major stroke in 1970. In 1972, following severe chest pains, he succumbed to a massive stroke.

CONCLUSION

Tracy Barnes moved beneath the radar through the most dramatic covert events that the CIA was involved in between 1953 and 1963. Rather than being the "corporate liberal" that parts of Evan Thomas's study make him out to be, Barnes was a daring, frequently "over-the-top," hard-core cold warrior. Barnes was arguably more directly involved with operations that included political assassination than was any other high-ranking CIA officer of his era. By comparison, the man who many of us have been most interested in over years of studying the assassination, William K. Harvey, is not even close.

Barnes went off on his own, to places in which he moved outside of a formal chain of command, more than once. He was bitter about the Kennedys following the Bay of Pigs and remained so for the rest of his life. Personalizing the tragedy of the "brilliant disaster," Barnes is quoted by Thomas as telling a friend late in his life that "Kennedy let me down." During the most critical time period in the narrative we are examining, he was head of a division of CIA that was the bureaucratic equivalent of a black hole, an area of CIA that we know far too little about, offering up opportunities for meetings of the kind that Lafitte records T engaging in.

Writing history is hard and precarious work, even when the source material being used is readily accessible and reasonably clear, much less when dealing with a record that has been truncated and veiled, as is the case with the topic of this book. Renowned scholars, dealing with archival material, regularly engage in deeply and passionately argued disputes about the meaning and importance of various strands of evidence. Historians climb out on limbs that they believe to be sturdy enough to bear the burden of the weight being placed on them. Sometimes, the limbs break.

One of the premier historical scholars of the past century, Charles Austin Beard, once remarked to a distinguished colleague of his: "What the hell do the historians think they are doing when they are selecting ten facts out of millions and gluing them together with adverbs?" Still, Beard and many other historians who have enhanced our knowledge of "the way the world works" over the years were able to isolate the most important parts of the narrative they worked with and make reasoned judgments about the validity of myriad sources. That difficult task has been accomplished by Hank Albarelli, and, in a much more modest vein, I hope to have added fruitfully to an important part of the larger story.

There is no "smoking gun" that proves Tracy Barnes to be the integrally important T in the plan that we can now begin to assemble from the writings of Pierre Lafitte and corroboratory research into the key people whom Lafitte named. Smoking guns are almost the historical equivalent of urban myths. They are rarely seen, at least in the way that the term is generally used. Strongly patterned evidence that points to reasonable conclusions is what can be reasonably expected from a successful historical inquiry. There is a powerfully coherent mass of evidence pointing in the direction of Tracy Barnes as the "T" in Lafitte's notes. If Barnes was not "T," then someone who was uncannily like Barnes was.

"CARETAKER" ANALYSIS
BY LESLIE SHARP

The objective of the *Lancelot Project* was the removal of President John F. Kennedy from the political scene—permanently and in a spectacular fashion. Paramount to the success of the operation was a guarantee that those behind the plot would never be brought to bear. The greatest threat to that anonymity was the potential arrest and subsequent identification of the assassin or assassins, so aside from the requisite technical skills, the criteria for their selection had been a history of entrenched service to those within the hierarchy of the conspiracy— assassins they could trust. At the core of that trust was a record of intense loyalty and a shared ideology that the conspirators could rely on. These were not merely hired guns. In exchange, of course the shooters were guaranteed significant compensation, but more critical was the assurance that as soon as Kennedy was annihilated, they would be spirited out of Dallas into virtual oblivion.

To that end, the strategist of *Lancelot* devised a set of foolproof deflections during the first forty-eight hours following the shooting of President Kennedy while the killers fled. Drawing from a handbook of magic tricks, the insertion of a patsy, a pigeon, into the drama—one who would be arrested within hours of the crime while the murderers left Texas—was the diversion of choice. Enter Lee Harvey Oswald.

Hundreds upon hundreds of books and thousands of essays and articles have been dedicated to the man who didn't live to see his twenty-fifth birthday. No effort is being made here to reinvent his history or question his likely grooming since adolescence to fulfill any number of roles for the US intelligence apparatus. Nor is it argued that he was entirely innocent on November 22, 1963. For instance, his known associates, Thomas Eli Davis, Jr. and Jack Ruby, are highlighted in this investigation. The reader may then ask why more pages are not dedicated to Lee Oswald.

The answer may be found in the synonymous terms "patsy," "pigeon," "scapegoat," understood in the collective as *one who is sacrificed to take the blame for a crime; one whose role is to distract investigators* while the criminals go "scot-free."

Even in death, Oswald continued to fulfill the critical function of diversion for almost six decades. Millions still fail to fully understand the coup in Dallas because, for many, Lee Harvey Oswald continues to be the central focus of research into the cold case. Even those insisting on his utter and complete innocence have, to a degree, perpetuated the deleterious effect the patsy has had on the pursuit of truth. Committed to interrupting that cycle, this investigation avoided the pitfalls and considered Oswald's cameo performances in the broadest context of the drama. Who cast him in the role, and who could maneuver him onto stage at the right time? It was evident from Lafitte's records that *caretaker* was key.

In his 1963 datebook, the project manager records the word *caretaker* on seven separate occasions. Initially, the logical candidate seemed to be George de Mohrenschildt, widely referred to as the "handler" of LHO. De Mohrenschildt and his wife, Jeanne, were in Dallas through March 1963, prior to departing for a stopover in Washington, D.C., before an extended stay in Haiti and surrounding islands, so it might seem pointless to pursue *caretaker* any further than the Russian-born oil exploration consultant with a known history of intelligence service to the highest bidder.

However, because Lafitte resumed focus on *caretaker* in the fall, as evidenced in his datebook—when we know from official records and testimony that George and Jeanne spent the last half of 1963 concentrating on suspect business deals in the West Indies—we returned to the datebook to follow the path of *caretaker* with more diligence.

The first mention is on March 7, just days after Lee Oswald was introduced to Ruth Hyde Paine in the home of Socony Mobil Oil chemist Everett Glover. Everett had known both Ruth and her estranged husband, Michael, through Madrigal choir practices and performances, a passion shared with Hungarian-born Fr. Ralph March, who cofounded Our Lady of Dallas, the Cistercian Abby located in Irving, Texas. Fr. March also served on the faculty of the University of Dallas, located on the campus of the Abby, during the tenure of President Robert Morris, the head of the regional chapter of the ultraconservative John Birch Society (JBS) and legal counsel to General Edwin A. Walker. (Morris's history has been pursued in depth earlier in this book.) Michael Paine testified that out of curiosity, he attended a John Birch meeting in October at the invitation of a JBS advocate who was part of the Madrigal choir.

During his own testimony before the Warren Commission, Everett Glover claimed that while planning a party with his roommates from Socony Mobil, including German born Volkmar Schmidt, *it occurred to him* that his friend

Ruth—whose interest in the Russian language and culture had been a frequent topic of conversation—might like to meet the Oswald couple. Glover elaborated during testimony that during the previous weeks he had been playing doubles tennis with his friend Sam Ballen. The two had only recently caught up with each other at the home of the director of Graduate Research Center of the Southwest, Lauriston Marshall. (The significance of GRCSW is explored in a separate essay of the appendix.)

Over drinks that evening, the two men had agreed to challenge Ballen's close friends, George and Jeanne de Mohrenschildt, to a series of doubles tennis matches. It was through these encounters that Glover was quickly introduced to Marina Nikolayevna Oswald at a small dinner gathering in the home of the de Mohrenschildts, and from there, the idea of a party in his own home in February was seeded. The circumstances of the fairly impromptu party were innocuous enough on the surface. But that gathering, known to researchers as the *Magnolia party*, launched what would be one of the most serendipitously "innocent" relationships in the saga of the plot to kill the president.

Critical to grasping the undertow of the introduction of the Paines to the Oswalds is the revelation that both Glover and Volkmar Schmidt are named in Pierre Lafitte's datebook, first on October 16, just one week after a pivotal meeting for *Lancelot* was held in D.C.; and eight days later, October 24, *Volkmar* appears again in an entry that includes "*O. Caretaker*" and "*Ilse [Skorzeny] with T - ?*"

* * *

During testimony, Michael Paine stated that the John Birch Society meeting he attended with another friend from Madrigal choir practices was held the same evening of the infamous incident with Adlai Stevenson when he was spat upon in Dallas. Paine speculates that it was sometime in November. However, Wesley Liebeler, commission attorney, sets the record straight when he said, *For the record I think the record should indicate that Mr. Stevenson was in Dallas on or about October 24, 1963.* It was in fact October 24.

The full context of the exchange is worth considering:

Mr. LIEBELER - Are you a member or have you ever attended any meetings of the John Birch Society?

Mr. PAINE - I am not a member. I have been to one or, I guess chiefly one meeting of theirs.

Mr. LIEBELER - Where was that?

Mr. PAINE - That was in Dallas?

Mr. LIEBELER - When?

Mr. PAINE - That was the night Stevenson spoke in Dallas.

The CHAIRMAN - When?

Mr. PAINE - The night Stevenson spoke in Dallas, U.N. Day.

Representative FORD - Was that 1963?

Mr. PAINE - Yes.

Mr. LIEBELER - Would you tell us the circumstances of your attendance at that meeting and what happened?

Mr. PAINE I had been seeking to go to a Birch meeting for some time, and then I was invited on this night so I went. It was an introductory meeting

Mr. DULLES - On the 9th of November?

Mr. PAINE - It was November something, I don't know what, a Wednesday or Thursday night.

Mr. LIEBELER - For the record I think the record should indicate that Mr. Stevenson was in Dallas on or about October 24, 1963.

Liebler asks Michael a few more questions and then commission member Dulles, the former Director of the CIA, made a point of interjecting:

Mr. DULLES - May I ask, did you go out of curiosity rather than sympathy or rather how did you happen to go?

Mr. PAINE - I am not in sympathy.

Mr. DULLES - So I gathered.

And with that, Dulles relieved Paine of any taint of animosity toward John Kennedy.

Also intriguing to this series of datebook entries, Lafitte is either writing from the Ritz Hotel in Madrid, Spain, or he is identifying a meeting held there, and possibly both, on October 23 and 24.

* * *

The following abbreviated Oswald time line, juxtaposed with chronologically relevant notes from the Lafitte datebook, indicates that *caretaker* served as an indispensable link between Oswald—perhaps both Lee and Marina—and those who were advancing the assassination plot, including Lafitte himself.

Interspersed in the Oswald time line, in the left column, are references to Ruth Paine's interactions with Marina as well as Lee; interspersed in the datebook entries on the right are references to Lee and Marina and several other key characters and events that at first seemed independent of *caretaker*, until the references are considered in the context of the overall plot.

ABBREVIATED OSWALD TIMELINE	SELECT LAFITTE DATEBOOK ENTRIES
January 1963 Everett Glover reconnects with Sam Ballen at the home of the dir. of Graduate Research Center of the Southwest, Lauriston Marshall.	
Glover and Ballen launch a series of doubles tennis matches with Ballen's good friends George & Jeanne de Mohrenschildt.	
Feb 13 de Mohrenschildts host a dinner attended by Marina Oswald and Everett Glover.	
Feb 22 Lee and Marina Oswald attend a dinner party at the home of Everett Glover and Volkmar Schmidt where they are introduced by Glover to Ruth Paine.	
March 2 The Oswalds move to 214 West Neely Street.	
March 9–10 LHO takes photographs of the home of Gen. Edwin Walker.	March 7 **(Caretaker) -- T**

March 11 "The Militant" publishes a letter signed L.O.	
March 12 Ruth Paine visits Marina Oswald at the new apartment. LHO orders a rifle from Klein's Sporting Goods of Chicago.	
	March 13 **Caretaker** T - Dallas Office
	March 19 **Caretaker**
March 25 LHO retrieves the rifle and revolver at the P.O.	
	March 26 McWillie - Tues with Davis - Oswald (Note: it is possible this is in reference to global weapons dealer Victor Oswald who is known to have been in the New Orleans area periodically.)
March 31 Marina photographs LHO with rifle.	
April 6 LHO last day at Jaggers-Chiles-Stovall.	
	April 7 Walker - Lee and pictures-Planned soon Can he do it? Won't. [possibly reads: 'Wait']

April 10 LHO allegedly fires shot into the home of Gen. Walker.	
April 12 LHO decides to move to New Orleans.	
April 24 Ruth Paine drives LHO to bus station.	
May 9 LHO hired by Reily Coffee Co. New Orleans.	
May 11 Ruth Paine and Marina Oswald arrive in New Orleans.	
July 11 Ruth Paine invites Marina to live with her.	May 23 Ask T about Oswald Magazine?
July 19 LHO is fired from Reily Coffee Co. and files unemployment.	
	July 23 Oswald -- wife M.- Where?
	August 26 Oswald -- bank? M -- meet T.

September 20 Ruth Paine returns to New Orleans. Marina decides to move back to Irving for the birth of her baby.	September 4 Hotshot Walker **(Caretaker)**
September 23 Ruth Paine and Marina Oswald depart for Texas.	September 22 Oswald -- Mex City Gaudet?
	September 24 --Oswald D/T (Labadie / Florida) W.J.
September 25 LHO departs New Orleans for Mexico City.	
	September 26 -O traveling- Let T know -Madrid -
September 27 LHO arrives Mexico City; allegedly makes first visits to Cuban and Russian embassies.	September 27 Oswald Comercia Hotel - to meet with Tom D. at Luma T. says <u>yes</u>.
September 28 LHO allegedly returns to Russian and Cuban embassies.	
September 29 LHO allegedly attends bullfight in Mex City.	September 29 Tom at embassy Done
September 30 LHO allegedly phones Cuban and Russian embassies; buys a bus ticket to Laredo, TX.	
October 2 LHO departs Mexico City for Dallas.	

October 4 LHO applies for work at Padgett Printing in Dallas.	October 3 **-Caretaker -** 10:30
	October 6 Oswald issue (!) [check] with **Caretaker . . .**
October 12 LHO visits Marina at Ruth Paine's home.	
October 14 Ruth Paine drives LHO to Dallas; Ruth learns that TSBD is hiring.	
October 15 LHO applies at TSBD.	
October 16 LHO starts work at TSBD.	October 16 Volkmar - (Glover) (K.C. Stanley)
	October 24 Ritz Madrid w/T **(O. Caretaker)** Volkmar Ilse with T.--?
Nov 11 LHO spends Veteran's Day at the Paines.	
Nov 12 LHO notifies FBI Agent Hosty to leave his family alone.	November 14 Crichton w/ T. **(Caretaker)**
Nov 15 Marina Oswald tells Lee not to come to the Paines.	

Nov 21 LHO arrives at the Paine home to spend the night. Nov 22 LHO departs the Paine home with neighbor and work colleague Buell Wesley Frazier.	

Initially, this visual exercise established the high probability that *caretaker* was Ruth Paine, possibly in league with her husband, Michael.

However, and despite volumes of research into her personal history that led researchers over the years to conclude both she and Michael had connections to US military contractors and intelligence agencies, Ruth's day-to-day responsibilities as mild-mannered busy mom who was even considering a part-time position at St. Mark's in Dallas presented a challenge. Regardless of persistent and reasonable claims that she was in direct contact with figures in the highest echelons of intelligence, including one degree removed from DCI Allen Dulles, we had to ask whether it was necessary, let alone feasible, for her to be meeting directly with those whose focus was not simply the positioning of Oswald—which was but one compartment of the plan—but the entire operation. The rationale for face-to-face meetings between Ruth and the project's hierarchy was missing from the equation.

From that perspective, more serious consideration was given to the possibility that there was someone else in play, someone acting as Ruth's handler, someone who was the ultimate *caretaker* of the role to be filled by the patsy. And with that realization, interest in FBI Special Agent Bardwell Dewitt Odum—known personally to the Paines prior to November 22 by their own admission—was revived. "The Ubiquitous Bard" was elevated to prime candidate for *caretaker*.

* * *

In a July 1998 volume of the *The Fourth Decade*, a highly regarded publication focused on the assassination, researcher Raymond F. Gallagher presented a brilliant exposé of Special Agent Odum titled "The Ubiquitous Bard." According to Gallagher, from the moment Odum ascended the stairway to the 6th floor of the TSBD to witness the recovery of the alleged murder rifle, he was an ever-present fixture in advancing Oswald as the lone gunman.

Less than an hour after the rifle discovery, Bard Odum, along with Lt. Day of the Dallas Police Department, was photographed leaving the depository building with the alleged rifle used by an alleged assassin from the sniper's nest. Lt. Day later stated that en route to headquarters, SA Odum had used his car radio to contact the Dallas FBI office and described the rifle. As Gallagher pointed out in 1998, there didn't seem to be a record of this communication, but there is no doubt that early descriptions of the rifle set in motion rampant confusion as to the official identification of the alleged weapon.

Odum, an agent of the federal government, was at the DPD headquarters only briefly before dashing to the Texas Theater, where a suspect in the shooting of a Dallas police officer was about to be apprehended. It has yet to be explained what prompted Odum to attend that particular arrest in the middle of what should have been the most aggressive manhunt in the nation's history. Why would his boss, SAC Gordon Shanklin, pull one of his prize protégés from the search for Kennedy's assassin to pursue a local shooting, unless, of course, Shanklin had already been advised that Lee Oswald would not only be charged with gunning down Officer J.D. Tippit, but that he would soon be charged with the assassination of Kennedy.

Once Oswald was in custody at the Texas Theatre, Odum, instead of tracking federal arrests being made in critical hours of the assassination, inexplicably spent another hour and a half in pursuit of the Tippit shooting along with nearly a dozen DPD staff. Federal detentions in the Dallas area during that twenty-four-hour period—persons of interest to the Feds since the spring of 1963—stand out: Jean Rene Souetre and Michel Mertz and possibly Michel Roux.

Rather than being ordered to question Souetre and or Mertz or Roux, Odum seems focused on Tippit's murder, even taking time to interview Helen Markham, who had witnessed a young male fleeing the scene. In another rarely heralded essay published in the *Fourth Decade* in 1997, researcher Tom Wallace Lyons summed up Odum's early influence over the Tippit investigation, asserting that Odum sowed the confusion that contributed to Markham being labeled as an inconsistent, unreliable witness for decades to come.

In another noteworthy timeline, while Odum is biding time in Oak Cliff, pursuing a case that was technically outside his jurisdiction, Lee Oswald's various addresses were being nailed down at the school book depository. Meanwhile, Oswald was being driven to police headquarters in Car Number 2 under the custody of Jerry Hill and his colleagues. According to Bill Simpich, another researcher who has long recognized that the elusive Bard demands close scrutiny, Jerry Hill had been on the sixth floor of the depository building when Mannlicher-Carcano shells were found and reported as a match to the rifle that Bard

Odum escorted to police headquarters. Either the police department and the FBI were stretched thin that afternoon, or this was one of numerous serendipitous coincidences that would unfold in the next few days.

Once Lee Oswald was identified as AWOL during an alleged formal roll call of depository employees, and once his addresses were known, including that of the Paines, Odum seems to have finally returned his keen eye to the assassination, and with every subsequent step he took, the profile of the lone nut commie suspect was advanced. By December 2, he was responsible for the transfer of a fragment of a bullet retrieved from the wall of General Edwin Walker's study to Washington, D.C., for comparison against fragments from Dealey Plaza. In light of the September 4 Lafitte datebook entry, which reads *Hotshot – Walker (Caretaker)*, we're forced to consider the possibility that Odum knew more about the Walker incident than has ever been contemplated.

* * *

Bardwell "Bard" Dewitt Odum, known to many as "Hart," and called "Bob" by Michael Paine, was born in Fort Worth in 1918, the oldest of four brothers. He received a Doctor of Jurisprudence from the University of Texas, where he was a track and field star, in 1940. His 2010 obituary makes no mention of military service in spite of the pending war, indicating that instead, he joined Hoover's FBI in 1942. More significantly, there is no specific mention in his obituary of the investigation of the century, the assassination of the president of the United States, which he clearly played a key role in. Retiring from the FBI in 1968, Odum took up law practice and became chief counsel for Gibson Discount Corp, dealers in wholesale jewels.

His brother, Harold G. Odum, was a well-known Presbyterian minister in San Angelo, Texas, from 1957 to his retirement in 1986; another brother, William Thomas, was a successful architect in Dallas. It was the history of his youngest brother, Arthur Milton, that opened yet another avenue of the mystery of Bard's ubiquitous assignments during the assassination investigation.

According to Arthur's 2017 obituary, "At the height of the Cold War, with the Cuban missile crisis barely in the rearview mirror, the President of the United States was looking for a person to administer a highly classified interagency intelligence-sharing program. After careful consideration, the President appointed a young, up-and-coming United States Foreign Service officer who had just returned from a State Department assignment in Venezuela." Official records indicate that Arthur had concluded his tour as Vice Consulate in Maracaibo in

September 1963. But before pursuing the significance of his posting in one of the hotspots of US diplomacy in Latin America, according to the obituary, "Prior to entering the Foreign Service, Arthur had served for four years in the US Navy as the custodian of classified intelligence on Soviet nuclear capabilities . . . Arthur quickly impressed the intelligence community in Washing with his ability to serve as the intelligence liaison between the director of the CIA, the Secretary of State, the Secretary of Defense and the White House. As Cold War tensions mounted, the need for skillful diplomacy became a national priority."

Many assassination experts are aware that on Kennedy's desk the morning he prepared to fly to Texas was an explosive memorandum to advise the president that a significant cache of arms had been discovered near Maracaibo, Venezuela, with Fidel Castro's "name all over them." Records indicate that the cache had been stored outside Maracaibo sometime in August 1962, a significant time frame for our interests in light of the machinations of Georgia-based arms dealer Mitchell WerBell III during the fall of 1962 and into February '63. Pierre Lafitte is clearly interested in WerBell, mentioning him in intriguing circumstances on five occasions during the first two months of '63. Government records documented WerBell's effort beginning in late July 1962 to secure the endorsement of Central and South American dictators, including Romulo Betancourt of Venezuela, for his personal choice of replacement of Castro.

WerBell aside, the coincidence that Arthur Odum was in Maracaibo throughout 1962 to the end of September 1963, if not weeks later, cannot not be dismissed out of hand, nor can his notoriety as the perfect liaison between CIA and the Defense Department be ignored, not in light of brother Bardwell's extraordinary impact on the investigation of the assassination by perpetuating from the outset Oswald's legend as a Marxist in support of Castro's regime in Cuba.

Adding to the mystery is Arthur Odum's particular expertise in intelligence pertaining to the Soviet Union, along with the history of his older brothers, Rev. Harold Odum, who spent weeks at a time on an annual basis proselytizing in Russia, and Bard "Hart" Odum, who was in hot pursuit of a former defector to the Soviet Union.

The moment Arthur departed Venezuela for D.C., he was immersed in Russian language training, presumably a skill set required for his new, *highly classified intelligence-sharing* assignment. Details of that assignment remain elusive; however, we do know that Arthur eventually joined Ambassador Llewellyn Thompson for Thompson's second stint in Moscow. In a twist of fate, it was under Ambassador Thompson's watch in 1962 that Marina Oswald had been issued a passport to emigrate with Lee to the US. Thompson was called to testify before the

Warren Commission, shining additional light on Oswald's time in the Soviet Union. Arthur's brother, SA Bard Odum, who was on the ground in Dallas at the time of the assassination, was not.

* * *

The aforecited circumstantial evidence still was not sufficient to confirm that Bard Odum was *caretaker*, so we turned to what in the Lafitte material might persuade us further. The answer was John Alston Crichton, *Lancelot* project's man on the ground in Dallas who had the credential, the impetus, and the connections to ensure the escape of the real assassins. The patsy, Lee Harvey Oswald, was essential to his success.

It was Crichton who arranged for his friend, Sun Oil geologist and Russian-born Latvian native Ilya Mamantov, to provide translation for Marina, the traumatized wife of Lee Oswald, on the afternoon of November 22. It was Bard Odum who navigated his way in the early days of the investigation to "handle" Marina's version of her husband's complex history. And it was Bard's acquaintance, and some might argue friendship, with Ruth Paine that smoothed his path. The behind-the-scenes hand-off of Marina to Ilya Mamantov, who is notorious for having mistranslated Marina's statements regarding the rifle, was well underway.

Ilya Mamantov's Warren Commission testimony skirts around his good friend Jack Crichton except to acknowledge that Crichton phoned him just before 5:00 p.m. to let him know that the Dallas police needed a Russian translator. His recall of the afternoon contradicts his wife's account that a convoy of government-type cars pulled up on Mockingbird Lane at approx. 12:20 p.m., minutes before the assassination in Dealey Plaza. After his death in 1991, Ilya's decades-old version of the events of that Friday was challenged by widow Sondra's emotionally charged recollection. She had never before spoken openly of what she witnessed that day.

Ilya insisted under oath that he had been in his dentist's clinic that Friday afternoon, was startled to hear Oswald's name, and phoned the FBI around 4:30 p.m. to advise that he was familiar with the Oswald couple. Within the hour, he was in the DPD headquarters prepared to translate for the Russian wife of the man who had been arrested some three hours earlier for shooting a police officer. Oswald had not been arraigned for the assassination of Kennedy.

However, as noted in an Endnote of this book, Sondra Mamantov had acute memory of watching her husband being driven from their home on Mockingbird

Lane in a three-vehicle motorcade some ten minutes prior to the assassination in Dealey. She was home for lunch, and only when her son came into the house unexpectedly, having been dismissed from school just after news of the assassination, did she realize that Kennedy had been shot. Her version of events advanced the credible assertion of Roberta Pew, the wife of Sun Oil president Jack Pew, that it was Col. Jack Crichton who organized Ilya's trip to police headquarters.

Author Mark North, in his 1991 exposé of FBI Director J. Edgard Hoover, *Act of Treason: The Role of J. Edgar Hoover in the Assassination of President Kennedy* rereleased in 2011 by Skyhorse Publishing: ". . . A U.S. Army . . . colonel in intelligence was feeding information to the FBI within an hour of Oswald's arrival at the police station." Although North, who draws from Antony Summers's *Conspiracy*, doesn't name the colonel, we have sufficient cause to consider two possible candidates: Col. Brandy Brandstetter, or Dallas resident Jack Crichton of the 488th Military Intelligence Unit. It is reasonable to believe that FBI agent Bard Odum would have been in direct contact with either (or both) of these men during this period, implicating them in the same critical phase of the *caretaking* of Marina Oswald.

* * *

Returning to Raymond Gallagher's exceptional research and subsequent astute insight into Bard Odum's role, combined with that of author Bill Simpich, the following is a truncated version of just how enmeshed the FBI agent was in guaranteeing that Oswald alone would be charged with Kennedy's death: there was no conspiracy, there was no "coup" other than a blow to the president's head.

After transferring the rifle from the "scene of the crime" to DPD headquarters, witnessing the arrest of Oswald at the Texas Theatre, and following a stop-off to interview a witness in the Tippit shooting, Odum either cooled his heels the rest of the afternoon, or pursued leads that were not documented or have not been released. We do know from records that he ended up with shells and slugs from the Tippit scene in his pocket.

We also know with certainty that within twenty-four hours of the assassination, Odum played a role in yet another attempt to cement Oswald's guilt. Again, author Bill Simpich: "[Wallace] Heitman had a close colleague—Bardwell Odum . . . while Heitman specialized in working with the Russians and the Cubans as a valued CIA liaison for the Dallas office, Odum was a senior criminal specialist and a favorite of Dallas FBI chief Gordon Shanklin. Heitman was the man who met Eldon Rudd on the tarmac the night of the assassination. Rudd was delivering documents provided to him by CIA Mexico City chief Win Scott—a photo of the Mystery Man that Scott allegedly believed was Oswald . . . ."

Simpich reminds us that J. Walton Moore, agent in charge of the CIA's Dallas office, was a college roommate of Wallace Heitman. It was Moore who introduced George de Mohrenschildt to the returned "defector," Oswald, and Moore and de Mohrenschildt shared a friendship with Texas oilman and former WWI Col. Lawrence Orlov, who is named in the Lafitte datebook.

CIA agent Heitman's buddy, SA Odum, was teamed up that evening with James Hosty, the agent assigned to Oswald since his return from the Soviet Union and infamous for having destroyed an alleged note from Oswald in the weeks prior to the assassination. Odum was the only agent to later claim that Hosty's story about the Oswald note was erroneous. Ruth Paine soon changed her assessment of the note to align with Bard's by insisting that the note was yet "another lie" told by Lee.

When the photos arrived from Mexico City, after cropping any vestiges of the embassy building behind the image of a man in the photo that they intended to present to Marina for identification, the Hosty/Odum team proceeded to the motel in Garland, north of downtown, to confront her. Enter Marguerite Oswald, who ran interference that night and refused to allow Odum to interrogate either of the two women.

Despite those seeming early unpleasantries, a photo of the Bard facing Marina who is cradling her newborn, attests to the FBI agent's persistence. It also reveals that Ilya Mamantov was no longer her translator. The woman in the middle of the photo has been identified as a skilled Russian translator. Apparently, Ilya had served his purpose.

Over the ensuing months, while CIA's Heitman relentlessly pursued a very vulnerable Marina, pressuring her to confirm the latest official version of the investigation, whatever version that was, Bardwell would have *cordial visits* with Ruth Paine and Michael at least ten more times. In fact, Ruth referred to Bardwell as her "primary contact"; Freudian slip perhaps, or, it is also possible that both she and Michael were always kept in the dark.

Researcher Gallagher additionally draws attention to Ruth's testimony, which indicates that Agent Odum was involved in the seizure of Lee's wedding ring—a ring that in the following decades would serve as centerpiece of the Sixth Floor Museum, ensconced in a plexiglass case positioned dead center in the passageway through the main floor. The ring has been a nuanced symbol advancing the pathos of the lone gun assassin in the minds of millions upon millions of visitors to the Dealey Plaza over decades. Odum also pursued employees at the Texas Employment Commission responsible for placing Oswald in several jobs. One of those TEC employees made a permanent move from the area she had lived in for decades within months of Odum's interviews. Some suggest she was terrified. Also, it was Odum who ordered construction of a replica of the alleged bag that concealed the alleged weapon, from materials found in the depository shipping room, to show to Wesley Buel Frazier, the Paines' neighbor and Lee's ride to work the morning of November 22. There can be little doubt that Bard was hell-bent on perpetuating the case against the patsy, Lee Oswald.

Researcher/author Simpich also references records that indicate the confusion facilitated by Odum around the identification of a Minox camera discovered in the Paines' garage, discrepancies that were fueled by Michael Paine's sudden realization that the camera was his. Simpich then reminds us of perhaps the most intriguing fact relevant to the pursuit of the real *caretaker*: SA Odum and Oswald had shared the same Irving barber, Cliff Shasteen. Absent the official records of Odum's work schedule throughout 1963 to determine to whom he may or may not have been assigned, Shasteen provides perhaps the single most solid clue in support of the hypothesis that Odum was the Oswald *caretaker* named by Lafitte beginning in March 1963.

* * *

In 2002, researchers Tink Thompson and Gary Aguilar tracked down Odum to ask about an FBI summary memo of interviews of those who witnessed the "magic bullet," the projectile that was alleged to have penetrated both John Kennedy and the man sitting in the jump seat of the limousine in front of the president, Texas Governor John Connally. The memo includes a statement by O. P. Wright, a former policeman working at Parkland Hospital when the bullet (known as Warren Commission Exhibit #399) was discovered. Wright insisted that the bullet in question was pointed tip and not rounded, as is the bullet housed in the National Archives.

During the 2002 interview, Odum disavowed the memo, insisting that he was never in possession of the "magic" bullet, despite FBI Director J. Edgar Hoover's memo indicating unequivocally that his agent in Dallas, Bardwell Odum, was included in the provenance of what was the most phenomenal piece of evidence in support of the *lone gunman* theory central to the function of "the patsy." The ease with which Odum challenged his ultimate superior, FBI Director Hoover whom he had served for over two decades, is telling.

The Odio Incident

Germane to evidence presented throughout this book, the *caretaker* analysis concludes with SA Odum's pursuit of claims made by Cuban-born Silvia Odio, a young woman who testified that someone whose appearance was similar to Lee Oswald visited her home in the Casa Linda neighborhood of Dallas along with two Cubans in late September 1963. It was Odio's testimony that launched a decades-long controversy over whether Lee Oswald was in Mexico City in late September in pursuit of a visa to Cuba, or standing on her doorstep.

Lafitte's records have put closure to that debate, but she continues to intrigue. Odio, whose uncle was exiled from Cuba living in New Orleans, was engaged in an affair with a Catholic priest in Dallas, who was perhaps in the shadows of attempts to restore the church's dominance over Cuban politics; she was socially and emotionally mentored by an ultraconservative Dallas socialite, Lucille McConnell, who happened to also be in love with the priest; she took shelter in the home of a prominent Dallas family, McConnell's friends, with interests intertwined with oilman Clint W. Murchison. And, Odio's Dallas address in September '63 was 1081 Magellan Circle, a stone's throw from the home of the Ferenc Nagy family.

Nagy was the registered president of Permindex Corporation, notorious in assassination research as being of service to the CIA, and having invited New Orleans businessman Clay Shaw on board as director. Clay Shaw's *close associate*, David Ferrie, ironically lived in the quiet neighborhood of Broadmoor, just five hundred yards from Silvia's uncle, Augustin Guitart, a physics professor at Xavier University who resided at 3694 Louisiana Avenue Parkway. In hindsight, had FBI agents Odum and Hosty done their homework and tapped into their resources in New Orleans, including SA Bartlett and SA Rice, who might have been slightly curious of the coincidence (the former having been a pivotal figure in the provenance of the magic bullet), they might have uncovered a connection. Instead, Silvia's testimony before the Warren Commission served only to compartmentalize and confuse, deflecting attention from any legitimate pursuit of anyone other than the patsy.

Despite Odum's follow-through with Silvia Odio's claims, including at least one interview with her, Odum was never called to testify before the Warren Commission on at least this aspect of the investigation. However, as revealed in the following snippet of her testimony before the commission, in a scene worthy of the film *The Godfather,* Odum hovered:

Mr. LIEBELER. Did you say that you also started working at a new job that same day?

Mrs. ODIO. No, sir.

Mr. LIEBELER. But you had been working on the day that you did move?

Mrs. ODIO. I started working initially the 15th of September, because it was too far away where I lived in Irving. I started the 15th of September, I am almost sure of the 15th or the 9th. Let me see what day was the 9th. It was a Monday. It was the 9th, sir, that I started working at National Chemsearch.

(Special Agent Bardwell O. Odum of the Federal Bureau of Investigation entered the hearing room.)

Mr. LIEBELER. This is Mr. Odum from the FBI. As a matter of fact, Mr. Odum was the man that interviewed you.

Mrs. ODIO. I remember. He looked very familiar.

Mr. [LIEBELER]. What is the name?

Mr. [sic] **ODIO.** I interview so many people, it slips my mind at the moment.

Agent Odum left the hearing room . . .

Little more can be said about the high strangeness of Federal Bureau of Investigation Special Agent Bardwell Dewitt Odum leaving the Warren Commission hearing room without being invited to testify.

NOTES ON THE APPOINTMENT AND CALL DIARIES OF ALLEN DULLES, 1962–1963
BY ALAN KENT

Princeton University, the alma mater of legendary one-time director of the Central Intelligence Agency Allen Dulles, houses a fascinating collection of material compiled by and about Dulles. Among the most interesting sources of information are the appointment and call diaries of Dulles, which are available—more or less—for the years 1939–1974, per Princeton's text. Dulles died in 1969, so I assume that the last figure is in error, unless Dulles possessed even greater powers than his admirers credit him with. Here I will be examining the records of some of Dulles's doings during 1962–1963. This time period encompasses the formal end of Dulles's long intelligence career—as is well-known, Dulles was escorted out of the Kennedy government after the CIA's dicey performance prior to and during the Bay of Pigs invasion—and the assassination of the man who escorted him, President Kennedy.

Dulles formally left his position as DCI in November 1961, but by January of the following year he began to create a new position for himself, one in which he had scarcely less influence within a circle of powerful friends than he had enjoyed at the head of CIA, and arguably even less accountability. As Dulles biographer David Talbot wrote: "In truth, the Kennedy purge had left the ranks of Dulles loyalists at the CIA largely untouched. Top Dulles men like Angleton and Helms remained on the job. And the 'Old Man's' shadow knights never abandoned their king . . . Dulles had been deposed, but his reign continued."

Before delving into an examination of some of the patterns and specific detail revealed by this material, a common-sense caveat should be made: Dulles was a very intelligent and devious man, who was quite capable of arranging communications and meetings that would fall outside the records that he and whatever secretarial person or persons he employed over the years created. One example of this is the strange meeting Dulles attended on April 15, 1963, with retired Army general Lucius D. Clay and a (still) mysterious anti-Castro exile, Paulino Sierra Martinez. We know about this meeting today due to CIA monitoring of Sierra's whirlwind 1963 activities, but there is no hint of the meeting to be found in Dulles's appointment diaries. It is also the case that more than a few contacts that Dulles had during this time period are redacted, either wholly or in part. Sometimes the redactions are present in the familiar form of a crude crossing out, and others are simply listed as being "redacted."

No doubt, some of Dulles's contacts, particularly so soon after his departure from a long reign as DCI, would have qualified as "national security" matters, as that category was broadly interpreted at the time. There are, however, more of these redactions than would seem necessary for the communications of a man who was nominally a private citizen at this time of his life. The operative term here, though, is "nominally." Because the record of his '62–'63 contacts shows that—with the exception of the absence of meetings with foreign dignitaries and intelligence chiefs that occurred frequently during his time as DCI—Dulles was still doing business.

1962

January 1962 was a pivotal time in the history of CIA, and in Dulles's life. He was removing himself from the position at the head of the organization, and transferring information and advice to his successor, John McCone. As would be expected, there was much communication with Dulles's most trusted contacts. Jan. 8, a note from a message left asks him to "Please call Cord Meyer," and an afternoon appointment with Meyer was arranged. Jan. 9 featured a lunch with Tracy Barnes, a meeting with CIA Counterintelligence head Jim Angleton, and an evening visit by Sen. Prescott Bush. On Jan. 10, Mrs. Tracy Barnes invited Mrs. Dulles to lunch, and a call from former Deputy Director of CIA Gen. Charles Cabell. Cabell invited Dulles to attend a get-together later in the month, celebrating Gen. Cabell's achievements, prior to Cabell cleaning out his office and moving on as of Jan. 31. On Jan. 15, Angleton met with Dulles at Allen's home. On Jan. 16, an interesting call from Tracy Barnes took place. "Mr. Barnes said they hoped to have 'it' to go tomorrow for Mr. McCone. Mr. Dulles will take 'it' in pieces." Dulles had a 3:45 appointment with McCone on this day, and (presumably) a meeting with the new DCI on the following day in which "it" was presented to McCone.

Jan. 17 brought a phone call from another man who had recently been "retired" from the Kennedy administration, former Chief of Naval Operations, Admiral Arleigh Burke. Burke's call was regarding a weekend meeting of the "Defense Committee." Burke and Dulles would communicate frequently about this shared membership over the next few months, very likely a reference to the developing Center for Strategic and International Studies (CSIS), which was officially inaugurated in September, just before the Cuban Missile Crisis. Jan. 19 was a busy day for the former DCI. Calls from Barnes and Cord Meyer were recorded, as well as a call from a Dulles favorite, E. Howard Hunt. Hunt's call referred to a "news item," and the contents of the call were redacted. Five separate phone calls placed to Dulles on Jan. 19 were fully redacted. A Jan. 22 call from a "Col. White" had to do with something referred to as the "deer incident" . . .

February 1962 had few entries in Dulles's diaries, but March and April show a good deal more activity. A March 23 note refers to (Redacted), who will be in town "next week." "What time will be convenient?" asks Dulles's secretary. On March 28, Angleton's head of the Research and Analysis Department of CIA CI, Raymond Rocca, called, to discuss the "Hohenlohe papers" with Dulles. These papers, which were circulating in a truncated form in the early 1960s, covered a late-World War Two relationship Dulles had developed with Maximilian von Hohenlohe, a Nazi courier, with whom Dulles, then in OSS, was attempting to broker an agreement for a Nazi surrender. This business was not sanctioned by anyone of authority in the US government, and Dulles was understandably nervous about allegations that he had been flirting with treason. On March 30, (Redacted) called to seek an appointment with Dulles, and to remind Allen that his time in Washington was "very limited."

April 3 featured a lunch appointment with Frederick Praeger, the owner of a publishing company with which CIA had a long-standing relationship. Praeger would pitch books he wanted to publish, which comported with Agency interests, but which were not economically feasible to publish, and the Agency would frequently subsidize the publication and marketing of these books. Cord Meyer had been involved in this previously, and Tracy Barnes and his assistant at the Domestic Operations Division, Howard Hunt, would be involved with the Praeger operation. As is often the case during this period of time, Dulles seems to have been actively involved with Agency business from which he was supposed to have been separated.

In April '62, Dulles had appointments with important active CIA station head Bronson Tweedy and another appointment with one of Dulles's Agency favorites, Tracy Barnes. In the wake of the Bay of Pigs fallout, Barnes was busily staking out his Agency future, while his fellow participants in the "fiasco" were shown the door. April 23 brought a call from Agency legend Henry Hecksher regarding an "article on Indonesia," and a call from Barnes, who said he had decided to "do nothing for the time being." (A great many of the Dulles calls were monitored for content by Dulles's secretary. Some were not and are specifically designated "not monitored.") On April 25, DCI McCone issues a dinner invitation to Dulles. McCone and Dulles would communicate and meet frequently over the next few months. April 30 brought a call from head of CIA's Far Eastern Division, Desmond Fitzgerald. Fitzgerald and Dulles discussed the "situation in Laos." That situation involved CIA opposition to President Kennedy's policy of attempted neutrality between competing factions in that country, a policy Kennedy had laid down soon after taking office, amidst a powerful barrage of military and intelligence advice to him to intervene forcefully in Laos.

The close Dulles-McCone relationship, and Dulles's frequent "informal" consulting with key Agency personnel on matters concerning US foreign policy, brought forth a caustic evaluation from veteran diplomat W. Averell Harriman. Harriman spoke with Kennedy aide Arthur Schlesinger in May 1962. Harriman told Schlesinger that JFK's policy of Laotian neutrality was being "systematically sabotaged by the military and the CIA." "McCone and the people in the CIA want the president to have a setback," Harriman contended. "They want to justify the [interventionist] position CIA took five years ago. They want to prove that a neutral solution is impossible, and that the only course is to turn Laos into an American bastion." McCone, who largely shared the Dulles perspective, "has no business in the New Frontier," railed Harriman, who clearly believed, as David Talbot suggests, that Kennedy's purge of the CIA had not been sweeping enough. In 1963, Dulles would accurately inform a newspaper columnist who had authored a critical piece on CIA operations that "Since my retirement, there have been few important policy changes, and I am wholly in support of its new chief and of its recent work."

Nineteen sixty-two would continue to be an "active" year for Dulles, as reflected in his appointment and call diaries. He began to meet regularly with his old friend and former Agency kingpin Frank Wisner, who had suffered a great deal of emotional anguish during his last few years at CIA, and had retired from the Agency in '62. Dulles met journalist and Agency asset Isaac Don Levine on June 13. On July 13, Dulles also met "Mr. Wyatt," likely Mark Wyatt, an old-boy Agency operator from the late 1940s, and a man who would be tasked with the unenviable job of supporting Bill Harvey in Rome, after Harvey's RFK-led exile following the Cuban Missile Crisis.

Summer meetings with long-time Agency asset Perkins McGuire and State Department clandestine operator Robert Murphy, as well as continued meetings with McCone, filled Dulles's schedule. McGuire, former Assistant

Secretary of Defense for Supply and Logistics, appears multiple times in the papers of Otto Skorzeny and, per the research of historian Ralph Ganis, was the US government contact who authorized the clandestine use of Skorzeny's training camps by US Army special forces. Multiple meetings with Dulles's protégé, Angleton, at times with Howard Hunt in tow, and continued frequent contact with Ray Rocca occurred during 1962. Some of the Rocca calls were redacted. In a particularly striking illustration of Dulles's continued sway within CIA, on Oct. 8, Dulles requested certain OSS records from the new Far Eastern station head, William Colby. Records that Dulles probably had no right to have at the time. Colby's first response was to "request an autographed picture of AD."

Dulles continued to communicate regularly with close associate William A. M. Burden during 1962 and early 1963. Burden, the great-great-grandson of the founder of the Vanderbilt wealth, railroad baron Cornelius Vanderbilt, who maintained a business office at a New York City address (630 Fifth Avenue) in which Dulles was also ensconced, ran the gamut of US national policy and prime corporate positions. Burden served on the boards of the Hanover Bank, Lockheed Aircraft Co., and CBS during his lengthy career. He had been a director of the Council on Foreign Relations and founded a family investment firm that bears his name today. During the Second World War, he had been a Special Assistant for Research and Development to the Secretary of the Army Air Force.

Following a heavy campaign contribution to the 1956 Presidential campaign of Dwight Eisenhower, Burden was granted an ambassadorship to Belgium, a position he held from 1959 to 1961, during the period of time that the former imperialist power was struggling to hold on to the remnants of past wealth and national glory. After the ascension to power in the Congo of charismatic leader Patrice Lumumba, Burden strongly felt the threat that Lumumba's independence posed to Belgium's longtime preeminence in the mineral-rich Congo and was lobbying his longtime friend Dulles for action against Lumumba in 1959.

Dulles, Burden, and the State Department's C. Douglas Dillon led the charge to persuade President Eisenhower to take serious action against Lumumba, culminating in an August 1960 "direct approval" by Eisenhower of Dulles's backing of a plot to assassinate Lumumba. While the US-Belgian war to eliminate the Congolese leader moved forward in 1960–61, journalist James Phelan would report receiving a postcard from the Congo, mailed by his friend and clandestine source Pierre Lafitte, who was engaged in . . . something in that embattled country at the time.

1963

In 1963, Dulles maintained some of the same contacts, but there were noticeable differences. Part of this was his interest in preparing the book that would be published under his name in the fall of the year, to be titled *The Craft of Intelligence*. Dulles spent time going over galleys for the book and in communication with his publisher, a longtime friend, Cass Canfield, of Harper and Row. Dulles also spent a great deal of time with the men who effectively "ghosted" the book: Howard Roman, whose wife Jane Roman was part of Jim Angleton's shop at CIA Counterintelligence; *Fortune* magazine reporter Charles Murphy; and E. Howard Hunt, then working for Tracy Barnes at DOD. Dulles tapped renowned CIA analyst Sherman Kent for research and used Frank Wisner as a sounding board. There was less communication with Angleton on the record than there had been in 1962, and far less communication with Tracy Barnes. In light of the notes made by Pierre Lafitte, the timing of some of the contacts Dulles had with these men will be examined shortly.

Tracy Barnes phoned on April 1, but Dulles was not available. Barnes "will call again," the notation reads. But he would not contact Dulles on his business phone for some time. On April 17, dinner was had with Jim and Cicely Angleton. On April 24, Angleton phoned Dulles. On April 23, the November visit of JFK to multiple Texas cities was announced by Lyndon Johnson. May through August '63 were "light" as far as calls and appointments went. A couple of meetings with Wisner, and an appointment with Praeger were recorded. Angleton phoned on June 28. Lafitte datebook entries during this time period suggest the possibility that Pierre visited New York City, and that he had planned meetings with Charles Willoughby and Ilse Skorzeny, although we do not know when these entries were written. Dulles took a long vacation to Colorado in July, likely aligned with Aspen Institute's summer schedule. July and August were very light in recorded communications by/with Dulles.

June 12 featured an evening reception for Deputy Secretary of Defense Roswell Gilpatric and his wife. Dulles had been invited by Secretary of Defense Robert McNamara and Joint Chiefs of Staff Chairman Maxwell Taylor, who had organized the reception. This is as good a place as any to note that both McNamara and Taylor highly respected Allen Dulles. Taylor would serve with Dulles on the board of a major Wall Street investment firm—Nation-Wide Securities—prior to assuming a role in Mexico City with Canadian-based Mexican Light and Power, and after he served as Kennedy's Joint Chief. Nationwide was heavily invested in military contractors. McNamara, interviewed by author Noel Twyman in 1994, took care to absolve Dulles from any possible involvement in the assassination of President Kennedy. "McNamara made a very specific point that in his view it was impossible that Allen Dulles and Richard Helms were behind the Kennedy assassination," wrote Twyman. "He reiterated several times that Richard Bissell, Allen Dulles, and Richard Helms had been or were still his close personal friends; that he knew them like brothers . . ." Such was the aura of institutional respectability that surrounded Dulles during his lifetime.

September and October, as reflected by the appointment and call diaries, heat up considerably for Dulles. Meetings with Arleigh Burke, Cord Meyer, Wisner, and Sam Papich from FBI are recorded, as well as a dinner with former President Eisenhower. September 19 features a very strange bit of clandestine . . . something. Following a call from Howard Hunt, an entry reads: "Mrs. Nickerson, Montreal, said she had been 'instructed' to give 'very urgent' material to Mr. Dulles, person- ally." "Dulles in N.Y." "Subsequently, letter and package were delivered."

September also brought a Dulles meeting with the board of Calvin Bullock, Lt., and an agreement to address that board subsequently. The Bullock group, headed by close Dulles associate Hugh Bullock, was one of the top invest- ment-management firms in the United States and, at various times during this period, featured the chairman of General Dynamics (and former Army Secre- tary) Frank Pace, Gen. Maxwell Taylor, Admiral R.B. Carney (Chief of Naval Operations during the Eisenhower administration), and President of Columbia University Grayson Kirk on its Board of Directors. No doubt, the degree to which Dulles remained plugged in to strands of national policy during his "retirement" from CIA was of interest to the Bullock people . . .

As of September 17, it appears from datebook entries that Pierre Lafitte and his wife, Rene, are in New York City for a brief stay. This follows a September 16 entry in which Pierre wrote, "Set-up complete." On October 2, another very odd entry appears in Dulles's phone log. "Mr. Hunt – Figure AWD interested in is '42." This may, of course have to do with Dulles's recently published book, but it is unusual and looks to be coded communication from Hunt to AD.

The record of an October 10 phone call to Dulles was redacted—blacked out—with the only surviving markings being exclamation marks on both ends of the blackout, certainly a provocative look. Dulles met with Papich of FBI on this date, as well as having lunch with Frank Wisner. On October 11, the nota- tion "Two calls redacted" appears. This comes two days after a lengthy Lafitte datebook entry in which Pierre lays out what looks to be a great many particulars that pertain to the upcoming assassination of Kennedy. On October 16, Dulles signed a copy of *Craft of Intelligence* for "Bob Nichols," presumably the financial reporter for the *Los Angeles Times*, Robert Nichols, which aligns with reports that

Dulles made a whirlwind, forty-eight-hour DC/LA round trip jaunt, landing him in DC Thursday, October 17. On October 18, Angleton calls Dulles, for the first time in nearly four months.

As noted, Lafitte, in a critically important datebook entry dated October 17, wrote, "JA call yest. Says High-level gathering in D.C. Lancelot – GO – OK . . ."

On October 19 and 20, there are no recorded communications with Mr. Dulles. On October 17, a Dallas newspaper had announced the arrival of Dulles for book promotional events, and a Dulles address at the Dallas Council on World Affairs scheduled for October 28. One does not need to speculate unduly to come to the conclusion that something of clandestine importance was being attended to during this time period by Mr. Dulles. In light of this meshing of calls and activity, it may not be surprising that "by October 1963, Dulles felt confident enough to speak out against Kennedy's foreign policy in public, ignoring the Washington etiquette that deemed it bad form to criticize a president whom you had recently served," as Talbot writes.

Prior to the arrival of Dulles in Texas, two phone calls from the previous month should be noted. On September 17, Dulles's secretary phoned Canon Martin of St. Albans school and regretfully informed him that, through an error, AWD would be unable to fulfill a previously scheduled October 24 commitment at the renowned D.C. private school, due to the fact that Dulles had an overriding scheduled appearance in Houston on that date. Mr. Martin "was very kind" and said that he planned to call Mrs. Wilkinson, with whom the initial arrangement had apparently been made.

Either Martin, or Dulles's secretary, phoned Mrs. Wilkinson, who expressed surprise at the cancellation, saying that "she couldn't understand how the error had occurred, since she had a letter from Harper's confirming the date and she also knew that AWD had to be in Princeton on the evening of October 24 . . ." Mrs. Wilkinson said she would attempt to change the date of the Dulles appearance to October 31. "We are to call . . . if this date is satisfactory . . . although there is a possibility the date cannot be changed," wrote Dulles's secretary. The following day, Dulles agreed to an appearance at a book fair at St. Albans on October 31. In the context of Dulles's forthcoming trip and other significant time-line events, it seems likely that Dulles's priorities for October were distinctly different from what they had been months before.

On October 25, Dulles arrived in Houston for the first leg of his Texas book promotional tour. Dulles's Texas itinerary—Houston to Ft. Worth to Dallas—would mirror the schedule of President Kennedy less than a month later. The Texas visit, presumably due to an invitation from his old Dallas friend Neil

Mallon, was the only "noncoast" appearance Dulles would make in support of the book. Talbot writes: "Dulles often used speaking engagements and vacations as cover for serious business, and his detour through Texas bears the markings of such a stratagem." Also on October 25, Lafitte noted, "Call JA Wash D.C. - O says - done - Oswald set in place - call Walker & others."

Dulles would deliver the promised address to Mallon's DCWA, after spending the 27th in Ft. Worth, with only a speech made to the "Friends of the Fort Worth Library" recorded in his diaries. He returned to Washington, D.C., on October 29. On Monday, October 28, and on the following day, Lafitte—who moved easily between his home in New Orleans and Dallas in 1963—entered only the words "Lancelot Planning" in his datebook. Detailed planning for the forthcoming murder of JFK was on the agenda.

Dulles began November '63 with a meeting with Frank Wisner, and a two-hour visit to the Tunisian Embassy on November 5. On November 12, he resumed an old pattern, having lunch with Howard Roman. November 13 featured a meeting with NASA's golden boy, Wernher von Braun, who had smoothly moved from providing creative expertise for Adolf Hitler's rocket technology to doing the same for the American military establishment during the height of the Cold War. On November 14, Tracy Barnes called AD, for the first (recorded) time since April 1 of '63. The description of the call notes that the two men discussed "the Praeger project," and that, in itself, would not seem surprising, since Barnes was handling contact with the CIA-subsidized publisher by that time, and since Dulles was still in frequent contact with Praeger.

If, however (as I have argued elsewhere), Tracy Barnes was the mysterious "T" in Lafitte's datebook, it is striking that this call was made to Dulles on the day in which "T" engaged in what was an extremely important meeting regarding the rapidly approaching murder of JFK. On November 14, "T" met personally with a crucial cog in the "on-the-ground" planning for the Dallas event: Jack Crichton, a man whom Dulles's old friend Col. Albert Haney would describe as being a vitally important part of the JFK assassination. Barnes would contact Dulles again on November 18, the day in which a threat against the life of President Kennedy was uncovered in Tampa, Florida.

Dulles was addressing a Brookings Institution breakfast meeting on November 22, 1963, in Williamsburg, Virginia. After the Dallas shooting, he headed immediately to the northern Virginia countryside, where he would spend the weekend at a top-secret CIA facility known officially as Camp Peary, but referred to within CIA as "The Farm." As CIA director, Dulles had created what Talbot describes as "a comfortable home" at The Farm. As an active participant in numerous Agency affairs two years after his forced "retirement," Dulles was still welcome there. As former House Assassinations Committee investigator Dan Hardaway told Talbot: "The Farm was basically an alternative CIA headquarters, from where Dulles could direct ops." It is not entirely clear from Hardaway's quote whether he was referring to Dulles's role in the Agency when he had been formerly in charge, or what was, in 1963, a continuation of his power and influence by less formal means. As has been strongly suggested by a journey through Dulles's contacts and activities during 1962 and 1963, there seems to have been little substantive difference between the two time periods, at least not to Mr. Dulles and his acolytes.

November 26 brought a call from President Lyndon Johnson, who was very interested in appointing Dulles to the investigative body that would become known as the Warren Commission. Dulles graciously accepted the position as one of the seven commissioners who would oversee the inquiry, a position that Dulles confidant William Corson later told author Joe Trento that Dulles had "lobbied hard for." Dulles told Johnson that "I would like to be of any help." Dulles's protégé Richard Helms, then CIA Deputy Director of Plans, would allegedly tell historian Michael Kurtz that he had personally persuaded LBJ to appoint Dulles, but it is doubtful that the president needed much persuading on this count.

Dulles would throw himself into the job, becoming the commissioner who attended the highest percentage of WC sessions. Dulles began preparation for the establishment slant that he would bring to the Commission quickly. A December 2 phone contact shows Dulles requesting multiple copies of Isaac Don Levine's *The Mind of an Assassin*, Levine's study of the Kremlin-dispatched murderer of Leon Trotsky. Readers will remember from the epilogue of this book the datebook entry penned by Pierre Lafitte on November 28, 1963: "Levine will deal with Marina . . ."

December 5, 1963, is a date that resonates historically, both on the surface, and in the backstory provided by the datebook of Pierre Lafitte. The first meeting of the Warren Commission was held, on a day in which Dulles spoke with DDP Richard Helms, and Lafitte recorded the essence of a personal conversation with CIA Counterintelligence head James Angleton in a datebook entry: "JA (Close out Lancelot)," with a reference to "T," as well.

Allen Dulles would take the stage as the most active member of the Warren Commission, with the intent of wrapping up the investigation of Kennedy's assassination without drawing undue attention to personnel or operations connected to CIA. Dulles would chat with Angleton on December 11—a "power call" day in which Dulles also talked with Prescott Bush and Dick Helms—confirming a dinner meeting between the two men on December 12, a meeting that likely had to do with the same topic of discussion that occupied Angleton when he spoke with Lafitte a week before. In mid-December, Dulles would be communicating again with CIA DCI McCone, this time pointing toward a forthcoming California meeting.

Among the many portions of Dulles's call and appointment diaries that are blacked out, a December entry stands out as being particularly odd. On December 6, a day in which Dulles had one more of the frequent conversations he enjoyed during this time period with Frank Wisner, an entry reads: "REDACTED reported that a group of Air Force officers had planned to try to impeach President Kennedy before next re-election. AWD advised he report to FBI . . . REDACTED." As is the case with many of Dulles's calls and plans during the period of time that he was supposedly out of power, one would like to know more about this. Who made the allegation, where did this person get the information, and whether the word "impeach" should be taken literally, or whether it masks another activity that might have been considered. But neither Allen Dulles, nor those he moved within close proximity to, were concerned with abstractions such as the "right to know." Dulles moved quietly down back channels of a world he helped to create, and we do the best we can with what is left to us of his life and times.

ENRIQUE ERNESTO PUGIBET:
A TIMELY VISIT TO DALLAS
BY ALAN KENT

In 1967, Allen Eli Wright was housed in a federal prison in Leavenworth, Kansas, the culmination of a fascinating life of high-level crime. Wright had worked as a diamond smuggler and had been involved in a variety of often sophisticated scams. Beyond these activities, he moved in some high-level and dangerous circles throughout his adult life. When arrested in connection with a half-million-dollar diamond swindle in 1959, he hinted to authorities that he had information about "underground activity in Cuba, Panama, Mexico, and other South American countries and was close to the President of Nicaragua, with whom he was involved in an oil refinery deal . . ." Claims of this nature are sometimes made by criminals who are facing possible confinement, but Wright was indeed an interesting fellow. The same FBI document that gave us the above information closed with this: *"In July 1960, while still under bond, he volunteered the information contained in [unintelligible letters] B 3162730 which was the earliest indication of Soviet Missile activity in Cuba that we are aware of."*

Wright knew people of importance, people who were involved in covert operations with agencies of the United States and other countries. A December 1962 memo from the chief of CIA's Miami Field Office to the chief of CIA Contact Division informs us that the MFO had received a December 18 call from Joseph Merola, "notorious racketeer, gun runner and ex-convict." Merola, part of the large network of criminal types who also served as informants to US intelligence agencies, called to report that ". . .a US national, Allen Eli Wright, had arrived in town from Mexico and stated that Julio Couttilenc of the Mexican Secret Service had informed him that the 'Number 2 Man' of the Soviet Embassy in Moscow was interested in defecting." The CFO (Justin F. Gleichauf) checked with JMWAVE to see if there was information on Wright and Couttolenc and found that both names were listed. Gleichauf quickly requested that Merola set up an appointment with Wright, which he apparently did.

Wright arrived in Gleichauf's office accompanied by Chester Gray, "a well-known con man and racketeer." Gray's actual name was Chester Zochowski, another person with high-level contacts, who would become involved in deals with Mitchell WerBell. Wright outlined the story as he had heard it from Couttilenc, adding that Couttilenc "had been on the payroll of General Trujillo and also on the payroll of General Somoza as an informer on matters of interest to the governments involved . . ." Wright closed his discussion with Gleichauf—who appeared very interested in Wright's story—by indicating that he would be interested in some remuneration from the US government for his services, also mentioning that he was "in trouble with a branch of the US government, possibly Secret Service, and that a kind word might not be amiss . . ." Gleichauf closed the memo with this: "P.S. As of 1500 hours on 18 Dec., a phone call from Julio Couttilenc to Wright indicates that the individual [the potential defector] is still available and interested."

Further information on Wright, highlighted in FBI files, shows him to be "promoting a deal in Panama which depends on the United States Government making a loan to Panama for the purpose of constructing a hydro-electric dam" in 1961, a plan in which he was purportedly involved with Gulfport, Mississippi, Mayor R.B. Meadows, Jr., and attempting to "work a confidence scheme" involving the operation of a still in the Dominican Republic. Regarding the latter project, "New Orleans files reflect that investigation was conducted in 1961 concerning ALLEN ELI WRIGHT, FBI # 362873B, reported to have been an alleged former FBI agent [!] who was in the Dominican Republic on April 11, 1961, in company with the Dominican Consul General of New Orleans." Among his many other designations, Wright is described in this document as being "a big hoodlum from Houston, Texas."

Clearly, Wright was more than a swindler and a crook. He had moved in and around the security services and intelligence agencies of multiple governments. He knew who to contact, and how to do so. He wanted favors, monetarily and otherwise, and was willing to leverage information to achieve that goal. There is much more that could be said about Wright, who appears to have led a life that was worthy of a movie, but I want to move back to 1967, when a great many epochal events were taking place in the United States, including the investigation into the assassination of President Kennedy by New Orleans District Attorney Jim Garrison. Garrison, who was quite understaffed for such a lofty quest, was being helped by numerous private citizens. While this "help" sometimes took the form of infiltration of his operation by interested parties, Garrison did have the benefit of assistance from a handful of dedicated, serious researchers. Among them was former FBI agent William Turner, who was also a first-class investigative reporter, working for *Ramparts* magazine in the 1960s. In '67, Turner was contacted by the wife of prison inmate Allen Eli Wright. In a July 16, 1967 letter to Garrison, Turner wrote, "Mrs. Wright claims her husband has indicated to her that he has information bearing on the assassination . . . he wants to talk to someone from your office or Ramparts . . ."

Whether, or to what degree, Garrison or his staff took interest in Wright is unknown. Reference checks through multiple sources related to Garrison's investigation reveal no mention of Wright. At the time in question, Garrison's office was being inundated with offers of information, which he and his staff were ill-prepared to examine carefully. Much of the information was of dubious quality, and it is likely that an offer from a Leavenworth Prison inmate was tossed into that category. If so, Garrison probably missed out on a significant piece of information.

Later, in the 1970s, another investigative reporter who possessed formidable resources, Bernard Fensterwald, had the opportunity to talk with Allen Wright, and to document the essence of what Wright had tried to tell Garrison. Researcher Mary Ferrell—who developed a close relationship with Fensterwald—was given Fensterwald's notes pertaining to his conversation with Wright. In one of her extensive chronological files, Ferrell records Fensterwald's summary. "An FBI informer," Allen Wright, alleged that an Ernesto Puijet [*sic*] "checked into the Stoneleigh Hotel in Dallas on November 19, 1963." "Puijet" was, according to Wright, a French gunman for hire who was posing as a cattle rancher. Wright asserted that "Pujiet" was in Dallas on November 22, 1963. There does not appear to be an "Ernesto" or "Ernest" Pujiet involved in anything like what we will see that this person of interest is involved with. But "Ernesto Pugibet" fits the description given by Wright very well. (As an aside, I have worked through some of Fensterwald's notes. He was not a secretarial-quality transcriber.)

Pugibet was—like Allen Wright—a person of interest to FBI and CIA. From a documentary study focusing on him, utilizing multiple trusted FBI informants as well as statements from Pugibet himself, we find that he had been a member of the French resistance during the Second World War—as an "anticommunist," he would emphatically declare to investigators, had been a naturalized citizen of Mexico from 1947 on, and had worked for the Mexican Ministry of Agriculture and also the notorious Mexican Federal Security, on the "Communist squad." While going through the United States—he would say on a mission for the Ministry of Agriculture—in 1959, he was deported from the US after being convicted of a crime "involving moral turpitude."

A source within the Mexican government advised US authorities that Pugibet had been charged in the past on various occasions with "crimes of fraud and abuse of confidence." When, on October 23 and October 28, Pugibet voluntarily spoke to personnel at the US Embassy in Mexico City, he stated that he had been referred there by "a mutual acquaintance," Colonel Roscoe B. Gaither, a Mexico City attorney. In fact, Gaither was not a run-of-the-mill lawyer. He was a highly connected international figure who represented oil companies in Venezuela and Mexico, among other countries, and he was the founder of the Papantla Royalties Corporation. His intervention on Pugibet's behalf is an indication that Pugibet had developed important connections.

Pugibet told embassy personnel that he had a background that included training in protection, and that he was closely associated with the Chief of the Presidential Staff of Mexico, General Jose Gomez Huerta. He added the information that he had been advised by a friend of his "who is Director of Presidential Security on the staff of the Mexican President, Arturo Wollfer" that during a visit of the Mexican President to Washington, D.C., the Chief of Security of the United States Secret Service, one Sr. Bauman (phonetic) had shown Wollfer a card with a photograph of Pugibet thereon, a card which had the designation "Communist and possible bomb-thrower." The skewed spelling of the Secret Service head's name no doubt referred to the head of Secret Service during the Eisenhower administration, U. E. Baughman.

Pugibet had friends in both high and low places. An important FBI report, written in 1961 by Bureau agent Henry Thomas, notes Pugibet's booking in Dallas in 1958 on a worthless check charge. Dallas County Sheriff's office records from this time period describe Pugibet as claiming to be a cattleman, a confirmation of the information about Pugibet given by Wright. He was described by "a source" as "the biggest crook in the world." On entirely another level, FBI informant NY-T-2 described Pugibet as a one-time agent of Dominican Republic dictator Rafael Trujillo.

* * *

One of Pugibet's Dallas-based friends who bridged the gap between "high and low" was Norman (Roughhouse) Rothman, a well-known operative of Santo Trafficante Jr. Pugibet is connected to Rothman in several FBI documents. Significantly, Thomas writes: "It is to be noted that information concerning the subject has been set forth in various reports in the case entitled: 'Norman Rothman; IS-DR; RA-DR, Bureau file 97-3487.' Pertinent information from this investigation . . ." And that is where the sentence, and any further reference to Pugibet and Rothman, stops. What appear to be pages later—not formally redacted, just missing—lead to a non-sequitur finish. It is relevant to the inquiry into Pugibet to note that both of the specific FBI Rothman files cited by Thomas have to do with Rothman's dealings with the Trujillo government in the Dominican Republic.

One more story emerges from the truncated Thomas report, this one both stunning and relevant to our inquiry. Pugibet was apparently involved directly in a political assassination. FBI informant NY T-1, a prized and protected FBI source, "advised one Pugibet killed Jose Almoina Mateos, former secretary to Trujillo, in Mexico, in May 1960." NY T-1's detailed account "regarding the assassination of Jose Almoina Mateos, former Private Secretary to Generalissimo Trujillo in Mexico, in May 1960" claimed that two individuals presently being held by Mexican police on suspicion of the murder of Almoina, namely Artemio Servado Molina and Francisco Quitana Valdes, did not kill Almoina. NY T-1 said Almoina was killed by Pugibet, "who is now working for the Dominican Military Intelligence Service (SIM)." NY T-I stated that Pugibet was directly involved in the murder and that he either "drove the car, did the actual shooting, or he was the third man in the plot."

We know from a coalescence of evidence that Pierre Lafitte was ensconced in the Stoneleigh Hotel on November 19–20, 1963, conducting meetings and making calls in furtherance of the final stages of the plot that felled President Kennedy. We know that Ilse Skorzeny was there as well, among others who were close to the ongoing plot. I contend that if a man with the lengthy résumé of Enrique Ernesto Pugibet, a highly connected criminal who had been directly involved in a political assassination, checked into the Stoneleigh on November 19 and remained through November 22, as alleged by a man who was extremely well-connected himself, and this sequence of events turned out to be coincidental, the bounds of coincidence would have been stretched almost to the breaking point.

When Allen Wright gave this information to Bernard Fensterwald—years after he had attempted to give it to Jim Garrison—there was no hint of the use of the Stoneleigh as an assassination planning venue in any record that could be accessed. Wright clearly knew something of importance, and Pugibet clearly was involved in some way in the assassination of President Kennedy.

If Pugibet was involved, what was his likely role? And on whose behalf was he acting in Dallas? Does he connect to groups or persons of interest in our investigation? These are all important questions, and, while they cannot be answered definitively at this point in time, I believe that some reasonable assertions can be made. Let's start by suggesting that November 19—three days before the planned assassination of JFK—is awfully late for a shooter to be arriving on the scene. Although we cannot be certain, it appears from inferential evidence in the Lafitte datebook that Jean Souetre and his team of assassins arrived in the Dallas area a week or so prior to November 22.

It has been suggested that in a well-planned operation, gunmen participating in a high-level assassination would want to arrive on the scene a couple of weeks prior to the planned event in order to thoroughly familiarize themselves with the "lay of the land." While there seems no doubt that the plot managed by Lafitte was thoroughly planned out, there is also a certain sense of flux as the final steps are taken during October and November 1963. Still, three days is probably too short a time for a shooter who is participating in a crime of this magnitude. Although Pugibet had been in and around Dallas before, I will lean on Pugibet likely being used in some auxiliary role. Recall that "NY T1" was not certain whether he had acted as a shooter or in another capacity in the murder of Trujillo's secretary three years earlier.

In noting that Pugibet was apparently tied with Norman Rothman, and his involvement with the anticommunist strain of French resistance forces in Europe during World War Two, we point in the direction of two of the factions that coalesced in the 1963 murder of JFK. While the resistance forces in Nazi-occupied France were, of course, acting in opposition to Germany, there was a good deal of slipperiness among individuals and groups who were involved. According to Albarelli, Pierre Lafitte participated in OSS-run missions in Nazi-occupied France and Belgium. On the other hand, he "reportedly had dealings with Henri Dericourt, double-agent extraordinaire, who sold drugs and black market goods for François Spirito . . ." And Lafitte was to align himself with Waffen SS Colonel Otto Skorzeny, as part of a French unit that assisted the Nazi occupation of France.

There were many others besides Lafitte who played both ends, while attempting to profit thereby. It was a nasty business in a nasty war. It may be of interest that Pugibet hooked up with Mexican brothers and arms dealers Alfred J. Miranda and Ignatius Joseph Miranda, operating with them during the late 1940s and throughout the 1950s. The Miranda brothers, who founded the military supply company American Armament Corp. in 1933, were alleged to have been pro-Nazi during World War Two. It may also be of interest that the name Enrique Ernesto Pugibet appears in a file listing compiled by the Interagency Working Group on Nazi War Crimes, housed at the National Archives. I would be interested to ask Ralph Ganis whether his Skorzeny archival collection contains any references to Pugibet, The Miranda brothers, or American Armament.

Norman Rothman is a thread that leads us down a more certain path. Among the multiple FBI reports involving Rothman with the Dominican Republic (referenced earlier in the Thomas report), a particularly informative one deals with Rothman's associates involved in a large jewelry theft ring in the late 1950s, and also with a Rothman interest in playing some sort of role for the Trujillo government in the late 1950s. Rothman's partners in the moving of stolen jewelry include figures we have already come across, such as Allen Wright's companion Chester Zochowski (the fellow who later partnered with Mitch WerBell); and Joseph Merola, Wright's friend, who played both sides, informing on Wright. Given Rothman's affiliation with Pugibet, I think we may be a bit closer to understanding the path by which Wright came to know of Pugibet's timely visit to Dallas in 1963.

Rothman cuts far deeper than his role in running large heists. Author Peter Dale Scott, citing sources as diverse as Kaplan and Dubro's study *Yakuza*, Alan Block's works, Bruce Cumings's *Origins of the Korean War*, the McClellan Hearings on organized crime, and Walter Sheridan's biography of Jimmy Hoffa, paints a rich tapestry. Describing the evidence for a formerly unnamed network (Operation X, as Scott calls it) trading in weapons and drugs that encompassed individuals connected over the years with both organized crime and US intelligence agencies—including the Federal Bureau of Narcotics—Scott lays out the interconnected milieu that we see a part of in our examination of the murder of President Kennedy:

> . . . CIC (China), a subsidiary of Donovan's World Commerce Corporation, was the firm that employed mob figure Sonny Fassoulis, at the urging of army colonel (and FBN agent) Garland Williams, to procure arms for Taiwan in the period of private procurement before the Korean War. From 1946 on, Major-General Charles Willoughby . . . used Japan's dope-dealing yakuza gangs to break up left-wing strikes and demonstrations, just as CIA backed the Corsican Guerinis in Marseille . . . Like Operation Underworld before it, "Operation X," with FBN agents at its center, operated both within and outside the CIA, and particularly with the military. This arrangement continued.
>
> In the late 1950s, US Army Colonel Jack Y. Canon, a veteran of the Willoughby-yakuza operations in Japan, penetrated Castro's guerrilla operation against Batista in Cuba . . . . Associated with Canon in Cuba was

a US Marine reservist, Gerry Patrick Hemming . . . . With Hemming was another Marine reservist, future Watergate burglar Frank Sturgis . . . Castro appears to have accepted the services of Canon, Hemming, and also Sturgis, because of their ability to procure surplus or allegedly stolen US military supplies for his troops. Hoffa and mob casino operator Norman Rothman both were part of this arms flow, for which in exchange Castro initially selected Sturgis, a Rothman associate, to be his liaison in 1959 with the Havana casinos . . . ."

Rothman, of course, was well known as being the 1950s operator of Havana's San Souci casino, a joint venture with Santo Trafficante, Jr. As Scott notes, Rothman also was said to have a piece of the Trafficante/Meyer Lansky-owned Tropicana casino, an operation that employed Jack Ruby's close friend Lewis McWillie as a manager in 1959. According to an FBI informant, Ruby would later be active in arranging illegal-arms flights to Cuba, piloted by Rothman associate and CIA contract operator Eddie Browder.

Without dot-connecting ourselves into oblivion, I think that it is reasonable to see a long stretch of military, intelligence, and organized crime figures whose names we recognize: Willoughby, Canon, McWillie, Trafficante, Ruby, et al. Pierre Lafitte moved comfortably in this world, associating with Lansky associates Amleto Battisti y Lora and Paul Mondolini in Cuba, and Santo Trafficante in Florida and Cuba. And Dallas's Norman Rothman, associated closely with Ernesto Pugibet, was directly centered in this milieu. Pugibet was a foot soldier, and there is much that we don't know about him, but we can reasonably assert that he played some role in the assassination of JFK and that we can, at least in a general sense, speak to his derivation: the path to his arrival at the Stoneleigh Hotel at such a critical time in US and world history. His role may have been small, or it may have been larger than we know, but he was there. He played a part in the history we are attempting to gather and set out.

THE GATHERING NETWORK
BY ANTHONY THORNE

In 1935, Frederick Seitz, a physicist at the University of Rochester, marries Elizabeth "Betty" Marshall. Seitz finds work as a research physicist at General Electric in 1937 and begins a career supporting military and corporate interests. Betty Marshall helps Seitz research a book on state-of-the-art physics. Lauriston Marshall, Betty's brother, is a physicist in the US Department of Agriculture, and Seitz remains close to their family.[1]

In 1939, Frederick Seitz becomes an associate professor at the University of Pennsylvania and meets Detlev Bronk, the future president of Rockefeller University. Seitz receives a letter from DuPont Laboratory, asking if he can visit their laboratory to discuss scientific problems and remains a DuPont consultant for the next 35 years. When World War II breaks out in Europe, Seitz assists munitions experts at Frankford Arsenal in producing bullets and researching armor penetration. The professor also consults on a ballistics laboratory for the Naval Reserve. Seitz's book *The Modern Theory of Solids* is published by Rockefeller University in 1940. It is acclaimed as a classic and advances the study of atomic physics.[2]

In June 1940, Carnegie Institute President Vannevar Bush helps create the National Defense Research Committee (NDRC), a group that enlists civilian scientists to work in university laboratories for the war effort. The NDRC is tasked with spending large amounts of government money on military research and creates numerous laboratories, including the Radiation Laboratory at the Massachusetts Institute of Technology (MIT). Lauriston Marshall, who had done pioneering work on radar systems, joins the Radiation Laboratory in 1940 and serves as its division director during the early years of WW2. Marshall manages a team of scientists doing classified work for the government, and Seitz gives technical assistance. In June 1941, the NDRC is replaced by the Office of Scientific Research and Development (OSRD), with Vannevar Bush as director. As the war intensifies, the OSRD is granted nearly unlimited budgets for its projects. Bush appoints physicist Lloyd Berkner as his assistant, until Berkner becomes occupied by radar duties during the war.[3]

When Vannevar Bush and the OSRD oversee the Manhattan Project in 1943, Seitz joins the project.

Marshall continues to manage scientific teams when the OSRD makes him the chief of its Operational Research Section in the Pacific Ocean Areas. After the war, Seitz is tasked by Henry Stimson to research German science of interest to the US military and industry. Seitz joins the Field Intelligence Agency, Technical (FIAT), and continues to work for the government. In 1946, The Federation of American Scientists produces a book on issues surrounding the atomic bomb, *One World Or None*. Seitz's essay, "How Close is the Danger?," warns of the continuance of the Soviet threat.[4]

In July 1946, Vannevar Bush becomes chairman of the Joint Research and Development Board (JRDB), a postwar replacement for the OSRD, and Berkner joins as Bush's Executive Secretary. Within a few years, the JRDB falls victim to bureaucratic infighting and is dissolved. Its eventual successor, the Defense Science Board (DSB), refocuses the scientific community's interest in dedicated military spending. Seitz joins the DSB as a consultant. In early 1949, Berkner becomes special assistant to Secretary of State Dean Acheson, and the coordinator for Foreign Military Assistance Programs. While in the State Department, Berkner also heads the Foreign Assistance Correlation Committee (FACC), where he works with Lyman Lemnitzer.

In the Spring of 1949, when the Soviet Union attempts to jam Voice of America radio broadcasts, government official James E. Webb contacts Berkner, a radio engineer by trade, and asks him to formulate a response using the military's network of academic advisors. Berkner assembles scientific personnel for the Cold War psychological warfare Project TROY at MIT in 1950 with Walt Rostow and completes a four-volume report for the State Department. On the TROY staff, Berkner includes Clyde Kluckhohn and Jerome Bruner, two ex-Office of War Information staff from Harvard University. Berkner's TROY report observes that up-to-date knowledge of foreign scientific developments is crucial to the work of American scientists and in a classified appendix, "Science Intelligence," suggests that American scientists should be covertly recruited for spy and intelligence work.

In March 1951, Vannevar Bush discusses the formation of a psychological warfare agency with Allen Dulles. Lloyd Berkner joins the newly formed Psychological Strategy Board with Dulles the following month. Berkner's completion of Project TROY establishes an ongoing relationship among the State Department, the CIA, and scientific/academic figures at MIT and Harvard. Berkner joins MIT's Center for International Studies (CENIS), a CIA-funded research body set up jointly by MIT and Harvard to allow Project TROY staff and managers to continue working on national security goals during the Cold War. CENIS members include Max Millikan, Assistant Director of the CIA, and Richard Pipes, who will join the Committee on the Present Danger in 1976. While Berkner participates in top-level government and intelligence discussions, Seitz does laboratory work studying how computers can be used for military purposes during the Korean War.[5]

Vannevar Bush and Lloyd Berkner work closely alongside Dulles for the next few years, as Berkner serves as a consultant to the National Security Resources Board. In April 1952, when Dean Acheson sets up a Panel of Consultants on Disarmament with J. Robert Oppenheimer, Vannevar Bush and Dulles are part of the panel. Berkner takes part in a May 1952 meeting at Princeton University with Dulles, Walt Rostow, and C.D. Jackson to discuss psychological warfare planning. Those same participants—Dulles, Berkner, Rostow, and C.D Jackson—return to Princeton in May 1954 to discuss economic strategies for the Cold War, where they are joined by Richard Bissell of the CIA. After their work on the disarmament panel, Dulles maintains a close friendship with Vannevar Bush. Bush had personally designed the pipe that the CIA director habitually smokes, and Dulles mentions it in letters to Bush, asking his friend to visit if he is ever in Washington. In 1954, Seitz becomes the Chairman of the American Institute of Physics, then starts work with NATO in Europe, establishing an air defense laboratory.[6]

In August 1955, Frederick Seitz attends the Atoms for Peace meeting of scientists in Geneva and views a demonstration by physicist Vladimir Veksler. Seitz is dismayed by the progress made by the Soviets and urges the Department of Defense to invest in a high-energy physics program.[7]

Also in 1957, Lloyd Berkner joins the President's Science Advisory Committee with Seitz. Berkner had joined the board of Texas Instruments (TI) that same year, and personnel from Texas Instruments occupy much of the GRCSW management through the decade that follows. (In 1963, GRCSW board members J. E. Jonsson and Eugene McDermott are chairmen of Texas Instruments, and Sol Goodell, the GRCSW Assistant Secretary, had worked as an attorney for Texas Instruments after WW2. Texas Instruments President Cecil Green is on the GRCSW Advisory Council and later joins his fellow TI founders on the board.) In 1958, Seitz helps NATO create a Naval research unit, and Berkner is made Chair of the Space Studies Board. In that role, Berkner will encourage cooperation with foreign scientists as a method of informally gathering scientific intelligence for the State Department and CIA. The same year, Joshua

Lederberg, a colleague of Seitz and Berkner, wins the Nobel Prize for his work in genetics.[8]

In 1959, Detlev Bronk offers Seitz the position of science advisor to NATO. Seitz accepts and is made a Foreign Service Officer with the Department of State. He receives security clearances for his position.[9]

Frederick Seitz accepts a consultantship with United Aircraft in 1960. At the beginning of the Kennedy administration, Charles Tyroler II, director of the Democratic Advisory Council, is president of Quadri-Science, Inc., a research and development company. In 1961, Tyroler hires Joshua Lederberg as a consultant.[10]

In early 1962, Arleigh Burke and other Cold War hawks make plans to establish the Center for Strategic and International Studies (CSIS). The cosecretary of the Institute is David Abshire, son-in-law of Admiral George Anderson. Within months, Anderson will be in charge of the US blockade of Cuba during the Cuban missile crisis. Abshire is a PhD graduate from Georgetown University, and James Horigan, Dean of the Graduate School, encourages Abshire to locate CSIS at Georgetown.[11]

In January 1962, Berkner notifies National Academy of Sciences President Detlev Bronk that he is leaving the SSB to join the GRCSW as president. Frederick Seitz is nominated president of the National Academy of Sciences (NAS) in July 1962. At NAS, Seitz inherits a staff, and his Executive Officer is S. Douglass Cornell from the Pentagon's Research and Development Board. In late 1962, when Berkner becomes president of the Graduate Research Center of the Southwest (GRCSW), Detlev Bronk joins Berkner on the Board of Directors. Frederick Seitz also becomes a member of the GRCSW. Lauriston Marshall and Berkner will continue working on scientific projects together for the next few years.[12]

On September 4th, 1962, CSIS opens its doors at Georgetown. Arleigh Burke and David Abshire begin making plans for a conference to be held by CSIS in early 1963. The planning continues during the Cuban missile crisis the following month. On January 23rd, 1963, CSIS begins a three-day conference in the Hall of Nations at Georgetown University, with Henry Jackson and Walt Rostow as headline speakers. James Schlesinger, future Secretary of Defense, attends as an economist. CSIS documents the discussions in a book intended to act as a guide for government as to where CSIS thinks the economy, Cold War, and country should be going. The book appears in December, shortly after JFK's murder in Dallas.[13]

Lloyd Berkner, now established at the GRCSW, had also served as a project member on the Gaither Report, working under Harry Truman's former Secretary of Defense, William C. Foster. Foster was another statutory member of the Psychological Strategy Board and was a longtime associate of Ralph Stohl, the GRCSW's vice president for Administration, secretary and treasurer. Stohl had previously worked as the Director of Administration for the US Government, and in 1947, he had signed off on the creation of the National Security Council and the CIA. From 1953 to 1955, Stohl was the Director of Domestic Security Programs, with Air Force Colonel Sidney Rubenstein working as a member of Stohl's staff. Rubenstein helped manage the American Society for Industrial Security (ASIS), a military/industrial group with board members from Boeing, Lockheed, and General Dynamics. ASIS often hosted Allen Dulles as speaker, and ASIS member George R. Wackenhut would later bring ex-FBI members with him from ASIS onto the board of the Wackenhut Corporation.[14]

GRCSW fixture Stohl had sworn William C. Foster into office in 1951, and the two men maintained connections in and out of government for the rest of the decade. Foster, an engineer by trade, deals regularly with the Pentagon's Research and Development Board. After leaving government, Foster becomes executive vice president of Olin Mathieson Chemical Corporation in 1955, and Stohl joins him at Olin Mathieson as a manager, working as Foster's assistant. With numerous government contracts, Olin Mathieson is an attractive destination for retiring high-ranking military figures seeking lucrative positions in big business. Foster codirects the Gaither Report committee in 1957 with Robert Sprague, after Ford Foundation President H. Rowan Gaither falls ill. Foster and Allen Dulles are also long-standing members of the Business Advisory Council. In the late 1950s, Foster and Olin Mathieson send overseas intelligence reports to the CIA, with Foster often communicating with Dulles. Foster's associate Stohl—like Stohl's fellow GRCSW member Bryghte Godbold, a former Korean War commander who had served as a Pentagon advisor—gives the Center additional connections to the military establishment in Washington.[15]

In 1964, Seitz becomes president of the Defense Science Board (DSB), heading an advisory group of Cold War scientists, industry R&D experts, and hawkish military figures who undertake studies for the Department of Defense. Under Seitz's leadership, the DSB promotes new weapons research and an increase in military expenditures. Texas Instruments and other major contractors benefit from DSB recommendations for years afterward, and members of those companies work with the DSB to produce reports recommending further weapons research and investment. In October 1965, John S. Foster Jr. (no relation to William C. Foster) is appointed director, Defense Research and Engineering. In November 1966, Foster, Jr., asks the DSB to list companies undertaking useful R&D programs for the Department of Defense. The eventual DSB report nominates 16 defense contractors, including Texas Instruments. Foster, Jr., previously director of Lawrence Livermore Laboratory, is also a member of the American Defense Preparedness Association (ADPA), a group devoted to maintaining the defense industrial base. For his first five years in office, Foster, Jr.'s assistant director, working alongside him in government, is Norman Augustine. Foster, Jr., will later work as a defense consultant, join the Committee on the Present Danger, then serve as DSB chairman for three years. Norman Augustine will later become under secretary of the Army, and then eventually the CEO of Martin Marietta and Lockheed Martin.[16]

In the late 1960s, as NAS President, Seitz also participates in plans to create the Office of Technology Assessment (OTA), a group that will advise on critical future trends in science and engineering. When the organization is finally established, Seitz collaborates on OTA reports, urging further military investment. During the Reagan administration, Congressman Jack Brooks (who was in the Dallas motorcade when JFK was killed) leads an investigation into the DSB, calling it an "old boy network" of defense employees and weapons contractors.[17]

The Defense Science Board defends the interests of the military-industrial complex for the next half-century, with DSB studies urging further investment in weapons systems. Future CIA heads R. James Woolsey, Jr., and John Deutch become recurrent members and join DSB task forces with other high-ranking figures from industry and government. DSB member Richard Garwin works with GRCSW members Bronk and Seitz in the Office of Science and Technology, then assists the National Academy of Science's Committee on Ballistic Acoustics. As part of the NAS study, Garwin examines audio recordings from the day of JFK's assassination and argues against the HSCA's claim of multiple gunmen. At the end of the 1980s, Norman Augustine joins with the DSB to warn of the impact of declining weapons investment as the Cold War draws to a close. The warnings will be heard by associates in government, the military, and the armaments industry. A new strategy will be required to navigate the changing security environment, and to determine what path the network should take as the new century approaches.[18]

NOTES FOR "THE GATHERING NETWORK"

[1] Seitz's career is discussed in depth in his well-illustrated autobiography *On the Frontier: My Life in Science*, a book that dives deep into some areas and carefully glides across others.

[2] *On the Frontier: My Life in Science*, p. 115, DuPont visit, p. 132, Frankford Arsenal, pp. 137–138. *The Modern Theory of Solids*, Frederick Seitz (International Series in Physics), McGraw-Hill Book Co, 1940.

[3] See *Five Years at the Radiation Laboratory*, p. 20, *Endless Frontier*, pp. 111–135.

[4] See Lauriston Marshall obituary, by Frederick Seitz, published in *Physics Today*, Volume 33, Issue 3, March 1980, p. 100. Seitz's essay is featured in One World or None, written with Hans Bethe, p. 116.

[5] Project TROY is discussed in "'Truth Is Our Weapon': Project TROY, Political Warfare, and Government-Academic Relations in the National Security State," by Allan A. Needell, Diplomatic History Vol. 17, No. 3 (Summer 1993), pp. 399-420 (22 pages), Oxford University Press. The founding of CENIS, with a membership list including Berkner, appears in Global TV - New Media and the Cold War, by James Schwoch, University of Illinois Press, 2009, p. 63. According to Schwoch, CENIS received a $875,000 grant from the Ford Foundation in August 1952. Also see Science, Cold War and the American State: Lloyd V. Berkner and the Balance of Professional Ideals, pp. 155–181.

[6] See *Science, Cold War and the American State: Lloyd V. Berkner and the Balance of Professional Ideals*. For Allen Dulles's comments about Vannevar Bush's pipe, see LETTER TO DR BUSH FROM ALLEN DULLES, November 19, 1958, CIA-RDP80R01731R000400290001-0

[7] see "Atoms for Peace, Scientific Internationalism, and Scientific Intelligence," *Osiris, Vol. 21, No. 1, Global Power Knowledge: Science and Technology in International Affairs* (2006), pp. 161–181, University of Chicago Press

[8] The staff of the GRCSW are covered in the Graduate Research Center of the Southwest 1963 Annual Report, June 30th, 1963, Dallas, Texas. A diverting, nearly week-by-week chronology of the Center is available at Graduate Research Center of the Southwest (GRCSW)/Southwest Center for Advanced Studies (SCAS) Collection, GRCSW/SCAS Chronology, 1961-1969 by Al Mitchell, Folders 1-6, Box 1, Series I, The University Archives, Special Collections Department, Eugene McDermott Library, The University of Texas at Dallas.

[9] *On the Frontier: My Life in Science*, pp. 241–242.

[10] *On the Frontier: My Life in Science*, p. 242. Lederberg letters about Quadri-Science detailed at The Joshua Lederberg Papers, Letter from Joshua Lederberg to Ralph E. Lapp and Charles Tyroler, Quadri-Science, Inc., 1st Dec. 1961, NLM ID: 101584906X19113, and Letter from Joshua Lederberg to Charles Tyroler, Quadri-Science, Inc., 7 February 1962, NLM ID: 101584906X19114.

[11] *Strategic Calling*, pp. 3–5.

[12] See *Science, Cold War and the American State: Lloyd V. Berkner and the Balance of Professional Ideals.*

[13] *Strategic Calling*, pp. 22–26. The CSIS essay collection is National Security - Political, Military and Economic Strategies in the Decade Ahead.

[14] Berkner, see *Science, Cold War and the American State: Lloyd V. Berkner and the Balance of Professional Ideals*; ASIS is detailed at REQUEST TO ADDRESS THE AMERICAN SOCIETY FOR INDUSTRIAL SECURITY, 1030, 16 SEPTEMBER 1958, April 10, 1958, CIA-RDP80B01676R003200170022-7

[15] Foster's biography through this period is usefully detailed in a lecture given by him in 1960. See The American Industrial Complex, William C. Foster, Industrial College of the Armed Forces, 1960, which concludes with a statement by Foster about the importance of the defense industrial base. For additional biographical details on Foster and Olin Mathieson, see LETTER TO ALLEN DULLES FORM GORDON GRAY [*sic*], September 18, 1957, CIA-RDP80B01676R001100090054-4 ; Foster sending intel to Dulles, LETTER TO MR. WILLIAM C. FOSTER FROM ALLEN W. DULLES, October 31, 1959, CIA-RDP80R01731R000200100018-4 ; Olin Mathieson attractive to ex-military, WASHINGTON CALLING . . . THE POSTWAR MERGER, by Marquis Childs, United Features Syndicate, April 20, 1956, reprinted at CIA-RDP68-00046R000200020050-1 . Godbold's life is detailed in Bryghte D. Godbold: An Oral History Interview, Conducted by Bonnie Lovell, Dallas, Texas, 2002, Goals for Dallas Oral History Project Interview: 311.

[16] *On the Frontier: My Life in Science*, pp. 294–295. DSB report.

[17] *On the Frontier: My Life in Science*, p. 303. Discussion of the Defense Science Board, with comments by Jack Brooks, is available at US Government publishing office, SENATE Friday, July 22nd, 1983, GPO-CRECB-1983-pt15-3, 20483-20498, statement of Senator David Pryor; and Favoritism and Bias within the Defense Science Board and other Military Advisory Panels, Hearing Before a Subcommittee of the Committee on Government Operations, House of Representatives, Ninety-eighth Congress, First Session, September 22, 1983.

[18] see ABC News. "Expert Discounts JFK 'Second Gunman' Theory," January 8, 2006.

BIBLIOGRAPHY

Abshire, David M, and Richard V. Allen. *National Security: Political, Military and Economic Strategies in the Decade Ahead, Center for Strategic Studies,* Georgetown University, 1963.

Masters, Dexter, and Katharine Way. *One World or None,* Whittlesey House, London 1946.

Needell, Allan. A. *Science, Cold War and the American State: Lloyd V. Berkner and the Balance of Professional Ideals,* Harwood Academic Publishers, 2000.

Seitz, Frederick. *The Modern Theory of Solids,* New York and London: McGraw-Hill Book Co., Inc., 1940.

Seitz, Frederick. *On the Frontier: My Life in Science, American Institute of Physics,* Woodbury, NY, 1994.

Schwoch, James. *Global TV: New Media and the Cold War,* University of Illinois Press, 2009.

Smith, James Allen. *Strategic Calling: The Center for Strategic and International Studies, 1962–1992,* Center for Strategic and International Studies, Washington, D.C, 1993.

Zachary, G. Pascal. *Endless Frontier: Vannevar Bush, Engineer of the American Century,* MIT Press, 1999.

GOVERNMENT AND INDUSTRY

Favoritism and Bias within the Defense Science Board and other Military Advisory Panels, Hearing Before a Subcommittee of the Committee on Government Operations, House of Representatives, Ninety-eighth Congress, First Session, September 22, 1983.

Five Years at the Radiation Laboratory, Massachusetts Institute of Technology, Cambridge, 1947.

Graduate Research Center of the Southwest 1963 Annual Report, June 30th, 1963, Dallas, Texas.

Graduate Research Center of the Southwest (GRCSW)/Southwest Center for Advanced Studies (SCAS) Collection, GRCSW/SCAS Chronology, 1961-1969 by Al Mitchell, Folders 1-6, Box 1, Series I, The University Archives, Special Collections Department, Eugene McDermott Library, The University of Texas at Dallas.

ARTICLES

ABC News. "Expert Discounts JFK 'Second Gunman' Theory," January 8, 2006.

Krige, John. "Atoms for Peace, Scientific Internationalism, and Scientific Intelligence," *Osiris*, Vol. 21, No. 1, *Global Power Knowledge: Science and Technology in International Affairs* (2006), pp. 161–181, University of Chicago Press.

Needell, Allan A. "'Truth Is Our Weapon': Project TROY, Political Warfare, and Government-Academic Relations in the National Security State," *Diplomatic History* Vol. 17, No. 3 (Summer 1993), pp. 399-420 (22 pages), Oxford University Press.

Seitz, Frederick. Lauriston Marshall obituary, *Physics Today*, Volume 33, Issue 3, March 1980, p. 100.

Anthony Thorne is a filmmaker and historian living in Melbourne, Australia.

ACKNOWLEDGMENTS
H. P. ALBARELLI JR.

To my cowriters—Leslie Sharp, my best and wonderful friend and muse; and my Blues buddy Alan Kent, whose depth of knowledge of the assassination of Kennedy is surpassed by very few—heartfelt thanks.

Many other people unselfishly assisted the author in writing this book. They are former CIA asset in New York, Cuba, and Mexico City, Viola June Cobb; three of June's CIA handlers who must remain anonymous; Doug Valentine, a very brave soul; Malcom Blunt, for expert advice; Damien Albarelli, David Albarelli, and Nicole Albarelli Centellas, the best children a man can have; Michael J. Briggs, another great book editor; my friend, Michael J. Petro; Jeanne-Marie Thomas Byron, a friend and a very, very brave woman; Tammy and Samantha Ryea; Dick Crandlemire, a great editor; Kris Newby, a friend, a great researcher and writer; David Gill for great backup research; Ashley Crout, an excellent editor; attorney Steve Rosen for always expert advice; Ran Daniel, whose insights proved significant; author Peter Janney; and Charles d'Autremont, a good friend.

My great friends, the de Marchi family: Xavier, Valerie, and Luigi at the Café de Paris Bakery in Indian Rocks Beach, Florida, who provided me with the world's finest pastries and much-needed coffee; Serena Hazard for being a good friend and for solving several perplexing FBI enigmas; Dan Luzadder; Joe Taglieri; John Strain; Margot Kiser; J. P. Mahoney, my best friend, who sadly couldn't hold on until this book was completed. Last, but far away from least: Kathleen R. McDonald, who never once flinched through this difficult ordeal. And there is Buddy, who has never let me down, who has stayed with this book better than I have and traveled over eight thousand miles with me and never once complained.

And especially: Tony Lyons, Skyhorse publisher; and Hector Carosso, director of special projects for Skyhorse. Tony and Hector were more than patient with my occasional slowness and always fully supportive. And author Dick Russell, who, years ago, planted all the seeds needed, and more, for this book to take root. And last, my first mentor, writer Robert Moore Williams, who told me long ago, when I was only twelve years old, "Write, write, write, and then rewrite and write more."

LESLIE SHARP—ADDENDUM

Hank's unexpected passing in June 2019 created a void, professional and personal, for so many, but in his wake was a network of friends and colleagues who, in testament to his and their integrity and humanity, took up the gauntlet and helped get this book into print.

First, immeasurable thanks to Hector Carosso, the Skyhorse editor without whom this project would have languished, and whose innate kindness and sensitivity not only held the deal together, but made the final phase bearable (if not almost pleasant); and to Skyhorse publisher Tony Lyons, who, under challenging circumstances, made the wisest decisions for *all* concerned because, ultimately, his role was to protect this project. Peace and thanks to author Peter Janney for keeping the plates spinning during a delicate phase; to Dick Russell for remaining open-minded to the question of authenticity; and to Mark Crispin Miller for enduring an early and very rough draft of the manuscript. And hat tip to Albuquerque attorney Jeffrey Myers, by coincidence a student of WWII history and SS Otto Skorzeny, who listened patiently and then quietly and firmly encouraged, "hang in there."

In the months following Hank's loss, I also had the good fortune to engage with another of his valued confidants, Alexander Foyle who proceeded over the ensuing months to encourage completion of Hank's project, adding doses of humor at just the right moments. Hank would also be the first to say that this effort is further indebted to former University Press of Kansas Publisher Michael Briggs, who served selflessly as advisor and became a valued friend along the way. Both men are a credit to their professions.

A unique thanks to a relatively new friend of Hank's, an experienced researcher in New Orleans with the mind of a seasoned detective who, for two years, wouldn't accept from us anything short of what he would have expected from Hank. Early on, Hank said, "Trust me, our investigation will be better for this man's contributions." And Hank left another gift, the friendship of Ran Daniel, whose generous and mind-expanding perspectives kept the batteries charged. I know why Hank was so fond of him.

The Work has also benefited from the camaraderie and the challenges posed by Hank's other research comrades, including Stu Wexler, Paul Brancato, Robert

Ward Montenegro, Larry Haapanen, John Beviliqua, among others; and researcher/author J. Gary Shaw, who entered our sphere not having engaged with Hank directly, but whose prescience in the 1970s can now be further confirmed. Shaw's decades-long quest for justice in the cold case murder investigation of John Kennedy puts to shame those who engage in parlor games. Thank you to Bill Simpich, who has been on so many of the right trails, it's difficult to count. Tom Scully and Linda Minor, I stood on your shoulders; and thank you to Australian filmmaker and historian Anthony Thorne, who recognizes that the story isn't over. Blessings to Kris Milligan of TrineDay Press, a self-effacing, truly independent publisher.

Music, Hank's first career, is a common denominator among a number of members of the assassination community, and what a great talent is professional drummer Alan Dale, director of the respected Assassination Archives and Research Center. His early interest in this project kept the wheels turning, and I'm a huge fan. Thanks as well to musician Steve Vitoff, a professional writer, for helping me maintain perspective and for fixing several tricky paragraphs; to the incomparable Dick Waterman for a brief interlude into his and Hank's music past (and that photo of Janice!); and sincere gratitude to jazz aficionado, saxophonist Charles Drago whose loyalty to Hank and faith in this project never wavered.

There are no bounds to my appreciation for the support of Milicent Cranor, senior editor at WhoWhatWhy.org, whose refreshing wit never failed to offset the stress, and who offered the cliff notes of her unparalleled expertise in an area of the assassination I avoided for decades. I'm not saying I fully understand it now, but I'm confident Mili does. Blessings to Hank's friend Kathleen for offering countless hours of solace into the wee hours; to Barbara Gus for listening actively during escapes to our favorite haunts in Santa Fe; to Kim for being Kim; and to dearest Sarita, the first comforting presence in the intense minutes following the PA announcement that President Kennedy was dead—our shared experiences in the Texas Panhandle during the Cold War and on November 22, 1963, prompted me to head down the twisty road to this book.

On Hank's behalf as well, it's impossible to reduce the contribution of library *research angels* to a cliché, "they were just doing their jobs." Without exception, I encountered grace and patience: from Dublin and Kilkenny, Ireland, to Seattle and Tucson; Austin to Midland to Dallas to Amarillo and Santa Fe; Tulsa to St. Louis and Columbia MO, Abilene KS, West Lafayette, Chicago, and Boston, and of course the Kennedy Library at Columbia Point, so I offer each and every one a blanket high praise. And to all of the authors and researchers dedicated to uncovering the facts, thank you for providing hundreds of thousands of pages of research from which to draw, especially those available at the highly searchable websites, Mary Ferrell Foundation and Assassination Archives and Research Center.

A special thanks is reserved for Walter Terzano, a gifted private detective who has investigated the assassination for decades and was present at the incubation of my role in Hank's project. Over the following six years, Terzano freely shared his insight into a long-ignored myriad of unresolved ambiguities, complexities, and possibilities. He never hesitated to push back against the legitimacy of the primary source material on which this book is based.

Thanks to my brother Larry, whose kindness overrode the skepticism that comes with a fine mind, and who, in spite of suspecting that Lee Harvey Oswald shot John F. Kennedy, provided unconditional psychological and practical support for my contribution to the project; and to Sydney—historian, progressive activist, and my beautiful sister who some sixty-five years ago established my high bar.

And last, because he's also first, James O'Hara—poet and student of British colonial history and its impact on his motherland, Ireland—who believed in this quest from the beginning and who for forty years kept me nourished on all levels, carried more weight of this project than anyone should have asked, and whose keen intellect and humor continue to challenge me daily, thank you.

Finally, unlimited gratitude to Pete Sattler—whose still waters of talent, knowledge, and commitment run deep; and Alan Kent—there simply aren't enough words, so I won't try.

To Hank—*You knew. You always knew.*

ALAN KENT—ADDENDUM

When I first contacted Hank Albarelli, in 2013, we began sharing research material and—much more importantly—developing a trusting bond. I learned of the unique primary source materials that the Lafitte family trusted him with, and the width and depth of a great many other important research paths that Hank walked down. Little did I know that the book the reader has begun would be the final outcome of his efforts, or that it would be completed in the manner that would come to pass, many years later.

In addition to the acknowledgements so ably laid down by Leslie Sharp, I would very much like anyone who is beginning this evidentiary adventure to know that Leslie has been a wonderfully supportive partner during the process of tying a bow on the story that Hank began many years ago. In point of fact, given some health-related problems I experienced last year, she has performed "above and beyond," as they say, engaging in a disproportionate amount of "heavy lifting," as we moved toward the completion of this project. She has done so with consummate skill, and a continual fine spirit. I have never heard from her anything resembling a complaint.

While Hank, Leslie, and I have been and are distinctly different personalities in many ways, we always united on the most significant matter: pulling the myriad threads of the story told herein together as tightly as the evidence would allow, in an effort to finally—decisively, as the book's title boldly proclaims!—get the history behind one of the most significant "deep events" in American history right. Which, given nearly 60 years of a flood of data and perspectives on the murder of President Kennedy, is no simple task.

Finally, I would like to thank two researchers in particular from whom I (and many others) have learned much over the years, and whose methodological rigor hopefully is reflected between the covers of this book. While neither of these scholars will likely agree with every perspective within, Peter Dale Scott and Larry Hancock have performed so much valuable work in this field, and have been so resolutely supportive of serious research, that it would be an intellectual crime of sorts not to credit them for all they have accomplished.

As for the fountainhead of this book, Hank Albarelli, his passing two years ago left a void that will never be filled. Leslie and I can only hope to have finished what he began in a manner that he would have approved of. As we have moved through numerous areas over the past several months in search of the cleanest and clearest presentation of the evidence and insights that Hank left to us, a frequent exchange between us became almost a mantra: "It's Hank's book!" And so it is. We go forward, in his memory.

ORGANIZATIONAL AND CHARACTER MAPS
BY PETE SATTLER

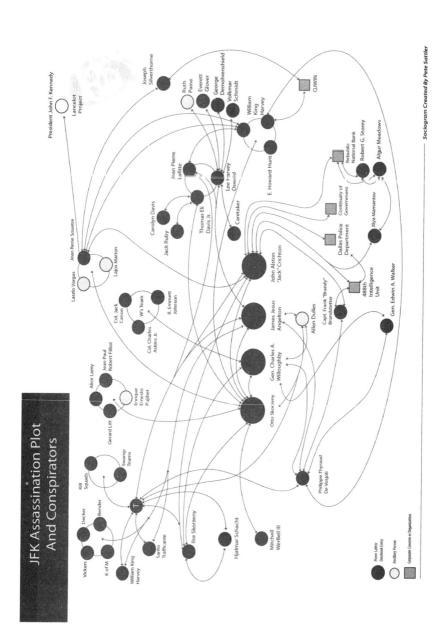

JFK Assassination Plot And Conspirators

Sociogram Created By Pete Sattler

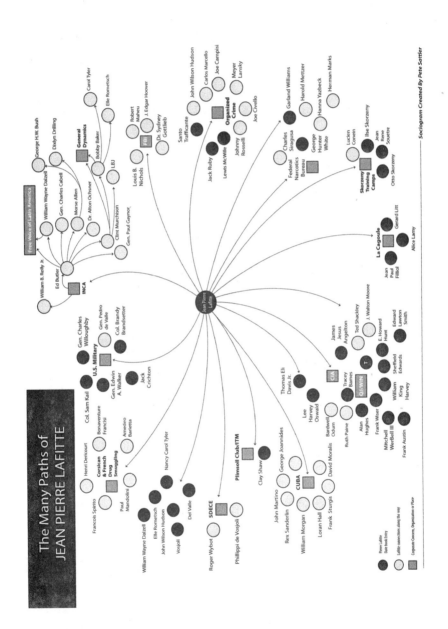

The Many Paths of
JEAN PIERRE LAFITTE

Sociogram Created By Pete Sattler

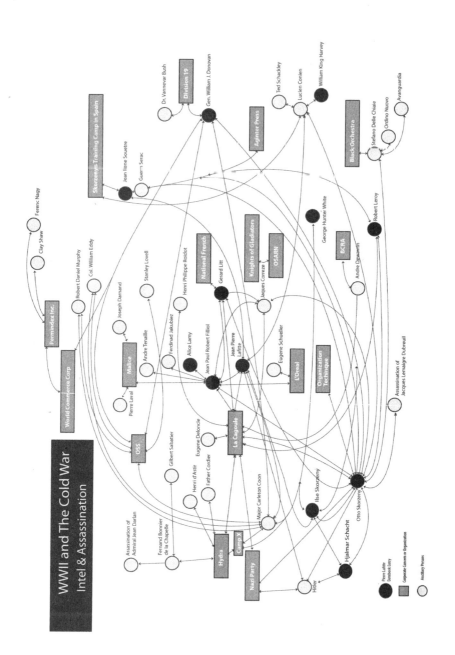

WWII and The Cold War
Intel & Assassination

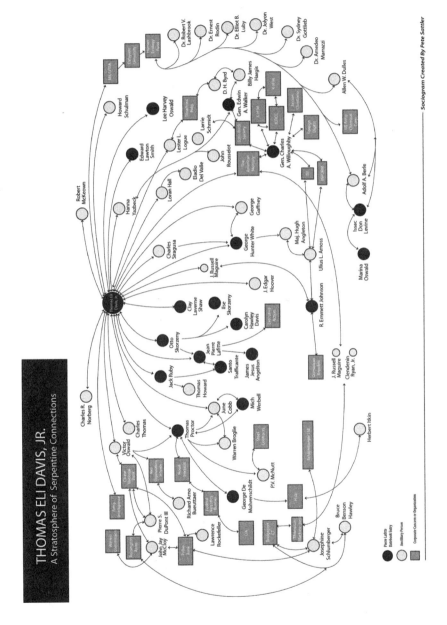

THOMAS ELI DAVIS, JR.
A Stratosphere of Serpentine Connections

Sociogram Created By Pete Sattler

COAUTHOR'S STATEMENT ON THE PROVENANCE AND AUTHENTICITY OF THE LAFITTE DATEBOOK
BY LESLIE SHARP

During our initial phone conversations and email exchanges, Hank Albarelli walked me through his pursuit of the private papers of Pierre Lafitte, one of the central characters of this investigation. With time, I came to appreciate the implications of one item from the collection in particular, the 1963 datebook maintained by Lafitte.

By early 2018, Hank had dictated the text of a series of daily entries from the datebook to which he had been allowed periodic access. He then followed up with a selection of screenshots of pages for me to get a sense of this exclusive evidence.

In November, he flew to London to take possession of the physical datebook for the purpose of filming the initial segment of what was to become a six-to-eight-part documentary based on *Coup in Dallas*. He had not initiated authentication himself because he knew the chain of custody of the Lafitte records firsthand; however, he recognized that the proposed authentication process would provide compelling visuals that could advance public knowledge of these exclusive revelations of the plot to assassinate President Kennedy. Following careful deliberation and with caveats and nondisclosures in place established by the owner(s) of both the datebook and other samples of handwriting, Hank was permitted to proceed for the sole purpose of the documentary. He provided the London-based professional handwriting/document analysts whose clientele include the British Secret Service, as well as a renowned international ink expert, access to the datebook, and the first hours of footage for the documentary were captured.

Hank then flew to Dallas, where we met, and I had the opportunity to study the datebook cover to cover. My first reaction was a mixture of awe and skepticism, both of which I did not hesitate to share with Hank. The datebook itself is in near immaculate condition given its age: the cover is well preserved although it is clearly not "new"; the paper is discolored by age, but, with the exception of several dog-eared pages, there are no watermarks, stains, cigarette burns, etc., that one might expect in a nearly sixty-year old document. It has been well cared for. The ink and pencil that the author used varies from day to day. Some entries written in lead pencil are quite faded. The handwriting varies, as well: some days it seems the author is in a rush, others he or she is writing very deliberately, and other days, the handwriting is nearly illegible. Once I adjusted to the likelihood that the author, and those who preserved the datebook over the ensuing decades, was fastidious, I determined that this instrument and the contents therein are either a brilliant fraud, or a miraculous find. All of these reactions I shared with Hank as they surfaced, and periodically resurfaced. He understood entirely.

Eventually, preliminary reports were submitted by the experts in London, but Hank did not own those reports. Unfortunately, the documentary contract lapsed just weeks before Hank fell ill, and the outstanding issue—more handwriting samples—remained unresolved. It is my understanding that the preliminary reports from the analysts are currently in the hands of those who financed the authentication. Attempts to reignite the collaboration effort, and release those reports to the public, have been unsuccessful thus far.

* * *

After Hank passed away, I experienced levels of doubt and uncertainty equal to the most severe critic and spent months as devil's advocate, turning every stone in a deliberate and somewhat unpleasant effort to prove that the datebook is *not* authentic. I suspect, having firsthand knowledge of aspects of Hank's access to the material, I've probably considered more possibilities than even the most cynical.

- During one phase, I realized that the timeline Hank left in his Frank Olson book, *A Terrible Mistake*, reflects dates tied to the Lafitte material that sometimes contradicted my understanding of the trajectory of events. It was unsettling at best. However, ironic as it might sound, I also know that Hank was hopeless when it came to recall specific years/ dates in his own personal history. He had to use his fingers to count back the decades to his high school graduation, when he first went to work for the Carter administration, when he joined the staff at SEIU, so the discrepancies can be explained somewhat, but insufficient to argue authenticity. But I also knew that Hank spoke often of his concern that less scrupulous journalists would hound his sources, or worse, subject them to threat, and I concluded that the imprecision in certain detail was deliberate. Some might call his tactic obfuscation, but I'm now satisfied it was a prudent approach given the sensitive nature of his investigations.

- I also asked, could Hank have been duped? That possibility simply did not resonate. In my relatively informed opinion, Hank would never have subjected himself to ridicule were the datebook to be determined the equivalent of the "Hitler Diaries." His professional pride was not false, but it was a strong component of his character. He would not be a victim of fraud.

- Of deep concern were those parties in a position to confirm the provenance but refused to cooperate; every feasible effort to secure a definitive statement has gone unfulfilled. These refusals may speak to a desire to not be associated with this volatile record, or they may be a psychological mechanism to avoid the label "conspiracist" by associating with this project. I came to the conclusion that the refusals to confirm the provenance do not prove that the datebook is fraudulent.

- Similarly, when approached for even the most general statement regarding the process involved in handwriting analysis, the London professional would only state that he remains under a Nondisclosure Agreement and could not comment; a simple "in general, I was not fully satisfied that the datebook is authentic" would have sufficed. I determined, objectively, that the absence of his endorsement of authenticity is not evidence of fraud.

During a lengthy interview with an American-based handwriting/document analyst who is considered an expert in the field and is called to testify in significant document fraud cases, I was advised that in general, unless he had close to one hundred distinct samples of handwriting for comparison, he would not consider putting his professional stamp on an evaluation. I appreciated the argument because this issue was similar to the one alleged to be the reason that London refused to produce a final report on the Lafitte datebook. The American expert added that unless a case goes to court before a judge who respects the credentials required for such an audit, handwriting analysis is not always considered an exact science, and, depending on the motivation, in this field it is easy to pay for an assessment that produces the desired outcome of the paying party.

We know from records that for dubious reasons, Pierre Lafitte was on the move periodically over decades, which added to stress that also impacted his penmanship. As Hank noted, his sources explained that Pierre experienced at least one mild stroke before turning sixty. On the question of inconsistencies in Pierre's handwriting, Texas native and author J. Gary Shaw, a first-generation Kennedy assassination expert who founded the ASK conference series, cofounded the JFK Assassination Information Center, a former board member of the Assassination Archives and Research Center, close colleague of research luminaries Penn Jones, Mary Ferrell, and Bud Fensterwald, and the first to track Jean Rene Souetre when others couldn't even pronounce the name, opined: *"In the early 1960s, I was a partner in a construction management firm and I always kept a 'gimme' date book handy. In it, I recorded 'to-do's,' names, addresses, phone numbers, etc. At times I found it necessary to jot down a note while driving which was not always neat and tidy.*

I have studied the contents of the datebook for more than two years and find it persuasive for similar (although more in-depth) reasons outlined by Dick Russell. For the record, I was not introduced to Hank's source(s) for the datebook and other material, so I can only speak to the provenance from my personal experience, through Hank: I was present when he placed phone calls to his source(s); I have emails that reference their responses to his specific questions, e.g., *Was Stoneleigh Hotel in Dallas where your family stayed?*; I have emails that indicate Hank had recently met with them to take possession of additional documents; I was in frequent communication with him while he was in London taking possession of the datebook and the subsequent filming of the first round of authentication; and I have held additional documents from the Lafitte collection including postcards, keepsakes, and personal notes. Therefore, I am satisfied, objectively and to the most reasonable degree of certainty under the circumstances, that the provenance is what Hank said it was, and that the datebook is authentic.

PIERRE LAFITTE DATEBOOK
SELECT ENTRIES AND IMAGES

- Cover [Sweet Foods . . .]
- Inside Front Cover — Hitler stamp, Reich coin; Lincoln penny with hole
- Jan 11 — WerBell-Conein . . .
- Jan 18 — Harvey here FL training . . .
- Feb 5 — WerBell guns . . . in desert with Proctor . . .
- Mar 26 — McWillie . . . Davis – Oswald . . .
- April 7 — Walker Lee and pictures . . . can he do it? . . .
- April 21 — Carol T Dallas . . .
- April 30 — Walker Souetre in New Orleans . . .
- May 10 — T says . . .
- June 7 — Else and W. wife . . . John "W-H" . . .
- June 16 — Ella acting classes . . .
- June 18 — Willoughby meet . . .
- June 25 — Nickel deposits . . . Skorzeny . . .
- July 2 — Ella R. - Q . . .
- July 28 — George/OS talk . . . to Stockdale about P. Graham . . .
- July 31 — passports for Rometsch . . .
- Aug 16 — Antoinnes . . . Joannides . . .
- Aug 21 — Talk Joannides . . . King . . .
- Aug 23 — JA says Ella R sent . . .
- Sept 12 — Askins . . .
- Sept 14 — Canon . . .
- Sept 16 — See J. Dallas . . . T says L.O. . . .
- Sept 22 — Oswald – Mex city Gaudet? . . .
- Sept 27 — Algur . . . Ilya . . . Oswald- Comercia Hotel meet Tom D. . . .
- Sept 28 — Bowen & Hudson – Mex . . .
- Sept 29 — Tom at embassy . . .
- Oct 2 — Askins Willoughby . . .

- Oct 3 — Caretaker
- Oct 6 — Oswald issue! . . .
- Oct 9 — OSARN . . .
- Oct 17 — JA call yest. Says high-level . . .
- Oct 18 — ask OS re Ella . . .
- Oct 25 — Call JA . . . O says . . . Oswald set in place . . .
- Oct 28 — Lancelot Planning
- Oct 29 — Lancelot Planning
- Oct 30 — QRTS . . . Ruby – Wilson-H . . .
- Nov 5 — Meet with Crichton . . . Lancelot go
- Nov 7 — 11·30 meet Warsaw . . .
- Nov 8 — Silverthorne . . . Call T . . .
- Nov 9 — on the wings of murder . . .
- Nov 10 — Dallas-Meadows B. W/T . . .
- Nov 11 — Terry says . . . J. Crichton . . .
- Nov 12 — Souetre Mex City . . .
- Nov 13 — Lamy coming . . .
- Nov 14 — Crichton w/T. caretaker . . .
- Nov 15 — Nov 22 Willoughby backup . . .
- Nov 17 — Jack C. grates and span . . .
- Nov 19 — Dallas Souetre to go . . .
- Nov 20 — Lamy – Filiol . . . call Storey . . . DeM . . . Frank B. . . .
- Nov 21 — Willoughby team – Canon . . .
- Nov 23 — Silverthorne . . . Jeans gone out . . . coup di grace . . .
- Nov 24 — Red . . . airport . . .
- Nov 26 — DC NYC JJA . . .
- Nov 27 — Call J. . . .
- Nov 28 — Levine will deal . . .
- Dec 4 — Canon home . . . shells-Souetre . . .
- Dec 5 — JA – close out Lancelot . . . T . . .
- Dec 12 — Holdout here

1 9 6 3

EAT BETTER . . . FOR LESS
SERVE

SWEET LIFE

Delicious FOODS

SWEET LIFE HAS VARIETY

PHONES for your convenience

from Springfield & North - RE 2-3131
from Hartford & South - CH 9-7681
from Northern Conn. - NA 3-2451
from New Haven - SP 7-5416

Friday, January 11, 1963

Friday, January 18, 1963

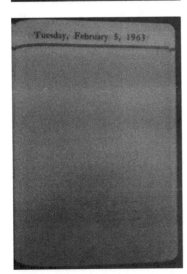

Tuesday, February 5, 1963

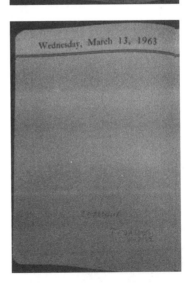

Wednesday, March 13, 1963

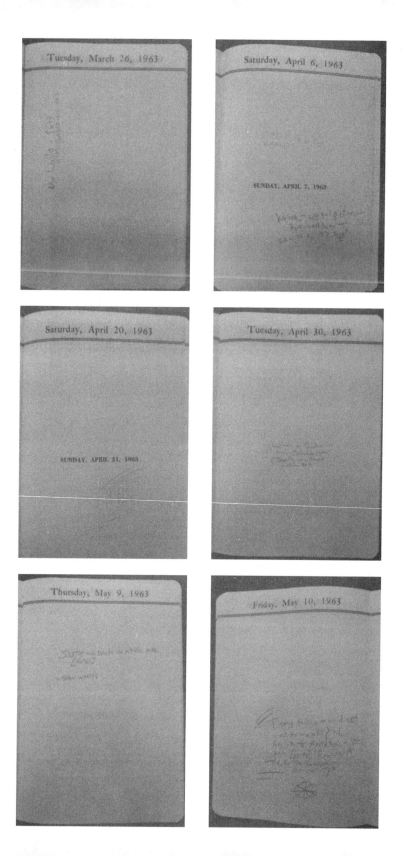

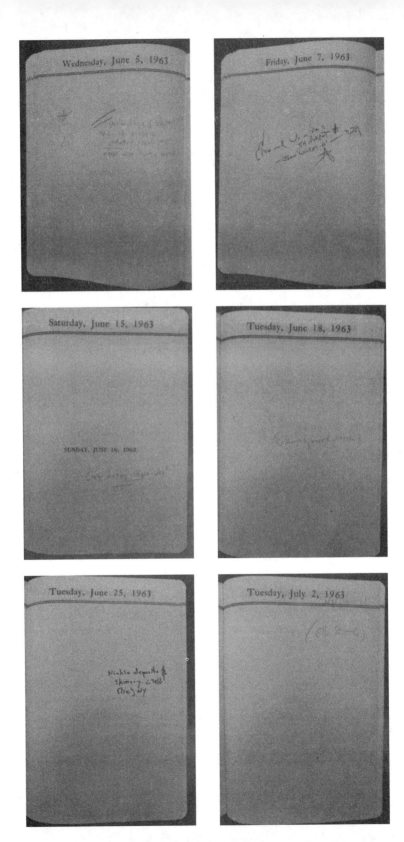

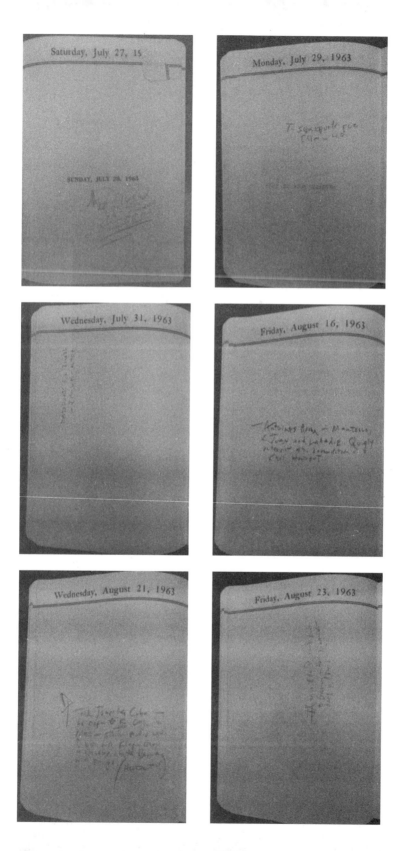

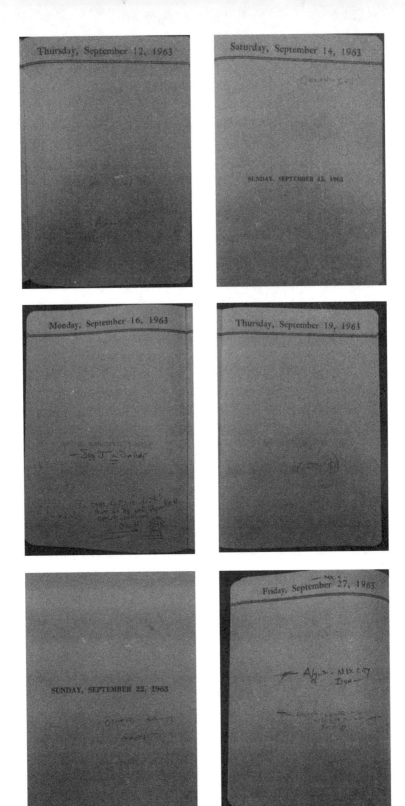

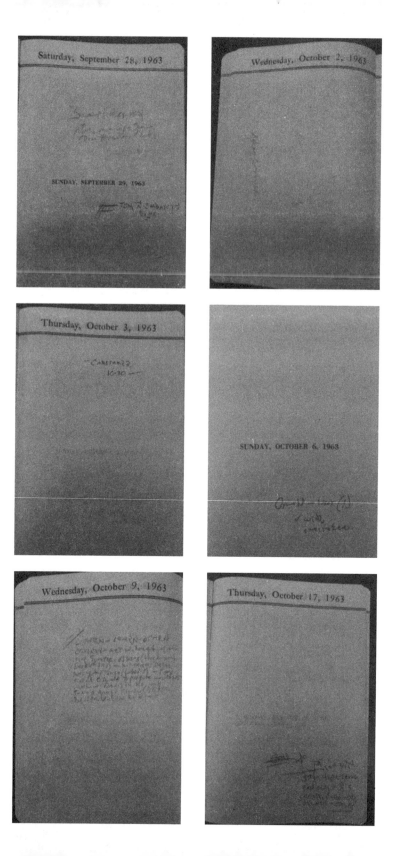

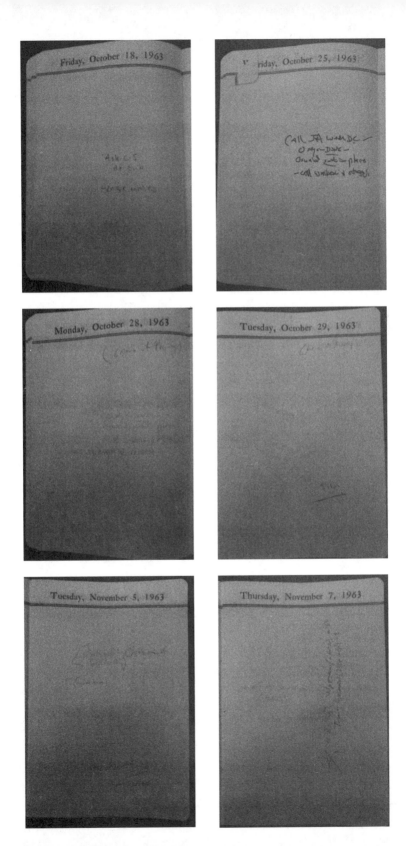

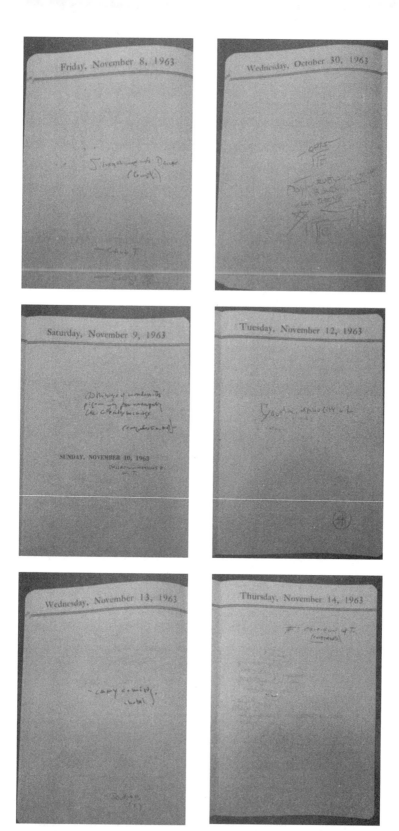

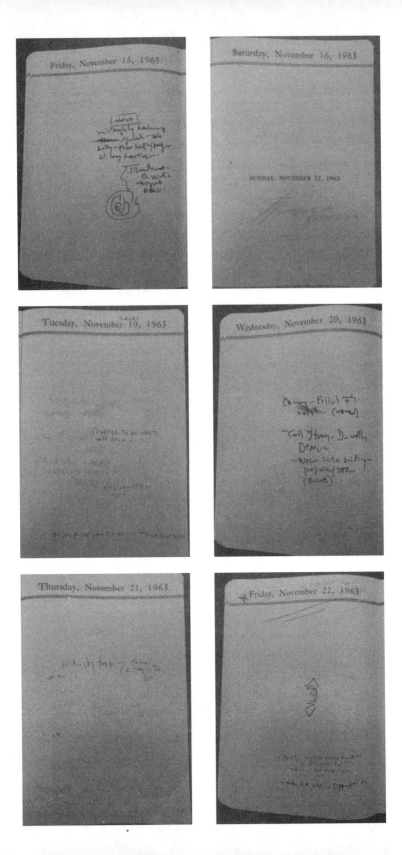

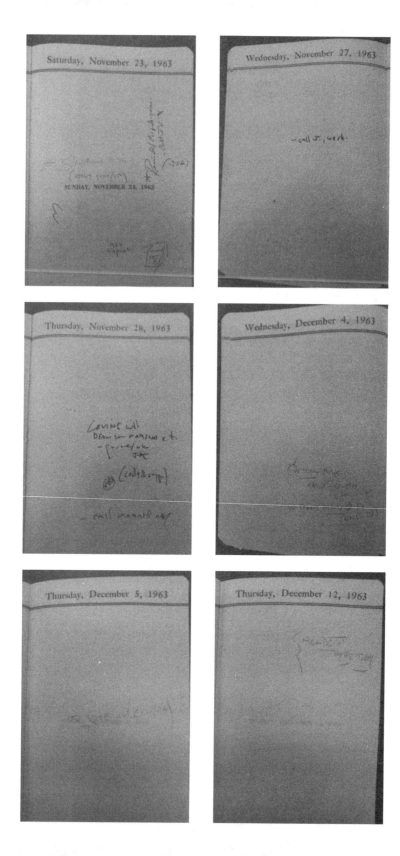

NOTES

CHAPTER 1: WWII, SPECIAL OPS, AND ASSASSINATIONS

Pierre Lafitte Datebook, 1963, Lafitte Family Estate. [Used with express permission 2005–2019.]

Alias name "Mornard": Fernand Bonnier used the alias "Mornard" on his fake passport in late 1942. Resulting data from using program HPASTH-1 on this area of research.

de Montmorency, Alec, "Who Ordered the Death of French Admiral Darlan?" *The Barnes Review*, May 1997, Volume III, Number 4.

Paul Gluc letters to FBI Director Hoover—author's FOIA to FBI, 2015. See Mary Ferrell Foundation website.

March 13, 1975 Letter to FBI: FBI 62-109060, JFK HQ File, Section 178, Mary Ferrell Foundation, online archive. This letter was translated for the author by Clodie François and Kathleen R. McDonald.

Léon Degrelle: In 1974, Degrelle delivered the following speech, venue unidentified; however, film footage proliferates contemporary on-line neo-Nazi websites. "I sometimes made huge mistakes. But what actually is a mistake in politics? And when I look back, I have only one sentiment: an enormous regret. Regret that we did not succeed, that we were not able to create this European world which would be the master of the universe for all time, which made the white race the first race, with the great mastery of the spirit. . . . And when we see what there is on the other side, what 30 years of the others' victory has given, this anarchy in the world, this rout of the white world, this desertion throughout the universe; when we see in our own countries the decay of morals, the fall of the fatherland, the fall of the family, the fall of social order; when we see this appetite for material goods which has replaced the great flame of the ideal which animated us, well then, truly, between the two we chose the right side. The small, miserable Europe of today, of this impoverished Common Market, cannot give happiness to men. Consumer society poisons humanity rather than elevating it. . . . So, for our part, we dreamed of something great, and we have only one desire, that this spirit be reborn. And with all my might, up to the last moment of my existence, I will fight for this. So that what was our struggle and our martyrdom, will one day be the resurrection."—Léon Degrelle, *We Dreamed of Something Marvelous.*

Oswald Emald Mosley: Having served on the Western Front during World War I, Oswald Mosley, 6th Baron of Ancoats entered the world of politics, serving as a British MP from 1918 to 1924 and from 1926 to 1931, when he founded the British Union of Fascists. The party initially reflected his admiration for the Italian dictator Benito Mussolini, but became heavily influenced by Nazism.

OSS 201 File on Carleton Coon, NARA, Washington, D.C.

Borghese and Angleton: James Angleton constructed the first building blocks for his long career in CIA counterintelligence in the waning days of the Second World War, as an OSS operative negotiating with enemy forces in an attempt to secure a solid anti-communist foundation in postwar Italy. Angleton concocted "Plan IVY," an Italian counterpart of Allen Dulles's beneath-the-radar canoodling with Nazi SS General Karl Woolf, "Operation Sunrise." Jefferson Morley writes: "The goal of Angleton's Plan IVY was to convince Borghese not to join any plans for a 'scorched earth' retreat." As part of a last-ditch Axis effort in early 1945, German plans envisaged Italian troops razing a large part of northern Italy, while retreating to a zone of resistance in Austria. Angleton made contact with Borghese and offered him protection from Italian partisans who were planning to assassinate the "Black Prince," if he and his "Decima Mas" soldiers would lay down their arms. Borghese and his men did so on April 26, 1945. Angleton would subsequently protect Borghese, allowing him to build anticommunist forces in postwar Italy. "In Rome, Angleton installed Borghese in an OSS safe house on via Archimedes . . . As Angleton later explained, he had saved Borghese's life because he thought the US government had a 'long-term interest' in retaining his services . . . thanks to Angleton, Borghese survived to become titular and spiritual leader of postwar Italian fascism . . . Imbued with fascist sympathies and anti-communist passion, Angleton channeled his convictions into Anglo-American hegemonic ambition." (*The Ghost: The Secret Life of CIA Spymaster James Jesus Angleton*, Jefferson Morley, St. Martin's Press, 2017, pp. 22–27).

Jean Pierre Lafitte, a.k.a. Jean Martin, while in New Orleans in 1963 observing Lee Harvey Oswald, employed the surname "Voituriez" for conducting covert work for the CIA. Additionally, the surname that Fernand Bonnier employed, "Mornard," was also used as an alias by Lafitte on several occasions in the 1960s. —Lafitte family records.

Murphy on Giraud: Murphy, Robert, *Diplomat Among Warriors*, Doubleday & Company, Inc., New York, fourth printing, February 1965.

La Cagoule, Filliol, background and assassination: Brunelle, Gayle K. and Finley-Croswhite, Annette, *Murder in the Metro: Laetitia Toureaux and the Cagoule in 1930s France*, Louisiana State University Press, Baton Rouge, 2010.

Jean Paul Robert Filliol (also spelled "Filiol"): Jean Filliol was born in Bergerac (Dordogne Perigord), France. His parents were of very modest means; his grandparents, on both sides, were village farmers. His mother's maiden name was *Emery*. Like Lee Harvey Oswald, Filliol quit high school before finishing. He became a papermaker for Laroche-Joubert. He was becoming a fierce patriot at the same time and quit the Protestant Church of his parents. He then became a Catholic who faithfully attends Mass weekly and attends Sunday school sessions regularly. About this same time, he joined the French army and was on active duty for about two years. When he was discharged from the Army, he moved to the Paris area and worked for a paper mill, Hachette de Colombes. He was ambitious and aggressive and became commercial manager at the company's Quai de Javel headquarters. Dissatisfied and bored, he left the company in October 1935 and formed his own papermaking brokerage firm. At about this same time, Filliol embarked on his radical, fascist activities.

Filliol, Correze, and US Department of Justice, OSI sources: For an excellent and comprehensive look at Filliol see blog at: devirisillustribusblog.wordpress.com/; Thierry Meyssan, "The Secret History of L'Oréal," Voltaire.net.org, 17, June 2017; 3 March 2004; "L'Oréal Official Investigated by US Over Pro-Nazi Past" by Steven Greenhouse, *New York Times*, June 20, 1991; Coignard, Sophie and Guichard, Marie-Therese, *French Connections: Network of Influence*, Algora Publishing, New York, 2000; Bar-Zohar, Michael, *Bitter Scent: The Case of L'Oréal, Nazis, and the Arab Boycott*, Dutton Books, New York 2000; Brandon, Ruth, *Ugly Beauty,* Harper Collins, New York, 2006.

Reinhard Heydrich: Acclaimed historians Robert Paxton and Michael Marrus write, "The most important rival to the military authority in Occupied France was the police. The Security Police was a subdivision of the RSHA (Reichssicherheitshauptamt), the gigantic Reich Security Division of Heinrich Himmler's SS (Schutzstaffel) [of which Otto Skorzeny was a revered member], under the direct command of Reinhard Heydrich in Berlin . . . the miniature version set up in Paris and modeled on its Berlin headquarters was familiarly known as the 'Gestapo' or the 'SD' (Sicherheitsdienst). . . . As early as 31 July 1941, Hermann Goring wrote to Heydrich, 'carry out all necessary preparations with regard to the organization and financial matters for bringing about a complete solution of the Jewish question in the German sphere of influence in Europe.' It was however the conference of Nazi leaders in Berlin at 56–58 Am Grossen Wannsee, that systemized the new Nazi policy of outright extermination and set the wheels in motion. . . [January 20, 1942]. The Wannsee meeting was convoked by Heydrich, head of the RSHA and Himmler's deputy in the SS. Representatives from the Reich's Four-Year Plan, the Interior Ministry, the Foreign Office, the Justice Ministry, various occupation authorities, the Nazi party, and of course, the SS were present. . . . Later that spring, during a visit to Paris, Heydrich urged the French to create a special police and security force, 'outside the administration.'" —Marrus, Michael Robert and Robert O. Paxton, *Vichy France and the Jews*, Stanford University Press, 1995.

Secret Report, *OSS Activities in Corsica*, September 12 to October 5th, 1943, Carleton S. Coon, Major, AUS.

Gerard Litt: Lafitte datebooks, 1962 and 1963.

Aginter Press and Yves Guillou and Robert Leroy: Lafitte private papers 1964, 1965.

Bale, Jeffrey, "The 'Black' Terrorist International: Neo-Fascist Paramilitary Networks and the 'Strategy of Tension' in Italy, 1968–1974" – BA (University of Michigan) 1977, MA (University of California at Berkeley) 1987 – A dissertation submitted in partial satisfaction of the requirements for the degree of Doctor of Philosophy in History in the Graduate Division of the University of California at Berkeley. Bale, particularly in his deeply researched second chapter, "The International Background," delves deeply into the European and US right wing milieu that is embedded at the core of this book.

Ferraresi, Franco, *Threats to Democracy: The Radical Right in Italy After the War*.

Prince Junio Valerio Borghese: The Coup known as Golpe Borghese, like all Italian Politics, is an extremely complex affair. It has Fascist elements but is also linked to Gladio, the Mafia, P2 Masonic lodge, and American intelligence. It can be understood, if at all, in all these contexts together. Gladio itself is very complex, linked to, and perhaps mirroring, events as far-spread as the Condor Years in South America, and the Grey Wolves (active from Turkey to China and today perhaps superseded to some extent by ISIS). See *Portrait of a Black Terrorist*, Stuart Christie; *The Beast Reawakens* Martin Lee (pp. 187–188); *Puppet Masters* by Philip Willan, (pp. 90–120). —Ran Daniel, researcher, writer and research associate of H. P. Albarelli Jr.

Julius Evola: Evola (1898–1974) was an Italian philosopher, an advocate of an elitist, idealist variety of Fascism, or some might say Nazism. Influenced by Plato, Nietzsche, Oswald Spengler, Evola espoused an antidemocratic and anti-Semitic return to semimystical forms of Medieval Chivalry. During the war, Evola met Mussolini immediately after the latter was rescued by Skorzeny. He may also have met Skorzeny there, but this is unconfirmed. His vision inspired Count Valerio Borghese, who wrote an introduction to Evola's book *Men Among the Ruins*, and also international terrorist (still living today) Stefano Delle Chiaie.

In 2017, there was a resurgence of interest in Evola's work, and President Donald Trump's advisor Steve Bannon and also "Putin's Rasputin," Aleksandr Dugin, should be cited among the thinkers of the Right who have been influenced by Evola.

Intriguingly, his name also appears in works of fiction such as Umberto Eco's *Foucault's Pendulum* and Peter Levenda's "Lovecraft Code" —Ran Daniel, researcher, writer and research associate of author H. P. Albarelli Jr.

A portentous January 1968 affidavit: Translation of sworn testimony by Jacques Godard of Aginter Press. Bruges 27 January 1968; Godard born Courbevoie (suburb of Paris) 25 August 1935.

William A. Eddy Assassination Proposal: Memorandum to Col. Willian Donovan from W.A. Eddy, 26 August 1942, NARA microfilm cited in article by Eléony Moorhead, "The OSS and Operation TORCH: The Beginning of the Beginning," *Tempus: The Harvard College History Review*, Vol. X, Issue 1, Summer 2009.

Tunander, Ola, "Democratic State vs. Deep State: Approaching the Dual State of the West" from *Government of the Shadows, Parapolitics and Criminal Sovereignty*.

Christie, Stuart, "Portrait of a Black Terrorist," Black Papers No. I, *Anarchy Magazine*.

"In Spain, Delle Chiaie met Otto Skorzeny and Yves Guerin-Sac, a leader of the French OAS. From Spain mercenary groups were organized to help 'friends' in Southern Africa and Latin America. Delle Chiaie worked for Skorzeny, who was perhaps under contract to the Spanish government, Delle Chiaie's job being to murder opponents of Spanish fascism in Spain and outside [including US]. He has been charged in connection with the *Italicus* murder. The gun which killed Alessandrini during the Calvi investigation has been traced to him." —Harris, Geoffrey, *The Dark Side of Europe: The Extreme Right Today*, New Edition, Edinburgh University Press, Edinburg, 1994.

Memorandum titled "Secret Report on Area S" to Mr. Joseph Scriber from Major C. S. Coon, February 27, 1944. The secret report was sent to OSS director Donovan and Joseph Scribner, deputy director of the OSS, Washington, D.C.

"OSS Used Poison Against Germans," Washington AP report, *Beckley Post-Herald*, 9 March 1977, Wednesday, p. 10.

German Human Experimentation with Drugs, SS Papers captured by Boris Pash's ALSOS Mission, 1945–1946. [Author's files.]

Lucien Conein: Some readers may recall that for decades now reports have persisted that Lucien Conien was photographed in Dallas, Texas, on November 22, 1963. These reports are erroneous and the man in the photo has been identified as not being Conien, who is believed to have been in Vietnam at the time. —H. P. Albarelli Jr.

Assassination Manual: CIA, 1954, author's FOIA to CIA, 2009. Note: this manual had not been published internally by the CIA in 1953.

Heinz Krug: German rocket scientist, who had been a part of Von Braun's team at
Peenemunde and was to take a major part in Egypt's missile program, disappeared
on September 11, 1962. There are two versions of his disappearance and death. In
both versions, the Israeli Mossad orchestrated the deed. One version, put forward by
Dr. Ronen Bergman in his book *Rise and Kill First*, says Krug was abducted by
Israeli agents, taken to Israel, and interrogated and eventually killed there. The other
version, put forward by Dan Raviv and Yossi Melman in their article "The Nazi
Who Became A Mossad Hitman," says he was lured to a forest outside Munich and
murdered there by Skorzeny, on the orders of Skorzeny's Mossad handlers.

These conflicting versions may underscore the difficulty of understanding Skorzeny's
personality and motives. Was he an unrepentant Nazi, an opportunistic mercenary,
or a madman? Or perhaps all three? —Ran Daniel, researcher, writer and research
associate of author H. P. Albarelli Jr.

CHAPTER 2: HOLDING COMPANIES, INTEL OPS, AND THE COLD WAR

Otto Skorzeny Private Papers, Ralph Ganis, 1946–1956; Pierre Lafitte Datebook,
1960–1962, Author's page copies, 2016.

Park Report: Report to Clayton Bissell, MG, GSC, from Richard Park, Jr., Colonel,
GSC, 12 March 1945; MID Recs, NA-RG 165, WFRC, folder 334, OSS, 3-6-43.
UMC.

Confidential letter to US Secretary of State Dean Acheson from Paul T. Culbertson,
Madrid, Spain, May 9, 1949. CIA/Nazi War Crimes Disclosure Act, 313425,
National Archives, Washington, D.C.

King, Jr., Henry T., "Robert H. Jackson and the Triumph of Justice at Nuremberg,"
Case Western Reserve Journal of International Law.

Gil, Joaquín, "War makes for strange bedfellows: An exiled Spanish Socialist tells how
he warmed to his Nazi boss in Argentina." Spain: El País, 02 Aug 2013.
www.english.elpais.com/elpais/2013/08/01/inenglish/1375364409_371574.html.

Irujo, José María, "Este Greco me lo regaló Franco." Spain: El País, 07 Sept 2013
www.elpais.com/cultura/2013/09/06/actualidad/1378485841_999198.html.

The Great Salad Oil Swindle, Norman Miller. Tino De Angelis, a New York-based commodities trader who bought and sold vegetable oil futures contracts around the
world. In 1962, De Angelis started a huge scam, attempting to corner the market
for soybean oil, used in salad dressing. In the aftermath of the salad oil scandal,
investors in 51 banks learned that he had bilked them out of about $175 million in

total ($1.2 billion in year 2000 dollars). Miller won a Pulitzer Prize in 1964 for his
reporting on the De Angelis story.

The World Commerce Corporation: Anthony Cave Brown, examining a letter written
by WCC President Frank Ryan to General Lucius Clay, contends that the primary
function of WCC was to aid in building up the post-WW2 productive capacity of
Germany as a bulwark against a potentially encroaching Soviet Union, and that may
well be the case.

Prof. Peter Dale Scott, who has studied the assassination of President Kennedy for
decades, offers a potent hint of a deeper clandestine reality, which bespeaks important connections with the narrative of this book: ". . . George White's closest CIA
contact, James Angleton, was still working for the US Army at this time (1947),
reporting to future Army G-2 and DIA chief William Quinn. And when White
turned up in Italy to meet with his former OSS boss William Donovan, Donovan
was not working for CIA, but for the elusive World Commerce Corporation, a private intelligence service representing wealthy Americans like Nelson Rockefeller . . .
CIC (China), a subsidiary of Donovan's World Commerce Corporation, was the
firm that employed mob figure Sonny Fassoulis, at the urging of army colonel (and
FBN agent) Garland Williams, to procure arms for Taiwan in the period of private
procurement before the Korean War." —Sharp & Kent, coauthors.

German Nationalist and Neo-Nazi Activities in Argentina,
    www.cia.gov/readingroom/home Document No.
    CIA-RDP62-00865R000300030004-4.

Johannes Bernhardt: Special Collection / Nazi War Crimes Disclosure Act /
    www.cia.gov/readingroom/home Document No. 519a6b2a993294098d51187b.

Permindex:
Memorandum For: Chief, Commercial Staff
Subject: Permindex – World Trade Center
Signed, Cord Meyer, Jr., Chief, International Organization Division
(see pages 3 & 4) https://www.maryferrell.org/showDoc.html?docId=157805#relPageId
    =1&search=Ferenc_Nagy%20Permindex
Alfonzo Rodriguez: a.k.a. Earl Williamson, a.k.a. Wallace Growery was station chief in
    Madrid in 1951 as Otto Skorzeny positioned himself in the Spanish capital to begin
    his service to the CIA and his lucrative work for not only himself and wife, Ilse, but
    Johannes Bernhardt's Sofindus, and the World Commerce Corporation. Rodriguez,
    who had served in Bill Donovan's OSS during the war, would have been the boss of
    Al Ulmer, whom many researchers will recognize as having gone into private busi-
    ness with Win Scott, the former Station Chief in Mexico City at the time of the

assassination of JFK. According to records, in 1944 Rodriguez was posted by the Army Counter Intelligence Corps to the OSS, including stints in London and Tangier, where he was vice counsel, affording him ample opportunity to encounter dubious characters named in this investigation. His obituary reads, "After the war, he was assigned to Costa Rica and served as station chief during the revolution there. He was deputy chief of the CIA's Latin American division in the late 1940s and served in Madrid and Mexico during the 1950s. He was part of the task force that worked with anti-Castro forces in Miami after the attempted invasion of Cuba at the Bay of Pigs. He concluded his career at the CIA as Director of Training."

James Noel: Close agency colleague of Rodriguez, James Noel was the CIA Station Chief in Havana at the time of the failed attempt at the Bay of Pigs. In late 1959, Noel had received instructions from Col. J. C. King, chief of the Western Hemisphere for the agency, to prepare an analysis of the political situation in Cuba. Intended for a specific audience in the government hierarchy, King wanted Noel to report that Fidel, under the influence of his closest collaborators, had been converted to Communism and was preparing to export the revolution throughout the hemisphere to spread the war against capitalism. King then recommended actions to "solve the Cuban problem, including consideration of eliminating Castro." Director Dulles then passed on King's memorandum to the National Security Council, which signed off on "Operation 40," to address the "Cuban" problem. Presided over by VP Richard Nixon, the group included NSA Gordon Gray. The direct Task Force was headed up by Tracy Barnes, whom we encounter in a significant essay in our appendix focused on the identity of a major player in Pierre Lafitte's datebook, coded "T." Tracy Barnes's team included Gerry Droller, a.k.a. Frank Bender, an egocentric agent at Central Intelligence who appears on a significant date in the 1963 Lafitte datebook. Also named in the datebook is Jack Crichton, among a cadre of Texas oilmen including future president George H.W. Bush that Richard Nixon had assembled to gather necessary funds for the task force.

CHAPTER 3: THE PROJECT MANAGER AND THE PATRON

Pierre Lafitte, Datebook 1963, copyright [Lafitte] Family, permission for use from [Phen] Lafitte, Miami, Florida, 2011, 2016, 2017.

Lafitte had been arrested: "Plimsoll Chef Pleads Innocent," *New Orleans States-Item*, 22 December 1969; "January Trial Ordered for Club Manager," *New Orleans States-Item*, 23 December 1969; author's Lafitte/Martin Briefing Book, 2003–2015; selected pages from Pierre Lafitte's letters from 1962, 1963, 1964; notes from his proposed "novel"; and conversations with members of Lafitte's family, New York,

New Hampshire, Florida; George Hunter White Datebooks, 1944–1970, Perham Foundation, Sunnyvale, California.

"On May 10, 1963 . . .": It is well to note that on the day following the entry of this directive from "T," Ruth Paine and Marina Oswald arrived in New Orleans. For extended analysis that explores the likely identity of "T," see the essay included in the appendix titled "A Well Concealed 'T.'"

Author's interviews with former CIA-TSS Chemical Division chief Sidney Gottlieb, January–March, 1999.

". . . one escapes the effort.": The one publicly available photo of Pierre Lafitte appeared in a 1955 syndicated newspaper article written by well-known journalist Bob Considine. The *Considine* article was circulated widely, and its prominence at the time may have exempted it from Helm's directive. Instead, per the author's recollection of having seen family photos of Lafitte taken around this time period, the photo appears to have been altered.

Former FBN officer: Harney, L. Malachi, *The Narcotic Officer's Notebook.*

Inquiry re: Lafitte deportation on behalf of Sen. Thomas Hennings, FBI # 66-18621-269. Bernard Fensterwald.

Author's 1997 interview with Col. Albert Haney, Florida.

"Author Dick Russell, in 1992 . . .": Russell, Dick, *The Man Who Knew Too Much*, Carroll and Graf, 1992, p. 558.

In late fall 1962 government status report on the ordeal of Christ, Anderson and Suzminski: Item 8. Other operational efforts to secure the release of the men are in progress. We have avoided keeping Mrs. Christ fully [informed] on the specifics of the efforts being made, as she tends to be critical of the Agency and of the fact that she is unaware of any significant interest in the case in the Executive Branch of Government. —Weberman, A. J. and Michael Canfield, *Coup d'Etat in America.*

Christ, Andersona, and Szuminski prisoner exchange: The circumstances of the actual release of Christ, Anderson, and Szuminski did not involve a dramatic rescue from the walls of the dreaded Isle of Pines Prison, but instead, a multimillion-dollar food and pharmaceutical "contribution" to Castro and a highly orchestrated prisoner exchange. Associated Press published a news report on November 17, 1962, that FBI agents in NYC confiscated a small arsenal of explosives and incendiary devices at a Manhattan jewelry manufacturing shop owned by Cuban-born Jose Garcia Orellana. The report alleges that the weapons were supplied by a Cuban husband-wife diplomatic team (Jose Gomez Abad and his wife Elsa) who were posted at the United Nations. Within three days of arrest, the couple was flown out of Idlewild Airport bound for Mexico City under diplomatic immunity. A third member of the Cuban UN mission, Roberto Santiesteban Casanova, was being held along with Garcia Orellana and twenty-two-year-old Carmen Duero y Cabrera, who worked part-time in Orellana's shop. A subsequent FBI report on the raid indicates that a "Fair Play" [for Cuba] card with an associated phone number was in Garcia Orellana's possession at the time of his arrest. Garcia, who had become a naturalized American citizen for having served in the US military during WWII, had never concealed his support of the Casa Cuba Club, a refuge for Cuban exiles living in New York.

According to author Pierre Huss, *Red Spies in the UN*, after the arrest and hearings for Garcia Orellana, Santiesteban Casanova, and Cabrera during which all three entered not guilty pleas, the case quickly seemed to be forgotten. Writes Huss, "Nothing more was heard about the Cuban saboteurs for the next four months [in spite of what is alleged by the FBI to have been a plot on a massive scale to create bedlam and destruction], except for one unconfirmed report that Attorney General Robert F. Kennedy had visited Santiesteban in the Federal House of Detention in New York City to discuss a 'trade' with him. At the time, the Government was negotiating with Cuba for the release of US nationals and others involved in the calamitous Bay of Pigs invasions." This is an obvious reference to the aforementioned "Other operational efforts to secure the release of the men are in progress. We have avoided keeping Mrs. Christ fully [informed] on the specifics of the efforts being made . . . . she is unaware of any significant interest in the case in the Executive Branch of Government." Huss continues, "There had been talk, too, that besides the drugs and medical supplies that Castro was seeking in the exchange, he also wanted the release of the three saboteurs. On April 22, 1963, the release became a reality. The three Cubans were given their freedom to return to Cuba. Along with them, the Government threw into the bargain a fourth Cuban prisoner, Francisco 'The Hook' Molina . . ." Molina's 20 years to life sentence for a violent shoot out during which he killed a young Venezuelan girl had been commuted, overnight, by NY Governor Nelson Rockefeller. Huss concludes, "The prisoners' release was granted on the ground 'that the state department had suggested to the Department of Justice that it would be in the national interest if the three defendants were released."

Jose Orellana Garcia: April 22, 1962, the family of Jose Orellana Garcia was making preparations in their small NY apartment for his homecoming party following his five-month incarceration on charges for what they were convinced was a staged raid. As told to coauthor Leslie Sharp, the FBI agents who had been keeping the family apprised of the US Attorney General's promise to allow Jose to return to his life in Manhattan were, at the eleventh hour, involved in a frantic last-minute change in plans. When the agents knocked on the door, Jose was not with them. Over the next hour, the agents would leave and reenter the apartment, taking phone calls that were obviously related to complications. In retrospect, Jose's family realized that the last-minute negotiations involved Robert F. Kennedy himself. Less than an hour later, the agents advised Jose's wife that the Department of Justice had decided that Jose would not be allowed to remain in America and they were ordered to pack only what she and her two young daughters ages twelve and seven could carry. Jose's wife, a US citizen, became distraught at the prospect of leaving her mother and other family members behind. According to witnesses, she was given less than an hour to make a decision, "join your husband or he leaves the United States on his own and you and your daughters may never see him again." Under extreme emotional stress, she and her daughters hurriedly gathered the meager belongings, and within two hours the agents had delivered them in a US government vehicle to Idlewild International Airport. This coauthor has been told that among the three men who boarded the flight with Jose and his wife and daughters was a man who had a partial arm, fitting the description of Francisco "The Hook" Molina. While government records reflect the negative impact that David Christ's imprisonment in Cuba made on his wife and six children, thereby posing a myriad of national security risks, a postscript to the Garcia Orellana family story bears reporting, as well. Jose was greeted with a hero's welcome in Havana, but his wife found it impossible to adjust to Castro's restrictive regime and soon returned to the US with her young daughters—one of whom was as devoted to her father, Jose, as only daughters can be. The girls never saw their father again. —author's interview with anonymous.

John Martino: author Larry Hancock, citing HSCA travel receipts provided by John Martino's wife: "He was in New Orleans on September 27, and spoke in various Texas cities on October 1–3, returning to New Orleans on October 4, before going home to Miami . . ." As Hancock made clear, Martino's sole claim to participation in the JFK assassination was that he acted as a courier, moving money. Given Martino's travel schedule, it is striking that Pierre Lafitte, a long-time acquaintance of Martino's, jotted in his datebook on September 30, 1963, "Money from Dallas."

Lafitte-Greenspun operation: "Pierre Lafitte, an undercover investigator hired by the Las Vegas Sun, impersonated a big-time racketeer and was able to bribe county and state officials to secure protection for his pretended operations. In a tape-recorded conversation with [Nevada] Lt. Gov. and Democratic National Committee member Clifford Jones, Lafitte, using the name Louis Tabet, told Jones he'd 'taken care of the county' and named several county officials whom he had agreed to pay off. Jones replied 'You're with the right people. I talk for the state.' Tabet asked Jones for help in obtaining a gambling license, despite his admitted criminal record ('a few things when I was young—a little narcotics, bootlegging, murder, manslaughter' (!)) When assured that Tabet had no recent convictions, Jones told him, 'you're all right, but not until after the first of the year, when [Gubernatorial candidate Vail] Pittman takes office.' Following the *Las Vegas Sun's* exposure of the exploits of 'Louis Tabet,' Jones resigned his position on the Democratic National Committee . . ."

Testimony of Theodore Shackley [Halley] on QJ/WIN: Church Committee, 8/19/75, NARA #157-10002-10084.

QJWIN as program: ". . . that cryptonym had been used for a larger program that dates as far back as the early 1950s. Under this program, we know that there were at least two—and probably more—QJ/WIN 'offices.' Very little about this far-flung QJ/WIN program has been declassified."—John Newman.

Newman, John M., *Countdown to Darkness: The Assassination of President Kennedy* Vol. Two, CreateSpace, 2017, p. 282.

Hanna Yazbeck and Edward Lawton Smith: CIA files, see Mary Ferrell site.

Author's [Albarelli] interviews with daughter of Edward Lawton Smith, Canada, March–April 2017.

Bill Dalzell and Edward Scanell Butler: Butler was appointed executive director of the Information Council of the Americas (INCA) in 1961, an organization established by Dr. Alton Ochsner with the financial help of Texas oilman Clint Murchison to prevent Communist revolutions in Latin America. As intimated previously, Murchison had been a frequent host to FBI Director J. Edgar Hoover as well as William Reily's friend, Senator Joe McCarthy at the Hotel Del Charro in La Jolla, California. The views of Dallas-based oilmen on whom many politicians and government officials relied financially were aligned closely with their friends in politically powerful positions. According to Anthony Summers, *The Secret Life of J. Edgar Hoover*, Murchison's political instincts were of the far, far Right. He was a fervent supporter of states' rights, reportedly funded the anti-Semitic press, and was a primary source of money for the American Nazi Party and its leader, Lincoln Rockwell, who considered Edgar [Hoover] "our kind of people." Butler also cofounded the short-lived "Free Voice of Latin America" with William Wayne Dalzell, who had recently organized Friends of Democratic Cuba in New Orleans. According to a CIA document dated October 19, 1967: DALZELL, William Wayne: "One of the incorporators of Friends of Democratic Cuba. Had three contacts with DCS New Orleans, November 1960 and January-February 1961." There are conflicting accounts as to the true origins of FDC, including claims of direct involvement of former FBI agent Guy Banister, whom readers will recognize from the Garrison investigation in New Orleans; regardless, it is apparent that the FDC had caught the attention of James Angleton. According to A. J. Weberman, *Coup d'Etat in*

America, "On March 30, 1961 ANGLETON sent CSCI-3/764,414 to Sam Papich regarding the Friends of Democratic Cuba." ANGLETON had either generated or had seen this document. It stated: 1. Reference is made to Bureau Memoranda dated January 20, 1961, and February 7, 1961, both titled "Frente Revolucionario Democratico (FRD). . . . The Friends of Democratic Cuba was incorporated January 6, 1961, in New Orleans, Louisiana, with offices in the Balter building for the purpose of collecting funds to assist Cubans in opposition to Castro." (It should be noted that the field office of the CIA, headed by Lloyd Ray, who was known personally to William Dalzell according to his interview during the Garrison investigation—located in the Balter building. Dalzell advised during that same interview that he also was acquainted with Stephen Lemann, attorney for Freeport Sulphur, alleged to have been the paymaster for the agency in New Orleans according to a memo stored away in Garrison's files.

On Wednesday, April 17, Pierre Lafitte made the following entry: "Dalzell – K money for Drilling." Three days earlier, Lafitte's entry reads, "Delong meet with T. Cuba." We have reason to believe that "Delong" is a reference to the patent holder of various designs of heavy equipment for the oil industry, Leon Delong; we know that Dalzell had been attempting to raise money in New Orleans for another of his oil-related schemes, and we know that he had been employed briefly in Odessa, Texas, by Dixilyn Drilling the same year that the West Texas oil company invested in the "Julie Ann," one of the first floating, self-contained platform rigs with jack-up legs for off-shore drilling designed by Texan R. G. LeTourneau. An oil industry manufacturing magnate, LeTourneau had been in joint ventures with Delong. The "Julie Ann" was the fifth such jack-up rig based in Longview, Texas (the first two being commissioned by Zapata Oil founded by George H. W. Bush who held extensive contracts with LeTourneau). Three months later, on July 17, Lafitte wrote "-Dalzell crazy? (Rene says ignore his antics.)" Bill Dalzell had been in psychiatric care the summer of 1963.

LATIN AMERICAN DIVISION/DDO, June 29, 1977. George V. Lauder, Acting Chief Latin America Division: "Latin American Division Task Force Report of Possible Cuban Complicity in the John F. Kennedy Assassination." www.documents.theblackvault.com/documents/jfk/NARA-Oct2017/NARA-Nov9-2017/104-10506-10028.pdf.

- Memo for the Record by Henry Hecksher, 10 July 1963 Washington, D.C. Meeting with ARTIME (BOX 18). ARTIME related events prior to the Bay of Pigs invasion. Manuel RAY had just arrived in the U.S. from Cuba. He enjoyed strong Department of State support. It was his intent to get the U.S. to withdraw support from the FRD and to obtain control over the training camps himself.

VARONA's and CARILLO's intention was to see the FRD go down. Hecksher said he masterminded RAY's defeat and RAY knew it.

- Memo to C/FI from William Harvey, 27 June 1963
  "As far as ZRRIFLE aspects this op, which have been covered under the QJWIN authorization for security reasons and with which Fletcher Knight is fully familiar, except for one precautionary line, aspects of this case have been terminated and need no longer be considered part of this project."

- Memo by Henry D. Hecksher on AMWORLD Meeting in Washington 7 to 10 Nov 1963 Subj: Dr. La Saga (BOX 18) LaSaga was the MRR delegate in the U.S. while ARTIME was imprisoned in Cuba (following the Bay of Pigs invasion). ARTIME demoted LaSaga. LaSaga described by Hecksher as one of the most intelligent men he had ever met. It was LaSaga's firm position that while President Kennedy was in power it would be impossible to defeat CASTRO.

- "In 1959 he furnished information to our QJWIN California office. . . but has not since cooperated with us. N.B. He has the back-ground and talent for the matter we discussed but it is not known whether he would be receptive." Hanna YAZBECK lived in Beurit and worked for QJWIN's office intennittently during the past 10 years (dates not given- possibly 51-61). YAZBECK's chief bodyguard from 50–58 (not named) was a convicted murderer. The bodyguard was murdered. States that YAZBECK has an available pool of assassins.

CHAPTER 4: SUICIDES AND CALL GIRLS

"Grant Stockdale Killed," article in *Evening Independent*, St. Petersburg, Florida, Monday December 2, 1963, p. 1A.

McDermott, John B., "Stockdale Into Irrational Mood." *Miami Herald Reporter.*

Author's [Albarelli] interviews with Connie Larsson, Arlington, Virginia, November-December, 2015.

Mollenhoff, Clark, ". . . U.S. Capitol May Be Rocked by Story of Exotic Mystery Woman." *Des Moines Register*, October 26, 1963.

Kilgallen, Dorothy, "The Novotny Story." *Washington Post.*

". . . took up a gun and shot himself to death." *Time* magazine, November 15, 1971.

www.archives.gov/files/research/jfk/releases/docid-32263513.pdf.

Memorandum from FBI Director J. Edgar Hoover to FBI officials Tolson, Belmont, DeLoach, Rosen, and Sullivan, November 7, 1963.

FBI Urgent Teletype to J. Edgar Hoover and FBI SAC Washington D.C. Field Office [WFO] from SAC, Baltimore, Maryland, November 8, 1963.

FBI Memorandum to Mr. Belmont from A. Rosen, Subject: Ellen Rometsch, Internal Security-East Germany, October 27, 1963.

Rometsch Case 1964: FBI Master File, Subject: Ellen Rometsch, File No. 105-122316, Volumes 1 to 4.

FBI Memorandum to Mr. DeLoach from M.A. Jones, Subject: Ellen Rometsch: Request for Summary by the White House, February 21, 1964.

FBI Memorandum to Mr. Mohr from C. D. DeLoach, re: Ellen Rometsch and Robert G. Baker, December 7, 1964.

Joesten, Joachim, *The Case Against Lyndon B. Johnson*, 1967, typed pages, CIA document Number 1079-405c, September 1976. This document in part reads: "Leading American newspapers frequently, if coyly, alluded to the malodorous 'moral aide' of the Baker affair, which was strenuously [*sic*] suppressed in all investigations. The New York Times, for instance, on March 22, 1964, published a dispatch for Phoenix, Arizona, that began with this paragraph: 'Call girls and Bobby Baker and motels' have become the symbols of Washington under President Johnson, Sen. Barry Goldwater charges today . . . '"

Joesten continues, "Less than two weeks before Kennedy's death, The New York Herald Tribune, in an article on the 'Secret Rules of Inquiry' governing the Baker investigation, reported on Nov. 10, 1963: 'It is an open Washington secret that when the 'sex angle' was introduced into the Baker case by revelations that a beautiful German model had been sent home after reported (and denied) affairs with Washington politicians, it scared almost as many people in Washington as when the Russian missiles in Cuba pushed the US to the brink of nuclear war.' This was a reference to Elly Rometsch who had been bundled out of the United States, on August 21, 1963, by the FBI after she had been boasting a little too indiscreetly about her intimate relationship with top government officials. What had aroused the FBI into frantic action was not a concern about the morals of the nation's leaders but knowledge that Elly Rometsch hailed from East German, a Communist country. With the impact of Britain's Profumo scandal still fresh in everybody's mind, J. Edgar Hoover wasn't going to take any more chances . . . The deep secrecy about the Rometsch ouster was maintained even for some weeks after the Baker scandal had broken early in September 1963."

"David Talbot: Grant Stockdale": Started by John Simkin, May 26, 2007 12:20 PM; online JFK Assassination Debate, Education Forum.

FBI files on Ellen and Rolf Rometsch, Volume I and Volume II, Privately published. The many and extensive FBI documents concerning Ellen Rometsch are heavily redacted, some seemingly absurdly so. The files remain in this redacted state to date.

"As long as this Soviet-dominated apparatus exists in the United States, there will remain among us an aggressive force of dedicated fanatics, constantly at work to destroy the American way of life. It is a beachhead of subversion within our Nation." —J. Edgar Hoover, Director, Federal Bureau of Investigation. "The Communist Conspiracy Must Be Destroyed!" New Orleans: copyright 1963 by *The Independent American*, Tax Fax No. 49 (published by Kent and Phoebe Courtney).

The Fourth Decade, Volume 5, No. 3, March, 1998.

Des Moines Register: Aviation pioneer William Boeing founded his aircraft company in 1916, which formed the basis of what is now claimed to be the oldest commercial airline in the US, United Airlines. The board of United would later include news mogul, Gardner Cowles, Jr., chairman of Cowles Communication of Des Moines, which owned the *Des Moines Register* and employed Clark Mollenhoff. Boeing would later dub one of their 747s the "Gardner Cowles." Cowles had been a founding member of the Cold War propaganda campaign, Crusade for Freedom, conceived by Frank Wisner, who was head of the CIA's Office of Policy Coordination and as referenced, the mastermind of Operation Mockingbird. The first chairman of the Crusade had been Gen. Lucius Clay, military governor of occupied Germany, and the effort enjoyed the strong support of John Jay McCloy, who had served as high commissioner of West Germany. About the Crusade, General Dwight Eisenhower said in a speech given on Labor Day, 1952, "To destroy human liberty and to control the world, the Communists use every conceivable weapon—subversion, bribery, corruption, military attack! Of all these, none is more insidious than propaganda. Spurred by this threat to our very existence, I speak tonight—as another private citizen, not as an officer of the Army—about the Crusade of freedom. This crusade is a campaign sponsored by private American citizens to fight the big lie with the big truth." Thus was the milieu surrounding Mollenhoff.

"The Washington Cover-Up" Program at Georgetown University, November 1962.

http://ukrweekly.com/archive/pdf2/1962/The_Ukrainian_Weekly_1962-42.pdf.

"Anti-Communist League Holds 7th Conference in Washington." April 1974.

https://www.ukrweekly.com/archive/1974/The_Ukrainian_Weekly_1974-17.pdf.

Memorandum for: Chief, SR/OPS, Subject: Reported Settlement of Zch/OUN/B Headquarters from Munich to Washington, D.C. ". . . Resettlement of the group from Germany to the United States is reportedly being done with the approval of

"American Intelligence" and U. S. Congressional circles. . . . Among those to be resettled in the United States reportedly are Yaroslav STETSKO and his wife, and Ivan KASHUBA."

CHAPTER 5: JACKS-OF-ALL-TRADES

Otto Skorzeny private archives 1961–1964, Ralph Ganis, North Carolina.

Lafitte Datebook: Pierre Lafitte, 1963. H. P. Albarelli Jr., London, England.

Thomas Eli Davis, U.S. State Department files, 1963–1964; Thomas Eli Davis Case File, 1961–2007, H. P. Albarelli Jr.

Tom Davis and State Department: Department of State Incoming Telegram, Limited Official Use. Control 6690, From: Tangier, Action: SECSTATE 59 PRIORITY,

INFO: RABAT 33, DECEMBER 9, 1963 NOON, Rec'd: December 10, 1963, 3:13 PM, Copy to CIA.

FBI Airtel, TO: Director, FBI and SAC, Los Angeles (105-14523), FROM: SAC, Detroit (105-9046) (RUC), Subject: Thomas Eli Davis, III, June 28, 1963.

Lee Harvey Oswald and Howard Loeb Schulman, Tangier: FBI Memorandum, To: Deputy Assistant Secretary for Security, Department of State, From: John Edgar Hoover, Director, Subject: Lee Harvey Oswald, December 20, 1963.

US Ambassador to Spain Robert Woodward and the Department of State Inter-American Affairs: Ambassador Robert Woodward was an old hand in the department of Inter-American Affairs, one of the more influential government agencies during World War II, coordinated by Lawrence Rockefeller's brother, Nelson Rockefeller. George de Mohrenschildt is said to have worked for Rockefeller at the time.

Serving alongside Robert Woodward at Inter-American affairs were fellow diplomats Edwin M. Martin and Thomas C. Mann. The three career diplomats leapfrogged as Assistant Secretary of State for Inter-American Affairs: 1960–61 Thomas Mann; 1961–62 Robert F. Woodward; 1962-64 Edwin M. Martin; and 1964–65 Thomas Mann. President Lyndon Johnson's policy for all of Latin America became known as the Mann Doctrine. Some authors speculate that this was Mann's reward for his handling of the crisis in Mexico City following the assassination in Dallas. (It should be noted that Mann succeeded career diplomat Robert C. Hill as American Ambassador to Mexico. Hill, as noted in the introduction of this book, was a close family friend of the author.)

Ambassador Woodward's Inter-American Affairs colleague, Edwin M. Martin, was an economist who participated in the mobilization of the US economy for World War II. As such, he held a key post on the War Production Board, whose members included executives from Remington Arms, Underwood Typewriter, and the Bullard Corp.—all of Bridgeport, CT. The WPB worked in lockstep with Paul McNutt's War Manpower Commission. As noted, Schlumberger periodically employed contract soldiers of fortune, including Thomas Eli Davis, who seems to exemplify the profile that US oil companies turned to for less than legitimate projects. Schlumberger's major research and development division was located in Ridgefield, CT, less than an hour from Carolyn's hometown. It was McNutt's law partner, Thomas Proctor, who was the intended recipient of Tom Davis's letter, downplayed by Ambassador Woodward.

In 1962, Edwin Martin had spearheaded President Kennedy's task force during the Cuban Missile Crisis and would have been privy to the administration's internal and highly controversial views on all things relating to rumors of a Communist threat from Cuba, originating in the Soviet Union. Martin was an experienced intelligence operative, having served as Bill Donovan's Deputy Chief of Division in the OSS, which placed him in close proximity to Donovan's chief of security, Arthur van Beuren, a founding member of Previews, Inc., the NYC-based business front used by Otto's wife, Ilse Skorzeny, beginning in 1957. Ilse of course would have been flying in and out of Madrid during this period, ostensibly pursuing a global real estate career.

All three career diplomats—Woodward, Martin, and Mann—served in government roles heavily influenced by Latin American specialist and longtime close friend to the Rockefeller brothers, Adolf Berle. Berle was so fond of Thomas Mann that he referred to him as "Tommy," and about Robert Woodward he wrote, "At all events, he knows the score . . . he understands the democratic forces as well as the governmental forces." And Berle shared a passion for economics with Edwin Martin, advising President Kennedy, while Martin chaired the Cuban Missile Crisis Task Force. Reflecting on those years, in his oral history, Berle shared a conversation he had with Jack Kennedy regarding, in particular, the State Department. According to Berle, Kennedy once observed, "These fellows really object to my being President," and continued to confide in the elder statesman that he was "entirely disillusioned about the old pros in the State Department, their capacity to deal with situations." It was Berle, along with Allen Dulles, who set in motion the human experiments conducted by the Human Ecology Foundation, including those at the Lafayette Clinic in Detroit, where Tom Davis was a victim.

Date Book 1963, Pierre Lafitte, Copyright Lafitte Family, 2009. Custodian: Phen Lafitte, Miami, Florida. Specific permission granted to the authors to quote from the datebook.

Notes regarding conversations between H. P. Albarelli Jr. and Ralph Ganis concerning Thomas Eli Davis, Jr., July–August 2015; link analysis report on Thomas Eli Davis, Jr. and Carolyn Hawley by Leslie Sharp, New Mexico and Dallas, Texas.

Note: According to Seth Kantor, Davis was first arrested in Algiers on November 22, 1963, while attempting to sell guns to anti-Algerian terrorists; he was released, again according to Kantor, through efforts of QJ/WIN.

Russell, Dick, *The Man Who Knew Too Much*. Readers should note the extraordinary coincidences between Thomas Davis's life and Russell's chief subject, Richard Case Nagell.

Carolyn Davis: Interviews with author, 2005, Connecticut.

Viola June Cobb: Interviews, Albarelli with Cobb specific to Thomas Davis were conducted in February–March 2015 in Indian Rocks Beach, Florida, and New York.

Victor Oswald bio: Operation Safehaven report on Baquera, Kusche and Martin S.A. in Spain. 3 pp. July 1945; see also XL 13247 Safehaven report on Baquera, Kusche, and Martin (BAKUMAR), German-controlled Spanish customs and shipping agents.

Willie Palm: "A Relative Responds" by Mark Bridger, *Dealey Plaza Echo*, Vol 13, Number 1, March 2009.

Proctor lawsuit against Bronston: *Evening Herald News*, 4 February 1967, p. 2.

"Thomas Eli Davis, Jr. Recruits Mercenaries in Los Angeles" — excerpt from *A Secret Order* by H. P. Albarelli Jr. (pp. 320–323): The FBI individually interviewed every man that attended Davis's Tahitian Village gathering. Detailed statements taken from each man reveal a number of interesting things said during the meeting. William Henry Wade, a Korean War veteran who had traveled from his home in Wilmington, North Carolina, for the meeting, stated that Davis told the group that he was seeking to hire men "who would represent the US government in Haiti" and that "either the US government or CIA was not actually behind his movement to overthrow Duvalier in Haiti, but that they would not turn their back until they saw how it turned out." Wade also told the FBI, "We were to be picked up to go to Haiti at the Los Angeles International Airport in a C-119 on or before Friday, May 24, 1963, and flown to some base in the United States where we would then leave for Haiti." Additional statements taken from participants revealed that Davis appeared to be privy to very timely and highly classified information about Haiti, including knowledge about a US Naval ship off the coast of Haiti that was allegedly not known to anyone but a few intelligence officers. According to another FBI report, Davis told a former paratrooper and ranger who attended the meeting that "he had served in Korea and that he had already visited Haiti." Davis told the man that "he had met a man in Mexico who had given him $25,000 for this purpose" [invasion of Haiti]. Despite the many FBI agent-hours and investigation into Davis's activities in California, nothing came of it, and Davis and his wife were allowed to leave the US for Europe and Morocco within weeks.

Congressional Record: Proceedings and Debates of the . . . , Volume 107, Part 14

Remington Arms: Bridgeport-based Remington Arms' parent company was the Du Pont Corporation. The daughter of Pierre S. du Pont III, named as an investor in Sam Bronston's project set in Spain, Jane a.k.a. Leit, married Dallas independent oilman Barron Ulmer Kidd Jr. in May 1963 in what was the social event of the season in Delaware. The "Ulmer" in Barron Kidd's name is in honor of his grandfather, Marvin Ulmer, who served as Mayor of Midland, Texas—the heart and soul of the US oil industry—in the 1940s. Mayor Ulmer was responsible for establishing the Midland Air Force Base. There is no evidence to date that the Ulmers of West Texas were related to CIA agent Al Ulmer—who was based in Madrid as Otto Skorzeny found his footing both with Franco and with the CIA. However, Barron Kidd Oil Co.—whose patriarch was living in the same Turtle Creek condominium high-rise in Dallas as Frank "Brandy" Brandstetter of the 488 Military Intelligence, in 1963—was among the first occupants of Dallas architect T. E. Stanley's office building located at 3707 Rawlins in the Oaklawn neighborhood in April 1963. This was also the first office space in Dallas for NY based Previews, Inc., employer of Ilse Skorzeny and Herschel V. Williams of Sikorsky's Tolstoy Foundation.

The investments of Henry S. du Pont, III—father of Leit du Pont Kidd of Dallas by the summer of 1963—included Sam Bronston's CIA-backed film project in Spain. That operation brought du Pont into a circle with Victor Oswald—an arms dealer who trafficked in explosives, suggesting they were already acquainted—and by osmosis, du Pont at the very least knew of Otto Skorzeny; headquarters of Du Pont Corp's Remington Arms was in the Hawley's Connecticut National Bank; Carolyn Hawley and her new husband, Tom Davis, traveled to Madrid with an introduction to Victor Oswald from Thomas Proctor, legal counsel to Bronston on the project partially financed by Leit Kidd's father, Henry du Pont. The likelihood cannot be dismissed easily that the Rawlins' address in Oak Lawn—which housed both Barron Kidd Oil and Previews Inc. (providing cover for Ilse's presence in Dallas)—may have been essential to the implementation of Otto's assassination strategy—once he had signed off on plans he received by November 5. While Carolyn was in London, Paris, and then Madrid (in a meeting with Victor and Otto), Ilse was in Dallas.

A decade after the assassination, E. I. du Pont de Nemours & Co. employed a young Dallas investment expert, Garry Weber. His office was in the Meadows Building, as were those of Lester Logue, Remington Arms, and D. H. Byrd's wife, Mattie. Weber's mother was, later, a contract agent for the Turtle Creek travel agency that handled travel for the national associations of petroleum engineers and of petroleum geologists in the 1970s. A favored destination of the ASPE and the ASPG was the Canary Islands, the Spanish archipelago off the coast of northwest Africa, and haunt of Fort Worth oilman Sid Richardson, who is known for his ventures with Clint W. Murchison, a collaborator with Otto Skorzeny since the early 1950s. Mrs. Weber's office was within three blocks of the Rawlins St. office building, where Kidd Oil and Previews Inc. had occupied a majority of space. Her coagent, Mitzi Calder, was married to independent oil producer Bruce Calder, the best friend of George de Mohrenschildt, who sublet the space leased by George in the Republic National Bank while he was "out of the country." Both men were known to stroll into the offices of the Turtle Creek travel agency on occasion. Once Garry Weber was elected to the Dallas City Council, he became instrumental in the creation of the Sixth Floor Museum, custodians of the "sniper's nest" and responsible for how the City of Dallas—the scene of the crime and of the coup—would display the tragic history of November 22, 1963.

CHAPTER 6: LONG SHADOWS

Based on a transcribed interview with an unnamed source in Tampa, Florida, and with Viola June Cobb, May–April 2014, Indian Rocks Beach, Florida. The source was a longtime and close associate of Trafficante; June Cobb was a CIA asset in Havana, as well as later, for nearly six years, in Mexico City, Mexico. She encountered Trafficante twice in Cuba, once in the presence of Che Guevara and the other time with William Alexander Morgan, who was executed by Che on March 11, 1961, at Cabana Prison in Havana. Said Cobb, "I met Ruby once in the company of a Dallas businessman, Raymond Cortez, who falsely claimed to be an attorney. The businessman had come to attempt to talk with Che and Fidel about land reform efforts. They never met with him. . . . I suspected he was with an intelligence group, but, of course, didn't ask. I ran into the businessman again in Mexico City where he owned a shoe factory. I had no idea who Ruby was until much later, after the assassination." Cobb had no knowledge about Otto Skorzeny other than conventional news accounts about his wartime exploits; however, she did hear constant reports and rumors about assassination activities originating out of Spain: "There were constant whispers about assassinations, constant. So often I mostly didn't pay attention. Of course, after Kennedy was killed, Mexico City was abuzz with chatter, everywhere. You couldn't get into a taxi without hearing something new. People seemed to know about Oswald almost right away. There was no lack of news there. The few people I encountered with the Agency made a concerted effort to not talk about it."

Information from Santo Trafficante's immunized testimony before the HSCA on November 14, 1977, John Wilson Hudson, pp. 49–51.

CIA-FBI FOIA documents: Memorandum to J. Edgar Hoover, FBI Director from Richard Helms, Deputy Director, Plans, CIA, Subject: WILSON, Carlos John. DOB: 29 December 1916, POB: Liverpool, England, Reference: OUT 85657, 28 November 1963.

WILSON, CARLOS JOHN, AKA WILSON-HUDSON, JOHN, WILSON, JOHN HUDSON. https://www.maryferrell.org/showDoc.html?docId=55932 #relPageId=2&search=John_Wilson%20Hudson.

John Wilson-Hudson: To underscore the potential significance of Wilson-Hudson to the investigation into the 1963 assassination of President Kennedy: Memorandum For: Director of Central Intelligence, From: John H. Waller, Inspector General, Subject: Jack Anderson Reference to 28 November 1963 CIA Cable. ". . . The dissemination was based on a 27 November 1963 cable from London . . . raising a question as to his [John Wilson-Hudson's] reliability . . . " The undated memo was from the CIA IG to Director of Central Intelligence George Herbert Walker Bush. www.maryferrell.org.

United States. Congress. House. Select Committee on Assassinations. Investigation Of the Assassination of President John F. Kennedy: Hearings before the Select Committee on Assassinations of the US House of Representatives, Ninety-Fifth Congress, Second Session. Washington : US Govt. Print. Off., 19781979.

> (734) A memorandum from the deputy director of plans of the CIA to the FBI provided additional information about John Wilson Hudson. (670)
> A "usually reliable source" reported on August 8, 1951, that Carl John Wilson Hudson was a Spanish citizen of British descent residing in Chile and a contact of Bert Sucharov, a suspected Soviet agent in Santiago, Chile.
> (671) Wilson was born in Liverpool, England, on December 29, 1916. (672) After arriving in Chile in 1939, in his capacity of journalist Wilson reportedly be n "a one-man crusade against the British Government." (673) Anogfiar source described as "usually reliable" and "whose information was evaluated

as "possibly true" reported in 1952 that Wilson was "very probably an intelligence agent." (674)

(735) It was also reported by a "usually reliable source" that on June 18, 1959, Carl John Wilson, a British journalist, sent a cable to the British Parliament and the British Trade Union Federation claiming he had confirmed that the U.S. military attachés in the Caribbean were providing military advice to dictators. In this cable, Wilson reportedly protested these actions "in the name of humanity." (675) Another report from another "usually reliable source" stated that Wilson was involved in a planned attack from Cuba on Puerto Cabezas, Nicaragua, during the weekend of June 27–28, 1959. (676) Associated Press reported on July 1, 1959, that the Cuban home of Capt. Paul Hughes was raided, leading to the seizure of:

A large arms cache and air-sea invasion plans and the detention of two other Americans, a British journalist, several Cubans, and nearly 200 would be members of an expeditionary force against the regime of Nicaraguan President Luis Somoza. (677)

The article stated that "the British subject was identified as Carl John Wilson, a freelance journalist who had been in Havana several weeks." (678)

(736) The committee was unable to locate John Wilson Hudson. In response to the committee's inquiries, the Metropolitan Police in London, England, contacted unspecified government agencies, but these efforts were unsuccessful. (679) It has been alleged that Hudson is dead. (680) Analysis.

(742) It has not been possible to corroborate the allegation that Ruby visited Trafficante at Trescornia. John Wilson Hudson was not located, and Trafficante denied any such meeting, although he did recall an individual fitting Hudson's description. José Verdacia also recalled a British journalist who was at Trescornia.

The District of Columbia against *Canadian Javelin Ltd.*, John C. Doyle, Raymond Balestreri, Sarto Fournier, Manuel Paredes, *Jean V. Allard* and P. J. DeSantis.

New England Counsellor F. Payson Todd (Rowley Massachusetts) with Ralph L. Loomis. Oct. 1960.

SETH KANTOR was with President John F. Kennedy's press entourage when the president was assassinated in Dallas, and Kantor spent many years investigating the background of Jack Ruby. He published *Who Killed Jack Ruby?* in 1978, calling into question the Warren Commission's report, particularly as it pertained to Ruby's potential involvement in the assassination plot. He also published a book on Nazi saboteurs living in the United States. Seth Kantor died in 1993 at the age of 67. The cause was cardiac arrest, the hospital said.

NICKEL: New feats in speed and power came from the development of the first jet engines during World War II and into the 1950s. These new engines created high-pressure gas jets by using rapidly spinning turbines to compress air and eject it through exhaust nozzles. The fast-spinning turbines reached high temperatures and stresses and once again required new metal alloys to withstand these forces. Nickel was used as a strengthening agent in many of these alloys. Similar needs for stress and temperature resistance prompted the use of nickel-containing alloys in the burgeoning space race. Rocket engines have similar engineering demands as jet engines due to the high temperature and pressure of exhaust gases, and they also must endure extreme vibration caused by the combustion of rocket fuels. The early space industry used nickel in conjunction with other high-strength materials like titanium to create new classes of superalloys capable of withstanding the turbulence of space flight.

Gray, James A.,"Big Nickel." *Maclean's*, October 1, 1947. www.archive.macleans.ca /article/1947/10/1/big-nickel.

"Review of Soviet Petroleum Industry Technology and Equipment (S-3426)," www.cia.gov/readingroom/home DOC_0000307673.

Pease, Lisa, "David Atlee Phillips, Clay Shaw and Freeport Sulphur." (This article first appeared in *Probe* magazine [Vol. 3, No. 3, March–April 1996] and can now be found in The Assassination.) Excerpts: Nickel Mining in Cuba, Processing in New Orleans According to Cuban lawyer Mario Lazo, whose firm represented Freeport Sulphur in Cuba, the Nicaro project was conceived just two months after Pearl Harbor. The strange Cuban nickel-cobalt ore required a special extraction process. Freeport had developed a new chemical process—and Washington approved the financing—to aid the development of nickel (used in the manufacturing of steel) for the war effort. The Nicaro nickel plant cost American taxpayers $100,000,000. At one point, the plant produced nearly 10 percent of all the nickel in the free world. New Orleans became home to a special plant Freeport set up just outside the city to process the nickel-cobalt ore. When the Moa Bay Mining project was conceived, Freeport Nickel, a wholly owned Freeport Sulphur subsidiary, put up $19,000,000 of $119,000,000 to develop the Cuban nickel ore. The rest of the money came from a group of American steel companies and major automobile makers. (Freeport's pattern of putting in a small portion of total cost is a recurrent one.) $44,000,000 of the original funds went into Louisiana for the development of the New Orleans nickel processing facility at Port Nickel. Batista, Castro, and the Moa Bay Mining Company . . . Freeport versus Kennedy: The Stockpiling Investigation Already reeling from its losses over Castro's appropriation of the Moa Bay plant, Freeport found itself under attack from a new quarter: a Senate investigation into stockpiling surpluses, requested by President Kennedy himself. In 1962, President Kennedy asked Congress to look into the war-emergency stockpiling program, stating it was "a potential source of excessive and unconscionable profits." He said he was "astonished" to discover that the program had accumulated $7.7 billion worth of stockpiled material, exceeding projected needs by $3.4 billion. Kennedy also pledged full executive cooperation with the investigation, mentioning specifically $103 million in surplus nickel. The Senate pursued an investigation into stockpiling surpluses. Special attention was paid to three companies in which the Rockefeller brothers had substantial holdings: Hannah Mining, International Nickel, and Freeport Sulphur. A December 18, 1962, headline in the *New York Times* read, "U.S. Was Pushed into Buying Nickel, Senators Are Told." The article opened with this: "A federal official told Senate stockpile investigators today that the US Government got a bad deal in a 1957 nickel purchase contract with a potential $248,000,000 obligation."

Jesse Vickers: Born March 25, 1907, Atlanta, Georgia; wife Mirtus Vickers, in 1949 was investigated concerning purchase of a plane reportedly used in an attempt invasion of Dominican Republic. Prosecution declined. Vickers owned Airport Sales Company, Inc. . . . In 1950, informational received that Vickers was involved in a scheme to purchase arms on behalf of Caribbean Region for use against Dominican Republic. This scheme did not pass planning stage.
See also: www.maryferrell.org/showDoc.html?docId=134372#relPageId=6&search=Jesse_Vickers.

Catherine (Mrs. W. Randall) Taaffe: Memorandum from Director, FBI to Director CIA: Mrs. Catherine Taaffe, 06/19/60.

https://www.maryferrell.org/showDoc.html?docId=42396#relPageId=2&search=Catherine_Taaffe.

Summers Jr., Harry G., "JFK and Vietnam: an interpretation that makes him politically correct?" *Baltimore Sun*, March 15, 1992. www.baltimoresun.com/news/bs-xpm-1992-03-15-1992075129-story.html.

Birtie, Jr., Andrew, "The Campaigns of World War II – World Warr II Commemorative Series Pamphlets, Sicily."

The Federal Reserve Hoax. Vennard, Wicliffe B. —A standard work on the Fed, originally published in 1963, explains just how the Fed was created and how it has perpetrated at least 100 acts of treason against the United States and her people. Includes a foreword by Lt. Gen. Pedro A. del Valle and a chapter by populist

Congressman Louis McFadden. Also explains how bankers have become an invisible world government. Softcover, 364 pages, indexed, $18.95, advertised in Willis Carto's "Special Report on the Bogus Budget from American Free Press," 2011. Louis McFadden is widely considered one of America's most outspoken anti-Semites of his era who endorsed the *Protocols of the Elders of Zion*.

Foreign Intelligence Digest: That same year the director of the FBI, J. Edgar Hoover also wrote for the magazine. The title of the article by J Edgar Hoover, then director of the FBI, in December 1957 was "God and Country or Communism." In it he wrote about the atheists (here: materialists): "These materialists deny the existence of God. They deny the existence of the soul, of immortality, and values derived from unchanging moral principles. Reality, the materialists maintain, consists only of matter. These people, as I stated, are not Communists; yet they are preparing mental soil for the seeds of communism. Their pernicious doctrine of materialism, fed to young Americans as something new and modern, readies the minds of our youth to accept the immoral, atheistic system of thought we know as communism."

Brussell, Mae. "The Nazi Connection to the John F. Kennedy Assassination: Evidence of link between Nazis still in operation after World War II to the still unsolved murder of John F. Kennedy," published in *The Rebel*, January 1984.

CHAPTER 7: THE GENERALS, THE TEAMS, AND THE KILL SQUADS

Merwin Hart: article by Victor H. Bernstein, "Employee Tells What Went on in Merwin Hart's Office," *The Nation*, May 23, 1943.

"As we know now, Willoughby and Skorzeny met . . . ": In 1953, CIA operative Miles Copeland, then formally employed by contracting firm Booz Allen Hamilton in Cairo, Egypt, but acting as an adviser to Egyptian President Nasser was privy to the genesis of one Skorzeny-Willoughby meeting. Nasser was attempting to modernize his military forces and to instill needed discipline, and reached out to Skorzeny through American contacts. Copeland later wrote: "He (Skorzeny) was approached in a routine manner, then at a higher level, then through a personal visit from a certain well-known Major General of the American Army . . . ": —*The Game of Nations, The Amorality of Power Politics, Simon and Schuster*, 1969, pp. 87–88.

"As readers may suspect . . . ": The other "German gentleman" referred to here, per a part of the previous communications between Dulles and Willoughby, was very likely Gen. Hans Speidel, Rommel's chief of staff.

Pierre Lafitte Datebook, 1963; letter(s) to George Hunter White, 1964–1965.

"Many respected historians . . . ": Willoughby's contemporary critics also realized his mixed record of intelligence collection and dissemination, as well as his tendency toward personal puffery. When, after his retirement, the General launched a broadside against his critics (accusing them of offering "aid and comfort to the enemy," among other charges leveled), the response was rapid and vigorous. The highly respected journalist and military correspondent Hanson Baldwin replied: "As an intelligence officer, General Willoughby was widely and justly criticized by Pentagon officials as well as in the papers. His . . . article is as misleading and inaccurate as were some of his intelligence reports. . . . ": Kluckhohn, "Heidelberg to Madrid . . . " ibid.

Spas T. Raikin: *A Secret Order: Investigating the High Strangeness and Synchronicity in the Kennedy Assassination.*

Frank Ryan: *Relieved of Command*, Times-Picayune.

"In 1947, Willoughby appointed Canon . . . ": *The Korean War in Asia: A Hidden History.*, ed. Tessa Morris-Suzuki. p. 176.

Seagrave, Sterling and Peggy, *Gold Warriors: America's Secret Recovery of Yamashita's Gold*, pp. 110–111.

"Dr. Hargis and Gen. Willoughby Elected to International Committee." Foreign Intelligence Digest, June 29,1962. www.macarthurmemorial.org/31/Library-Archives.

Caufield, Jeffrey H. M.D., *General Walker and the Murder of President Kennedy: The Extensive Evidence of a Radical-Right Conspiracy.* Caufield covers the core of 1963 maneuverings by rightist revolutionaries Joseph Milteer, General Walker, General Willoughby, General del Valle, et al., pp. 137–198.

Date: 01/14/1963, From: Legat, Bonn (105-4174), Subject: Edwin A. Walker

". . . In addition the REDACTED information which was furnished under the caption "International Neo-fascism" stated that the same generally reliable source had reported that a conference of international fascists is to take place in Malmoe, Sweden, during 1963. This conference reportedly will serve to bring together the views on Jewish question of REDACTED of Coventry, England, and REDACTED of London." https://archive.org/details/foia_John_Birch_Society_Legat-Bonn-1 https://archive.org/details/foia_John_Birch_Society_Legat-Bonn-1

"Report of Detective Lochart P. Gracey, Jr. to Detective Sergeant C. H. Sapp, Intelligence Unit, City of Miami Police Department, April 10, 1963," Available in Harold Weisberg Collection, Hood College, jfk.hood.edu.

"Oswald' participation in the incident . . . ": Caufield thoroughly covers the details of
this period of time in his Chapter 14, "The Walker-Hargis National Speaking Tour
and the Walker Shooting Incident, Spring 1963," pp. 374–417.

"Confirmation of author Peter Kross's source . . . ": Kross, in *"JFK: The French Connection,"* p. 263, reports that "it is believed" that Jean Souetre and associates met with
both William King Harvey and General Walker during Souetre's visit to the Western Hemisphere in the spring of 1963. When this author queried him on his source
for that information—not of insignificant value!—Kross responded: "I'm sorry to
say that it has been many years since I wrote that book and for the life of me, I cannot remember the source of the question you are asking. All I can say is that I did
not make up what I wrote . . ." If Kross dropped the ball in sourcing his chronicle of
Souetre's '63 visits, it should be said that he is a well-respected researcher, who was
dealing with a great deal of evidence, both documentary and oral history. It is likely
that his source at the time requested anonymity. Be that as it may, confirmation of
one part of the Souetre story from Pierre Lafitte's writing leads me to suspect that
the other part—Souetre's meeting with Harvey (who is mentioned several times in
the '63 datebook)—is likely accurate as well.: Peter Kross email to Alan Kent,
August 26, 2019.

"James Angleton sincerely believed . . . ": Angleton particularly—as well as his Agency
mentor and protector, Allen Dulles—is an example of the reality that extreme right-
wing paranoia at the height of the Cold War was not limited to people who lacked
education. A Yale man and a published poet, Angleton could complain (in a 1940
letter to Ezra Pound) that the American press favored London over Berlin: "Everything is definitely British, and the Jews cause a devil of a stink. Here in New York
will be the next great pogrom, and they do need about a thousand ghettos in America. Jew, Jew and Jew, even the Irish are losing out." (Morley, *The Ghost: The Secret
Life of CIA Spymaster James Jesus Angleton*, p. 11). Historian Bruce Cumings, who
researched the right-wing dynamic in the 1950s in great depth, wrote: "Walter
Bedell Smith, among the most powerful men in the CIA and the director before
Dulles, was, according to [historian Stephen] Ambrose, 'about as right-wing as a
professional Army officer was ever likely to get' telling Eisenhower once that he
thought Nelson Rockefeller was a Communist. James Angleton, head of counterintelligence, was probably to the right of Smith. . . . " (Cumings, *The Origins of the
Korean War*, Vol. One,: p. 126). Author David Talbot writes: "Angleton was known
to loathe President Kennedy, whom he came to regard—in his alcohol fueled paranoia—as an agent of the Soviet Union. If the Soviets had launched their doomsday
missiles, he darkly muttered to reporters late in his career, the Kennedys 'would have
been safe in their luxury bunker, presumably watching World War Three on

television, while the rest of us would have burned in hell.'" (Talbot, *Brothers: The Hidden History of the Kennedy Years*, p. 275).

Escalante, Fabian, *The Secret War: CIA covert operations against Cuba 1959-62*.

CHAPTER 8: THE SKORZENYS

Smith, Stuart. *Otto Skorzeny: The Devil's Disciple*.

Eisenberg, Dan. *Re-emergence of Fascism*.

"U.S. Investors Seek Land in Australia," *Sydney Morning-Herald*, May 26, 1969.

In an news article, long buried, the wife of Col. Herschel V. Williams, daughter of a prominent Missouri politician, is photographed sitting behind Senator Joseph McCarthy during a day's hearing giving a "thumbs up" to her good friend Joe McCarthy.

Ganis, Ralph. *The Skorzeny Papers* Ganis, p. 318.

Adams, Jefferson, "Historical Dictionary of German Intelligence."

Hull, Mark M., *Irish Secrets: German Espionage in Wartime Ireland 1939–1945*.

Carter, Carolle Jr., *The Shamrock and the Swastika: German Espionage in Ireland in WWII*.

Mullins, Gerry. *Dublin Nazi No. 1: The Life of Adolf Mahr*.

Lee, Martin. *The Beast Reawakens: Fascism's Resurgence from Hitler's Spymasters to Today's Neo-Nazi Groups and Right-Wing Extremists*.

O'Reilly, Terrance. *Hitler's Irishmen*.

Weale, Adrian, *Renegades: Hitler's Englishmen*. Pimlico, Revised edition, January 1, 2002.

Jewish Telegraph Agency, Vol. XXX.

O'Donoghue, David, "State within a State: the Nazis in neutral Ireland," *History Ireland*, Ireland's History Magazine, Issue 6 (Nov/Dec 2006). O'Donoghue is also author of "The story of German radio's wartime Irish service" (Belfast, 1998), and "The Irish Army in the Congo 1960–1964: the far battalions" (Dublin, 2005).

O'Driscoll, Mervyn, Ireland, West Germany and the New Europe, 1949-73: Best Friend and Ally?

Sedar, Irving & Harold Greenburg, *Behind the Egyptian Sphinx; Nasser's Strange Bedfellows*.

An Sionnach Fion: Irish News, Politics and Culture,

"Gun, The IRA And The War of Independence," October 7, 2018. First published 20th-century / Contemporary History, Features, Issue 6 (Nov/Dec 2006), The Emergency, Volume 14.

Von Bulow, Mathilde, *West Germany, Cold War Europe and the Algerian War (New Studies in European History.*

O'Halpin, Eunan, *Defending Ireland: The Irish State and Its Enemies since 1922.*

"The Men in the Trojan Horse: Allen Dulles Heads Our Intelligence, World's Largest," by Dr. Singer. Available www.cia.gov/readingroom/home Document No. RDP70-00058R000100100033-3.

Wieviorka, Olivier, and Jane Marie Todd, *The French Resistance.*

"The Flying Boats of Foynes," *History Ireland.*

"The CIA stayed silent on allegations it was involved in IRA gunrunning," *Irish Independent,* January 19, 2017.

"New evidence on IRA/Nazi links," *History Ireland.*

Operation Harvest: "From 1957 to 1960 I simultaneously organized an army in India and another in the Congo, supplied and advised both the Algerian FLN and the French OAS, and thanks to my Irish sheep I was also able to take an interest in the activities in the IRA." —Otto Skorzeny.

In direct contrast to these mocking protestations by the SS Commando, authors Irving Sedar and Harold Greenberg asserted as early as 1960 that "Skorzeny's reputation as a military commando, political mastermind, and leading figure of the Fascist International, has spread across four continents. He is one of the key conspirators in an international clandestine organization of exiled Nazis whose chief objective is to keep alive the ideology of National Socialism and to work from abroad for the strengthening and resurrection of a united Germany in its new bid for world power. This sinister network of neo-Nazi intrigue operates from the heart of the German colony in Madrid, and its activities extend to Dublin, Rome, Bonn, Berlin, Communist East Germany, the Soviet bloc, Asia, Africa, the Caribbean as well as North and South America. . . . He continued to Dublin, which has now replaced Madrid as his base of operations, and purchased a large farm outside the Irish capital. From there, he is in constant contact with Bonn and Cairo." In 1956, just months before Skorzeny began his quest for Irish visas, the Irish Republican Army (IRA) launched "Operation Harvest," an overtly ambitious guerrilla effort that was meant to secure the political unity of Ireland by force of arms. It was waged against the backdrop of a "thaw" in international relations and drew inspiration from successful anti-colonial guerrilla struggles in Algeria and Cyprus.

We know with certainty how deeply involved were Otto Skorzeny and those identified by Pierre Lafitte in the Algerian uprisings, so any assessment of the Irish
campaign that began in December 1956 should be considered in context and timing. The start of Operation Harvest also coincided with the 1956 insurgency in
Hungary against Russian domination. Irish Republicans, legitimately, were quick to
point out the hypocrisy of those who praised the armed revolt of the Hungarians but
condemned the Irish resistance fighters. During the '50s, the British had been ruth-
lessly suppressing anticolonial revolts in Kenya, Malaya, and Cyprus, and while
their colonial empire was crumbling, their conceit that they were still a supreme
military power remained. Suez burst that bubble, and we know that Skorzeny was
heavily involved there, as well. It was in the wake of that British humiliation in
Egypt that Operation Harvest was launched in Ireland. By the end of 1957, there
were several hundred IRA members interred in Dublin, Belfast, and other British
prisons, and there were 125 internees in the Curragh Camp in County Kildare, only
miles from where Otto and Ilse would set up camp in 1959. In a world of struggles
for national self-determination, it was clear that the Irish struggle remained unfin-
ished business. The lull that followed the end of the campaign in 1962 proved
illusory, and six years later the nationalists and republicans of the Six Counties rose
up, never to retreat again.

Adamson, OBE, Dr. Ian, *The Hidden History of Herr Hoven.*

O'Donoghue, David, *The Devil's Deal: The IRA, Nazi Germany and the Double Life of
Jim O'Donovan.*

Biddescombe, Perry. *SS Hunter Battalions: The Hidden History of the Nazi Resistance
Movement 1944–45* (Revealing History), Tempus (November 15, 2006).

Robert Schacht: The application that Oswald completed for entry to the Albert Schweitzer College was a drab three-page questionnaire. On page one, Oswald supplied
basic personal information along with the request to attend the semester commenc-
ing April 12, 1960, and ending on June 27, 1960. The form was signed and dated on
March 19, 1959. There are no indications as to how Oswald knew the start and end
date of the semester. The most logical answer is that the pamphlets Oswald had
been receiving and that Nelson Delgado thought might be from a church were informational pamphlets about the college. Yet negating that is George Michael Evica's
fruitless search for evidence that any advertising took place through which Oswald
may have been sent such material. Additional confirmation that no such advertising
existed came via an interview by Evica with Reverend Leon Hopper that took place
in 2003. Hopper told Evica that recruitment to Albert Schweitzer College was
almost always through personal contact, and because of this, Stephen Fritchman
could have been the direct source.

The second page of the college application had to be completed in duplicate with one copy going to Dr. Robert H. Schacht at an address in Providence, Rhode Island, and the other to the college itself . . . Consider that he shared his surname with Hitler's finance wizard, Hjalmar Schacht. Hjalmar was born in Tingleff, Schleswig-Holstein, Prussia (now part of Denmark), to William Leonhard Ludwig Maximillian Schacht and Constanze Justine Sophie von Eggers, a native of Denmark. However, he was raised largely in the US, and his full name was Hjalmar Horace Greeley Schacht with his middle name a nod to the famed American Universalist journalist.

Schacht was related by marriage to Prince Guitare de Spadafora, an Italian industrialist who sat on the board of Centro Mondiale Commerciale (CMC). Clay Shaw, the only man ever tried over the assassination, stated that he joined the CMC board in 1958. The company had been kicked out of Switzerland under a cloud of suspicion that it was a CIA front. It thereafter set up shop in the friendly environs of Johannesburg. . . . —Greg Parker, reopenkennedycase.org.

Frank Healy: Alias used by Francis Parker Yockey, who ensconced himself in the small village of Brittas Bay south of Dublin in the late winter, early spring of 1948, to pen his fascist screed, "Imperium." Yockey relied on the clearly Irish alias Frank Healey to travel freely.

CHAPTER 9: DALLAS . . . LAY OF THE LAND

Mussolini Receives the Browning Pilgrims: "When Mr. Mussolini notified the American ambassador that he would be pleased to receive us, the Chargé d' Affaires ad interim, Alexander Kirk, called to inform us and to instruct us in the niceties of such a reception. His visit was followed by a special messenger from the Italian 'Ministero degli Affari Esteri' bearing a very large envelope with a gold seal. In Italian the Secretary had informed us that 'the Chief of the Government'—as Mussolini is invariably called—'would receive us at 19:45 in the Palazzo Venezia.' It was a memorable day. The Browning Pilgrims had been given an audience by the Pope at one and now at 7:45 we were being accorded a private reception by Mussolini. It thrills Americans to see Mussolini as he leaves his home in his automobile . . . but to see him intimately at close range was exciting and unforgettable . . . since our return to America, Mr. Mussolini has shown his further interest in Baylor Browning Collection and this pilgrimage by sending his autographed photograph in large cabinet size to be placed in the Browning Library" —Baylor Bulletin: "Browning Interests" by A. Joseph Armstrong, Ph D., Litt.D.

Crichton, Jack and E. J. Anderson, *The Middle East Connection (Yemen).*

Earl Cabell: Cabell's activity on behalf of the anticommunist organization included a trip to Munich, Germany, during which time he was a featured speaker on the Office of Policy Coordination's Radio Free Europe. Indeed, Cabell saw the "evils of communism" and weighed in to halt it. On his return, Cabell participated in the founding of the Texas chapter of Ike's Crusade for Freedom and was joined by, among others, Dallas patriots Neil Mallon, D. H. Byrd, Everett DeGolyer, Lewis MacNaughton, Jake Hamon, Robert G. Storey, Jr., Paul Raigorodsky, and a rather obscure name in the annals of Kennedy research, oilman Barron Kidd.

According to Anthony Summers in *Official and Confidential: the Secret Life of J. Edgar Hoover* . . . "By a secret agreement, even before the inaugural, Allen and Billy Byars, another oilman friend of Edgar's—arranged to finance Eisenhower's Gettysburg farm. They also funneled money to him 'for his share of the farming operation.' Byars subsidized Mamie Eisenhower's brother-in-law Gordon Moore, by establishing a racing stable on his land." Texas oilman Billy Byars, a native of Tyler, along with Algur Meadows, Jack Crichton, Tyler native Joe Zeppa of Delta Drilling, and others, is named in Otto Skorzeny's papers. Byars was an annual guest of Clint Murchison's at the Hotel Del Charro, along with FBI Director J. Edgar Hoover.

NATION-WIDE SECURITIES, One Wall Street, New York: The small board of NY firm, Nation-Wide Securities—whose investments focused on industries tied to the military—enjoyed the prestige for members such as DCIA Allen Dulles, Gen. Maxwell Taylor prior to and following his stint as President Kennedy's Chief JCS, Ret. Gen. Frank Pace—former Sec Army, CEO General Dynamics and board of Continental Oil and CBS, and RB Carney, former CNO, board of Bell Helicopter and president of Bath Iron Works, whose Washington, D.C., headquarters were shared with the National Petroleum Council, which in 1963 was presided over by Jake Hamon, Dallas oilman and friend of George de Mohrenschildt, Algur Meadows, Clint Murchison, Paul Raigorodsky, others on the periphery of the Skorzeny milieu. Following his first retirement, Gen. Taylor had been persuaded to take over the helm of Mexican Light & Power in Mexico City from former NATO ambassador William H. Draper, Jr., who wanted to return from Mexico City in 1960 to head of the country's first independent nuclear companies, Combustion Engineering. Taylor's board in Mexico City included A. H. Dean, a partner at the Dulles brothers' law firm, Sullivan & Cromwell. Draper returned to the West Coast and joined his old friends for form equity firm DGA, friends he had cultivated while with the Special Representatives to Europe (NATO), Ret. Gen. Horace R. Gaither of the RAND Corporation, and Ret. Gen. Fred L. Anderson, the man who recruited petroleum engineer Paul Raigorodsky to oversee the US petroleum interests in Europe. (Draper was a significant financial supporter of the political campaigns of George H. W. Bush; his son followed suit and was a "Pioneer" for George W. Bush's run for president. Draper Sr. was also a longstanding member of the American Society of Magicians.)

Cord Meyer, Jr.: CIA officer Cord Meyer's father, founder of NY development concern, Cord Meyer Development Co., was an avid promoter of aviation and served as the regional commander of the Civil Air Patrol, created in December 1941 by NY Mayor Fiorello H. LaGuardia, Dir. Office of Civil Defense, along with aviation enthusiasts around the country including David Harold Byrd of Dallas. Other potential ties between Meyer senior and our story include his role on the board of Home Insurance Co. of New York along with R. W. Dowling, Jr., board member of Hilton Hotels and a deep history with military contractor General Dynamics (identified in this book related to the TFX scandal involving Bobby Baker, lobbyist and close aid to Lyndon Johnson) and Henry C. Brunie, president of Empire Trust, whose board included Dean Mathey, professional mentor to Jack Crichton of Dallas. In addition to an obvious association with Empire Trust, Cord Meyer senior was also on the board of Windsor Trust, which had been merged into Empire Trust in the early 1900s.

In 1953, DCIA Allen Dulles determined that the agency needed one large, secure campus that would be home to a rapidly growing intelligence apparatus. He selected the New York architectural firm Harrison & Abramovitz. According to Richard Brownell's *"Designing America's Spy Headquarters"* (available online at "Boundary Stones," blogs.weta.org), "It took three years to finalize the exact location, secure federal funding for the purchase of the land, and confirm the architectural firm that would design the building. The contract went to New York firm Harrison & Abramovitz. Known for designing large public projects and some well-known New York skyscrapers, the firm had recently completed work on the United Nations complex and Lincoln Center in New York . . . Although the contract to begin the work was signed on July 5, 1956, the final blueprints for the headquarters building were not approved until March 1958. . . . The cornerstone for the CIA headquarters was laid by President Dwight D. Eisenhower on November 3, 1959. Construction was formally completed in 1963 but staffing of the 1.4 million square-foot complex was fully completed by May 15, 1962." Brownell fails to identify that Harrison & Abramovitz was an architectural firm of choice for a number of buildings in the Rockefeller family's Rockefeller Center complex. In 1953, the same year that Dulles conceived the idea for Langley, architectural firm Harrison & Abramovitz had initiated plans for the new headquarters of Republic National Bank of Dallas, which opened its doors in 1955. No doubt the plans for Republic and Langley were housed under one roof at Harrison & Abramovitz for a number of months if not several years. Harrison & Abramovitz chose Gill & Harrell as their local architect of record for the Republic National Bank building project. In 1964, an addition to Republic National opened, designed by Harrell & Hamilton, a firm that interviewed Lee Harvey Oswald in early 1963. (The legend that George de Mohrenschildt's friend Sam Ballen walked Oswald to the Republic National Bank likely related to RNB tenant Harrell & Hamilton, or George and Sam's good friend, independent oilman Bruce Calder, who was subletting George's lease in the building.) The following words of Karl Hoblitzelle, chairman of the board for Republic National Bank from 1945 to 1965, are set in bronze at the Ervay Street entrance: "*This building is dedicated to the principle that no institution can long endure unless it serves faithfully and unselfishly its country, its state and community.*"

"Jaworski Reportedly Had Role in Setting Up C.I.A. Aid Conduit," *New York Times*, November 6, 1973. *www.nytimes.com/1973/11/06/archives/jaworski-reportedly-had-role-in-setting-up-cia-a-id-conduit-amount.html.*

Simpich, Bill. "The JFK Case: The Twelve Who Built The Oswald Legend."

Empire Trust Co. of NY and London: Empire established roots in Texas in early 1912 as the primary investor in the Texas Land and Development Co. and the Staked Plains Trust straddling the High Plains and the Texas Panhandle. Minor Cooper Keith, founder of United Fruit Company, was also the president of Empire Trust at the time. Keith's name and that of United Fruit Company will be familiar to students of the history of the US Government interference, on behalf of corporate interests, in the politics of Central America for decades. Jack Crichton, who would be brought on board Empire Trust around 1952 by H. C. Brunie, then president of Empire, would become a director of Dorchester Gas, a petroleum-related company established in the Texas Panhandle growing community of Amarillo. On the board of Dorchester was D. H. Byrd, the owner of 411 Elm, which he leased to Texas School Book Depository. (It is inconceivable that Byrd was not in possession of both his building's specs and the city drawings of Dealey Plaza.) Expediency insists that Jack Crichton spent time overseeing the interests of Empire's Staked Plains Trust while tending to Dorchester's drilling operations. See *The Texas Land and Development Company: A Panhandle Promotion, 1912–1959.* B.R. Brunson. University of Texas Press; First Edition (June 1970). Amarillo, a bastion of the John Birch Society in the late '50s and early '60s, quietly boasted the presence of Pan-Tex, a DuPont-funded nuclear weapons finishing plant servicing Los Alamos during and after the Manhattan Project, the only one of its kind in the country to date. Amarillo was also selected by Bell Helicopter as the site of their expanding operation. On Feb. 26, 1968, the first helicopter from the Vietnam War arrived in Amarillo via truck to Bell's hangars at Amarillo Air Force Base.

Jones, John Price and Paul Merrick Hollister, *The German Secret Service in America.*

Premier Petro Chemical Company: "President of Premiere and a stockholder will be Sylvester Dayson, who joined Meadows in the formal announcement. Dayson was president of Premiere Oil Refining Company at Longview prior to its sale several years ago and since has been active as an individual in the petroleum business. There is no financial connection between Premiere Petrochemical and Premiere Oil Refining, which now is owned by Western Natural Gas Co., Houston. Other Premiere Petrochemical stockholders are these Dallas men: Lewis W. MacNaughton, DeGolyer & MacNaughton senior chairman; Roland S. Bond and R. H. Venable, independent oilmen; D. Harold Byrd, president of Byrd Enterprises; and Frederick R. Mayer, president of Exeter Drilling Co. Other stockholders are these Tyler men: Joe Zeppa, Delta Drilling Company president; B. G. Byars and Watson Wise, independents. J. R. Rogerson, formerly Monsanto Chemical Co. vice president at El Dorado, Arkansas, will be executive vice president of Premiere Petrochemical. He will headquarter in Houston. Edward Kliewer, Jr., Dallas attorney, will be secretary and general counsel." Financing the new company was First National Bank in Dallas, which also worked with several other Dallas banks. First National Bank's incoming president Robert H. Stewart, III who was a board member of the Murchison - Wynne Great Southwest enterprise that built 6 Flags Over Texas, was responsible for keeping LTV somewhat solvent in the mid-1960s as well as instrumental in the myriad of loans that both he and Murchison secured for Bobby Baker prior to the F-111 scandal.

Ilya and Sondra Mamantov: All that survives of an in-depth interview with Sondra Mamantov, the wife of Ilya, is the detail seared into memory supported by a single personal letter detailing the exchange, which was penned by the interviewer several years later. Sondra Mamantov, clearly in a state of grief after the recent death of her beloved Ilya, an emotion that might serve as a catalyst to purge one's conscience, told her friend of over ten years that she watched as a black *government-looking* vehicle, one of three that had pulled up in front of their East Mockingbird during lunchtime Friday, November 22, drove off with her husband in the backseat. At the time, she was employed by Frito-Lay, a company located less than a mile from her house, which enabled her to dash home for a nice lunch. On that day, she remembered that she had left her office around 12:10–12:15 p.m., arriving at the house on Mockingbird well before 12:30 p.m. She explained to the interviewer that she was startled to see the small motorcade pull away. Although she and Ilya were US citizens at that point, she was worried that he might have been picked up for deportation. She rushed inside and began searching for a note that Ilya might have left. Sometime between 12:35 and 1:00 p.m., her son arrived home from school, unexpectedly. It was only then that Sondra became aware that President Kennedy had been assassinated in Dallas. Alleged assassin Lee Oswald was not arrested at the Texas Theatre until after 1:00 p.m.

Why was Ilya needed by anyone to translate Russian a good 45 minutes before a suspect was arrested? Sondra's assertions established that Ilya was not home at the time the official record claims; that Ilya was picked up at his house, not by a Dallas patrol car, but by a black vehicle accompanied by two other black vehicles that she believed to be government-related; and that Ilya was picked up an hour and a half prior to Oswald's arrival at police headquarters. It was later revealed to the interviewer that Ilya's employer, Jack Pew of Sun Oil, was privy to the incident because according to Pew's wife, Jack had a call from "that army guy" earlier than previously claimed. The army guy wanted to determine if Ilya would be available to translate for Oswald's wife. Thus far, there is no corroboration of Sondra's claims. However, researchers accept that Jack Crichton of the 488th was behind the recommendation of Pew's employee, Ilya Mamantov, as a suitable translator for the young widow. (A side note: years later Sondra told the same interviewer, "I cannot introduce you to Mary Ferrell [by then the godmother of assassination records], I just cannot." She continued, "but," and she paused ". . . I could introduce you to Ruth Paine.")

LTV stock trades on November 22, 1963: A note about the inspired inside stock purchase made by James Ling and D. H. Byrd in October 1963: Ling and Byrd, directors of LTV, purchased 132,600 shares of LTV stock for around $2 million, through an investment vehicle (the Alpha-Omega Corp.) that the two used for such speculation. This extraordinary move was made at a time in which aerospace issues were near the bottom of the stock market, amidst rumors of upcoming defense budget cuts. The Ling-Byrd purchase was nearly 100 times that of any other inside purchase in aerospace issues during this period. Ling and Byrd were to be rewarded handsomely when the first major prime defense contract of the Johnson Administration went to LTV, for the construction of the Navy A-7 Light Attack plane. That contract was let in February 1964, and at the time, the *New York Times* estimated that the contract "could run into more than a billion dollars." In fact, the $2 million investment by Byrd/Ling was worth $26 million by 1967. Of even greater importance, the award led to the ascendance of LTV into the top tier of US defense-related companies. During the 1960s, as the Vietnam War continually sucked an ever-greater amount of funding from the US economy, LTV would consistently be among the top ten aerospace companies in dollar volume of prime contracts. Prior to the assassination of JFK, LTV had experienced a rough couple of years. Joan Mellen once wrote that the company was in danger of "going under," which is not accurate. But there were some serious problems. When I went through the personal papers of

Byrd, I culled some internal LTV material that he had kept. Looking through it, it's obvious that the directors of that company were not pleased with the moves that they perceived Kennedy to be making. It's an interesting look inside the corporate world of a company that depended on international tension for their business to thrive. Given what we know about Byrd and his corporate and political affiliations—as well as his ownership of the building that was home to the Texas School Book Depository—I find it unlikely that the massive stock purchase that he and Ling put through was simply a shot in the dark.

Byrd sat on the board of Dorchester Gas Producing Company with Jack Crichton, among other significant contacts. He was one of the closest backers of Lyndon Johnson, which he bragged about in his strange little autobiography (which, much like his personal papers, makes no mention of the year 1963), and he and his wife were involved in Texas-based organizations with the Cabells and LBJ's vice-presidential military aide Howard Burris. His trip to Africa during the time of the assassination, via the von Albersleven company "Safariland" is suspicious, and his subsequent placement of a TSBD window in a special place in his home—the trophy room—is bizarre. As has also been mentioned, he employed Mac Wallace in a high-security position at Temco during the late 1950s, and Wallace would go on to work at Ling Electronics in California during the '60s. Whether or not one believes that Wallace played any role in the assassination, the employment of a convicted murderer in companies that depended on government business for their income is extraordinary. While Joan Mellen's biographical treatment of Wallace may well debunk several pet theories about Wallace, she demonstrates clearly that he was a part of Lyndon Johnson's small empire of usable people, and she is not in doubt that Wallace's employment at Temco and Ling Electronics was had at the behest of LBJ.

DeGolyer-MacNaughton: The petroleum industry engineering firm warrants an entire chapter when covering the history of petroleum not only in Texas, but the globe. Time does not permit an in-depth study, so for now we can only periodically underscore the reverence they were accorded in the industry.

The Meadowses as art collectors: During one of his first trips to Spain to meet with Skorzeny in late 1951, Meadows learned of the Prado Museum in Madrid. Upon his first visit there, he became most interested in the works of the old Spanish masters. By early 1953, he had purchased a large number of masterpieces, which eventually ended up at SMU. In 1964, Meadows began collecting paintings by French Impressionists and post-Impressionists, with encouragement from his second wife. Many of these works were eventually donated to the Dallas Museum of Art after Meadows's death. In 1965, Meadows bought nearly 400 pieces of original art from the family of French artist, Jean Despujols, who had died earlier that year.

Scott, Peter Dale, *Dallas '63: The First Deep State Revolt Against the White House*. Bookstore. Series edited by Mark Crispin Miller, Sep 29, 2015.

Frederick R. Mayer: Born in Youngstown in 1928, Mayer attended Texas Day school, graduating from Phillips Exeter Academy in 1945 and later earning a bachelor's degree from Yale University in 1950. In September 1953, Mayer founded Exeter Drilling Company and by November was operating one rig in Texas. A year later, Mayer's drilling operations were moved to the Denver-Julesburg Basin . . . He served as Chairman of the Governing Board of the Yale University Art Gallery and director of the American Petroleum Institute, the National Petroleum Council, and the Independent Petroleum Association. An avid art collector, he was also commander in the Confrérie des Chevaliers du Tastevin, a membership he shared with Texas Governor Alan Shivers. (Pierre Lafitte would be inducted into the New Orleans chapter of the Confrérie des Chevaliers in 1968.) Mayer was president of the Continental Emsco Co., Dallas, a manufacturer and distributor of oil and gas drilling equipment, for 33 years until his retirement in 1964. Mayer also served as director of the Texas Mid-Continent Oil Association, as past president of Petroleum Equipment Suppliers Association, and as a former member of the National Petroleum Equipment Suppliers Association. In addition, Mayer was a member of the Dallas Park Board and the Transit Board. He is a former president and chairman of the board of the Dallas Museum of Art and Friends of the Public Library. He is an honorary member of the Dallas Citizens Council. On July 22, 1963 Mayer signed on as Chairman of the Board of the newly formed H. L. Hunt Foundation As noted previously, Jack Crichton is listed as one of the six additional members of the Hunt Foundation board. Searcy Ferguson, another member of the foundation board was a successful independent oil and gas operator, brilliant trial lawyer and champion debater, extemporaneous orator, astute and proficient banker, generational Texas rancher, a professional gambler, and well-known card shark.

Garry Weber: Before establishing his own brokerage firm, Dallas native Garry Weber, who a decade later would be elected to the Dallas City Council, was a broker for Delaware-based E. I. du Pont de Nemours. The firm handled the sale of stocks for several area military contractors. When the city determined that the alleged sniper's window on the 6th floor of the Texas School Book Depository represented a quandary that needed to be managed from a public relations viewpoint, it created a board to oversee what could be a blight on the city in perpetuity. The result was the Sixth Floor Museum. Among the first members of the board of the museum was Garry Weber. In an odd coincidence for those who study such things, Weber's mother was a contractor for a travel agency located in the Turtle Creek Village complex, two blocks off Rawlins St., that also contracted a former Pan Am stewardess and wife of

Bruce Calder, close friend of both George de Mohrenschildt, from whom he sub-
leased an office space in Republic National Bank, and Sam Ballen. It was Calder
who on one occasion walked into the travel agency to have a word with his wife, and
with him was the imposing figure of George de Mohrenschildt. The travel agency
would later land the exclusive contract for arranging trips for the American Society
of Petroleum Engineers and the American Society of Petroleum Geologists, whose
preferred destination was the Canary Islands off the coast of Spain as well as
Acapulco, Mexico.

The Meadows Building: The landmark building passed into the hands of the heirs of
Algur Meadows, who died on June 10, 1978, following a strange automobile accident
that occurred fifteen months after the alleged suicide of George de Mohrenschildt in
Manalapan, Florida, on the day George had initiated interviews related to the assassination of President Kennedy. Worth noting, George's good friend Sam Ballen was
responsible for setting up the interview with journalist Jay Epstein, and he was
among the first to be notified that his friend was dead. The phone call reached Ballen while he was in Austin, TX, attending a Texas Railroad Commission meeting.
The commission in essence regulated America's petroleum industry. In February '78,
Algur and his second wife, Elizabeth, attended what was locally viewed as a serious
kerfuffle in the life of Palm Beach society, the first ball hosted by the new charity in
town, the Knights of Malta. The story made the *New York Times,* "France, America
Glamour and Controversy meet at the Malta Ball." Elizabeth Meadows was captured
in a photo, widely circulated, dancing with another prominent Dallas oilman who
spent time in PB, William Moss. Among the rest of the Texas contingent at the
Knights of Malta Ball were Lupe and John Murchison, the son and daughter-in-law
of Clint Murchison, whom our reader will recognize from very early in this chapter
(along with Ret. AF Gen. Nathan Twining, Murchison sat on the board of Holt,
Rinehart & Winston, publishers of *Field and Stream* magazine, which many associate with the evidence surrounding Oswald's alleged purchase of the alleged rifle that
was alleged to have been used on Kennedy).

Also in the Texas contingent in Palm Beach that evening were Houston socialites
Joanne and Robert Herring. Joanna—who joined the Texas Minutemen at age sixteen—had replaced her husband, Robert Herring, as honorary consul at the
Consulate-General of Pakistan in Houston, a title that opened doors for the infamous launch of arming the Mujahideen against the Russians as memorialized in
investigative journalist George Crile's *Charlie Wilson's War.* As mentioned previously, Joanna was appointed honorary consul to Morocco.

The honorary guest of the previous ball, Al Meadows, would attend, Prince Edouard
de Lobkowicz, whose title, according to the *Times,* was actually Austro-Hungarian,

and his wife, Françoise, and such starring players as Prince Jean-Louis de Faucigny-Lucinge, Prince Guy de Polignac and his wife, Gladys, and Archduke Robert Von Habsburg and his wife, Margherita. The Archduke opined that the town had changed considerably from his alligator-shooting days thirty years ago. Algur Hurtle Meadows died four months later.

Joseph Zeppa: Joe Zeppa, in 1963, sat on the board of Petroleum Reserves, along with a senior vice president of Itek—a company that might be familiar to assassination experts as having analyzed the Zapruder film for Dan Rather's CBS exposé in the 1970s. Petroleum Reserves' offices were located in the International Building at 630 Fifth Ave. in the heart of the Rockefeller Center. The International Building at 630 Fifth was also the home of British Intelligence (MI6) in the US and the address chosen by Allen Dulles, when, following the disaster of the failed invasion of Cuba, he was dismissed by President Kennedy. Prior to his own role with Petroleum Reserves during the late 1940s, Everett DeGoyler had served as director of conservation with the Office of the Coordinator for National Defense and then as assistant deputy director of the Petroleum Administration for War.

"Amerasia Case." Dictionary of American History. Retrieved February 26, 2019 from *encyclopedia.com.*

Barron Kidd Jr.: Kidd was the namesake of his grandfather, Marvin Ulmer, who served as Mayor of Midland, Texas, in the 1940s. Marvin was the driving force behind the founding of the highly regarded Midland Air Force Base. There is no evidence to date that the Ulmers of West Texas were related to Dan Ulmer of Tyler, Texas, and his brother, CIA station chief Al Ulmer, named elsewhere in this book. Ulmer served as station chief in Madrid in the 1950s and was familiar with Jere Wittington, the agent who was assigned to "watch over" Otto Skorzeny in Madrid.

Adolphus Tower tenants included Sam Passman, Abraham Zapruder's attorney in the negotiations with *Life* for the original film. A nearby tenant in the tower was J. Sowell, who later moved into 3707 Rawlins, where he was listed under his given name as well as the company name, Delhi Properties. It is reasonable to believe that Sowell's company was associated with Murchison's Delhi-Taylor Oil, although he should not be confused with the Sewell family that is directly related to Murchison. There is reason to believe that Clint Murchison secured an early copy of the Zapruder film. The 16mm copy could prove beyond a reasonable doubt that the original Zapruder film was altered. It should also be noted that Hugh Jamison, the founder of Jamison Labs, which was the first to handle the original Zapruder film, was the direct next-door neighbor of Robert G. Storey, Jr., in the Lakewood area of Dallas.

628   Coup in Dallas

J. Sowell, who moved office from the Adolphus Tower to 3707 Rawlins, had been a
groomsman for Barron Ulmer Kidd when Kidd married Pierre du Pont's daughter in
May 1963. Barron Kidd Oil and related companies, Previews Inc., and J. Sowell /
Delhi Properties, were among the first tenants of the building. In 1979, Carol Wesley Rogers, daughter of Wesley G. Rogers, married fifty-one-year-old Donald Arthur
Byrd. A Dallas native, Don Byrd joined the city's police department in March 1951.
He was promoted to detective in '54 and lieutenant in '57, a post he held on the day
that John Kennedy was assassinated. Following training with the Federal Bureau of
Narcotics, Lieutenant Byrd joined the Special Operations Division of the department reporting directly to Captain W. P. "Pat" Gannaway. Byrd oversaw twenty-two
officers of Gannaway's Vice Squad. Gannaway claimed to have initiated a roll call at
the Texas School Book Depository within an hour of the assassination, erroneously
establishing that because Lee Harvey Oswald was the *only* employee who had left
the building prior to the arrival of authorities, a pursuit to tie Oswald to the rifle
found in the sniper's nest was warranted. Several hours later, Gannaway advised the
media that Oswald had been in the Soviet Union and had married a Russian
girl. The patsy had been effectively identified.

Don A. Byrd: According to official records obtained by the House Select Committee on
Assassinations, Lt. Byrd was involved in the 1962 investigation into bookmaking
and related crimes of John Eli Stone—an associate of Mafia boss Joe Civello—
whom the reader will recall was eventually indicted in Wichita Falls, TX, by a
federal prosecutor on behalf of Attorney General Robert F. Kennedy. Don
Byrd's boss, Pat Gannaway, would a year later declare in an interview with the *Dallas Morning News* that organized crime had not taken hold on his watch. Following a
somewhat meteoric rise through the ranks, including filling the role that Gannaway
vacated when he retired as head of Special Operations Division, Don Byrd became
the Chief of the Dallas Police in 1973, where he served until retirement in '79. He
then ran for and was elected sheriff of Dallas County, a post he filled from '81 to
'84. Byrd planned on reelection, but one evening, following a party at Reunion
Square hosted by oilman Ray Hunt (another son of H. L. Hunt), Byrd was driving
down Preston Road not far from the Rawlins St. address when he careened off
course, causing a serious accident. He was charged, and although he was acquitted at
trial, his law enforcement career was over.

Hidden History of Plano, Texas (History Press, March 16, 2020).

Graduate Research Center of the Southwest: Former Texas Governor Alan Shivers must
be recognized as having fought Kennedy's stance on the Texas Tidelands case on
behalf H. L. Hunt and Clint Murchison and their fellow independent oilmen while
he served as governor in Austin. Although he was not a resident of Dallas, Shivers

was a member of boards around the city including St. Mark's School, where Ruth Paine taught part-time, as well as the newly formed Graduate Research Center of the Southwest, through which Sam Ballen, close friend of George de Mohrenschildt, was first introduced to Everett Glover of Mobil Oil, named in the Lafitte datebook. GRCSW was established by defense contractor Texas Instruments' founders, including Eric Jonsson, who would replace Earle Cabell as Mayor of Dallas in 1964. TI was located in Richardson, not far from Collins Radio, and in the precinct of JP Larry Johnston. Jonsson made both announcements at the Trade Mart relating to Kennedy's condition, opining, "I feel the way I did the day of Pearl Harbor." His research center cohosted the luncheon along with the Dallas Assembly. Members of the advisory board of GRCSW were on the welcoming committee for the Dallas leg of Kennedy's Texas trip. The significance of all this, including the sheer coincidence that it was through Lauriston Marshall, Everett Glover, and Sam Ballen that things were set in motion for Oswald to meet Ruth (and Michael) Paine and end up working at the Texas School Book Depository building: it is important to understand this milieu to grasp why Dallas was the optimal setting for the assassination and cover-up. That office building in question was developed by and housed the Wynne family law firm and business interests. Marina would be spirited away to the Wynne's 6 Flags hotel, where Ilya Mamantov would serve as her translator at the urging of Jack Crichton, of whom much has been written and much has been speculated. Unless the "ground-up" efforts either integrate these facts—and hundreds more that cannot logically be left on the cutting room floor—or explain sufficiently their insignificance, I would worry we are not as close to resolution of the investigation as some would suggest. For a thorough analysis of GRCSW, see appendix essay, "The Gathering Network" by Anthony Thorne.

Robert Allan Shivers: In a speech before a large gathering of oil and gas industry-related Texans during Kennedy's campaign for president, Shivers was seen to mock then-Senator Kennedy for his alleged immaturity and lack of understanding that, simply stated, oilmen owned the nation's petroleum resources onshore and off. During those years, Shivers also took comfort in the support paid him by oilman Clint Murchison in his fight to maintain segregation in his state. And it was Shivers who, in 1951, organized the "Shivercrats," attracting disgruntled Democrats in support of Republican General Ike Eisenhower for president; the contemporary foothold of the Republican Party in Texas began there and then. Shivers also served for over a decade on the board of Dresser Industries, presided over by Allen Dulles's good friend Neil Mallon.

Biffle, Kent, "Allen Dulles Looks Behind Red Moves." *Dallas Morning News*, October 29, 1963.

Marshall Lauriston: Lauriston was born of missionary parents in Canton, China, in 1902 and received his PhD in physics from Univ. of California Berkeley, followed by a varied career including with the Radiation Laboratory at MIT and the Office of Scientific Research & Development. In 1961, Marshall was invited to join the Graduate Research Center of the Southwest, founded by Erik Jonsson, Cecil Greene, and Eugene McDermott, cofounders of the highly profitable military contractor Texas Instruments, based in Dallas. The idea for the graduate research center germinated in the late '50s, and by February 14, 1961, GRCSW was officially chartered as a privately funded, basic research institution to aid the southwestern region of the United States in the advancement of graduate education in the natural sciences. It was Jonsson who waited for the arrival of President Kennedy at the Grand Hall of the Dallas Trade Mart, to no avail. Jonsson's Texas Instruments/GRCSW had underwritten a significant portion of the cost of the luncheon in honor of Jack and Jackie Kennedy, affording the two entities the right to determine the location. Erik Jonsson would be elected mayor of Dallas in 1964.

J. Walton Moore: A few days before his death, George de Mohrenschildt told author Edward Epstein that he had been contacted by the head of DCS in Dallas, J. Walton Moore, in 1961, several months prior to Lee Oswald's return from the Soviet Union and briefed about Oswald. De Mohrenschildt was a frequently used source of Moore's, dating back into the late 1950s. Moore would later dissemble when testifying about his contacts with de Mohrenschildt, stating that he had seen George infrequently in the 1960s, but de Mohrenschildt's wife, Jeanne, called Moore up on this, claiming that she and George quite frequently dined with Moore and his wife. While it is often stated in the literature that Barnes was "Moore's boss" from his perch as head of DOD, this assertion cannot be proven. Still, the overlap between DOD and the DCS seems strong enough to suggest that as a likelihood. Moore occupies a unique and very interesting position in the story of the Kennedy assassination. De Mohrenschildt told Epstein that he "would never have contacted Oswald in a million years if Moore had not sanctioned it." When de Mohrenschildt first made contact with Oswald, he arrived in the company of a CIA informant, Col. Laurence Orlov. Orlov, a longtime oilman and acquaintance of de Mohrenschildt's, was also an informant for Moore at DCS in Dallas, as well as being a social companion of Moore's. Joan Mellen writes: "It seems apparent that J. Walton Moore . . . had set up the meeting between de Mohrenschildt and Oswald." And, it could well be added, if what de Mohrenschildt told Epstein about a 1961 contact from Moore regarding Oswald is accurate, Moore would seem to be on a short list of people who were involved very early on in maneuvering Lee Oswald.

Moore, an ex-FBI man, as well as an OSS agent during his service in the Second World War, had joined CIA in 1948, being assigned to Domestic Contacts at that time. By the 1960s, Moore was exceptionally well known and respected within CIA. A friendly and personal letter from then-Deputy Director of CIA Gen. Charles Cabell is in the record. Cabell, addressing Moore as "Walt," thanked him for his hospitality during a recent (1960) Cabell visit to Dallas. Late in Moore's career, a note in his personnel file shows that the Houston-based DCS office was upgraded in status, the New Orleans DCS office was placed under the Houston office in Agency command structure, and both offices were subordinate to the Dallas office, still headed by Moore. After the assassination of Kennedy, Moore would pop up periodically during times of intense interest in the assassination. In 1976, with the HSCA investigation into Kennedy's death about to begin, Moore—still in the position in Dallas with DCS that he had occupied since 1948—wrote to the head of that division, asking for help in handling "the exposure of [Clay] Shaw's connections with CIA." When de Mohrenschildt died from gunshot wounds in 1977, Moore clipped the news stories reporting the death and sent them to the chief of CIA's Domestic Contact Division. On a cover sheet over a *Dallas Times-Herald* article that stated that the HSCA had uncovered "new, unproven evidence on Oswald's ties with CIA, FBI," Moore wrote, "Nothing new, is there?" Moore's Agency files also feature a detailed account of the story of Gilberto Policarpo Lopez (December 1963), a young man whose late 1963 travels parallel those of Lee Oswald. Lopez moved suspiciously before and after the assassination of President Kennedy— attempting to get a visa to Cuba in Mexico City in the fall of 1963 and boarding a plane from Texas headed for Mexico City in the immediate aftermath of the assassination. A note from CIA DD/P Richard Helms to Win Scott at the Mexico City CIA station is also in Moore's files. The note is suggestive of Lopez being involved in a highly compartmentalized intelligence operation. Beyond the particulars of the Lopez story, the significance for our interest is that Moore is being entrusted with highly sensitive information pertaining to an investigation of the murder of President Kennedy, information that was not widely shared within CIA. J. Walton Moore was not "regular folks" in CIA by the 1960s; he was something out of the ordinary—particularly for an employee whose record reflects no obvious advancement for nearly 30 years.

Warren Report supplements. 11/23/64. *Washington Evening Star.*

Warren Caster: According to his 1964 WC testimony, Caster seemed not to know who the employees were who worked in the shipping area of the TSBD. By 1995, however, that had changed significantly: *It soon became apparent that a suspect had been arrested and he was named as Lee Harvey Oswald. Warren knew him and he told me:*

"I used to see him frequently, eating his lunch in the lunchroom, but he was a weird sort of guy and he kept himself to himself." (The second floor lunchroom was close to Warren's office.) The last time Warren could recall having seen Oswald was two days before, when Oswald had been one of that small group of TSBD employees who were examining Warren's two newly purchased rifles before returning to work after their lunch break. And this: One important question that I almost forgot to ask Warren was who he thought had killed the President that day. Warren replied in a very positive tone: "To sum it all up, I think Lee Harvey Oswald alone killed President Kennedy. Why? I just can't speculate except to say that he really was some kind of nut!"—Interview with Rick Caster (no relation) published 1995, found at reopenkennedycase.forumotion.net.

CHAPTER 10: D'AFFAIRE KENNEDY

The authors would be very remiss if the work of researcher and writer Mae Brussell was not highlighted. Indeed, it was Brussell that partially led us in the right direction. Thank you, Ms. Brussell.

Brousse: Influential member of the Committee of the Association of Mayors of France and Overseas, in charge of the Youth and Sports Commission, member of the steering committee of the Council of European Municipalities, he joined the Algerian War and became head of the SAS of Masséna. Opposed to the Algerian policy of France, he was the animator of the first "French Algeria" maquis, in the territories of Mostaganémois, with as companions Sheikh Si El Hadj Tekouk Ben Tekouk Senousssi, Captain Souetre, commandos of the air, and René Villard, Algerian civil leader of France-Résurrection. Arrested, placed in solitary confinement, he escaped and went into exile. Its troops, civilians and soldiers, fervent nationalists, were chosen, with the young Nation group, to take part in the preparation and the launching of the putsch of the generals in April 1961. After the failure of the military coup, France-Résurrection organized itself clandestinely and became one of the spearheads of the French resistance in Algeria against the abandonment policy of the French government. Even before André Brousse de Montpeyroux joined Marshal Salan in hiding in Algiers, his main assistants, civilians and soldiers, including René Villard, were brutally shot. The arrest of General Salan sounded the death knell for the OAS; André Brousse de Montpeyroux then resumed the hard roads of exile, being divided between Europe and Black Africa. Between 1963 and 1965, we will still see him at the head of Berber troops in the mountains of Kabylia. Hunted by all the police forces in France, he refused the 1967 amnesty law, invigorating his faith in a Spanish monastery in the valley of Los Caidos. A few breaths later, he returned to France, taking into account his state of health but continued, more than ever, to beat the countryside and to strike out his truths by the pen, after having done it by the sword.

Report of the Warren Commission on the Assassination of President Kennedy. United States. Warren Commission.

Kross, Peter. *JFK: The French Connection.*

West, Nigel, *Encyclopedia of Political Assassinations.*

"New Suspect in JFK Slaying-A French Terrorist." *National Enquirer*, November 22, 1983. www.jfk.hood.edu/Collection/Weisberg%20Subject%20Index%20Files/N%20Disk/National%20Enquirer/Item%2094.pdf.

Root, Waverly, "Headed by Skorzeny? Neo-Nazis Linked to Algeria French." *The Washington Post.* www.cia.gov/readingroom/docs/SKORZENY,%20OTTO%20%20%20VOL.%202_0139.pdf.

Duffy, David, "Is This The Man Who Killed JFK?" *The National Enquirer.*

www.jfk.hood.edu/Collection/Weisberg%20Subject%20Index%20Files/N%20Disk/National%20Enquirer/Item%2094.pdf.

"Dr. Alderson furnished a small snapshot of four men taken in Petite, France, in the early 1950s. He identified the man first from left in the photograph as Souetre. He could not identify the other three men. Dr. Alderson stated that he had contacted the Select Committee soon after its inception and furnished them the information pertaining to Souetre's activities of November 22 (which he had learned upon visitation of FBI soon after assassination), also furnishing a copy of this photograph. The committee's response, he said, was that they would enlarge the photograph, age Souetre, then compare him to photographs of individuals in Dealey Plaza on November 22, 1963." —excerpts from interview notes with Dr. Lawrence Alderson, by author researcher J. Gary Shaw. Shaw is the author of *Cover-Up* (1976) and coauthor with Dr. Charles Crenshaw of *JFK: Conspiracy of Silence* (1992). In the 1990s, he served as codirector of the JFK Assassination Information Center in Dallas. Recorded July 23, 2007.

The United States District Court for the District of Columbia: Gary Shaw, Plaintiff v. Department of State, et al, Defendants www.archive.org/stream/nsia-SouetreJean/nsia-SouetreJean/Souetre%20Jean%2063_djvu.txt.

EPILOGUE—NOTES

Finder, Joseph, "Ultimate Insider, Ultimate Outsider," NYTimes April 12, 1992, Section 7, Page 1 of the National edition.

Rose, Jerry D., "Plain Talk About Isaac Levine" State University College, Fredonia, New York. *The Fourth Decade*, January 1995, Volume 2, Number 2.

Walter Krivitsky: https://spartacus-educational.com/SSkrivitsky.htm.

Kern, Gary. *A Death in Washington: Walter G. Krivitsky and the Stalin Terror.*

FBI Memorandum [3-31-64], Subject Lee Harvey Oswald to Mr. Sullivan from Mr. Branigan.

124-10129-10137: No Title. www.maryferrell.org/showDoc.html?docId=145702&relPageId=2.

FBI Memorandum, New York, New York, April 1, 1964: Lee Harvey—Internal Security—Russia—Cuba. Mary Ferrell Collection.

Hobsbawm, Eric. "Uncommon People: Resistance, Rebellion and Jazz."

Scott, Peter Dale. *Deep Politics and the Death of JFK*, University of California Press, 1993, p. 55; for further detail on this intelligence-drenched milieu operating both pre and post-assassination, see Scott's *Crime and Cover-up: The CIA, the Mafia, and the Dallas-Watergate Connection*, Open Archive Press, 1993, pp. 35-36.

Loftus, John and Mark Aarons, *The Secret War Against the Jews: How Western Espionage Betrayed the Jewish People.*

"The new buzz term has me thinking some—simply put, I'll take all the TRUTH I can get. If it's branded 'deep truth' I know that it's simply partial truth blended to fit some theory wacky or not. When folks have to redefine truth then we should be mindful that what we are getting are twisted facts. Truth served folks like Roosevelt, JFK, RFK, and Carter quite well. They all would have been suspicious of what's going on today. Like Carter once observed: "The actual truth serves everyone well." —H. P. Albarelli Jr.

Mann, William, "How Buchanan Made Trump Possible." *The Week*, July 26, 2019.

John Hudson, "Exclusive: Think Tank Fires Employee Who Questioned Ties to Donald Trump," ForeignPolicy.com. May 20, 2016.

Aram Roston and Joel Anderson, "The Moneyman Behind the Alt-Right," *BuzzFeed News*, July 27, 2017.

Bokhari, Allum and Milo Yiannopoulos, "An Establishment Conservatives' Guide to the Alt-Right." *Breitbart News*. www.breitbart.com/tech/2016/03/29/an-establishment-conservatives-guide-to-the-alt-right/.

America First Policy Institute: "The Resurrection of America First," www.americafirstpolicy.com.

"Burt Reynolds Roy Cohn Ben Stein and More!" *Penthouse Magazine*, July 1981.

Manuel Roig-Franzie, "The Swamp Builders: How Stone and Manafort helped create the mess Trump promised to clean up," *The Washington Post*, November 29, 2018.

Gary Sargent, "Opinion: The repulsive worldview of Trump and Bannon, perfectly captured in one poll," *The Washington Post,* March 17, 2017.

Alex Gibney, "Meet the Leader of the Eliot Spitzer's Smear Campaign, *The Atlantic*, October 13, 2010.

CIA Cryptonyms, Mary Ferrell Foundation, maryferrell.org/php/cryptdb.php?bigram.

DeCamp, John W, *The Franklin Cover-up: Child Abuse, Satanism, and Murder in Nebraska.*

Roy Cohn, recorded interview by James A. Oesterle, March 24, 1971, Robert F. Kennedy Oral History Project of the John F. Kennedy Library Oral History Program.

United States District Court Southern District of New York.

United States v. Brian Kolfage, Stephen Bannon, Andrew Badolato, and Timothy Shea. www.justice.gov/usao-sdny/press-release/fire/1306611/download.

In the United States District Court for the District of Columbia.

United States of America v. Paul J. Manafort, Jr. and Richard W. Gates III www.justice.gov/file/1007271/download.

In the United States District Court for the District of Columbia.

United States of America v. Roger Jason Stone, Jr. www.justice.gov/file/1124706/download.

A WELL-CONCEALED "T"—ESSAY NOTES

Biographical information on Tracy Barnes is both voluminous, and . . . woefully inadequate. As a legendary figure in intelligence circles who was involved at a very high level in well-known CIA escapades, Barnes's name is very familiar. But there has been no biographical treatment of him of the kind that his peers Dulles, Angleton, or Helms have had. The closest thing to a biography of Barnes is Evan Thomas's justly respected study *The Very Best Men: Four Who Dared: The Early Years of the CIA*, in which Thomas profiled Frank Wisner, Richard Bissell, Desmond Fitzgerald, and Barnes. Thomas was granted access to CIA sources that, in some cases, are still not available to researchers. The book is a fine, well-written resource, but it should be noted that historian John Newman nails Thomas for his reliance on two major sources—Jake Esterline and former CIA DD/P Richard Bissell—in regard to one

636　Coup in Dallas

particular story involving a 1960 assassination plot against Raul Castro. Thomas's reliance on these men—rather than on Church Committee testimony—"obscures the CIA's responsibility for approving a plot that they had conceived" (Newman, *Countdown to Darkness*, pp. 182–183). This story involves an authorization by Barnes, once again acting for DDP Bissell. One would be curious to know how many more such exculpatory errors pertaining to Barnes and others might have crept into the book . . . There is also the previously mentioned chronological gap in Thomas's Barnes story that encompasses precisely the time span that readers of this piece would be most interested in . . . The story of ARRB's quest to obtain the detailed personnel records of Barnes and other CIA royalty is told in NARA #104-10332-10022. These records are still not available to any degree.

[#]

Another subject of interest to ARRB staffers and to Kennedy assassination researchers is William K. Harvey, whose desired operational files are still being held tightly. If these files ever become available, I believe that—among many other fascinating bits—we will see evidence of Harvey, John Roselli, and others working in Florida with a man Harvey referred to as "Maceo" during the latter part of 1962 and the beginning of 1963, probably in greater detail than has been available to researchers. These people were engaging in operations against Fidel Castro, which are referred to in the 1967 CIA IG Report on plots to assassinate Castro. Corroboration in later writings of Pierre Lafitte, utilized by H. P. Albarelli in his *A Terrible Mistake: The Murder of Frank Olson and the Cia's Cold War Experiments,* and in the contemporaneously written January 1963 datebook entries of Pierre Lafitte, strongly suggest that the mysterious "Maceo," noted in the IG Report, was "Frank Maceo," one of over thirty aliases Lafitte employed over the many years of his unique career.

The Psychological Strategy Board is addressed by John Prados, in his *Safe For Democracy: The Secret Wars of the CIA,* and—sporadically—in the brilliantly researched study of the International Rescue Committee and concurrent projects by Eric Thomas Chester, *Covert Network: Progressives, the International Rescue Committee, and the CIA.* Chester cites a seminal offering in the papers of William Donovan, "The Role of the Psychological Strategy Board." . . . A good general overview of PSB is found in Scott Lucas's "Campaigns of Truth: The Psychological Strategy Board and American Ideology, 1951–1953," *The International History Review,* May 1996. Lucas notes the breadth and ambiguity of the PSB's mission, citing PSB head Gordon Gray's disinclination to give a precise definition of the term "psychological operation." . . . A very recent study of the links between the PSB and CIA mind-altering experiments during the time that Barnes served under Gray at PSB—and sometimes was the acting head of PSB in Gray's absence—is "Murky Projects and

Uneven Information Policies: A Case Study of the Psychological Strategy Board and CIA" (Susan Maret, *Secrecy and Society*, Vol. 1, No. 2, 2018).

[#]

Peter Kornbluh and Kate Doyle's "CIA and Assassinations: The Guatemala 1954 Documents," a comprehensive summary of assassination-related documents generated by the CIA's PBSUCCESS operation, is essential . . . Larry Hancock, who began his exploration into the Kennedy assassination with a short monograph, has blossomed into a first-class historian, specializing in covert operations in the context of geopolitical warfare, and he has focused a good deal of attention on Barnes's career over the past few years. His Appendix "Barnes, Hunt and Friends," in *Someone Would Have Talked,* is a succinct summation of many of the strands of Barnes's career that should raise eyebrows. Hancock makes use of the work of researcher Pat Speer, who has delved as deeply as the available record will allow into myriad biographical sources on Barnes, and into the Domestic Operations Division of CIA. Hancock's *Nexus: The CIA and Political Assassination* is an outstanding study of the culture and typology of CIA assassination planning. There is much on PBSUCCESS, and useful information about Barnes, traveling from the Guatemalan operation to the Bay of Pigs . . . In reference to one term that appears to have originated around the Guatemalan coup, "K Squad," which referred to groups specifically tasked with the execution of political enemies, complementary use is found in Lafitte's 1963 datebook. An August 22, 1963, meeting between Lafitte and George Joannides, then chief of the Psychological Warfare branch of the CIA's JMWAVE station in Miami, had taken place in a New Orleans location, and Lafitte wrote: "Talk Joannides Cuba – refers to K Organization in Mexico – similar setup now . . ." On October 9, 1963, Lafitte would write—in the context of "Lancelot" (the name given to the plot to kill President Kennedy)—" . . . kill squads Dallas." An earlier entry, around the time that the final phase of the plot appears to be beginning—April 12, 1963—features Lafitte writing "Willby soldier kill squads." The entry, which also references the ongoing "Congress of Freedom" meetings that had just taken place in New Orleans (and at which multiple speakers took the podium to advocate violence, not to mention what was likely discussed in the hallways), refers to Gen. Charles Willoughby, who would play an integral part in the plot, in part by providing a shooting team. "K Squads" "Kill Squads" "K Organization." All referring to teams of murderers, and all harking back to the assassination plots that Barnes approved in Guatemala.

[#]

As mentioned in the text, CIA historian Michael Warner offers up an important assessment of the ferocious battles over the historical record of the Bay of Pigs operation in "The CIA's Internal Probe of the Bay of Pigs Affair: Lessons Unlearned." . . . A unique and well-researched study of the vital importance to Agency hard-liners in putting forth "their" view of the Bay of Pigs—and in the process casting stones at JFK—is Simon Willmetts's "The Burgeoning Fissures of Dissent: Allen Dulles and the Selling of the CIA in the Aftermath of the Bay of Pigs."

The much-overlooked story of Wayne January's dealings with representatives of the Houston Air Center in the purchase of a DC-3 in late November 1963 is told by Matthew Smith in three books. Full details of the story emerged after the death of January in 2004, but the accounts given in *Say Goodbye to America*, *Vendetta*, and *Conspiracy: The Plot to Stop the Kennedys* are all worth reading. I obtained the same FAA file on the plane as Smith had and verified numerous details of the story as told by January to my satisfaction. Hancock also looks closely at the January story in the latest edition of *Someone Would Have Talked*. Again, Kennedy's alleged cowardice—traitorous cowardice in the estimation of many of the most fervent Cubans and some of their Agency backers—is paramount in the story. While Smith's interpretation of the foreknowledge of the assassination of JFK can be questioned (he believed that the DC-3 played a part in the assassination scenario; I am inclined to see the Cuban pilot's words to Wayne January as part of the knowledgeable "noise" that Hancock has documented, rather than an admission of active participation), the story is well worth our time, in my opinion . . . For what it is worth, it appears as though the best candidate for the Cuban pilot were Antonio Soto, who was involved in 1963 and 1964 with paramilitary operations being conducted by Barnes's old asset Rip Robertson. For cutting-edge research into Soto and a great many names not previously examined, see Larry Hancock and David Boylan's paper "Wheaton Names/Who Knew?," available online via Hancock's blog. And I believe, based on a detailed overlay of information given by January about the Air Force Colonel involved in the purchase of the plane and relevant biographical information, that the representative of the Houston Air Center was very likely Col. Joe Shannon, an American pilot who flew at the Bay of Pigs and was a full-fledged CIA officer by 1961. Research is ongoing . . .

[#]

Information about the collection of individuals related to CIA Domestic Contacts and/or J. Walton Moore who appear in Lafitte's 1963 datebook and could well have provided Barnes with cover for assassination planning can be had in Nancy Wertz Weiford's *The Faux Baron: George de Mohrenschildt*, and (with arguably deeper documentary research) in Joan Mellen's *Our Man in Haiti: George de Mohrenschildt and the CIA in the Nightmare Republic*. . . . Significant data from the personnel files of J. Walton Moore, as well as information about Moore's knowledge of the Gilberto Lopez case, are available in the research papers donated by John Armstrong to the W. R. Poage Legislative Library at Baylor University. Armstrong's material is available online. Search for: "TAB: J. Walton Moore, Box 1, Notebook 1.". . . A deep examination of this specific milieu, and numerous other significant threads surrounding the world of Lee Oswald based on terrific documentary research, can be had by reading through Bill Simpich's twelve-part series *The JFK Case: The Twelve Who Built the Oswald Legend*, available on the website of the Assassination Archives and Research Center, https//aarclibrary. org . . . An older but still quite valuable piece dealing with the CIA's Domestic Operations Division at the time Tracy Barnes was in charge is Seymour Hersh's "Hunt Tells Of Early Work For A CIA Domestic Unit," based on a two-year-long *New York Times* investigation headed by Hersh, released in 1974 . . . Highlights from William Davy's April 1995 interview with Victor Marchetti can be found in Davy's "Let Justice Be Done: New Light On the Jim Garrison Investigation." . . . As is the case with many of the angles highlighted in this essay, the stellar work of a great many lay historians who have posted over the years in the two incarnations of the Education Forum should be perused. Examining the hard work of many minds is often preferable to reliance only on "established" sources, although—as a counsel of perfection—the research generated by all of these efforts should be balanced.

[#]

A standard source for anyone who has researched the Kennedy assassination over the past several decades is the groundbreaking *The Man Who Knew Too Much*, Dick Russell's study of the sad story of Richard Case Nagell—and a million associated characters and organizations. Russell's work has educated and inspired dozens who find ourselves returning repeatedly to his book. There is much information about many of the most significant players in the story told here. The footnotes alone are worth "the price of admission."

CARETAKER—ESSAY NOTES

Like Marina Oswald, Silvia Odio was offered refuge and comfort throughout her ordeal. Her friend Lucille McConnell, who actively supported the Cuban exile community, had introduced her to the founder of Texas Industries, Ralph Rogers. His son, Jack, was particularly supportive of the attractive young Cuban, and she eventually moved into the Rogers home for an extended period. There has been speculation that one of the three men who appeared on her doorstep on Magellan Circle that September evening was Thomas Eli Davis, Jr. Without venturing too far afield, is it possible that the men looking for a supplier for weapons knocked on the wrong door? Were they looking for Ferenc Nagy, who lived less than 300 yards from Odio?

Although few who study him carefully would confuse Tom Davis with Oswald, the possibility lingers that Silvia met Tom, until one studies the evidence provided us by Lafitte. Davis was in Mexico City, with his wife, Carolyn, as was Lee Harvey Oswald, on the dates in question. However, the high strangeness of Davis's death by electrocution in a quarry located outside Chico, Texas, leaves this tale in limbo. That quarry was owned by Texas Industries, founded by Silvia's host, Ralph Rogers, with major investment from Texas oilman Clint Murchison.

Several years prior, the psychiatrist who in 1963 had guided Silvia through the trauma induced by her recollection that possible suspects in the assassination may have been at her house just weeks prior moved offices. His new address was 3707 Rawlins, Oak Lawn Plaza, Oak Lawn neighborhood of Dallas, the previous address of Ilse Skorzeny's cover, Previews Inc.

Gallagher, R. F., "The Ubiquitous Bard," The Fourth Decade, Volume 5, Number 5, July 1998. Available online Harold Weisberg Collection, Hood College, jfk.hood.edu.

Simpich, Bill, "The Twelve Who Built the Oswald Legend" Assassination Archives Research Center, February 2018. https://aarclibrary.org/bill-simpich-the-twelve-who-built-the-oswald-legend/.

Timeline of the Life of Lee Harvey Oswald by W. Tracy Parnell. jfkasassination.net.

1963 Datebook, Pierre Lafitte.

DULLES—ESSAY NOTES

"Princeton University . . . ": The Allen Dulles Appointment and Call Diaries: https://findingaids.princeton.edu/collections/MC019/c012.

"As Dulles's biographer David Talbot wrote . . . ": The Devil's Chessboard: Allen Dulles, the CIA, and the Rise of America's Secret Government, David Talbot, HarperCollins Publishers, 2015, p. 428 . . . Talbot's study is among several that have examined Dulles's life and the growth of CIA in the post-WW2 era, but it is arguably the deepest and most sophisticated examination of Dulles personally and of the Agency he constructed.

"One example of this is the strange meeting . . . ": Devil's Chessboard, pp. 458–462 . . . For a nuanced interpretation of the 1963 activities of Paulino Sierra Martinez—which does not, however, in my opinion, lessen the strangeness of the Dulles-Clay-Sierra meeting—see *Dallas '63: The First Deep State Revolt Against the White House*, Peter Dale Scott, Open Road Media, 2015," pp. 152–160

"These papers, which were circulating . . . ": Talbot, op. cit., pp. 31–36, covers Dulles wartime dance with Prince Hohenlohe.

"Brought forth a caustic evaluation . . . ": Talbot, op. cit., pp. 442–443.

"McGuire, former Assistant Secretary of Defense . . . ": *The Skorzeny Papers: Evidence for the Plot to Kill JFK*, Ralph Ganis, Hot Books, 2018, pp. 197–198.

"Dulles continued to communicate regularly . . . ": Talbot, op. cit. pp. 377–378.

"McNamara, interviewed by author Noel Twyman . . . ": *Bloody Treason: The Assassination of John F. Kennedy*, Noel Twyman, Laurel Publishing, 1997, pp. 499–513.

"In light of this meshing of calls and activity . . . ": Talbot, op. cit., p. 8.

"Dulles's confidante William Corson . . . ": *The Secret History of the CIA*, Joseph J. Trento, Carroll and Graf, 2005, p. 269 . . . Corson, who had commanded Dulles's son in the Marine Corps during the Korean War, was utilized by Dulles as an investigator during Dulles's stint with the Warren Commission and came to believe that the assignment Dulles had given him—involving Jack Ruby—might have been designed to "go nowhere." "Allen Dulles had a lot to hide," Corson told Trento.

"Dulles's protégé, Richard Helms . . . ": *The JFK Assassination Debates: Lone Gunman Versus Conspiracy*, Michael L. Kurtz, University Press of Kansas, 2006, p. 173 . . . Kurtz, while a well-accredited academic historian, has been questioned regarding some claims in his books that are sourced to imprecisely cited interviews with people who had, in some cases, spoken "on the record" to no one but Kurtz. We will not enter this area of controversy here, as the material he sources to an interview with Helms is quite plausible and does not affect the argument presented in this paper in any event.

PUGIBET—ESSAY NOTES

Documents pertaining to Allen Eli Wright and associates:

NARA # 1994.05.17.08:24:18:250005; # 104-10074-10133 (Wright background); # 124-10202-10343 (Wright background); # 124-90115-10030 (Chester Zochowski); # 104-10074-10133 (Wright-Gleichauf meeting).

Letter from Bill Turner to Jim Garrison, July 16, 1967, JFK Assassination Records, National Archives, Papers of Jim Garrison, Investigative Files Received From New Orleans District Attorney Harry Connick, Box 10 (Bill Turner, Ramparts).

Summary of notes from Bernard Fensterwald interview with Allen Eli Wright, Mary Ferrell Chronologies, Entry #7730.

Documents pertaining to Enrique Ernesto Pugibet and associates: Dallas County Sheriff's Office data on Pugibet, (incl. "Friend, Norman Rothman, Dallas Texas,") accessed by Lee Farley, posted on Education Forum, Sept. 13, 2013.

NARA # 124-10300-10078 (Thomas FBI memo).

(Information on Roscoe Gaither) No Decision / Leagle.com.

NARA # 124-10226-10267 (Rothman, Zochowski, Merola, Trujillo); # 124-10226-10244 (Pugibet, Miranda brothers).

Scott, Peter Dale, *Deep Politics and the Death of JFK* 1993, pp. 177–179.

Albarelli Jr., H. P., A *Terrible Mistake: The Murder of Frank Olson and the CIA's Secret Cold War Experiments,* 2009, (Lafitte) pp. 432–438.

BIBLIOGRAPHY

BOOKS

Adams, Jefferson, "Historical Dictionary of German Intelligence." Lanham, Maryland: Scarecrow Press, September 1, 2009.

Albarelli Jr., H. P., *A Secret Order: Investigating the High Strangeness and Synchronicity in the Kennedy Assassination.* Oregon: TrineDay, 2013.

Albarelli Jr., H. P., *A Terrible Mistake: The Murder of Dr. Frank Olson and the CIA's Secret Cold War Experiments.* Oregon: TrineDay, 2005. [Revised Edition: Albarelli Private Papers.]

Ambrose, Stephen E., *Ike's Spies: Eisenhower and the Espionage Establishment.* Jackson: Banner Book, University of Mississippi, 1981.

Askins, Charles. *Unrepentant Sinner: The Autobiography of Colonel Charles Askins.* Boulder: Paladin Press, 1991.

Baker, Bobby with King, Larry L., *Wheeling and Dealing: Confessions of a Capitol Hill Operator.* New York: W. W. Norton & Company, Inc., 1978.

Baker, Russ, *Family of Secrets. The Bush Dynasty, America's Invisible Government, and the Hidden History of the Last Fifty Years.* London: Bloomsbury Press. 2008.

Belin, Jean, *My Work at the Sûreté.* London: George G. Harrap & Co., Ltd., 1950.

Bernadac, Christian, *Dagore les carnets secrets de La Cagoule.* Editions France-Empire, Paris, 1977.

Biddescombe, Perry. *SS Hunter Battalions: The Hidden History of the Nazi Resistance Movement 1944–45* (Revealing History), Stroud, UK: Tempus Publishing Ltd. (November 15, 2006).

Bridger, Mark, "A Relative Responds." *Dealey Plaza Echo*, Vol 13, Number 1, March 2009.

Brown, Anthony Cave, *The Last Hero: Wild Bill Donovan.* New York: TIMES BOOKS, 1982.

Carter, Carolle Jr., *The Shamrock and the Swastika: German Espionage in Ireland in WWII.* Palo Alto: Pacific Books, 1975.

Caufield, Jeffrey H. M.D., *General Walker and the Murder of President Kennedy: The Extensive Evidence of a Radical-Right Conspiracy*. Moreland Press, First Edition, September 2015.

Chalou, George C., editor, *The Secret War: The Office of Strategic Services in World War II*. National Archives, Washington, D.C. 1992.

Christie, Stuart, "Portrait of a Black Terrorist." Black Papers No. I, *Anarchy Magazine*. London: Refract Publications 1984, first edition, and 1972, second edition.

Cirules, Enrique, *The Mafia in Havana: A Caribbean Mob Story*. Melbourne: Ocean Press, 2010.

Coon, Carleton S., *A North African Story: The Long Mislaid Diary-Account of a Harvard Professor of Anthropology Turned Cloak-and-Dagger Operative for General Donovan and His OSS 1942–43*. Ipswich, MA: Gambit, 1980, First Edition.

Corson, William R., *The Armies of Ignorance*. New York: Dial Press, 1997.

Crichton, Jack and E. J. Anderson, *The Middle East Connection (Yemen)*. Bloomington: Author House 2005, 12-09-04.

Crutchley, Peter,"How Did Hitler's Scar-faced Henchman Become an Irish Farmer?" BBC Digital & Learning NI, 30 December 2014, Northern Ireland.

de Montmorency, Alec, "Who Ordered the Death of French Admiral Darlan?" *The Barnes Review*, May 1997, Volume III, Number 4.

De Vosjoli, P. L. Thyraud, *Lamia*. Boston – Toronto: Little, Brown and Company, 1970.

Deitche, Scott M., *The Silent Don: The Criminal Underworld of Santo Trafficante Jr*. New Jersey: Barricade Books, 2007.

Denton, Sally and Roger Morris, *The Money and the Power*. New York: Alfred A. Knopf, 2001.

Dorman, Michael, *Payoff: The Roll of Organized Crime in American Politics*. New York: David McKay & Co., 1972.

Dulles, Allen Welsh, *From Hitler's doorstep: the wartime intelligence reports of Allen Dulles, 1942–1945*. University Park, Pa.: Pennsylvania State University Press, 1996.

Eisenberg, Dennis, *Re-Emergence of Fascism*. South Brunswick, NY: A. S. Barnes, January 1, 1967.

Escalante, Fabian, *The Secret War: CIA covert operations against Cuba 1959–62*. Melbourne: Ocean Press, 1995.

Ferraresi, Franco, *Threats to Democracy: The Radical Right in Italy After the War.* Princeton NJ: Princeton University Press, 1996.

Fetherling, George, *The Book of Assassins.* New York: Random House of Canada, Nov 16, 2011.

Foley, Charles. *Commando Extraordinary: the Remarkable Exploits of Otto Skorzeny.* Costa Mesa: Noontide Press [Willis Carto]; 1st edition (March 1, 1992).

Ganis, Maj. Ralph. *The Skorzeny Papers: Evidence for the Plot to Kill JFK.* New York: Hot Books (June 26, 2018).

Hancock, Larry, "Someone Would Have Talked." Mary Ferrell Publishing, 2010.

Hancock, Larry, *Nexus: The CIA and Political Assassination.* JFK Lancer Production; Illustrated edition (October 12, 2011).

Harney, L. Malachi, *The Narcotic Officer's Notebook.* Springfield: Charles C. Thomas Publications, Ltd., 1971, first edition.

Hemmer, Nicole, *Messengers of the Right: Conservative Media and the Transformation of American Media.* Philadelphia: University of Pennsylvania Press, 2018.

Hersh, Seymour M., *The Dark Side of Camelot.* New York: Back Bay Books, Little, Brown and Company, 1998.

Hull, Mark M., *Irish Secrets: German Espionage in Wartime Ireland 1939–1945.* Dublin: Irish Academic Publishing, 2004.

Joesten, Joachim, *The Case Against Lyndon Johnson in the Assassination of JFK.* Munich: Dreschstr. 5, Selbstverlag, 1967.

Jones, John Price and Paul Merrick Hollister, *The German Secret Service in America 1914–1918.* Boston: Small Maynard & Co., March 19, 2012.

Kantor, Seth, *The Ruby Cover-Up.* New York: Zebra Books, Kensington Publishing Corp., 1978.

Kern, Gary, *A Death in Washington: Walter G. Krivitsky and the Stalin Terror,* New York: Enigma Books; (October 1, 2003) Revised, Updated edition (October 1, 2004).

King, Jr., Henry T., "Robert H. Jackson and the Triumph of Justice at Nuremberg." *Case Western Reserve Journal of International Law,* Case Western University, School of Law, Volume 35, Issue 2, 2003.

Kornbluh, Peter and Kate Doyle, "CIA and Assassinations: The Guatemala 1954 Documents." Washington, D.C.: National Security Archive, The George Washington University www.nsarchive2.gwu.edu/NSAEBB /NSAEBB4/index.html.

Kross, Peter, *Operation Torch and the Assassination of Admiral Jean Darlan*. Warfare History Network, July 20, 2015.

Kurtz, Michael L., *The JFK Assassination Debates: Lone Gunman Versus Conspiracy*. Lawrence, KS: University Press of Kansas, 2006

Lee, Martin. *The Beast Reawakens: Fascism's Resurgence from Hitler's Spymasters to Today's Neo-Nazi Groups and Right-Wing Extremists*. Routledge, Oct 12, 1999.

Loftus, John and Mark Aarons, *The Secret War Against the Jews: How Western Espionage Betrayed the Jewish People*. New York: St. Martin's Press, 1994.

Luther, Craig W.H., PhD, and Hugh Page Taylor, *For Germany: The Otto Skorzeny Memoirs*. San Jose: R. James Bender Publishing, 2005.

Mellen, Joan, *Our Man in Haiti: George de Mohrenschildt and the CIA in the Nightmare Republic*. Oregon: TrineDay, October 22, 2012.

Mellen, Joan, *The Great Game in Cuba. CIA and the Cuban Revolution*. New York: Skyhorse Publishing; Reprint edition (February 16, 2016).

Messenger, David A., *Hunting Nazis in Franco's Spain*. Baton Rouge: Louisiana State University Press, 2014.

Michael, George (2012). *Lone Wolf Terror and the Rise of Leaderless Resistance*. Nashville, Tennessee: Vanderbilt University Press, 2012.

Miller, Norman C., *The Great Salad Oil Swindle*. Baltimore, MD: Penguin Books, 1965.

Morley, Jefferson, *Our Man in Mexico: Winston Scott and the Hidden History of the CIA*. Lawrence, KS: University Press Kansas, 2008.

Morley, Jefferson, *The Ghost: The Secret Life of CIA Spymaster James Jesus Angleton*. New York: St. Martin's Press, 2017.

Mudd, Roger, *The Plan to Ge: Washington, CBS, and the Glory Days of Television News*. New York: Public Affairs, 2008.

Mullins, Gerry. *Dublin Nazi No. 1: The Life of Adolf Mahr*. Dublin, Ireland: Liberties Press, March 1 2015.

Murphy, Robert, *Diplomat Among Warriors*, New York: Doubleday & Company, Inc., fourth printing, February 1965.

Nellor, Edward K., *Washington's Wheeler Dealers: Broads. Booze & Bobby Baker*. New York: Bee-Line Books, 1967.

Newman, John M., *Countdown to Darkness: The Assassination of President Kennedy* Volume II (Volume 2), January 19, 2017 CreateSpace Independent Publishing Platform (January 19, 2017). www.jfkjmn.com /countdown-to-darkness-the-assassination-of-president-kennedy -volume-ii/.

North, Mark, *Act of Treason: The Role of J. Edgar Hoover in the Assassination of President Kennedy*. New York: Carroll & Graf Publishers, Inc., 1991.

O'Donoghue, David, *The Devil's Deal: The IRA, Nazi Germany and the Double Life of Jim O'Donovan*. Dublin, Ireland: New Island Books (October 1, 2010).

O'Driscoll, Mervyn, *Ireland, West Germany and the New Europe, 1949-73: Best Friend and Ally?* Manchester, UK: Manchester University Press, 1st edition (January 10, 2018).

O'Halpin, Eunan, *Defending Ireland: The Irish State and Its Enemies since 1922*. Oxford, UK: University Oxford Press (November 16, 2000).

O'Reilly, Terence, *Hitler's Irishmen*. Cork, Ireland: Mercier Press, Ltd., 2008.

Phelan, James, *Scandals, Scamps and Scoundrels: The Casebook of an Investigative Reporter*. New York: Random House, 1982.

Plokhy, Serhii, *The Man with the Poison Gun: A Cold War Spy Story*. New York: Basic Books First Edition, December 2016.

Prados, John, *Safe For Democracy: The Secret Wars of the CIA*. Chicago: Ivan R. Dee Publishing, (February 16, 2009).

Price, David H., *Cold War Anthropology: The CIA, the Pentagon, and the Growth of Dual Use Anthropology*. Durham: Duke University Press, 2016.

Price, David, H., *Anthropological Intelligence: The Deployment and Neglect of American Anthropology in the Second World War*. Durham: Duke University Press, 2008.

Price, David H., *Threatening Anthropology*. Durham: Duke University Press, 2004.

Riebling, Mark, *Wedge: From Pearl Harbor to 9/11: How the Secret War Between the FBI and CIA Has Endangered National Security*. New York: Touchstone Book, Simon & Schuster, 1994, and 2002, Second edition.

Russell, Dick, *The Man Who Knew Too Much*. New York: Carroll & Graf, Three Editions: 1992, 1993, 2003.

Scott, Peter Dale, *American War Machine: Deep Politics, the CIA Global Drug Connection, and the Road to Afghanistan* (War and Peace Library). Lanham, Maryland: Rowman & Littlefield Publishers; 1st edition, November 16, 2010.

Scott, Peter Dale, *Dallas '63: The First Deep State Revolt Against the White House*. New York: Open Road Integrated Media LLC, 2015.

Scott, Peter Dale. *Deep Politics and the Death of JFK*. Berkley: University of California Press, 1993.

Seagrave, Sterling and Peggy, *Gold Warriors: America's Secret Recovery of Yamashita's Gold*. Brooklyn - London: Verso, 2003.

Sedar, Irving & Harold Greenburg, *Behind the Egyptian Sphinx; Nasser's Strange Bedfellows.* Boston: Chilton Company – Book Division, First Edition (January 1, 1990).

Shaw, J. Gary and Larry Ray Harris, *Cover-Up: The Governmental Conspiracy to Conceal the Facts About the Public Execution of John Kennedy,* Paperback, (1976).

Simpich, Bill, "The JFK Case: The Twelve Who Built the Oswald Legend" (Part 6: White Russians Keep An Eye On Oswald In Dallas), Assassination Archives and Research Center.

Skorzeny, Otto, *My Commando Operations: The Memoirs of Hitler's Most Daring Commando.* Atglen, Pennsylvania: Schiffer Publishing, 1995, p. 334.

Smith, Matthew *Conspiracy: The Plot to Stop the Kennedys.* Citadel Press Publishing, First Edition (July 1, 2005).

Smith, Matthew, *Say Goodbye to America: The Sensational and Untold Story Behind the Assassination of John F. Kennedy.* Edinburgh, UK: Mainstream Publishing, March 1, 2004.

Smith, Matthew, *Vendetta, The Kennedys.* Edinburgh, UK: Mainstream Publishing, January 1, 1993.

Smith, Richard Harris, *OSS: The Secret History of America's First Central Intelligence Agency.* Guilford, Conn: The Lyons Press, 1972, 2005.

Smith, Stuart. *Otto Skorzeny: The Devil's Disciple.* Osprey Publishing (September 18, 2018).

Stern, John Allen, *C. D. Jackson: Cold War Propaganda for Democracy and Globalism.* Lanham, Maryland: University Press of America, 2012.

Summers, Anthony, *Official and Confidential: The Secret Life of J. Edgar Hoover.* New York: G. P. Putnam's Sons, 1993.

Talbot, David, *Brothers: The Hidden History of the Kennedy Years.* Free Press; 1st edition (May 8, 2007).

Talbot, David, *The Devil's Chessboard: Allen Dulles, the CIA, and the Rise of America's Secret Government.* New York: HarperCollins, 2015.

Thomas, Kenn and Lincoln Lawrence, *Mind Control, Oswald & JFK: Were We Controlled?* Kempton, IL: Adventures Unlimited Press, 1997. Original edition, Lawrence, Lincoln, *Were We Controlled?* University Books, January 1, 1967.

Trento, Joseph J., *The Secret History of the CIA.* New York: Carroll and Graf, 2005.

Twyman, Noel, *Bloody Treason: On Solving History's Greatest Murder Mystery: The Assassination of John F. Kennedy*: Muller Point, NY: Laurel Publishing, December 1, 1997.

Vaughan, Hal, *FDR's 12 Apostles, The Spies Who Paved the Way for the Invasion of North Africa*. Guilford, Conn: The Lyons Press, 2006.

Vennard, Wickliffe B. Sr., *The Federal Reserve Hoax: The Age of Deception*. Boston: Forum Publishing; 8th edition, January 1,1960.

Verrier, Anthony, *Assassination in Algiers: Roosevelt, Churchill, de Gaulle, and the Murder of Admiral Darlan*. New York: W.W. Norton & Company, 1990.

Von Bulow, Mathilde, *West Germany, Cold War Europe and the Algerian War (New Studies in European History*. Cambridge, UK: Cambridge University Press (August 22, 2016).

Waller, Douglas, *Wild Bill Donovan: Spy Master Who Created the OSS and Modern American Espionage*. New York: Free Press, 2001.

Warner, Michael, "The CIA's Internal Probe of the Bay of Pigs Affair: Lessons Unlearned." Studies in Intelligence Winter (1998-1999).

Weale, Adrian, *Army of Evil: A History of the SS*. Botston: Dutton Caliber; Reprint edition (September 3, 2013). Author of articles: Irish Volunteers in German Service.

Weale, Adrian, *Renegades: Hitler's Englishmen*. London: Pimlico, Revised edition, January 1, 2002.

Welford, Nancy, *The Faux Baron: George de Mohrenschildt. An Aristocrat's Journey from the Russian Revolution to the Assassination of John F. Kennedy*. CreateSpace Independent Publishing Platform; 1st edition (October 18, 2014).

Wieviorka, Olivier, and Jane Marie Todd, *The French Resistance*. Boston: Belknap Press: An Imprint of Harvard University Press (April 25, 2016).

Wilmetts. Simon, "The Burgeoning Fissures of Dissent: Allen Dulles and the Selling of the CIA in the Aftermath of the Bay of Pigs." Wiley Online Library, March 27, 2015. www.onlinelibrary.wiley.com/doi /full/10.1111/1468-229X.12097.

Yeadon, Glen and John Hawkins, *The Nazi Hydra in America: Suppressed History of a Century*. Progressive Press, First Regular Edition (October 31, 2008).

ARTICLES

Adamson, OBE, Dr. Ian, *The Hidden of Herr Hoven*. February 2016. www.ianadamson.net/the-hidden-history-of-herr-hoven/.

Altweg, Al, "The Howard Corp. Unique in Banking." *Dallas Morning News*, March 10, 1963.

Altweg, Al, . . . *the veil of secrecy was lifted from "The Howard Corp" et al. by officers of the Republic National Bank of Dallas. Dallas Morning News,* Business Ed., Feb 1964.

Anderson, Nicola, "The CIA stayed silent on allegations it was involved in IRA gunrunning." *Irish Independent,* January 19, 2017.

Ayoob, Massad, "The Gunfights of Col. Charles Askins, Jr." *American Handgunner,* Nov-Dec 1999.

Bale, Jeffrey, PhD, "General del Valle, et al.: "The Black Terrorist International: Neo-Fascist Paramilitary Networks and the 'Strategy of Tension' in Italy, 1968–1974." Dissertation, University of California at Berkeley, 1994.

Bernstein, Victor H., "Employee Tells What Went on in Merwin Hart's Office." *The Nation,* May 23, 1943.

Biffle, Kent, "Allen Dulles Looks Behind Red Moves." *Dallas Morning News,* October 29, 1963.

Birtie, J., Andrew, "The Campaigns of World War II – World Warr II Commemorative Series Pamphlets, Sicily." www.history.army.mil/html /books/072/72-16/index.html.

Bokhari, Allum and Milo Yiannopoulos, "An Establishment Conservatives' Guide to the Alt-Right." *Breitbart News,* March 29, 2016. www.breitbart .com/tech/2016/03/29/an-establishment-conservatives-guide-to-the-alt-right/.

Brussell, Mae. "The Nazi Connection to the John F. Kennedy Assassination: Evidence of link between Nazis still in operation after World War II to the still unsolved murder of John F. Kennedy." www.worldwatchers.info /November 22, 1981. Also published in *The Rebel,* January 1984.

Coogan, Kevin, "The Defenders of the American Constitution and the League of Empire Loyalists: The First Postwar Anglo-American Revolt Against the 'One World Order.' "2006 essay available online: https://web.archive.org/ web/20060823103720/http://www.iisg.nl/research/coogan.doc.

Davy, William, "The Friends of Democratic Cuba." Back Channels Fall/Winter 1993/4.

Duffy, David, "Is This The Man Who Killed JFK?" *The National Enquirer,* November 22, 1983.

Evans, Emyr Estyn, "Celtic Racialist and Nazi Spymaster in Dublin before the Second World War." cited by Dr. Ian Adamson OBE at www.ianadamson .net/the-hidden-history-of-herr-hoven/.

Finder, Joseph, "Ultimate Insider, Ultimate Outsider." *New York Times,* April 12, 1992, Section 7, Page 1 of the National edition.

Gallagher, R. F., "The Ubiquitous Bard." The Fourth Decade, Volume 5, Number 5, July 1998. Available online Harold Weisberg Collection, Hood College, jfk.hood.edu.

Gibney, Alex, "Meet the Leader of the Eliot Spitzer's Smear Campaign." *The Atlantic*, October 13, 2010.

Gray, James A.,"Big Nickel." *Maclean's*, October 1, 1947. www.archive .macleans.ca/article/1947/10/1/big-nickel.

Harwood, Richard, "Business Leaders Are Tied to CIA's Covert Operations." *Washington Post*, February 18, 1967.

Harwood, Richard, "CIA Reported Ending Aid to Some Groups," *Washington Post*, February 22, 1967.

Higgins, Trumbull, review of "MacArthur: 1941–1951" by Charles A Willoughby and John Chamberlain. *Commentary Magazine*. June 1955.

Hobsbawm, Eric. "Uncommon People: Resistance, Rebellion and Jazz." Abacus. New Ed edition. December 2, 1999.

Hudson, John, "Exclusive: Think Tank Fires Employee Who Questioned Ties to Donald Trump." ForeignPolicy.com. May 20, 2016.

Jewish Telegraph Agency, Vol. XXX Monday, Feb 4, 1963 NY, NY.

Kilgallen, Dorothy, "The Novotny Story." *Washington Post*, June 28, 1963.

Kluckhohn, Frank, "Heidelberg to Madrid – The Story of General Willoughby." *The Reporter*, August 19, 1952.

Lauder, George V., Acting Chief, Latin American Division, "Latin America Division Task Force Report of Possible Cuban Complicity in the John F. Kennedy Assassination." June 30, 1977. *The Black Vault*. www.documents .theblackvault.com/documents/jfk/NARA-Oct2017/NARA-Nov9-2017 /104-10506-10028.pdf.

Mann, William, "How Buchanan Made Trump Possible." *The Week*, July 26, 2019.

Manuel Roig-Franzie, "The Swamp Builders: How Stone and Manafort helped create the mess Trump promised to clean up." *Washington Post*, November 29, 2018.

McDermott, John B., "Stockdale Into Irrational Mood." *Miami Herald Reporter*, December 1963.

Mollenhoff, Clark, ". . . U.S. Capitol May Be Rocked by Story of Exotic Mystery Woman." *Des Moines Register*, October 26, 1963.

Morris-Suzuki, Tessa, "Democracy's Porous Borders: Espionage, Smuggling, and the Making of Japan's Transwar Regime." *The Asia-Pacific Journal*, Japan Focus, Oct. 2, 2014 and Oct. 12, 2014.

O'Donoghue, David, "State within a State: the Nazis in neutral Ireland." *History Ireland*, Ireland's History Magazine, Issue 6 (Nov/Dec 2006).

Pease, Lisa, "Clay Shaw and Freeport Sulphur." (This article first appeared in *Probe* magazine, Vol. 3, No. 3, March–April 1996, and can now be found in The Assassination.)

Pirre-Gosset, Renee and Nancy Hecksher [translator], *"Conspiracy in Algiers, 1942–1943."* Whitefish, MT: Kessinger Publishing, March 1, 2007 (first published, New York: The Nation, 1945).

Root, Waverly, "Headed by Skorzeny? Neo-Nazis Linked to Algeria French." *Washington Post*, February 26, 1962. https://www.cia.gov/readingroom /docs/SKORZENY,%20OTTO%20%20%20VOL.%202_0139.pdf.

Rorty, James, "The Native Anti-Semite's 'New Look': His Present 'Line' and His Prospects." *Commentary Magazine*, October 1955.

Rose, Jerry D., "Plain Talk About Isaac Levine." State University College, Fredonia, New York. *The Fourth Decade*, January 1995, Volume 2, Number 2.

Roston, Aram and Joel Anderson, "The Moneyman Behind the Alt-Right." BuzzFeed News, July 27, 2017.

Sargent, Greg, "Opinion: The repulsive worldview of Trump and Bannon, perfectly captured in one poll." *Washington Post,* March 17, 2017.

Simkin, John, "E. Grant Stockdale." The Education Forum, JFK Assassination Debate, online site, June 11, 2004.

Singer, David, "The Men in the Trojan Horse: Allen Dulles Heads Our Intelligence, World's Largest." Available

Sotos, MD, John G., "Botulinum Toxin in Biowarfare." JAMA Network, June 6, 2001; 285 (21):2716.

Sudol, Stan, "Nickel Closest Thing to a True 'War Metal.'" Originally published in *Northern Life*, Greater Sudbury's community newspaper on February 23, 2007; reproduced in *Republic of Mining*, February 2009.

Summers Jr., Harry G. "How We Lost." Published in *The New Republic*, April 28, 1985.

Summers Jr., Harry G., "JFK and Vietnam: an interpretation that makes him politically correct?" *Baltimore Sun*, March 15, 1992. www.baltimoresun.com/news/bs-xpm-1992-03-15-1992075129-story.html

www.cia.gov/readingroom/home Document No. RDP70 -00058R000100100033-3.

www.jfk.hood.edu/Collection/Weisberg%20Subject%20Index%20Files /D%20Disk/Davy%20William/Item%2001.pdf.

www.jfk.hood.edu/Collection/Weisberg%20Subject%20Index%20Files /N%20Disk/National%20Enquirer/Item%2094.pdf.

Wertz, Nancy, "William Gaudet - Make Room for the Man at the Front of the Line." Kennedy Assassination Chronicles, Volume 5, Issue 2.

ADDITIONAL ARTICLES

"Robert D. Murphy, Diplomat, Dies at 83," *New York Times*, January 11, 1978.

"Amerasia Case." Dictionary of American History. Retrieved February 26, 2019 from *encyclopedia.com*.

"Frank Ryan, Relieved of Command." *Times-Picayune* (New Orleans, Louisiana) Sunday, June 25, 1961, p. 28.

"Grant Stockdale Killed." *Evening Independent*, St. Petersburg, Florida, Monday December 2, 1963.

". . . [Charles William Thomas] took up a gun and shot himself to death." *Time* magazine, November 15, 1971. www.archives.gov/files/research/jfk/releases/docid-32263513.pdf.

"U.S. 'Profumo' Scandal Reported to Break." *The Blade*, Toledo, Ohio, Monday, October 28, 1963, p. 7.

"Washington Cover-Up." Program at Georgetown University. Jersey City: *The Ukrainian Weekly Section*, November 3, 1962.

"Anti-communist League Holds 7th Conference in Washington." *The Ukrainian Weekly Section*, April 20, 1974. www.ukrweekly.com/archive/1974/The_Ukranian_Weekly_1974-17.

Congreso Annual—INFORMATION

Internationales Comité Zur Verteidigung der Christlichen Kultur
Comité International de Défense de la Civilisation Chrétienne
Internaciónal de Defensa de la Civilización Cristiana
International Committee for the Defence of Christian Culture
Internacional de Defesa da Civilização Cristã
—MacArthur Library and Archives, Norfolk, Virginia.

"Dr. Hargis and Gen. Willoughby Elected to International Committee." *Foreign Intelligence Digest*, June 29, 1962.

"Gun, The IRA And The War of Independence." *An Sionnach Fion: Irish News, Politics and Culture,* October 7, 2018. First published 20th-century / Contemporary History, Features, Issue 6 (Nov/Dec 2006), The Emergency, Volume 14.

"Hitler's Bodyguard Skorzeny Lives in Ireland; Says He is No Nazi." *Daily Express,* London, August 17, 1960.

"U.S. Investors Seek Land in Australia." *Sydney Morning-Herald*, May 26, 1969.

"The Flying Boats of Foynes." *History Ireland*, Ireland's History Magazine, Issue 1 (Spring 2001).

"New evidence on IRA/Nazi links." *History Ireland*, Ireland's History Magazine, Issue 2 (March/April 2011).

"Jaworski Reportedly Had Role in Setting Up C.I.A. Aid Conduit." *New York Times*, November 6, 1973. *www.nytimes.com/1973/11/06/archives/jaworski -reportedly-had-role-in-setting-up-cia-a-id-conduit-amount.html*.

"New Suspect in JFK Slaying-A French Terrorist." *National Enquirer*, November 22, 1983.

www.jfk.hood.edu/Collection/Weisberg%20Subject%20Index%20Files /N%20Disk/National%20Enquirer/Item%2094.pdf.

"BROWNING INTERESTS." *Baylor Bulletin*, 1931 Second Series, edited by A. Joseph Armstrong, Ph D., Litt.D.

AUDIO

Kupcinet, Irv, "At Random." Chicago, IL: Museum of Broadcast Communications, 360 North State Street, 2nd Floor.

Morley, Jefferson, "WHAT JANE ROMAN SAID: A Retired CIA Officer Speaks Candidly About Lee Harvey Oswald." www.maryferrell.org/pages /Unredacted_-_Episode_11.html.

LAFITTE ARTICLES, POST-ASSASSINATION

"The Gourmet Pirate." *Time Magazine, Nation*, December 19, 1969.

"Plimsoll Chef Pleads Innocent." *New Orleans States-Item*, December 22, 1969.

"January Trial Ordered for Club Manager." *New Orleans States-Item*, December 23, 1969.

"Lafitte Trail Postponed Indefinitely." *New Orleans States-Item*, January 12, 1970.

ARCHIVAL SOURCES

National Archives and Records Administration: JFK Assassination Records Collection, College Park, Maryland: www.archives.gov/research/jfk.

Mary Ferrell Foundation: www.maryferrell.org.

Assassination Archives and Research Center: www.aarclibrary.org.

The Harold Weisberg Collection: Hood College, Frederick, Maryland, www.jfk.hood.edu.

Allen W. Dulles Papers: Digital Files Series 1939-1977, Princeton University, Princeton, New Jersey. www.catalog.princeton.edu/catalog/11446359.

Charles Andrew Willoughby Papers, Hoover Institution Library and Archives, Stanford University, Stanford, California: www.hoover.org /library-and-archives.

MacArthur Library and Archives, Norfolk, Virginia. www.macarthurmemorial .org/31/Library-Archives.

Parish Library of Management & Economics, Purdue University, West Lafayette, Indiana.

DeGolyer Library, Southern Methodist University, Dallas, Texas.

The Black Vault. https://www.theblackvault.com/documentarchive /www.cia.gov/readingroom/home vault.fbi.gov.

ADDITIONAL BOOKS

Black, Edwin, *IBM and the Holocaust: The Strategic Alliance Between Nazi Germany and America's Most Powerful Corporation*. London: Little, Brown and Company, 2001.

Bower, Tom, *The Paperclip Conspiracy*. Boston - Toronto: Little, Brown and Company, 1987.

Colby, Gerard with Charlotte Dennett, *Thy Will Be Done - The Conquest of the Amazon: Nelson Rockefeller and Evangelism in the Age of Oil*. New York: HarperCollins Publishers, 1995.

Hunt, Linda, *Secret Agenda*: *The United States Government, Nazi Scientists, and Project Paperclip, 1945 to 1990*. New York: St Martin's Press – A Thomas Dunne Book (January 1, 1991).

GOVERNMENT PUBLICATIONS AND REPORTS

Report of the Warren Commission on the Assassination of President Kennedy. New York: McGraw-Hill Book Co, 1964.

Annual Report of the Securities and Exchange Commission by United States Security and Exchange Commission, 1962.

Federal Reserve Records of WWII: Civilian Agencies.

US Bureau of Mines Bulletin Issue 630.
   www.documents.theblackvault.com/documents/jfk/NARA-Oct2017
   /NARA-Nov9-2017/104-10506-10028.pdf.

GENERAL REFERENCE

Moody's Bank and Finance Manual, John Moody and Company publisher.
Moody's Industrial Manual, John Moody and Company publisher.
Who's Who in America, published by Marquis Who's Who.
Who's Who in the Southwest, published by Marquis Who's Who.
Who's Who in Great Britain, published by Bloomsbury Press UK.
The Handbook of Texas, compiled by the Texas State Historical Association
   www.tshaonline.org/handbook.

INDEX